Words and Life

In philosophizing, I have to bring my own language and life into imagination. What I require is a convening of my culture's criteria, in order to confront them with my words and life as I pursue them and as I may imagine them; and at the same time to confront my words and life as I pursue them with the life my culture's words may imagine for me: to confront the culture with itself, along the lines in which it meets in me.

Stanley Cavell

Words and Life

Hilary Putnam

Edited by James Conant

Harvard University Press
Cambridge, Massachusetts
London, England

Copyright © 1994 by the President and Fellows of Harvard College
Printed in the United States of America
Third printing, 1996

First Harvard University Press paperback edition, 1995

Library of Congress Cataloging-in-Publication Data

Putnam, Hilary.
 Words and life / Hilary Putnam ; edited by James Conant.
  p. cm.
 Companion v. to: Realism with a human face.
 Includes bibliographical references and index.
 ISBN 0-674-95606-0 (cloth)
 ISBN 0-674-95607-9 (pbk.)
 1. Realism—History. 2. Science—Philosophy—History.
 3. Philosophy—History. 4. Philosophy. I. Conant, James.
 II. Title.
 B835.P88 1994
  149′.2—dc20   93–39799
            CIP

Preface

The essays that James Conant has selected for the present volume have been mainly written in the last four years; in this respect this volume differs from its companion volume *Realism with a Human Face* (Harvard University Press, 1990), which consisted largely of papers written in the early 1980s. Yet there is a continuity between the two volumes. The preface to *Realism with a Human Face* explained that the view of truth I put forward in *Reason, Truth, and History* (1981)—the view that a statement is true if and only if acceptance of the statement would be justified were epistemic conditions good enough—was not "emphasized" in the papers in that volume, although metaphysical realism—the view that truth involves a fixed correspondence (a correspondence relation which is one and the same no matter what sort of statement is under consideration) to a fixed set of "objects" and "properties"—was repeatedly attacked. That much might be said to be even more true of the papers in this volume, since I no longer defend that theory of truth at all, while, as in the earlier volume, I continue to argue that metaphysical realism is not the friend of common-sense realism that it claims to be, and that, in many ways, metaphysical realism and the fashionable antirealisms stand in a symbiotic relation; philosophical illusions require one another for sustenance. Indeed, all the ideas listed in the last paragraph of the preface to *Realism with a Human Face* are as central to this volume as they were to the earlier volume (these were "that the fact/value dichotomy is untenable, that the fact/convention dichotomy is also untenable, that truth and justification of ideas are closely connected, that the alternative to metaphysical realism is not any form of skepticism, that philosophy is an attempt to achieve the good"). I also remarked that these ideas "have been long associated with the American pragmatist tradition" and that both James Conant and I want that tradition "to be more widely understood in all its manifold expressions"; the essays in Part III of the present volume continue the effort to realize that goal.

Nevertheless, there are significant differences, some of which will be evident from a glance at the table of contents, starting with the fact that the previous volume had only one historical section, while the present volume begins with three consecutive such sections. More significant, in my own view at least, are two other facts about these essays. One is the fact that the essays on "ethics and aesthetics" in the earlier volume were primarily attacks on the fact/value dichotomy, whereas the essays in Part III ("The Inheritance of Pragmatism") of the present volume, while continuing the criticism of that dichotomy, go on to develop a positive view of the nature of social/ethical problems which I (together with Ruth Anna Putnam, the co-author of two of these papers) find in the writings of John Dewey. I say "social/ethical" rather than simply "ethical" because, as I remark in Chapter 8 ("Pragmatism and Moral Objectivity"), it is a feature of Dewey's approach to blur the distinction: when we have solved a problem in our communal life, we may not know—or care—whether it was an "ethical" problem or not, and also because I would be the last person to claim that the social ethics that I so much admire in Dewey is all there is to ethics. The other fact is that many of the papers in the present volume (for example, those in Part VI, "Mind and Language," as well as Chapters 14 and 15, "Realism without Absolutes" and "The Question of Realism") attack illusions associated with the rhetoric of "cognitive science." Indeed, even the papers in Part I ("The Return of Aristotle") are concerned to attack the idea that intentionality, the directedness of thought to objects, is either to be reduced to facts of physics or to be "eliminated" as an illusion, and readers of the papers in Part I may want to look ahead at Chapter 24 ("Why Functionalism Didn't Work") as they read those papers. If there is a single unifying theme in this volume, it may well be the attack on a certain set of prejudices—prejudices which pretend to be "scientific," but which confuse respect for science with uncritical acceptance of a materialist ideology.

I should like to say a word here about the reason for the "historical sections." I am convinced that the history of philosophy is not only a history of gaining insights—and I do think philosophers gain insights—but also a history of neglecting, and even actively repressing, previously gained insights. It will be clear to the reader, I believe, how that view informs Part I ("The Return of Aristotle") and Part III ("The Inheritance of Pragmatism"). But what in the world, some may ask, is Part II ("The Legacy of Logical Positivism") doing here? Am I saying that there were, after all, real insights in logical positivism? Was not logical positivism the chief expression in this century of the very scientism that I am concerned to attack?

To those questions my answers are, respectively, "yes" and "no." There were real insights in logical positivism. Some of those insights are to be found in the course of Hans Reichenbach's profound examination of the question "In precisely what sense is relativistic physics a refutation of the Kantian view that Euclidean geometry is synthetic *a priori*?" in *Relativity Theory and Apriori Knowledge*. And even if the attempts of some positivists to deductively "vindicate" induction failed, the investigations that resulted from those attempts represent the beginnings of modern formal learning theory, as I point out in Chapter 7 of the present volume, "Reichenbach and the Limits of Vindication."

More important, some of the crude philosophical ideas that are rampant today—claims that neurobiology has solved the problem of intentionality, for example, or that the computer model of the mind has enabled us to answer metaphysical and epistemological questions—are more extreme (and cruder) versions of scientism than logical positivism ever was. Many philosophers think that *because* they have "refuted" a straw man version of logical positivism—refuted a doctrine that never actually existed in the form they describe—they cannot themselves possibly be guilty of the charge of scientism. (The real logical positivists, for example, did not need Thomas Kuhn to tell them that observation terms are "theory laden"—they had been saying that, in those very terms, since the early 1930s. And—see Chapter 6, "Reichenbach and the Myth of the Given"—far from accepting the idea of the given, they were its keenest critics.)

In saying there were real insights in logical positivism, I am not defending the verifiability theory of meaning, or the identification of cognitive value with predictive value, or the sharp fact/value dichotomy that characterized that tendency. But it is important to see why logical positivism *really* failed, for example, to see that positivism has a deep problem in refuting the charge of solipsism (this is the gravamen of Chapter 4, "Logical Positivism and Intentionality"); that some philosophers have failed to see this is evidenced, I believe, by the current revival of the "disquotational theory of truth"—that is, of a redundancy theory of truth coupled with an "assertibility conditions" account of understanding. (See Chapter 13, "Does the Disquotational Theory of Truth Solve All Philosophical Problems?" as well as Chapters 16 and 17, "On Truth" and "A Comparison of Something with Something Else," for an explanation of this remark.)

Finally, I want to say a word about the fourth and the seventh parts of this volume. Part IV is not exactly "historical," although it does try to rescue Wittgenstein from persistent misinterpretations; rather it consists of papers in which I believe I have *learned* from Wittgenstein, though not from the stock Wittgenstein who has a "use theory of meaning" and a "disquotational theory of truth." Indeed, the first paper in the section, Chapter 12 ("Rethinking Mathematical Necessity"), simultaneously corrects the way I myself misread Wittgenstein's philosophy of mathematics in the past (for example, in "Philosophy of Mathematics: Why Nothing Works," Chapter 28 of this volume), and presents a way of thinking about the issue that I find attractive; similarly, Chapters 14 and 15 ("Realism without Absolutes" and "The Question of Realism") correct the commonplace idea that Wittgenstein was an "antirealist" and begin to work out a way of thinking that I intend to follow up in the coming years. Finally, the papers in Part VII, although grouped together because in one way or another they all have to do with science and the impact of the idea of science on philosophy, also continue the antireductionist and broadly pluralistic themes of the preceding parts of the book.

Hilary Putnam, 1994

Contents

Introduction by James Conant

Any philosophy that can be put in a nutshell belongs in one.

Hilary Putnam

In a number of the essays in this volume, the author discourages us from taking a certain view of his thought. He says that what he is offering should not be taken for a philosophical *theory* in the traditional sense. He is not setting forth a *position*, but attempting to sketch a *picture* (sometimes one he deplores, sometimes one he recommends as a corrective to some coercive alternative picture); and he has some things to say about what pictures are and how to use and abuse them. He also goes out of his way, at various points, to explain what he now finds misleading about this or that label he has in the past applied to his own views, saying that he has now discarded the label because he no longer wishes to invite the impression (which the label made irresistible) that his rejection of one philosophical thesis was meant to imply his endorsement of its traditional antithesis.

Even if the reader were eager to conclude that the author is quite mistaken about all this—that he is as deep in questionable theses and theories as he ever was—the reader would still be hard put to conclude that the essays here all form part of a single system. Not only were they written at different times and for very different occasions,[1] but often one essay will devote itself to tearing out individual pieces from the overall puzzle that another happily assumes still remain firmly in place. Thus some essays clearly represent earlier, and others later, way stations along a single winding journey of thought.

Having thus cautioned the reader not to expect from this introduction an overview of the author's system, I will now proceed to proffer a handful of nutshells, each of which affords (I hope) some glimpse of—but none of which contains—the philosophy of Hilary Putnam.

Putnam and Baudelaire

I have tried more than once to lock myself inside a system, so as to be able to pontificate as I liked. But a system is a kind of damnation that condemns us to perpetual backsliding; we are always having to invent another, and this form of fatigue is a cruel punishment. And every time, my system was beautiful, big, spacious, convenient, tidy and polished above all; at least so it seemed to me. And every time, some spontaneous unexpected product of universal vitality would come and give the lie to my puerile and old-fashioned wisdom . . . Under the threat of being constantly humiliated by another conversion, I took a big decision. To escape from the horror of these philosophical apostasies, I arrogantly resigned myself to modesty; I became content to feel; I came back and sought sanctuary in impeccable naïveté. I humbly beg pardon of academics of every kind . . . for only there has my philosophic conscience found rest.

> Charles Baudelaire, "The Universal Exhibition of 1855"

In recent years, Putnam appears to have taken "a big decision"—not unlike the one Baudelaire reports himself as having taken, and for not altogether dissimilar reasons. Putnam has become increasingly disenchanted with putting forward new philosophical "positions" of his own (or revamping ones to which he was previously committed), and increasingly concerned with articulating his dissatisfactions with the prevailing forms of orthodoxy in Anglo-American philosophy (some of which he himself was instrumental in ushering on to the scene). Investigating the sources of these dissatisfactions has become an abiding preoccupation of his recent work. But this preoccupation has, in turn, led to a more positive and constructive concern—a concern not only with the structure and history of the philosophical controversies which he himself has participated in, but also, more generally, with the nature of philosophical controversy *überhaupt*: with what fuels it and with what might allow it to attain and confer satisfaction. This shift in the focus of his work has only gradually become fully explicit and self-conscious. The shift is reflected in a change in the tone of his work: from the authoritative tone of someone explaining the solution to an outstanding problem (functionalism, the causal theory of reference, and so forth) to the unhurried tone of someone who is concerned above all to convey an appreciation of the *difficulty* of the problems. The change in philosophical voice is from that of someone who is excited to be able to announce that we are on the verge of a revolution (in our thinking about the nature of mind or language or whatever) to that of someone who has become distrustful of such an-

nouncements and impressed with how—to paraphrase one of
Putnam's heroes[2]—those who are unfamiliar with the history of a
problem (even its *recent* history) are condemned to repeat that history.

None of the essays in the present volume begins by announcing a
solution to a long-standing philosophical problem. This is not to say
that Putnam has come to despair of the possibility of making progress
in philosophy. But his conception of the form in which he himself is
able to contribute to the achievement of such progress has evidently
undergone some transformation. Several of the essays in this volume
begin with a historical prelude (often in order to illustrate how a popular contemporary "solution" to a philosophical problem is a disguised version of a much older proposal).[3] Some of the essays begin
on an autobiographical note (tracing the development perhaps of
Putnam's own present, usually ambivalent, attitude to a particular
philosophical school, author, or doctrine).[4] Some of them begin with
a dialectical overview of a philosophical controversy (often in order to
try to bring out how the crucial presuppositions are ones which both
parties to the dispute share).[5] The proximate goal of these essays
therefore is not to attempt to have the last word about a philosophical
problem, but rather to give the reader a sense of the *shape* and the
depth of the problem—of how, for example, in a particular philosophical dispute, thesis and counter-thesis bear one another's stamp
and how each of the pair comes with its own false bottom, hiding the
true dimensions of the problem from view.

The opening remarks of Putnam's most recent work suggest he has
come to see in stretches of the history of philosophy a version of
Baudelaire's vision of a kind of damnation that condemns one to perpetual backsliding:

> The besetting sin of philosophers seems to be throwing the baby out
> with the bathwater. From the beginning each "new wave" of philos-
> ophers has simply ignored the insights of the previous wave in the
> course of advancing its own . . . I want to urge that we attempt to
> understand, and to the extent that it is humanly possible overcome,
> the pattern of "recoil" that causes philosophy to leap from frying
> pan to fire, from fire to a different frying pan, from different frying
> pan to a different fire, and so on apparently without end.[6]

The essays collected in the present volume should be read as additional piecemeal contributions to such a project of attempting to understand—and, to the extent that it is humanly possible, overcome—this characteristically philosophical oscillation from one source of excessive heat to another.

Many of the essays in the present volume offer criticisms (and, in some cases, official recantations) of views that Putnam himself has previously held. Indeed, in many cases, what is under indictment is a philosophical view which not only continues to be widely associated with Putnam's name (generally because he either originated or helped to originate it), but which also continues to exert considerable influence within analytic philosophy. Every essay here seeks in some way to bring into sharper focus an "unexpected product of universal vitality" whose existence "gives the lie" to some piece of wisdom to which Putnam himself was previously strongly attracted. Thus, if there is a single over-arching doctrine—a single teaching which underlies every essay here—it would seem to be that one's ability to make progress in philosophy depends, above all, on one's continuing willingness to reexamine the grounds of one's philosophical convictions.

The parallel between Putnam's (most recent) metamorphosis and the one which Baudelaire reports extends not only to the resolve no longer to lock oneself inside a system, but also to the resolve arrogantly to resign oneself to modesty and return to "sanctuary in impeccable naïveté." In Chapter 14, "Realism without Absolutes," Putnam formulates the problem which that essay seeks to address in the following terms: "The difficulty is in seeing how such a move in the direction of deliberate 'naiveté' can possibly help after three centuries of modern philosophy, not to mention a century of brain science and now cognitive science. The problem now is to *show the possibility* of a return to what I called 'deliberate naiveté' . . . it seems to me that that is the direction in which we need to go." Putnam is here describing a philosophical move which he finds in Wittgenstein and which he himself wishes to emulate. It is, he says, a move which seeks to head off our tendency, when philosophizing, to repudiate our ordinary ways of talking and thinking ("we can't actually *see* physical objects, all we really see are appearances"), and to restore our conviction in such ways of thinking and talking.

Before we further explore what is involved in cultivating such a "deliberate naiveté" in philosophy, we need some further sense of the nature of Putnam's dissatisfaction with traditional forms of philosophical sophistication; and we might as well begin at the beginning.

Aristotle *after* Wittgenstein?

I never thought that Anaxagoras, who said that such things were directed by the Mind, would bring in any other cause for them . . . This wonderful hope was dashed as I went on reading and saw that the man made no use of Mind, nor gave it any responsibility for the management of things, but mentioned as causes air and ether and water and many other strange things. That seemed to me much like saying that Socrates's actions are all due to his mind, and then in trying to tell the causes of everything I do, to say that the reason I am sitting here is because my body consists of bones and sinews . . . If someone said that without bones and sinews and all such things, I should not be able to do what I decided, he would be right, but surely to say that they are the cause of what I do, and not that I have chosen the best course, even though I act with my mind, is to speak very lazily and carelessly. Imagine not being able to distinguish the true cause from that without which the cause would not be able to act as a cause!

> Socrates, *Phaedo*

Some problems won't go away. The topic of Socrates' quarrel with Anaxagoras—whether when "I act with my mind" the true cause is something in my body—is one such problem. It recurs in the pages that follow in a number of guises, perhaps most provocatively in the guise of a quarrel between Aristotle and contemporary cognitive science—a quarrel in which Putnam always awards the last word to Aristotle.

The opening essay of this volume begins with the question whether the subject of Aristotle's *De Anima*, the *psyche*, is to be identified with what we now call "the mind." Here is how Putnam explains the motive behind this sudden departure on his part into matters of classical philology:

In this century people talk as if the mind is almost a self-evident idea. It is as if the phenomena themselves required us to classify them as mental or physical in the way we do. Yet the present notion [of mind] is not very old, or at least its hegemony is not very old. The words *mind* and *soul*, or their classical ancestors, the Latin *mens* and the Greek *psyche*, are of course old. The habit of identifying notions which are actually quite different leads us to think that therefore the present notion of the mind must be equally old, but nothing could be more false . . . My hope is that whatever our interest in the mind—whether as philosophers or as psychologists or as "cognitive scientists" or just as curious and puzzled human beings—we may find that this bit of intellectual history may also have the benefit of making

usual ways of thinking about our "mental phenomena" seem less
coercive.

Putnam goes on to argue that nothing in Aristotle's thought corresponds to "the mind." Aristotle's notion of *psyche* is considerably
more comprehensive, and his notion of *nous* much narrower, than the
modern notion of mind. *Psyche* is the "form" (which Putnam para-
phrases, somewhat controversially, as the "functional organization")
of the whole living human organism (encompassing digestion and reproduction, as well as desire and thought); while *nous* is an exclusively intellectual faculty (which Putnam paraphrases, less controversially, as "reason") which does not encompass either sensation or
desire. Putnam's preoccupation with these matters derives from his
interest in wanting to show that the mind/body problem is of relatively recent vintage. Hence the significance he attaches to the following observation: "One can generate questions about how *nous* is related to body, how *psyche* is related to body, and so on, within the
Aristotelian system; and Aristotle says things about those questions
(for example, he says 'active *nous*' is separable from body but the *psyche* as a whole is not), but one cannot find the modern 'mind/body
problem.'"
      One of the aims of the essay as a whole is to argue that "each pre-
vious period in the history of Western thought had a quite different
idea of what such a term as 'mind' or 'soul' might stand for, and a
correspondingly different idea of what the puzzles were that we
should be trying to solve." Thus, along the same lines, Putnam goes
on to develop a claim about the relation between our contemporary
views and those of Thomas Aquinas, this time focusing on the question where to locate the faculty of *memory*. Here, too, Putnam argues
that we tend to read our contemporary conceptions back into our predecessors. We read the idea that memory is a mental faculty back into
earlier writers because "it has come to seem such a central function of
the mind to us." To us it seems simply *obvious* that memories are in
the mind. Whereas, Putnam claims, Aquinas's view was that—unless
they happened to be in the process of being actively recalled—it was
obvious that memories were in the body (that is, the brain). This
fact—that the answer to this question seemed as obvious to Aquinas
as it now does to us—helps prepare the way for one of the conclusions
of the essay: "If there is one value which a historical survey of what

has been thought on these matters can have, it is to caution us against thinking that it is obvious even what the questions are."

Putnam has an additional interest, however, in giving us a brief tour of the history of thought about (what we now call) "the mind." It is his conviction that there is not only something arbitrary and accidental about our contemporary philosophical way(s) of drawing the contours of the realm of the mental, but also something coercive and confused:

> The *nous*/body distinction that Aquinas would have drawn is not at all the same as the modern mind/body distinction. Yet, when I think about it, it doesn't sound worse than the modern one! *Is it* obvious that there is something called the mind whose contents include all of my memories, whether I am actively recalling them or not, but whose functions do not include digestion and reproduction? Or are we in the grip of a picture whose origins are somewhat accidental and whose logic, once examined, is not compelling?

Putnam's claim that neither Aristotle nor Aquinas drew the modern mind/body distinction may not come as a shock, especially in light of the widely disseminated notion that it is, above all, Descartes who should get credit for first elaborating the distinction in its modern form. On one influential version of this story, Gilbert Ryle traces (in order then to criticize) what he takes to be the modern idea of mind— the idea that the mind exists in the body as a ghost in a machine— back to Descartes's conception of *res cogitans* (and of its relation to *res extensa*). Putnam, however, wishes to contest the standard account in three respects, claiming (1) that the modern notion of the mind is of even more recent vintage—its origins should be traced to developments within the history of *empiricist* thought; (2) that the standard account fails to interest itself sufficiently in certain developments internal to the history of the modern notion of the *body*—the reason the mind/body problem has come to seem so intractable is that the ghost has received all the blame while the machine has escaped suspicion; and (3) that the direction of progress in our thought about the relation of mind to body lies in large measure in a *return* to Aristotle—a recovery of a moment in the history of thought prior to the rise of modern science. I will briefly review each of these claims.

Putnam suggests that the source of our contemporary puzzles about the nature of mind should in part be traced to the emergence of a

conception of mind according to which the paradigmatic mental phenomena are sensory. For Aristotle and Aquinas, it was reason *(nous)*
which was most unlike body, while sensation was held to be "clearly
on the side of matter and body". Descartes, according to the interpretation that Putnam favors, held that sensations were modes neither of
res cogitans nor *res extensa*, but of that organic unity known as the
human being (or, in Descartes's technical vocabulary, "the substantial
union of mind and body").[7] Sensations, Descartes thought, have a
dual ontological status, possessing both a corporeal and a mental aspect. In this respect, Descartes's conception appears to stand poised
halfway between that of Aristotle (who locates sensation firmly within
the body) and that of Hume (who locates it firmly within the mind).
Putnam argues that there is a sense, nonetheless, in which Descartes
should be placed squarely within "the tradition that goes back to Aristotle, the tradition of thinking of sensations as 'material.'" For the
features of sensation which most preoccupied the empiricists—for example, their affinity with images—belonged for Descartes to their corporeal aspect. For Descartes, insofar as they were considered under
this latter aspect, sensations were "material images in the body rather
than 'mental' phenomena in the Cartesian sense" (where the term
"Cartesian" is now taken by Putnam to name a conception of mind
Ryle opposes rather than one Descartes espouses). Thus our contemporary philosophical conception of the mind remains in the thrall of a
post-Cartesian "Cartesian" picture.

In this same essay, after reviewing some of his own earlier arguments for functionalism, Putnam writes:

> What interests me when I read the writing of my former self is how
> obvious it seemed to me that the mind/body problem concerned, in
> the first instance at least, *sensations*, and how the "usual arguments
> for dualism" were all arguments against identifying sensations with
> anything physical. Nor was I alone in this impression . . . Everybody
> "knew" the mind/body problem had to do with whether sensations
> were material or not. Obviously something had happened in philos-
> ophy—at least among English-speaking philosophers—between
> Descartes's time and ours to bring this about.

What happened? Without reviewing the steps by which Putnam arrives at his conclusion, let me jump to the end of the story. The real
villains turn out to be Berkeley and Hume:

Since British empiricism virtually identified the mind with images (or "ideas" as they were called in the seventeenth century), *we* have come to think of images as paradigmatically "mental," and—unless we are materialists—as immaterial . . .

Berkeley did not think the world consisted *only* of "ideas," however . . . There were, for Berkeley, also the *subjects* of the "ideas" . . . the world consists of "Spirits and their Ideas" . . . For Hume, however, a Spirit is nothing but a bundle of Ideas . . . With Hume's step of identifying the mind with a "collection" (that ambiguous word!) of sensations and feelings and images, the transformation of the mind/body problem into what I knew it as in 1960, and into what my teachers and my teachers' teachers knew it as, was complete.

The mind/body problem has become (among English-speaking philosophers) the problem of the relation of these apparently immaterial sensations (now thought of as the paradigm of the "mental") to the physical world.

After a brief interlude of relative lucidity, English-speaking philosophy, Putnam claims, "reverted to its traditional empiricist way of conceiving mind/body issues." The reversion was due to the advent of logical positivism (and the concomitant decline of idealism and pragmatism), the interlude of lucidity to the English-speaking world's first try at assimilating Kant's philosophy. Putnam credits Kant not only with launching a powerful *ad hominem* critique of the British empiricist tradition, but also with having addressed to that tradition "the central Kantian question." Putnam's first crack at formulating this question (in Chapter 1) runs as follows: if I confine myself to the sort of description of the nature of thought which is appropriate to a scientific discipline (such as empirical psychology)—that is, if I describe the phenomena as a sequence of representations ("images or words with certain causes and effects")—then how am I to discover that I am dealing with a *rational* being ("that I am dealing with something which has truth, value, freedom, and meaning, and not just causes and effects")? Later in this volume, Putnam reformulates "the central Kantian question" as follows: how can an investigation (say, into the nature of thought) which confines itself to examining the realm of natural law—that is, the realm of entities governed by lawlike relations of cause and effect—ever bring within its view the realm of freedom (the realm in which we act and think and mean what we say)?

As Putnam sees it, the crucial aspect of the shift from Aristotle's
conception of *psyche* to our present conception of mind is the shift in
the respective underlying conceptions of *nature*.[8] On the modern conception, the mind is anything but at home in the natural world. It has
been cut adrift and is in search of some form of accommodation. The
only place in the body where the mind might still seem to belong is "in
the head"—somewhere between the ears—but it can also seem as if
there isn't quite enough room in such cramped quarters for both it
and the brain. Aristotle's conception of nature, by contrast, is one in
which our mental capacities are at home—one according to which
body and mind "fit" together. Thus Martha Nussbaum and Putnam
(in "Changing Aristotle's Mind," Chapter 2) write: "The soul is not a
thing merely housed in the body; its doings are the doings of the body.
The only thing there is one natural thing . . . the soul's natural and
best home is in the body . . . It is not in the body as in a prison, nor is
it impeded by it from some better mode of cognition . . . The body's
matter fits it, *does its actions,* through and through."

At this point, some readers may find themselves thinking: however
difficult the questions may appear in their contemporary form, surely,
going back to Aristotle can't be the answer. As we all know, you can't
just turn back the clock. Myles Burnyeat has leveled a scholarly version of this charge against Nussbaum and Putnam.[9] Due to (what
Burnyeat presumes to be) their unfamiliarity with the truly alien (and
hopelessly pre-scientific) character of Aristotle's thought, Nussbaum
and Putnam seem to fail to realize that Aristotle cannot help them
with their dissatisfactions with contemporary philosophy of mind. In
particular, according to Burnyeat, they fail to realize (1) that Aristotle
cannot avail himself of the modern conception of nature; (2) that we
moderns, of course, cannot do without the modern conception of nature; (3) that the modern conception of nature cannot accommodate
Aristotle's conception of mind; and (4) that therefore we have no
choice but to "junk" Aristotle.[10] The second essay in this volume is a
response to Burnyeat. The strategy is essentially to reply (1) that a
good philosophy of mind doesn't need to presuppose an up-to-date
physics; (2) that thus we can accept Aristotle's views on the nature of
mind without undermining our commitment to modern physics; (3)
that the modern conception of nature cannot accommodate the *modern* conception of mind either; and (4) that the modern conception of
mind is forced on us not by the rise of modern science, but by a phil-

osophical understanding of what science has shown us—that the modern conception of nature (which is so inhospitable to mind) is the legacy not of modern science but of modern metaphysics.

Nussbaum and Putnam do indeed differ substantially with Burnyeat over some fundamental questions in the interpretation of Aristotle.[11] They attribute the crux of their dispute with him, however, not to differences over questions of scholarship, but rather to differences over questions of metaphysics. They take Burnyeat to be a victim of an endemic form of post-scientific common sense. They enter the following remark of Burnyeat's as evidence on behalf of this claim: "To be truly Aristotelian, we would have to stop believing that the emergence of life or mind requires explanation."[12] Nussbaum and Putnam's rebuttal takes the form of suggesting that Burnyeat's sense of the inappropriateness of looking for philosophical assistance from Aristotle is forced on him by (1) his conception of what we (sophisticated moderns) should be prepared to count as a real (that is, scientifically respectable) *explanation* of the "emergence of mind"; (2) his thinking that only a post-Aristotelian physics can supply the resources for "explanations" in this freighted sense of the word; and (3) his (British empiricist) assumption "that *of course* the 'emergence of mind' (as if it were clear what that is!) requires explanation." Nussbaum and Putnam locate the virtue of Aristotle's conception precisely in its ability to make such a project of "explaining" the "emergence of mind"—the necessity of which Burnyeat is so reluctant to stop believing in—no longer seem obligatory. Aristotle, on their reading, offers us a view of our powers of mind that no longer makes it seem puzzling that such powers are natural to us. Aristotle's "solution" to the problem takes the form of trying to show us that there is no problem of the sort which we imagined. But it may be thought that Nussbaum and Putnam manage here to sidestep one charge of anachronism only to face another. For Burnyeat's charge (that their reading of Aristotle requires him to have *per impossibile* mastered the teachings of modern physics) may seem to give way to the charge that, on their reading, Aristotle must have already mastered the teachings of the later Wittgenstein. This time, however, Nussbaum and Putnam plead guilty as charged: "We suggest that Aristotle's thought really is, properly understood, the fulfillment of Wittgenstein's desire to have a 'natural history of man' . . . As Aristotelians we do not discover something behind something else, a hidden reality behind the complex unity that we see and are. We find what we are in the appearances. And Aristotle tells us that if we attend properly to the appearances the dualist's questions never get going."

The modern conception of nature saddles us with an unbridgeable dualism of the mental and the physical, or—as Putnam tends to prefer to put it—of the intentional and the nonintentional. The response to this dualism which the essays in this volume are most concerned to criticize is the fashionable one of attempting to eradicate it by simply eliminating one of its two poles (that is, by attempting to reduce the intentional to the nonintentional). Putnam thinks that the varieties of this response currently available on the philosophical market tend simply to paper the problems over with sheaves of unfulfilled (and probably unfulfillable) promissory notes.[13] (Hence his enthusiasm for John Dewey's quip that the old soul/body or mind/body dualism still survives in a scientific age as a dualism between "the brain and the rest of the body.")[14] Philosophical reductionists tend to rush on to the stage promising to make the mind disappear by dissolving it in matter—by bringing it within the fold of (what Putnam, following McDowell, calls) "disenchanted nature"—but, at the end of the performance, we're left staring at the same props that were sitting on the stage at the outset.

Putnam sees the two most popular current trends in the philosophy of mind—reductionism and eliminativism—as instances of the characteristic way in which modern philosophy attempts to bridge a dualism by overcoming the appearance of a gulf.[15] Nussbaum and Putnam propose an alternative to these trends which they call "an Aristotelian attitude" to the problems:

> When the computer revolution burst upon the world, it was widely expected that computer models would clear up the nature of the various sorts of "intentional" phenomena. In effect, people expected that a reductive account of the various subheadings included under the chapter heading "intentionality" would sooner or later be given. Now that this has not proved so easy, some thinkers . . . are beginning to suggest that it is not so bad if this can't be done; intentionality is only a feature of "folk psychology" anyway. If a first-class scientific account of intentional facts and phenomena cannot be given, that is not because scientific reductionism is not the right line to take in metaphysics; rather it is because there is, so to speak, nothing here to reduce. The "Aristotelian" attitude, in the present context, is that both attitudes are mistaken; that intentionality won't be

reduced and won't go away . . . we can have nonreductionism and the explanatory priority of the intentional without losing that sense of the natural and organic unity of the intentional with its constitutive matter that is one of the great contributions of Aristotelian realism.

Putnam argues, later in this volume, that one source of our contemporary perplexities is our tendency to think of the mind as *inside* the head, as some kind of an *organ* with which we think. This leads to a picture in which the primary relation between mind and world is a causal one: the world first causally acts on the mind, providing it with mere (nonconceptual) sensory input, which the mind then processes into output of the appropriate (conceptualized) form. On this picture, there is always a gap between mind and world which stands in need of mediation: "this picture . . . is disastrous for just about every part of metaphysics and epistemology. The key element responsible for the disaster is the idea that there has to be an 'interface' between our conceptual powers and the external world; our conceptual powers cannot reach all the way to the objects to themselves."

Two of the chapters in this volume, "Realism without Absolutes" and "The Question of Realism," are concerned to argue for a conception of the relation of mind and world on which the appearance of such a gap—and hence the need for some mediating interface—need not arise in the first place. The first of these papers urges a philosophy of mind and language which does not leave us uncomfortable with the idea that the mind is not inside (or outside) the head. The essay's primary target is the assumption that "seeing an object is a two-part affair"—of which the first part occurs outside the head (as a physical interaction between the object, light rays and the eye), and the second part inside the head (as processing in the brain/mind). Part of the solution, Putnam urges, lies in seeing that the mind is implicated throughout the whole affair, and thus accommodating ourselves to a conception of mind on which "the mind is neither a material nor an immaterial organ but a system of capacities."[16] "The Question of Realism" urges a philosophy of perception and conception which does not leave us uncomfortable with the idea that our perceptual and conceptual powers "reach all the way to the objects themselves."[17] The second half of the paper takes a step in this direction by arguing against the assumption that "thinking is essentially a matter of manipulating symbols" (which have no intrinsic relation to what is outside the head). The first half of the paper, to which I will now turn, is concerned with why some contemporary philosophers have come to believe that "representing the world as it is" is something we cannot do. It is in these pages that Putnam distances himself most from his own earlier formulations of internal realism.

A Mirage of Impotence

The great difficulty here is not to represent the matter as if there were something one *couldn't* do.

> Ludwig Wittgenstein, *Philosophical Investigations*

Putnam's reasons for not wishing his arguments against a particular philosophical thesis to be construed as arguments in favor of its antithesis—his increasing reluctance to take sides in the current debates (between realists and antirealists, for example)—are perhaps most illuminatingly discussed in "The Question of Realism." The essay is in large measure a contribution to an ongoing effort on Putnam's part to distance himself from the views of Richard Rorty.

Both Putnam and Rorty have been concerned to criticize metaphysical realism on the grounds that it involves an illicit appeal to the idea that we can "stand back" from our current forms of thought and language—that we can, as Putnam was once fond of putting it, "step outside our skins"—and thereby compare our thought and language with the world (seen "from a God's-eye point of view") in order to ascertain whether the former adequately "represents" the latter. We should instead, Putnam has written, "accept the position we are fated to occupy":[18] one of being unable to "stand back" from our thought and language. This way of putting the matter encourages the idea that what we need to do is resign ourselves to our inability to surpass some limit (imposed on us by the nature of our thought or our language or our "practices")—a limit which metaphysical realism misguidedly imagines we can surpass. Thus Putnam has endeared himself to Rorty (and others) with pronouncements such as the following: "The important thing, it seems to me, is to find a picture that enables us to make sense of the phenomena from within our world and practice, rather than to seek a God's-eye view."[19]

Given his enthusiasm for such pronouncements (which can be found throughout Putnam's work), Rorty professes himself to "have long been puzzled" by what keeps him and Putnam apart. In a recent article (which is devoted to identifying the points at which he and Putnam diverge),[20] Rorty begins by listing—in the form of passages drawn from Putnam's work—five points on which he "wholeheartedly concurs with Putnam." Here, by way of a sample, are the first two passages which Rorty cites:

(1) Elements of what we call "language" or "mind" penetrate so deeply into what we call "reality" that the very project of representing ourselves as being "mappers of something language-independent" is fatally compromised from the start. Like Relativism, but in a different way, Realism is *an impossible attempt* to view the world from Nowhere [my emphasis].[21]

(2) [We should] accept the position we are fated to occupy in any case, the position of beings who *cannot have a view of the world* that does not reflect our interests and values, but who are, for all that, committed to regarding some views of the world—and, for that matter, some interests and values—as better than others [my emphasis].[22]

I have drawn attention to the idea, present in each of these passages, that the flaw in metaphysical realism lies in its attempting to do something "impossible"—in its striving after "a view of the world" which "we cannot have." Since Putnam is no longer fully able to concur with himself on either of these points (with which Rorty wholeheartedly concurs), he is able to locate the point at which he first begins to diverge from Rorty at an earlier juncture than Rorty himself does.

Putnam himself was formerly quite happy to express his rejection of metaphysical realism in terms of the idea that we run up against a certain kind of limit beyond which thought or language is unable to carry us—in terms therefore of an impossibility claim, a claim to the effect that there is something we *cannot* do. We cannot view the world in *this* way. Putnam formulates the putative impossibility in "The Question of Realism" as follows: It is impossible to stand outside our thought and language and compare our thought and language, on the one hand, with the world, on the other. This formulation seems to invite us to consider a particular possibility (viewing the world in this way, rather than some other way) and to conclude that *that* is something that cannot happen.

Putnam now wishes to identify this way of expressing one's rejection of metaphysical realism as already succumbing to the decisive move in the philosophical conjuring trick. Rorty's skepticism about the possibility of representation is a result of his failure to ponder what is at issue in his own talk of "impossibility":

> I think the trouble . . . comes when one does not properly explore the sort of "impossibility" which is at issue when one concludes—with Rorty—that such a guarantee is indeed impossible. What I want to emphasize is that Rorty moves from a conclusion about the unintelligibility of metaphysical realism (we cannot have a guarantee—of a sort that doesn't even make sense—that our words represent things outside of themselves) to a skepticism about the possibility of representation *tout court*. We are left with the conclusion that there is no metaphysically innocent way to say that our words *do* "represent things outside of themselves." Failing to inquire into the character of the unintelligibility which vitiates metaphysical realism, Rorty remains blind to the way in which his own rejection of metaphysical realism partakes of the same unintelligibility. The way in which skepticism is the flip side of a craving for an unintelligible kind of certainty (a senseless craving, one might say, but for all that a deeply human craving) has rarely been more sharply illustrated than by Rorty's complacent willingness to give up on the (platitudinous) idea that language can represent something which is outside of language.

We pass from the (metaphysical realist's) perception of us as being *able* to step outside of our skins to a perception of us as being *unable* to do so. We now see ourselves as forever sealed *within* our skins: confined, as it were, to *our* forms of language and thought. Rorty, Putnam now thinks, trades on such a sense of confinement (one which Putnam's own earlier formulations of "*internal* realism" helped to some extent to encourage).[23] This sense of confinement—of being trapped inside something (language, thought)—draws its life, Putnam now suggests, from the temptation to express the failure of metaphysical realism in terms of the idea that there is something we cannot do.

Putnam's overarching concern in "The Question of Realism" is to take issue with Rorty's claim that the collapse of metaphysical realism carries with it the moral that certain commonplace notions about representation—in particular, "the whole idea that our words and thoughts sometimes do and sometimes do not 'agree with' or 'correspond to' or 'represent' a reality outside themselves"—ought to be rejected as entirely empty.[24] The commonplace which Putnam is most concerned to rescue is the one Wittgenstein expresses as follows: "When we say, and *mean*, that such-and-such is the case, we—and our meaning—do not stop anywhere short of the fact."[25] Rorty can hear this remark—about our words not stopping anywhere short of the fact—only in the metaphysical realist's way. Putnam sees Rorty as representative of much contemporary philosophy in being unable to recover a (naive) pre-philosophical sense of the uses to which certain words (the ones most overworked in philosophy) can be meaningfully put in ordinary discourse—our sense (before we fell into philosophical perplexity) that thoughts can be about the world, that language can represent the world, that our beliefs can be justified by how things stand in the world. It can come to seem, after a little philosophy, that one can assent to such platitudes only if one does so advisedly when speaking with the vulgar[26] (strictly speaking, the world is well lost).[27] Putnam takes Rorty's inability to construe these platitudes in a metaphysically innocent way to be an indication that his thought continues to be controlled by the very picture he is concerned to reject.

In "A Comparison of Something with Something Else," Putnam also contests Rorty's claim that Rorty is following in Wittgenstein's footsteps:

> Wittgenstein never suggests that our ordinary ways of talking and thinking—our *ordinary* talk of "following a rule," or our *ordinary* talk of "seeing as," or our *ordinary* talk of "understanding"—are shown to be mere *mythology* by the fact that our accounts of what it is to follow a rule, or to see something as a duck, or to understand a sentence run thin . . . We walk on thin ground, but we do walk. Rorty, on the other hand, does suggest that even ordinary talk of objectivity, or rational acceptability, or truth is somehow mythological.[28]

Putnam sees the metaphysician as having hijacked words such as "language," "thought," and "world," depriving us of a clear view of the ways in which we ordinarily call upon them (when we're not under the pressure of philosophy). He quotes in this connection[29] Wittgenstein's remark that "if the words 'language,' 'experience,' 'world' have a use, it must be as humble a one as that of the words 'table,' 'lamp,' and 'door.'"[30] Putnam sees his aim as that of trying to recover the original humble uses of these words—the uses we are able to put them to before they become harnessed to the metaphysical stories we tell ourselves when we seek to answer questions such as "how does language hook on to the world?" Under the pressure of such a question, the connection between language and world takes on the appearance of a puzzling *achievement,* needing explanation; in giving such explanations, we are led to sublime the senses of our ordinary words. Thus Putnam writes in "The Question of Realism": "While I agree with Rorty that metaphysical realism is unintelligible, to stop at that point without going on to recover our ordinary notion of representation (and of a world of things to be represented) is to fail to complete that journey 'from the familiar to the familiar' that is the true task of philosophy."

On Putnam's view, what is representative about Rorty's way of rejecting metaphysical realism is his picture of what our philosophical options are; they are essentially exhausted by the following two choices (which Putnam finds equally unattractive): (1) rehabilitate some version of metaphysical realism, or (2) give up on the (naive) idea that beliefs can be justified by how things stand in the world (and opt for either some sort of coherence theory or some form of skepticism). Rorty opts for a version of (2). For Rorty, "representation" is the name of a metaphysically suspect relation between language and world. The only relation which Rorty is prepared to countenance between the world and sentences (or thoughts, or beliefs) is a causal one. Putnam wants to trace such an insistence (upon keeping thought and belief from entering into anything but causal relation with the world) to the idea that the collapse of metaphysical realism carries in its train a *discovery*—a discovery about the relations in which thought and world can and cannot stand to one another.

What conjures up the appearance that we have made an important discovery (about the nature of the relation of thought and world) is our inclination to express our rejection of metaphysical realism in the form of an opposing thesis. That is, we take ourselves to have discovered that metaphysical realism is *false;* thus we (naturally) conclude that its negation is true. Putnam believes he can now head off certain widespread misunderstandings concerning his own views (misunderstandings which he freely admits that he himself is partially responsible for encouraging) by drawing his reader's attention to *how* he wishes to express his rejection of metaphysical realism, questioning not its truth but rather its *intelligibility.*[31] If the problem with metaphysical realism is that in the end we find that we are unable to make sense of its thesis, then we should be equally unable to make sense of its antithesis. If we can rescue either member of the pair from unintelligibility we should be able to rescue its opposite number as well; if we wish to conclude that one member of the pair is unintelligible, we lack the option to affirm the truth of the other. "If the notion of an absolute point of view is unintelligible, then not being able to speak from the absolute point of view is no incapacity."[32]

Rorty professes to accept Putnam's arguments concerning the incoherence of metaphysical realism; but he goes on to formulate what these arguments show in terms of a very general claim about what we cannot do (compare thought and language, on the one hand, with the world, on the other). It is this transition—from a demonstration of the incoherence of a philosophical position (concerning the relation between thought and world) to a substantive eye-opening conclusion—which Putnam now seeks to call into question. Putnam's initial way of putting the worry in "The Question of Realism" takes the following form: "If we agree that it is *unintelligible* to say 'We sometimes succeed in comparing our language and thought with reality as it is in itself,' then we should realize that it is also unintelligible to say 'It is *impossible* to stand outside and compare our thought and language with the world.'" Putnam thinks he detects an ambivalence in Rorty's (and his own former) attitude to the central thesis of metaphysical realism. Putnam sees Rorty as wanting, on the one hand, to argue that what the metaphysical realist says is nonsense, and yet wanting, on the other hand, to be able to grasp the thought which the metaphysical realist is *attempting* to express—at least to be able to grasp it with sufficient clarity to draw substantive consequences from its failure. The crucial mistake here, from Putnam's point of view, is the idea that we can make out what it is that a piece of nonsense is trying to say (if it were only able to say it). If Rorty really were able to grasp the thought behind metaphysical realism sufficiently clearly to be able to draw substantive consequences from its failure, then clearly it would not be nonsense. Conversely, if what the metaphysical realist is trying to say really is *unintelligible,* then nothing follows (from the fact that it is empty) about what kinds of things are or are not possible. Putnam summarizes this point in "The Question of Realism" as follows: "Rorty seems to be telling us of an Impotence, in the way the physicist tells us of an Impotence when he says 'You can't build a perpetual motion machine,' but it turns out on examination that the Impotence is a mirage, or even less than a mirage—that it is chimerical."

As long as we continue to conceive of the failure of metaphysical

realism in terms of our *inability* to attain a certain ("non-perspectival") standpoint, we continue "to remain in the grip of the metaphysical realist's picture" (even if we imagine that we are rejecting it).

Rorty, however, may seem to be less open now to an objection of
this form from Putnam than he perhaps once was. For Rorty has
become increasingly disinclined to formulate the charge against metaphysical realism in terms of a complaint about its intelligibility.
He has moved instead to expressing the issue in terms of whether realism presents us with a vocabulary which enables us to "cope better"
or not:

> I should not speak, as I sometimes have, of "pseudo-problems," but
> rather of problematics and vocabularies that might have proven to
> be of value, but in fact did not. I should not have spoken of "unreal"
> or "confused" philosophical distinctions, but rather of distinctions
> whose employment has proved to lead nowhere, proved to be more
> trouble than they were worth. For pragmatists like Putnam and me,
> the question should always be "What use is it?" rather than . . . "Is
> it confused?" Criticism of other philosophers' distinctions and prob-
> lematics should charge relative inutility, rather than "meaningless-
> ness" or "illusion" or "incoherence."[33]

To charge the metaphysical realist's conception (of what it would be
to represent the world as it is) with relative inutility, as Rorty now
proposes, would seem to presuppose its intelligibility. It makes sense
to dismiss something on such a ground only if one has first ascertained
what "it" is. Ordinarily, when one responsibly levels such a charge,
one takes oneself to know what has been proposed (for example, representing the world in such-and-such a way) and to have concluded
that it is *that* which one deems lacking in utility. Such a charge presupposes the applicability of the question: In what respect is the item in
question lacking in utility? (Rorty seems to want to answer here: Let's
not worry about exactly how it is lacking in utility; it is just lacking in
utility *altogether,* so let's move on to something else. But such a response seems to cut the concept of "utility" free from its ordinary
moorings. It appears to be functioning as a mere pretext for drawing
the conclusion Rorty is after anyway.) If what the metaphysical
realist's vocabulary brought to light (contrary to his original inten-
tions) was that we really cannot do something which we would like to
do (and which it does make sense to think we might be able to do), it

is not evident that the distastefulness of this insight would, in and of itself, constitute a sufficient reason for rejecting the vocabulary which made this insight available. If the point is a *fully intelligible* one—if what has been brought to light is a *genuine* impotence—we need to understand why we should blind ourselves to this discovery and deprive ourselves of the resources for expressing it. Our simply finding a discovery inconvenient or oppressive is not generally considered an intellectually defensible reason for wishing no longer to attend to it. Its "lacking in utility" (whatever that means) might be such a reason. But when Rorty turns to the task of giving principled reasons for being suspicious of metaphysical realism, considerations of relative utility do not seem to be what is at issue. Rorty's original disenchantment with metaphysical realism, in his earlier writings—and not obviously *only* his earlier writings[34]—was expressed in the light of an appreciation of the confused character of its demand (that we be able to represent the world in a certain way)—a sense, on Rorty's part, that there was something wrong with this demand.[35] Rorty now wants a way of dismissing metaphysical realism that does not even commit him to the claim that it is in some way "confused." He now just wants to be able to conclude—through a vague appeal to what helps us "cope better"—that, since the vocabulary of the metaphysical realist forces us into a skeptical problematic (the upshot of which is that "we cannot represent the world as it is"), we are better off chucking that vocabulary altogether.

From Putnam's point of view, this is progress in the wrong direction. To cite "relative inutility" as one's reason for eliminating the term "representation" from one's lexicon, as Rorty now does, is to fail to explore the character of the frustrations it seemed to impose on us. It is the expression of a desire to just run away from the whole irritating issue as fast as possible, so that one doesn't have to think about it any more. The presumption behind such an approach is that the best direction in which to run will be the one which allows one to get as far away as possible from the terms—the "vocabulary"—of the original problem. The reason such impatience is philosophically disastrous, Putnam thinks, is that the problem lies not simply with the "vocabulary" of the metaphysical realist, but with what becomes of that vocabulary in his hands. Rorty continues to allow the metaphysical realist to hold the concept of representation hostage to certain ("metaphysically inflated") demands and then—despairing of a satisfying outcome to the metaphysical realist's demands—gives up on the ordi-

nary concept along with its metaphysically sublimed counterpart. For
Putnam, any satisfying diagnosis of both what is compelling and what
is confused about metaphysical realism requires an appreciation of
how the metaphysical realist's employment of the concept of representation superficially mimics the grammar of the ordinary concept while
completely draining it of its content. A recovery of the ordinary concept depends upon seeing how the metaphysical realist only appears
to continue to employ that concept meaningfully. An insight into the
emptiness of metaphysical realism is therefore, for Putnam, the only
way to escape its seductive coils. Only when metaphysical realism has
been made to disappear completely does it cease to cast a shadow.

Putnam thus traces Rorty's inclination to give up on the whole idea
of representation to the hold that the metaphysical realist's picture
continues to exert on him even as he tries to escape from it. In "The
Question of Realism," as part of an attempt to diagnose where he
thinks Rorty goes wrong, Putnam suggests that Rorty and the metaphysical realist share a certain "craving": "Why is Rorty so bothered
by the lack of a *guarantee* that our words represent things outside of
themselves? Evidently, Rorty's craving for such a guarantee is so
strong that, finding the guarantee to be 'impossible,' he feels forced to
conclude that our words don't represent anything. It is at this point in
Rorty's position that one detects the trace of a disappointed metaphysical realist impulse." This is tied to a refrain which runs throughout the essays collected here: "Metaphysics . . . frequently appears
disguised as the rejection of metaphysics."[36] The essays in this volume
devoted to logical positivism (in Part II) and to contemporary trends
in philosophy inspired by cognitive science (in Part VI) are largely concerned to document various instances of metaphysics disguised as the
overcoming of metaphysics. Putnam suggests, at a number of junc-
tures, that this remarkable robustness of metaphysics—its capacity to
return to life and haunt its undertakers—is due to the depth of a craving which expresses itself through the metaphysical impulse: "a craving for an unintelligible kind of certainty (a senseless craving, one
might say, but for all that a deeply human craving)." Putnam calls this
craving a form of "intellectual yearning" which is "deeply rooted" in
us. Whatever one thinks about this as a claim about *us,* it is difficult
not to credit Putnam's claim that he finds this craving to be deeply
rooted in himself. His attitude toward the craving seems to be as ambivalent as it is complex, regarding it with both respect and suspi-

cion—as the expression of something noble in the human spirit, and as the wellspring of persistent deep confusion.

Neither Naked nor Dressed

One can . . . say that "I shall know a good solution when I see it"— and in that respect . . . [philosophical] problems are like riddles . . . I can recognize, even before I have . . . a way of deciding . . . such questions (and in that way fixing their sense), that . . . [some proposed answer] is *not* the answer. But *what* it's not, is only as yet a form of words. The rejection of an answer, like the question itself, seems not quite to grasp its own sense, seems to exist, as it were, on borrowed sense, on an advance from the solution to the problem.
Cora Diamond, "Riddles and Anselm's Riddle"

Of the essays collected here, the one which represents the most striking departure in Putnam's recent thought is probably "Rethinking Mathematical Necessity" (Chapter 12).

In a previous striking departure from his earlier views, in a paper entitled "There Is at Least One A Priori Truth,"[37] Putnam had sought to argue that there are, after all, a priori truths (in exactly the sense that a still earlier Putnam and W. V. Quine had famously been concerned to deny that there could be). At least one truth is unrevisable, Putnam declared, in the sense that it would never be rational to give it up. Putnam's candidate for such an a priori truth was the minimal principle of contradiction, the principle that not every statement is both true and false. Putnam's strategy was to try to argue that there are no circumstances under which it would be rational to give up this principle, and therefore that it provides us with an example of at least one "absolutely, unconditionally, truly, actually a priori truth."[38] Putnam adduced in the course of the paper a number of arguments[39] purporting to show that the principle of minimal contradiction plays a role in our reasoning which is "prior to anything that might be offered as an explanation of its truth," and hence also prior to anything which might count against its truth.[40] Putnam had been concerned to argue therefore that at least one logical law (the minimal principle of contradiction) represented an absolutely unrevisable a priori truth. Putnam has, in this volume, continued to retain his hostility to the idea that the laws of logic are simply empirical truths, but he has substantially modified his strategy for arguing against such an idea. In "Rethinking Mathematical Necessity," Putnam now wishes to claim that the question whether such a principle (for example, the minimal principle of contradiction) can be revised or not is one which we are simply unable to make any clear sense of.[41]

In "Rethinking Mathematical Necessity," Putnam asks us to consider the following riddle: "A court lady once fell into disfavor with the king. (One easily imagines how.) The king, intending to give her a command impossible of fulfillment, told her to come to the Royal Ball 'neither naked nor dressed.'"[42] Putnam goes on to divulge the solution to the riddle (she came wearing a fishnet) and to ask us to compare it to certain philosophical questions (concerning the revisability of the laws of logic). He then goes on to remark: "Concerning such riddles, Wittgenstein says that we are able to give them a sense only after we know the solution; the solution bestows a sense on the riddle-question. This seems right."[43] This remark comes at the end of a paper in which Putnam attempts to distance himself from some of Quine's views (another abiding preoccupation of this volume as a whole) and in which he advances some rather surprising claims—some unorthodox interpretive claims about how to understand a tradition of thought about logic, as well as some provocative philosophical claims about what is involved in attempting to think the negation of a logical truth. His concern here is to attack the view (which he and Quine made popular) that the laws of logic are—at least in principle—revisable and to defend a conception of logical necessity which he (now) claims to find in later Wittgenstein.

Putnam says at the outset of the paper that he presently sees contemporary philosophy as faced with two equally unsatisfying alternatives—alternatives he associates with the names of Carnap and Quine, respectively: a linguistic conventionalism, on the one hand, according to which the laws of logic are analytic truths, and a naturalized epistemology, on the other, according to which they are synthetic a posteriori and hence not dissimilar in kind to ordinary empirical truths (only—so the mixed metaphor goes—far more deeply entrenched in our web of belief). After canvassing these standing alternatives, Putnam turns his attention to what he calls "a very different line of thinking—one which goes back to Kant and Frege." He continues: "This line is one I believe Carnap hoped to detranscendentalize; and in Carnap's hands it turned into linguistic conventionalism. My strategy in this essay will be to suggest that there is a different way of stripping away the transcendental baggage, while retaining what I hope is the insight in Kant's and perhaps Frege's view, a way which has features in common with the philosophy of the later Wittgenstein rather than with Carnap."

The paper is typical of a number of the essays in this volume in seeking to offer a heterodox account of some chapter drawn from the recent history of philosophy, not only in order to set the historical record straight, but also out of the conviction that important philosophical lessons remain hidden from view by Whiggish textbook accounts of philosophy's recent past. Elsewhere in this volume, Putnam tries to rescue Peirce, James, Dewey, and Reichenbach from the fate of having to remain the figures who—according to historians of philosophy's recent past—they're supposed to be. In each case, Putnam's revisionist reading comes with a philosophical punchline he wishes to commend to our attention. "Rethinking Mathematical Necessity" is, however, perhaps the most ambitious of these revisionist exercises, in that (at least with respect to their thought about logic) Putnam wants to redraw the portraits of four different philosophers: Kant, Frege, early Wittgenstein, and later Wittgenstein. More specifically, Putnam's aim is to try to trace the roots of Wittgenstein's later views on the nature of "grammatical propositions" through a tradition of thought about logic which begins with Kant and runs through Frege and the *Tractatus*. This is how Putnam outlines the first part of the story he wants to tell:

> What interests me . . . is to be found in *The Critique of Pure Reason* . . . as well as in Kant's *Logic,* and that is the repeated insistence that illogical thought is not, properly speaking, thought at all . . .
>
> It is this that brought home to me the deep difference between an *ontological* conception of logic, a conception of logic as descriptive of some domain of actual and possible entities, and Kant's (and, I believe, Frege's) conception. Logic is not a description of what holds true in "metaphysically possible worlds" . . . It is a doctrine of *the form of coherent thought.* Even if I think of what turns out to be a "metaphysically impossible world," my thought would not be a thought at all unless it conforms to logic.
>
> Indeed, logic has no metaphysical presuppositions at all. For to say that thought, in the normative sense of *judgment which is capable of truth,* necessarily conforms to logic is not to say something which a metaphysics has to *explain.* To explain anything *presupposes* logic; for Kant, logic is simply prior to all rational activity.

Putnam then goes on to trace this conception of logic (as the form of coherent thought) through Frege, the *Tractatus,* and the later

Wittgenstein. We are thus offered a capsule history of an entire tradition of philosophical thought about logic—one which Putnam thinks has been unjustly neglected (despite the prestige of its original proponents). The historical component of the essay can be summarized in the following seven claims: (1) Kant held that illogical thought is not, properly speaking, a kind of thought at all; (2) Frege inherited this view from Kant; he held that the laws of logic prescribe "the way in which one ought to think if one is to think at all";[44] (3) Frege held another view of logic as well—one according to which the laws of logic are the most general laws of nature; (4) these two views of logic are in tension with one another; (5) the early Wittgenstein's view (that the propositions of logic are *sinnlos*) should be read as attempting to resolve this fundamental instability in Frege's philosophy;[45] (6) the *Tractatus* shows that Kant's and Frege's formulations of the Kantian insight (that illogical thought is impossible) do not meet the conditions which they themselves wish to impose on coherent thought; and (7) Wittgenstein's early and later works represent different attempts to address and resolve this problem.

After developing these historical claims, Putnam goes on to propose that there is an important idea which is developed and refined within this tradition of thought which he himself wants to argue for—the idea that logical truths do not have negations that we are able to understand. The negation of a logical proposition involves a form of words which presents us with a mere appearance of sense. It is not that such "propositions" present us with a coherent thought that we are able to grasp and then reject as false; rather, "we are simply unable to make sense" of these propositions. We are unable to formulate them in such a way as to allow the question of their truth or falsity to arise.[46] As Putnam puts it at one point: "the negation of a theorem of logic violates the conditions for being a thinkable thought or judgment."[47] Putnam says he wants to follow the later Wittgenstein in trying to tease this idea free from its original setting in Kant's and Frege's ("metaphysically inflated") accounts of the unrevisability of the laws of logic:

> My suggestion is not . . . that we retain . . . [the] idea of a nature of thought (or judgment, or the ideal language) which metaphysically guarantees the unrevisability of logic. But what I *am* inclined to keep from this story is the idea that logical truths do not have negations

that we (presently) understand. It is not, on this less metaphysically inflated story, that we can say that the theorems of logic are "unrevisable"; it is that the question "Are they revisable?" is one which we have not yet succeeded in giving a sense.

Putnam, following up certain suggestions of Cora Diamond's, thinks we should compare the question "Are the laws of logic revisable" to the king's command to the court lady that she appear before him "neither naked nor dressed." We are only able to give the king's words a sense once we know the solution to the riddle. Similarly, Putnam wants to say of the question "Are the laws of logic revisable?" that it too seems not quite to grasp its own sense.[48] Its sense is "borrowed," as Cora Diamond puts it, "on an advance from the solution"—on an advance, that is, from the specification of a wider setting which enables us to discern a pattern of sense in the riddle's question (and thus determine *what* question it is that these words form). When we first hear them, the words of the riddle—as they stand—appear to enunciate a paradox. A good solution gratifies us by dissipating the sense of paradox. We recognize the solution to a riddle by its capacity to suddenly make sense of what appeared to be (and, in a sense, until that moment, was) nonsense. For something to count as a solution it has to fit snugly into place and gratify our expectation that this was what these words were trying to express all along. This is just what Putnam thinks we have not yet succeeded in doing for our philosophical talk about "revising" logic: "A question may not have a sense . . . until an 'answer' gives it a sense, ... I want to suggest that, in the same way, saying that logic may be 'revised' does not have a sense, and will never have a sense, unless some concrete piece of theory building or applying *gives* it a sense."

There is a parallel here between Putnam's criticisms of Quine's (and his own former) views about logical necessity and his criticisms of Rorty's (and his own former) views about metaphysical realism. In both cases, Putnam wants to show how an apparently exciting philosophical thesis—about the *impossibility* of doing one thing (representing the world as it is in itself) or the *possibility* of doing another (revising a law of logic)—borrows its aura of intelligibility from the very position it wishes to reject as unintelligible. Putnam quotes the following famous remark (about the revisability of the laws of logic): "Any statement can be held true come what may, if we make drastic enough adjustments elsewhere in the system. Even a statement close to the periphery can be held true in the face of recalcitrant experience by pleading hallucination or by amending certain statements of the kind called logical laws. Conversely, by the same token, no statement is immune to revision."[49] In the closing pages of "Rethinking Mathematical Necessity" Putnam argues that the "cans" in these famous sentences of Quine's "are not intelligible 'cans.'" If Rorty's postulation of an inability on our part derives from a mirage of the impotence of human knowledge (to transcend the conditions of thought or language), Quine's postulation of an ability on our part (to revise the laws of logic) derives from a mirage of the omnipotence of future experience (to overturn *any* statement). As things stand, we have no clearer conception of what it would be to entertain the falsity of a logical law, Putnam thinks, than we have of what it would be to view the world from a God's-eye point of view—not because the laws of logic are "unrevisable," but because we have not yet given sense to our talk of "revisability" in this context. We have heard the riddle many times, but we have yet to hear something which has that power to dissipate the appearance of paradox which is the touchstone of a good solution.

The Interpretation of Wittgenstein

For Wittgenstein, philosophy comes to grief not in denying what we all know to be true, but in its effort to escape those human forms of life which alone provide the coherence of our expression. He wishes an acknowledgment of human limitation which does not leave us chafed by our own skin, by a sense of powerlessness to penetrate beyond the human conditions of knowledge.

Stanley Cavell, "The Availability
of Wittgenstein's Later Philosophy"

The one philosopher whose name occurs at some point or other in almost every essay in this volume is Wittgenstein. Often Putnam will digress from the main argument of an essay for a paragraph or two in order to clear up some point about the interpretation of Wittgenstein's thought. Putnam's dissatisfaction with the standard interpretations of Wittgenstein is tied to his sense that Wittgenstein seeks a form of "acknowledgment of human limitation" which is not haunted by *skepticism*.

Putnam—employing a terminology which is bound at first to confuse some readers—suggests that, from Wittgenstein's point of view, philosophers such as Rorty, Quine, Carnap, and Donald Davidson (all of whom, each in their own way, take themselves to be attempting to defeat skepticism) are really at bottom advocating *"forms* of skepticism." Skepticism, in this sense, is an instance of what Putnam calls a *metaphysical picture*—one which he sees informing not only the classical forms of philosophical despair over the possibility of knowledge (conventionally known as "skepticism"), but equally the various classical (and often mutually opposed) strategies of allaying that despair (such as rationalism and empiricism, foundationalism and coherentism, and so forth). Putnam takes skepticism, employing here a terminology which he borrows from Cavell, to be the expression of a natural human disappointment with the reach of knowledge. Putnam sees the position of thinkers such as Rorty (who insists upon our confinement within—our fatedness to—*merely* human forms of knowledge) as marked by such a sense of disappointment. Here is Putnam's explanation of Cavell's use of the term "skepticism":

> In the conventional usage, skepticism is the denial of knowledge. It is traditionally supposed to be easy to tell who is and who isn't a skeptic (the skeptic says, "You don't have any knowledge," or "You don't know what is going on in any one else's mind," or "You don't have any empirical knowledge," right?); and traditional metaphysical realism and positivism are seen as alternative *answers* to skepticism. How can answering skepticism be tantamount to skepticism? In the case of positivism, it is not hard to see how. The positivist's strategy can be described thus: *to concede the correctness of almost everything the skeptic says* (e.g., we don't have any moral knowledge, we don't know anything about other people except their behavior, we don't know that there are any objects except our own sense-data and constructions therefrom) in the hope of keeping back from the skeptic the claim to some minimal sort of "scientific knowledge." In the case of metaphysical realism, it is true that we are alleged to know more than the skeptic (in the conventional sense of the term) or the positivist would admit that we know, but this knowledge . . . is knowledge of a "true world" which has little resemblance to our quotidian world of common sense objects and fellow passengers to the grave. In sum, both the "skeptic" and his "opponents" deny the primacy and reality (or better, the primacy of the reality) of the life world. The ordinary human world is what they are one and all skeptics about; skepticism . . . is a perpetual dissatisfaction with

the human position . . . It is this downgrading of the human position, this aspiration to be outside our own skins . . . that Cavell calls "skepticism."[50]

Putnam sees Cavell's use of the term "skepticism" as helping to highlight the difference between two alternative ways of acknowledging human limitation: the metaphysician's way (which leaves us feeling there is something we cannot do—we cannot step outside our own skins) and Wittgenstein's way (which seeks to leave us not feeling "chafed by our own skin," haunted by "a sense of powerlessness to penetrate beyond the human conditions of knowledge"). On this reading of Wittgenstein, what is most significant is the perception— shared by both the traditional skeptic and the antiskeptic—that our natural state is one of being sealed within our skins. (Where the traditional skeptic and antiskeptic differ is over how incurable our natural condition of confinement is.)

The readings of (both early and later) Wittgenstein which Putnam (now) wishes to take issue with are all readings which understand Wittgenstein to be calling upon us to acknowledge the existence of certain *limits* (the limits imposed on thought by the logical structure of language, or the limits imposed on knowledge by the contingent nature of our forms of life). Wittgenstein (according to the readings Putnam opposes) shows us how to acquiesce in—rather than chafe against—these limits. Most of the readings of Wittgenstein which are presently in circulation (however much they may otherwise differ from one another) are of this variety, counseling us to resign ourselves to our inability to transcend the conditions of human knowledge. The readings of Wittgenstein's *Tractatus* and *Philosophical Investigations* that Putnam himself (now) urges are ones which take Wittgenstein to be concerned to show that the limit against which, in our philosophizing, we (imagine ourselves to) chafe is an illusory limit. On this reading of Wittgenstein (as Putnam puts it in "The Question of Realism"), "we cannot know the world as it is 'in itself' . . . not because the 'in itself' is an unreachable limit, but because the 'in itself' doesn't make sense."

Toward the end of Chapter 12, "Rethinking Mathematical Necessity," Putnam writes: "If it makes no sense to say or think that we have discovered that . . . [logic] is *wrong*, then it also makes no sense to offer a reason for thinking it is not wrong. A reason for thinking . . . [logic] is not wrong is a reason which excludes nothing. Trying to justify . . . [logic] is like trying to say that whereof one cannot speak thereof one must be silent; in both cases, it only looks as if something is being ruled out or avoided." Putnam here connects the central topic of "Rethinking Mathematical Necessity" (is illogical thought a kind of thought?) with the question how one should interpret the famous closing line of the *Tractatus:* "Whereof one cannot speak, thereof one must be silent." Putnam suggests that that line should not be read as debarring us from being able to say something. It should not be read as telling us that there is something we cannot do—a limit we cannot overstep. The contrapositive of that line is: "Whereof one may speak, thereof one can speak."[51] Putnam's reading of the line therefore suggests that if we are faced with a silence at the end of the book, this is so simply because (although there has been a great deal of noise) nothing has been said. Proponents of the standard reading of the *Tractatus* take the silence which is alluded to here to be one that guards the ineffable. What Wittgenstein is here drawing our attention to, they tell us, is the unsayable. These commentators hear this line (which speaks of silence) noisily declaring a substantive thesis: there are certain things which cannot be said and concerning them we must remain silent. What Putnam hears this line calling our attention to is: a silence.

Here is how Putnam (in Chapter 3) characterizes "the special kind of distance that the Wittgenstein of the *Tractatus* puts between himself and his own propositions":

> Wittgenstein tells us, both in his prefatory remarks and at the end of the *Tractatus,* that his own theory is nonsense (*unsinn*), and although some have seen this repudiation as weakened, if not altogether cancelled, by the Tractarian claim that there are things that one can "show" but not "say" . . . , others have argued (correctly to my mind) that it is an overuse of the "say/show" distinction to hold that the metaphysical propositions of the *Tractatus* are, at the end of the day, really supposed to express truths, or even thinkable thoughts.

On the reading of the *Tractatus* which Putnam favors, what happens is *not* that we (1) succeed in conceiving of an extraordinary possibility (illogical thought), (2) judge "it" to be impossible, (3) conclude that the truth of this judgment cannot be accommodated within (the logical structure of) language because it is about (the logical structure of) language, and (4) go on to communicate these discoveries—by putting into words (under the guise of only "showing" and not "saying" "it") just what it is that cannot be said. Rather, what happens is that we are lured up all four of these rungs of the ladder and then: (5) urged to throw the *entire* ladder (all four of the previous rungs) away. On this reading, first we grasp that there is something which cannot be; then we see that it (that which we grasped concerning what can and what cannot be) cannot be said; then we grasp that if it can't be said it can't be thought (that the limits of language are the limits of thought); then we grasp that there is no "it" in our grasp (that that which we cannot think we cannot "grasp" either). The ladder we climb is one which draws us into an illusion of occupying a certain sort of a perspective— a perspective from which we take ourselves to be able to survey the possibilities which undergird how things are with us, holding our ne- cessities in place—a perspective from which we can view the logical structure of the world "from sideways on."[52] But the point of the work as a whole is to show us—that is, to lead us up a ladder from the top of which we are able to see—that the "perspective" that we thus occupy is only an illusion of a perspective. So the only "insight" that the work imparts to its reader, in the end, is one about the reader himself: that he is prone to such illusions.[53]

Elsewhere in this volume one finds equally concrete suggestions about how one should read later Wittgenstein. In Chapter 13 Putnam picks a quarrel with the (widely accepted) view that in *Philosophical Investigations* Wittgenstein advances a "use-theory of meaning." Put- nam points out that in the famous passage in which Wittgenstein is supposed to have identified meaning with use what Wittgenstein actu- ally says is: "For a *large* class of cases—though not for all—in which we employ the word 'meaning' it can be defined thus: the meaning of a word is its use in the language."[54] Putnam then goes on to declare that it is a misreading of this (or any other) remark of Wittgenstein's to interpret it as proposing a theory of meaning: "The famous remark that, in a large class of cases, we may say that the meaning of a word is its use in the language is not a *theory* of meaning (although it is the expression of a point of view from which one can question whether it makes sense to ask for a 'theory of meaning,' in any sense in which a 'theory of meaning' might be metaphysically informative)." There is an evident parallel between the readings Putnam favors of the *Tractatus* and of the *Investigations:* in each case, the "theory" which has been attributed to the work (by most commentators) constitutes precisely the philosophical point of view which the work is most concerned to undermine. The commentators have mistaken the bait for the hook: the "theory" (which has been attributed to the work) is, indeed, according to Putnam, *in play* in the work—not as its doctrine, but as an expression of the philosophical temptation which the work as a whole seeks to enable us to overcome.

There is a sense therefore in which Putnam thinks that the bulk of the contemporary secondary literature on Wittgenstein has simply failed to encounter Wittgenstein's thought. His complaints about this body of secondary literature are perhaps most emphatic in Chapter 13. Putnam there discusses a cluster of interpretations of Wittgenstein's later work (variants of which were first proposed by Michael Dummett and Saul Kripke) which take Wittgenstein's interest in what he calls "language-games" to be an attempt to supplant truth conditions with assertibility conditions as the fundamental concept of a theory of meaning. Two recent versions of such an interpretation, those of Paul Horwich and Michael Williams, are accused of offering what Putnam calls a "positivist interpretation" of Wittgenstein:

> On Horwich's view, as on Williams', a language-game is to be understood as consisting of sentences for which . . . there are "assertibility conditions." These conditions specify that under certain observable conditions a sentence counts as true or at least "confirmed." (Think of these conditions as stipulating that under certain observable conditions we are allowed to utter certain noises, or write certain marks, and also to expect certain observable events or certain reactions from others . . . The key idea (as in positivism) is that if you know under what conditions a statement is confirmed, you understand the statement . . .
>
> The assumption that underlies this picture is that the use of words can be described in terms of what speakers are allowed to say and do in observable situations. "Use" is a theoretical notion, and there is a standard way of describing the use of expressions in an arbitrary language-game. Let me call this *the positivistic interpretation of Wittgenstein.* A very different interpretation . . . is the following: the use of the words in a language-game cannot be described without using concepts which are related to the concepts employed *in* the game . . .
>
> *Understanding a language-game is sharing a form of life.* And forms of life cannot be described in a fixed positivistic metalanguage,

whether they be scientific, religious, or of a kind that we do not have
in Western industrial societies today.

Putnam wants to argue that Wittgenstein's interest in investigating
(what *Philosophical Investigations* calls) "the use of concepts" is not
to be interpreted as an interest in providing a reductive naturalistic
description of human linguistic activity (in terms of, say, dispositions
to produce marks or noises under specifiable circumstances). On
Putnam's reading, Wittgenstein's aim is, on the contrary, to try to help
us to see what it is (about thought or language) that inevitably eludes
the grasp of such a description.

Here, once again, Putnam sees Wittgenstein as following in Frege's
footsteps. Thus, in Chapter 16, we find Putnam saying that contemporary attempts to naturalize the notions of truth and meaning are vul-
nerable to the very same arguments "that Frege deployed against the
naturalism and empiricism of *his* day." Frege is concerned to argue
against someone he calls "the psychologistic philosopher of logic."
The psychologistic philosopher of logic maintains that the laws of
logic are empirically established generalizations about our inferential
habits. The sense in which it is "impossible" for us to deny a law of
logic is construed on this account as a psychological fact about us: we
cannot help but think in this way. Frege wants to show the psychologistic logician that his account is unable to make sense of the
idea that two judgments can *disagree* with each other. This is how
Putnam (in Chapter 16) summarizes Frege's argument against the psychologistic logician's account: "On such an account, we cannot genuinely disagree with each other: if I produce a noise and you produce
the noise 'No, that's wrong,' then we have no more disagreed with
each other than if I produce a noise and you produce a groan or a
grunt. Nor can we agree with each other any more than we can disagree with each other: if I produce a noise and you produce the same
noise, then this is no more *agreement* than if a bough creaks and then
another creaks in the same way."[55] Frege's argument against the psychologistic logician flows from his commitment to the Kantian conception of logic—for which Putnam confesses much fondness in
Chapter 12—which holds that the laws of logic set forth the most
general principles of thought (which prescribe how we must think if
we are to think at all). The possibility of judgment, on Frege's (Kantian) account, is tied to the ability to discern relations of agreement
and disagreement between propositions; and it is the principles of

logic which provide the framework within which such discernment operates. The underlying claim which fuels Frege's argument[56] is that one can recognize two judgments as being in conflict with each other only if the framework of logic is already firmly in place: the criteria by which we are able so much as to recognize (let alone adjudicate) an instance of disagreement presuppose the availability of this shared framework. The psychologistic logician's employment of the notion of "disagreement" is one in which the ordinary notion of "disagreement" must be drained of virtually all its sense. The psychologistic logician (if he does not wish to presuppose the very notion of "logical contradiction" which he is attempting to explain) must restrict himself to a notion of "disagreement" according to which disagreement is simply some form of causal incompatibility, that is, a species of difference which does not in any way involve the idea of *logical* conflict. But if the noises we and others make merely differ from (or are merely causally incompatible with) one another (and nothing further concerning their logical relation to one another can be said), then they are no more in disagreement with one another than are the moos of two different cows or the shapes of two different snowflakes. As long as his account labors under this restriction, the psychologistic logician has deprived himself of the resources for discerning *any* sort of logical structure in our utterances. The only sort of structure which such an empirical (psychological) investigation can hope to uncover is a structure of *causal* (as opposed to logical) relations. The psychologistic logician, Frege concludes, is unable to bring within his view the activity of judgment; all he can study are the relations which obtain among the various marks and noises we make.[57]

Putnam sees the later Wittgenstein as accepting the spirit of this argument while altering the letter of it. The Fregean claim which Wittgenstein accepts is that any purely "naturalistic"[58] account of thought (or language) will simply drain thought (or language) of its normative resources (for example, its capacity to express agreement and disagreement), leaving us (as the psychologistic logician does) with a structure of marks or noises in which we are unable to discern the expression of a judgment. The letter of Frege's argument, however, undergoes some modification. Putnam sees talk about "the fundamental nature of the laws of logic"—as that which provides the framework within which agreement and disagreement are possible— giving way, in the later Wittgenstein, to talk about "sharing a form of life." Thus Putnam is able to take Wittgenstein's famous remark that "to imagine a language-game means to imagine a form of life"[59] to be directed against the very conception of what a language-game is (a game of making noises in certain observable circumstances), which serves as the point of departure for the standard (Dummett/Kripke) interpretation of the *Investigations*. What belongs to a language-game, for Wittgenstein, is not simply the sounds we utter in certain isolated circumstances; rather "what belongs to a language-game is a whole culture."[60]

Pictures and Philosophy

It is true that we can compare a picture that is firmly rooted in us to a superstition; but it is equally true that we always eventually have to reach some firm ground, either a picture or something else, so that a picture which is at the root of all our thinking is to be respected and not treated as a superstition.

Ludwig Wittgenstein, *Culture and Value*

In Chapter 8, "Pragmatism and Moral Objectivity," Putnam says that what he thinks is most "worth taking seriously" in the work of the American pragmatists is their "appeal to the primacy of practice." He tries to bring out what he takes the philosophical force of such an appeal to be by reconstructing various lines of thought he finds in their writings in terms of a series of "indispensability arguments." The targets of these arguments are philosophical views which attempt to impugn ways of talking and thinking which lie at the foundations of our ordinary practice on the grounds that these ways of talking and thinking fail to meet certain (metaphysically imposed) standards of "rationality" or "objectivity." The aim of these indispensability arguments is to demonstrate that these philosophical views can be seen to founder in incoherence. Putnam takes this strain of thought in the classical pragmatists to represent an important bond between their teachings and those of Wittgenstein.

Putnam has taken to referring to those ways of talking and thinking which are fundamental to our practices—the integrity of which Wittgenstein, the American pragmatists, and now Putnam himself are all concerned to uphold—as involving "pictures." This terminology may confuse the reader since Putnam's favorite pejorative term of philosophical criticism in this volume is (to say of someone that he or she is) "in the grip of a picture." How can pictures be so good and yet, at the same time, so bad?

The final section of Chapter 13 is entitled "Pictures and Philosophy." It closes by quoting Wittgenstein's remark that "a picture which is at the root of all our thinking is to be respected." It opens as follows:

> Consider the sentence "Caesar crossed the Rubicon." I think it is undeniable, as a fact about the lives we actually lead, that our ordinary linguistic practice in connection with such a statement is deeply informed by a "realist" picture . . . That the statement is just something we "utter" in response to *present-day* (or even present and future) "assertibility conditions" is an idea infinitely remote from our actual form of life . . . our "realism" (note the small "r") about the past, our belief that truth and falsity "reach all the way to" the past, and "do not stop short," *is* part of a picture, *and the picture is essential to our lives.*

Part of the point of describing the kind of realism which "is essential to our lives" (which lies "at the root of all our thinking") as a *picture* is to distinguish it from a fully developed philosophical view. Putnam draws our attention to the lower-case "r" here in his employment of the term "realism." One might well wonder: how much philosophical progress can there be in shifting the "r" in one's Realism from the upper to the lower case? Putnam draws attention to this orthographic detail in order to contrast the realist picture (which "our linguistic practice is deeply informed by") with Realism understood as a metaphysical conception—an interpretation of the nature of reality which is in competition with, say, idealism or empiricism. Putnam wants to claim that the picture which informs our lives is not seen for what it is if it is seen as a "position" situated in this space of competing interpretations. In the first chapter of *The Many Faces of Realism*, Putnam describes the relation between Realism and realism in roughly the following terms: under the pressure of philosophical scrutiny, we attempt to defend the realism implicit in our linguistic practice by calling upon the services of Realism.[61] We thus enter the labyrinth of competing metaphysical interpretations and are unable to find our way back out.

At the end of an essay in Putnam's earlier collection of papers, entitled "A Defense of Internal Realism," the following remarks occur:

I don't think it is bad to have pictures in philosophy. What is bad is to forget they are pictures . . .

Now, the picture I have sketched *is* only a "picture" . . . On the other hand, metaphysical realism is only a "picture." At a very abstract level, the debate between metaphysical realism and idealism is a standoff. Each side can truthfully say to the other, "You don't have a theory!"

In spite of this, I think that the idealist "picture" calls our attention to vitally important features of our practice—and what is the point of having "pictures" if we are not interested in seeing how well they represent what we actually think and do? . . .

Recognizing such [vitally important features of our practice] . . . is part of what might be called "rejecting 'realism' in the name of the realistic spirit." It is my view that reviving and revitalizing the realistic spirit is the important task for a philosopher at this time.[62]

This passage raises a number of questions. Why don't the metaphysical realist and the idealist each have a theory? What is the "realistic spirit" (the revitalization of which is *the* important task for a philosopher at this time)? What does it mean to reject "'realism' in the name of the realistic spirit"?

The materials for formulating an answer to the first question have already been touched upon: we've seen (through his exchange with Rorty) that Putnam's complaint about metaphysical realism is not that it is false, but that we are unable to make sense of it. Before attempting to answer the second and third questions, however, we should note that the concluding lines of the above passage allude to an article by Cora Diamond entitled "Realism and the Realistic Spirit."[63] That article is an extended exegesis of the following remark of Wittgenstein's: "Not empiricism and yet realism in philosophy, that is the hardest thing."[64] What is initially puzzling about the remark is the occurrence of the word "yet": Not empiricism *yet* realism. Ordinarily, empiricism is thought to be opposed to realism. Empiricism names a philosophical attitude which seeks to stay close to the surface of experience and to minimize the significance—or altogether deny the intelligibility—of that which lies beyond experience. Whereas realism, in contemporary philosophical parlance, names a philosophical attitude which seeks to go beyond the surface of experience and emphasize the significance of that which is independent of human thought and experience. Thus some commentators have read Wittgenstein's remark as if what he must have meant were: "Not empiricism *ergo* realism."

Wittgenstein's remark would suggest, however, that he is after a sense of "realism" according to which empiricism is a species of realism. Diamond writes, "The suggestion appears to be that empiricism is something we get into in philosophy by trying to be realists but going about it in the wrong way."[65] What does Wittgenstein mean by "realism" here?

Diamond goes on to consider some nonphilosophical uses of the term "realism":

> We may tell someone to "be realistic," when he is maintaining something in the teeth of the facts, or refusing even to look at them. Or again if he knows what the facts *ought* to be, either from a theory or wishful thinking, and will not take the world to be something capable of shaking his belief. We also speak of realism in connection with novels and stories; and here again we often have in mind certain kinds of attention to reality: to detail and particularity . . . We expect in a realistic novel something you might call a phenomenalism of character: it is built up out of observed detail, and in a sense there is nothing to it over and above what we are shown . . . once we look outside philosophy, the idea of connections between what is *there* called 'realism' and what we associate with empiricism becomes less puzzling . . .
>
> Magic, myth, fantasy, superstition: in different ways are terms used in making contrasts with realism . . . with this non-philosophical use of "realism" there is a connection with empiricism, with its characteristic attempts to banish from philosophy (or from our thought more generally) myth, magic, superstition of various sorts, or what it sees as that.[66]

The context of Wittgenstein's remark bears out Diamond's interpretation. Wittgenstein contrasts realism with "obscurantism" and "moonshine."[67] This helps us to see how empiricism could be a species of realism, but it still leaves it somewhat obscure what Wittgenstein is after in calling for something which is "not empiricism and yet realism." If empiricism is, after all, a form of realism, then what has he got against it?

A clue to an answer is to be found in Wittgenstein's remark about what is not to be treated as a superstition. The wrong kind of realism—or better: a misfired attempt at realism—will lead us to treat even that which should be respected *as* superstition. Empiricism is, in this sense, an expression of the realistic impulse run amok. In its eagerness to uncover every form of moonshine, it is unable to see even in good money anything but counterfeit currency. Putting these two remarks of Wittgenstein's together, we thus arrive at the suggestion that the problem with empiricism is that it leads us to treat a picture which is at the root of all our thinking—and which is to be respected—as superstition. This still leaves us with the question: *how* does it do this? By way of answering this question, Diamond develops a contrast between "the metaphysical spirit" and "the realistic spirit."[68] The characteristic activity of the metaphysical spirit, she says, is *a laying down of* (metaphysical) *requirements* (about what must be the case in order for something—reference, determinacy of sense, knowledge of other minds, and so on—to be possible). In the thrall of the metaphysical spirit, when one does finally turn to the task of looking and seeing, what one sees is refracted through the lens of the requirements one has imposed (about what *must* be the case). The realistic spirit seeks to reverse the order of procedure and place the activity of looking (at what we do and how we talk) first:

> The laying down of philosophical requirements, the characteristic activity of the metaphysical spirit, may be contrasted with looking at the use, looking at what we do. Thus, for example, there is on the one hand what we might lay down, in some philosophical theory, as essential to rule-following, to something's being in accordance with a rule; in contrast there is description of the face, the physiognomy, of what we call "obeying a rule" in everyday life, of all that belongs to that face. The philosophical theory lays down, without looking, what must be present in following a rule, while Wittgenstein's talk of what is possible is entirely different . . . The important thing then is not what answer you give, but your willingness to look, i.e. your not laying down general philosophical conditions.
>
> Only if we understand Wittgenstein's aim in relation to metaphysical requirements will we see the point of his urging us to look at what we do. We shall get a wrong idea of the sense in which philosophy "leaves everything as it is" if we ignore that aim . . . The sense in which philosophy leaves everything as it is is this: philosophy does not put us in a position to justify or criticize what we do by showing that it meets or fails to meet requirements we lay down in our philosophizing.[69]

We are now in a better position to understand Putnam's remark that what he is doing might be called "rejecting 'realism' in the name of the realistic spirit." It is a rejection of forms of realism which—in the name of what *must* be—obscure our view of "what we actually think and do." Forms of (metaphysical) realism which lead us to treat a picture which lies at the root of all our thinking as a superstition are to be rejected for misrepresenting the role such a picture actually plays in the physiognomy of our practice. We have, for example, seen Putnam urge against Rorty that a preoccupation with metaphysical realism can leave one unable to recover a clear view of our ordinary talk about what is the case. Our ordinary picture of what we mean when we say "such and such is the case"—our picture that what we mean does "not stop anywhere short of the fact"—is to be respected and not treated as a superstition. We have also just seen Putnam urge something similar with respect to the picture implicit in our ordinary discourse about the past (against an analysis of such discourse in terms of assertibility conditions).

In Chapter 13 Putnam sums up his discussion of this topic as follows: "As Wittgenstein himself puts it (in the *Lectures on Religious Belief*), a picture can have human weight. That truth is not *just* 'disquotational,' that truth genuinely depends on what is *distant,* is part of a picture with enormous *human weight.*" Here is the passage from Wittgenstein's *Lectures on Religious Belief* to which Putnam is alluding:

> "God's eye sees everything"—I want to say of this that it uses a picture.
>
> I don't want to belittle . . . the person who says it . . .
>
> We associate a particular use with a picture . . .
>
> What conclusions are you going to draw? . . . Are eyebrows going to be talked of, in connection with the Eye of God? . . .
>
> If I say he used a picture, I don't want to say anything he himself wouldn't say. I want to say he draws these conclusions.
>
> Isn't it as important as anything else, what picture he does use? . . .
>
> The whole *weight* may be in the picture . . . When I say he's using a picture, I am merely making a *grammatical* remark: [What I say] can only be verified by the consequences he does or does not draw . . .
>
> All I wished to characterize was the consequences he wished to draw. If I wished to say anything more I was merely being philosophically arrogant.[70]

Wittgenstein says that when he speaks of "the person using a picture," he doesn't want to say anything the person himself wouldn't say.

What is being proposed therefore is a discipline of *description*[71] (of accurately characterizing the consequences the person himself does and does not draw). The suggestion would seem to be that we will miss what weight the picture has in this life if we attempt to bypass this task of description in favor of immediately turning to explore some question which the picture appears to force upon us. Putnam comments:

> Wittgenstein is saying here that to say the religious person is using a picture is simply to describe what we can in fact observe: that religious people do employ pictures, and that they draw certain consequences from them, but not the same consequences that we draw when we use similar pictures in other contexts. If I speak of my friend as having an eye, then normally I am prepared to say that he has an eyebrow, but when I speak of the Eye of God being upon me, I am not prepared to speak of the eyebrow of God. But the impressive thing here is not what Wittgenstein says, but the limit he places on his own observation. Pictures are important in life. The whole weight of a form of life may lie in the pictures that that form of life uses.[72]

The consequences the religious person draws (that is, actually draws in his life with the picture) may not be "the consequences that we draw when we use similar pictures in other contexts." It is this fact about the pictures which inform our lives that allows the ways of the metaphysical spirit and the realistic spirit to diverge. If we consider the picture itself without first surveying the intricacies of its use, we may be led to ascribe to the person who uses the picture the belief that God has eyebrows.

Wittgenstein's suggestion here is that there are two ways to consider the use. One way involves simply looking and seeing how the picture informs the life. The pattern of its use may be quite unperspicuous and, indeed, perhaps completely invisible to someone in whose life such a picture plays no role and who is unable to imagine what a life informed by such a picture would be like. Another way of considering the use is first to consider the picture in, as it were, a vacuum. Wittgenstein suggests that this second way will lead to our seeing the use *through* the lens of a certain construal of the picture. When one turns from the picture to the question of its application, one's view will be shaped by certain requirements (derived from one's prior consideration of the picture) which are laid down as conditions for the appropriate application of the picture. In the absence of any other way of seeing how the picture might inform our practice, our initial consideration of the picture will tend to favor an excessively *literalistic* construal. This leads us to fill in the picture in particular ways. Our understanding of what it is for the picture to have application is now controlled by our antecedently filled-in version of the picture. We come to have a view of what it would be *really* to have the eye of God upon one, next to which any other application of the picture seems, at best, a wildly figurative and misleading form of expression.

This is one way into metaphysics: understanding the application of a picture (which informs our practice) by being (unwittingly) *guided by the picture itself* (considered, that is, in abstraction from its actual role in use). When one allows oneself to be so guided, one arrives at a mistaken conception of what attachment to the picture entails and hence of what its role in informing use *ought* to be. One is led to insist that this (religious) person is *committed* to such and such (an ontology which permits him to quantify over divine eyebrows!) whether *he* realizes it or not. A refusal of interest on his part in certain questions (about, say, whether God has eyebrows)—while he wishes to continue to allow the picture to play a role in his life—can then appear (to someone whose view of the use is guided only by the picture) to be a failure on this person's part to reflect sufficiently on the nature of his commitments.[73] This example has been chosen by Wittgenstein because—in moving from an observation of a person's inclination (under certain circumstances) to call upon the words "the eye of God is upon me" to an insistence on ascribing to him an ontology which includes divine eyebrows—the confusion it illustrates is of a relatively transparent character. The importance of the example lies in its structural affinities with less transparent instances of such confusion. The significant cases in philosophy are the ones in which we are unable to see that—in laying down certain requirements—we have been misled by a picture in our language which forces itself upon us.

Wittgenstein's most famous and influential remark about pictures and philosophy is the following: "A *picture* held us captive. And we could not get outside it, for it lay in our language and language seemed to repeat it to us inexorably."[74] Taken in isolation, this remark can encourage the idea that what Wittgenstein thinks about pictures is that they are simply a bad thing. Thus we arrive at the standard reading of Wittgenstein's view of pictures and philosophy: what is involved in freeing oneself from a picture (which holds one captive) is doing away with it altogether—achieving a "pictureless" view of things. After discussing various passages about pictures (including the one above) from Wittgenstein's *Lectures on Religious Belief,* Putnam remarks:

> These remarks seem to go totally against the idea that Wittgenstein was against pictures as such. When Wittgenstein attacks philosophers for being in the grip of a picture, the usual reading of this is that Wittgenstein opposes pictures—that pictures are bad. But Wittgenstein in his lectures during the 1930s repeatedly praises pictures in two ways: he praises them as good ways of explaining the meaning of words[75] . . . and, moreover, he speaks of pictures as having "weight," or of pictures' being "at the root of all one's thinking." Evidently, then, if certain philosophers are attacked by Wittgenstein for being in the grip of a picture, . . . what is wrong is not that pictures are bad.[76]

So it seems that we need to distinguish between simply "using a picture" and "being in the grip of a picture." It is not that "pictures are bad"—indeed, they can be indispensable (can lie at the root of all our thinking)—but that, under the pressure of philosophy, we are inevitably misled by them. The pictures which "lie in our language" are essential to how we represent things, and yet they lead us into perplexity when we call upon them, in our philosophizing, to play a role—in particular, an explanatory role—they cannot bear up under. Thus Putnam writes: "Was not Wittgenstein telling us to reject *all* pictures? . . . As Cora Diamond has pointed out . . . , the fact that a picture is not an 'explanation' doesn't mean that the picture is *wrong.*"[77] In the essay of Diamond's which Putnam refers us to at this point,[78] we find this:

> That it can be misleading is not to say that we should really give up using the picture, stop talking that way. It is no accident that we do; no mischievous demon has been at work in our language putting in misleading analogies which the philosopher can simply discard when he has seen through them. To give up thinking and talking in such terms would be to give up the life in which these figurative expressions do have an application (just as giving up the picture of our "inner" mental life would be giving up the kind of life in which that picture is applied).[79]

This is how Putnam glosses Diamond's remark about what would be given up if we were to give up our picture of human beings as having an "inner" mental life: "Suppose . . . that I were to be convinced that *other people* were just logical constructions out of my sense data (or, alternately, that talk about other people is just a game that is just useful for predicting *my* future sense-impressions); this would make an *enormous* difference to my life. (The whole question of *hurting* other people would be 'displaced'; and so would the whole question of companionship.)"[80]

Many philosophers nowadays are inclined to view talk of an "inner mental life" as an outdated remnant of Cartesian metaphysics. Of course, we often employ turns of phrase that presuppose such a picture of the "inner"—we talk about her feeling of pain being something that happens *in* her—but that is because ordinary language is shot through with Cartesian metaphysics. Commentators therefore conclude that Wittgenstein is hopelessly at odds with himself in wishing to free us from a Cartesian conception of the inner while wanting, at the same time, to insist that philosophy should not interfere with ordinary language.[81] Is Wittgenstein at odds with himself?

Of course, *within philosophy*, discussions about "the inner life" are shot through with a full-blown Cartesian metaphysics—a conception of the inner as a self-standing private *realm*, completely independent of the ("outer") public realm. Realism about the inner thus comes to seem to involve a commitment to private mental *entities* (and thus our ontology begins to swell again). Now if anyone is famous for attacking such a conception of the inner it is certainly Wittgenstein. The question whether Wittgenstein is at odds with himself (in his attachment to ordinary language) boils down to the question whether the picture implicit in our language is one which, in and of itself, commits us to such a (metaphysical) conception of the inner. Diamond's previous remark alludes to the following passage from *Philosophical Investigations*: "*Certainly* all these things happen in you.—And now all I ask to understand is the expression we use.—The picture is there. And I am not disputing its validity in any particular case.—Only I also want to understand the application of the picture. The picture is *there;* and I do not dispute its *correctness*. But *what* is its application?"[82] Wittgenstein affirms here just what the standard interpretation has him denying: the correctness of the picture. He is not disputing its validity in any particular case (in which it occurs in ordinary conversation). What he says he wants to understand is the application of the picture. It is, he thinks, the unhappy coincidence of two factors which brings about our confusion here: (1) the complex and unperspicuous nature of the application the picture actually has in our lives; and (2) the comparatively straightforward (until one tries to make sense of it!) metaphysical picture of an inside and an outside which the picture itself (considered in abstraction from its use) invites. The passage continues:

> There is a picture in the foreground, but the sense lies far in the background; that is, the application of the picture is not easy to survey . . .
>
> In numberless cases we exert ourselves to find a picture and once it is found the application as it were comes about of itself. In this case we already have a picture which forces itself on us at every turn,—but that does not help us out of the difficulty, which only begins here . . .
>
> A picture is conjured up which seems to fix the sense *unambiguously*. The actual use, compared with that suggested by the picture, seems like something muddied . . .
>
> In the actual use of expressions we make detours, we go by side-roads. We see the straight highway before us, but of course we cannot use it, because it is permanently closed.[83]

What we need to see—the sense, that is, which our talk (about what goes on "inside" someone) actually has—lies far in the background, while the picture, which lies in the foreground, *forces itself on us* at every turn, railroading our view of the grammar of our talk about the inner. Wittgenstein tries to bring this out through the following example: "'While I was speaking to him I did not know what was going on in his head.' In saying this, one is not thinking of brain-processes, but of thought-processes. The picture should be taken seriously. We should really like to see into his head. And yet we only mean what elsewhere we should mean by saying: we should like to know what he is thinking. I want to say: we have this vivid picture—and that use, apparently contradicting the picture, which expresses the psychical."[84] A conflict arises between the picture and things we ordinarily say. The actual use seems to contradict the way in which the picture invites us to understand the sense of our everyday talk of the inner. Misled by the picture, we lay down requirements as to what would count as *really* seeing inside someone's head. We make the picture "vivid." Thus we come to be in the grip of a (literalistic) view of what it would be for the picture to apply, compared with which any other use of the picture seems merely figurative. It comes to seem as if we lay claim, in our ordinary discourse, to forms of knowledge which we are, strictly speaking, unable to attain. In ordinary language, when we say we should like to see into his head, what we mean, Wittgenstein says, could also be expressed by saying: we should like to know what he is thinking. This is something that sometimes we do know. Sometimes we know what another person is thinking. In this (ordinary) sense, we can sometimes see into someone's head. The conception of the inner the picture forces on us leads us to a conception on which all we can ever see is the *outside* of another person's head.[85] We see the straight highway before us, but it is closed to us: the road is blocked—so it seems to us, when held captive by the picture—because the outside of his head is in the way, obscuring our view of the inside. It is not that Wittgenstein thinks that there *is*—that is, that sense can be made of our picture here of—a permanently closed highway. What he thinks is, rather, that we are induced to picture such a highway to ourselves.[86] We need therefore, in a sense, to distinguish between two pictures: the picture implicit in our practice and the filled-in version of the picture. It is the former which is to be respected. It is the latter which holds us captive and which eventually induces us (through our misdirected attempts to free ourselves from its grip) to treat the former as a superstition.

Our view of what it would be to speak properly about the inner is thus controlled by a particular way in which the picture has been filled in (so as to include a view of a closed highway before us). We thus conclude: properly speaking, we can never know what's going on inside of someone. We are left feeling (once again) that there is something we cannot do. We cannot see inside another person. The resulting conception of the inner (as radically private) saddles us with the threat of skepticism concerning other minds. In an attempt to escape skepticism, we resort to various strategies. We give up on the highway and try (what seem to us to be) circuitous back roads: we concede that we can never have direct knowledge, but we comfort ourselves with the thought that we can still have *indirect* knowledge of another person's mind. No (nonmagical) sense, though, can be made here of the idea (which the filled-in picture imposes on us) of direct knowledge. But the comforting possibility of indirect knowledge derives its (appearance of) sense from its participation in a contrast with the idea of direct knowledge. Thus we do gradually come to see, in our philosophizing, that there is no highway here (open or closed), but the realization comes too late: we conclude that there are no roads to another mind. We are left now with a picture of an inner realm so remote that there is no route—direct or indirect—from the outside in. So, in the end, in search of a way out of our problem, (rightly) unwilling to settle for a radically private realm accessible to only one person, we decide to throw away the picture of an inner world altogether. We come to look upon our ordinary idioms (which involve talk about the inner) as just so many expressions of metaphysical confusion. Hence we begin our search for a philosophically respectable substitute (perhaps in terms of assertibility conditions) for the ordinary idiom.

"Rejecting 'realism' [about the inner] in the name of the realistic spirit" therefore, for Putnam, does *not* mean: simply subtracting from the Cartesian conception (of the relation of the outer and the inner) the idea of an independent private mental realm, and thus abandoning ourselves to one side of the Cartesian dualist's divide. This simply leaves us with a hollowed-out public realm in which the human body can no longer be seen as *expressive* of anything inner. (This way of rejecting realism about the inner leaves us continuing to conceive of the human body as something which screens—rather than expresses—the human soul, but then concluding that there is nothing behind the screen). The same (filled-in, literalized) picture of the inner continues to control our thought when we "recoil"[87] from Cartesianism into anti-Cartesianism—into, that is, some form of phenomenalism about what the subject of meaningful talk about "the inner" (henceforth permanently consigned to scare quotes) must, in the end, *really* consist in (something which is to be constructed out of elements drawn exclusively from one side of the divide). The realistic spirit aims to recover the role that talk about the inner plays in our lives. "Rejecting 'realism' [about the inner] in the name of the realistic spirit" therefore means rejecting a metaphysically loaded conception of the relation of the inner and the outer (as two independent realms, the metaphysically private and the inexpressively public), while treating with respect a picture of the inner which has great weight in our lives (and in which the inner and the outer are inextricably entangled and intimately interdependent).

The Weave of Our Life

Metaphysics without ethics is blind.
> Hilary Putnam, *Meaning and the Moral Sciences*

In Chapter 8, "Pragmatism and Moral Objectivity," we learn that Putnam sees both Wittgenstein and the American pragmatists (especially James and Dewey) as helping to revive a claim which was central to the ancient Greek tradition of thought about ethics: "only the virtuous have an adequate idea of what virtue is" and "the person who does not engage in the *practice* of virtue cannot have a fully adequate idea of what virtue is." The arguments which Putnam himself advances for this claim are indebted to the manner in which "something like this traditional view has been defended in a well-known series of papers by John McDowell."[88] McDowell's own arguments (offered in part as an interpretation of Wittgenstein) were directed, in the first instance, against non-cognitivist theories of ethics—theories which "hold that ascriptions of value should not be conceived as propositions of the sort whose correctness . . . consists in their being true descriptions of the world."[89] According to non-cognitivists, the application of any concept to the world is governed solely by its "descriptive content"—that component of the concept which is free of any evaluative connotations. They held that it should, in principle, be possible to analyze any moral concept into two discrete components: a descriptive element and an evaluative element. For any moral concept, that is, one should be able to fashion a new concept which could pick out just the same features of the world while lacking any prescriptive force. The thrust of McDowell's arguments against this view turned on the claim that it is impossible to understand a moral concept unless one is able (at least imaginatively) to *share in the evaluative perspective* within which such a concept has its life. This is how Putnam summarizes the claim:

> McDowell . . . argued that there is no way of saying what the "descriptive component" of a word like "cruel" or "inconsiderate" is without using a word of the same kind; as McDowell put the argument, a word has to be connected to a certain set of "evaluative interests" in order to function the way such [an] . . . ethical word functions, and the speaker has to be aware of those interests and be able to identify imaginatively with them in order to apply the word to novel cases or circumstances in the way a sophisticated speaker of the language would.
>
>   For example, someone who has studied how the word "cruel" is used without performing such an act of imaginative identification could predict that the word would be used in certain obvious cases, for instance, torture. But such a person would be baffled by the fact that some cases which seemed (from the same external point of view) to be cases of "kindness" would be described by us as "subtle forms

of cruelty," and by the fact that some cases of what he or she would describe as cruelty would be described by us as "not cruel at all under the circumstances." The attempt of non-cognitivists to split words like "cruel" into a "descriptive meaning component" and a "prescriptive meaning component" founders on the impossibility of saying what the "descriptive meaning" is without using the word "cruel" itself, or a synonym.[90]

In order to allow it to resonate with other aspects of Wittgenstein's thought, Putnam tends to paraphrase this claim of McDowell's (that in order to use an ethical concept one must allow oneself to identify imaginatively with the interests which guide its application) as the claim that one cannot acquire an ethical concept unless one participates (at least imaginatively) in the form of life in which such a concept has its evaluative point. When Putnam claims (echoing Wittgenstein) that "understanding a language-game is sharing a form of life," he is extending the application of the point McDowell makes about ethical concepts to *all* of our concepts. In order to grasp the point of a concept one must have a sense of what it would be to be caught up in the whole fabric of activity into which the thread of the concept's use is woven. A concept can be thought of as "a pattern which recurs, with different variations, in the weave of our life."[91] Putnam's claim that "the use of the words in a language-game cannot be described without using concepts which are related to the concepts employed *in* the game" is therefore, in a certain sense, a generalization of the ancient Greek claim about virtue: "the person who does not engage in the *practice* of virtue cannot have a fully adequate idea of what virtue is."

Putnam (again following McDowell) points out that we are quite likely to find the counterpart of the ancient Greek view of virtue a perfectly plausible thing to say about *music:* "the person who does not engage in musical practice cannot have a fully adequate idea what great music is." The reason the Greek theory of virtue has seemed attractive to some thinkers as a theory about virtue has in part to do with the way in which (at least certain) ethical concepts appear similar in this respect to musical concepts. Yet it is precisely this aspect of (at least certain) ethical concepts which has inclined certain philosophers (preoccupied with the goal of describing the world in terms of "maximally non-perspectival" concepts) to impugn the "objectivity" of concepts of virtue. Putnam argues in "Pragmatism and Moral Objectivity" that what can be seen to be a relatively perspicuous feature of our aesthetic concepts and some of our concepts of virtue (the ways in which they are woven into the texture of a practice) is in fact a feature of all of our important concepts. Early in the essay, he develops this point briefly in connection with the concept of intelligence:

> An unintelligent person might not care about losing or gaining in intelligence; but an unintelligent person does not have a good idea of what intelligence *is*. What makes this example relevant . . . is that an ancient tradition in ethics, the Greek tradition, did in fact think that virtue was in these respects like intelligence; it held, on the one hand, that only the virtuous have an adequate idea of what virtue is, and that those who have an adequate idea of what virtue is do not *ceteris paribus* wish to lose their virtue. Perhaps most people do not believe any longer that the Greek tradition was right; but it is not clear that this disbelief is based on some piece of "scientific knowledge" that we have gained in the meantime.

Putnam tries to turn the tables on the non-cognitivist by arguing that all of our concepts are, in a sense, tied to concepts of virtue. The non-cognitivist argues that those concepts which are closely tied to action—that is, which are used centrally in answering questions concerning how we should act—are unsuited to the (scientific and philosophical) task of describing the furniture of the universe. The non-cognitivist seeks to sort our concepts into two categories: those which are (exclusively) "world-guided" and those which are (in addition) "action-guiding." His reservation about ethical concepts is that their evaluative component—the component which implies that we *ought* to act in a certain way—renders them incapable of depicting the world "as it really is." Putnam wants to argue not only that the normative and descriptive dimensions of our paradigmatically ethical concepts are hopelessly entangled (and cannot be separated into distinct "components"), but that, upon careful reflection, essentially the same point can be seen to apply to our most fundamental epistemic and scientific concepts as well. Individual essays in this volume (especially those on philosophy of language, philosophy of mind, and philosophy of science) develop this point with respect to different concepts (instrumental rationality, truth, warranted assertibility, reference, confirmation, and so on). If there is a single sentence somewhere in this volume which comes closest to summing up the collective burden of the numerous individual arguments threaded through this volume as a whole, it is therefore probably the following: "Many of our key notions—the notion of understanding something, the notion of something's making sense, the notion of something's being capable of being confirmed, or infirmed, or discovered to be true, or discovered to be false, or even the notion of something's being capable of being stated—are normative notions, and it has never been clear what it means to naturalize a normative notion."[92]

If there is a single overarching theme in this volume it is that, on the one hand, without appeal to our basic cognitive values (consistency, coherence, simplicity, instrumental efficacy, and so on) we are not in a position to make philosophical sense of most of our adult activities in life (practical or theoretical), while, on the other hand, in most of our philosophizing about those activities we tend to lose sight of the ways in which "these values are arbitrary considered as anything but a part of a holistic conception of human flourishing."[93] Putnam sees this overarching theme as, in turn, closely tied to what he takes to be the heart of Wittgenstein's teaching: namely, that it is only through a perspicuous representation of the practices in which they are embedded that we can command a clear view of any of our concepts (moral or scientific, logical or theological). "What determines our judgment, our concepts and reactions, is . . . the whole hurly-burly of human actions, the background against which we see any action."[94] Putnam sees the most characteristic manifestation of the metaphysical impulse as lying in its tendency to attempt to grasp our concepts in isolation from the surroundings—the whole hurly-burly of human actions—in which they have their life. Each essay in this volume, while sympathetically acknowledging the felt pressure of such an impulse, seeks to recover some particular concept from a condition of metaphysically imposed isolation and to restore it to the surroundings in which it is at home.[95]

Notes

1. Most (about two thirds) of the essays in this volume were written between 1989 and 1993. Quite a few of them have not been published before. Those essays which are of less recent vintage have been selected either in deference to popular demand or because they are presupposed by one (or more) of the other essays in the volume. The oldest of them ("Reductionism and the Nature of Psychology") dates to 1974.

2. "Those who cannot remember the past are condemned to fulfill it." George

Santayana, *The Life of Reason* (New York: Charles Scribner's and Sons, 1909), vol. 1, chap. 12.

3. Putnam's favorite version of this sort of point concerns the ways in which the history of logical positivism continues to be reenacted. He argues that some of the central research programs of logical positivism have been revived in forms which obscure the fact that they run into the same deadends as their predecessors (and often for the same reasons). He argues in Chapter 16, "On Truth," and Chapter 13, "Does the Disquotational Theory of Truth Solve All Philosophical Problems?" that contemporary analyses of truth (in terms of disquotation) and meaning (in terms of assertibility conditions) run into some of the same problems positivist theories of truth and meaning foundered on. In Chapter 20, "Artificial Intelligence: Much Ado about Not Very Much," and Chapter 24, "Why Functionalism Didn't Work," he sketches a similar point with respect to the parallels between certain contemporary research programs in artificial intelligence and certain efforts of the positivists to formulate an inductive logic.

4. See in this connection the three essays on the views of Putnam's former teacher Hans Reichenbach (Chapters 5–7).

5. Most notable in this regard perhaps are Putnam's discussions (especially in Chapters 14–17, "Realism without Absolutes," "The Question of Realism," "On Truth," and "A Comparison of Something with Something Else") of the relation between Richard Rorty's views and the views of those whom Rorty seeks to oppose.

6. "Sense, Nonsense, and the Senses" (The Dewey Lectures, forthcoming, 1994), p. 1.

7. Putnam's reading of Descartes is indebted to a pair of articles by Paul Hoffman. In "The Unity of Descartes's Man," *Philosophical Review*, 95 no. 3 (July 1986), Hoffman argues that "substantial union" for Descartes refers not only to a union of two substances but to a product of such a union which is itself a substance. The substantial union of mind and body constitutes that genuine individual *(ens per se)* known as the human being. In "Cartesian Passions and Cartesian Dualism," *Pacific Philosophical Quarterly*, 71 (1990), Hoffman argues that sensations are modes of the (substance) human being which (though themselves simple modes of a genuine unity) bear both a mental and a corporeal aspect.

8. Thus, in Chapter 14, we find Putnam arguing against "reductive forms of naturalism" and in favor of what he calls "a sane naturalism." Putnam opposes "a sane naturalism" to what he calls a "disenchanted naturalism." Putnam here (and elsewhere in this essay and in "The Question of Realism") is taking his lead from John McDowell's John Locke Lectures, *Mind and World* (Cambridge: Harvard University Press, 1994). McDowell writes: "Modern science understands its subject matter in a way that threatens . . . to leave it disenchanted, as Weber put it in an image that has

become a commonplace . . . According to the picture I have been recommending, our sensibility yields states and occurrences with conceptual concepts . . . Even though the logical space that is the home of the idea of spontaneity cannot be aligned with the logical space that is the home of ideas of what is natural in the relevant sense, conceptual powers are nevertheless operative in the workings of our sensibility, in actualizations of our animal nature, as such . . . this can seem to express a nostalgia for a pre-scientific world-view, a call for a re-enchantment of nature . . . If we rethink our conception of nature so as to make room for spontaneity, even though we deny that spontaneity is capturable by the resources of bald naturalism, we shall by the same token be rethinking our conception of what it takes for a position to deserve to be called 'naturalism' . . . The rethinking requires a different conception of actualizations of our nature. We need to bring responsiveness to meaning back into the operations of our natural sentient capacities as such . . . for Aristotle the rational demands of ethics are autonomous; we are not to feel compelled to validate them from outside an already ethical way of thinking. But this autonomy does not distance the demands from anything specifically human . . . They are essentially within reach of human beings. We cannot credit appreciation of them to human nature as it figures in a naturalism of disenchanted nature, because disenchanted nature does not embrace the space of reasons . . . we can return to sanity if we can recapture the Aristotelian idea that a normal mature human being is a rational animal, with its rationality part of its animal, and hence so natural, being, not a mysterious foothold in another realm." In one of the notes to Chapter 14, Putnam writes: "Although I do not wish to hold McDowell responsible for my formulations in the present lecture, I want to acknowledge the pervasive influence of his work."

9. M. F. Burnyeat, "Is an Aristotelian Philosophy of Mind Still Credible?" in Essays on Aristotle's "De Anima," ed. Martha Nussbaum and Amalie Rorty (Oxford: Oxford University Press, 1992), pp. 15–26. Burnyeat's article is written in criticism of a reading of Aristotle which was originally advanced independently by Nussbaum and Putnam—by Nussbaum in Aristotle's "De Motu Animalium" (Princeton: Princeton University Press, 1978) and by Putnam in "Philosophy and Our Mental Life," in Mind, Language, and Reality, Philosophical Papers, vol. 2 (New York: Cambridge University Press, 1975). "Changing Aristotle's Mind," Chapter 2 of the present volume, is their co-authored response to Burnyeat's criticisms.

10. Burnyeat writes: "My hope is that a historical inquiry into what Aristotle believes about the physical basis of animal life will bring about a sense that the other half of Cartesian dualism, the matter half, remains intact in all of us. Our conception of the mental may be open for discussion and revision, but our conception of the physical is irreversibly influenced by the demolition of the Aristotelian philosophy through Descartes and others in the sev-

enteenth century . . . Aristotle's philosophy of mind is no longer credible because Aristotelian physics is no longer credible, and the fact of that physics being incredible has quite a lot to do with there being such a thing as the mind/body problem as we face it today . . . Aristotle has what is for us a deeply alien conception of the physical. If we want to get away from Cartesian dualism, we cannot do it by traveling backwards to Aristotle, because although Aristotle has a non-Cartesian conception of the soul, *we* are stuck with a more or less Cartesian conception of the physical. To be truly Aristotelian we would have to stop believing that the emergence of life or mind requires explanation. We owe it above all to Descartes that that option is no longer open to us. Hence all we can do with the Aristotelian philosophy of mind . . . is what the seventeenth century did with it: junk it. Having junked it, we are stuck with the mind body/problem as Descartes created it, inevitably and rightly so" ("Is an Aristotelian Philosphy of Mind Still Credible?" pp. 16, 26).

11. In particular, they accuse Burnyeat of seeing "no way of reading Aristotle but in a Frank Baumian way, and no way in which Aristotle *could be* relevant to anything we're interested in today": "In the world of Frank Baum, matter—the straw in the Scarecrow's head . . .—can have the property of . . . being the location of thoughts and feelings without having any other particularly relevant properties . . . On Burnyeat's reading of Aristotle, we are *all* like the Scarecrow."

12. Burnyeat, "Is an Aristotelian Philosophy of Mind Still Credible?" p. 26.

13. The closing pages of Chapter 1 of this volume ("How Old Is the Mind?") touch on two reductionist projects which are discussed in further detail in a number of the essays which follow. In the context of attempting to offer a historical diagnosis of the powerful appeal of such projects, Putnam expresses considerable skepticism about two booming philosophical research programs he himself originally helped to launch: (1) causal theories of the referential powers of the mind and (2) computational analyses of interpretive rationality. His doubts about the former, he says, stem from their reliance on "an ancient (in fact, an Aristotelian) notion of efficient causation which is no more clear than reference itself"; his doubts about the latter stem from his inclination to think that "human interpretive rationality is deeply interwoven" in the rest of the fabric of human rationality, and his further inclination to think that it is impossible to construct an algorithmic model of prescriptive rationality in general. The former topic is taken up by the chapters in Part V of this volume, the latter by those in Part VI.

14. John Dewey, *Democracy and Education* (New York: Macmillan, 1916), p. 336. Quoted by Putnam in Chapter 15.

15. I am allowing myself here to echo formulations of Putnam's (in Chapter 14) which, in turn, echo formulations of John McDowell's. Here is an example of the kind of passage from McDowell's Locke Lectures (about mod-

ern philosophy's response to dualisms) that Putnam is drawing on: "modern philosophy addresses its . . . dualisms in a characteristic way. It takes its stand on one side of a gulf it aims to bridge, accepting without question the way its target dualism conceives the chosen side. Then it constructs something as close as possible to the conception of the other side that figured in the problems, out of materials that are unproblematically available where it has taken its stand. Of course there no longer seems to be a gulf" *(Mind and World)*.

16. See Chapter 14, note 6. In this connection, both here and in Chapter 15, Putnam expresses an indebtedness to John McDowell's "Putnam on Mind and Meaning," in *The Philosophy of Hilary Putnam, Philosophical Topics,* 20, no. 1 (Spring 1992), pp. 35–48. Both essays are in large part a response to this paper. Taken together, these two essays can also be read as an extended commentary on Wittgenstein's remarks in §§605–607 of *Zettel* (Berkeley: University of California Press, 1970), beginning with Wittgenstein's remark that "one of the most dangerous of ideas for a philosopher is . . . that we think with our heads or in our heads."

17. Putnam claims that we can find the seeds of such a philosophy of perception in the writings of William James and John Austin and its full flower in those of Wittgenstein and McDowell.

18. *Realism with a Human Face* (Cambridge: Harvard University Press, 1990), p. 28.

19. *Representation and Reality* (Cambridge: MIT Press, 1988), p. 109.

20. Richard Rorty, "Putnam and the Relativist Menace," *Journal of Philosophy,* 90, no. 9 (September 1993), 443–461.

21. *Realism with a Human Face,* p. 28.

22. Ibid., p. 178.

23. Gary Ebbs has suggested that certain misunderstandings and criticisms of Putnam's view are "encouraged by Putnam's unfortunate use of the word 'internal' to characterize his realism. For this word suggests that there is an 'external' alternative to internal realism, a legitimate perspective from which internal realism looks like an optional view . . . But this reaction rests on a failure (or refusal) to understand Putnam's realism . . . from Putnam's point of view, metaphysical realism is a thesis which has no genuine content. There is no legitimate perspective from which internal realism looks like an optional view of the relationship between our concepts of truth and rational acceptability" ("Realism and Rational Inquiry," in *The Philosophy of Hilary Putnam,* p. 26).

Putnam writes in "His Reply to Gary Ebbs": "I agree with Ebbs that the connotations of the word 'internal' have proved unfortunate; which is why, in later writings, I have tended to speak of 'pragmatic realism,' or simply 'realism with a small "r"'" (ibid., p. 353).

24. Putnam's criticisms (in Chapter 15) of remarks of Rorty's about represen-

tation ("we should give up the idea" that "our beliefs represent the world accurately") are provoked in large part by Rorty's essay "Pragmatism, Davidson, and Truth," as are the criticisms in Chapter 14 of Rorty's views on reference (we should give up the idea that there is a genuine relation of reference between words and objects in the world). Rorty's essay is in *Truth and Interpretation,* ed. E. LePore (Oxford: Basil Blackwell, 1986).

25. *Philosophical Investigations* (Oxford: Basil Blackwell, 1953), §95.

26. Rorty writes: "I have urged that we continue to speak with the vulgar while offering a different philosophical gloss on this speech than that offered by the realist tradition" ("Putnam and the Relativist Menace," p. 444).

27. See Rorty's essay "The World Well Lost," in *Consequences of Pragmatism* (Minneapolis: University of Minnesota Press, 1982).

28. In the portion of this passage I have omitted, Putnam writes: "On this, there is a beautiful paper by Cora Diamond, 'Realism and the Realistic Spirit.'" I discuss below what Putnam takes from this paper.

29. In Chapter 15, "The Question of Realism."

30. *Philosophical Investigations,* §97. Quoted by Putnam in Chapter 15.

31. Rorty is not the only philosopher to read Putnam's earlier attacks on metaphysical realism—as set forth, for example, in his essays "Realism and Reason" (in *Meaning and the Moral Sciences* [Boston: Routledge and K. Paul, 1978]) and "Models and Reality" (in *Realism and Reason* [New York: Cambridge University Press, 1983])—as underwriting the conclusion that "the whole idea of representing something external to language has collapsed." Putnam now goes out of his way therefore in "The Question of Realism" (and elsewhere) to emphasize that the aim of his earlier essays had been to argue not that metaphysical realism was false, but that it was *incoherent*—a form of words masquerading as a thesis: "What is common to all versions of . . . metaphysical realism is the notion that there is—in a philosophically privileged sense of 'object'—a definite Totality of All Real Objects and a fact of the matter as to which properties of those objects are the Intrinsic Properties and which are, in some sense, perspectival. The chief aim of the essays of mine that Rorty cites was to argue that this metaphysical kind of realism is 'incoherent.' I did not mean by that that it is inconsistent in a deductive logical sense, but rather that when we try to make the claims of the metaphysical realist precise, we find that they become compatible with strong forms of 'antirealism.' Thus attempts at a clear formulation of the position never succeed—because there is no real content there to be captured. My aim in those essays, therefore, was not to argue for the truth of a metaphysical counter-thesis (one which could be identified with the negation of metaphysical realism), but rather simply to provide a *reductio ad absurdum* of metaphysical realism by teasing out the consequences of it own presuppositions."

32. Putnam, "Reply to Carolyn Hartz," in "Replies and Comments," *Special Issue on the Philosophy of Hilary Putnam, Synthese,* 34, no. 3 (May 1991), 404.

33. "Putnam and the Relativist Menace," p. 445. Rorty offers this passage as a response to a parallel Putnam draws between Rorty and Carnap centering on an observation about the "scorn" with which "Rorty rejects a philosophical controversy" (*Realism with a Human Face,* p. 20). In the sentence preceding this passage Rorty writes: "There *is* a tone of Carnapian scorn in some of my writings . . . and there should not be." Rorty has missed Putnam's point here. What he does in this passage is propose to express his scorn in a different way. Putnam's point was not about whether Rorty charged a philosophical view with confusion or with relative inutility. The point was not about which terms of criticism were applied, but about *how* they were applied. Putnam was drawing attention not to whether Rorty's terms of criticism resembled Rudolf Carnap's, but to whether his *tone* did. His point was about the *dismissiveness* of Rorty's tone—his eagerness to dismiss a philosophical controversy before having taken the trouble to ascertain carefully what should be rejected in it and what should not. The parallel between Carnap and Rorty had to do with their shared desire to be able to cut themselves free from certain philosophical knots without first having to take the trouble to untangle them. The fundamental difference between Rorty and Putnam lies in their respective views of whether it is possible without further ado just to cut oneself free from certain philosophical controversies, and whether anything—and, if so, how much—is to be gained by carefully examining the structure of such controversies.

34. Rorty still often expresses his dissatisfaction with traditional philosophical positions in terms of a worry about their intelligibility. Consider, for example, the following remark (about skepticism) from the introduction to his most recent book: "From a Darwinian point of view, *there is simply no way to give sense* to the idea of our minds or our language as systematically out of phase with what lies beyond our skins [my emphasis]" (*Objectivity, Relativism, and Truth* [Cambridge: Cambridge University Press, 1991], p. 12).

35. One might want to question Rorty's recent claim that *now* his real reason for wishing to discard talk of representation is simply its relative inutility (and has nothing to do with his formerly thinking that such talk was in some way confused). What we have here is a change in rhetoric which seems to suggest—but in no way corresponds to—a change in view. For Rorty continues to counsel us to speak, in the course of our ordinary dealings, with the vulgar. This shows that he does think that such talk has sufficient relative utility to be retained for certain purposes. Rorty counsels us to retain this way of talking but to do so advisedly. Evidently, he thinks it "lacks utility" with respect to some further purpose. The inescapable

conclusion here is that Rorty thinks that we have philosophically compelling reasons to discard such ways of talking in certain limited contexts *despite their practical utility* in other contexts. The relative inutility of such ways of talking comes into play for Rorty when we turn to the task of making general theoretical pronouncements about the relation of language and world. To try to respond here that what this shows is that *for philosophical purposes* such ways of talking lack relative utility—aside from seeming to rely upon a strikingly unpragmatist separation of the philosophical from the practical—is just to try to hide behind a notion of "philosophical utility." What does a failure to bake philosophical bread come to for Rorty other than a failure to make certain kinds of sense? The philosophical inutility of metaphysical realism's talk of representing the world as it is in itself—to go no further than the considerations adduced in Rorty's own writings—would seem to lie precisely in the ways in which such talk is inherently confused. Rorty can say that he now prefers to speak of "relative inutility" rather than of "incoherence" or "confusion," but it is hard to see how this new way of speaking on his part amounts to anything more than a misleading surrogate for his old way of speaking.

36. See Chapter 13, "Does the Disquotational Theory of Truth Solve All Philosophical Problems?"

37. Collected in *Realism and Reason*, pp. 98–114. Putnam's paper is followed by a note in which he writes that the paper which precedes the note is actually only "a first draft of a paper I never finished." In the note Putnam goes on to complicate, and to some extent retract, the view put forward in the body of the paper. The note is followed by a "Note to supersede (supplement?) the preceding note." This document seems to retract other aspects of the main paper and some of the preceding note's retractions. Some of Putnam's remarks in these appendixes anticipate aspects of the line of thought he elaborates in this volume.

38. Ibid., p. 101.

39. Here is an example of one: "The statement . . . 'This sheet of paper is red and this sheet of paper is not red' . . . simply asserts what *cannot possibly* be the case. And the reason that 'when I open the box you will see that the sheet of paper is red and the sheet of paper is not red' does not count as a prediction, is that we know—know a priori—that it *can't possibly* turn out to be the case [my emphases]" (ibid., p. 105).

40. Putnam summarizes the conclusion of the paper as follows: "The idea is that the laws of logic are so central to our thinking that they define what a rational argument is. This may not show that we could never change our mind about the laws of logic, i.e. that no causal process could lead us to vocalize or believe different statements; but it does show that we could not be brought to change our minds *by a rational argument* . . . [The laws of logic] are presupposed by so much of the activity of argument itself that it

is no wonder that we cannot envisage their being overthrown . . . by rational argument" (ibid., p. 107).

41. This development is anticipated to some extent by the last sentence of the "Note to supersede (supplement?) the preceding note" tacked on to the end of his earlier paper: "if it is always dangerous to take on the burden of trying to show that a statement is absolutely a priori, . . . it is not just dangerous but actually wrong to make the quick leap from the fact that it is dangerous to claim that any statement is a priori to the absolute claim that there are no a priori truths" (ibid., p. 114).

42. In his telling of it here, Putnam has revised the original Grimms' fairy tale (referred to by Wittgenstein) "The Peasant's Wise Daughter."

43. Putnam acknowledges a debt here to Cora Diamond's "Riddles and Anselm's Riddle," chap. 11 of *The Realistic Spirit* (Cambridge: MIT Press, 1991), for the riddle, for drawing the (unpublished) Wittgenstein passage in question to his attention (quoted by Diamond on p. 267), and for her discussion of it.

44. Gottlob Frege, *The Basic Laws of Arithmetic* (Berkeley: University of California Press, 1967), p. 12.

45. The last three claims are summarized by Putnam as follows: "While I would not claim that Frege endorses this view of Kant['s], it seems to me that his writing reflects a tension between the pull of the Kantian view and the pull of the view that the laws of logic are simply the most general and most justified views we have. If I am right in this, then the frequently heard statement that for Frege the laws of logic are . . . [the] 'most general laws of nature' is not the whole story . . . At times it seems that their *status,* for Frege as for Kant, is very different from the status of empirical laws. (It was, I think, his dissatisfaction with Frege's waffling on this issue that led the early Wittgenstein to his own version of the Kantian view.)"

46. I am here simply allowing myself to paraphrase some of Putnam's own remarks. His considered view, however, is considerably more nuanced than these formulations suggest. The nuance arises from the fact that Putnam does not use the terms "sense" and "meaning" as synonyms. Putnam writes: "The word 'sense' in questions like 'In what sense do you mean that?' is much more flexible than the word 'meaning' as used in philosophers' talk of 'translation manuals' and 'recursive specifications of meaning.' To use an example due to Charles Travis, suppose someone paints the leaves on my Japanese ornamental tree (which has copper-colored leaves) green. If someone who doesn't know what happened remarks that my tree has 'green leaves,' is that right or wrong? We may reply that it all depends on what sense we give to 'green leaves'; but I don't think this shows that either 'green' or 'leaves' has two *meanings*. Rather it shows that given the (dictionary) meanings of the words, we do not always know what a particular sentence *says* (if anything). The content of a token sentence

depends on the meaning of its words in the language, but it also depends on a multitude of features of the context" (*The Philosophy of Hilary Putnam*, p. 375).

Putnam wants to claim that we are not at present in a position "to give sense" to the *assertion* of the negation of a law of logic. But he does not take this to entail that the denial of a law of logic "has no meaning." He wishes, for example, to regard sentences which contain such denials as sub-sentential components as meaningful. He therefore wishes to drive a wedge between a sentence's "having a meaning in the language" and our being able to make sense of the sentence as the assertion of a *claim*: "Thus when I suggested that Frege was attracted to and Wittgenstein actually held the position that the negation of a law of logic violates the conditions for being a thinkable thought or judgment, I was not excluding contradictions from 'meaning' in the sense of well-formedness in the language, or saying that they have no use at all . . . My point was rather that a contradiction cannot be used to make an intelligible claim" (ibid., p. 376). Putnam offers, by way of example, a pair of historical cases in which he thinks we should say that, at a certain time, certain sentences "had a meaning in the language" but that they did not (yet) express "understandable claims": "someone says, before anyone has succeeded in conceiving of a coherent alternative to Euclidean geometry, that a plane triangle may have two right angles as base angles. I think it is fair to say that we would not find this *intelligible* in that cognitive situation. Learning Riemannian geometry enables us to *give sense* to those words; that doesn't mean that we are *stipulating a new meaning* for one or more of the words of the sentence in question. It means that we can now see how that sentence can be used to make a claim, whereas before we could not. We understand 'in what sense' such a triangle is possible. Similarly, 'Momentum is not exactly mass times velocity' once had no sense; but it is part of Einstein's achievement that the sense he gave those words now seems inevitable. We read old physics texts homophonically for the most part; certainly we do not say that 'momentum' used to refer to a different quantity, but rather that the old theory was wrong in thinking that momentum was exactly *mv*. So this is not a case of giving a word a new meaning in the language. But that does not alter the fact that the use to which we put the words (the sense we have given them) was not available before Einstein. Even if we decide to say that the sentence "had a meaning in the language" even before Einstein, that does not mean that it was *understandable*—understandable as a *claim*—before Einstein" (ibid., p. 375).

Putnam wants to say that when we declare—in a misplaced spirit of fallibilist humility—that "the laws of logic may turn out to be wrong," we have not (yet) succeeded in giving those words a sense any more than the pre-Riemannian geometer or the pre-Einsteinian physicist would have been in a position to make sense of the sentences in the above examples as assertions of intelligible claims.

Putnam is famous for having argued against the idea (as put forward, for example, by Thomas Kuhn and Paul Feyerabend) that Newton's and Einstein's theories are incommensurable with one another because the fundamental theoretical terms (such as mass) have all undergone a *change in meaning*. Putnam can be seen in the above quotation as trying to recover the kernel of truth (which was misexpressed in terms of an incommensurability thesis) underlying the views of those theorists of scientific change who were so impressed by the radical character of scientific revolutions. While continuing to stand by his earlier arguments (for rejecting the thesis that the terms "momentum," "mass," and "velocity" all underwent a change in meaning in the shift from Newton to Einstein), Putnam makes it clear here that he does not take those arguments in any way to preclude him from agreeing with what (he now thinks) was perfectly sound (but misexpressed) in Kuhn and Feyerabend: namely, the thought that the Newtonian physicist would not have known how to make sense of the claim that "momentum is not exactly mass times velocity"—that it was only with Einstein that we learned how to understand those words as making a fully intelligible claim.

47. Putnam, on his present view, thus seems to be wedded to the idea that the negation of a proposition of logic is worse off than the (unnegated) proposition of logic. There is, for Putnam, a significant asymmetry between a logical proposition and its negation: the question of the truth of a logical proposition makes sense, whereas the parallel question about its negation (in ordinary circumstances) does not; the former meets the conditions of being a thought and the latter does not. This aspect of Putnam's view aligns him, one might have thought, much more closely with Kant and Frege than with the *Tractatus* or the later Wittgenstein. For further discussion of this and related questions which arise in connection with Putnam's account in "Rethinking Mathematical Necessity," see my "Search for Logically Alien Thought," in *The Philosophy of Hilary Putnam,* pp. 115–180.

48. See Wittgenstein, *Philosophical Grammar* (Berkeley: University of California Press, 1978), p. 455.

49. These sentences (which Putnam reproduces without supplying a reference, assuming that all educated readers know these lines by heart) are from Quine's essay "Two Dogmas of Empiricism," in *From a Logical Point of View* (Cambridge: Harvard University Press, 1980), p. 43.

50. "Introducing Cavell," Preface to *Pursuits of Reason: Essays in Honor of Stanley Cavell,* ed. Ted Cohen, Paul Guyer, and Hilary Putnam (Lubbock: Texas Tech University Press, 1993), pp. vii–viii. In *Renewing Philosophy* (Cambridge: Harvard University Press, 1992), Putnam expands on this: "Cavell sees all of Wittgenstein's work as concerned with the problematic of skepticism, but skepticism in a very wide sense. The skeptic in Cavell's

enlarged sense may indeed not be a skeptic in the usual sense at all. Rather then professing to doubt everything or to relativize everything, he may claim to have a grand metaphysical solution to all our problems. But for Cavell the pretense that there is a grand metaphysical solution to all of our problems and skeptical or relativistic or nihilistic escape are symptoms of the same disease. The disease itself is the inability to accept the world and to accept other people . . . Something in us both craves more than we can possibly have and flees from even the certainty that we do have. It is not that relativism and skepticism are unrefutable. Relativism and skepticism are all too easily refutable when they are stated as positions; but they never die, because the attitude of alienation from the world and from the community is not just a theory, and cannot be overcome by purely intellectual argument. Indeed, it is not even quite right to refer to it as a disease; for one of Cavell's points is that to wish to be free of skepticism is also a way of wishing to be free of one's humanity. Being alienated is part of the human condition, and the problem is to learn to live with both alienation and acknowledgment" (pp. 177–178).

51. This is obscured by the David Pears and Brian McGuinness translation of the *Tractatus* (London: Routledge, 1961), which introduces into this sentence the idea that there is something which "we must *pass over* in silence." It is further obscured by their translation of the previous sentence. Where Wittgenstein says the reader "must overcome [or defeat]" the propositions in this book, Pears and McGuinness have: "He must *transcend* these propositions."

52. This is a phrase of John McDowell's which (as the reader of this volume will discover) Putnam has grown fond of; see McDowell's John Locke Lectures, *Mind and World,* and McDowell's "Non-Cognitivism and Rule-Following," in *Wittgenstein: To Follow a Rule,* ed. S. Holtzman and C. Leich (London: Routledge, 1981), p. 150.

53. I have partly constructed this paragraph from sentences taken from my "Search for Logically Alien Thought" (which discusses these issues in more detail).

54. *Philosophical Investigations,* §43.

55. Putnam's reading of Frege and my summary of it below are indebted to Thomas Ricketts' "Objectivity and Objecthood: Frege's Metaphysics of Judgment," in *Synthesizing Frege,* ed. L. Haaparanta and J. Hintikka (Dordrecht: D. Reidel, 1986).

56. *The Basic Laws of Arithmetic,* pp. 12–25.

57. Here, again, Putnam sees Frege (and *a fortiori* Wittgenstein) following in Kant's footsteps. In Chapter 1 Putnam summarizes a similar point (about how the activity of judgment eludes the gaze of empirical psychology) offering it, on this occasion, as an exposition of Kant: "Here is an example to illustrate what Kant had in mind. If I think, 'There are cows in Rumania,'

then regarded as an event in the material universe, what I have produced is a list or sequence of words—noises, or subvocalizations, or images in my mind, or whatever. If I utter (or think) not the sentence 'There are cows in Rumania,' but the mere list of words *There, are, cows, in, Rumania,* I also produce a sequence of words—one with different causes and effects to be sure. But the difference between judging that there are cows in Rumania and producing a mere list of noises seems to be something over and above a mere difference in the causes and effects in the two cases. The judgment is, in Kant's terminology, an act of *synthesis.* And the problem about which, according to Kant, empirical psychology cannot tell us anything is the problem of understanding synthesis."

58. I am allowing myself here to follow Putnam's (somewhat inconsistent) use of this term. Throughout most of the essays in this book "naturalistic" is employed as a label for various forms of (what Putnam in some of his more careful moments calls) "reductive naturalism": empiricism, behaviorism, positivism, psychologism, eliminativism, and so on. As mentioned above, Putnam also sometimes uses the label "disenchanted naturalism" to name the enemy in order to leave room for the claim that the view he himself endorses is a ("sane") form of naturalism—one which allows nature to encompass (rather than exclude) normativity and intentionality.

59. *Philosophical Investigations,* §19.

60. Ludwig Wittgenstein, *Lectures and Conversations on Aesthetics, Psychology, and Religious Belief* (Berkeley: University of California Press, 1966), p. 8.

61. *The Many Faces of Realism* (La Salle, Ill.: Open Court, 1987), chap. 1.

62. *Realism with a Human Face,* pp. 40, 42.

63. *The Realistic Spirit,* chap. 1.

64. Ludwig Wittgenstein, *Remarks on the Foundations of Mathematics,* 3rd ed. (Oxford: Oxford University Press, 1978), p. 325.

65. *The Realistic Spirit,* p. 39.

66. Ibid., pp. 39–40.

67. Wittgenstein, *Remarks on the Foundations of Mathematics,* pp. 201–202. For further discussion of Wittgenstein's remark, see *The Realistic Spirit,* pp. 41ff., and the appendix to Diamond's "Wittgenstein, Mathematics, and Ethics," in *The Cambridge Companion to Wittgenstein,* ed. Hans Sluga and David Stern (London: Cambridge University Press, 1994).

68. *The Realistic Spirit,* pp. 18–22.

69. Ibid., pp. 21–22.

70. Wittgenstein, *Lectures and Conversations on Aesthetics, Psychology, and Religious Belief,* pp. 71–72.

71. Putnam writes: "Mary Warnock once said that Sartre gave us not arguments or proofs but 'a description so clear and vivid that when I think of his description and fit it to my own case, I cannot fail to see its application.'

It seems to me that this is a very good description of what Wittgenstein was doing, not just in the private language argument, but over and over again in his work" (*Renewing Philosophy*, p. 74).

72. Ibid., p. 156.

73. If the person lacks a perspicuous view of the way in which the picture informs his own practice, he may himself become puzzled whether he is entitled to the use he makes of it. He may thereby be drawn into viewing the possibilities of use in the same way—through the lens of the picture considered in abstraction from its use. He will thus be led either into conflict with himself (through his continued reliance on the picture—unless, that is, he changes his life) or into (what Wittgenstein calls) "superstition" (into insisting that God *does* have eyebrows, and only a heathen sinner would deny it!).

74. *Philosophical Investigations*, §115.

75. Putnam is here alluding to a discussion in Wittgenstein's *Lectures and Conversations on Aesthetics, Psychology, and Religious Belief*: "In general there is nothing which explains the meanings of words so well as a picture" (p. 63).

76. *Renewing Philosophy*, pp. 156–157.

77. Chapter 13, last paragraph.

78. "The Face of Necessity," chap. 9 of *The Realistic Spirit*.

79. *The Realistic Spirit*, p. 259. Diamond immediately goes on to develop this point in connection with the topic of her paper—the picture of necessity implicit in everyday mathematical practice: "To give up altogether the pictures that mislead us when we talk as philosophers about proof and reasoning would be to give up—not Platonist mathematics—but mathematics, reasoning, inference, what we recognize as making sense, as human thinking. The picture of a necessity behind what we do is not then to be rejected, but its application looked at" (p. 259).

80. Chapter 13, penultimate paragraph. The passage continues: "As Cavell puts it, skepticism about other minds can be (and, in a way, often is) a *real* problem, while skepticism about 'middle-sized dry goods' is an utterly unreal problem." The allusion here is to the discussion of the asymmetry between skepticism about other minds and skepticism about the external world in Part IV of Cavell's *The Claim of Reason* (Oxford: Oxford University Press, 1979).

81. This question (whether Wittgenstein can, without inconsistency, uphold the integrity of our ordinary talk of the inner) forms the topic of an exchange between John McDowell and Crispin Wright. Here, again, there is a considerable affinity between Putnam and McDowell—this time with respect to their readings of Wittgenstein's remarks about pictures. See McDowell's "Intentionality and Interiority in Wittgenstein," in *Meaning Scepticism*, ed. Klaus Puhl (Berlin: Walter de Gruyter, 1991).

82. *Philosophical Investigations,* §§423–424.

83. Ibid., §§422, 425–426.

84. Ibid., §427.

85. Wittgenstein writes: "We are thinking of a game in which there is an inside in the normal sense. We must get clear about how the metaphor of revealing (outside and inside) is actually applied by us; otherwise we shall be tempted to look for an inside behind that which in our metaphor is the inside" ("Notes for Lectures on 'Private Experience' and 'Sense Data,'" in *Philosophical Occasions, 1912–1951* [Indianapolis: Hackett, 1993], p. 223).

86. Putnam's views on these matters are (as therefore is also my summary of them—especially at this point) indebted to Peter Winch's article "Wittgenstein, Picture, and Representation," in *Trying to Make Sense* (Oxford: Basil Blackwell, 1987).

87. Here again, I am allowing myself to echo Putnam echoing McDowell.

88. The papers by McDowell which Putnam has in mind here are "Virtue and Reason," *Monist,* 62 (1979); "Are Moral Requirements Hypothetical Imperatives?" *Proceedings of the Aristotelian Society,* suppl. vol. 52 (1978); and "Non-Cognitivism and Rule-Following."

89. McDowell, "Non-Cognitivism and Rule-Following," p. 141.

90. *Renewing Philosophy,* p. 86.

91. Wittgenstein, *Philosophical Investigations,* p. 174.

92. Chapter 12, last paragraph.

93. *Reason, Truth, and History* (New York: Cambridge University Press, 1981), p. 136.

94. Wittgenstein, *Zettel,* §567.

95. I am indebted to Stanley Cavell, Cora Diamond, Martin Stone, and Lisa Van Alstyne for comments on a previous draft of this introduction.

I

The Return of Aristotle

1. How Old Is the Mind?

In this century people talk as if the mind is almost a self-evident idea. It is as if phenomena themselves required us to classify them as mental or physical in the way we do. Yet the present notion is not very old, or at least its hegemony is not very old. The words *mind* and *soul,* or their classical ancestors, the Latin *mens* and the Greek *psyche,* are of course old. The habit of identifying notions which are actually quite different leads us to think that therefore the present notion of the mind must be equally old, but nothing could be more false. This is worth knowing as a fact of intellectual history, of course, but my hope is that whatever our interest in the mind—whether as philosophers or as psychologists or as "cognitive scientists" or just as curious and puzzled human beings—we may find that this bit of intellectual history may also have the benefit of making usual ways of thinking about "mental phenomena" seem less coercive.

Let us begin, as one so often does, with Aristotle. Aristotle's *De Anima* is often considered (rightly, I believe) the first work on psychology—indeed, it virtually gives the subject its name. But is Aristotle's subject, the psyche, to be identified with what we call the mind? (*Psyche* is often translated "soul," so we could also ask whether the psyche is to be identified with what we call—or have called—the soul.)

The answer, known to those of you who have read Aristotle, is no. Aristotle's *psyche* is the "form," or I would say the organization to function, of the whole organized living body. Its nature is that of a capacity. (A capacity is described as a "first actuality" in the standard translation of Aristotle's text; perhaps the thought is that the "primary realities," as one might also render "first actuality," are capacities to *do* things.) Among the activities of the psyche (activities listed by Aristotle) are those we would regard as physical (digestion and

3

reproduction). These activities are the "second actualities." But our capacity for reproduction and our capacity for digestion are obviously not part of what we nowadays call mind. If the Aristotelian *psyche* corresponds to any contemporary notion it is to the extremely up-to-date notion of our "functional organization," as I have argued elsewhere,[1] not to the present popular notion of the mind.

Aristotle has other notions, other distinctions; do any of these quite correspond to *our* mental/physical distinction? There is, for example, the famous notion of *nous* (reason). But the *nous* is much more restricted than the mind. The "passions," the natural desires for affection (at least for physical affection), for sustenance, for comfort, as well as the vindictive and aggressive feelings and the vanity and desire for admiration that are a part of our makeup, are none of them part of the *nous*. (In Plato's tripartite division of the soul, the passions were themselves a section and the *nous* was a different section.) The ordinary sensations of sight or hearing are also not part of the *nous*. (Sensation did not come to be considered part of the mind until very late. In fact, during the last two or three hundred years, especially in English-speaking countries, the mind has been virtually identified with sensation.) In Aristotle's system, visual sensations occur in the sense of sight itself, auditory sensations in the sense of hearing itself.

A point that is puzzling, or at least one that I find puzzling, is just how information from the senses gets integrated with general principles from the *nous;* such integration is required as much by Aristotle's account of theoretical reasoning as by his account of practical reasoning. But Aristotle does not describe the faculty that performs this task *(unless it is the "common sense"?).* He recognizes the need for an integrative agency, and locates it in the region of the heart. At any rate, one can generate questions about how *nous* is related to body, how *psyche* is related to body, and so on, within the Aristotelian system; and Aristotle says things about those questions (for example, he says "active *nous*" is separable from body but the psyche as a whole is not), but one cannot find the modern "mind-body problem."

Similar points can be made about the medieval conceptions. Aquinas had an elaborate psychology,[2] but it does not divide things up as we now do. The senses, in Aquinas' scheme, produce representations in the passive imagination, which Aquinas (using an Aristotelian term) calls *phantasmata* (not fantastic things, but perceptions). Like Aristotle, Aquinas considers these sensory images to be material (although not in a modern reductive sense—there is no talk of neurons or of computer circuitry in the brain, of course). To modern ears, this conception of the sensory images as something virtually on a level with body is, perhaps, the strangest feature of the classical way of thinking. Since British empiricism virtually identified the mind with images (or "ideas" as they were called in the seventeenth century), *we* have come to think of images as paradigmatically "mental," and—unless we are materialists—as immaterial. Yet for the classical thinkers it was reason—*nous*—that was unlike body, and sensation that was clearly on the side of matter and body. (In Aquinas' psychology the *phantasm* is explicitly described as "material," from which the intellect extracts an "intellectual species" or—to make one of those oversimple equations I warned against—a concept.)

One of the most difficult questions to answer about these models is the exact location of *memory*. It has come to seem such a central function of the mind to us that we tend to read it back into earlier writers. And until you actually look for it, you don't become aware of how very different thinking about memory was, just as thinking about sensation was very different. Earlier writers distinguished two kinds of memory. One kind is memory of things you can understand or see with your intellect once you've figured something out (for example, the Pythagorean theorem, or that the essence of being human is being rational). Once you've figured out one of these intellectual truths and come to grasp it, you can recall it, and it's in your *nous* itself. But if I have an ordinary memory of something that happened to me (say, that I ate eggs for breakfast) or of a fact about myself (my name is Hilary Putnam), where is this stored? Certainly not in the active *nous*. Neither Aristotle nor Aquinas is explicit about this, but I think that the following position might be ascribed to both of them: if I am not actively now recalling the episode or the fact, then the memory trace is not in my *nous* at all. Aquinas already knew that the brain and not the heart was the seat of the intellect; although it sounds strangely contemporary, the view that "brain traces" are memories which are not actively being recalled might well have been perfectly acceptable to him.

Aquinas explicitly denies that you can think properly without a body. He rejects the theology according to which the body is simply a kind of drag on the soul which corrupts it, drives it down, and makes it sinful. God, he believed, was a good workman. He made this body and this soul for each other; without one the other doesn't really work. If this interpretation is correct, then when I remember my name or what I had for breakfast, something in my brain activates my passive imagination and produces a *phantasm* (one from the inside instead of the outside); my *nous* acts on this *phantasm* and obtains conceptual information from it.

I said this view sounds contemporary, and up to a point it is. A modern materialist who does not trouble himself to distinguish between mind and brain might feel that such a view was virtually just common sense. But notice that it is not quite the common-sense view. The contemporary "common-sense" view is that it is obvious that memories are in the mind; what is still regarded as a difficult question is whether they are *identical* with brain traces or only *correlated* with brain traces. The view I have been attributing to Aquinas is that it is obvious that memories are in the body (the brain); when they are not actively being recalled, they are not "mental" at all. The *nous*/body distinction that Aquinas would have drawn is not at all the same as the modern mind/body distinction. Yet, when I think about it, it doesn't sound worse than the modern one! *Is it* obvious that there is something called the mind whose contents include all of my memories, whether I am actively recalling them or not, but whose functions do not include digestion or reproduction? Or are we in the grip of a picture, a picture whose origins are somewhat accidental and whose logic, once examined, is not compelling?

The fact that the passions and the episodic memories (as opposed to memories of general principles, like the principles of geometry or logic) are not part of *nous,* of the part of the mind which Aristotle considered to be immaterial, sheds light on a controversy concerning the doctrines of Maimonides as well as on some vexed interpretative questions concerning Descartes. Although in his doctrinal writings (his great commentary on the Talmud) Maimonides avows belief in immortality, in his work of pure theoretical philosophy, the *Guide to the Perplexed,* he qualifies this notion in such a way that Strauss,[3] in particular, has wondered whether Maimonides believed in *personal* immortality at all. Some of the things Maimonides writes lead Strauss to think that, in Maimonides' view, only reason, "active *nous,*" is indestructible. If the active *nous* does not contain such things as memory of the episodes in my life, my knowledge of who I am, my desires (insofar as they do not stem from reason alone), and so on, then even if it be true that active *nous* is not destroyed when I die, this is not what anyone ordinarily thinks of as me, Hilary Putnam, surviving my bodily death. I don't wish to assert that Strauss's interpretation is right; but the very presence in medieval philosophy of this distinction between survival of the *nous* and survival of the *individual* illustrates how very different the immaterial part of the soul, as a medieval philosopher would have termed it, is from what we today call the mind.

The problem in Descartes to which I alluded is the problem of reconciling the statement that I am essentially a mind (a "thing that thinks"), which we find in the *Discourse* and the *Meditations,* with the statement in Descartes's letters that I am not my mind alone but rather an organic unity of my mind and my body. One possible way of reconciling the two statements would be to interpret the *I* that is my mind as simply the active thinking consciousness—there is no evidence at all that Descartes has an "unconscious mind"—and the *I* that is the organic unity as the whole self, including my memories, standing dispositions, and sensations. (Hoffman[4] has argued that in Descartes's view sensations were material images in the body rather than "mental" phenomena in the Cartesian sense, and Hoffman takes this to support reading Descartes's view of the *self* as a true organic unity view. Note that if Hoffman is right, Descartes is, among other things, continuing the tradition that goes back to Aristotle, the tradition of thinking of sensations as "material.")

Humean Minds and Post-Kantian Minds

When I wrote my first paper on the mind-body problem, "Minds and Machines,"[5] I argued that a "logical analogue" of the problem arises for Turing machines, and that "all of the questions of 'mind-body identity' can be mirrored in terms of the analogue." To do this, I imagined a machine which is capable of generating scientific theories, and which accepts theories that satisfy certain criteria ("assuming it is possible to mechanize inductive logic to some degree"). "In particular, if the machine has electronic 'sense organs' which enable it to scan itself while it is in operation, it may formulate theories concerning its own structure and subject them to test," I wrote. I imagined the machine discovering "I am in state A when and only when flip-flop 36 is on." Here "I am in state A" was supposed to be *observation (introspective) language for the machine:* that is, the command that the machine print out "I am in state A" when it is in state A is "hard-wired" into the machine, while "flip-flop 36" (machines had flip-flops and not circuit chips in those days) is supposed to be *theoretical language for the ma-*

chine. "Flip-flop 36" was described as a "theoretical term" which is "partially interpreted in terms of observables." I went on to assert:

> Now all of the usual considerations for and against mind-body identification can be paralleled by considerations for and against saying that state A is in fact *identical* with flip-flop 36 being on.
>
> Corresponding to Occamist arguments for "identity" in the one case are Occamist arguments for identity in the other. And the usual arguments for dualism in the mind-body case can be paralleled in the other: for the machine "state A" is something directly observable; on the other hand "flip-flops" are something it knows about only via highly sophisticated scientific inferences—How *could* two things so different *possibly* be the same?[6]

What interests me when I read the writing of my former self is how obvious it seemed to me that the mind-body problem concerned, in the first instance at least, *sensations,* and how the "usual arguments for dualism" were all arguments against identifying sensations with anything physical. Nor was I alone in this impression. A glance at the various anthologies on the mind-body problem reveals that it was just about universal in those years. Everybody "knew" the mind-body problem had to do with whether sensations were material or not. Obviously something had happened in philosophy—at least among English-speaking philosophers—between Descartes's time and ours to bring this about.

What had happened was the impact of British empiricism, and in particular the empiricism of Berkeley and Hume. The classical view was based, as I have said, on Aristotle, for whom there was something in common between my perception of the object and the object itself—exactly *what* is a difficult question of interpretation, and I don't think that Aristotle really worked it out. I think that when you try to read more into Aristotle's theory you are already creating your own theory rather than his. But at the least he says that the Logos (sometimes translated "Form") of the external thing enters into my mind in perception, minus, of course, the matter. I don't have a chair in my head if I look at a red chair, but I do somehow have the form, chair. Perceptions, according to the classical reading of *De Anima,* produce *phantasmata* in us (in our "passive imagination," in Aquinas' system), and these *phantasmata* were identified with what were later called "sense impressions" or even with mental "images." (Martha Nussbaum has argued[7] that this reading is actually a misreading, and that *phantasmata* are by no means always images; but this question is far too difficult to discuss here.) At any rate, the Aristotelian view holds that the "form" of the external thing is somehow connected both with the external thing whose form it is *and* with the *phantasm* produced in me by seeing or touching or hearing or smelling or tasting the thing. When I see a chair, the very "form" of the chair is in some way in me.

Descartes, however, argued that in the case of the so-called secondary qualities (texture, color, and so on), it is a mistake to confuse the sense in which a mental image can have one of those qualities with the sense in which a material object can do so. When I have a mental image or a sense impression of a red, smooth table, I may call the image smooth and I may call the table smooth; but there are two concepts (or "forms") of *smooth* involved here, not one. Similarly with *red*. In the case of the primary qualities—the "extension" of the material object, its size and figure—Descartes did, however, retain the classical view that these are present in the mind *and* in the object, that (in this respect) I have the very form of the object within my own mind (though not, of course, its matter). Now Berkeley pointed out that an image can no more be literally three inches long than it can be literally red in the way a physical object is red. In Berkeley's view—which became the almost universal view—a mental image or a sense impression has no ordinary property in common with matter: no physical length, no physical shape, no physical color, no physical texture, and so on. Of course, this is not how Berkeley himself would have put it. Berkeley would rather have said that the only red we know is the red we directly experience—which, in his view, is the red of the "idea," the sense impression or image; that the only smooth we know is the smooth we directly experience, the smooth of the "idea"; that the only extension we know is the extension we directly experience, the extension of the "idea"; and he notoriously went on to conclude that the whole notion of a realm of matter distinct from and responsible for our "ideas" is a philosopher's mistake.[8]

Although the philosophical world as a whole did not follow Berkeley into that immaterialism, it did follow Berkeley in concluding that (contrary to the classical tradition) sense impressions and images were totally immaterial. From Berkeley's time until very recently it has been a minority view that, say, pains or visual impressions could possibly be identical with physical events or processes. The mind-body problem has become (among English-speaking philosophers) the problem of the relation of these apparently immaterial sensations (now thought of as the paradigm of the "mental") to the physical world.

In Germany, however—and German philosophy was the dominant philosophy in the whole non-English-speaking world until very recently—a different evolution took place. The dominant influence was Kant. Kant's views are extremely difficult, and I will touch on only one or two issues here. Kant addresses both what we today would call the problem of the nature of the mind—that is, problems of theoretical psychology—and problems of the nature of the self. (Most of his readers have tended to ignore the distinction between these two sorts of problems in Kant's writings.) There is, in Kant's system, a distinction between the self of pure subjectivity—the Berkeleyan "Spirit," which is always subject, always "I," and never object (the "transcendental unity of apperception," in Kant's jargon)—and the empirical self, the self Hume found whenever he introspected. On the side of mind, there is a similar duality (although it is a mistake, I believe, to simply identify the two dualities in Kant). There are the mental processes we can study empirically, the laws of association and so forth; and there are mental processes, processes of "synthesis" as Kant calls them, whose nature Kant says we will "probably" never be able to discover. The fact that Kant uses the word "probably" is one of the reasons that I think it unwarranted simply to identify the faculty of synthesis with the transcendental self. (That we cannot discover the nature of the transcendental self is not just a matter of "probability" for Kant.)

Note that Kant does not say there are two "substances"—mind and body (as Descartes did). Kant says, instead, that there are "dualities in our experience" (a striking phrase!) that refuse to go away. And I think that Kant was, here as elsewhere, on to something of permanent significance.

If the discussion of the mind-body problem in this country has changed since 1960, it is largely because of the present centrality of computers and computer-suggested metaphors to our modeling of mental processes. And, oddly enough, the effect of this change has been to bring post-Kantian topics and concerns back into English-speaking analytic philosophy in a massive way. (I say back into, because they were concerns of English-speaking philosophy at the turn of the century—it was with the decline of pragmatism and idealism and the rise of logical positivism that English-speaking philosophy reverted to its traditional empiricist way of conceiving mind-body issues.) Today we see the term *intentionality* (borrowed from Brentano) everywhere. A popular book on the computer model, Margaret Boden's *Minds and Mechanisms,* formulates its task in highly Kantian language as "providing a richer image of *machines* that suggests how it is that subjectivity, purpose and freedom can characterize parts of the material universe."[9] Evidently, the nature of the mind-body problem is once again undergoing a shift. The paradigmatic question is no longer "Is pain identical with stimulation of C-fibers?" but rather is "How can subjectivity, purpose, and freedom characterize parts of the material universe?" It is the Kantian mind rather than the Humean mind that we now want to understand.

The reason for this is simply that computer models lend themselves more naturally to speculating about these Kantian topics than they do to speculations about the nature of sense-data. But what are the Kantian topics?

Kant was concerned about the following puzzle: when I describe a thought as an empirical psychologist might (Kant was thinking of Humean psychology, but the point he was making has not become outdated), I describe it as a sequence of representations—images or words with certain causes and certain effects. I may find out a great deal of value by doing this. But there is one thing that I can never discover as long as I stick to this approach, namely, that I am dealing with something which has truth-value, freedom, and meaning, and not just causes and effects. That's the central Kantian question.

Here is an example to illustrate what Kant had in mind. If I think, "There are cows in Rumania," then, regarded as an event in the material universe, what I have produced is a list or sequence of words—noises, or subvocalizations, or images in my mind, or whatever. If I utter (or think) not the sentence "There are cows in Rumania," but the mere list of words *There, are, cows, in, Rumania,* I also produce a sequence of words—one with different causes and effects, to be sure. But the difference between judging that there are cows in Rumania and producing a mere list of noises seems to be something over and above a mere difference in the causes and effects in the two cases. The judgment is, in Kant's terminology, an act of *synthesis*. And the problem about which, according to Kant, empirical psychology cannot tell us anything, is the problem of understanding synthesis.

I myself think that Kant was right, but his claim remains intensely controversial today. Ken Winkler has written of Berkeley that "like some other great philosophers" he "thought that philosophy would end with him; what made him great is not that he ended it, but that he made it even harder to avoid."[10] One of the "other great philosophers" Winkler had in mind must have been Kant. The problem Kant raised here has indeed proved hard to avoid.

The Problem of Synthesis Today

The question that Kant bestowed on us as his legacy is just what the key question about the mind actually is. What should puzzle us more: that we have sensations or that we have "propositional attitudes"? The problem of synthesis has taken a number of forms in contemporary philosophy and "cognitive science." One form is a heated discussion over whether the study of the semantical properties of thought is a topic for psychology (in the widest sense) at all.

Two philosophers who have argued for many years that it is not are Wilfred Sellars and W. V. Quine. Sentences (whether I say them or write them or just think them in my mind) do, indeed, have semantical properties. The sentence "There are cows in Rumania" has the property of being true, for example, and it contains words which denote the set of cows, the extended individual we call Rumania, and the set [(x,y)| x *is spatially contained in* y]. The properties of truth and denotation, mentioned in the previous sentence, are paradigmatic examples of semantical characteristics. But the explication of these semantical characteristics is not a problem for psychology at all. Truth and denotation are not in any way derivative from the mind; they are rather derivative from language. According to Quine, "Immanent truth, a la Tarski, is the only truth I recognize."[11] (For a discussion of the influence of Tarski's work on Quine see my "A Comparison of Something with Something Else.")[12] The way to define *truth* and *denotation* has been found by Alfred Tarski, in his famous "definition of truth." Sellars thought he himself had shown us how to understand denotation and other semantical notions in linguistic terms. Chisholm, on the other hand, has argued that it is extremely implausible to think that certain signs are "language" apart from their relation to a mind.[13]

Philosophers and cognitive scientists who do think the nature of meaning is a problem for psychology have many different ideas as to how and why it is so, and correspondingly many different programs for tackling the problem. One school of thought, based at MIT, holds that there is an innate "language of thought."[14] This innate language, "Mentalese," is thought of as having the structure of a classical (or

"Fregean") symbolic logic—complete with quantifiers, and so on. The meaning (or "content") of a thought is somehow determined by the way that thought is coded in "Mentalese." This "content" determines the "conceptual role" of the item—how it is related to the outputs of various hypothetical "modules" or "mental organs" that Fodor postulates, but it does not determine its external world reference. Reference (and truth) are problems for philosophy rather than for psychology, on this view. (So Kant is partly right; part of what makes thought thought—that it refers to external things—cannot be seen as long as we stick to a "methodologically solipsist" perspective, and psychology, according to Fodor, must be methodologically solipsist.)

Certain other philosophers hold that the key problem *is* the problem of reference, and that this problem can, in principle, be solved by a kind of social psychology. The reference of a term (at least in basic cases—and the program of this school is to start with these basic cases and understand reference in other cases as derivative in some way from these) is determined by the way the term, or rather the speaker's or the community's use of the term, is causally linked to external things. The word *cat* refers to cats because cats have figured (in a certain "appropriate" way) in interactions which have led us to use the word *cat* as we do. "Reference is a matter of causal chains of the appropriate type" might be the slogan of this group.

The problem these philosophers face (I would say it is an insuperable problem) is to say why and how a certain kind of causal connection between the characteristics of a thing and the use of a word brings it about that the word refers to that kind of thing, and to say what that certain kind of causal connection is without using any "semantical" word (any word which presupposes the notion of reference) in the characterization. Since studying the sort of causal connection in question involves looking at groups of speakers rather than individual speakers, a science that answered these questions would have to be a social psychology rather than an individual psychology; and since the causal connection involves real external things, things which are not in the heads of the speakers, it would not be a methodologically solipsist psychology, not even in a communitarian sense of *methodological solipsism* (a solipsism with a *we* instead of an *I*). Notice that if reference is essential to minds and the causal theory is even partly on the right track, then what makes a mind a mind is, in large part, the way it is hooked up to an external environment—a striking shift away from the British empiricist perspective!

Aristotle and MIT

A causal theory of the referential powers of the mind cannot remain at the level of talk about "causal chains of the appropriate type," however. To persist there is not just to be guilty of vagueness, but to rely on an ancient (in fact, an Aristotelian) notion of efficient causation which is no more clear than reference itself. When we say, for example, that our encounters with cats are what have caused us to use the word *cat* as we do, we are relying on the old notion of cause-as-what-explains; what we mean is that events involving cats are what *explain* the fact that we use the word as we do. But to use an unreduced notion of explanation in a theory of reference would be to explain the obscure in terms of the more obscure.

To avoid use of an unreduced notion of explanation while keeping the program will certainly be difficult. For a start, one might hope to eliminate vague talk of "the way we use the word '_____'" by actually constructing a model of the use of language. Some people say: "Well, we might somehow build a computer model—not just of the individual human but of the entire linguistic community in its environment. And when we get through with this huge model, it will somehow enable us to classify the causal chains that connect the subroutines inside the head of the speaker with external things and events." The only way one can think of doing this today is with the aid of the computer analogy; thus the MIT program of a computer model of the "language organ," including a "semantic level of representation," would itself be one part of the larger program sketched by the causal theorists of reference. This would be a model of the use of language in a methodologically solipsist sense, the use insofar as it is contained inside the head of the individual speaker. In addition, of course, one would have somehow to classify the "causal chains" that connect these uses (subroutines inside the head of the speaker) with external things and events. The entire program might be called sociofunctionalism—the program, that is, of giving a model of the functional organization of a whole language-speaking community in its semantic relations to an environment.

This program hardly sounds more realistic than that other ancient program, the program of inductive logic: an algorithm which reproduces human scientific competence. But there is more wrong than just lack of realism. (After all, the devotees of this program would be content with progress in this direction; they do not seriously expect the entire program ever to be carried out, any more than—they would say—the entire program of physical science, the program of completely modeling the basic laws of nature, has to be carried out to justify physics as an activity.)

The difficulty is rather as follows. There *are* causal constraints on interpretation—we do expect some of the things speakers say to be "about" things they causally interact with, and we have some idea of the kind of causal interaction (for example, perceptual interaction) which is likely to be relevant. I interpret the speaker of a jungle language when I look at what he is seeing and touching and hearing, and I would assume that a lot of his words refer to the things he perceives. But we do not always interpret speakers as if they were referring to whatever it is that caused them to introduce the word or locution they are using. How difficult interpretation can become! An example from the history of chemistry and metallurgy is instructive. In his great history of metallurgy, Cyril Smith has pointed out that the properties of the oxygen molecule do not really enter into the explanation of a number of the properties of metal calxes: what enters is rather the properties of the valence electrons of the metal itself. He once jokingly expressed this by saying, "Phlogiston *does* exist; it's valence electrons!" We don't say that, however. We say instead, "That's a nice joke but there really isn't any such substance as phlogiston."

The question I want to ask is, "*Why* doesn't *phlogiston* denote valence electrons?" The simple answer would be that the causal chain connecting valence electrons to the properties of calxes and thence, via human perception of those properties, to (the invention of phlogiston theory and) the use of the word *phlogiston* isn't "of the appropriate type." But isn't this the typical kind of causal chain in the case of a theoretical term in physics? An entity is responsible for the observable behavior of something or other, and observation of that behavior leads to the introduction of a theory containing a term which refers to that entity—refers to it even though typically we didn't get the properties of that entity exactly right when we first made up the theory.[15]

Another less simple answer—a better one—is that the causal chain is there, all right, but interpreting *phlogiston* as denoting valence electrons would falsify central beliefs of the people who used the term (as they thought) referentially. But look! Taking the word *electron*, as Bohr used it in 1900, to refer to electrons *also falsifies central beliefs of the people, including Bohr himself, who used it "referentially."*

Bohr believed in 1900 that electrons had trajectories—had both position and momentum all the time. So he had centrally false beliefs about electrons. Yet we regard it as reasonable, nonetheless, to interpret his 1900 word *electron* as referring to what we now call electrons. And so did Bohr. By keeping the same word when he developed quantum mechanics, he treated his own sequence of theories as a sequence of better and better theories about the same things. (In Husserlian language, he treated electrons as an "ideal pole," a kind of ideal object about which we get convergent knowledge, even though what we say about them at any given time is not exactly right.)

This illustrates that causal constraints on reference have to be balanced against other constraints in the actual practice of interpretation. Interpreting someone is not something you can reduce to an algorithm. You can't do it by just looking at what he perceives, or looking at the phenomena he is trying to explain, or looking at all of this plus his beliefs, or rank-ordering his beliefs in terms of which are more or less central. We do manage to interpret one another; otherwise hermeneutics would be impossible and conversation would be impossible. But it takes all of the intelligence we have to do it.

To say what is an "appropriate kind of causal chain" we would have to have a *normative* theory of interpretation as a whole, not just a description of certain kinds of "causal chains." For interpretation (like theory formation in empirical science) is a holistic matter. What I'm leading up to is the *holism of interpretation.* In truth, a survey of interpretative rationality is as Utopian a project as a survey of scientific rationality.

There is one last element, and again I'm giving the case for Kantian pessimism. To ask what someone's—say, Jones's—words are about, how to interpret them, is a *normative* question. The question should not be confused with the question of what Jones would *say* his words are about, because very often speakers give terrible answers. (When you ask explicit semantical questions, as linguists know who have worked with native informants, the first rule is not to let them know what you want to find out. For once the informant knows what you want to learn, you'll get ruined data. People will tell you, "Yes, we talk this way and not that way," and it will be absolutely wrong.)

Nor is Fodor's project—the project of saying what words have the same "content" and what words have different "content" without looking at the causal chains connecting those words to the external world—any better off.[16] To attempt this is just to engage in theory of interpretation while throwing away a large part of the data (the data about the external correlates of the representations being processed by the brain); this won't make the task easier—rather it will make it impossible! But what if the task *is* impossible? The task of physics, as we said before, may also be impossible to fulfill, yet we are content, and rightly so, with partial success. Could not the "sociofunctionalist" view be correct in principle even if it cannot be carried out in practice?

For a long time this is what I myself believed.[17] But it now seems to me that there is an important difference between the two cases. What is analogous to the task of physics, perhaps, is the task of describing how the human brain actually works (either at a neurological or at a computational level). Progress certainly has been made in doing this— as an example of exciting work using computational models one thinks of the work of the late David Marr.[18] But the task of giving a computational analysis of meaning or reference seems to resemble this task less than it resembles the task of formalizing scientific reasoning (inductive logic). These latter two tasks—formalizing interpretation and formalizing nondemonstrative reasoning—are normative, or partly normative, in a way in which simply modeling how we actually see or think or interpret is not.

A correct model of how the brain works might, in the Utopian limit, actually predict what people will say about what a word refers to and about whether a phrase is or is not a good paraphrase of a given expression as used in a particular context. But if the question is not "Do most people think that *phlogiston* refers to valence electrons?" but is instead "*Does phlogiston* refer to valence electrons?"; or if the question is not "Do most people think that the phrase 'justifiably believes, what is in fact true, that . . . ' is a reasonable paraphrase of the verbal phrase 'knows that . . . '?" but is instead "*Is* 'justifiably believes, what is in fact true, that . . . ' a *correct* paraphrase of the verbal phrase 'knows that . . . '?"; then, as I said before, we are asking a normative question. We are asking for an algorithmic or computer version of a normative account of interpretative rationality; and I, for one, see no reason to think this is possible. Indeed, if (as I believe) human interpretative rationality is deeply interwoven with human rationality in general, then constructing an algorithmic model of interpretation would presuppose constructing an algorithmic model of prescriptive rationality in general—and this is surely impossible for human minds to do, for Gödelian reasons among others.[19]

To close, we are back with the question Kant raised: the question, in

contemporary rather than Kantian terms, whether the nature of semantical characteristics of representations is a problem for descriptive
science at all. One great twentieth-century philosopher who would
have answered "no" to this question—and not because he thought the
question was answered by the work of Alfred Tarski—was Ludwig
Wittgenstein. But his philosophy is both too complex and too close to
my own time for me to attempt to survey here.

Perhaps it is enough if I have succeeded in indicating that the question of those "dualities in our experience" which don't seem to go
away is still very much with us. If there is one value which a historical
survey of what has been thought on these matters can have, it is to
caution us against thinking that it is obvious even what the questions
are. For part of what we have seen in this survey is that each previous
period in the history of Western thought had a quite different idea of
what such a term as *mind* or *soul* might stand for, and a correspondingly different idea of what the puzzles were that we should be trying
to solve.

Notes

1. See my *Philosophical Papers,* vol. 2, *Mind, Language, and Reality* (New
   York: Cambridge University Press, 1975).
2. T. Aquinas, *On Being and Essence,* translation and interpretation by Joseph Bobik (Notre Dame, Ind.: University of Notre Dame Press, 1965).
3. L. Strauss, "The Literary Character of the Guide to the Perplexed," in *Per-
   secution and the Art of Writing* (Chicago: University of Chicago Press,
   1952), pp. 38–95.
4. P. Hoffman, "Cartesian Passions and Cartesian Dualism," *Pacific Philosophical Quarterly,* 71, no. 4 (December 1990), 310–333.
5. In my *Philosophical Papers,* vol. 2, *Mind, Language, and Reality* (New
   York: Cambridge University Press, 1975).
6. Ibid., p. 363.
7. M. Nussbaum, "The Role of *Phantasia* in Aristotle's Explanation of Action," in *Aristotle's "De Motu Animalium"* (Princeton: Princeton University Press, 1978), pp. 221–270.
8. Berkeley did not think the world consisted *only* of "ideas," however. The
   mind was not (as it became for Hume) just a collection of sense impressions, images of the imagination, memory images, conscious feelings, and
   so on. There were, for Berkeley, also the *subjects* of the "ideas." *Subjectivity* is irreducible in Berkeley's system. My "I," my "self," is a "spirit" (in
   Berkeley's terminology), and the world consists of "Spirits and their Ideas."

The two categories of Spirit and Idea are correlative in this system; a Spirit is described by saying what its Ideas are, and Ideas, to be completely described, must be assigned to the proper Spirit. For Hume, however, a Spirit is nothing but a bundle of Ideas. (Whether this solves the problem of subjectivity or conceals it by hiding it behind the notion of a bundling relation has been argued by philosophers for centuries.) With Hume's step of identifying the mind with a "collection" (that ambiguous word!) of sensations and feelings and images, the transformation of the mind-body problem into what I knew it as in 1960, and into what my teachers' teachers knew it as, was complete.

Incidentally, it is with Hume that memory gets classified as a part—or rather a faculty—of the mind: the faculty "by which we repeat our impressions" in such a way that they retain "a considerable degree of their first vitality." Calling memory a faculty of course raises more questions than it answers; but Hume's chapter "Of the Ideas of the Memory and Imagination" occupies less than two pages of his two-volume *Treatise*. See *A Treatise of Human Nature*, 2nd ed., ed. B. A. Selby-Brigge (New York: Oxford University Press, 1978). Here Hume follows Augustine rather than Aristotle.

9. M. Boden, *Minds and Mechanisms: Philosophical Psychology and Computational Models* (Ithaca: Cornell University Press, 1981).
10. G. Berkeley, *A Treatise concerning the Principles of Human Knowledge*, ed. K. Winkler (Indianapolis: Hackett, 1982).
11. W. V. Quine, *Theories and Things* (Cambridge: Harvard University Press, 1981).
12. See Chapter 17 of this volume.
13. The following letter by Chisholm (from a famous correspondence between Sellars and Chisholm) illustrates the opposing views:

August 24, 1956

DEAR SELLARS,

The philosophic question which separates us is, in your terms, the question whether

(1) "_____" means p

is to be analysed as

(2) "_____" expresses (thought) t and t is about p.

I would urge that the first is to be analysed in terms of the second, but you would argue the converse. But we are in agreement, I take it, that we need a semantical (or intentional) term which is not needed in physics.

How are we to decide whether (1) is to be analysed in terms of (2), or conversely? If the question were merely one of constructing a language, the answer would depend merely upon which would give us the neatest language. But if we take the first course, analysing the meaning of noises and marks by reference to the thoughts that living things have, the "intentionalist" will say: "Living things have a funny property that ordinary physical things don't have." If we take the second course, there could be a "linguisticist" who could say with equal justification, "Marks and noises have a funny kind of characteristic that living things and other physical things don't have."

Where does the funny characteristic belong? (Surely it doesn't make one whit of difference to urge that it doesn't stand for a "descriptive relation." Brentano said substantially the same thing, incidentally, about the ostensible relation of "thinking about," etc.) Should we say there is a funny characteristic (i.e., a characteristic which would not be labelled by any physicalistic adjective) which belongs to living things—or one which belongs to certain noises and marks?

When the question is put this way, I should think, the plausible answer is that it's the living things that are peculiar, not the noises and marks. I believe it was your colleague Hospers who proposed this useful figure: that whereas both thoughts and words have meaning, just as both the sun and the moon send light to us, the meaning of words is related to the meaning of thoughts as the light of the moon is related to the light of the sun. Extinguish the living things and the noises and marks wouldn't shine any more. But if you extinguish the noises and marks, people can still think about things (but not so well, of course). Surely it would be unfounded psychological dogma to say that infants and mutes, and animals cannot have beliefs and desires until they are able to use language.

In saying, "There is characteristic . . ." in paragraph 2 above, I don't mean to say, of course, that there are abstract entities.

I don't expect you to agree with all the above. But do you agree that the issue described in paragraph one is an important one and that there is no easy way to settle it? . . .

Cordially yours,

RODERICK M. CHISHOLM

This correspondence appears under the title "Correspondence on Intentionality," in *Concepts, Theories, and the Mind-Body Problem*, ed. by H. Feigl, M. Scriber, and G. Maxwell, Minnesota Studies in the Philosophy of Science, 2 (Minneapolis: University of Minnesota Press, 1958), pp. 521–539.

14. J. Fodor, *The Language of Thought* (New York: T. Y. Crowell, 1975).

15. See my "Explanation and Reference" and "Language and Reality," in *Phil-

osophical Papers, vol. 2, *Mind, Language, and Reality* (New York: Cambridge University Press, 1975).

16. See Chapter 21 of this volume. Fodor has subsequently gone over to a causal theory of reference.

17. See my "The Nature of Mental States" and "Philosophy and Our Mental Life" in *Philosophical Papers,* vol. 2.

18. D. Marr, *Vision: A Computational Investigation into the Human Representation and Processing of Visual Information* (San Francisco: W. H. Freeman, 1982).

19. See Chapter 22 of this volume.

2. Changing Aristotle's Mind

With Martha C. Nussbaum

We take up arms together in response to an attack. It is an attack on our interpretation of Aristotle and, through that, on the credibility and acceptability of Aristotle's views of soul and body. Myles Burnyeat, in his paper "Is an Aristotelian Philosophy of Mind Still Credible?" discovered in various things that we had written separately a shared view of Aristotle: namely, a defense of the Aristotelian form-matter view as a happy alternative to materialist reductionism on the one hand, Cartesian dualism on the other—an alternative that has certain similarities with contemporary functionalism.[1] Burnyeat argues "that the Putnam-Nussbaum thesis is false, and that its falsehood is of more than historical interest." Aristotle's view of mind, he argues, cannot be defended as we defend it, since, properly interpreted, it is wedded to, it "cannot be understood apart from," a view of the material side of life that we can no longer take seriously. Indeed, we cannot even know what it would be to take it seriously. Burnyeat develops an alternative interpretation of Aristotle in the context of the theory of perception, defending a reading that he also claims to be that of Philoponus, Aquinas, and Brentano. He then argues that this interpretation does have the consequence that Aristotle is wedded to the unacceptable view of matter. Aristotle's philosophy of mind, therefore, must be "junked"; and, "having junked it, we are stuck with the mind-body problem as Descartes created it."

This co-authored paper represents a stage in an ongoing dialectical exchange. Burnyeat's paper responded to our earlier work, and we now respond to him—with a revision and expansion of an argument first produced and circulated in 1984. We allude throughout to the 1984 text of Burnyeat's paper, which has now circulated widely in typescript, and was published in 1992 as an unfinished work in progress.[2] Although the debate is bound to continue, we hope that this stage of it states the issues sufficiently clearly that the reader will be able (in the words of that peaceable philosopher Parmenides) to "judge by reason the very contentious refutation."

First we shall talk briefly about Aristotle's motivating problems—why these are not the problems from which the classic mind-body debate begins, and what significance this has for the understanding of his attitude toward material reductionism and material explanation. Then we shall look at the texts, defending against Burnyeat an interpretation that distinguishes Aristotle both from materialist reductionism and from the Burnyeat interpretation, according to which perceiving and so on require no concomitant material change, and awareness is primitive. We shall go on to defend Aristotle's position philosophically, as a tenable position even in the context of a modern theory of matter. Explain the doings of natural beings "neither apart from matter nor according to the matter"—so Aristotle instructs the philosopher of nature (Ph. 194^{a}13–15). So: with "cannon to right" of us and "cannon to left," we shall try to forge a middle path that will not, as Burnyeat thinks it must, end up in the "valley of death."

Aristotle's Problems: Explanation, Nature, and Change

We have chosen the title "Changing Aristotle's Mind." This paper was first written for a conference entitled "Aristotle's Philosophy of Mind and Modern Theories of Cognition."[3] The first change we wish to make in Aristotle's mind is to point out that, properly speaking, he does not have a philosophy of mind. This fact has been pointed out before. Nussbaum has discussed the issue in "Aristotelian Dualism: A Reply to Howard Robinson." Putnam discusses it in Chapter 1 of this volume, "How Old Is the Mind?" Others have also discussed it.[4] But it still bears repeating: for only if we understand Aristotle's starting-points and problems can we accurately assess his solution.

The mind-body problem, the problem with which Burnyeat says we are "stuck," the problem with which he believes any contemporary functionalist must "inevitably and rightly" begin, starts from a focus on the special nature of mental activity—therefore from just one part of the activity of some among the living beings. It attempts to characterize that specialness. Whether the answer defended is Cartesian, reductionist, functionalist, or of some still other sort, the starting-point is the same. It is the question, How are we to speak about (conscious) awareness and about those aspects of our functioning that are thought to partake in awareness or consciousness? Aristotelian hylomor-phism, by contrast, starts from a general interest in characterizing the relationship, in things of many kinds, between their organization or structure and their material composition. It deals with the beings and doings of all substances, including all living beings (plants, animals, and humans alike), all nonliving natural beings, and also all nonnatu-ral substances (i.e., artifacts). It asks some very global and general questions about all these things, and two questions in particular.[5]

First, it asks: How do and should we explain or describe the changes we see taking place in the world? In particular, which sorts of entities are the primary subjects or "substrates" of change, the things that persist through changes of various sorts, on which our explanations of change are "hung"? Aristotle holds, plausibly (appealing to ordinary discourse and practices), that any coherent account of change must pick out some entity that is the "substrate," or underlying persistent thing, of that change, the thing to which the change happens and which persists itself as one and the same thing throughout the change. His first question, then, is: What are those primary substrates?

Second, he asks: How do and should we answer "What is it?" ques-tions asked about the items in our experience? What accounts give us the best stories about the identities of things, as they persist through time? What is it about individuals that makes them the very things they are? And what is it (therefore) that must remain one and the same, if we are going to continue to regard it as the same individual?

Aristotle shows that these two questions are held closely together in our discourse and practices. For any good account of change will need to single out as its underlying substrates or subjects items that are not just relatively enduring, but also relatively definite or distinct, items that can be identified, characterized as to what they are. On the other hand, if we ask the "What is it?" question of an item in our experi-ence, one thing we are asking is, what changes can that item endure and still remain what it is? One reason why "a pale thing" is a bad answer to the "What is it?" question asked about Putnam, while "a human being" is a good answer, is that Putnam can get a suntan in Spain without ceasing to be himself; whereas if an orangutan got off the plane we would suspect that someone had done Putnam in.

Aristotle seems to argue, then, that an answer that fails to deal with one of the questions will fail, ultimately, to do well by the other. Mat-ter might look at first like the most enduring substrate, in that it per-sists through the birth and death of horses, human beings, trees (see

Metaph. 983^{b} 6–18). But if it is not a "this"—a definite structured item that can be picked out, identified, and traced through time—it is not in the end going to be a very good linchpin for our explanations of change and activity.[6] Indeed, in natural substances at least, matter clearly falls short even earlier on. For the matter of a tree does not in fact stay the same as long as this tree exists; it changes continually. In general, no list of particular materials will give us a substrate as stable and enduring as the form or organization of the tree, since that organization stays while the materials flow in and out. That is the nature of living things—to be forms embodied in ever-changing matter. By the same token, the organization characteristic of the species has the best claim to be the essential nature, or what-is-it, of the thing, since it is what must remain the same so long as that thing remains in existence. If it is no longer there, the identity of the thing is lost, and the thing is no more. When Putnam returns from Spain, he will have assimilated a great deal of fine Spanish food; and this will have produced matter that he didn't have before he left. Nussbaum will still regard him as the same person, and treat the new bits of matter as parts of him. But if the being who got off the plane had changed in functional organization, and now had the organization characteristic of the aforementioned orangutan, not of a human, she would call the police.

These are complex issues. We have only alluded schematically to some of our more detailed treatments of them. But we think that even this brief account shows a profound difference between Aristotle's motivations and those of most writers on the "mind-body problem." He does not appear to give awareness or the mental any special place in his defense of form. He has a broad and general interest in identity and explanation, and he defends the claim of form over matter with respect to his whole broad range of cases, in connection with these two questions. These are not outmoded philosophical questions; nor is Aristotle's way of pressing them at all remote from the methods and concerns of modern inquiries into substance and identity. Fine contemporary philosophers such as David Wiggins and Roderick Chisholm[7] share Aristotle's belief that the form-matter question can and should be posed in this very general way, in connection with worries about identity and persistence, before we go on to ask what special features the cases of life and mind might have in store for us. Although one of these thinkers defends the Aristotelian position and the other attacks it, neither believes that our possession today of a theory of matter different from Aristotle's alters in a fundamental way the manner in which these questions should be posed, or makes the Aristotelian reply one that we cannot take seriously.[8]

In replying to Burnyeat, then, we think it important to point out that when Aristotle argues against materialist reductionism he could not possibly be relying on the "primitive" nature of intentionality, or on the inexplicable character of life and mind—for the simple reason that his defense of form is meant to apply (as are Wiggins' similar defense of form and Chisholm's mereological essentialism) across the board to all substances, whether or not they have "mind," or even life. Both of us, when characterizing Aristotle's general line of antireductionist argument, used an artifact as our example, in order to make this point perfectly clear. And we also, for the sake of argument, expressed the example in terms of a modern theory of matter, in order to show that it is independent of premodern views. Let us recall the example briefly. We asked the question, why does a bronze sphere of radius r pass through a wooden hoop of radius just slightly greater than r, while a bronze cube of side $2r$ will not pass through? We argued that—no matter whether one thinks in terms of lumps of Aristotelian stuff or in terms of plotting the trajectories of the atoms characteristic of bronze and wood—the relevant answer to this "why" question will not in fact be one that brings in facts specific to the materials (the bronze and wood) in question. The relevant answer will appeal to general formal or structural features, features that can be given in terms of geometrical laws without mentioning matter—though of course any existing cube or sphere must always be realized in *some* suitable matter. The geometrical explanation remains the same no matter whether we make the cube and sphere of bronze, or wood, or plastic (all of which will, of course, very much change an account on the material level, whether in terms of stuffs or of atom-charts). The formal account, therefore, is *simpler* and more *general* than the material account; and while the material account omits the *relevant* features and includes many irrelevant features, the formal account introduces only the relevant features.[9]

In short, Aristotle thinks matter posterior to form because of a general view about the nature of scientific explanation—and *not* because matter cannot do a certain special task, the task of "explaining mind." We believe that these general arguments against reduction are still sound, although we are also convinced that the case for nonreduction can be bolstered by further arguments where the functions of life are concerned. So we think that any view of Aristotle that criticizes his antireductionism on the grounds that mind must be explained in such and such a way in our scientific age risks failing to come to grips with Aristotle.

We are not clear about how Burnyeat would confront the more general Aristotelian arguments, which are explicitly designed to hold whether one uses an ancient or a modern theory of matter. He says cryptically that he does fault them on "strong independent grounds"; but he does not develop this thesis. We think it will be important for him, if he wants to "junk" Aristotle on form and matter, to say how and why he "junks" this general argument, or why, if he does not "junk" it, he feels confident that Aristotle's whole "philosophy of mind" can be "junked" anyhow. In short: beginning where Aristotle begins helps to see exactly why Aristotle feels that the mind-body problem (or rather, the *psuchē*-body problem, which is his closest analogue to that problem) can be bypassed and should not arise. We shall study Aristotle's antireductionism with this in mind.

One further point deserves emphasis before we charge in. Aristotle's general arguments against reductionism pertain to all substances, living and nonliving, as we said. At least one of these substances is altogether immaterial and unchanging. Another group consists of artifacts, whose principle of motion lies outside themselves. Living beings are a subgroup of the class of natural substances. These are defined in *Ph.* 2.1 as "things that have within themselves a principle of change and of remaining unchanged." In two passages Aristotle tells us that, of necessity, if something is a changing thing it is also a material thing.[10] In *Metaph.* 1026^a2–3, he writes: "If, in fact, all natural things are accounted for in the same way as the snub [Aristotle's stock example of the inseparability of a form, and its account, from a suitable material substrate]—for example, nose, eye, face, flesh, bone, in general animal, leaf, root, bark, in general plant—for the definition of none of these is without change, but they always have matter—then it is clear how one must seek and define the what-is-it in natural things." Lest we be hesitant on account of the conditional (*not*, however, a hesitant conditional, but one with an emphatic indicative antecedent), *Metaph.* Z11 asserts the point unconditionally about animals, in a passage to which we shall return in our next section: "For the animal is a perceptible thing, and it is not possible to define it without change, therefore not without the bodily parts' being in a certain condition" (1036^b27ff.). The inferential pattern in both passages suggests that Aristotle makes an intimate—indeed a necessary—connection between change and materiality. The commentary ascribed to Alexander of Aphrodisias, in fact, takes things all the way to identity, writing on both passages, "By change, he means matter" (512.21 and 445.5).[11] Before

Christianity and Cartesianism separated movement from matter, it was apparently taken for granted that change is something that goes on in materials, and indeed that what matter is is the vehicle of change.

We believe that this is still a reasonable position (although we do not go so far as to *identify* change with matter). In our conception, any being that undergoes change is a material being. We cannot prise these two things apart, even in thought, without incoherence. From this it follows that any account that properly gives the what-is-it of such a being must make mention of the presence of material composition— and, as our Z11 passage suggests, of the presence of a material composition that is in some way *suitable* or *in the right state*. This tells us that on pain of incoherence we cannot describe the natural functions that are the essential natures of animals and plants without making these functions (even if only implicitly) embodied in some matter that is suitable to them: matter that is not simply an inert background, but the very vehicle of functioning itself.

All of this is supposed to be true of all the essential beings and doings of natural substances;[12] *a fortiori* (apparently) of the beings and doings of living creatures; *a fortiori* (one might suppose) of perceiving. But there are problems to be dealt with before we can arrive securely at that conclusion. So we turn from the preliminary skirmishing and prepare for the battle.

Perceiving Is an Enmattered Form

Our argument in this section will have two parts. First, we shall give an account of how we understand and, in general, defend Aristotle's antireductionism. Here we shall try to show that Burnyeat has not accurately characterized our position, and that in one important respect Nussbaum's position has shifted since the 1978 work that Burnyeat cites. Then we shall argue that the psychological activities of living beings, such as perceiving, desiring, and imagining, are realized or constituted in matter, are in fact the activities *of* some suitable matter; and that the relationship between form and matter is one of constitution or realization, not of either identity or mere correlation.

Antireductionism

Burnyeat ascribes to us two views—both about Aristotle and about mind in general—that seem hard to put together. First, that the relation between life-functions and matter is purely contingent: "psychological states . . . must be realized in *some* material or physical set-up, but it is not essential that the set-up should be the flesh and bones and nervous system of *Homo sapiens,* rather than the electronic gadgetry of a computer." Second, that we can state, in material terms, sufficient conditions for the occurrence of psychological processes, such as perception of colors and properties. These are supervenient on material changes, and even if we cannot state the material sufficient conditions now, we can always work toward such an account. There will eventually be an efficient-causal account with no gaps in it.

This puzzles us: for our argument for saying that the link between form and matter was contingent is one that gives us good reasons *not* to think that sufficient conditions will be forthcoming on the material level. It is that living creatures, like many other substances, are *compositionally plastic.* The same activity can be realized in such a variety of specific materials that there is not likely to be *one* thing that is just what perceiving red *is*, on the material level. In our substance examples, the fact that matter continually changes during a thing's lifetime gave us reason to say that matter fails to be *the nature of the thing;* in these examples of life-activity a different and further sort of variability blocks us from having the generality that would yield adequate material explanations. We shall return to this point later. There are numerous passages in Aristotle that make it, in a general way. ("We must speak of the form and the thing *qua* form as being each thing; but the material side by itself must never be said to be the thing"; *Metaph.* 1035ª7–9, and cf. also *PA* 640ª33ff., ᵇ23ff., 641ª7ff., *DA* 1.1.403ª3ff., cf. below, *Ph.* 2.2.) We originally illustrated the point, as we have said, through the example of a bronze sphere, whose doings were explained not by alluding to its specific materials but by speaking of its geometrical properties.

Now, however, we must concede that in her 1978 book Nussbaum did suggest that, although the material account would not have a high degree of generality across cases, we could still, in particular cases at least, give material sufficient conditions for action, belief, perception, and desire—and that we would need to do so, if we wanted to have a genuine causal explanation of actions. This was supposed to be so on the grounds that the logical connections among perception (or belief), desire, and action invalidated these as genuinely explanatory Humean causes of the action.[13] Nussbaum has, however, recanted and criticized this view in two subsequently published papers—"Aristotelian

Dualism" and "The 'Common Explanation' of Animal Motion,"[14] the latter known to Burnyeat before he wrote the paper we discuss here. In "The 'Common Explanation'" (later revised and expanded as Chapter 9 of *The Fragility of Goodness*) she argues that the *sort* of logical connection the intentional *explanantia* have with one another does not really disqualify them from acting as genuine *causes* of the *explanandum,* the action. Aristotle stresses this independence in several ways,[15] and it is all the independence he needs. Indeed, so far from being incompatible, the logical and causal connections are closely linked. It is because what this *orexis* is is an *orexis* for object O, and because what the creature sees before it is this same O, that the movement toward O can be caused in the way it is, by the *orexis* and the seeing. Suppose a dog goes after some meat. It is highly relevant to the causal explanation of its motion that its *orexis* shall be for meat (or this meat) and that what it sees before it it shall also see *as meat.* If it saw just a round object, or if its *orexis* were simply for exercise, the explanatory causal connections that produce the action would be undermined. The dog might for some other reason not have gone for the meat, while having the same desire and belief: in this sense the desire and belief are independent of the goal-directed motion. But their close conceptual relatedness seems very relevant to their causal explanatory role.

Nussbaum then went on to argue that the physiological account *could not,* for Aristotle, provide a causal explanation of an animal action. First, as we have already mentioned here, the connections we might find between a desire for meat and certain concrete bodily changes will lack the generality requisite for Aristotelian explanation. Second, and this is what we want to stress here, the physiological feature, *just because* it lacks both the general and the particular conceptual link with the action, links which the intentional items, perception (belief) and desire, do possess, lacks the sort of *relevance* and *connectedness* that we require of a cause when we say, "This was the thing that made that happen." In other words, to use Aristotle's terminology, it could not be a *proper cause* of the action.[16] All this suggests that we shall never be in a position to explain action (or indeed presumably the perceptions and desires that cause it) from the bottom up; it is not simply that we do not have the realizing descriptions in each case. If we did have them, they would not have the right sort of explanatory linkage with the *explanandum* and with the other *explanantia.* So we believe that these intentional features are irreducible, and not explicable in terms of material states and activities. We argue for finding this view in Aristotle, and we believe it to be a compelling and largely correct view.[17]

Material Embodiment

Burnyeat holds that in Aristotelian perception, becoming aware is a primitive phenomenon that has no associated material change:

> No physiological change is needed for the eye or the organ of touch to become aware of the appropriate perceptual objects. The model says: the effect on the organ *is* the awareness, no more and no less . . . Not merely is there no deduction from physiology to perception, not merely are there no physiological sufficient conditions for perception to occur, but the only necessary conditions are states of receptivity to sensible form: transparent eye-jelly, still air walled up in the ear, intermediate temperature and hardness in the organ of touch. When these have been specified, the material side of the story of perception is complete.

In other words, there is in perception a transition from potential to actual awareness that is not the transition of any materials from one state to another. There is psychological transition without material transition. Becoming aware is neither correlated with nor realized in the transitions of matter. It is this feature that is thought to have the consequence that Aristotle's view is not to be taken seriously by us moderns. Let us examine the thesis, and then this inference.

We now wish to make two preliminary distinctions and two dialectical concessions. First, it is one thing to hold that perception cannot be explained "from the bottom up," quite another to hold that it is not accompanied by or realized in any material transition. We hold the first, but deny the second. For something to be a causal explanation of something, as we and Aristotle both suppose, far more is required than that it be true and truly linked with the item in question. As we have already said, we believe that our sort of "functionalism" (the next section will show that Putnam now dissociates himself from functionalism for reasons that bring him even closer to Aristotle) is not only not committed to explanation "from the bottom up," but is built on the denial of this possibility.

Second, we find that Burnyeat's argument at this point takes a peculiar turn. For suddenly we find little reference to Putnam and Nussbaum, and copious reference to an article by Richard Sorabji.[18] Burnyeat takes our position to be committed to Sorabji's account of what the physiological change involved in perception is: that in perception the sense-organ actually takes on the quality of the object perceived, becoming red, or hard, or whatever. He calls this Sorabji position "a piece of essential support" for us in the area of perception. Having argued against this view and in favor of a view according to which the eye's becoming *aware* of red does not require its *going red,* he thinks he has damaged our view (and Sorabji's more general thesis, which we do accept) that the becoming aware is realized in (constituted by) a material transition. But it is one thing to argue against a particular story of what the physiological change is, quite another to establish that there need be no physiological change. (Aquinas, as we shall see below, argues like Burnyeat against the Sorabji physiological story, yet takes it as so evident as not to require argument that each act of perception is of necessity accompanied by *some* physical change *(immutatio)* in the sense-organs.)

Now the dialectical concessions. We shall grant Burnyeat his criticism of Sorabji's physiological thesis, and so forgo that concrete story as to what the physiological change is. We are not sorry to give that up. Indeed, it would be unwelcome to us if Aristotle *did* insist on a monolithic account of what the physiological realization of perception always *consists in,* since we have ascribed to him the view that there *need not be one thing* that it (physiologically) consists in. What we do want to ascribe to Aristotle on the physiological side will become clear in a moment.

Second concession: we grant as well that it is important that perception is not the type of change that Aristotle (speaking strictly)[19] calls a *kinēsis;* it is, rather, the actualization of a potential. This is why we have been using the rather mysterious word "transition" instead of the word "change." (Aquinas is not so cautious.) Still, the point is: it does not follow that this transition is not at every point of necessity accompanied by *some material transition.* (Matter has potentialities too, clearly; and these too can be actualized.) We shall argue that it is; indeed, with Sorabji, we believe that the most precise way of characterizing the relationship is that it is a transition *realized in* the matter. The *psuchē* does nothing alone; its doings are the doings *of* the organic body. Perceiving is an activity in matter.[20]

Burnyeat's position is a slippery one to attack, since he is prepared to grant that perception has necessary material conditions, and that these are conditions of the sense-organs. Many of the passages in which Aristotle asserts that the *psuchē* or its activities are "not without matter" could indeed be understood in this weaker way. We shall now, however, bring forward several that are not so ambiguous.

Exhibit A: *De Motu Animalium,* Chapters 7–11[21]

Burnyeat's analysis of perception rests on the evidence of *De Anima* alone. And of course this is a major text, where perception is concerned. On the other hand, it seems especially unwise to regard it as *the* central text, when discussing this particular problem. For Aristotle himself makes a distinction between two types of writings on psychology, according to which the *De Anima* will, on the whole, discuss psychological matters structurally, without reference to their material accompaniments, and another group of treatises will handle the relationship between psychology and physiology. Thus in *DA* 3.10, discussing the way in which desire produces bodily movements, he writes, "But as for the equipment *(organōi)* in virtue of which desire imparts movement, this is already something bodily *(sōmatikon)*—so we shall have to consider it in the 'functions common to body and soul'" (433^{b}18ff.).[22] There follows a brief summary of the argument of the *De Motu Animalium*. The rubric *ta koina psuchēs kai sōmatos erga* will be discussed below, when we analyze Exhibit B: for it appears to be a general title for the *Parva Naturalia* taken as a group, with the *De Motu* added. Meanwhile, we wish to suggest only that this passage shows any silence on Aristotle's part, in the *De Anima,* about the physiology of psychological processes to be a deliberate strategy, indicating his commitment to nonreductionism about psychological explanation, but showing nothing at all about the issue that divides our view from Burnyeat's. It is not surprising that he should be silent about what he has deferred to another treatise; and someone who wants to find out his view on the problem needs to look closely at that other treatise.

Moreover, since Burnyeat seems inclined (see below, Exhibit C) to grant something like our position where *desire* is concerned, it is worth pointing out that the *De Motu* cannot be read as treating desire and perception asymmetrically. The treatment of the physiology of desire is more obscure than that of the physiology of perceiving, and seems to involve reference to the somewhat mysterious *sumphuton pneuma;* by contrast Aristotle (as also in Exhibit B) treats perceiving as the clearest and simplest case of physiological realization. But both

are treated perfectly symmetrically, as interlocking elements in a single causal process.

The general approach of the *De Motu,* where physiology is concerned, can be clearly seen from the passage in Chapter 10 that introduces the *pneuma:* "According to the account that gives the reason for motion, desire is the middle, which imparts movement being moved. But in living bodies there must be some *body* of this kind" (703ª4–6). In other words, it is psychology, unreduced, that gives us the reasons for, or explanations of, the (voluntary) movements of animals. But since we are dealing with embodied living creatures (and not, for example, with the activities of gods), we know, too, that we will discover *some* physiological realization for the psychological process in each case.

Let us now look at the situation where perception is concerned—and the complex interaction between perceiving and desiring that results in animal movement. At the opening of Chapter 7, Aristotle asks the question: how does it happen that cognition of an object is sometimes followed by movement and sometimes not? He answers: because sometimes the animal has a desire for the object it apprehends, and also a feasible route toward getting it through movement, and sometimes not. He describes the complex ways in which different forms of cognition (including *aisthēsis, phantasia,* and *noēsis*) interact with different forms of desiring, in order to produce the resulting action (the famous "practical syllogism"). In the second half of the chapter, however, he turns to a further question: how *can* such psychological processes actually set a large heavy animal body in motion? The answer seems to be: because these processes are themselves functions of and in the body; and they easily and naturally cause other bodily movements that end up moving the limbs. In a famous simile, Aristotle compares animals to automatic puppets, and also to a certain sort of toy cart. In both cases, even a small change in a central part of the mechanism can bring about large-scale and obvious changes in other parts. And such changes (warmings and chillings in the region of the heart above all) are the physiological concomitants of perception and the other forms of cognition, as well as of desire.

We propose to look very closely now at the central text in which this thought is expressed, first interpreting it in what seems to be the most natural and straightforward way, then trying out Burnyeat's position, to see whether it can possibly be made to fit. We shall quote it in Nussbaum's translation, with one difference: the pivotal word *al-*

loiōsis ("alteration") will remain untranslated. Numbers have been inserted for ease of reference in the subsequent discussion:

(1) The movement of animals is like that of automatic puppets, which are set moving when a small motion occurs: the cables are released and the pegs strike against one another; and like that of the little cart (for the child riding in it pushes it straight forward, and yet it moves in a circle because it has wheels of unequal size: for the smaller acts like a center, as happens in the case of the cylinders). For they have functioning parts that are of the same kind: the sinews and bones. The latter are like the pegs and the iron in our example, the sinews like the cables. When these are released and slackened the creature moves. (2) Now in the puppets and carts no *alloiōsis* takes place, since if the inner wheels were to become smaller and again larger, the movement would still be circular. But in the animal the same part has the capacity to become both larger and smaller and to change its shape, as the parts expand because of heat and contract again because of cold, and alter *(alloioumenōn).* (3) *Alloiōsis* is caused by *phantasiai* and sense-perceptions and ideas. For sense-perceptions are at once a kind of *alloiōsis,* and *phantasia* and thinking have the power of the actual things. For it turns out that the form conceived of the pleasant or fearful is like the actual thing itself. That is why we shudder and are frightened just thinking of something. All these are affections *(pathē)* and *alloiōseis.* (4) And when bodily parts are altered *(alloioumenōn)* some become larger, some smaller. It is not difficult to see that a small change occurring in an origin sets up great and numerous differences at a distance—just as, if the rudder shifts a hair's breadth, the shift in the prow is considerable. Further, when under the influence of heat or cold or some other similar affection an *alloiōsis* is produced in the region of the heart, even if it is only in an imperceptibly small part of it, it produces a considerable difference in the body, causing blushing and pallor, as well as shuddering, trembling, and their opposites. (701^{b}2–32)

What this *seems* to say, we claim, is that the animal moves as it does because of the fact that its psychological processes are realized in physiological transitions that set up movements that culminate in fully-fledged local movement.

(1) Puppets and little carts move as wholes, just as the result of a change in a central part; this is the way animals also move. For they are equipped with a functional physiology (*organa* in the sense of suitable equipment), their tendons and bones being rather like the strings and wood in the puppets.

(2) But there is a difference. The puppets and carts move simply by a push-pull mechanism that does not involve a (physiological) qualitative change, an *alloiōsis*. Animal parts, however, do undergo such *alloiōseis*, namely changes of shape and size in the parts resulting from heatings and chillings.

(3) These *alloiōseis* are brought about by perception and imagining and thinking. For perceptions just *are (ousai)*, are realized in, such *alloiōseis*. And although this seems less clear where *phantasia* and thinking are in question, still, the fact that these two produce results similar to those produced by perception shows that the case *is* similar. Just imagining or thinking of something can chill you.[23] And all these are experience and *alloiōseis*.

(4) When an *alloiōsis* takes place, some parts become larger, others smaller. And this has consequences at a distance.

Now it appears that *alloiōsis,* in this passage, is Aristotle's word for what we have called the material transition. He tells us, both here and in subsequent chapters, that such *alloiōseis* of necessity accompany perceiving and imagining; and Chapter 10 completes the picture where desire is concerned. Furthermore, the material transition is not just a concomitant, it is what perception *is*. Nussbaum has argued that this "is" must be understood (as elsewhere in Aristotle) to indicate material realization or constitution, not full identity. For Aristotle's commitment to explanatory nonreductionism is plain in the treatise as a whole, and there is no sign that a complete causal account could be given on the material level. None the less, the material transition is linked far more closely with psychological activity than Burnyeat's account permits. Whatever the *ousai* means, it clearly means that the material change is intrinsic to what goes on when perceiving takes place, and necessary for a full explanation of animal motion. There are some unclarities about the physiological story: it is not fully clear, for example, whether the *alloiōsis* is the heating (chilling) or the closely linked change of shape. But in a sense the very vagueness of the story is its strength, where our view is concerned. For we would not want Aristotle to suggest that sufficient conditions for motion could be given by mentioning materials alone. The story here is far more pleasingly reticent than the one Sorabji told. But it does show that psychological transitions are, for Aristotle, material transitions, *and* that this embodied status is necessary for the explanation of perception's causal efficacy.

Subsequent chapters confirm this general picture. Chapter 8 argues, once again, that certain heatings and chillings are the necessary concomitants of certain perceptions; the argument is extended to memory. And now we are given a way of handling Burnyeat's point that perceiving is not a *kinēsis*. For we are told that the bodily parts are crafted in such a way as to have by nature the capability of making these transitions—so the transition in question will be the realization of a natural capability, just the sort of transition from potency to actualization that Burnyeat is after on the psychological side. (He seems to suppose that material changes are all *kinēsis;* but matter has its potentialities too.) Chapter 9 argues that the complexity of animal movement requires something like our central nervous system: a central bodily location for stimulus-reception and the initiation of response. The area of the heart is defended by arguments presupposing the general psychological picture we have outlined. Chapter 10 fleshes out the picture where desire is concerned, introducing the *pneuma.* Chapter 11 assures us that desire is not necessary for any and every animal motion: some movements of parts are produced by *phantasia* alone, without *orexis;* and some systemic movements (e.g., digestion, the functions of sleep) go on without either perception or desire.[24]

Where can Burnyeat dig in here? It seems to us that he cannot deny that the *alloiōseis* in the crucial parts of the cited passage are material transitions, without making the passage as a whole so riddled with ambiguity as to be hopeless. Nor can he deny, it seems to us, that this natural reading of the passage is consistent with *De Anima*'s insistence that perceiving is an *energeia,* and also consistent with Aristotle's overall nonreductionism about the explanation of animal motion. Our account, based on the passage, is not reductionistic, and it does not propose to build up intentionality from matter. The best hope for Burnyeat's reading, we believe, would be to claim that the *alloiōseis* in question here are material transitions associated not with *all* perceiving, but only with a special sort, the perceiving of the object of desire or avoidance. In other words, it is not perception itself that is realized in matter, it is perception-cum-desire. It is only in so far as desire enters the picture that the body enters it also.

We have already said that we believe this severing of perception from desire to be very peculiar and *ad hoc,* given the symmetry with which *De Motu* treats the two. Furthermore, the passage indicates that it has been talking about changes connected with the cognitive side of the animal's functioning, saving desire for more detailed discussion in Chapter 10. *DA* 3.12 tells us that the most essential function of perception in animal life is to present to the animal's awareness objects of pursuit and avoidance, so that it can survive (434^{b}9–27). So the fact that Aristotle does not spend much time talking about what happens when the animal gazes at a mountain or smells a rose or hears a symphony is hardly surprising: animals' perceiving is eminently practical, and their awareness of motivationally irrelevant parts of the world is bound to be limited. (This would presumably be true of humans too, except insofar as we have *nous* in addition.) So an account focused, like Burnyeat's, on the intentionality of awareness, and one that, like ours, combines an interest in intentionality with a concern for its physical embodiment, should be expected to focus on the very same cases, the cases that Aristotle himself stresses here: namely, cases in which animals become aware of motivationally salient features of their environment. The same things that are the objects of awareness in Burnyeat's view will be, in ours, both objects of awareness and occasions for material transition.

We conclude that the *De Motu* provides very powerful evidence that Aristotle conceives of both perceiving and desiring as thoroughly enmattered. Their activity is accompanied, of necessity, by a transition in matter.[25]

Exhibit B: *De Sensu*, Opening

We have already mentioned the fact that the short treatises to which we give the title *Parva Naturalia* (together with *De Motu*) are referred to by Aristotle himself as "functions shared by soul and body," *koina psuchēs kai sōmatos erga* (*DA* 433^{b}19–20). The opening of the first of these short works, which is of course the treatise *On Perception and Perceptibles*, gives reasons for thinking that the entire range of functions to be discussed in these treatises are "shared" or "common" in this way:

> It is evident that the most important functions, both those shared by animals with other creatures and those peculiar to animals, are shared by the soul and the body, e.g., perception and memory, and emotion and appetite and in general desire, and in addition to these pleasure and pain . . . That all the enumerated items are shared by soul and body is not unclear. For all happen with perception: some as its corruptions and privations. That perception comes to be for the soul through body *(dia sōmatos)* is evident, both from argument and apart from argument.

Perception, then, is taken to be the clearest case of something that is a "common" or "shared" function. Can this passage be read as weakly as Burnyeat requires, so that perception is "common to soul and body" just in case it has necessary conditions of receptivity in the sense-organs? We think not. To say that a function *(ergon)* is shared by (the "common function" of) both soul and body must be to say that they both *do* it, are both active and acting together. Alexander takes it this very natural way: "The activities *(energeiai)* of living beings are shown to be shared by soul and body," in that they are all linked to perception; and "he takes it as evident that perception is an activity *(energeia)* that is shared by soul and body" (2.16ff. Wendland).[26] Soul and body are *active together:* we would say, not only together but indissolubly, as one thing. Similarly, a later passage (441^b15ff.) says of touching, construed as the activation of a potential, that it is a "*pathos* in the wet" as it is affected by the dry; we suppose that the dry affects the wet materially, producing a material change. We cannot see how to read this Burnyeat's way: that the only *pathos* present is just the becoming aware. As in *De Motu,* Aristotle is saying that the matter undergoes something. And we note that, here as in *De Motu,* he seems to treat perception as an especially clear case of embodiment, not more problematic than desire, but less so.

Furthermore, if this passage is read in Burnyeat's way, an essential contrast disappears. If being a "common function" means only that the function has some material necessary conditions, then everything, including thinking, is a common function. Thinking too, in the animal organisms that have it, has material necessary conditions: for it never takes place without *phantasia,* which is itself embodied (see Exhibit C below).[27] But we notice that Aristotle does not in fact include thinking among the functions that are said to be common to body and soul. It is perfectly clear that he means to distinguish it from all these—presumably because its activity is not the *activity of* a bodily organ or organs, an activity realized in suitable matter. (Aquinas reads the contrast this way, as we shall see.)

Exhibit C: *DA* 403^a5ff.

Our next passage takes up this very point. In the first chapter of *De Anima,* Aristotle says, "It appears that the soul suffers and does most things not without body, like getting angry, being confident, desiring appetitively, in general perceiving, but thinking seems to be especially its own thing. But if this is *phantasia* or not without *phantasia,* then even this could not be without body."

Here we have a dialectical passage, but nonetheless one that introduces a distinction that is developed and never effaced in the rest of the text. The way perceiving is "not without matter" is different from the way thinking is. The latter turns out to have necessary conditions, but no organ and no correlated and realizing change of the organ or organs. The former, as Aristotle will go on to say later in this passage, is a *logos enhulos,* a structure realized in matter.

In his paper Burnyeat grants something close to this (although it is difficult to tell exactly how much) for anger, the example that Aristotle goes on to discuss in detail, and for a range of similar examples. He makes, however (as we have already mentioned in discussing Exhibit A), a strong contrast between "the emotional" and "the cognitive side of our mental functioning." Body may be involved in the former in something like the way we say; it is not involved in the latter. We find no such contrast, here or elsewhere; and we believe that the passage does not even permit this, for perception is explicitly named in the sentence we have quoted as one of the things in question that the soul "suffers or does," *paschei* or *poiei,* "not without body." It is true that the passage (which is somewhat loosely structured) goes on to focus on a narrower group of cases—"anger, mildness, fear, pity, confidence, joy, love, hatred"—asserting of all these that the body "suffers something" along with them (403ª16–18). But this is not because perception is not included in the conclusion of the general argument: the connection of perception with material change has been plainly asserted earlier, in the passage we cite. If anything, it is because perceiving is, here as in *De Sensu,* taken, along with *phantasia,* to be an especially clear and obvious case of bodily involvement, whereas desire is far less obvious: notice, for example, that Aristotle's remarks about thinking take the bodily status of *phantasia* for granted. (The need to devote special attention to desire stems, no doubt, from Aristotle's background in the Academy; for Plato persistently puts perception on the side of body, with no hesitation. But desire receives a variety of different treatments, being body in the *Phaedo,* soul in the *Republic,* immortal soul in the *Phaedrus* and *Laws.*) There is no reason, then, to suppose that the general conclusion of the passage applies only to the "emotional" and not to the "cognitive" side of the animal's psychology.[28]

In fact, we can go even further: neither here nor elsewhere does Aristotle even make Burnyeat's sharp distinction between the cognitive and the emotional. Desire and emotion are treated throughout the corpus as forms of selective intentional awareness. Even where appetite is concerned, Aristotle criticizes Plato's treatment of hunger, thirst, and so forth as blind urges impervious to conceptions and beliefs. Only the plant-like self-nutritive aspect of our make-up *(to phutikon)* is unaware and unreasoning, "in no way partaking in *logos*." But "the appetitive and in general the desiderative partake in *logos* in some way"—as is shown, he says, by the success of moral advice and education *(EN* 1102ᵇ29–1103ᵃ1). And when he actually gives analyses of the emotions in the *Rhetoric,* it emerges that (presumably unlike appetites) they are, so to speak, less "commonly animal" than perceiving is. For all require and rest upon belief, and a belief is actually one component of an emotion in each case.[29] The view that emotions are more animal, more bodily, than perceiving is actually a view unknown in the ancient world, though common enough in modern times.[30] If ancient thinkers make any distinction of the sort, it goes the other way: animals are always considered perceiving creatures, but frequently denied the emotions. So it would appear that an account of Aristotle's psychology that splits emotion off from perception, making one an activity of matter and the other immaterial, is both false to Aristotle's text and in a more general way anachronistic.

We can see the closeness of emotion and cognition in the very passage before us. For instead of making Burnyeat's distinction between cognition and emotion, Aristotle makes the emotions forms of cognitive awareness. For when Aristotle uses expressions of the form "*x, y, z,* and in general *(holōs)* A," what he means by this is that *A* is a genus of which *x, y,* and *z* are some of the species. (For three excellent examples, see *Metaph.* 1026ᵃ2–3, quoted above, and *De Sensu*'s opening, Exhibit B.) So unless this passage is exceptional, Aristotle is actually treating emotion as a type of perception, a selective cognitive awareness of an object or objects in the world.[31]

The proper conclusion, Aristotle's conclusion, is that all these, perceiving, desiring, emotion, are formulae in matter *(logoi enhuloi).* Even though the structure of the passage moves from a broad class which explicitly includes (and subsumes other items under) perception to a narrower group of *pathē* whose members are all emotions, its conclusion is evidently what Aristotle has in other words asserted already about perception and *phantasia*—and it can be regarded as an expansion of that assertion, applying it to the more controversial case of desire. All these processes, then, are *logoi enhuloi,* formulae in matter, of which a proper sample definition would be, "A certain movement of a body of such and such a sort—or of a part of it or of a particular faculty, caused by this for the sake of this" (403[a]25ff.).[32] The good natural scientist should, Aristotle concludes, treat the various psychological functions as common functions, giving priority to the formal account of (for example) anger as a form of intentional awareness, but also saying as much as possible about the physical doings involved.[33] (This, of course, is what Aristotle does for perception in the *De Sensu,* for both perception and desire in the *De Motu.*) The good scientist deals "with everything that makes up the doings and affections of a body of this sort and matter of this sort" (403[b]11–12). On Burnyeat's reading, perceiving is not the doing *of* any matter at all, since the matter is not active.

Exhibit D: *De Anima* 2.1.412[b]4–25

If it is necessary to say something general *(koinon)* about all soul, it would be the first actuality of a natural organic body. Therefore it is not appropriate to inquire whether the soul and the body are one—just as it is not appropriate in the case of the wax and its shape, and in general *(holōs)* the matter of each thing and that of which it is the matter . . . (The soul) is the what-it-is-to-be for a body of a certain sort: just as, if a tool, for example an ax, were a natural body, then its being an ax would be its being *(ousia),* and the soul is this. When this is separated from it, there would no longer be an ax except homonymously—but as things are it is an ax . . . And one can also examine what has been said by considering the parts. For if the eye were an animal, its soul would be the power of sight. For that is the being of an eye, according to the account (for the eye is the matter of sight)—in the absence of which there is no eye, except homonymously, as with the stone eye and the painted eye. One must then apply what has been said of the part to the whole of the living body. For there is an analogy: as the part to the part, so the whole of perception to the whole of the perceiving body, as such.

This is a central theoretical statement of Aristotle's hylomorphic view. We believe that it makes little sense on Burnyeat's reading, while on ours it is exactly what one would expect Aristotle to say. For on Burnyeat's reading, the relationship between soul and body is *not* that between the wax and its shape: matter merely supplies background conditions for transitions that are not carried out in and by the matter. The ax analogy, furthermore, would not be apt—for of course an ax cannot do anything without material transitions. And on Burnyeat's view, it of course makes a great deal of sense to ask whether soul and body are one; for if the body does not perform the soul's activities, there is an obvious sense in which they are not one, and the nature and extent of their unity is not at all evident. In fact, as we have said, the situation with perception, on Burnyeat's view, seems to be exactly the situation we have for *nous* alone, on our reading—body providing necessary conditions without doing the functions. And where *nous* is concerned, Aristotle plainly thinks that the question about unity and separation not only makes sense, but is important. On our interpretation, on the other hand, the wax analogy and the ax analogy are apt; and the question about unity really *is* one that the Aristotelian ought to repudiate as ill formed. The soul is not a thing merely housed in the body; its doings are the doings of body. The only thing there is one natural thing.

To summarize: perception, desire, and the other "very important things" mentioned by Aristotle in *De Sensu* 1 are activities of the soul realized in some suitable matter. There will be no explanatory independence to the material side, and yet a scientist may legitimately investigate it in the cases before him, as Aristotle does in the *De Motu* and the *Parva Naturalia*—provided that he does not present what he does as a reduction or a complete explanation.

In *Metaphysics* Z11, Aristotle mentions a philosopher known as Socrates the Younger, who wishes to argue that animals are just like the sphere: they may need to be realized in some materials or other whenever they exist, but this realization is not part of what they are, and need not enter into their definition. Aristotle accepts this move up to a point, apparently: for he seems to grant that in both cases there is a certain plasticity of composition. But he then distinguishes the cases. In the case of animals, to take away the matter is "to go too far—for some things just are this in this, or these in such and such a condition" (1036^b22ff.). The point seems to be that although every actual sphere is embodied, the geometrical properties that make a sphere do not depend on the component materials' having any particular properties, except perhaps a certain rigidity. The functional essence of a living being like an animal (whose essence it is to be a perceiving creature) *does* require mention of material embodiment, in that its essential activities are embodied activities. Just as "snub" applied to a nose directly imports a reference to material composition, so too does "perceiving creature"—in a way that "sphere" does not. We feel that Burnyeat's interpretation assimilates Aristotle to Socrates the Younger, and does not allow sufficient room for the all-important distinction between sphere and animal that pervades Aristotle's thought about life.[34]

Why We Don't Have to "Junk" Aristotle

Burnyeat goes wrong at the very beginning—wrong in a way that corrupts the way he sees contemporary issues, not just the way he reads Aristotle. It is because he is in the grip of what Husserl called the "objectivist" picture—the picture according to which Newton (or, as Husserl would have it, Galileo) discovered for us what external objects really are (they are what is described, and, "in themselves," no more than what is described, by the formulae of mathematical physics)—that he sees no way of reading Aristotle but a Frank Baumian way, and no way in which Aristotle *could be* relevant to anything we are interested in today.

Who on earth is Frank Baum? You mean you've forgotten? The author of the Oz books, of course! You remember the Tin Man and the Scarecrow? In the world of Frank Baum, matter—the straw in the Scarecrow's head or, perhaps, the sack that contains the straw—can have the property of "seating," or being the location of, thoughts and feelings without having any other particularly relevant properties. Some scarecrows don't think thoughts and have feelings, and one scarecrow magically does, and that's all one can say about it. On Burnyeat's reading of Aristotle, we are *all* like the Scarecrow. We have already indicated why, in our view, this is a misreading of Aristotle. But our reply to Burnyeat would be incomplete if we did not indicate why his account of the present metaphysical situation, although a commonly accepted one, is not one *we* can accept.

The view that has ruled since the seventeenth century is that there is obviously such a thing as "the mind-body problem as we face it today," in Burnyeat's phrase. His conception of this problem is expressed in the statement "To be truly Aristotelian, we would have to stop believing that the emergence of life or mind requires explanation." Putting aside "life," the key idea here is that *of course* the "emergence of mind" (as if it were clear what that is!) requires explanation, and, on Aristotle's view (the Frank Baum theory), it obviously doesn't. So let's forget that silly magical world that Aristotle lived in and get down to the real business of explaining the "emergence of mind."

If we may be forgiven for bombarding the reader with examples of great and near-great philosophers who have found this description of the present problem situation less than coercive (think of this as a softening-up bombardment in the artillery sense, rather than as an appeal to authority!), note that not only "Continental" philosophers and phenomenologists have rejected the idea that "matter" is such a clear notion, and also rejected the idea that tables and chairs and human bodies and such are obviously "matter" in the sense of being *identical* with physicists' objects, but so, likewise, have such great "analytic" philosophers as Wittgenstein and Austin. Coming to our own day, Kripke has pointed out (in conversation with Putnam) that if tables were "space-time regions," as Quine claims, then such modal statements as "this very table could have been in a different place now" would not be true, and similar arguments show that the relation between this table and its "molecule slices" cannot be *identity* unless we are willing to abandon our common-sense modal beliefs (or reinterpret "this would have been the same table" as meaning "this would have been a *counterpart* of this table" in the David Lewis sense of "counterpart").[35] Reverting to Austin, we note that the burden of *Sense and Sensibilia*[36] was that the way philosophers use "material object" is *senseless*. The Strawson of *Individuals*[37] certainly doubted that the relation between *me* as a bearer of "P-predicates" (intentional states, and other attributes of a person) and my body can even be *stated* in the terms Descartes "stuck" us with! So much for "we are stuck with the mind-body problem as Descartes created it"! End of preliminary bombardment.

Now for the cavalry charge. If "explaining the emergence of mind" means explaining how the brain works, how "memory traces" are laid down, how the "representations" from the right eye and the "representations" from the left eye are processed to "compute" the three-dimensional layout in front of the viewer (as in the work initiated by Hubel and Wiesel,[38] and extended and modified by David Marr[39] and others), how the various areas of the left lobe collectively function as the "speech center" (in humans who have not developed speech in the right lobe as the result of massive and early damage to the left lobe), etc., then—as long as this work is not understood in a reductionist way, as telling one what "seeing a chair," or "remembering where

Paris is," or "thinking there are a lot of cats in the neighborhood" *is*—why on earth should an "Aristotelian" object to it? Does one still have to believe that integration takes place in the region of the heart to be an "Aristotelian"? On the other hand, if "explaining the emergence of mind" means solving Brentano's problem, that is, saying in *reductive* terms what "thinking there are a lot of cats in the neighborhood" *is,* and what "remembering where Paris is" *is,* etc., why should we now think that *that*'s possible?[40] If an Aristotelian is one who rejects that program as an unreasonable program for metaphysics, then yes, we *are* "Aristotelians."

The insight of Putnam's "functionalism" was that thinking beings are *compositionally plastic*—that is, that there is no necessary and sufficient condition expressible in the language of physics for being even a *physically possible* (let alone "logically possible" or "metaphysically possible") occurrence of a thought with a given propositional content, or of a feeling of anger, or of a pain, etc. *A fortiori,* propositional attitudes, emotions, feelings are not *identical* with brain states, or even with more broadly characterized first-order physical states.

When he advanced his account, Putnam pointed out that thinking of a being's mentality, affectivity, etc., as aspects of its *organization to function* allows one to recognize that all sorts of logically possible "systems" or beings could be conscious, exhibit mentality and affect, etc., in exactly the same sense without having the same matter (without even consisting of "matter" in the narrow sense of elementary particles and electromagnetic fields at all). For beings of many different physical (and even "nonphysical") constitutions could have the same functional organization. The thing we want insight into is the nature of human (and animal) functional organization. The question whether that organization is centrally located in the "body" or in suitable stuff of some totally different kind loses the importance it was thought to have, in this way of thinking.

It was at this point that Putnam (and Nussbaum) cited Aristotle. Thinking of the *psuchē* as our organization to function permitted Aristotle to separate questions about specific material composition (which he at times discusses) from the main questions of psychology.

Putnam also proposed a theory of his own as to what our organization to function is, one he has now given up; but this theory we did not, of course, attribute to Aristotle. This is the theory that our functional organization is that of a Turing machine. Putnam has now given this up because he believes that there are good arguments to show that mental states are not only compositionally plastic but also *computationally plastic,* that is, reasons to believe that physically possible creatures which believe that there are a lot of cats in the neighborhood, or whatever, may have an indefinite number of different "programs," and that the hypothesis that there are necessary and sufficient conditions for the presence of such a belief in computational, or computational-cum-physical, terms is unrealistic in just the way the theory that there is a necessary and sufficient condition for the presence of a table statable in phenomenalist terms is unrealistic: such a condition would be infinitely long, and not constructed according to any effective rule, or even according to a noneffective prescription that we can state without using the very terms to be reduced.[41] Putnam does not believe that even all *humans* who have the same belief (in different cultures, or with different bodies of background knowledge and different conceptual resources) have in common a physical-cum-computational feature which could be "identified with" that belief. The "intentional level" is simply not reducible to the "computational level" any more than it is to the "physical level."

What then becomes of Burnyeat's problem of "the emergence of mind"? Some philosophers[42] now wave the word "supervenience" around as if it were a magic wand. Materialists should never have claimed that propositional attitudes are reducible to physical attributes, they say; they should only have said they are *supervenient* on them. In one sense this is right, but in another sense it is simply papering over the collapse of the materialist worldview. For, after all, if Moore's theory of the Good in his *Principia Ethica* (he claimed that the goodness of a thing is supervenient on its "natural" characteristics) is a *materialist* view, then hasn't "materialist" lost all meaning?

When the computer revolution burst upon the world, it was widely expected that computer models would clear up the nature of the various sorts of "intentional" phenomena. In effect, people expected that a reductive account of the various subheadings included under the chapter heading "intentionality" would sooner or later be given. Now that this has not proved so easy, some thinkers (though not Burnyeat) are beginning to suggest that it is not so bad if this can't be done; intentionality is only a feature of "folk psychology" anyway. If a first-class scientific account of intentional facts and phenomena can not be given, that is not because scientific reductionism is not the right line to take in metaphysics; rather it is because there is, so to speak, nothing here to reduce. The "Aristotelian" attitude, in the present context, is that both attitudes are mistaken; that intentionality won't be reduced and won't go away.

That claim—the claim that "intentionality won't be reduced and won't go away"—has sometimes been called "Brentano's thesis," after the philosopher who put it forward with vigor over a century ago. But Brentano himself did not merely have a negative thesis; his positive view was that intentionality is, so to speak, a *primitive phenomenon,* in fact *the* phenomenon that relates thought and thing, minds and the external world.

This positive view may seem to follow immediately from the negative one; but there is a joker in the pack. The joker is the old philosophical problem about the One and the Many. If one assumes that whenever we have diverse phenomena gathered together under a single name, "there must be something they all have in common," then indeed it will follow that there is a single phenomenon (and, if it is not reducible, it must be "primitive") corresponding to intentionality. But this is not an assumption we wish to make. We want to follow Wittgenstein's advice and *look:* look to see if there *is* something all cases of thinking, say, "there are a lot of cats in the neighborhood" do have in common. If, as Putnam tries to show, there is not any isolable, independently "accessible" thing that all cases of any particular intentional phenomenon have in common (let alone all cases of "reference" in general, or of "meaning" in general, or of "intentionality" in general), and *still* these phenomena cannot be dismissed as mere "folk psychology," then we are in a position which does not fit any of the standard philosophical pictures: not the picture of intentionality as a phenomenon to be reduced to physical (or, perhaps, computational) terms, not the picture of intentionality as "primitive" (not if "primitive" means "simple and irreducible"), and not the picture of intentionality as just a bit of "folk psychology."

Is such a philosophical attitude compatible with Aristotle, however? Many standard accounts of his methods certainly do not suggest a philosophical attitude that gives up many of the traditional assumptions about appearance and reality; that gives up, for example, the assumption that what is real is what is "under" or "behind" or "more fundamental than" our everyday appearances, that gives up the assumptions underlying the conventional statement of the problem we referred to as the problem of the One and the Many; or an attitude that gives up the assumption that every phenomenon has an "ultimate nature" that we have to give a metaphysically reductive account of. Are we not assimilating Aristotle to Wittgenstein?

Nussbaum has in fact argued (developing further some seminal work by the late G. E. L. Owen) that the philosophical attitude we recommend *is* Aristotle's; that his recommendation to "set down the appearances" and to preserve "the greatest number and the most basic" announces a refusal of Eleatic and Platonist reality-appearance distinctions and a determination to found philosophy on attention to the variety of experience.[43] In her discussion she explicitly compares Aristotle's concerns with Wittgenstein's.[44] She has also tried to show in detail, for the case of the explanation of animal motion, how Aristotle's account succeeds in doing just this.[45] She argues that Aristotle preserves the nonreducibility and also the experienced complexity of intentional phenomena such as perception, belief, and desire, criticizing both materialist reductionism and Platonist intellectualism for their inability to offer a causal explanation of motion that captures the richness and relevance of ordinary discourse about motion and action. We have mentioned some of these arguments earlier, and we shall not recapitulate further. But we wish to mention two issues on which the conclusions of these studies affect our argument here.

First, the position argued for in Nussbaum's "The 'Common Explanation'" makes it evident that our Aristotle is not guilty of the kind of reductionism with which Putnam now taxes functionalism. His opposition to materialist reductionism preserves the independence and irreducibility of the intentional and does not, as the modern functionalist would, seek to reduce these to independently specifiable computational states. There is no hint of any such enterprise (or even a desire for such an enterprise) in Aristotle; this is one reason that we prefer the phrase "organization to function" to the more common "functional organization," as more suggestive of the irreducible character of the intentional activities in question.

Second, Aristotle's account also seems free of the difficulty we have just found in Brentano, namely the tendency to treat all intentionality as a unitary phenomenon. In Aristotle we find instead a subtle demarcation of numerous species of cognition and desire, and of their interrelationships.

In sum: *if* the "emergence of mind" has to be "explained," and the only possibilities are (i) the Frank Baum theory (some matter is just *like* that) and (ii) a reductionist account—or, possibly, (iii) an "eliminationist" one—compatible with contemporary physics, and *if,* as Burnyeat claims, the Frank Baum account was Aristotle's (we are all like the Scarecrow), *then,* since modern physics has demolished the Frank Baum theory (in case anyone ever believed it), we are "stuck" with "our" problem—reductionism or "supervenience" (redefine "materialism" so that *everything* counts as materialism) or "eliminationism" (à la Dennett[46] or Quine[47] or the Churchlands[48]). But why should one believe the antecedent of this conditional?

Aristotle and Theodicy; or, Aquinas' Separated Souls Change Their Mind

If the interpretation of Aristotle defended by Burnyeat does indeed, as we have argued, force the text and neglect some unequivocal statements, if there is another interpretation that is both textually more sound and philosophically more powerful (we want you to believe the antecedent of *this* conditional!), then where does the rival interpretation come from, and why has it enjoyed such a long history? We find the history of this misreading so interesting that we cannot resist a brief digression.

In his earliest draft, Burnyeat called his view "the Christian view." Finding it in John Philoponus, Saint Thomas Aquinas, and Franz Brentano, he mentions as significant the fact that all three were "committed Christians." We agree with him that this fact is significant. For all three were not simply interpreters of the text of Aristotle; nor were they simply seekers after the best explanation of the functioning of living beings as we encounter them in this world. They were engaged in the delicate enterprise of Aristotelian theodicy—the attempt to use Aristotle's excellence and authority to bolster and flesh out a picture of the world that would be an acceptable foundation for Christian life and discourse. Such a thinker must give some story about the immortal life of the separated soul; this story will have to ascribe to it a cognitive functioning rich enough to support Christian hopes and beliefs concerning the life after death. It will also need to insist upon the gulf between the human soul and the operations of animal souls that are not to be immortal. All this has obvious implications for what the thinker will say about the operations of perception and other forms of cognition in the human organism in this world. It will begin to look sensible to veer away from Aristotle's insistence on the seamless unity of form and matter, toward a picture that makes this relation more fortuitous, less organic, characterized by a certain degree of independence or even opposition. And if the aim is theodicy, this sensible course is also perfectly legitimate.[49]

Brentano makes the complexity of his relation to Aristotle's text explicit. In the remarkable monograph *Aristotle and His World View* (recently translated by Rolf George and Roderick Chisholm),[50] he candidly announces that his aim in presenting his account of Aristotle as a thinker about theodicy is "to make this pessimistically inclined age aware of the resources of the optimistic world idea." And he grants that the theodicy he sets forth, which makes much of the cognitive powers of the separated soul, goes beyond the text: "It is indeed true that this view is not set forth in Aristotle's writings as explicitly as I have described and defended it here, for Aristotle unfortunately did not find time to write the intended detailed exposition of his metaphysics."[51] We reply with some astonishment that Aristotle surely found time to write quite a lot of detailed metaphysics, and that what he wrote simply does not agree with the picture mapped out by Brentano. When Brentano goes on to inform us that the "eschatology" implied in Aristotle's view of soul yields the doctrine that "In order that the number of those who inhabit the world beyond may increase to infinity, the human souls move one after the other from this world into the other"—*and* that this view has "remarkable agreements" not only with Christianity but also "with the religious doctrines of Judaism"[52]—we reply that these "agreements" are no accident, since that is where this allegedly Aristotelian view comes from. In the same passage Brentano defends the rapprochement with a reference to a statement by Theophrastus (*ap.* Porphyr. *De Abstinentia* 2.26) admiring the Jews as an "especially philosophical" people. We accept the compliment, but we deny the "remarkable agreement." If the concept of similarity is this elastic, it is about as useful as Nelson Goodman says it is.[53]

Theodicy, however, has its complexities. And the real point of this digression is to show how the greatest of the Christian interpreters of Aristotle, Saint Thomas Aquinas, was led by philosophy and theodicy together to reject Burnyeat's "Christian interpretation" and to adopt one that is very close to ours. The committed Christian must indeed endow the soul with powers such that it can enjoy a cognitively rich afterlife. But he or she must also satisfy two further demands: and here the balancing act begins. First, she must explain why, if the body's capabilities are *not* perfectly suited to fit with, *act along with,* the functions of soul, God did *not* make the body less arbitrary and more organic. And she must also explain the point of the resurrection of the body, an element of doctrine that causes notorious difficulty for the more Platonistically inclined among Christian philosophers. If the soul in its separated condition is well equipped to perceive and imagine and think—if there are no material transitions necessary for its good activity—then this promised event will be at best superfluous, at worst a divine blunder.

Aquinas never, in fact, adopted the entirety of the Burnyeat position. For although in his commentary on *De Anima* he does interpret the reception of form without matter in much the way Burnyeat says he does—awareness of red being a nonreducible intentional item—he consistently holds that each act of perceiving has material necessary conditions, *and* that these conditions are *changes in the sense-organs.* "For as things exist in sensation they are free indeed from matter, but not without their individuating material conditions, nor apart from a bodily organ" (*In II De Anima*, Lect. 5, n. 284).[54] Free from matter, in that I become aware of red without any sense-organ literally going red. But there is none the less some *concomitant necessary material change* in that organ. The *Summa Theologica* asserts this repeatedly, and unequivocally:

> But Aristotle insists that . . . sensing and the related operations of the sensitive soul evidently happen together with some change *(immutatio)* of the body, as in seeing the pupil is changed by the appearance of color; and the same is manifest in other cases. And so it is evident that the sensitive soul has no operation that is proper to itself; but all the operation of the sensitive soul is the operation of the compound. (I, q. 75, a. 3; cf. I, q. 75, a. 4: "sensing is not an operation of the soul by itself"; I, q. 76, a. 1, *et saepe*)

Furthermore, Aquinas consistently contrasts perceiving with thinking in a way that brings him very close to our interpretation: for while he says of both that in the human organism they have necessary material conditions (thinking requires phantasms which themselves are realized in matter)—and both are for this reason to be called forms of the human body—sensing is *the act of* (an activity embodied or realized in) a corporeal organ, and thinking is not:

> As the Philosopher says in *Physics* II, the ultimate of the natural forms, in which the investigation of natural philosophy terminates, namely the human soul, is indeed separate, but none the less in matter

. . . It is separate according to the rational power, since the rational power is not the power of any corporeal organ, in the way that the power to see is the act of the eye: for to reason is an act that cannot be exercised through a corporeal organ, in the way that vision is exercised. But it is in matter, inasmuch as the soul itself, whose power it is, is the form of the body. (*Summa Theologica* I, q. 76, a. 1, ad. I)

He holds, furthermore, that each operation of intellect in a human being, both during the acquisition of knowledge and in using knowledge once acquired, requires that the intellect address itself to sensory phantasms, which he takes to be realized in matter, modifications constituted by matter (*ST* I, q. 84, aa. 7, 8; q. 85, a. 1; q. 101, aa. 1.2; q. 76, a. 1). This has the consequence that in its natural operation even the human intellect is firmly linked to matter and has very specific material necessary conditions. The main difference between intellection and sensing is that sensing is an act of a bodily organ, accompanied of necessity by a change in that organ; intellect is the form of the body in a different and looser sense. We think that Aquinas has correctly understood Aristotle's distinction between "shared" functions (cf. "the operation of the compound") and non-shared functions that nonetheless have material necessary conditions.

In some earlier works Aquinas did, however, hold that the separated human souls, once out of the body, would have a mode of cognition superior to that of the embodied soul. And it is here that further thought about theodicy has prompted, as we see it, a turning-back to the true Aristotelian position.[55] For in the *Summa Theologica* he concludes that this cannot be so: that soul and body are so unified, so fitly and fully together in all their activity, that the separated soul has cognition only in a confused and unnatural way. With the death of the body, sensing and *phantasia* go; but then, he holds, all cognition of particulars and all modes of cognition built on this must go as well. But then the natural human way of cognizing must go: "To be separated from the body is contrary to the principle of its nature, and similarly to cognize without turning to phantasms is contrary to its nature. So it is united to the body so that it should be and act according to its nature" (*ST* I, q. 89, a. 1). What remains is only an imperfect cognition, "confusam in communi."

We must, then, conclude, Aquinas continues, that the soul's natural and best home is in the body: "The human soul remains in its being when it is separated from the body, having a natural fittedness and inclination towards union with the body" (*ST* I, q. 76, a. 1, ad. 6). It is not in the body as in a prison; nor is it impeded by it from some better mode of cognition; nor, even, is it simply *housed,* Baum-like, in the body. The body's matter fits it, *does its actions,* through and through. Asking the question whether the soul is *conveniently*—appropriately, suitably, aptly—united with the organic human body, he retails several dualist objections, and then replies; "Against this is what the Philosopher says in II of *De Anima:* 'The soul is the act of a natural organic body potentially having life'" (I, q. 76, a. 5, *sed contra*).

This change was prompted by theodicy. First, as we have said, by concern with the resurrection of the body. Second, and much more stressed in the text, by the desire to show that God and nature did not do things arbitrarily and badly where human life is concerned. If the human mode of cognition is different, in its embodiment, from that of God and the angels, still it is exactly suited to human life, life in a world of changing perceptible particulars. Matter is suited to its function, and cognition's embodied modes to the nature of cognition's worldly objects (*ST* I, q. 84, a. 7). We note that it seems to be a consequence of this general principle that *if* a modern theory of matter had displaced Aristotle's in such a way as to make his particular sort of hylomorphism untenable (which we deny), Aquinas would then have had to show how the new matter itself was perfectly suited and united to *its* form (a *new* hylomorphism) in such a way that relevance and elegance are preserved in the universe as a whole.

Here theodicy converges with good philosophy. Aquinas' God would not have made us like Baum's Scarecrow, because, like the philosopher who is concerned with adequate explanations, God wants things to fit together in a suitable and coherent way. He wants a world that yields good explanations, not bad ones. If the body contributed so little, it could not be anything but a mistake that a soul should be set up in one. And, we emphasize, not only a practical mistake, but a conceptual and philosophical mistake. For, having given the soul the sort of natural activity that, in its very nature, requires suitable matter for its fulfillment in activity, he would have failed to supply the suitable matter. So then, there just could not *be* those souls and those activities. The activities are forms in matter: take away matter and you cannot have *them.* The human soul would be a conceptually confused (not just physically handicapped) item. But God cares for conceptual fittedness, for explanatory relevance, for nonarbitrariness. He wants the function to be the reason why the matter is thus and so (*ST* I, q. 76, a. 5).

Of the Pythagorean view that "any chance soul" can turn up animating "any chance body," Aristotle writes: "Some people try only to say of what sort the soul is, but they determine nothing further about the body that is going to receive it . . . That is just like saying that one could do carpentry with flutes; for an art must have its appropriate tools, and the soul an appropriate body" (*DA* 408ª19ff.). (Notice how close Burnyeat's Frank Baum Aristotle is to the Pythagorean position.) This (religiously inspired) view, Aristotle says, is bad philosophy, since it makes the conceptual mistake of supposing you *could* have human life-activity without the embodiment of that activity in suitable matter. But you can't. It is an incoherent idea. If the person is banging around with a soft wooden musical instrument, then whatever she is doing, by definition it won't be carpentry. No more, by definition, can there be perceiving without *its* suitable embodiment. What these activities are in their nature is organically embodied forms: they require embodiment *to be themselves*. We think that Aquinas is taking this point, and attempting to save God from Pythagorean incoherence. The truly Christian view, says Aquinas, is one that makes God a good philosopher of nature, not a bad one, not one who tries to prise the activities apart from their constitutive matter. This view of embodied form he finds, as we do, in Aristotle.

Goodbye to Oz

We conclude: we can have nonreductionism and the explanatory priority of the intentional without losing that sense of the natural and organic unity of the intentional with its constitutive matter that is one of the great contributions of Aristotelian realism. We suggest that Aristotle's thought really is, properly understood, the fulfillment of Wittgenstein's desire to have a "natural history of man."[56] (It is also, in a different way, the fulfillment of Aquinas' desire to find that our truly natural being is the being that we live every day, and that God has not screened our real nature behind some arbitrary barrier.) As Aristotelians we do not discover something behind something else, a hidden reality behind the complex unity that we see and are. We find what we are in the appearances. And Aristotle tells us that if we attend properly to the appearances the dualist's questions never even get going. "It is not appropriate to inquire whether the soul and the body are one—just as it is not appropriate in the case of the wax and its shape, and in general the matter of each thing and that of which it is the matter" (*DA* 412^{b}6–9). If you attend in the appropriate way to the complex materiality of living things, you will not ask that question. The soul is not an "it" housed in the body, but a functional structure in and of matter. Matter is, in its very nature, just the thing to constitute the functions of life. (It is *not* a thing to which the functions of life can be *reduced*.) "Some things just are this in this, or these parts ordered in such and such a way" (*Metaph.* 1036^{b}22ff.). Or, to quote Frank Baum's heroine, "There's no place like home."[57]

Notes

1. Burnyeat in Nussbaum and Rorty, 1992, chap. 2. His references are to Putnam, 1975, and Nussbaum, 1978. He notes that Nussbaum refers to Putnam, and Putnam to Aristotle.
2. Nussbaum and Rorty, 1992.
3. At the University of Rochester in spring 1984.
4. Nussbaum, 1984; Putnam, 1988; see also the papers by Matthews and Wilkes in Nussbaum and Rorty, 1992. The arguments of Putnam (1988) summarized in Chapter 24 of the present volume.
5. See Nussbaum, 1983 and 1978, essay 1.
6. See *Metaph.* Z3, and the fine account of the argument in Owen, 1986.
7. Wiggins, 1980, and Chisholm, 1976.
8. An even stronger claim is made by Suppes (1974), who argues that Aristotle's theory of matter is *more* nearly adequate to recent developments in particle physics than the old atomic theory.
9. See Nussbaum, 1978, pp. 69–71; compare Putnam, 1975, pp. 295–298.
10. It is notoriously difficult to know where Aristotle wants us to place the necessity operator in claims like this, and whether he firmly grasps the difference. So we give the weaker form.
11. The commentary is clearly written in part by Alexander (the earlier books), in part by some later philosopher who is closely imitating Alexander; this section is from the later author, but may still derive from Alexander ultimately.
12. Thinking, of course, is an anomaly, here as elsewhere; see further discussion in this chapter.
13. Nussbaum, 1978, essays 1 and 3.
14. Nussbaum, 1984; see Nussbaum, also 1983, reprinted in 1986 as chap. 9, with changes.
15. First, he says that desire must be combined in the right way with perception in order for movement to follow. Second, he insists that the cognitive faculties must come up with a possible route to the goal, or else movement will not follow. Third, he makes it clear that the desire must be not just one

among others, but *the* one, the "authoritative" or "decisive" one—however we understand this. Fourth, he points out that even when all this is true there may be some impediment, in which case movement will not follow.

16. See *Ph.* 195^{b}3–4. The example is the relationship between Polyclitus the sculptor and the statue. Aristotle insists that not just any attribute of Polyclitus caused the statue: it was his skill of sculpting. So it is as sculptor (not as human being, or as father, etc.) that he is the cause of the statue. The point is that it is Polyclitus' skill that has the requisite conceptual connection with the production of the statue—although no doubt at every point he had many other properties, and at every point his body was in some suitable physiological condition. There is, Aristotle says, an intimate connectedness *(oikeiotēs)* to the one factor that is lacked by all the others.

17. We hold that while embodiment in some sort of suitable matter is essential to animals and their life-activities, the particular material realization is contingent. But caution is in order here. For Aristotle, the organic parts of animals—the heart, the eye, the hand, etc.—are *functionally defined:* the heart is whatever performs such and such functions in the animal, and a disconnected heart or hand is not, he repeatedly insists, really a heart or hand except in name. This means that we could perfectly well say that the life-activities of animal A are necessarily and not contingently realized in a heart, and eye, and so forth, *without ever leaving the formal (functional) level.* What would then be contingent would be the material realization of that organic function at a lower level. Aristotle is less consistent about the "homoiomerous parts," viz., flesh, blood, bone, etc. Sometimes he takes the same line about them—spilt blood is not really blood, etc.; and sometimes he gives a physiological formula for them, in terms of proportions of earth, air, fire, and water. So again, on the former line, we could say that an animal must have blood, without ruling out the possibility that some nonorganic stuff could play that same role in the animal's life. Aristotle's point is that this stuff would then *be blood:* and what would be contingent would be the relation between a certain lower-level chemical composition and being blood. The latter line—if the formulae are really meant as definitions—would imply that blood must be materially composed in such and such a way; but then, the fact that the animal is filled with *blood* would be contingent. We believe that Aristotle's line is the former line, and that the formulae should probably not be taken as definitions. For able discussion of this whole problem, see Whiting's paper in Nussbaum and Rorty, 1992, with which we are largely in agreement. For relevant passages, see *PA* 640^{b}34ff., 641^{a}18ff., *DA* 412^{b}18ff., *Mete.* 1.12, *GA* 734^{b}24ff., *GC* 321^{b}28, *Metaph.* 1036^{b}22ff., 1034^{a}6, 1058^{b}7, *Ph.* 193^{a}36ff., *Metaph.* 1035^{b}16, 1035^{a}18, *GA* 766^{a}8, *Pol.* 1253^{a}21, 24. The position implies that the Jarvik II *is* the heart of the person who receives it, that a transplanted cornea *is* the cornea of the recipient and a full-fledged part of his or her eye;

probably also that grafted or even artificial skin, bone, blood is that person's blood, etc.—just in case it does the function that defines each of these.

18. Sorabji, 1974. We refer to the strata of Sorabji's position that predate our original paper, not to the modified account included in Nussbuam and Rorty, 1992.

19. He does not, however, always make this distinction: sometimes he uses *kinēsis* as a very general word for change, covering both *kinēsis* and *energeia* narrowly construed. This is especially likely to be true in a work like *De Motu,* whose purpose is the general explanation of *kinēseis* of many sorts.

20. We *do* accept Sorabji's suggestion that the characterization of perception as "receiving the form" of the perceived object "without the matter" is primarily intended to bring out a contrast with plants—or, we would rather say, with nutritive and digestive activity in both plants and animals. In nutrition and related forms of being affected by the environment, the environmental material affects the animal by entering into it; in perception the animal gets in touch with the object without assimilating it. See Nussbaum, 1978, commentary on chap. 11, and essay 2, pp. 117ff.

21. On all this, see further details in Nussbaum, 1978.

22. On this passage and the *De Motu,* see Nussbaum, 1978, pp. 9ff.

23. Thinking, it turns out, is realized in the body *via* the concomitant *phantasia.*

24. Throughout the *De Motu* account, Aristotle focuses on physiological transitions in the region of the heart, since it is one of his primary purposes to establish the importance of this central "receptor"; he says less about transitions in the organs, but the conception of the heart area as receptor of stimuli and initiator of the movements that lead to local motion strongly suggests that there are some.

25. For further discussion of related passages, see Nussbaum, 1978, commentary.

26. See Alexander, 1901.

27. On *phantasia* and thinking, see Nussbaum, 1978, essay 5.

28. On some of the vicissitudes in Plato's position, see Nussbaum, 1986, chap. 7. On the interpretation of *pathē* in this passage, there are well-known arguments by Hicks, Rodier, and Hamlyn in favor of a broad interpretation. We note that Burnyeat himself produces evidence that Aristotle is prepared to call perceiving a *pathos.*

29. See for example *Rh.* 1385[b]13ff. on pity, 1386[a]22ff. on fear, both discussed in Nussbaum, 1986, interlude 2.

30. On emotions in ancient thought, see Nussbaum (1987).

31. Hicks in Aristotle (1907) reads the passage correctly, and finds the same view in the *De Sensu* commentary.

32. The word used is *kinēsis;* but, as we have said, Aristotle does use the word generically, so this need not rule out his believing that the movement involved is an *energeia;* moreover, he is alluding to the immediate context, in which the example is desiring, which he does not characterize as *energeia.*

33. Here we are sympathetic with the interpretation advanced by Modrak (1987), though we would insist more strongly than she does that the material account is not on a par with the formal account, and cannot be given independently.
34. To this extent our own use of an artifact example requires supplementation.
35. See Lewis, 1983, vol. 1, pp. 26–54.
36. Austin, 1962.
37. Strawson, 1964.
38. Hubel and Wiesel, 1962 and 1974.
39. Marr, 1982.
40. In this connection, see Putnam, 1988.
41. Ibid., chaps. 5–6 (summarized in Chapter 24 of the present volume).
42. For a review (and searching criticism) of these views see Kim, 1982, 1984.
43. Owen, 1961, reprinted in 1986; Nussbaum, 1982.
44. In the longer version of Nussbaum, 1982, that is Nussbaum, 1986, chap. 8.
45. Nussbaum, 1983, and also Nussbaum, 1986, chap. 9.
46. See Dennett, 1987.
47. See Quine, 1960.
48. See Paul Churchland, 1981, and Patricia Churchland, 1986.
49. We do not discuss Philoponus in this paper; but see Sorabji's paper in Nussbaum and Rorty, 1992.
50. Brentano, 1976.
51. Ibid.
52. Ibid.
53. Goodman, 1972.
54. In this section we are indebted to John Carriero and to his thesis (1984).
55. See Carriero, 1984, and Pegis, 1974; Carriero supplies references to *Summa Contra Gentiles*.
56. Wittgenstein, 1956, I, §141.
57. We owe thanks above all to Burnyeat, for provoking this reply; we are sure it will not end the debate. We are also grateful to the participants in the Rochester conference (see above n. 3), and especially to Robert Cummins, our commentator, for stimulating comments; and to John Carriero and Jaegwon Kim for discussion of the issues.

References

Alexander of Aphrodisias. 1901. In *Aristotelis "De Sensu,"* ed. P. Wendland; Commentaria in Aristotelem Graeca, vol. 3, pt. 1. Berlin: G. Reimer.
Aristotle. 1907. *De Anima,* translation, introduction, and notes by R. D. Hicks. Cambridge: Cambridge University Press; reprinted New York: Arno Press, 1976.

Austin, J. L. 1962. *Sense and Sensibilia.* Oxford: Clarendon Press.

Brentano, Franz. 1976. *Aristotle and His World View,* ed. and trans. Roderick Chisholm and Rolf George. Berkeley: University of California Press.

Carriero, John. 1984. "Descartes and the Autonomy of Human Understanding." Ph.D. diss., Harvard University.

Chisholm, Roderick. 1976. *Perceiving: A Philosophical Study.* Ithaca: Cornell University Press.

Churchland, Patricia. 1986. *Neurophilosophy: Towards a Unified Science of the Mind-Brain.* Cambridge: MIT Press.

Churchland, Paul M. 1981. "Eliminative Materialism and Propositional Attitudes." *Journal of Philosophy,* 78: 67–90.

Dennett, Daniel. 1987. *The Intentional Stance.* Cambridge: MIT Press.

Goodman, Nelson. 1972. "Seven Strictures on Similarity." In *Problems and Projects,* Indianapolis: Bobbs-Merrill.

Hubel, D. H., and T. N. Wiesel. 1962. "Receptive Fields of Single Neurons in the Cat's Striate Cortex." *Journal of Physiology,* 148: 579–591.

――― 1974. "Receptive Fields, Binocular Interaction, and Functional Architecture in the Cat's Striate Cortex." *Journal of Physiology,* 160: 106–154.

Kim, Jaegwon. 1982. "Psychophysical Supervenience." *Philosophical Studies,* 41: 51–71.

――― 1984. "Concepts of Supervenience." *Philosophy and Phenomenological Research,* 14: 153–154.

Lewis, David. 1983. *Philosophical Papers.* Oxford: Oxford University Press.

Marr, D. C. 1982. *Vision: A Computational Investigation into the Human Representation and Processing of Visual Information.* San Francisco: Freeman.

Modrak, D. 1987. *Aristotle: The Power of Perception.* Chicago: University of Chicago Press.

Nussbaum, Martha. 1978. *Aristotle's "De Motu Animalium."* Princeton: Princeton University Press.

――― 1982. "Aristotle." In *Ancient Writers,* ed. T. J. Luce, pp. 377–416. New York: Charles Scribner's Sons.

――― 1983. "The Common Explanation of Animal Motion." In *Zweifelhaftes in Corpus Aristotelicum: Studien zu einer Dubia. Akten des 9.ten Symposium Aristotelicum,* ed. P. Moraux and J. Wiesner. Berlin: De Gruyter.

――― 1984. "Aristotelian Dualism: Reply to Howard Robinson." *Oxford Studies in Ancient Philosophy* (ed. J. Annas), 2: 197–207.

――― 1986. *The Fragility of Goodness: Luck and Ethics in Greek Tragedy and Philosophy.* Cambridge: Cambridge University Press.

――― 1987. "The Stoics on the Extirpation of the Passions." *Apeiron,* 20: 129–77.

Nussbaum, Martha, and Amalie Oksenberg Rorty. 1992. *Essays on Aristotle's "De Anima."* Oxford: Clarendon Press.

Owen, G. E. L. 1961. "Tithenai ta phaenomena." In *Aristotle et les problemes de méthode,* ed. S. Mansion. Louvain: Publications universitaires de Louvain.

_____ 1986. *Logic, Science, and Dialectic: Collected Papers in Greek Philosophy.* London: Duckworth.

Pegis, A. 1974. "The Separated Soul and Its Nature in St. Thomas." In *St. Thomas Aquinas, 1274–1974: Commemorative Studies,* ed. Armand A. Maurer, vol. 1, pp. 131–158. Toronto: Pontifical Institute of Medieval Studies.

Putnam, Hilary. 1975. *Philosophical Papers,* vol. 2, *Mind, Language, and Reality.* New York: Cambridge University Press.

_____ 1988. *Representation and Reality.* Cambridge: MIT Press.

Quine, W. V. 1960. *Word and Object.* Cambridge: MIT Press.

Sorabji, Richard. 1974. "Body and Soul in Aristotle." *Philosophy,* 49: 63–89.

Strawson, Peter. 1964. *Individuals.* London: Methuen.

Suppes, Patrick. 1974. "Aristotle's Concept of Matter and Its Relation to Modern Concepts of Matter." *Synthese,* 28: 27–50.

Wiggins, David. 1980. *Sameness and Substance.* Cambridge: Harvard University Press.

Wittgenstein, Ludwig. 1956. *Remarks on the Foundations of Mathematics.* Cambridge: MIT Press.

3. Aristotle after Wittgenstein

In Book 3 of *De Anima,* Aristotle writes that "the thinking part of the soul, while impassible, must be capable of receiving the form of an object; that is, must be potentially the same as its object without being the object."[1] This idea is very difficult to interpret, and many interpretations have been offered through the centuries, and many continue to be offered today. But I do not pretend to be a specialist in classical philosophy; my aim here is not to interpret this doctrine of Aristotle's, but to try to understand the current relevance of the problem with which it seems to me that Aristotle was wrestling and of the intuitive idea that may have guided Aristotle in his treatment of that problem. Of course, even doing that much is, in a sense, "interpreting" Aristotle, but it will not require me to solve the problem of how Aristotle thought a form could be "in" the soul *minus* its matter.

The idea that knowledge of what is outside the mind (or outside of language) depends on something, call it the *form* of the object known, being able to exist (in different ways) both in the mind (or in language) and in the object may seem foreign to analytic philosophy, yet consider for a moment an equally difficult passage from Wittgenstein's *Tractatus.* I am referring to the famous (or notorious) 2.18, "What every picture, of whatever form, must have in common with reality, in order to be able to represent it at all—rightly or wrongly—is the logical form, that is, the form of the reality." (I have rectified the translation.)[2]

One difference between the two passages is that the passage in Wittgenstein's *Tractatus* attributes the same form to the reality pictured (*dem Abgebildeten*—2.16) and to the picture (*das Bild,* which Wittgenstein identifies with the proposition—*der Satz*), while the passage from Aristotle's *De Anima* says that the form of the object of knowledge is also in the mind (the *nous*), but does not say that in the mind it is the form *of* something, unless it is the mind itself (and, indeed, Aristotle does speak of the mind as "becoming the several groups of its objects"[3] in the same chapter. But presumably this is metaphor.

Another difference between the two theories, if one may call them that, is that the notion of "form" involved is quite different. For Aristotle, the form of a perceptible may be "hot," or its privation "cold," the form of a bronze sphere may be its shape, the form of a human being may be rational animality; and we are puzzled by Aristotle's theory because we don't understand in what sense (even in what metaphorical sense) the mind "becomes" hot or cold when it perceives something hot or cold, or in what sense the mind becomes spherical when it perceives a bronze sphere, or becomes a rational animal when it knows something about a man. For Wittgenstein, when he held the picture theory, the form of an object was the totality of its (abstract logical) possibilities of combination with other objects: to know the form of an object is to know the properties it could have and the relations it could bear to other objects. Similarly, to know the form of a fact is to know its abstract logical relations to other facts. This knowledge, however, is to be devoid of material content; it could be expressed simply by saying that there are F and G such that *a* is capable of having property F and of standing in relation G to *b*, etc. Moreover, the objects in the *Tractatus* are required to exist in all possible worlds, which means that they cannot really be "objects" in a vernacular sense. To make things even more confusing, for the sake of illustration Wittgenstein used as examples spatial objects and colored objects, which do *not* exist in all possible worlds, and thus cannot really be Tractarian objects at all. But, sticking with these misleading examples, it is clear that for Wittgenstein the sphericity of a bronze sphere is not what he would call its "form," although the shape of a bronze sphere is one of Aristotle's examples of what *he* means by *form*. For Wittgenstein, the facts that the sphere could have been in each of the other positions that it could have been in and that it could have stood in various relations to other objects, or suitably abstract counterparts of these facts, do constitute the "form" of the object.

In spite of these differences, it is worth insisting that Aristotle and Wittgenstein are both speaking to what we have come to call the problem of intentionality, that is, the problem of how either mind or language hooks on to the world. Aristotle takes the problem to be primarily one of how mind[4] can hook on to the world; Wittgenstein, initiating a linguistic turn, takes the problem to be how language can hook on to the world. But the problems are recognizably linked. Moreover, in spite of all the differences I have mentioned, there is a recognizably common intuition that they share; the intuition that mind and language could not hook on to the world if that which is to be hooked on to did not have intrinsic or "built-in" form.

What I wish to explore here are the ways in which that same idea reappears in contemporary discussion, and also the way in which certain reactions against that idea reappear in contemporary discussion.

Before going on, I shall mention, but only to put aside, one further difference between the Wittgenstein of the *Tractatus* and Aristotle, and that is the special kind of distance that the Wittgenstein of the *Tractatus* puts between himself and his own propositions. Wittgenstein tells us, both in the prefatory remarks and at the end of the *Tractatus,* that his own theory is nonsense *(unsinn),* and although some have seen this repudiation as weakened, if not altogether canceled, by the Tractarian claim that there are things that one can "show" but not "say" (for example, the logical form of a propositional sign shows itself but cannot be said in language), others[5] have argued (correctly to my mind) that it is a misuse of the "say/show" distinction to hold that the metaphysical propositions of the *Tractatus* are, at the end of the day, really supposed to express truths, or even thinkable thoughts. This very difficult and very important exegetical question is, fortunately, one that I do not have to get into. In any case, Wittgenstein did at one time accept the picture theory (for example, in the *Notebooks*), and Russell held a very similar view in his logical atomist period; and clearly Wittgenstein still thought the theory worth presenting, even if his purpose may have been primarily dialectical, when he wrote the *Tractatus.*

Today's Causal Theories of Reference

It may seem that both of these theories, Aristotle's and the much more recent theory that Russell and Wittgenstein once held, are now hopelessly out of date. Today the most commonly proposed answer to the question "how does language hook on to the world" invokes not the notion of form but the notion of *causal connection.* Different versions of this answer have been proposed in the United States by Jerry Fodor, Richard Boyd, Michael Devitt, and others, and in England by Simon Blackburn, and perhaps in a veiled way by Bernard Williams. Williams holds that some of our beliefs, although not all, refer to a reality which is "absolute," that is, independent of our human perspectives.[6] A feature of Williams' account of how knowledge of such an absolute reality is identified as such is that the characteristics which are ascribed to that reality by natural science (which alone describes reality as it is absolutely, according to Williams) are ones on which the beliefs of natural scientists *converge;* and a further crucial feature[7] is that this convergence in the beliefs of scientists is *explained* with the help of those very beliefs, that is, scientists come to have the beliefs in question because they represent "the way things (anyway) are." It is clear that what Williams is talking about is *causal* explanation; however, Williams' view is difficult to interpret, because Williams also holds that the very notion of "belief" may not be an absolute one.[8] In other words, Williams thinks that, although we have beliefs about the world as it is independently of our minds, beliefs which are *caused* by the very features of the world that they describe, *that* statement itself may be only "perspectivally" true and not "absolutely" true. Whether this idea is coherent is a question I cannot explore here.[9]

However, the popularity of the idea that causal connection—that is, efficient causation—can solve the problem of how language hooks on to the world is strange. For one only has to reflect on the properties of efficient causation to see that such conceptions are deeply problematic. Let me point out two features of the causal relation.

The first feature is that *we now think of events rather than objects as causes.* At one time it would have sounded perfectly all right to say that the parents are the cause of the child, but today we would say that the event of procreation (or something of that kind) is the cause of the event of the child's being born. (Some authors, e.g., Russell, speak of *states* rather than events as causes, but the points I am about to make are not affected by this.) The question "What are the causes and effects of this table?" makes no sense to us, although the question "What are the causes and effects of such and such an event involving the table?" makes sense. ("What is the cause of the table?" would, if regarded as intelligible at all, be regarded as a way of asking, "What is the cause of *the table's coming into existence?*"—i.e., what is the cause of an event.)

The second feature I shall remark on has been repeatedly called to our attention by Donald Davidson.[10] It has to do, in the first instance, not with causation but with the individuation of events, but if events are the arguments of the causal relation, then the theory of the individuation of events is of crucial importance for the analysis of causation. This feature is that the identity or non-identity of events cannot be simply read off from the identity or non-identity of the sentences we use to say that those events took place. We may use one sentence to describe a psychological event, say "John thought of all the work he had to do," and a different sentence to describe a brain event, but according to Davidson the two token events may be one and the same. Different descriptions—descriptions which are not logically equivalent—may be descriptions of one and the same event.

One reason for accepting Davidson's wide conception of individuation of events is this: if we say that any pair of different sentences (of the kind that describe happenings or events) describe *different* events, then events themselves begin to look suspiciously like ghostly counterparts of sentences. That is, events become things to which, on the one hand, we give exactly the same structure as sentences, but which, on the other hand, we put out into the world. The invention of such intermediaries is a piece of philosophical legerdemain. It may look as if such intermediaries provide a solution to the problem of how language hooks on to the world, but the solution turns out upon inspection to be just a form of the discredited "museum myth of meaning." For my purposes here, however, it is not necessary that one agree with Davidson that sentences which are not logically equivalent may describe one and the same event. It is enough for my purposes that we grant that at least in the case of sentences which *are* logically equivalent we should not speak of two different events. For example, assume the following two sentences are true:

(1) Someone gave me a pair of apples.
(2) Someone gave me an even prime number of apples.

We would not want to say that *the event of my being given a pair of apples* is a different event from my being given an even prime number of apples, given that the two sentences are logically equivalent in a wide sense (equivalent as a matter of mathematical fact).

You may be asking yourselves what the relevance of the two features I pointed out could possibly be, that is what relevance the features that (i) causation is a relation between events and (ii) that events may be described by different sentences, certainly by different sentences which are logically equivalent, and perhaps by different sentences which are not even logically equivalent, could have to the claim that causal connection is the "glue" that attaches extralinguistic reality to language.

The answer is that there is a direct relevance, but to show it properly would require a digression into what logicians call "model theory." I shall not show it properly today (a full treatment is given in the appendix of my *Reason, Truth, and History*), but I shall sketch the idea (using an illustration from the second chapter of *Reason, Truth, and History*).

In *Reason, Truth, and History* (1981), I considered the tenseless sentence "A cat is on a mat."

I also considered three mutually exclusive and jointly exhaustive cases, as follows:

(a) Some cat is on some mat and some cherry is on some tree.
(b) Some cat is on some mat and no cherry is on any tree.
(c) Neither of the foregoing.

And I defined two properties "cat*" and "mat*" as follows:

Definition of "cat*": x is a cat* if and only if case (a) holds and x is a cherry; or case (b) holds and x is a cat; or case (c) holds and x is a cherry.

Definition of "mat*": x is a mat* if and only if case (a) holds and x is a tree; or case (b) holds and x is a mat; or case (c) holds and x is a quark.

Now, in possible worlds falling under case (a), "A cat is on a mat" is true and "A cat* is on a mat*" is also true, because a cherry is on a tree and all cherries are cats* and all trees are mats* in worlds of this kind. Note that the actual world is a "case (a)" world.

In possible worlds falling under case (b), "A cat is on a mat" is true and "A cat* is on a mat*" is also true, because in worlds falling under case (b) "cat" and "cat*" are coextensive terms, and so are "mat" and "mat*."

In possible worlds falling under case (c), "A cat is on a mat" is false and "A cat* is on a mat*" is also false, because a cherry can't be on a *quark*.

Summarizing, we see that in every possible world "A cat is on a mat" and "A cat* is on a mat*" have the same truth value; that is to say, these two sentences are *logically equivalent* (even though, in the actual world, "cat*" refers to cherries and "mat*" refers to trees). In the appendix to *Reason, Truth, and History* I showed that a more complicated reinterpretation of this kind can be carried out for all the sentences of a whole language. It follows that *every* sentence about cats can be paired with a logically equivalent sentence of the same form about "cats*," although it is necessary for this purpose that we define "cat*" in a more complicated way, so that the set of cats* will have the same cardinality as the set of cats in every possible world. However, any term will do whose extension in each possible world has the same cardinality as the set of cats; thus, if in the actual world there are at least as many cherries as cats and as least as many trees as mats, we can construct an interpretation of the whole language under which the extension of "cat*" in the actual world is a subset of the set of all cherries of the same cardinality as the set of cats and the extension of "mat*" in the actual world is a subset of the set of all trees of the same cardinality as the set of mats. Now, imagine this to be done. Then for any sentence describing an event, say "A cat was on a mat at 12 noon on March 12th of such and such a year," there will be a *logically equivalent* sentence "A cat* was on* a mat* at 12 noon on March 12th of such and such a year" which is about quite different things—say about some bunch of cherries and trees and some complicated relation "on*."[11]

The relevance to the notion that causal connection is a sufficient explanation of how extralinguistic reality attaches to language is immediate. Let E be a cat-involving event that is causally connected to an utterance containing the term "cat." Then there is a description of the very same event E—a description of the very same logical structure, in fact—under which E is a cat*-involving event. Thus causal connection alone cannot explain why "cat" refers to cats and not to cats* (to some bunch of cherries).

Metaphysically speaking, the problem is this: we agreed to give up the idea that events have a *self-identifying structure*. (This is exactly what Davidson convinced most of us we must give up. And even those of us who are not convinced by Davidson would balk at saying that logically equivalent sentences describe *different* events.) But *unstructured* events, and a relation called "causation" between such unstructured events, cannot explain how *constituents* of events connect with subsentential parts of speech. (I do not believe that causation can account for the reference and truth value of whole unanalyzed sentences either, but I am not arguing that question here.) In short, what we are missing is precisely the notion that events have a *form*. Efficient causation, as presently conceived, will not provide us with enough *form*.

Aristotle and Wittgenstein Again

What I have just said looks like grist for the mill of a possible latter-day Aristotelian metaphysics. The natural Aristotelian response to the difficulties just canvassed is to say, "I told you so. You cannot do without the notion of *form*." I am not certain that Aristotle's ontology included events, but there is no reason why a latter-day Aristotelian might not say that just as things have form, so events also have form. Moreover, when we think about the difficulties I just described, it seems that an Aristotelian conception of form is much more suited to deal with them than is a Tractarian conception. Indeed, it is not clear how a Tractarian notion of form would help at all.

The problem I described arises because, in the very abstract sense of "form" that the Tractarian view requires, it just isn't *true* that different objects have different logical form. What the model-theoretic argument I described trades on, in fact—the technical name for this kind of argument is "a permutation of individuals argument"—is that, given an arbitrary permutation of the individuals in a universe of discourse, it is always possible to map propositional functions (that is, properties and relations) onto propositional functions in such a way that a "logical isomorphism" results: for example, if individuals *a* and *b* stand in a relation R, then the images of the individuals *a* and *b* under the permutation stand in the image of the relation R under the mapping. Of course, Wittgenstein (when he believed the Tractarian theory, for instance, when he wrote the *Notebooks*) might have replied that this occurs because our "individuals" are objects in the vernacular sense of object, that is, objects such as cats and trees and cherries (and even quarks); perhaps he would have said that this only shows that the true "objects" *must not be* empirical objects, that they must be such that any two different individuals of necessity have quite different logical form. If we could find objects that satisfied this description, then a permutation of individuals argument would be impossible. But the problem is that we haven't the faintest idea what a Tractarian object could possibly look like. (Of course, I am not the first to make this last remark.)[12]

For the Aristotelian, by contrast, the situation looks brighter. Aristotle's fundamental objects, the "substances," are living things (his paradigm substances), astronomical bodies, the artifacts that living things make, and (in a secondary sense) the forms of all of the foregoing. His forms are the scientifically and metaphysically fundamental characteristics of living things, the functions of artifacts (e.g., "cutting"), and also certain attributes of perceptibles, such as color, hot and cold, shape, and so on. This ontology keeps close links with a familiar and commonsensical ontology, even if (as worked up in the *Metaphysics*) it undergoes certain problematical transformations. Indeed, one of Aristotle's motives was to react against the Platonic theory of forms. It is true that the metaphor that Aristotle likes, that is, the metaphor according to which the form is "in" the object rather than "outside" it, or "apart" from it, is far from clear. (Which is why it is maddening when Aristotle's followers, up to the present day, simply repeat it as if it were self-explanatory.) Reasoning *a priori*, one might think that there was no reason to prefer one metaphor to the other. The bronze sphere *has* its shape, one might say, in the sense of the "has" of predication, F(*a*), and reading F(*a*) as "F" is "in" *a* only breeds confusion. But what led Aristotle to choose this metaphor was clearly a desire to think of forms not as quasi-divinities above the things that we experience, Realities in a sense of "reality" that relativizes the reality that we experience, but as properties and capacities of the things that we experience, and this was an attempt to develop a metaphysics that does justice to the world as we know it.

Another advantage of Aristotle's view is that, unlike the Wittgenstein of the *Notebooks*, he does not have to maintain that *everything* that we say (when our speech has significance) corresponds to a form. Some descriptions of things are descriptions of accidental properties of the things, or so highly artificial that they fail to reveal what the forms of those things are. If I define "cat*" and "mat*" in the highly complicated way I did before, and describe the fact that some cat is on some mat by saying "Some cat* is on some mat*," then I am simply not revealing the *form* of that event. In this last remark, I am not interpreting the historical Aristotle, but rather trying to guess what a latter-day Aristotelian philosopher might well say.

But I do not wish to suggest that simply reintroducing the notion of "form," and recognizing that not every description of a thing or event reveals what we might call the "form" or the "structure" or the "nature" of that thing or event, solves the problem of intentionality with which we began. Indeed, the very problem that puzzled us about Aristotle's theory still remains. One may well feel the attraction of the "intuition" that I described as being behind both Aristotle's theory and the Tractarian theory, that is, the idea that neither mind nor language could hook onto the world if what is referred to does not possess an "intrinsic" form of its own (although I will argue that we cannot finally accept that idea, put that way). But even if we could somehow make sense of the claim that objects and events have intrinsic form, there still remains the question of the relation between that form and the form of whatever it is that thinks about or represents the object. To say that the relation is identity, whether "identity" be taken literally or metaphorically, makes no sense.

In spite of my own skepticism about the enterprise of "explaining how language hooks on to the world,"[13] I have at times attempted to put myself in the frame of mind of a "latter-day Aristotelian," and to imagine what such a philosopher might say about this problem. (I find that such thought experiments are best conducted while taking my dog, Shlomit, on a walk in the woods and marshes of Arlington and Lexington.) When I performed this experiment, it occurred to me that a latter-day Aristotelian is in a different position than a latter-day Tractarian in the following respect: for the latter-day Aristotelian, the form is a *metaphysical* rather than a *logical* property—where "metaphysical" is not used pejoratively, and need not connote any transcendent realm, of course. By this, what I mean is that to give the form of, say, a living thing is to give the way it is organized to function, its capacities and functionings and the interrelationships among those capacities and functionings: in short, what it is capable of, and how it accomplishes what it is capable of. (Of course, this is only a part of the historical Aristotle's notion of form; if one accepts the doctrine of the Aristotelian four causes, then one will arrive at a still richer notion of form; but few present-day philosophers are willing to accept all that is involved in the Aristotelian doctrine of the four causes.)

What I am saying once again is that there is an enormous difference between taking the form of something to be the *metaphysically best description of its nature* and taking the form to be the *abstract characterization of the totality of its logical possibilities of combination with other objects.* As the model-theoretic arguments show, logic, at the abstract Tractarian level, does not do anything to distinguish one object from another. The idea that logic could do all the work of metaphysics was a *magnificent* fantasy, but fantasy it surely was.

Now, given this notion of form, one idea that might occur to a latter-day Aristotelian (while walking his dog) would be to *mimic* what logical atomism did, by simply substituting metaphysical form for logical form. In other words, just as logical atomism requires that, in a certain sense, the logical form of the proposition, of the representation, should be isomorphic to the logical form of the fact that is represented, so, one might say (if one is a latter-day Aristotelian who has taken account of the linguistic turn), that, in a certain sense, the metaphysical form of our descriptions needs to be isomorphic to the metaphysical form of the object represented, for reference to succeed. But let me say what I mean by this.

Speaking phenomenologically, we see propositions as imposing a certain kind of order on the world. (By speaking phenomenologically, I am, like Husserl, bracketing the question of the truth or falsity, or indeed the objective reference, of our propositions.) Certain verbs are causal verbs, certain parts of propositions are at least seen from within the language as denoting agents and others as denoting patients, certain words are seen as dispositional words, and so on. The metaphysical structure that our propositions project onto the world is what the world would copy in the best case, the case of the most successful and most complete reference, or so my "latter-day Aristotelian" would think.

Something like this idea, although in a much more schematic form, has indeed been proposed by David Lewis.[14] David Lewis believes that certain classes of things are intrinsically "natural," that is, intrinsically natural kinds, and that certain kinds of words are intended by us to be natural kind words, and that the constraint that determines how language hooks on to the world (when taken in conjunction with the familiar Davidsonian constraints having to do with charity in interpretation)[15] is that natural kind terms in our language (and perhaps other terms as well) should hook on to classes which have a high degree of this metaphysical "naturalness." This is a weaker form of what I just described as a possible latter-day Aristotelian metaphysics, which not only would require natural kind terms to hook on to classes which share a form, but also would require disposition terms to hook on to dispositions, etc. But Lewis' own application of his doctrine shows how suspicious such a doctrine is.

Lewis developed his doctrine in the course of replying to my argument (in *Reason, Truth, and History*) that the Brains in a Vat, the beings in a world in which all sentient beings are (and always were) brains in a vat (whose efferent nerve endings led to automatic machinery which supplied the right afferent nerve impulses to maintain the illusion that everything is just as it is in our own world), would not be able to say or think that they are brains in a vat. Lewis believes that his doctrine refutes this claim in the following way: if the Brains in a

Vat do use the words "vat" and "tree" in what they experience as speech and thought, then, in his view, those words do succeed in hooking on to real vats and real trees *even though the Brains in a Vat never have, in their entire history and in the entire history of their language, any differential interaction at all with real vats, real trees, or with properties and substances in terms of which real vats and real trees could be defined or at least described.* In short, it is precisely because no interaction at all is required for language to hook on to the world that, in Lewis' view, terms can refer to things with which we and our linguistic ancestors have never had the slightest contact. Of course, on any theory we can refer to *some* things with which we have not had the slightest contact, because we can describe them using terms for properties and things with which we have had contact; but the fact that even *this* is not necessary for reference on Lewis' view makes his account totally magical.

Still, there is reason to think that Aristotle himself might have made a similar criticism of Lewis' view. For it was no part of Aristotle's view that the mind can refer to universals with which it has had no contact. In fact, Aristotle says the contrary again and again. According to Aristotle, it is *experience* that "stabilizes the universal in its entirety within the soul."[16] On the other hand, although an Aristotelian would reject Lewis' account, in rejecting it he raises again the very problem that occasions all the difficulty: in just what sense can we say that, when we have "experienced" certain things sufficiently, the universal comes to be "in" the mind?[17]

A further difficulty for a neo-Aristotelian metaphysics, descriptive or otherwise, comes to mind. I have said that the strongest line for the neo-Aristotelian to take is to say that what enables reference to take place is a matching (mere isomorphism doesn't seem to be enough), some kind of a matching between the metaphysical structure our propositions project onto the objects and the metaphysical structure those objects actually have. The difficulty is that very often we have the structure of the things we refer to just dead wrong. For Aristotle, living before the successive scientific revolutions, this does not seem to have been a problem because he could assume that at a certain point we would just get the structure right. But in fact even the structure of something as familiar as water is something that we did not succeed in getting right for over two thousand years, and even today we have only a very approximate account of the structure of water. Aristotle himself regarded water as one of the elements, as did many of his contemporaries and many other people after them. Yet (*pace* Thomas Kuhn) this did not keep them from successfully referring to water. The requirement that to refer to something the representation must get the essential metaphysical properties right seems to be much too strong.

Do Substances Have a Unique Essence?

The greatest difficulty facing someone who wishes to hold an Aristotelian view is that the central intuition behind that view, that is, the intuition that a natural kind *has* a single determinate form (or "nature" or "essence") has become problematical. To be sure, some of the reasons it came to be regarded as problematical are themselves suspect. The familiar positivist claim that while it makes sense to ask for the essence of a concept (that is the "analysis" of the concept), it does not make sense to ask what the essence or nature of a *thing* is, is wrong on two counts. On the one hand, the notion that *concepts* have essences has been made problematical by many, largely successful, attacks on the positivists' analytic-synthetic distinction. Perhaps some concepts do have analytic definitions. I think it *is* analytic that a bachelor is an unmarried man. But the great majority of our concepts seem able to change their conceptual roles in the course of time[18]—and the kind of change I have in mind is not regarded as a change in the extension of the concept. For example, it was for a long time regarded as analytic that momentum is the product of mass and velocity; but when it was discovered that the product of mass and velocity was not conserved in elastic collisions and was not relativistically invariant, physicists began to say that the formula "momentum equals mass times velocity" was not exactly right, that momentum is only approximately mass times velocity (and then only when the velocity is small in comparison to the velocity of light). If the old definition "momentum is mass times velocity" was an analytic definition, physicists should feel that the acceptance of Einstein's corrected formula for momentum was a change in both the meaning and the extension of the concept. But it is clear that they do not. They feel that they are talking about the magnitude that they were always talking about, and that the former definition was simply not exactly right. Phenomena of this kind occur especially often when there are scientific revolutions. On the other hand, when a scientist says he is trying to "discover the nature" of something, say the nature of gold or the nature of water, he is hardly talking nonsense.[19] Such talk would, indeed, not make any sense if we did not have a long tradition of scientific investigation to give it substance; but we do have such a tradition.

Even if the positivist criticisms rested on doctrines which are themselves suspicious, there are still difficulties with the doctrine that every (kind of) substance has a determinate intrinsic form or essence. Imagine, for example, that someone asked the question, "Is it part of the essence of dogs that they are descended from wolves?" (Or, according to some theories, partly from wolves and partly from hyenas.) Is being a domesticated wolf-or-hyena modified by millennia of selective breeding the essence of doghood? The answer seems to be "yes" from an evolutionary biologist's point of view and "no" from a molecular biologist's point of view.

From an evolutionary biologist's point of view—and here one thinks of the writings of Ernst Mayr—species are essentially historical entities, very much like nations. Being a dog is being a member of a species somewhat as being a Frenchman is being a citizen of a nation; someone with characteristics very much like a Frenchman's might not be a Frenchman (he might be a citizen of Belgium, or of the United States), and something with characteristics very much like a dog's might not be a dog, because the population of interbreeding animals to which it belongs has enough distinctiveness *and enough genetic isolation* to count as a new species. Biology, on this conception, is the study of "populations," not of individuals; and it is part of the content of evolutionary theory itself that such populations are not always sharply distinguished from one another. How could they always be? For a new species to come into existence, it is necessary for a group of members of one species to become in some way genetically isolated, so that they form the nucleus of a new population. As Mayr has said, the evolutionary biologist's notion of a species is more or less the lay notion of a species, and it is not a defect of the notion of a species that some species do not have sharp boundaries (even if some philosophers continue to worry the question whether species are "individuals or sets," as though that were an important, or even a meaningful, question; one might wonder why no one asks whether *nations* are individuals or sets.) Note that the criterion (for species with sexual reproduction) that A and B are the same species if a normal member of A can successfully reproduce (and produce fertile offspring) with a normal member of B of the opposite sex does not work as a universal criterion. It can happen that populations A, B, C, D are such that members of A and members of B are capable of having fertile offspring, members of B and members of C are capable of having fertile offspring, members of C and members of D are capable of having fertile offspring, but members of A and members of D are not capable of having fertile offspring. The relation between populations—"a normal member of A can successfully reproduce (and produce fertile offspring) with a normal member of B of the opposite sex"—is not an equivalence relation. But, as I said, evolutionary biologists find the ordinary notion of a species not only useful but indispensable, just as students of government find the notion of a nation not only useful but indispensable, even if national boundaries are not always well defined. The similarities between the two notions are not accidental; both political science and evolutionary theory deal with history. Evolutionary theory seeks to understand the historical origins of the populations of animals that we see in the world, and to generalize about the mechanisms of population change; from this point of view, it is very much of the essence to know that dogs are descended from wolves.

From a molecular biologist's point of view, the situation is quite different. In molecular biology, animals are viewed simply as finished products; the molecular biologist is not concerned with where they came from or with what populations they belong to. From this point of view, having a certain kind of DNA is very much an essential property of a dog. It is not actually possible to give a necessary and sufficient condition for being dog-DNA (I am sure molecular biologists would be happy if it were), because, on account of the mechanisms of genetic variation that are beloved of evolutionary biologists, the DNA varies from one dog to the next, and is constantly changing. (Indeed, there can be almost as much similarity between the DNA of a dog and the DNA of a wolf or even of a cat as between the DNA of two dogs, when we look at the matter simply in terms of organic chemistry.) Nevertheless, one can, or one will soon be able to, make statements of the form "If something did not have such-and-such a kind of DNA, then it would not be a dog," and it is such statements, together with statements about how DNA and RNA are "expressed" in the living organism, that describe the essence or "nature" of dogs from the molecular biological point of view.[20]

These two different points of view can even lead to different decisions about counterfactual situations (at least they are now counterfactual, and likely to remain so for some time). If we suppose that technology becomes so advanced that it is possible to synthesize a whole dog, starting from chemicals on a shelf, say to synthesize a dog with exactly the DNA of my own dog, Shlomit, then, from a molecular biologist's point of view the resulting "synthetic dog" will count as a dog. (One is tempted to say that "synthetic dogs are dogs" will be an analytic truth for molecular biologists.) From the point of view of an evolutionary biologist, the situation is different. I suspect, in fact, that evolutionary biologists would not regard a "synthetic dog" as a dog at all. From their point of view, such a thing would simply be an artifact of no interest—unless, of course, it interbred either with natural dogs or with other synthetic dogs (and, in the latter case, became the start of the sort of "population" that evolutionary biologists study).

That different descriptions of the "nature" of a natural kind should lead to not quite coextensive criteria for membership in the kind is not in itself a new phenomenon, and is not limited to biology. In chemistry, for example, there have long been different definitions of "acid," which agree in all the ordinary cases but disagree about such exotic cases as single ions. And of course, the two views I have described are not the only points of view that we take toward dogs. To dog owners like myself, knowing that dogs are descended from domesticated wolves is of interest only insofar as it enables us to understand the behavior of dogs somewhat better. If it doesn't, then to tell me that I "don't know the nature of dogs" if I don't know that they are descended from domesticated wolves (or domesticated wolves and hyenas) is nonsense. And of course, millions of people know and have always known a good deal about the nature of dogs without having any idea that there is such a thing as DNA.

In conversation, Burton Dreben has pointed out a curious analogy between the possibility of taking these two points of view toward species and the different points of view that philosophers take toward the Brains in a Vat. In both cases, it seems that one is torn between simply looking at the "products," that is, the existing things with their actual present structure, and looking also at the "process," that is, the history of how the things came into being and came to have that structure. David Lewis' attitude toward the Brains in a Vat corresponds to the first of these points of view; for him, the salient fact is that their language (and the internal processing of the language) is exactly the same as our language (and our internal processing of our language). From that standpoint, how could the brains not be referring to trees when they think "tree" or to vats when they think "vat"? My own point of view, in this case, corresponds to the second of the points of view I described; given the history of the Brains in a Vat, and the utter absence of any interaction with the extra-Vat environment throughout that entire history, it makes no sense to me to describe them as referring to real trees and real vats. But fortunately we do not have to resolve that question here.

To avoid misunderstandings—unfortunately, they are very common—let me say as emphatically as I can that I am not saying that just *anything* can be regarded as the nature of a kind from some point of view or other. Not all points of view are rational, and not all rational points of view are sufficiently important to our lives with our language for us to feel that what it is necessary for someone who holds them to know about Xs justifies such a grand name as "the nature of Xs." Knowing the best way to wash a dog may be important for someone whose profession is washing dogs; but knowing the best way to wash a dog is not knowing the nature of dogs. Not just anything can be called the nature of dogs. On the other hand, it does seem that more than one thing can be called knowing the nature of dogs.

I am struck by the analogy between the limited relativity, the relativity to interests, of talk about the nature of Xs and the relativity pointed out long ago by Hart and Honoré[21] of talk about "the cause" to the point of view or the interests of the person using this expression. To use an example that I remember seeing in the literature in the 1960s, the answer to the question "What was the cause of the traffic accident?" given by a road engineer may be quite different from the answer given by the judge who sentences someone for speeding, and those answers—"The accident was caused by the fact that the curve was not banked," "The accident was caused by excessive speed"— may both be reasonable, may support counterfactuals, and so on. I remember discussing this some years ago with Richard Boyd, who remarked that while what counts as "the cause" of something may be relevant to interests, that something is the cause of something *given* those interests is absolute, and I am inclined to agree.

Talk of interests and points of view is, of course, intentional talk. It presupposes language users who are already in contact with a world, not minds in the abstract or languages in the abstract which have to somehow be related to a world, which have to, as we say, find a way to "hook on to" a world. Certainly, the Aristotelian insight that objects have structure is right, provided we remember that what counts as the structure of something is relative to the ways in which we interact with it. Intentionality and the structure of the world and the structure of language are all intimately related; but it seems that the hope of reducing the notion of intentionality to a metaphysical notion of structure (or "form") which itself has no intentional presuppositions is illusory.

Notes

An earlier version of this chapter was delivered as the S. V. Keeling Memorial Lecture for 1990–91 at University College London, March 12, 1991. The idea of discussing the viability of neo-Aristotelian metaphysics was inspired by conversations with John Haldane during my stay in St. Andrews in the fall of 1990. I am grateful for his companionship and stimulation, and look forward to his response. I am also grateful to Alva Noë and Eli Friedlander for helpful discussions about the *Tractatus*.

1. See Chapter 4 (429^a14–17).

2. Although "the reality" (in the sense of "the object represented") may seem awkward, it has two advantages over the Ogden translation—which has simply "reality": (1) it makes sense of the sentence, while the notion that each proposition has the logical form of (all of) reality makes no sense at all; and (2) in lectures given in English (see, in particular, Lecture 25 in Wittgenstein's *Lectures on the Philosophy of Mathematics*, ed. Cora Diamond [Chicago: University of Chicago Press, 1989]), Wittgenstein some years later used "a reality" in precisely this way (for example, he referred to a blue chair as "a reality").

3. See 429^b5.

4. However, Aristotle's notion of what is and what is not included in "mind" is not at all the same as the notion we have become used to since Descartes. On this, see Chapter 1 of the present volume.

5. See, in particular, James Conant's "Must We Show What We Cannot Say," in *The Senses of Stanley Cavell* (Lewisburgh: Bucknell University Press, 1989), and "Logical Aliens" in *The Philosophy of Hilary Putnam*, Philosophical Topics, 20, no. 1 (Spring 1992). See also Cora Diamond's "Throwing Away the Ladder: How to Read the *Tractatus*," in her *The Realistic Spirit* (Cambridge: MIT Press, 1991).

6. See Williams, *Descartes: The Project of Pure Enquiry* (London: Viking Penguin, 1990), pp. 236–249, 298–303, and *Ethics and the Limits of Philosophy* (Cambridge: Harvard University Press, 1985), pp. 136ff.

7. These features are, of course, reminiscent of Peirce, whom Williams credits with anticipating this account.

8. "There may be little reason to suppose that ['beliefs and theories and conceptions of the world'] could be adequately characterized in non-perspectival terms. How far this may be so is a central philosophical question. But even if we allow that the explanation of such things must remain to some

degree perspectival, this does not mean that we cannot operate the idea of the absolute conception. It will be a conception consisting of non-perspectival materials available to any adequate investigator of whatever constitution, and *it will also help to explain to us, though not necessarily to those alien investigators, such things as our capacity to grasp that conception.*" (*Ethics and the Limits of Philosophy*, p. 140, emphasis added.)

9. I argue that it is *not* coherent in *Renewing Philosophy* (Cambridge: Harvard University Press, 1992).

10. See "The Individuation of Events" in Donald Davidson's *Actions and Events* (Oxford: Clarendon Press, 1980).

11. The reader may wonder why we do not also have to reinterpret words referring to time—which will play a role in the sequel. The answer is that by a theorem of model theory known as the Beth Definability Theorem, the only circumstance under which it is impossible to find a model which generates a nonstandard interpretation for the other terms in the language while being standard on the words in a given class—in this case, the class of temporal expressions—is the circumstance in which the terms in question are explicitly definable in terms of the words in the given class alone. Since "cat," "mat," "on," etc., are not explicitly definable from temporal predicates alone, we are guaranteed that the nonstandard model—the model in which "cat" refers to cats*, "mat" refers to mats*, "on" refers to on*, etc.—does not have to be nonstandard on the temporal expressions. One last point, and we are ready to apply all this to our present concerns: it follows from the very weak principle that logically equivalent sentences describe the same events that the sentences "A cat is on a mat" and "A cat* is on a mat*" *describe the same event.*

12. It might seem that Wittgenstein could evade this whole problem by pointing out that the form that has to be shared (in the *Tractatus*) for representation to take place is the logical form of the *fact*, not the logical form of any *object*. But Wittgenstein did think that facts have objects as *constituents;* for example, an elementary fact might have the form Fab. But the "permutation of individuals argument" highlights a problem with this. Let Perm be any permutation of the objects. Define a two-place relation F′ by F′(x,y) if and only if F(Perm(x),Perm(y)). Then F(Perm(x),Perm(y)) and F′(x,y) are the same fact, in the Tractarian metaphysics; so which are the "real" constituents of this fact, x and y or Perm(x) and Perm(y)? The notion of a *constituent* of a fact was inherited by logical atomism from Russell's *earlier* metaphysics, and is, in fact, a quasi-Aristotelian element within the logical atomist picture.

13. The reasons for that skepticism are explained in many of the essays in my *Realism with a Human Face,* ed. James Conant (Cambridge: Harvard University Press, 1990).

14. See David Lewis, "Putnam's Paradox," *Australasian Journal of Philosophy,* 62 (1984), 221–236.

15. On these, see David Lewis' "Radical Interpretation," *Synthese*, 23 (1974), 331–344; reprinted in Lewis' *Philosophical Papers*, vol. 1 (Oxford: Oxford University Press, 1983).

16. See *Posterior Analytics* 100ᵃ7–8.

17. John Haldane has suggested—if I understand his view aright—that a neo-Aristotelian might hold that the universal, in its highest actuality, just *is* the act of thinking about the species, in the highest actuality of that act. But this suggestion invokes the very notion of *thinking about* something which it was the purpose of the account to explain!

18. What I say in this paragraph is expounded in much more detail in my *Representation and Reality* (Cambridge: MIT Press, 1988); see especially pp. 9–11 and 48–49.

19. On this, see *Representation and Reality*, pp. 34–36.

20. Bernard Williams would probably say that the molecular biological description "explains" (in principle) the phenomena described by evolutionary biology; at least, it is a constant theme of Williams' metaphysical writing that "physics" explains all the more "perspectival" truths of the other sciences. I can only say that this is the claim that Ernst Mayr, Stephen Gould, Richard Lewontin, and just about every recent philosopher of biology has been concerned to debunk. Williams might feel unscathed, because he might argue that the kind of reduction of all the other sciences to physics he envisages is not a definitional reduction, and is itself only "perspectival." Cf. n. 8, above.

21. See H. L. Hart and Tony Honoré, *Causation in the Law* (Oxford: Clarendon Press, 1959).

II

The Legacy of Logical Positivism

4. Logical Positivism and Intentionality

When "Freddy" Ayer asked me to contribute to his volume in the Library of Living Philosophers series I was delighted, and while the main topic of my contribution[1] was the sense (if any) in which it can be a "necessary" truth that water is H_2O, I devoted a section of that essay to problems that I saw with Ayer's account of the paradigm intentional notion, the notion of reference. Ayer ended his reply by saying that he could not satisfactorily meet my objections, and with characteristic modesty and good humor he added that it was only small consolation that, in his opinion, no one else could satisfactorily account for reference either. The thoughtfulness, fairness, and responsiveness of Ayer's entire reply reminded me of the way in which the same qualities were displayed in Carnap's reply to my contribution to his volume in the same series. These two replies—Carnap's and Ayer's—display the virtues of the philosopher who searches for truth, and who genuinely welcomes serious criticism, in a truly exemplary way. I treasure both of them, and they are bound up with my memories of those two wonderful philosophers.

Here I shall not review the difficulties I laid out in "Is Water Necessarily H_2O?" because those difficulties had to do with Ayer's own account of reference to mental particulars, an account which is closer to Russell's than it is to the main doctrines of logical positivism. Instead, I shall consider the treatment of intentional notions by the two principal leaders of the movement, namely, Rudolf Carnap and Hans Reichenbach.[2]

First, a word as to what I shall mean here by "intentionality." It has been said with justice that it is characteristic of analytic philosophy as a movement (and not just of logical positivism) to make the relation between thought and language (or between language and the understanding of language) a central—sometimes *the* central—question of philosophy. But, to pre-philosophical common sense at least, it would seem that any account of the relation between language and the understanding of language has to include some account of the relation between language and the world; and, taken in this way, the relation to be accounted for is just what Brentano and Husserl understood by intentionality. Moreover, this problem was known to Carnap, at least, before Carnap became a positivist; for in Carnap's doctoral dissertation, "Der Raum" ("Space"), there are admiring references to Husserl. Yet Brentano and Husserl believed that it was impossible to give a naturalistic account of intentionality, and logical positivism is avowedly naturalistic. So, how did Carnap come to think (and how did Reichenbach think) that a naturalistic answer to this problem (often called "Brentano's Problem" nowadays) had been given by logical positivism?

The general lines of the reply are well known: While the problem of the relation between language and our understanding of language remains a reasonable question for the positivists, and one to which they proposed answers, the idea that a part of the question is "the relation of language to the world" is rejected as a confusion. Brentano's Problem is one of the problems that Carnap would surely have dismissed as a "pseudo-problem." Whether it is or is not a pseudo-problem is a larger question than I can deal with here, except for some very brief remarks at the end; for the most part, what I wish to study is the more restricted question, do the reasons that the positivists gave for dismissing this question, or this family of questions, really work? And if they fail, just *how* do they fail?

Carnap and Solipsism

One way of seeing how these questions might seem to arise for the positivists, and how they attempted to dismiss them, is to consider the charge of "solipsism" that was often brought against Carnap's celebrated *Logische Aufbau der Welt*. On the face of it, such a charge might seem fully justified. For the "ontology" of the Aufbau, the domain over which the bound variables of the ideal language are intended to range, is *the reconstructor's past and present "elementary experiences."* When Carnap writes out an arbitrary synthetic statement in the ideal language, all it speaks about is Carnap's "elementary experiences." So, according to Carnap, the world consists of Carnap's "elementary experiences"—what is wrong with this argument?

According to Carnap, what is wrong is the following: it is true (Carnap thought at that time) that every cognitively meaningful statement either is a tautology or is expressible as a synthetic statement about "my" elementary experiences. (The idea—later to become explicit, and still later to be given up by Carnap—that any meaningful synthetic statement can be conclusively verified, and that its meaning is given by a description of the verifying experiences, is already implicit in this doctrine.) But, Carnap argued in the *Aufbau,* the "language of science" (i.e., the cognitively meaningful) can be rationally reconstructed in alternative and equally legitimate ways. (The "Principle of Tolerance" was already implicit in this claim.) If, in one reconstruction of the language, the "ontology" is "my" experiences, in another, equally admissible, reconstruction, the "ontology" might be physical objects. The adoption of one reconstruction or another is not a commitment to the noumenal existence of either elementary experiences or physical objects. Indeed, to know what the nominatum of a sign is is only to know how the sentences containing that sign receive truth values, and this can be displayed equally well by different rational reconstructions. The very term "ontology" is misleading, Carnap told me years later, and he was extremely critical of Quine for introducing it into analytic philosophy.

On Carnap's view, there are only two sorts of meaningful statements: one can make ordinary scientific statements within the ideal language (years later, when Carnap wrote "Empiricism, Semantics, Ontology," these become the "internal statements," the answers to the "internal questions," distinguished in that essay from both the senseless "external questions" of metaphysics and the meaningful "external questions" of pragmatics and syntax), and one can make syntactic statements about the various rational reconstructions, for example, "In the system of the Aufbau, the only primitive predicate is *Elementary experience X is remembered as similar to elementary experience Y.*" Confusing the latter sort of statement with statements of transcendent metaphysics, for example, "Only my elementary experiences really exist" is what gives rise to the charges of solipsism, idealism, materialism, and so on, that are constantly being brought against logical positivists on the basis of the character of their various (alternative) reconstructions of the language of science. Carnap's "solipsism" is a harmless "methodological solipsism" (that is, the adoption of one particular basis for the reconstruction from among a number of possible choices), not a bit of transcendent metaphysics.

The upshot is that the question of how all or any of these reconstructions relates to "the world" is a pseudo-question. For example, if

I adopt the *Aufbau* system, it is quite wrong to charge me with believing that only my own elementary experiences exist. For, if the question as to the existence of other people's experiences is meant as an ordinary internal question, then the answer is that other people, physical objects, and the experiences of other people all exist as a question of empirical fact (since these are all identified with various logical constructions out of my experiences, and the sentences about these constructions which translate "there are other people," "there are material bodies," and "there are experiences of other people" correctly state empirical facts in the system). On the other hand, if it is meant as an external question, then either the question is a syntactic question, answered by saying what the primitives of the system are, or it is a meaningless pseudo-question. The radical idea that the questions of classical philosophy are all illegitimate attempts to transcend the bounds of the language is present in the *Aufbau*, as it was, of course, in Wittgenstein's *Tractatus*, even if the *Aufbau* does not explicitly state a theory of meaning.

However, there is a major problem with all this—one which Carnap did not have the resources to deal in the *Aufbau* itself. The difficulty is the following: Carnap's reply to the charge of solipsism turns on the notion of "equally possible" (that is, equally correct) reconstructions of the language. But *what does "equally possible" mean?*

The problem is one with which Quine has wrestled in recent years (and one with respect to which he "vacillates" between different attitudes,[3] Quine tells us), namely, can one say that there are in some sense equally true descriptions of the world which are incompatible when taken at face value? If I reconstruct the language of science in the *Aufbau* way and then reconstruct it again on a physicalist basis, the two reconstructions will not simply be equivalent in the sense in which "equivalent" is used in standard logic.[4] Indeed, if we simply conjoin them, we may get *contradictions*.

To see the problem, suppose, *per impossibile,* that the program of "methodological solipsism" could really be carried out, and that thing sentences could be translated into sentences about (my) elementary experiences. If I define a physical object as a logical construction (in the sense of the *Principia,* which served as Carnap's model of rational reconstruction), and also (when I take physical objects as basic, in my "alternative" physicalistic reconstruction of the language of science) define my elementary experiences as logical constructions in the physicalist language, what will happen? In the "methodological solipsist" conceptual scheme, a physical object, say my desk, is a set of sets of sets . . . whose ultimate members are certain of my own elementary experiences. In the physicalist conceptual scheme, my elementary experiences are sets of sets of sets . . . whose ultimate members are certain physical objects. Given the axiom of foundation of set theory, conjoining the two schemes will lead to a contradictory set of statements. So the pressing question is: in what sense can two *incompatible* theories be "equally possible" reconstructions of the same language and the same science?

Even if one could somehow carry out the two constructions, the phenomenalist and the physicalist one, without using any explicit definitions, and the two resulting schemes were compatible, a problem would still remain. For, if we regard the "definitions" of the terms as mere conventions of abbreviation and not as parts of the systems, then the one system, *taken in unabbreviated notation,* and the other system, *likewise taken in unabbreviated notation,* simply speak about different things. One is a collection of truths about my experiences and the other is a collection of truths about physical objects. So in what sense are they both correct reconstructions of the same (unformalized) theory? And if the "definitions" are parts of the system, and not mere conventions of abbreviation, what does it mean to say they are "definitions"? *Exactly what* status is being claimed for them?

After the *Aufbau,* Carnap did develop the famous "verifiability theory of meaning" (which he always credited to Wittgenstein). In one way this does answer the foregoing questions: two reconstructions are equally correct,[5] assuming the verifiability theory of meaning, if they lead to the same predictions. (More precisely, for each sentence of the one, there must be a sentence of the other which is equivalent to exactly the same set of elementary experience sentences.) But—ignoring the fact that the demand for conclusive verification turned out to be too restrictive, and ignoring the fact that the program of phenomenalist reduction could not really be carried through—this solution only moves the difficulty to the metalanguage. For, if "prediction" means prediction of *my* elementary experiences, then reference to "my elementary experiences" enters into the whole system twice over. It enters once in one of the alternative rational reconstructions (the "methodological solipsist" one), and again, at the meta-level, in the criterion for the adequacy of rational reconstructions.

Can Carnap make the same moves as before at the meta-level? Can he say, "To be sure there is a methodological solipsist criterion for the adequacy of rational reconstructions, but there is an equally good physicalist criterion"? (Can he say that two reconstructions are equally adequate[6] if they predict the same observation sentences in thing language?)

Doubtless Carnap *would* say this. But let us go more slowly.

Suppose that Carnap had chosen to be a phenomenalist, but *not* a methodological solipsist in the *Aufbau*. Suppose, that is, that the "ontology" of the *Aufbau* had been the elementary experiences of *all* people, not just my elementary experiences. Then, whatever the virtues of the *Aufbau,* it would not have addressed the problem of intentionality that I described at the outset. For the assumption that we can *understand* the *Aufbau* would have presupposed that we can *refer to the experiences of other people. How* this is possible would not have been illuminated.[7]

Similarly, if the sense in which the various alternative reconstructions are "equally possible" or equally adequate is expressed physicalistically, say by saying that they are all equally good devices for making predictions about observable things, then again the problem will arise: *How are predictions about observable things understood?* How can statements about external objects so much as make sense? Again Brentano's Problem rears its ugly head. And it is here that we remember that Carnap does not *only* say that there are alternative, equally possible, reconstructions of the language; he also says that the methodological solipsist one has *epistemic priority.*

What this means, if it means anything, is that the methodological solipsist one is the one we can *understand;* that it is *by* seeing that they are in some sense "equivalent" to the methodological solipsist one that we understand the others. But at this point all illusion that the various ontologies are completely on a par vanishes. At bottom, the answer to Brentano's Problem is that we *don't,* in any substantive sense, refer to anything "external"; language is just a device for anticipating *my* experiences. To almost all present-day philosophers, of whatever persuasion, this will seem like retreating to solipsism—or solipsism plus the view that the real existence of the experiences of others is a "pseudo-question"—to avoid admitting that Brentano's Problem has not been either solved or dissolved.

Reichenbachian "Realism"

Although Reichenbach did not produce a book wholly devoted to epistemology until *Experience and Prediction* in 1938, the views laid out in that book had been sketched in a whole series of articles in the course of the preceding decade.[8] On the surface, those views look very "realist." Reichenbach insists that we observe physical things, not sense data, that unobserved physical things are not logical constructions out of observed things, that unobservables such as electrons and atoms are inferred entities, not logical constructions, and so forth. And at times Reichenbach likes to contrast his "realism" with Carnap's "positivism" and with what he sees as John Dewey's anti-realism with respect to theoretical entities. But things are not so simple.

They are not so simple because the claim that "we observe physical things, not impressions" has surprisingly little conceptual content for Reichenbach. For example, in *Experience and Prediction* Reichenbach holds open the possibility of constructing two languages:[9] a more "positivist" (in his sense) language, in which physical things (e.g., the tables and chairs that we see) exist only when I observe them and have only the properties that I observe them to have, and a language in which unobserved physical things exist (and I may decide that some of my observations about the physical things I observed were incorrect). Taking "physical thing" in the way the first language requires us to take it, physical things are virtually identical with the empiricist's "impressions," and, indeed, Reichenbach does sometimes call this first language "the language of impressions" or "the egocentric language." (Apparently my taking the thing that I see as a chair does not entail that it could exist unperceived, for Reichenbach, if my adoption of "the egocentric language" is a real possibility for me.) But even Reichenbach's notion of "realist language" is somewhat strange.

What Reichenbach holds is that, while I can construct my language so that inductive inferences to the existence and behavior of unobserved things are permissible, doing so requires the postulate that "unobserved things obey the same laws as observed things," and this postulate is a *convention*.[10] It is not an analytic sentence, to be sure, because certain empirical conditions have to be fulfilled or this postulate will lead to contradictions, but that *unobserved objects exist and obey the same laws as the observed objects **provided that** the observed objects behave in such a way that this assumption leads to no contradictions* is a pure stipulation. It is hard to see how someone who holds *this* view is entitled to berate Dewey, as Reichenbach does,[11] for (allegedly) denying the "independent existence" of the theoretical entities of science! (Although Reichenbach says that this view—that the inductive inference to unobservables depends on such a stipulation—was added after *Experience and Prediction* it is, in fact, clearly foreshadowed in that work; see pp. 145–146.)

The impression that Reichenbach's "realism" is hardly substantial is reinforced when one considers Reichenbach's view of truth. Briefly, he rejects the notion of truth as metaphysical. (He never considers a purely disquotational view, as far as I know, but I believe he would have found such a view uninteresting, as not providing us with any substantial notion we can use to *appraise* the sentences we utter and write for cognitive success.) The notion he proposes in place of the notion of truth, the only notion he has for measuring the cognitive success of an assertion, is the notion of *weight*, where the weight of a sentence is my estimate of the relative frequency of successful assertions in some appropriate reference class containing the sentence whose weight it is. (Weight is not itself a relative frequency, but a betting-quotient with respect to an unknown relative frequency, and, indeed, the reference class to be used in estimating the weight in question depends not just on the sentence whose weight I am assessing, but also on my total cognitive situation. Weight is, in effect, Reichenbach's frequentist substitute for Carnap's notion of "degree of confirmation.") Sentences are not true or false: it is just that I am justified in "betting" with them.

But what is all this "betting" for? Here Reichenbach is quite unambiguous: the whole purpose of inquiry is the prediction of experiences[12] (described, however, in thing language). But whose experiences? Is science concerned with finding strategies for predicting the experiences of other people? (In which case some ability to *refer* to the experiences of other people seems to be presupposed in the very notion of "science.") Or does my understanding of *my* language consist in my ability to successfully predict *my* experiences?

The fact is, Reichenbach never really faces this question. On the one hand, he does elsewhere[13] advocate choosing the narrowest possible basis for epistemology, which he considers to be the observable things available to one person at one single time, and this might seem to support the view that, in the last analysis, Reichenbach too has no notion of intentionality beyond the use of language to anticipate one's own experiences. But such a reading does not square with the following argument for rejecting "the strictly positivistic language": "Its insufficiency is revealed as soon as we try to use it for the rational reconstruction of the thought processes underlying actions concerning events after our death, such as are expressed in the example of the life insurance policies" (*Experience and Prediction,* p. 150). What Reichenbach simply does not face is this: if the "convention" that *there are times after my death, and events which occur at those times* (subject to the proviso mentioned above), is just a *stipulation,* and making such a stipulation is to be justified as a practical action, in terms of the "entailed decisions," as Reichenbach repeatedly tells us, then we are pushed back to the question of the character of the metalanguage in which these entailed decisions are to be discussed and evaluated. Is the metalanguage *already* a realist language? If it is, how, without an infinite regress, did I justify the choice of a realist metalanguage? If it is not, then how can I justify the choice of a realist object language, except purely as a means for more elegantly or economically (recall Mach's "economy of thought") making predictions about what I will experience while I am alive? If *that* is my justification for the choice of realist language, then I am in the same position as the positivist: I can *say* that I am buying the insurance policy for the sake of people who will live after I am dead, but that is itself a way of talking which is for *my* sake while I am alive. On the other hand, if my justification for the choice of realist language, the one I give in the metalanguage, is that it enables me to do things for the sake of people who will live after I am dead, and that is the "bottom line," then my metalanguage must clearly be a realist one.

The upshot of all this, I fear, is rather sad: I do not see that either Carnap or Reichenbach really thought through the problems involved in viewing language simply as a tool for the prediction of experiences. Perhaps the "problem of intentionality" *is* in some sense a "pseudo-problem," but if so, that is not something that the positivists succeeded in making clear.

Perception and Intentionality

Yet one should not leap to the conclusion that there is nothing "fishy" about questions like "How can we refer to things that are external to the mind?" For one thing, this question is suspiciously similar to that old stumper, "How can we know that there *exist* things external to the mind?" If I am asked, for example, how I know that my desk exists, and I do not immediately take the question to be a philosophical one, I will reply that I *see* it (or that I *saw* it, if the question should be put to me in the future). To get me to take the question as a philosophical one is, in part, to get me to conceive of the "possibility" that I might be mistaken, not just on the present occasion, but on all occasions, or on such a large number of occasions that the "general reliability of perception" is called into doubt. After such careful instruction, it will—if I am a normal philosophy student—seem flagrantly "question-begging" to answer the skeptical doubt of the existence of external things by saying "I see the desk." (Of course, if I am not a normal philosophy student but G. E. Moore, it may not seem question-begging, but that is another story.)

Once having been persuaded that there is a real question here, the philosopher (for that is what philosophy students are supposed to become) may try many different moves—too many to be listed here. He may—to cite just one possibility—produce a theory according to which perception is just a matter of the "existence of causal chains of the appropriate type" and a theory according to which knowledge is just a matter of having true beliefs which are caused in appropriate ways, and say that the skeptic has not *shown* that causal chains of the appropriate type for perception, and for knowledge of what I am perceiving, do not exist, and that this means that the skeptic has not shown that I do not *know* that I am seeing a desk. If the skeptic asks how I am supposed to even be able to *refer* to the desk in order to form true beliefs about it, the philosopher may try to produce a causal theory of reference as well. In this way a number of philosophical industries have gotten started, and all of them are extremely busy today.

In my last few sentences I indicated that the skeptic may well broaden the field of his skepticism from perception to intentionality, and, indeed, the two skeptical problems are closely linked, both logically and in the history of philosophy. For example, just as there is a common-sense "pre-philosophical" answer to "How do you know there is a desk there" ("I see it"), so there is a common-sense "pre-philosophical" answer to "How can you refer to external things such as the desk?" ("What's your problem? If I can see desks and handle them, surely I can learn what they are called.") And, as a matter of fact, the philosophers who discovered there was a "problem about intentionality" already knew, or took it as a matter of course that they knew, that there was a "problem of perception." And if the problem is not about reference to "external" things, in the funny sense of "external" in which everything except my own mind is supposed to be "external," but about reference to my own present, or past, or future experiences, there are similar pre-philosophical answers ("You mean there is a problem about how I can *expect* to have an experience?") which we must somehow come to distrust as "question-begging" before we can "see the problem" of intentionality.

I have argued elsewhere[14] that attempts to define reference in terms of patterns of efficient causation do not succeed, and that, in addition, the notion of a "cause" employed in such theories presupposes structures of causal explanation which themselves use many intentional notions.[15] There is not space here even to state these views of mine properly, let alone defend them, but for someone like myself, who sees the currently fashionable return to some mixture of materialism and empiricism as a dead end, it is natural to entertain the thought that there is a way around the problems I have been discussing which is not a matter of a straightforward "answer" to certain "questions." In a nutshell, the suggestion is, what if the common-sense pre-philosophical answer is the only answer? What if being convinced that it is not an answer to both questions (how do you know the desk exists? how can you so much as refer to the desk?) to say "I see the darn thing" is not coming to "see the problem" but falling into a deep confusion?

One way to try to show this would be to try to show that such "possibilities" as the possibility that I alone exist, and that I am a brain in a vat, are not real possibilities at all.[16] Another—one thinks of Wittgenstein's Private Language Argument—would be to try to show that the possibility of thinking about anything (let alone about "the nature of reference") presupposes the existence of public objects and public language. A philosopher who takes this line need not hold that the common-sense answers *are* "answers" to the philosopher's questions, as Moore did, or that they preempt the possibility of empirical scientific study of either perception or reference. Rather, what he should say is that the philosopher's questions gain their very sense from the supposition that certain possibilities make sense, and that once we see that we cannot consistently suppose that they do, we should also see that the enterprise of a "theory of the nature of intentionality" or of "the nature of perception" is an enterprise of answering questions we cannot understand we know not how. Note that if saying this is saying that the questions are "pseudo-questions," it is in a very different sense of "pseudo-question" than any that Carnap or Reichenbach had in mind. Their notion of a pseudo-question derived from the Machian (they called it "empiricist") idea that the whole purpose of cognition is prediction; the dissolution of the question of intentionality just suggested derives instead from an exploration of what Strawson called "the bounds of sense." Strawson was, of course, referring to Kant, and to the possibility of carrying on the Kantian enterprise of *exploring the presuppositions of cognition* without giving that enterprise a metaphysical interpretation.

Ludwig Wittgenstein was a philosopher who had a lifelong involvement with that task. His *Tractatus* excludes any "problem of how language relates to the world" by excluding the very idea of a metalanguage. This has been criticized from two directions. On the one hand, Carnap criticized it in his *Introduction to Semantics* (1942) on the grounds that one could add a disquotational definition of truth (in the style of Tarski) to *any* formal language. Whatever the merits of this criticism, it does not speak to our issue; for a purely disquotational definition of truth and reference does not speak to the problem of "the relation of the language to the world," as is shown by the thorough compatibility of such a view with Carnap's own "methodological solipsism." On the other hand, it would also be criticized by those who think, as Hartry Field once did,[17] that a definition of "primitive reference" can be given in terms of efficient causation. Here it may seem that Wittgenstein simply ignored a possibility; but in fact we know from his notebooks that he (like Kant) regarded it as absurd to think that we can understand how language connects with the world in terms of causal chains of appropriate kinds.[18] My purpose here is not to argue that he was right (although I have said that I believe he was); it is to point out that, if I understand his views correctly, then the *Tractatus* regarded the idea that there is a "problem of intentionality" as a confusion, but *not* for reasons which were anything like Carnap's and Reichenbach's.

Notes

1. "Is Water Necessarily H$_2$O?" reprinted in my *Realism with a Human Face* (Cambridge: Harvard University Press, 1990).

2. It should be noted, however, that Reichenbach disliked the label "positivism," and always referred to the movement to which he and Carnap belonged as "logical empiricism."

3. See Quine's "Reply to Roger F. Gibson, Jr.: Translation, Physics, and Facts of the Matter," in *The Philosophy of W. V. Quine*, ed. L. E. Hahn and P. A. Schilpp (La Salle, Ill.: Open Court, 1986).

4. For a discussion of philosophical uses of the notion of equivalence, see chap. 2, "Equivalence," in my *Realism and Reason, Philosophical Papers*, vol. 3 (New York: Cambridge University Press, 1983), pp. 26–45.

5. Strictly speaking this is only a criterion of *equal correctness* of reconstructions, and we also need a criterion of correctness. But Carnap would certainly say that a reconstruction is correct if (it is reasonable to suppose, given the imprecision and vagueness of ordinary unformalized scientific language, that) the reconstruction and what is reconstructed (unformalized scientific language) are equally correct in exactly the same sense.

6. Here see n. 7.

7. I do not mean to suggest that avoiding this problem was Carnap's motive for methodological solipsism; rather (possibly under the influence of Frege) he was moved to methodological solipsism by the belief that elementary experiences are "private" in a sense which implies that I *cannot* refer to the elementary experiences of other people—a view whose incoherence becomes obvious as soon as one tries to communicate it to another person.

8. For example, "Ziele und Wege der physikalischen Erkenntnis," *Handbuch der Physik,* vol. 4: *Allgemeine Grudlagen der Physik* (Berlin: Springer-Verlag, 1929), pp. 1–80; "Die philosophische Bedeutung der modernen Physik," *Erkenntnis,* 1, no. 1 (1930), 49–71; *Ziele und Wege der heutigen Naturphilosophie* (Leipzig: Felix Meincr, 1931); a review of Carnap's *Logische Aufbau der Welt* in *Kantstudien,* 38 (1933), 199–201. Translations of all of these are included in *Hans Reichenbach: Selected Writings, 1909–1953,* ed. Maria Reichenbach and Robert S. Cohen, 2 vols. (Dordrecht: D. Reidel, 1978).

9. Reichenbach calls these "Egocentric language" and "Usual language." See *Experience and Prediction* (Chicago: University of Chicago Press, 1938), pp. 135–145.

10. The conventional character of "extension rules" is stressed by Reichenbach in *The Rise of Scientific Philosophy* (Berkeley: University of California Press, 1951), pp. 266–267.

11. See Reichenbach's "Dewey's Theory of Science," in *The Philosophy of John Dewey,* ed. P. A. Schilpp (La Salle, Ill.: Open Court, 1939), pp. 159–192.

12. For example, in *Experience and Prediction,* "truth" is eventually rejected as a mere idealization of "weight," and "weight" is identified with *predictional value* (pp. 190–191).

13. See his "The Verifiability Theory of Meaning," in *Readings in the Philosophy of Science,* ed. Herbert Feigl and May Brodbeck (New York: Appleton-Century-Crofts, 1953).

14. See my *Representation and Reality* (Cambridge: MIT Press, 1989).

15. See "Is the Causal Structure of the Physical Itself Something Physical?" chap. 5 of my *Realism with a Human Face,* pp. 80–95.

16. See the opening chapter of my *Reason, Truth, and History* (New York: Cambridge University Press, 1981) for an attempt along these lines.

17. Hartry Field, "Tarski's Theory of Truth," *Journal of Philosophy,* 69 (July 18, 1972), 347–375.

18. I believe that one reason for this, in Wittgenstein's case as in my own, was the recognition that causal chains do not simply identify themselves as being causally explanatory, "of the appropriate type," etc., or, indeed, as consisting of "causes." Only when a language is already in place can we think of certain events as forming "causal chains of the appropriate type."

5. Reichenbach's Metaphysical Picture

I would like to begin by saying a word about Reichenbach's impact on my own philosophical formation. As an undergraduate at the University of Pennsylvania, I studied philosophy of science mainly with C. West Churchman, who taught a version of pragmatism informed by a substantial knowledge of and interest in the logic of statistical testing, and with Sidney Morgenbesser, who was himself still a graduate student, and logic and American philosophy with Morton White. My orientation on graduation was positivistic (although my knowledge of positivism came mainly from A. J. Ayer's *Language, Truth, and Logic*). I did a year of graduate work at Harvard in 1948–49 (studying mainly mathematics and mathematical logic), where I came under the influence of Quine's views on ontology and his skepticism concerning the analytic-synthetic distinction. At that point, I was in a mood that is well known to philosophy teachers today: it seemed to me that the great problems of philosophy had turned out to be pseudo-problems, and it was not clear to me that the technical problems that remained to be cleared up possessed anything like the intrinsic interest of the problems in pure logic and mathematics that also interested me. It was a serious question in my mind at that point whether I should go on in philosophy or shift to mathematics.

Within a few months of my arrival in Los Angeles in the fall of 1949 these philosophical "blahs" had totally vanished (although I did not lose my desire to pursue mathematics in some way, and eventually I succeeded in pursuing both fields simultaneously). What overcame my "philosophy is over" mood, what made the field come alive for me, made it more exciting and more challenging than I had been able to imagine, was Reichenbach's seminar, and his lecture course, on the philosophy of space and time. And it was not the technical details of Reichenbach's philosophy that did this, although I pondered those details with great excitement, but the sense of a powerful philosophical vision behind those details: the vision that I am going to sketch here.

A number of times some of my former students (and some who were not my former students) have complimented me on the fact that I have been willing to think and to write about the "big problems," and not just about technical problems. But this is something that Reichenbach instilled in me. Reichenbach taught me—by example, not by preaching—that being an "analytic philosopher" does not mean simply rejecting the big problems. Although Reichenbach was just as much of an empiricist as Ayer, empiricism, for Reichenbach, was a challenge and not a terminus. The challenge was to show that the great questions—the nature of space and time, the nature of causality, the justification of induction (and also, in other writings which I shall not discuss here, the question of free will and determinism, and the nature of ethical utterances)—could be adequately clarified within an empiricist framework, and not merely dismissed. In clarifying them, Reichenbach was guided by what many philosophers today would be comfortable calling a metaphysical picture (even if "metaphysics" was a pejorative term for Reichenbach himself). That Reichenbach had a "metaphysical picture" did not keep him from being an analytic philosopher at the same time: rather, it gave direction and motivation to his philosophical endeavors, and not just motivation but excitement. I felt that excitement, and it generated my own excitement for the subject. I think that every one of Reichenbach's Ph.D. students would say the same thing.

Reichenbach and Carnap

Although Reichenbach continues until this day to be lumped together with the Vienna Circle, his views, as he himself often insisted, differed in significant respects from those of the other leading representatives of logical empiricism. Throughout its existence, logical empiricism was characterized by a certain tension between its metaphysical and its antimetaphysical aspirations. On the one side, the antimetaphysical side, the self-image of the movement was that it represented the wholesale renunciation of metaphysics, that in the future metaphysical questions would be replaced by questions in the logic of science. Metaphysical questions which could not be so replaced would be seen to be unintelligible. In this way, it was believed, philosophical questions would for the first time become susceptible to objective resolu-

tion. On the other side, the metaphysical side, the great logical empiricists—the most famous example is Rudolf Carnap—produced "rational reconstructions of the language of science" which looked for all
the world like elaborate systems of metaphysics—or at least that is
how they looked to philosophers who did not join the movement.
Certain features of Carnap's *Logische Aufbau der Welt* have received
a great deal of attention in this regard—his phenomenalism, his logicism,[1] his doctrine of the "incommunicability of content," and the
"methodological solipsism" associated with that doctrine, have all
been extensively discussed. Indeed, the ontology and epistemology associated with the *Logische Aufbau der Welt* are now so widely known
that there is a tendency to assume that that metaphysical picture was
the metaphysics of logical positivism.

In the present essay, I want to describe a totally different metaphysical picture: the picture that Hans Reichenbach defended in his major
works, and particularly in *Experience and Prediction, The Philosophy
of Space and Time, Axiomatization of the Theory of Relativity,* and
The Direction of Time. I believe that that picture is of interest for at
least two different reasons. One is that, like Carnap's picture, it represents the work of a brilliant and philosophically ambitious mind. Even
if today one cannot accept either Carnap's or Reichenbach's solutions
to the problems of philosophy, their attempts represent contributions
of enormous value, and there is much to be learned from their study.
The second reason is that one does not properly understand logical
empiricism[2] itself if one simply identifies it with any of Carnap's successive programs of rational reconstruction. The fact that the movement had room for metaphysical visions as different as those of Carnap and Reichenbach is itself a fact that has to be appreciated if
simplistic pictures of "positivism" are to be overcome.

The first point at which the metaphysical picture in Reichenbach's
mature work stands in opposition to the metaphysical picture associated with Carnap's *Logische Aufbau* has to do with Reichenbach's
realism. To be sure, Reichenbach did not see this realism as presupposing traditional realist metaphysics in any way. He insisted that
the choice of "realistic language" is just that: a choice of a language.
He emphasized, however, that it was not an *arbitrary choice.*[3] He once
told me that he welcomed Carnap's shift from an *Eigenpsychische
Basis* (a phenomenalistic basis) to a physicalistic basis in *Testability
and Meaning* as an indication of convergence in their views, which is
also how Carnap saw the matter. But the discussion in *Experience and*

Prediction (henceforth cited as *EP*) reveals deep disagreements with Carnap in spite of this "convergence." For one thing, it turns out that what Reichenbach is thinking of is not the choice of *sense-datum language* versus "thing language"; it is, instead, the choice of a language in which I can speak of things as *existing when unobserved* ("usual language") as opposed to the choice of a language in which I can speak of things as existing only when they are observed by me ("egocentric language"). It is true that if "things" only exist when observed by me, and are ascribed only the properties that they appear (to me) to possess while observed, then these "things" will be, in a way, just as "phenomenal" as the empiricists' "impressions," and this is why Reichenbach, in the first part of *EP, identifies* the traditional empiricist problem of justifying the inference from "impressions" to "the external world" with the problem of justifying the inference from "observed things" to "unobserved things." He offers an account of this inference in Section 14 of that work; but that account, as he points out, assumes that one has already selected "usual language."[4] Reichenbach's inductive inference to the existence of unobserved things is not the *justification* for the choice of usual language—that is, for the decision to adopt a language in which I can ascribe properties to things that they do not appear to have, and in which I can ascribe properties to things at times when I do not observe them, and, indeed, when nobody observes them. The justification offered for that choice (*EP*, p. 150) is interesting: instead of making the usual argument that realist language enables us to formulate more successful scientific theories, Reichenbach argues that it makes nonsense of the *justification* of a great many ordinary human actions: "the strictly positivistic language . . . contradicts normal language so obviously that it has scarcely been seriously maintained; moreover, its insufficiency is revealed as soon as we try to use it for the rational reconstruction of the thought-processes underlying actions concerning events after our death, such as [are] expressed in the example of the life insurance policies. We have said that the choice of a language depends on our free decision, but that we are bound to the decisions entailed by our choice: we find here that the decision for the strictly positivistic language would entail the renunciation of any reasonable justification of a great many human actions."

What is striking, however, is that although Reichenbach does allow as possible the choice of an egocentric language in which I speak of the table I observe as existing only when I observe it, he rejects the idea that what I *really* observe are impressions. Instead (*EP*, p. 163), he warmly endorses Dewey's view in *Experience* and *Nature* that impressions are inferred entities (a view that goes back to Peirce's writings in the 1860s). In Reichenbach's view, what we observe are *things;* this is the correct description of what we might call the "phenomenology" of observation.[5] That the appearances of things may sometimes be deceptive, that I may mistake a shadow for a human figure, or whatever, does not show that we do not directly observe things; it shows simply that observation is corrigible. But, Reichenbach insists, it would be corrigible even if we did have such a thing as an "impression language." The idea that there can be any such thing as "incorrigible observation" is rejected. Even in the extreme case in which someone decides that he was simply hallucinating (or dreaming), Reichenbach would say that he observed a physical "thing" (counting events, and even states of one's own body, as "things"), namely a state of his own central nervous system, although he did not know that that was what he was observing.

For Reichenbach, to describe an observation using impression language—to say, for example, "I had the impression of a table," or "I had the impression of a flash of light"—is always to make an inference (*EP*, pp. 163–169). Thus the difference between Reichenbach's position and Carnap's is not just that Reichenbach adopted "thing language" as basic rather than "impression language"—after a certain point Carnap also shifted to taking "thing language" as basic—the decisive difference is that Carnap continued to regard impression predicates as a possible, although less convenient, observation basis for the reconstruction of the language of science, whereas Reichenbach insisted that it was a mistake to think of impressions as observed entities at all. Impressions are inferred entities. For Carnap, there remains, even after the turn to physicalism, a lingering tendency to think of sensations as "epistemologically primary"; for Reichenbach it is things that are epistemologically primary.

"Things" in a wide sense, however. For, as already remarked, events are also "physical things," and when Reichenbach develops his reconstruction of modern physics in his writings on relativity theory, the things which become fundamental are not the things we observe in everyday life, but the things we describe in our most basic physical theories.

Reichenbach and Kant

Although Reichenbach is justly famous for his decisive criticism of Kant's doctrine of the synthetic *a priori* as applied to the geometry of space and time, Reichenbach was by no means incapable of incorporating Kantian insights into his own philosophy.[6] One of the most important insights that Reichenbach takes from Kant[7] (even if he in one place credits it to Leibniz!),[8] but transforms, is the inadequacy of the traditional empiricist way of accounting for the existence of an objective time order. That account presupposed the truth of some form of subjective idealism. If everything that exists is a complex of sense impressions, then, many empiricists thought, it suffices to define an objective order for sense impressions. Such an order is implicitly defined by the following principles: (1) if an impression A is simultaneous with a memory image of an impression B, then A occurred after B; (2) if two impressions A and B are experienced simultaneously, then, of course, they occur simultaneously. But, as Kant saw, the case is different once one takes the "experiences" of the external senses to be experiences of things rather than of impressions; neither of these principles holds if "impression" is replaced by "physical thing or event." If A and B are things or events rather than impressions, then I cannot infer from the fact that an experience of A occurred simultaneously with a memory of an experience of B that B occurred or existed before A occurred or existed; and if an experience of A occurred simultaneously with an experience of B, I cannot infer that A and B occurred or existed simultaneously. This is clearest in the case of astrophysics (and Kant and Reichenbach shared, of course, a profound interest in astrophysics). If I observe an explosion of a supernova A before I observe the explosion of a supernova B it does not at all follow that the A explosion occurred before the B explosion; it may be that the A explosion occurred later but that it was so much nearer to me that the light from the A explosion reached my telescope before the light from the B explosion. Similarly, if I observe (or "experience") two astronomical events simultaneously, it does not follow that they happened simultaneously. There are, however, homelier examples that make the same point. One, which was used by Kant,[9] is the following: If I look at a building, I may observe the top of the building before I observe the bottom of the building, but I cannot infer that the top of the building existed before the bottom of the building did. But if I see a ship sailing down the river, and I first observe the ship passing under a bridge and then I observe the ship passing by a dock farther down the river, I do infer that the ship's being under the bridge temporally preceded the ship's passing the dock. The Kantian explanation is that my very conception of the ship as an object is bound up with a whole system of laws ("rules"), and given my total system of knowledge I am able to interpret the two experiences in the case of the ship as corresponding to the time order in which the events occurred. When I look at a building I apply a different part of my knowledge—different laws as well as different initial conditions—and I conclude that I am simply seeing in a different order things that have continued existence. Here Kant stresses a further causal consideration: I know that I can see the different parts of the building in any order I choose; but I cannot see the events in the case of the ship in any order I choose. Kant's conclusion is that it is only by interpreting my experiences with the aid of causal laws that I am able to understand them as giving me an objective world with objective time relations.

As an empiricist, Reichenbach does *not* follow Kant in holding that we do not have a notion of an object at all without a concept of causality. He does, nevertheless, agree that it is causal relations that determine what the correct ("objective") time order is. However, Reichenbach has a problem: As a good empiricist, he does not want to take the notion of causality as primitive. Yet he is convinced that one cannot simply take objective time order as primitive, that one must explain objective time order in terms of objective causal order. This leads Reichenbach to one of the most ambitious projects ever undertaken by an analytic philosopher, namely *to define causality without using temporal notions* so that he will be able to use the thus defined relation of causal precedence to define time order. In short, time order is to be reduced to causal order, and causal order is not to be taken as primitive, but to be explained. But explained using what notions?

Reichenbach's answer is that it is to be explained using the notion of *probability*.[10] In Reichenbach's metaphysical picture, the world consists of events, where an event might be either a macroscopic event or a microscopic one, say, a force-field's having a certain intensity at a certain space-time point. Imagine, now, that I am given a sequence of events: Suppose that I observe a sequence of astronomical events a_1, a_2, a_3, ... And let us suppose that I observe a second sequence of events, b_1, b_2, b_3, . . . , and that I notice a statistically significant relation between events in the first sequence and events in the second sequence. For example, suppose that I observe that the probability that an event in the b-sequence will have a certain property Q is much higher if the corresponding event in the a-sequence has a certain property P. Inductively projectible statistical relations are not always a sign that one event directly influences the other. It could be that, for example, the *a*-events and the *b*-events are effects of a common cause.[11] Moreover, even if there is direct causal influence between an *a*-event and the corresponding *b*-event, we do not yet know in which direction the causality goes, that is, whether a_1's being a P causally affects b_1's chances of being a Q, or whether it is the other way around. However, Reichenbach believed that there is a method of experimental intervention, which he calls "the method of the mark," by which one can determine when the statistical relation is directly causal (that is, by which one can rule out the hypothesis that the correlation is entirely explained by the presence of a common cause) and by which one can determine in which direction it goes. The idea is very simple: if the *a*-events are the causes (or partial causes) of the *b*-events, then small variations in the character of the *a*-events produced by an experimental intervention—Reichenbach calls such a variation a "mark" *(Kennzeichen)*—will bring about small variations in the character of the corresponding *b*-events.

Few contemporary philosophers of physics believe that Reichenbach's method succeeded. One difficulty is that the interpretation of an action as an "intervention" involves *already* knowing the direction of time/direction of causal processes, which is precisely what we are trying to determine. In *The Direction of Time*, Reichenbach tried to meet this objection by using thermodynamic criteria for irreversibility.[12] A further difficulty is the following: how can one know that the "small variation" in the *a*-event and the corresponding small variation in the *b*-event are not themselves effects of a common cause? If I myself "bring about" the variation in the *a*-events, this may be unlikely (but am I not appealing to causal knowledge when I say this?); but what if the "intervention" is nature's, and not a human experimenter's? Presumably, Reichenbach would reply that further experimentation could rule out the common cause hypothesis; discussing this might also involve the question of the adequacy of Reichenbach's theory of the counterfactual conditional.[13]

My concern here, however, is not with the success or failure of Reichenbach's program, but with the picture which inspired him. The picture is this: The world consists of events. Those events form various sequences,[14] and there are statistical relations among the events in those sequences. Those statistical relations indicate the presence of causal relations, and the detailed nature of the statistical relations fixes the nature of the causal relations.

From this point on, Reichenbach's procedure is well known to philosophers of science. If an event A causally influences an event B, then the event A (absolutely) temporally precedes the event B: the interval separating the events A and B is time-like.[15] If A does not absolutely precede B and B does not absolutely precede A, then the separation between A and B is said to be space-like. (Such events are simultaneous in at least one coordinate system, while events whose separation is time-like are simultaneous in no admissible coordinate system.) In terms of causal (absolute temporal) precedence, one can define the notion of *temporal betweenness* and this is the first step in the construction of a topology[16] for space-time.

With respect to the metric, as opposed to the topology, of space-time, Reichenbach's position was a sophisticated form of conventionalism.[17] The world as it is in itself does not have a unique metric; it does, however, have a unique topology, and this is defined, as just sketched, in terms of the causal relations (and ultimately in terms of the statistical relations) between the events of which the world consists.

Epistemology Again

At this point we may seem to have gotten very far indeed from the epistemological issues with which I started. The events of which I have been speaking are, for the most part, microevents, and thus very remote from observation. But here too there is a fundamental difference between Reichenbach's epistemological views and Carnap's. And this is true not only if one thinks of Carnap's approach in *Der Logische Aufbau der Welt,* but even if one considers Carnap's approach after the turn to "physicalism" (in "Testability and Meaning," and more completely in "Foundations of Logic and Mathematics").[18] Carnap's successive positions might be described as follows: In the *Logische Aufbau,* Carnap hoped to reduce all talk of physical things and events to talk of the subject's own impressions by the method of logical construction.[19] In "Testability and Meaning" the aim of reduction was still present, but with two changes: (1) Instead of taking impression predicates as the observation predicates to which all other descriptive predicates were to be reduced, Carnap took a collection of "observable thing predicates" as basic. Sentences without quantifiers in the observation vocabulary were eligible to represent what is given in experience. (2) Non-observation predicates were still to be reduced to observation predicates, but the allowed methods of reduction now included "reduction sentences," that is, operational definitions in a certain conditional form. Finally, in "The Interpretation of Physical Calculi," Carnap proposed to simply take theoretical terms as primitive and regard the adoption of a set of physical laws ("P-Postulates") as something to be justified on the following sorts of grounds: (a) an acceptable physical law is supposed to have observational consequences which are (as far as we know) true; and (b) in addition the set of laws is supposed to be simple, elegant, fruitful, and so forth. Physical laws and entities are, so to speak, *chosen rather than constructed or inferred,* according to late Carnap, but chosen subject to empirical constraints. Even in Carnap's last writings,[20] the whole content of the physical theory could be expressed by a single sentence in second-order logic which contains only observation predicates, the so-called Ramsey sentence of the theory.

In Reichenbach's view, in contrast, physical laws and entities are *inferred.*[21] An example of what Reichenbach was thinking of might be the following. If I see a paddle wheel spinning, I normally observe that something is hitting the paddle wheel: air or water, or perhaps someone is throwing stones at it. If I perform a demonstration which was very popular in the secondary schools of Europe at the end of the nineteenth century, and place a cathode inside one end of a glass tube and an anode inside the other end, replace the air in the glass tube completely with an inert gas, and then turn on the electric current, I will (if all goes well) observe a glowing ray (this is, of course, the basis for our present neon signs). An experiment which was also performed in the nineteenth century was to place a tiny paper paddle wheel inside the tube. It was discovered that if the wheel was light enough, the presence of the ray would cause the wheel to spin. This spinning could not be due to electromagnetism, because the wheel is made of paper. By an induction from the macroscopic phenomena I mentioned, we infer that therefore the ray consists of matter of some kind. Again, if I shoot a charged iron pellet through a magnetic field, I can observe that the pellet will be deflected from its usual trajectory by an amount which depends on the ratio of the charge on the pellet to its mass. If I put the glowing tube (this time without the paddle wheel) in a magnetic field, I can observe that the ray is also deflected, and, on the assumption that it consists of *charged* matter, I can infer the mass-charge ratio of the particles of which the ray consists. (Historically, this was one of the first determinations of the mass-charge ratio of the electron.) This is an example of an inference to the existence of what Reichenbach calls *illata,* inferred entities.

Whereas in the Carnap view (of the *Logische Aufbau* period, and even in the view of the "Testability and Meaning" period) the particles of which such a ray consists are logical constructions (*abstracta*, in Reichenbach's terminology), in Reichenbach's view they are inferred entities, and the inductive inferences by which we infer their existence are not different in kind from the inductive inferences that we find in, for example, Sherlock Holmes stories.[22] In fact, Reichenbach was famous for using Sherlock Holmes stories as the sources of his examples in his celebrated course on inductive logic.

Reichenbach's Vindication of Induction

If we picture Reichenbach's system as an arch, with the causal theory of time, the probability theory of causality, and the theory of the spacetime metric as one side, and the theory of the epistemological primacy of physical things and the inductive inferences to unobserved things and to *illata* as the other side, the keystone of the arch is his celebrated pragmatic vindication of induction (*EP*, pp. 339 ff.). To vindicate induction, Reichenbach first reconstructed all inductive inferences as inferences whose purpose is to estimate the limit of a relative frequency in an infinite sequence.[23] Induction, for Reichenbach, always means wagering ("positing") that the limit of the relative frequency in some sequence or other is approximately equal to the relative frequency observed in the so-far examined initial section of that same sequence. With "induction" so defined, it is a tautology that *if* a sequence possesses a limit at all, then continued use of the method of induction will enable us to eventually estimate it correctly, to within any preassigned accuracy.

To see why this tautology should be regarded as a vindication of induction, we make the following thought experiment (*EP*, pp. 358–359): Imagine that some method very different from induction leads to successful prediction, say, relying on a certain "clairvoyant." To say that the clairvoyant makes very successful predictions, say, that her predictions are true 85% of the time, is to say that the relative frequency in a certain sequence exceeds 0.85. But this is the sort of truth we can discover using the method of induction. Thus, Reichenbach concludes that induction will work in the long run if any method works.[24]

To recapitulate, then, for Reichenbach *probability* is the foundation of both metaphysics and epistemology. Metaphysically, probability is fundamental because it is the probability relations among the sequences of events in the world that give rise to causality, time, and space. Epistemologically, probability is fundamental because empirical knowledge is simply knowledge of probabilities. Even knowledge of observation sentences is considered to be probabilistic knowledge by Reichenbach (*EP*, pp. 183–188), because Reichenbach's fallibilism leads him to hold that no observation sentence is absolutely incorrigible, and with the advance of scientific knowledge we need to inquire into the probability that our singular observation judgments may be in error.

My aim here has not been to argue that Reichenbach succeeded in his magnificent attempt any more than Carnap succeeded in his. But I hope to have convinced you that it *was* one of the most magnificent attempts by any empiricist philosopher of this or of any other century, and I believe that the effort to understand it and to master its details will as richly repay us as the much greater effort which has been devoted to the study of Carnap's work has already repaid us.

Notes

1. By "logicism" I mean the desire, expressed by Carnap late in the *Logische Aufbau der Welt*, to eliminate empirical primitives from the system *entirely*. For a discussion of this feature, see Michael Friedman, "Carnap's *Aufbau* Reconsidered," *Nous*, 21, no. 4 (December 1987), 526–545.

2. Reichenbach refused to call himself a positivist, because he associated that term with phenomenalism. For this reason, when I am considering Reichenbach's contribution I use the term "logical empiricism," which is the term by which he himself always referred to the movement to which he belonged.

3. See *Experience and Prediction* (Chicago: University of Chicago Press, 1938), pp. 145ff. "In spite of our reference to a free decision, we should not like to say that the decision in question is arbitrary . . . If the languages in question are not equivalent, if the decision between them forms a case of a volitional bifurcation, this decision is of the greatest relevance: it will lead to consequences concerning the knowledge obtainable."

4. In particular, one must adopt a "postulate of the homogeneity of causality." This is described as one of a number of "postulates concerning the rules of language" (*EP*, p. 139), and shortly thereafter the choice between "egocentric language" and "usual language" is described as "a free decision." (Cf. n. 3.)

5. Although this view reminds one of Husserl, Reichenbach (*EP*, p. 163) finds an impeccably empiricist forerunner in Avenarius.

6. Indeed, Reichenbach's great book *The Theory of Relativity and A Priori*

Knowledge (Berkeley: University of California Press, 1965; English translation of *Relativitätstheorie und Erkenntnis apriori* [Berlin: Springer-Verlag 1920]), although a criticism of Kant's thesis of the apriority of geometry, is in many respects a neo-Kantian work.

7. "Kant saw very well the close relationship between time and causality. He saw that we discover time order by examining causal order." *The Direction of Time* (Berkeley: University of California Press, 1956), pp. 14–15.

8. Cf. Reichenbach's "Die Bewegungslehre bei Newton, Leibniz und Huyghens," *Kant-Studien,* 29 (1924), 421. After quoting Leibniz ("Time is the order of noncontemporaneous things. [Tempus est ordo existendi eorum quae non sunt simul.] It is thus the *universal* order of change in which we ignore the specific kind of changes that have occurred"), Reichenbach remarks, "This passage seems to me to represent a depth of insight into the nature of time that has not been equaled in the whole classical period from Descartes to Kant. Even Kant's theory of time (as formulated, for example, in the 'Second Analogy of Experience') does not attain Leibniz' perspicacity. Leibniz' characterization of time as the general structure of causal sequences is superior to Kant's unfortunate characterization of time as the form of intuition presupposed by causality."

9. In the Second Analogy, A193/B234; the interpretation of the Second Analogy is my own, but I believe it accords with Henry Allison's *Kant's Transcendental Idealism* (New Haven: Yale University Press, 1983), pp. 225ff.

10. In some of his writings on the subject, for example, "Die Kausalbehauptung und die Möglichkeit ihrer empirischen Nachprüfung", *Erkenntnis,* 3 no. 1 (1932), 32–64 (English translation, "The Principle of Causality and the Possibility of Its Empirical Confirmation," in Reichenbach's *Modern Philosophy of Science,* ed. Maria Reichenbach [London: Routledge and Kegan Paul, 1959]), Reichenbach, thinking of the deterministic case, identified causality simply with the existence of functional relationships (with the proviso that the relationships must be inductively projectible to unobserved cases). But the need to replace this deterministic notion of causality by a probability structure was already explained in his 1925 paper "The Causal Structure of the World and the Difference between Past and Future" (in *Hans Reichenbach: Selected Writings, 1909–1953,* vol. 2, ed. Maria Reichenbach and Robert S. Cohen [Dordrecht: D. Reidel, 1978]; this originally appeared in German in the *Sitzungsberichte der mathematisch-naturwissenschaftliche Abteilung der Bayerischen Akademie der Wissenschaften zu München,* November 1925, pp. 133–175).

11. For Reichenbach the above are the *only* possibilities; there cannot be an inductively projectible probability relation which *always* holds and which has no basis in a causal connection between the events related. (Two events' being effects of a common cause counts as a "causal connection"

for this purpose.) This might seem to be trivially wrong on the following ground: Suppose two sequences of events, a-events and b-events, both follow the same periodic law. Suppose, for simplicity, that every fifth a-event has property P and every fifth b-event has property Q. Then the probability that a b-event has property Q *given that* the corresponding a-event has property P is *one*, yet it may well be that the a-events and the b-events do not causally influence one another and do not have a common cause. Reichenbach might answer that, in this case, my prediction of the character of a b-event can also be made without using any knowledge of the character of the corresponding a-event: it is enough to know the character of the *four preceding* b-events. Perhaps it is when knowledge of the character of one or more a-events permits me to better predict the character of b-events ("better" in the sense of: better than I could do on the basis of the knowledge of earlier or later b-events) that Reichenbach would postulate causal connection—postulate it apparently *a priori,* judging by what he says in chap. 10 of *The Rise of Scientific Philosophy.* However, a case, in which one sequence is a "carbon copy" of another *could* also arise from a genuine causal connection; so the answer I have just suggested on Reichenbach's behalf does not satisfy me. (Moreover, a further counterexample to Reichenbach's claim might be this: Suppose the a-events are connected by a fortuitous relation of the kind just described—one that does not rest on any causal connection—to c-events, and the c-events *are* causes of the b-events. Then knowledge of the character of an a-event *may* enable me to better predict the character of the corresponding b-event whether or not there is any causal connection between the a-events and the b-events.)

12. *The Direction of Time,* p. 198. Note that the concept of entropy to which Reichenbach appeals itself involves *spatial* notions in its definition; but the spatial metric is explained by Reichenbach in terms which assume that time order has already been established. The difficulty that I am worried about is not determining the direction of time, given that the topology of time (= the structure of the causal net) has already been established; the problem is whether purely statistical relations *can* determine even the topology of time if no temporal notions are anywhere "smuggled in."

13. See *Nomological Statements and Admissible Operations* (Amsterdam: North Holland, 1954). The theory Reichenbach presents in this book presupposes the view I questioned in n. 11, that there cannot be a true but non-lawlike statement of the form: whenever an a-event has property P, the corresponding b-event has property Q. (In an unpublished note dating back to about 1954, Carnap also expressed skepticism as to the possibility of ruling out non-lawlike truths of this form.)

14. A problem which arises in connection with this picture is just what "sequence" means. Reichenbach does not mean *arbitrary* sequence: to see why not, let A be a random sequence of heads and tails produced by flipping a

coin, and let B be a second, causally independent sequence of heads and tails, also random. Let C be a subsequence of B which consists of heads and tails in exactly the order that they occur in A. (Every random sequence contains a subsequence which is a "carbon copy" of any sequence you like.) Then the probability that C is a head if the corresponding A is a head is one: but this is not because there is any causal connection between the A's and the C's. Reichenbach was aware of this objection, and in his lectures at UCLA he tried to rule it out by requiring that the sequences be "extensionally given." When I asked him what this meant, he explained that the probability relation we find must not be an artifact of the way the sequences are *defined*. But this raises the following problems: (1) It seems, then, that causal connections exist only between definable sequences of events (and with respect to definable attributes of the members of those sequences). This seems counterintuitive, and it raises a host of questions: for example, in what *language* must the sequences be definable? (2) What exactly is meant by a relation's being an *artifact* of the way something is defined? The intuitive idea is clear, but it seems difficult to capture in a definition. Reichenbach's theory of nomological statements, presented in the book cited in n. 13, may be designed to deal with this problem.

15. Strictly speaking, I should have written "time-like or light-like." Once the space-time metric has been constructed, one can identify a class of "fastest causal signals"; in our world, these are the signals that travel at the speed of light. In the customary metric of relativity theory, the world-lines of these fastest signals are considered neither time-like nor space-like.

16. To define such a topology, one may proceed as follows (here, let P, P', Q, and R be variables over point events and S a variable over sets of point events): define P *is a limit point of* S to mean that for every Q, R such that P is temporally between Q and R, there is a P' in S such that P' ≠ P and P' is temporally between Q and R.

17. For a discussion of this point see my "Refutation of Conventionalism," in my *Mind, Language, and Reality, Philosophical Papers*, vol. 2 (New York: Cambridge University Press, 1975).

18. Reprinted in *International Encyclopedia of Unified Science*, vol. 1, pt. 1, ed. Otto Neurath, Rudolf Carnap, and Charles W. Morris (Chicago: University of Chicago Press, 1938); see especially pp. 198–211.

19. Whether this was the principal *aim of the Logische Aufbau*, is, however, a matter of disagreement among interpreters. An alternative reading is that the phenomenalistic construction is offered as only one of a number of alternative reconstructions of the language, and the primary purpose of the work is to argue that it is only by being willing to formulate philosophical positions in terms of such reconstructions that we can see exactly what the issues are. Cf. the article by Friedman cited in n. 1.

20. See, for example, Carnap's "The Methodological Character of Theoretical

Concepts," in *The Foundations of Science and the Concepts of Psychology and Psychoanalysis,* ed. Herbert Feigl and Michael Scriven, Minnesota Studies in the Philosophy of Science, vol. 1 (Minneapolis: University of Minnesota Press, 1956).

21. There is, however, an element of choice in Reichenbach's view as well as in Carnap's: by adopting different coordinating definitions one can arrive at different but empirically equivalent metrics for space-time, for example. The inductive inferences needed to infer the existence of illata depend on these coordinative definitions, and thus rest on a certain element of convention. For a discussion of this element of Reichenbach's thought see "Equivalent Descriptions," in my *Realism and Reason, Philosophical Papers,* vol. 3 (New York: Cambridge University Press, 1983), and my essay cited in n. 17.

22. In a way, then, Reichenbach may have originated what was later called the "inference to the best explanation" account of scientific reasoning—an account which was often thought to constitute a *rejection* of logical empiricism!

23. Reichenbach idealized very long finite sequences as infinite sequences. I discussed this idealization and its bearing on Reichenbach's pragmatic vindication in my Ph.D. thesis, written under Reichenbach's direction in 1951. This has now been published as *The Meaning of the Concept of Probability in Application to Finite Sequences* (New York: Garland, 1990).

24. For a criticism of Reichenbach's vindication argument, see Chapter 7 of this volume.

6. Reichenbach and the Myth of the Given

Few philosophers any longer believe that phenomenal reports are incorrigible. I suspect that if you asked a graduate student on the street, "Who was responsible for overthrowing the view that reports of subjective experience represent absolutely certain knowledge?" he or she would probably name Wilfrid Sellars, whose profound monograph-length essay "Empiricism and the Philosophy of Mind"[1] has been praised by Richard Rorty[2] for providing us with a definitive refutation of "the myth of the given." However, an examination of that essay shows that questions of *certainty* play almost no role in Sellars' discussion. Here I want to discuss a lecture that was delivered four years before "Empiricism and the Philosophy of Mind" appeared, a lecture which contains the best discussion I know of this very question: Hans Reichenbach's "Are Phenomenal Reports Absolutely Certain?"[3] Reichenbach's lecture was given in a symposium entitled "The Experiential Element in Knowledge" with Nelson Goodman[4] and C. I. Lewis[5]—surely one of the most distinguished symposia of the second half of this century!—and it took the views of C. I. Lewis as its target.

Sellars on the "Myth of the Given"

For the sake of contrast, let me first say a word about Sellars' strategy in "Empiricism and the Philosophy of Mind." Unlike Reichenbach, Sellars was not a monistic materialist; although this is not mentioned in "Empiricism and the Philosophy of Mind" itself,[6] Sellars retains a dualistic element in his ontology. There are "raw feels," and "raw feels" are not reducible to brain states or anything of that kind. Nonetheless, there are strong points of agreement between Sellars' essay

115

and Reichenbach's earlier lecture. For example, Reichenbach and Sellars both claim that the sense-datum theorists postulated mental objects that we *perceive* when we have phenomenal experience (Berkeley's "ideas," or Hume's "ideas and impressions," or Russell's and G. E. Moore's "sense data"), when they should rather have inferred the existence of a special class of states that we are *in* when we perceive physical objects. According to both Reichenbach and Sellars, what we perceive are not our own phenomenal experiences but *things*, animals and vegetables and people and artifacts and hills and rivers, etc. When I look at a blue chair I am in a different state than I am in when I look at a red chair, or at something that is not a chair at all, a state of "seeing blue-chairly," to use Sellars' jargon; but I don't perceive my *state*. I perceive the blue chair. The idea that there is some "subjective thing" that I alone "directly perceive" is rejected.

However, Sellars' central argument is different from any argument to be found in Reichenbach's lecture, and although it presents a position which has considerable currency today, that position is one that I myself find problematic. The view in question is that there is an absolute gulf between what Sellars elsewhere calls "the space of reasons" and "the space of causes." (On Sellars' view) only a sentence, or a verbalized thought, can function as a *reason* for another sentence, or another verbalized thought. A phenomenal experience can *cause* me to utter or write a sentence, or think a verbalized thought, but it cannot function as a *reason* for that verbalized thought. Recently this position has come under criticism from John McDowell,[7] who has argued that this dualism of a space of reasons and a space of causes is as pernicious as the older dualism of inner world and external world, and leads us into the same predicaments. Nor, in McDowell's view, is it enough to say that a "token event" which is a reason under one description can also be a cause under a *different* description, as Donald Davidson does. What McDowell calls for is a conception in which phenomenal experiences can be intrinsically *both* reasons *and* causes; but the issues go very deep, and I think that it is a merit of the Reichenbachian arguments that I am going to describe that they do not require us to take a stand on these profound metaphysical issues.[8]

The main purpose of Sellars' essay, moreover, was to present a diagnosis of the predicament that traditional epistemology, and especially traditional British epistemology, thought that we were all in. Sellars suggests that the "sense data" (or "ideas," or "ideas and impression") beloved of generations of British epistemologists should be thought of as a *model* for certain parts of ordinary language psychology in the sense in which a collection of colliding billiard balls is sometimes used as a model for a perfect gas in physics. In reality, Sellars claims, the things being modeled, our phenomenal experiences, are not like the "sense data" of the model at all (just as the molecules of a gas are not really small billiard balls); experiences are not, for example, objects that we can perceive, but states that we are in, as I have already said. But *in the model* they are objects that we perceive as on a movie screen, and the model inevitably leads to the inference that in some way these objects are *between* us and the external world, since, after all, all that we *see* (in the model) are the objects on the movie screen. All the problems of traditional epistemology, such as the uncertainty as to whether there is an external world at all, and the problem of the very conceivability of the external world—all the problems familiar to a reader of, let us say, the first of Berkeley's Dialogues—immediately arise, within this model. Note, however, that the entire Sellarsian story—the division between a space of causes and a space of reasons, the "adverbial" account of phenomenal experience (that is, we "sense green-chairly" instead "seeing a green chair–shaped sense datum"), the idea, which I didn't mention, that the language of "thinks" is modeled on the language of "says," the explanation of the traditional sense-datum story as a "model" of the mind—note that none of this really has much to do with the question whether phenomenal reports are *certain* or not. Accepting the problematic dichotomy between the space of reasons and the space of causes may, perhaps, make it *easier* to suppose that phenomenal reports are corrigible; but the fact is that corrigibility issues are simply peripheral for Sellars. Sellars' concern (one that I applaud) is to defend a form of realism about perception, that is, to rehabilitate the idea that we directly perceive external things, not to show that phenomenal reports are corrigible.

Reichenbach and Wittgenstein on Moorean Certainty

In Reichenbach's lecture "Are Phenomenal Reports Absolutely Certain?" however, as the very title indicates, the question of the certainty of phenomenal reports is the entire subject, and this is the best single essay I know of in epistemology if *that*—the certainty of phenomenal reports—is the question.

Reichenbach begins by making it clear that he argues from an empiricist standpoint; that is, he rejects the very idea of a synthetic *a priori* element in knowledge; this is a standpoint he more or less[9] shared with his co-symposiasts Goodman and Lewis. He also rejects G. E. Moore's view that statements like "This is a hand"—Reichenbach describes them (p. 148) as "simple statements concerning our daily environment"—can be absolutely certain. Reichenbach's view is that such statements always imply predictions about the future, and *therefore* can always be overturned by future experience. This issue now seems more complex than such a straightforward argument allows, because, as Wittgenstein has pointed out, regarding *some* statements as non-veridical would undermine so *much* that is presupposed by the language game of empirical knowledge that it is not clear that we would be justified in any longer regarding the acceptance of *any* empirical statement as justified, let alone the negation of the statement in question. What I have in mind is not Moore's example, "This is a hand" (looking at one's own hand), but "Water has at some time boiled" (that is, there has been at least one occasion on which water has boiled), or "The earth has existed for a long time." That one might be warranted in concluding that either one these statements is *false,* that is, that what we observed in the past history of the world was never water boiling, or that there hasn't been much of a past history of the world, is very difficult to conceive. In the case of the former statement, if we are not allowed to suppose collective hallucination, or collective delusion on a massive scale, then the only remaining possibility seems to be to redescribe what we have called "boiling," that is, this bubbling behavior when the water is heated to a certain temperature, as something else. But the difficulty is that since this bubbling behavior when the water is heated is our paradigm of boiling, if we did this we would be subject to the charge that we had merely changed the meaning of "boiling."

On the other hand, if we say, "Well, we might have experiences as of waking up and discovering that all of our memories were a dream, or a hallucination, or something of that kind," then we have to face the question that Wittgenstein raises in *On Certainty,* namely the question *whether we would be justified* in coming to the conclusion that all of our memories had been a hallucination. Why should we not rather suppose *those* experiences—of discovering that all of our memories had been a hallucination—were a hallucination? I do think the following weaker thesis can be maintained, however, and it is sufficient for Reichenbach's purposes: in the case of any statement about the "external world," including "Water has sometimes boiled" and "The earth has existed for a long time," it does seem—precisely because we *do* base predictions about the future on these statements— that we can conceive of experiences such that *it would be problematic what to say* about the warranted assertibility of the statement if we had those experiences. The question Wittgenstein raised in *On Certainty,* as to whether propositions such as these are so "pivotal" that we cannot *now* conceive of circumstances under which we would *clearly be justified* in rejecting them is a fascinating one, but it can be put aside for the purposes of the present discussion. At any rate, neither Goodman nor Lewis would have challenged Reichenbach's rejection of Moore's view.

Reichenbach and the Uncertainties of Phenomenal Reports

As I have mentioned, Reichenbach devoted most of his lecture to the views of C. I. Lewis, and he begins with Lewis' view that a phenomenalistic language, or, to use Lewis' term, an *expressive language,* is possible. Reichenbach is skeptical; he doubts that we can, in fact, describe phenomenal experience without using language which is parasitic on ordinary thing-language; for example, if I say that I see a flight of stairs "optically speaking," or "subjectively speaking," then my description of my phenomenal experience is obviously parasitic on my description of a publicly observable thing, a flight of stairs. However, Reichenbach's strategy was not to keep Lewis' position from even getting stated (he allowed the plane to take off, as it were). Instead he said (p. 150), "Let us assume that this phenomenal language, as supposed by Lewis, can be carried through. Can we then maintain that there are absolutely certain report propositions formulated in phenomenal language? I will try to collect the arguments for and against Lewis' thesis of the existence of such propositions and, examining the pros and cons, attempt to arrive at a conclusion."

A defender of C. I. Lewis might, however, feel that by this time Reichenbach has already loaded the dice against Lewis with a remark that occurs a little earlier in the lecture (p. 149). "Yet these statements [Lewis' phenomenal reports or 'terminating judgments'] are synthetic. They inform us about something that is there, and do not merely give labels to the individual observation. They tell us, for instance, that what is there now resembles something I saw yesterday. They draw lines of comparison into the picture offered by experience." Here I can imagine that C. I. Lewis might have replied that if Reichenbach is saying that when I say that I have a blue chair–shaped sense datum in my visual field (or use whatever language I may choose to formulate the phenomenal report)—if Reichenbach is saying that when the phenomenalist utters such a report, or the man on the street does, if he ever talks that way—*part of what is meant* is "I am having the sort of experience that I have used these words to describe on earlier occasions, or that others have used these words to describe on earlier occasions," then Reichenbach is just wrong. It is not part of the literal meaning of "I have a blue chair–shaped sense datum in my visual field" that I have described any experience of mine by those words earlier (or even that I have earlier described any experience by the simpler sentences "I have a blue sense datum in my visual field" or "I have a chair–shaped sense datum in my visual field"). In support of this, one might argue that someone who knows no English, but only German, and who says "Ich habe ein blaues stuhlförmiges Sinnesdatum in meinem Sichtfeld" has uttered a sentence that has the same meaning as the English sentence "I have a blue chair-shaped sense datum in my visual field," but it would be absurd to say that the German sentence means that the speaker is having the sort of experience that on previous occasions he has described by using the words "blue" and "chair-shaped sense datum"; those words are no part of his vocabulary.

It seems to me, however, that this retort depends on a forced and uncharitable interpretation of Reichenbach's remark. Reichenbach need not be interpreted as claiming that, for example, "I have a blue chair–shaped sense datum in my visual field" *mentions* the words "chair-shaped," "blue," and "visual field." What I take Reichenbach to be saying is that, at least in the case of simple predicates such as "blue" and "chair," whether those be taken to be in phenomenalistic language or in physicalistic language, it is a *presupposition* of saying that something has one of those predicates—a presupposition of saying that something is blue, or something is a chair, or chair-shaped—that the thing in question is similar in relevant respects to the things to which that predicate has been applied in the past.

The more general principle would be something like the following: Let P be a non–compound predicate of the language whose meaning is learned by ostensive teaching, or from sufficiently many examples, and suppose further that one is not introducing P for the first time (that is, P is already a predicate in the language). Then the speech act of ascribing that predicate to something, of describing something as having P, presupposes that the thing in question is relevantly similar to things to which P has been applied in that language in the past.

It would be self-defeating to say, "This is a chair, but it is not similar in any respect to things which have been called 'chairs' in the past." If the presupposition is violated in a particular case, then construed as an utterance in which the predicate in question is supposed to be understood as it has always been understood in the language (and putting aside cases of metaphor and other figures of speech), we will be unable to regard the utterance as true; we shall have to regard the utterance as false, or perhaps as meaningless, depending on the particulars of the case. Of course, if we do bring figures of speech into the picture, then we may say that perhaps the utterance is true in the sense of being figuratively true, but I think we can safely put that question to one side when we are discussing phenomenal reports in the sense in which Lewis and Reichenbach used the term. They were not discussing the possibility of metaphorically communicating one's experience.

But what if one *does* intend one's utterance as a "dubbing"-event, that is, if one does not intend to be applying a predicate which already has an established use in the language, whether it be a public language or a "private" language, but simply intends to be *bestowing* a use on a predicate, say, "E"? Perhaps the simplest thing to say, if one does not want to go through a discussion of Wittgenstein's Private Language Argument, is that *even if* there were such a thing as a "private language," not *all* of the speech-acts performed by someone using that language could sensibly be taken to be "dubbing"-events; for the "private language" to be a language in any sense, the act of introducing a predicate should, in the normal case, be followed by further acts of *using* that predicate to make a claim; if on each occasion, when I say that something has the property E, I mean *not* that it has the property E in any sense that I have previously attached to "E," but that it has the property E in the sense of having the attribute that I am *now* attending to, then my various utterances of "This is E" will mean no more than "This is *thus*," and this is to say nothing. (Here, of course, I am mimicking a move in Wittgenstein's Private Language Argument, but I am sure that this is also what Reichenbach would have said about this possibility.)

In sum, if phenomenal predicates are to be genuine predicates, then they must be capable of figuring in reports in which they are used in a way that has already been established, used in a way that has already been exemplified in the language. They must, as Reichenbach said,

"draw lines of comparison into the picture offered by experience."
But in that case, they will carry the presupposition that I have described; the speaker, in making them, is committed to a claim which
goes beyond his present experience, even if that claim is not, if you
like, "part of the literal meaning" of his report, but a presupposition
of the possibility of making that report by means of those words. And
if that claim can be falsified by experience, then the report itself can be
undermined—shown to be, if not a downright lie, perhaps, confused,
or unintelligible, or senseless, or in some other way not determinately
true—by showing that the presupposition is false. Thus Reichenbach
is justified in holding that this presupposition must also be absolutely
certain if there are to be absolutely certain phenomenal reports.

C. I. Lewis' Three Arguments

The first Lewisian argument that Reichenbach considers is to the effect that it is conceptually impossible for a phenomenal report to be
wrong, because the very content of such a report is constructed by
removing every element that might be incompatible with later observations. As Reichenbach summarizes this argument (p. 150), "When
we discover that a report formulated in physical language is incompatible with later observations, we change its interpretation by reducing it to its phenomenal content; we say, for instance, 'Though it was
false to believe there was a flight of stairs, it remains true that there
was the phenomenon of a flight of stairs.' In other words, the method
by means of which we introduce the phenomenal reports seems to
guarantee their absolute certainty; we eliminate that component of the
original sentence which is falsified by later observation, and which
may be called its physical component, [and] thus we construct its phenomenal component as a residue exempt from doubt. Phenomenal
language is constructed by elimination of all physical implications; it
therefore appears plausible that the sentences of this language cannot
be disproved."

The second Lewisian argument might be called "the slip of the
tongue argument." According to this argument, although there are
sources of error even for our personal language, in the case of phenomenal reports these can be reduced to slips of the tongue. But slips
of the tongue (for example, in physicalistic rather than phenomenalistic language, saying "John" when I mean "Peter") do not matter, because (and again I quote Reichenbach summarizing Lewis' argument)

"we may use the words incorrectly, but they have at the moment we use them the correct meaning for us; the word 'John' at this moment has the meaning of 'Peter' for us, and, though a slip of the tongue may misinform other persons, it cannot deceive us who know what we mean" (p. 151).

The third argument is of a more mathematical kind (Reichenbach found it in a work by Russell),[10] and I recall that when the symposium took place at Bryn Mawr in 1952, it was Reichenbach's refutation of this particular technical argument that, perhaps, impressed the audience most, although I now think that the other points that Reichenbach raised are of more fundamental importance. The argument—defended by Lewis in his paper at the symposium, in fact—was that nothing can be *probable* unless something else is *certain*. The mathematical form of the argument is this: Suppose that a statement S is probable to a degree p. If the statement that S is probable to degree p is not itself certain, but only probable to a degree q, both p and q being less than 1, then the probability of S is "weakened" to the degree p·q; and if the statement that this probability is p·q is itself only probable to a degree r less than 1, the probability of S becomes weakened again to the product p·q·r, and so on. Here is Reichenbach's summary of this argument (p. 151): "If there is no certainty on any level, the ultimate probability of the event is a product of infinitely many factors each of which is smaller than 1 and which do not converge to 1, and thus the product is equal to zero."

It was necessary for Reichenbach to expose the fallacy in this argument because Reichenbach himself held a conception according to which there is only probability at every level. To be sure, Reichenbach did not claim that in order to make any statement at all I need to know the numerical probability of the statement; if that were the case, then to make any statement, I would have to know an infinite number of other statements of a quite complicated kind. Reichenbach's view was that we are sometimes justified in making statements without knowing even the approximate numerical value of their probability. This is frequently so in the case of observation statements; such observation statements are "blind posits," and all knowledge is ultimately based on blind posits. However, blind posits do not remain blind posits forever; with the passage of time, as we get more knowledge and put ourselves in a position to discover the errors that affect various sorts of observations, and the probability of the various kinds of error, we will (according to Reichenbach) eventually be able to assign a numerical probability to each blind posit. For a frequentist like Reichenbach, the probability of a statement is itself always a frequency, a frequency which depends upon the choice of an appropriate reference class of statements.[11] The statement that a statement has a certain probability is, thus, itself a claim about a frequency. Of course, the reference class itself may change as knowledge develops even though the same statement is being considered, just as the reference class an insurance company uses to estimate the probability that a certain building will catch fire may change as knowledge develops even though the same event is being considered. Thus the probability of a statement is not a *fixed* frequency; but at any given time the probability of a statement (in Reichenbach's sense) is a frequency in some reference class or other, and *the statement that a statement has a given probability* is, thus, itself an empirical claim. On this conception, every empirical statement that we make has a numerical probability, even if we do not know that numerical probability when we make the statement (even if the statement is a blind posit), and the statement that it has that probability is itself an empirical statement which has in turn its numerical probability. Russell's (actually Lewis') mathematical argument would be devastating for Reichenbach's view if it were correct. But Reichenbach has no difficulty in showing that it is incorrect.

As Reichenbach puts it (p. 152), "If q is the probability of the sentence s, 'The probability of the event is p,' then the probability of the event is not given by the product p·q, but by a more complicated formula . . . [which] requires knowledge about the probability of the event in case the sentence s is false. Let this probability = p′; then the probability of the event is equal to $q \cdot p + (1 - q) \cdot p'$. This expression need not be smaller than p, and can even be larger. . . . In fact, the infinite product p·q·r. . . . does not give the probability of the event, but supplies the probability that all these infinitely many sentences are true simultaneously; and such a probability is, of course, equal to 0. Thus the argument is invalid for mathematical reasons."

It should be noted that the interest of Reichenbach's refutation extends beyond the defense of Reichenbach's own view, put forward in *Experience and Prediction*,[12] that probability (or "weight") is the *only* meaningful predicate of sentences, and that we need to *replace* talk of truth and falsity with talk of "weight." In my opinion, there are many reasons for rejecting *that* view, not the least being this: if the weight of a sentence is, as Reichenbach says, a frequency, it must be a frequency of some *property*. Of *what* property? If the weight of a sentence is the frequency of *true* sentences in a reference class of sentences, then the existence of weight *presupposes* the existence of truth. If, on the other hand, it is only the frequency of sentences which will be accepted, that doesn't seem good enough, because being accepted is not a standing property of a sentence, but one which changes with time. Perhaps it is the frequency of sentences which will be accepted in the long run, or something of that kind; but if that is Reichenbach's thought, then his account would seem to presuppose something like a Peircean notion of truth, the notion of truth as what inquiry would converge to in the long run. Independent of all these questions, the value of Reichenbach's refutation of Lewis, however, is that it shows very simply that even if every statement we make to the effect that a synthetic statement is true, or very likely to be true, or true with a certain probability, etc., itself has a non-zero probability of being false, no paradoxical consequences will result. And a philosopher can perfectly well accept *this* claim of Reichenbach's without agreeing that probability should *replace* the notion of truth. (In any case, Reichenbach's idea that probability should replace truth is not even mentioned in this lecture.)

At this point in the lecture, Reichenbach does something very elegant. Having rebutted Lewis' attempt to appeal to the theory of probability to show that empirical knowledge would be impossible if there were not certainty at some level, Reichenbach now proceeds to make his own application of the probability calculus, in this case Bayes's theorem, to argue against Lewis that phenomenal reports must be capable of being tested by seeing whether other phenomenal reports, whose truth they lead us to expect, are or are not correct. The argument is extremely interesting—in my view, far more interesting than the more fashionable argument against the myth of the given that I reviewed at the beginning of this essay.

Reichenbach points out that a view like Lewis', a classical epistemological foundationalism of a phenomenalist kind, needs it to be the case that phenomenal reports are the *basis* on which we are able to assert thing-sentences, sentences which are corrigible. Indeed, the whole point of foundationalist epistemology, as the term "foundationalism" suggests, was to claim that what we know for certain, our phenomenal reports, can serve as the *foundation* for the rest of our knowledge. But phenomenalists do not think that phenomenal reports *deductively* imply sentences in thing-language. (Lewis' own position was that sentences in thing-language are equivalent to infinite conjunctions of sentences which say that if one were to have certain experiences, then one would have certain other experiences *with a certain probability;* and Lewis would have held that sentences of this kind can be rendered probable by observation reports in phenomenalistic language.) At any rate, if this sort of foundationalism is right, it must be the case that thing-sentences can be rendered probable by phenomenal reports, and these thing-sentences in turn (on any view) make certain other phenomenal reports probable. Leaving out the "middle man," we can say that phenomenal reports, while themselves absolutely certain according to the view under discussion, are supposed to make certain other phenomenal reports probable—statements about what we will experience in the future, for example, and also statements about what has been experienced in the past. And now Reichenbach offers the following argument (pp. 153–154):

"If the phenomenal sentence *a,* in a certain context, makes the phenomenal sentence *b* highly probable, whereas non-*a* would make non-*b* highly probable, then conversely the verification of *b* will make *a* highly probable whereas the verification of non-*b* would make *a* highly improbable. I refer here to the theorem of inverse probability known as Bayes' rule. It is true that the use of this rule requires a knowledge of quite a few probabilities, among which the antecedent probabilities play an important part; but the system of knowledge is elaborate enough to supply all of these probabilities, though perhaps sometimes only in the form of rough estimates. It follows, then, that any phenomenal sentence is capable of being tested in terms of other such sentences; and although the other sentences cannot completely verify, or falsify, the given sentence, they can verify it, or falsify it, to a high degree."

"I will call this *the argument from concatenation.* It shows that phenomenal sentences are not exempt from probability tests."

At first blush this argument may look question-begging. For this use of Bayes's theorem presupposes that direct observation does not confer the probability 1 upon the sentence *a;* if it does, then the sentence *a* will retain the probability 1 even if the probability of the actually observed *b relative to* the fact that *a* was observed was as small as you please, provided it was not actually 0. Reichenbach discusses this objection, and he illustrates the reasoning involved with an example within thing-language. The probability is very small that when I step upon the brake of my car, the car starts to speed up; but, Reichenbach points out, if such an experience actually occurred, I would not doubt my observation. I wouldn't conclude that I was mistaken in thinking that my car speeded up because the probability against the production of such an effect by a stepped-on brake pedal is very high. And then Reichenbach asks on Lewis' behalf (p. 154), "Would we not be willing to defend in a similar way any individual phenomenal sentence against the totality of other sentences?"

Against this rhetorical question, Reichenbach points out that my willingness to believe that my car did really speed up when I stepped on the brake pedal (against the prior probability that it would not) is accompanied by a belief that further observational evidence will support the speeding-up. One could ask other people whether they too saw the car speed up, one could investigate whether the foot was actually on the brake pedal, one could test whether the car speeds up again when the foot is again on the brake pedal, and one could inquire whether the sole of the shoe did not slightly press against the gas pedal and move it downward at the same time. According to Reichenbach, retaining an observation sentence against indirect evidence is always equivalent to predicting that the class of observation sentences will (if we investigate) be extended by future observations so as to turn the negative indirect evidence into positive evidence. (This is very much in the spirit of Peirce.)

In this example, to be sure, Reichenbach considered not phenomenal sentences but physical sentences; but, Reichenbach says (p. 155), "I do not see any reason why the procedure should be different in principle for phenomenal sentences. Retaining a phenomenal sentence against the indirect evidence derived from the total system of phenomenal sentences in which it is embedded is equivalent to assuming that the class of phenomenal sentences, on suitable experimentation, will be so extended as to supply positive evidence for the sentence." In this connection, Reichenbach introduces the notion of *inductive consistency*. Unlike deductive consistency, inductive consistency cannot always be achieved in the short run; but in what I have been describing as a Peircean spirit, Reichenbach holds that we should strive to attain it in the long run. So understood, as a regulative ideal, inductive consistency requires that we should not hold on to any sentence, not even to a phenomenal report, if the indirect probability of that sentence on all the other evidence converges to 0 as inquiry continues. If I say that I have had a certain experience, but all the indirect evidence makes it more and more and more probable as time goes by that I did not have that experience, then inductive consistency requires that at some point I should give up the claim to have had that experience.

But what does it mean to give up the claim that one has had an experience that one sincerely reported having? Must I plead a slip of the tongue? Here, Reichenbach makes the important point that to allow the notion of a "slip of the tongue" to become simply a wastebasket category, one into which we put *every* case in which, upon reflection, we realize that we made a report that was not true, is to deprive that notion of all psychologically explanatory content. "It is true," he writes (p. 156) "that there are situations in which we say 'John' and mean 'Peter', in which, therefore, at least subjectively the correct meaning can be said to exist. There are other situations, however, in which our attention is not fully focussed on our words, and for which we cannot maintain that any distinct meaning was attached to our words. These transitional situations play a greater part than is usually recognized." At this point, once again, Reichenbach is at least touching the terrain that Wittgenstein touched in the Private Language Argument. The idea that whenever I make a false phenomenal report I must have had a determinate "meaning" in mind, a proposition in my head, and I only failed to attach the correct words to the proposition, obviously depends on the picture of meaning as (to use Wittgenstein's language) an "aura" surrounding our words and determining their use in every context. Once we recognize that such a picture of meaning belongs not to empirical psychology but to a metaphysical parody of psychology, a metaphysical mechanics of thought, we see that Reichenbach's rejection of the idea that all misspeaking can be explained as "having the right meaning in mind 'at least subjectively' and failing to find the correct expression for it" was absolutely justified.

A Final Remark on the History of Analytic Philosophy

In sum, it seems to me that the arguments that Reichenbach brought against the whole idea of the incorrigibility of phenomenal reports—the idea that all predications "draw lines of comparison into the picture offered by experience" and thus have predictive import, the deep notion of "inductive consistency" as a regulative ideal, and the rejection of the "slip of the tongue" story as a universal explanation of the failure of such reports—are individually powerful and collectively add up to one of the masterpieces of the analytic tradition.

I have only one last point to make: Reichenbach's lecture was given in 1952, and thus after the appearance of both Quine's "Two Dogmas of Empiricism" and Wittgenstein's *Philosophical Investigations,* which I have alluded to a number of times in this essay. But *many of the ideas in this lecture can be found in Reichenbach's "Experience and Prediction" published in 1938!*[13] Today too many of our students have a picture of "logical positivism" as a collection of errors—phenomenalism, reductionism, neglect of the history of science, and so forth. That many of the people whom we lump together under that label (Reichenbach himself never accepted "positivist" as a label for his own philosophy, and called himself a logical *empiricist*) combatted those errors in the thirties, and often with arguments that are stronger than those marshalled against them today, is something they, regrettably, have not learned. I hope that this essay may have served in a small way to combat this mythological account of the history. It is time to deal *seriously* with logical empiricism as a movement and as a critical phase in the history of our own tradition, and to put to rest what may with justice be called "The Myth of Logical Positivism."

Notes

1. "Empiricism and the Philosophy of Mind," in *The Foundations of Science and the Concepts of Psychology and Psychoanalysis,* ed. Herbert Feigl and Michael Scriven, Minnesota Studies in the Philosophy of Science, vol. 1 (Minneapolis: University of Minnesota Press, 1956), pp. 253–329.

2. Cf. Richard Rorty's *Philosophy and the Mirror of Nature* (Princeton: Princeton University Press, 1979), e.g., p. xiii and p. 95.

3. *The Philosophical Review,* 61, no. 2 (April 1952), 147–159.

4. *The Philosophical Review,* 61, no. 2 (April 1952), "Sense and Certainty," 160–167.

5. *The Philosophical Review,* 61, no. 2 (April 1952), "The Given Element in Empirical Knowledge," 168–175.

6. Sellars' eventual dualistic position about "raw feels" is, however, anticipated in a paper with Paul Meehl in the same volume as "Empiricism and the Philosophy of Mind," cited in n. 1; see "The Concept of Emergence," pp. 239–252, esp. pp. 249–250.

7. These remarks are based upon an unpublished Whitehead Lecture that John McDowell delivered at Harvard in 1988.

8. A perhaps more mundane reason than McDowell's for being skeptical about the dictum that phenomenal experiences cannot be reasons but can only be causes is that we do seem to stand in certain cognitive relations to them. We can, for example, *pay attention* to them, and the nature of our attention is subject to criticism. For example, if I have an eye examination, I attend extremely carefully to whether the lines on the chart seem clearer

or less clear under various choices of lenses. Of course, saying that we can *attend* to our experiences does not commit me to the traditional view that we perceive our experiences (rather than the lines on the chart), and it certainly does not commit me to the view that we cannot directly observe anything but phenomenal experience. But I shall not deal further with this issue in the present essay; suffice it to repeat that the doctrine that whatever serves as the cause for our phenomenal reports cannot also be a reason for them is not one that I regard as simply a premise to be taken for granted in discussions of this issue.

9. I say "more or less" because there are well-known Kantian elements in Lewis' *Mind and the World Order;* they do not, however, affect the present discussion.

10. Bertrand Russell, *Human Knowledge* (London: Unwin, 1948), p. 414. What Russell actually held was that our premisses need to be "subjectively nearly certain."

11. See Ernest Nagel's discussion of the problems this raises for Reichenbach's philosophy of science in "Principles of the Theory of Probability," in *International Encyclopedia of Unified Science,* vol. 1, pt. 2, ed. Otto Neurath, Rudolf Carnap, and Charles W. Morris (Chicago: University of Chicago Press, 1955).

12. *Experience and Prediction* (Chicago: University of Chicago Press, 1938), pp. 187–192.

13. Ibid., pp. 163–187.

7. Reichenbach and the Limits of Vindication

Reichenbach's sense of the *need* for a justification of induction is poignantly expressed in the closing chapter of *Experience and Prediction*.[1] Reichenbach chides Hume, "He [Hume] is not alarmed by his discovery; *he does not realize that if there is no escape from the dilemma pointed out by him, science might as well not be continued*—there is no need for a system of predictions if it is nothing but *a ridiculous self-delusion*. There are modern positivists who do not realize this either. They talk about the formation of scientific theories, but they do not see that, if there is no justification for the inductive inference, *the working procedure of science sinks to the level of a game and can no longer be justified by the applicability of its results for the purpose of actions*. . . . If, however, we should not be able to find an answer to Hume's objections within the frame of logistic formalism, we ought to frankly admit that the antimetaphysical version of philosophy led to the renunciation of any justification of the predictive methods of science—led to a *definitive failure of scientific philosophy*" (p. 346, emphasis added). Indeed, Reichenbach suggests that not only "scientific philosophy" but life itself would be impossible if induction were not justifiable: "If we sit at the wheel of a car and want to turn the car to the right, why do we turn the wheel to the right? . . . if we should not regard the inductive prescription and consider the effect of a turn of the wheel as entirely unknown to us, we might as well turn it to the left as well. I do not say this to suggest such an attempt; the effects of sceptical philosophy applied in motor traffic would be rather unpleasant. But I should say a philosopher who is to put aside his principles any time he steers a motor car is a bad philosopher."

131

At the same time, Reichenbach insisted that Hume had successfully shown that:

"1. We have no logical demonstration for the validity of inductive inference.

2. There is no demonstration a posteriori for the inductive inference; any such demonstration would presuppose the very principles which it is to demonstrate."

"These two pillars of Hume's criticism of the principles of induction have stood unshaken for two centuries," Reichenbach tells us,[2] "and I think they will stand as long as there is a scientific philosophy."

If the inductive inference cannot be "demonstrated" to lead to successful prediction either deductively or *a posteriori,* and yet it can still be "justified," that "justification" must do something other than demonstrate that we will obtain successful predictions in the long run by relying on induction; what Reichenbach claimed to have shown was that *induction will lead to the goal of successful prediction in the long run if any method will do so.* Thus, Reichenbach contended, we can concede that Hume did prove 1 and 2 above—that is, Hume did show that there is no possibility of a deductive or an *a posteriori* proof that the goal of successful prediction can be reached by induction (or by any other method, for that matter); but this important discovery of Hume's does not preclude the possibility that there is a proof of the *conditional proposition* that induction will reach the goal *if* the goal is attainable at all. This way of reconstruing the notion of a "justification of induction" is so radical a departure from what had been sought by Hume's critics (or so the positivists thought) that Herbert Feigl thought one should give it a new name. A proof that induction will lead to success would be a *justification* of induction, in Feigl's terminology; a proof of the conditional proposition that it will lead to success *if success is attainable* would be a *vindication.*[3] And, like Reichenbach, Feigl argued that while induction cannot be *justified* (in the sense Feigl gave to that term),[4] nevertheless (he and Reichenbach had shown that) it can be *vindicated.* Moreover, both Reichenbach and Feigl held that *vindication is enough.* In *The Rise of Scientific Philosophy,*[5] Reichenbach employs a vivid analogy, "The man who makes inductive inferences may be compared to a fisherman who casts a net into an unknown part of the ocean—he does not know whether he will catch fish, but he knows that if he wants to catch fish he has to cast his net. Every inductive prediction is like casting a net into the ocean of the happenings of nature; we do not know whether we shall have a good catch, but we try, at least, and try by the help of the best means available." What makes induction "the best means available," according to Reichenbach, is that it is the only[6] method concerning which we can *prove* that it will lead to successful prediction if any method will. Since the possibility of the long-run success of induction is the necessary condition for the possibility of the long-run success of any method at all, we are rationally justified in using induction if we want successful prediction. "We should at least actualize the necessary conditions of success if the sufficient conditions are not within our reach."[7]

Given the magnificent grandeur of what Reichenbach claimed to have achieved—nothing less than to have provided the rational warrant for empirical knowledge which he believed we so desperately need—it is surprising that there is relatively little in-depth discussion[8] of Reichenbach's vindication argument in the literature, and most of that fails to address what seem to me to be the central issues. In the present contribution, I want to emphasize those issues, as I see them, and to assess the successes and the failures of Reichenbach's vindicatory strategy.

Reichenbach's Arguments

Reichenbach imagines an immortal inquirer who is engaged in sampling from an infinite population. For the sake of an example, let us imagine that balls are being drawn successively from an infinite urn, and that each ball is either red or black. The immortal scientist finds that 262 of the first 1,000 balls are black (let us say), that 2,489 of the first 10,000 are black, that 25,021 of the first 100,000 are black, . . . (Perhaps the limit of the relative frequency of black balls in the infinite series is actually .25.) Reichenbach's Rule of Induction tells the scientist to *keep positing that the limit of the relative frequency of the attribute he or she is interested in is approximately equal (to within any given preselected level of accuracy) to the frequency in the sample of cases so far examined.* (Thus, in our example, if the preselected level of accuracy is ".01," the scientist should "posit" that the limit of the relative frequency is .262±.01 when the first 1,000 have been examined, that it is .2489±.01 when the first 10,000 have been examined, that it is .25021±.01 when the first 100,000 have been examined, ...)

Now, if the relative frequency of the attribute the scientist is interested in approaches a limit at all, then, no matter what the degree of accuracy the scientist is using (±.01, in our example), the relative frequency with which the attribute occurs among the N members of the series so far observed will differ from that limit by less than the degree of accuracy (by less than ±.01) after N reaches a certain size (called "the point of convergence"). In other words, the scientist, using Reichenbach's Rule of Induction may make a finite number of mistakes "at the beginning," but *once the point of convergence has been passed all of the posits that scientist makes will be correct.* This is simply a consequence of the definition of the concept "limit" as applied to a series of relative frequencies. (In our example, if the limit of the relative frequency of black balls in the infinite sequence is actually .25, then the first "posit" was incorrect, and the subsequent ones were correct.)

But why does Reichenbach believe that all prediction problems can be reduced to estimates of limits of relative frequencies? Well, consider a case that might seem recalcitrant to such treatment. Imagine that the balls do not come out of the urn with a random distribution of colors at all. Instead, imagine that we see a black ball come out of the urn, then we see nine red balls, and then we see successive black balls until 90 percent of the observed balls have been black, after which we see successive red balls until 90 percent of the observed balls have been red, then successive black balls until 90 percent of the observed balls have been black . . . and so on. This series is such that it happens infinitely often that the relative frequency of black balls among the ones so far observed is .90 and infinitely often that the relative frequency of black balls among the ones so far observed is only .10. Clearly, in this series there is no "limit of the relative frequency" with respect to the attribute "black." But once we "tumble" to what is going on we will have no difficulty in predicting the color of any individual ball that may be examined in the future. Does this not show that successful prediction does not require the existence of limits of the relative frequency?

Reichenbach's strategy with cases like this[9] is to define a new attribute. Thus, suppose we have formulated a law which we believe to be the law obeyed by our sequence. (In the case of the example, the law would be that the sequence begins with a black ball followed by a "run" of red balls; and when there is a run of red balls the run always continues until a point is reached at which at least 90 percent of the balls which have been drawn are red, and as soon as this happens a run of black balls always begins; and when there is a run of black balls, the run always continues until a point is reached at which at least 90 percent of the balls which have been examined are black, and as soon as this happens a run of red balls always begins.) If the color of a ball is what it would be if the sequence followed our law, we say the ball has the attribute *C*, and otherwise that it has the attribute not-*C*. Then to know the *reliability* of our law, what we need to know is the relative frequency in the long run (that is, the limit of the relative frequency) of *C*. And only if such a reliability estimate can be made, Reichenbach argues, does our "law" give us any means of control over what happens. Thus all successful prediction depends on the existence of limits of the relative frequency, although not necessarily on the existence of limits of the relative frequency of the attribute we are ultimately interested in.

One obvious problem is that Reichenbach's vindication deals with success in *the infinite long run*. The relevance of such a vindication to the projects of us all-too-mortal members of a species which will not last forever in a universe which may not last forever is highly problematic! Although this is a problem Reichenbach himself discusses, it is not the problem I shall say much about here.[10] Here I will accept the idealization that Reichenbach works with, the idea of an immortal inquirer who wants to discover limits of the relative frequency (or methods for making successful predictions), and is willing to accept an arbitrarily long finite initial sequence of failures (or wrong posits).

Given this idealization, the position seems to be this. Reichenbach has shown that if successful prediction (in the indefinitely long run) is possible at all, then some limits of the relative frequency must exist and be capable of being estimated by us. (This is the argument I just reviewed.) And he has observed that it is a tautology that if there are limits of the relative frequency, then by using the Rule of Induction we shall eventually make correct posits about them (and no further incorrect ones, once the point of convergence has been reached). Does this not constitute precisely the vindication of induction that we were promised?

The Problem of the Consistency of Reichenbach's Rule of Induction

The problem with Reichenbach's vindicatory argument is so stunningly simple that it is surprising how little it has been discussed. The problem was, in effect, first pointed out by Nelson Goodman, although he did not refer to the issue of vindicating induction but instead pointed out that there was a prior issue, the issue of *saying what induction is.* Straightforward traditional formulations of the rule of induction—including Reichenbach's—*lead to inconsistent predictions.*

To see the bearing of this observation on Reichenbach's argument, consider the analogous problem of justifying a system of deductive logic. One cannot justify such a system merely by proving that all valid formulas in the appropriate vocabulary are theorems of the system. As it stands, such a result is not sufficient. (It is also not necessary, but that is not relevant here.)[11] It is not sufficient because this kind of "completeness" is trivially possessed by all *inconsistent* systems. Before we are impressed by a proof that "if S is valid, then S is a theorem of the system" we need to make sure (by a proof, if possible, and by "mathematical experience" otherwise) that the system in question is consistent.

The same thing is true in the case of *induction.* Reichenbach's celebrated conditional, "if successful prediction can be made by any method, it can be made by using the Rule of Induction," *needs to be supplemented by a proof that the rule of induction is consistent.* But, unfortunately, Reichenbach's rule is not consistent.

Perhaps Goodman's discovery has not been taken seriously enough by philosophers who have discussed Reichenbach's vindication of induction (it has, of course, been taken very seriously in other connections) because Goodman's predicate *grue*[12] is so "peculiar." But it is difficult to know how such "peculiar" predicates are to be ruled out, or what would be left of Reichenbach's argument if they were. The predicate C I used above is just as "peculiar" as "grue" (it takes a calculation to determine whether a given item in a series has to be red or black to have the attribute C); but *Reichenbach's demonstration that all successful prediction depends on the existence of limits of the relative frequency turns precisely on the fact that the rule of induction accepts predicates like C.* Certainly Reichenbach did not seem to appreciate the seriousness of the problem; in the English-language edition of his *Theory of Probability,*[13] he dismisses the problem with the strange remark that "with respect to consistency, inductive logic differs intrinsically from deductive logic; it is consistent not *de facto* but *de faciendo,* that is, not in its actual status, but in a form to be made."

Indeed, the problem is much more severe than the example given by Goodman would suggest. For the fact is that when we have observed some finite initial part of a sequence, the data we have obtained can always be reconciled with more than one possible universal hypothesis (this is a special case of the familiar "underdetermination of theory by evidence"). For example, if we have observed that the successive runs of red balls in a certain sequence have the lengths of the prime numbers up to 103, then using Reichenbach's Rule of Induction we might project the hypothesis[14] "the successive runs of red balls will always have the lengths of the successive prime numbers," but we might also project incompatible hypotheses (for example, the hypothesis that the sequence will repeat from the beginning once there has been a run of 103 successive red balls). In this respect, the inconsistency of Reichenbach's Rule of Induction is quite different from the inconsistency of a system of axioms. When a system of axioms is inconsistent, say a system of set theory, it sometimes takes a great deal of work to derive a contradiction from the axioms. And one might (it has been suggested, at any rate) seek to "localize" the contradiction by *modifying the propositional calculus* so that it will no longer be the case that from a single contradiction every formula of the system can be derived (I am thinking of the possibility of employing relevant logic instead of classical truth-functional logic). But in the case of Reichenbach's Rule of Induction, whenever the rule is employed to project a universal hypothesis, it can also be employed to project a directly inconsistent universal hypothesis; there is no need to derive one esoteric contradiction (perhaps involving "grue") and then employ the principle that from a truth-functional contradiction every assertion follows.

I confess that many times over the years I have wondered about what Reichenbach meant by saying that "[inductive logic] is consistent not *de facto* but *de faciendo,* that is, not in its actual status, but in a form to be made." I think that what he *must* have meant is this: to keep my inductions consistent, what I must do is *choose;* if I project the hypothesis that all the prime numbers will appear in order (as the lengths of "runs" of red balls), I must not simultaneously project any hypothesis which is inconsistent with that hypothesis *until* the projected hypothesis has been falsified. I may, of course, choose the "wrong" attribute to project initially; I may, to use Goodman's example, initially project "grue" rather than "green"; but the hypothesis that "all emeralds are grue" will be falsified as soon as green emeralds are examined after time *t,* and then I will (sooner or later) project the more useful attribute "green." (Or so Reichenbach might have thought.) Similarly, in terms of the example I used a moment ago, I may initially project the hypothesis that the series will repeat after a run of 103 red balls has occurred, but I will give up that hypothesis when I get a run of 107 red balls, and then I will (sooner or later) project the hypothesis that the lengths of the successive runs of red balls are the successive primes.

If this is what Reichenbach meant, however, it raises an interesting and very deep question: *What guarantee is there that the right hypothesis (or the corresponding attribute C) will ever be projected,* if there is a right hypothesis?

The Example of the Clairvoyant

One indication of Reichenbach's thinking here is the discussion of noninductive methods of prediction in *Experience and Prediction.* Reichenbach imagines an objector who argues that "there might be a clairvoyant who knows every event of a series individually, who could foretell precisely what would happen from event to event" (p. 358). And he replies that in such a case we could use induction to discover how reliable the clairvoyant was; in his classes on inductive logic at UCLA this was one of Reichenbach's favorite ways of illustrating his claim that induction must succeed if any method does.

This example, as it stands, does not speak to the problem of *consistency,* but it is easy enough to modify it so that it does. In my "Degree of Confirmation and Inductive Logic,"[15] I introduced a method in which "effective hypotheses" receive *priority rankings* based upon the time at which they are proposed. (I pointed out[16] that more sophisticated priority rankings are possible.) An effective hypothesis is one which says of each individual in a series whether it has some property *P;* and it does so *effectively* in the sense that it is possible to determine recursively whether the hypothesis implies that the individual in the nth place of the series is P or not-P (for $n = 1, 2, 3 \ldots$). Thus an effective hypothesis is one that we can actually compare with the data; we can calculate what the character of the members of the series is supposed to be, and see whether the predictions of the hypothesis agree with the facts as more and more individuals are observed. The following rules define the method (call it method I):[17]

1. Let $P_{t,M}$ be the set of hypotheses considered at time t with respect to a property M of the given series. That is, $P_{t,M}$ is a finite set of effec-

tive hypotheses each of which specifies for each member of the series whether or not it is M.

2. Let $h_{t,M}$ be the effective hypothesis *accepted* at time t (if any). That is, we suppose that, at any given time, various incompatible hypotheses have been actually suggested with respect to a given M, and have not yet been ruled out (we require that these be *consistent* with the data and with all other accepted hypotheses with respect to other series and other predicates). In addition, one hypothesis may have been accepted at some time prior to t, and may not yet have been abandoned. This hypothesis is called "the accepted hypothesis at the time t."

3. (Rule I:) At certain times $t_1, t_2, t_3 \ldots$ initiate an *inductive test* with respect to M. This proceeds as follows. The hypotheses in $P_{t,M}$ at this time t_1 are called the *alternatives*. Calculate the character (M or not-M) of the next individual on the basis of each alternative. See which alternatives succeed in predicting this. Rule out the ones that fail. Continue until (a) all the alternatives but one have failed; or (b) all the alternatives have failed (one or the other must eventually happen). In case (a) accept the alternative that does not fail. In case (b) reject all the alternatives.

4. (Rule II:) Hypotheses suggested in the course of the inductive test are taken as alternatives (unless they have become inconsistent with the data) in the *next* test. That is, if h is proposed in the course of the test begun at t_3, then h belongs to $P_{t_4,M}$ and not to $P_{t_3,M}$.

5. (Rule III:) If $h_{t,M}$ is accepted at the conclusion of any inductive test, then $h_{t,M}$ continues to be accepted as long as it remains consistent with the data. (In particular, while an inductive test is going on the previously accepted hypothesis continues to be accepted, as long as it is consistent with the data.)

It is built into method I that one cannot accept mutually inconsistent hypotheses (see 2 above). Yet, simple as method I is, it is easy to show that: (Completeness property of I:) *If h is an effective hypothesis and h is true, then, using method I, one will eventually accept h if h is ever proposed.*

Thus, modifying Reichenbach's argument, we have been able to show that there is a method which will converge to the right hypothesis if there *is* a right hypothesis (in a certain class), and which is not plagued with consistency problems. Extending this kind of argument to other (and larger) classes of hypotheses has become an important branch of inductive logic in recent years.[18] In this sense, Reichenbach's "vindicationist" strategy *has* borne fruit. But has induction really been vindicated?

Method II

Although the completeness property of method I is certainly an attractive one, it falls short of the vindication Reichenbach hoped for for several reasons. (1) Whether we will get successful prediction using method I depends on what effective hypotheses are actually proposed. To show that we can achieve successful prediction if successful prediction is possible at all, we would need to make sure that the immortal inquirer sooner or later considers *every* effective hypothesis. (2) As it stands, method I does not accept hypotheses like "the clairvoyant's predictions about the series are always right." Yet, although this hypothesis is not "effective" in the sense that we can *calculate* from it what the character of an arbitrary future member of the series must be, we do have a *procedure* for telling what it will be if this h is correct, namely, to ask the clairvoyant. To show that we can achieve successful prediction if successful prediction is possible at all, we would need to make sure that the immortal inquirer also considers (sooner or later) every hypothesis which leads to a procedure for telling what the character of a future member of the series will be, even if the procedure is not a calculation. (3) The assumption that humans cannot compute *nonrecursive* functions, which we have made throughout, would have to be justified without relying on induction. I shall defer discussion of (2) and (3) to the next section; in the present section we shall see how difficulty (1) can be met.

The problem is the following: if we could arrange all testable hypotheses in a single list, and then proceed to test hypotheses in the order in which they occurred in our list (in the way illustrated by method I), then we could ensure that if there is a correct testable hypothesis, sooner or later it would get accepted. However, the list must be a list of *different*, indeed of *incompatible*, hypotheses. To see why, suppose that two of the hypotheses in $P_{t,M}$ are in fact equivalent (or at least compatible), although we mistakenly believe that they are incompatible. Then, if they happen to both be true, the inductive test prescribed by Rule I will never terminate! I "ducked" this problem when I formulated method I by restricting the sets $P_{t,M}$ to sets of *incompatible* hypotheses; but, if our scientific language is rich enough to contain number theory, there will not be any effective method for telling whether an arbitrary pair of effective hypotheses *is* incompatible or not! This is an "undecidable problem" in recursion theory. Moreover, if an effective hypothesis has to make a prediction about *every* member of the sequence, there is no effective method for telling whether a hypothesis *is* "effective" or not; however, we can handle this problem by allowing all hypotheses of the form "(n)(the nth ball in the sequence is red if and only if $f(n) = 1$)," where f is a *partial* recursive function to count as effective; for the partial recursive[19] functions (as opposed to the general recursive functions) can be effectively enumerated.

However, Reichenbach's puzzling remark about inductive logic being "consistent not *de facto* but *de faciendo*, that is, not in its actual status, but in a form to be made," suggests that he was not thinking of proceeding in accordance with a *fixed* priority ordering of the hypotheses at all; he seems to have assumed his immortal inductive inquirer could simply rank order the hypotheses as he went along. But then, there will be no guarantee that the immortal inquirer will consider *every* hypothesis that could lead to successful prediction; and this is what Reichenbach's vindicatory argument assumes.

As I thought about this difficulty, it occurred to me that a present-day Reichenbachian, apprised of the surprising relevance of Gödel's and Church's work on undecidable problems to inductive logic (as Reichenbach himself, of course, was not),[20] might plausibly propose modifying method I by simply letting the sets $P_{t,M}$ be larger and larger subsets of the set of all hypotheses of the form "(n)(the nth ball in the sequence is red if and only if $f(n) = 1$)," where f is a computable (partial recursive) function (thus giving up the requirement that the sets $P_{t,M}$ consist of *incompatible* hypotheses), and then replace Rule I with the following rule:

(Rule I*:) At certain times t_1, t_2, t_3 . . . initiate an *inductive test* with respect to M. This proceeds as follows. The hypotheses in $P_{t,M}$ at this time t_1 are called the *alternatives*. Start calculating the character (M or not-M) of future individuals (not necessarily the *next* individual)[21] on the basis of each alternative. See which alternatives succeed in these predictions. Rule out the ones that fail. Continue until (a) the alternatives that have still not failed are *not known to be incompatible*; or (b) all the alternatives have failed (one or the other must eventually happen). In case (a) accept *all* the alternatives that have not failed. In case (b) reject all the alternatives.

Call the modified method "method II." Then if the immortal inquirer uses method II instead of method I he or she may, indeed, accept two or more mutually inconsistent hypotheses: but there is a useful strategy the immortal inquirer can follow to take care of this eventuality. This strategy, which is familiar to recursion theorists, is (1) to assign a priority ranking *without ties* to all hypotheses (so that the hypotheses within a single $P_{t,M}$ will be assigned different priorities, instead of being treated as a single "clump" as they were in method M); and (2) when the conjunction of two or more accepted hypotheses is discovered to be inconsistent, to continue to accept the one with highest priority (until and unless it becomes inconsistent with the data), and to reject other hypotheses in the set of inconsistent hypotheses, starting with the hypothesis of *lowest* priority, until consistency is restored. For example, if h_1, h_2, h_3 are all accepted (where h_1 has a higher priority than h_2, which in turn has a higher priority than h_3) and their conjunction has been discovered to be inconsistent, although the conjunction of the first two is not known to be inconsistent, then we would reject only h_3. Further, if one or more of the hypotheses that survive this process are rejected at a later time, then the inquirer is to reconsider hypotheses which were rejected because of their inconsistency with hypotheses which have now been falsified (that is, incorporate them into the next set $P_{t,M}$), unless they themselves have been falsified by the data in the meanwhile. If we add these rules to method II, our method has the attractive property: (Completeness property of II:) *If h is an effective hypothesis and h is true, then, using method II one will eventually accept h.*

Moreover, even though it can happen that at one time one does accept hypotheses which are inconsistent using II, this is rectified as soon as it is discovered. In this sense, II realizes Reichenbach's idea that "inductive logic. . . . is consistent not *de facto* but *de faciendo,* that is, not in its actual status, but in a form to be made."

The Limits of "Vindication"

At the beginning of the last section, I pointed out three reasons why the completeness property of method I falls short of the justification (or "vindication") Reichenbach hoped for: (1) Whether we get successful prediction using method I depends on what effective hypotheses are actually proposed. To show that we can achieve successful prediction if successful prediction is possible at all, we need to make sure that the immortal inquirer sooner or later considers *every* effective hypothesis. (2) Method I does not accept hypotheses like "the clairvoyant's predictions about the series are always right." Yet, although this hypothesis is not "effective" in the sense that we can *calculate* from it what the character of an arbitrary future member of the series must be, we do have a *procedure* for telling what it will be if this *h* is correct, namely, to ask the clairvoyant. To show that we can achieve successful prediction if successful prediction is possible at all, we need to make sure that the immortal inquirer also considers every hypothesis which yields a procedure for telling what the character of a future member of the series will be, even if the procedure is not a calculation. (3) The assumption that humans cannot compute *nonrecursive* functions, which we have made throughout, has not been justified. Difficulty (1) has now been dealt with. What can we say about (2) and (3)?

Difficulty (3) can be subsumed under (2) in the following way: If it turns out (contrary to what we now believe) that there is a method by which humans (or idealized immortal counterparts of human inquirers) can compute nonrecursive functions, then those procedures, whatever they may be, can be incorporated in a hypothesis of the kind envisaged under difficulty (2), a hypothesis to the effect that a procedure P will always tell us what the character of a future member of a series will be ("tell us" by a method other than algorithmic calculation). Thus we can confine our attention to (2).

The general form of hypotheses like the one about the clairvoyant is: "If you do X and get result Y, then the *n*th member of the sequence will be M" (where X must depend on *n*). The problem is that it is impossible to know how such hypotheses can be "enumerated" when we do not know in advance what predicates they may contain. Indeed, even if we restrict attention to so-called observation predicates, how can we know what the limits to human powers of observation are? The answer might seem simple, and perhaps it *is* simple, *if we are allowed to use empirical knowledge, knowledge obtained by induction,* but Reichenbach agrees with Hume that "there is no demonstration a posteriori for the inductive inference; any such demonstration would presuppose the very principles which it is to demonstrate." Clearly, a "vindicatory" argument any of whose premises requires a "demonstration a posteriori" would be unacceptable for the same reason.

Again, I believe that Reichenbach's attitude would be that *completeness* of our inductive method, like consistency, is "not *de facto* but *de faciendo*." If the immortal observer learns at some point that there are more predicates needed for prediction, or even more observation predicates, than he suspected, he can simply enlarge his language and adjust his inductive method accordingly. Formally, this means that method II will be enlarged by allowing the sets $P_{t,M}$ to contain hypotheses of the form "If you do X and get result Y, then the nth member of the sequence will be M" if such hypotheses are proposed, in addition to containing larger and larger subsets of the set of all effective hypotheses. (It also means that the *language* to which method II is applied is not fixed once and for all.) And again one can obtain a completeness property which says that *If h is a hypothesis of the form specified* ["If you do X and get result Y, then the nth member of the sequence will be M"] *and h is true, then, using method II, one will eventually accept h if h is ever proposed,* while still keeping the completeness property that *If h is an effective hypothesis and h is true, then, using method II one will eventually accept h.*

If we confine attention to hypotheses which have the form of universal laws (that is, if we put aside for the moment the more general question of *confirming statistical laws* which interested Reichenbach), does this not give us everything Reichenbach claimed?

There is no question that these completeness properties of certain inductive methods are of great theoretical interest. As I have already mentioned, a whole little "industry" has developed to study them. And this is certainly a success of Reichenbach's vindicatory strategy, even if the details are much more complicated that Reichenbach anticipated.

It is not, however, a complete success. Reichenbach's argument about the clairvoyant already has a feature that should now be conspicuous: the immortal inductive inquirer only considers the clairvoyant hypothesis *if he or she encounters a clairvoyant.* That is, Reichenbach does not really attempt to describe a method by which the immortal inquirer will (in the long run) arrive at successful prediction if successful prediction is possible (which was his announced goal); what he really describes is a method by which the immortal inquirer will arrive at successful prediction *if anyone else does* (and the immortal inquirer learns about it). But is this not enough?

Well, it would be enough *if the immortal inquirer could be sure that what methods other people use are independent of the method the immortal inquirer chooses.* But there is no reason to believe that this will be the case.

The problem is this. Reichenbach, in effect, says to the immortal inquirer, "You have nothing to lose (in the long run) by using the Rule of Induction. Using it will only increase your chances of successful prediction; for if either you yourself or anyone else thinks of a way of getting successful prediction, then you will get successful prediction too." In effect, Reichenbach claims that induction is the *dominant strategy*. But if the policies followed by the other inquirers are influenced by the policy choice of our immortal inducer, then the immortal inducer may conceivably *fail* to achieve successful prediction in the long run (and everyone else may fail as well), *even though someone—perhaps our immortal inquirer—would have achieved successful prediction if our immortal inquirer had not used induction!* The reason is that, as we have seen, the immortal inquirer cannot be sure of testing *all hypotheses that could conceivably lead to successful prediction* (or at least, the immortal inquirer cannot do this without relying on empirical laws confirmed by induction). The hypotheses that the immortal inquirer tests depend on what other people do. But, then, it could be the case that if the immortal inquirer had not used induction someone else would have thought of a method which is not even describable in the language of the immortal inquirer as it presently stands, and whose reliability will, therefore, never get tested in the inductive way that Reichenbach describes, because the immortal inquirer's choice of induction brought it about that this method was not even thought of. Indeed, if the immortal inquirer had not been a believer in induction, he himself might have thought of such a method, or been persuaded by someone else to use it. In sum, there is no proof that induction is the dominant strategy, when the policies used by other inquirers are not independent of the policy choice of the immortal inquirer.

In plain empirical fact, belief in the superiority of any method, belief that any method is identical with "science," does certainly effect the methods and the hypotheses that occur to other people. Thus there is no reason at all to believe in the independence assumption which Reichenbach's argument (in a hidden way) requires. If we did not believe in induction, it is certainly logically possible that other methods would be tried—and logically possible that they would succeed—that will never get tried (and hence never get tested) in the actual world. In short, there is a logically possible world in which (immortal) people use induction and fail to make successful predictions, although those same people *would have made* successful predictions if they had not used induction (using a method which was never tried in that world—never tried *because* induction was persisted in instead). Thus, there is no deductive proof that induction will succeed (even in the long run) provided that successful prediction is possible at all, and no deductive proof that using induction is the dominant strategy.

Finally, a word about the problem to which my own Ph.D. dissertation was devoted, the problem of extending Reichenbach's "justification of induction" (that is, the vindicatory argument) to "the finite case." All of the positive results I have sketched here depend on the availability of unlimited future time; thus it seems clear that even the partial results in the direction Reichenbach wanted that I have been able to obtain in the form of completeness properties for various inductive methods have no analogues in the finite case. (My own attempt, in the dissertation, at a justification for the finite case was invalidated by the discovery of the inconsistency of the Rule of Induction.)

But even if Reichenbach's aim of deductively vindicating induction has turned out to be an unattainable one, the discussion of Reichenbach's argument leads into profound depths. My own present stance is partly like Wittgenstein's. I agree with Wittgenstein that "the 'law of induction' can no more be *grounded* than certain particular propositions concerning the material of experience,"[22] and I further agree that "[the language game] is not based on grounds. It is not reasonable [*vernünftig*] or unreasonable. It is there—like our life." Where I perhaps differ with Wittgenstein is in finding attempts like Reichenbach's of permanent value nonetheless.

Notes

1. *Experience and Prediction* (Chicago: University of Chicago Press, 1938), pp. 346ff.
2. Ibid., p. 342.
3. See Herbert Feigl, "De Principiis Non Disputandum . . . ? On the Meaning and the Limits of Justification," in *Philosophical Analysis,* ed. M. Black (Ithaca: Cornell University Press, 1950), pp. 119–156. In another article ("Some Major Issues and Developments in the Philosophy of Science of Logical Empiricism," in *The Foundations of Science and the Concepts of Psychology and Psychoanalysis,* ed. Herbert Feigl and Michael Scriven, Minnesota Studies in the Philosophy of Science, vol. 1 [Minneapolis: University of Minnesota Press, 1956], pp. 3–37), Feigl writes (p. 29), "In some of my early papers I had been groping for this sort of solution of the problem of induction, and I think I came fairly close to a tenable formulation in the paper of 1934 [Feigl means "The Logical Character of the Principle of Induction," *Philosophy of Science,* (1935), 20–29]. But with genuine ap-

preciation I credit the late Hans Reichenbach with the independent discovery and the more elaborate presentation of this solution."

4. Reichenbach, it should be noted, did not use Feigl's terminology; he speaks of his purported demonstration of the conditional proposition simply as a "justification" of induction.

5. Published by the University of California Press in 1951; see pp. 245–246. Reichenbach employs the same analogy in *Experience and Prediction,* pp. 362–363.

6. Actually, Reichenbach has a problem with *uniqueness.* As he himself points out (*Experience and Prediction,* p. 354), "Now it is easily seen not only that the inductive method will lead to success, but that every method will do the same if it determines as our wager the value $h_n + c_n$ where c_n is a number which is a function of n, or also of h_n, but bound to the condition $\lim c_n = 0$. . . . all such methods must converge asymptotically. The inductive principle is the special case where $c_n = 0$." Reichenbach has two strategies for dealing with this problem; one is to argue that there is less "risk" in choosing the value $c_n = 0$ because "any other value may worsen the convergence" (p. 355); this is clearly fallacious, since the choice of $c_n = 0$ may also "worsen the convergence." The other strategy is to say that (for the immortal inquirer) the choice is "not of great relevance, as all these methods must lead to the same value of the limit if they are sufficiently continued" (p. 356).

7. *Experience and Prediction,* p. 362.

8. One of the few philosophers to devote sustained attention to Reichenbach's argument was Max Black. See his *Language and Philosophy* (Ithaca: Cornell University Press, 1949).

9. See, for example, *Experience and Prediction,* 358.

10. I attempted to meet this objection to Reichenbach's vindication argument in my Ph.D. thesis, published as *The Meaning of the Concept of Probability in Application to Finite Sequences:* (New York: Garland, 1990), in the series Harvard Dissertations in Philosophy, edited by Robert Nozick. For reasons given in the "Introduction Added Some Years Later" to that work, and developed at greater length here, I no longer regard my attempt as successful.

11. It is not necessary because we have learned to live with the fact that a good system may be incomplete, and indeed incompletable, for Gödelian reasons. But this point is not to my purpose here; my point here is that completeness, even when attainable, is no virtue unless the system is *consistent.*

12. "Now let me introduce another predicate less familiar than 'green.' It is the predicate 'grue' and it applies to all things examined before t just in case they are green but to other things just in case they are blue. Then at time t we have, for each evidence statement asserting that a given emerald is green, a parallel evidence statement asserting that that emerald is grue. And

the statements that emerald *a* is grue, that emerald *b* is grue, and so on, will each confirm the general hypothesis that all emeralds are grue." Nelson Goodman, *Fact, Fiction, and Forecast,* 4th ed. (Cambridge: Harvard University Press, 1983), pp. 74–75.

13. Published by the University of California Press, 1940.

14. Here and in what follows, when I speak of "projecting a hypothesis using the Rule of Induction" what I mean is estimating the "reliability" of that hypothesis by using the Rule of Induction applied to an appropriate attribute *C*.

15. Reprinted in my *Philosophical Papers,* vol. 1, *Mathematics, Matter, and Method* (New York: Cambridge University Press, 1975), pp. 270–292.

16. Ibid., pp. 283–284.

17. These are given in the paper cited in n. 15, pp. 279–280.

18. See Peter Kugel, "Induction, Pure and Simple," *Information and Control,* 33 (1977), 276–336; D. Osherson and S. Weinstein, "Identification in the Limit of First Order Structures," *Journal of Philosophical Logic,* 15 (1986), 55–81; D. Osherson and S. Weinstein, "Paradigms of Truth Detection," *Journal of Philosophical Logic,* 18 (1989), 1–42; D. Osherson, M. Stob, and S. Weinstein, *Systems That Learn* (Cambridge: MIT Press, 1986).

19. Partial recursive functions are functions which are computable, but not necessarily defined on all integers. (In general, whether a partial recursive function is defined on a given integer is an unsolvable problem.) Partial recursive functions which *are* defined on all integers are called "general recursive."

20. For the relevance of Gödel's and Church's work on undecidable problems to inductive logic see, in addition to the literature cited in n. 18, my "Trial and Error Predicates and a Solution to a Problem of Mostowski," *Journal of Symbolic Logic,* 30, no. 1 (1965), 49–57; E. M. Gold, "Limiting Recursion," *Journal of Symbolic Logic,* 30, no. 1 (1965), 27–48; the paper cited in n. 15; and my "Reflexive Reflections," *Erkenntnis,* 22 (1985), 143–153.

21. The reason for changing "the next individual" to "future individuals" is that, since we do not require the functions *f* to be total, an effective hypothesis may not in fact predict anything about the character of one or another individual. Also it may take an arbitrarily long time to compute what a hypothesis does predict about a given individual, if it does make a prediction; thus the fact that the user of this method *goes on forever* (i.e., is immortal) is essential.

22. *On Certainty,* §499.

III

The Inheritance of Pragmatism

8. Pragmatism and Moral Objectivity

The papers presented at the conference where this paper was originally read resulted from the happy idea of bringing together philosophers used to dealing with issues of justice, issues about what constitutes flourishing for an individual or for a society, feminist issues and development issues, and also some people who, like Martha Chen, have first-hand knowledge of what those issues mean in the lives of the women and men of developing countries. (Some of us, like Amartya Sen, fell into both of these categories.) This paper, like the others, was and is intended to contribute to the discussion of those issues. If it ended up being more "abstract" than most of the others, that is not because the author got "carried away" by a particular line of abstract thought. Rather, it is because it was my conviction, as well as the conviction of the organizers of the conference, that positions on the "abstract" question of moral objectivity have real world effects. In one of his major works,[1] Jürgen Habermas repeatedly expresses the conviction that Max Weber's conclusion that modern scientific rationality requires us to accept it as a *fact* that there can be no such thing as a rational foundation for an ethical position, and that we are "committed to a polytheism of ultimate values," is both wrong on intellectual grounds and disastrous in its effect on the "life-worlds" of ordinary women and men. Of course no one can tell just how much influence a wrong philosophy has in contributing to such real world effects as the instrumentalization of human beings and the manipulation of their cultures; nevertheless, to show that the justifications which are offered for ethical skepticism at a philosophical level will not stand up to examination, that the foundations of the idea that there is no rationality beyond purely instrumental rationality are in trouble, *may* help to combat that instrumentalization and that manipulation. This was also the conviction of John Dewey, whose philosophy I discuss in the fifth and sixth sections of this paper, throughout his long philosophical life. And it was in that spirit that I decided (and was in fact encouraged) to devote my paper to the "abstract" issue of moral objectivity.[2]

But not *every* defense of moral objectivity is a good thing. We live in an "open society," a society in which the freedom to think for oneself about values, goals, and mores is one that most of us have come to cherish. Arguments for "moral realism" can, and sometimes unfortunately do, sound like arguments against the open society; and while I do wish to undermine moral skepticism, I have no intention of defending either authoritarianism or moral apriorism. It is precisely for this reason that in recent years I have found myself turning to the writings of the American pragmatists.

In my case, turning to American pragmatism does not mean turning to a metaphysical theory. Indeed, the pragmatists were probably wrong in thinking that anyone could provide what they called a "theory of truth," and Peirce was certainly wrong in thinking that truth can be defined as what inquiry would converge to in the long run. What I find attractive in pragmatism is not a systematic theory in the usual sense at all. It is rather a certain group of theses, theses which can be and indeed were argued very differently by different philosophers with different concerns, and which became the basis of the philosophies of Peirce, and above all of James and Dewey. Cursorily summarized, those theses are (1) *antiskepticism:* pragmatists hold that *doubt* requires justification just as much as belief (recall Peirce's famous distinction between "real" and "philosophical" doubt); (2) *fallibilism:* pragmatists hold that there is never a metaphysical guarantee to be had that such-and-such a belief will never need revision (that one can be both fallibilistic *and* antiskeptical is perhaps *the* unique insight of American pragmatism); (3) the thesis that there is no *fundamental* dichotomy between "facts" and "values"; and (4) the thesis that, in a certain sense, practice is primary in philosophy.

The pragmatists did not only have an interesting set of very general theses, however. Contrary to the way James and Dewey in particular are often painted, they all had intricate arguments—arguments which are still not well known among analytic philosophers, and in the present essay I wish both to describe and also to build upon some of those arguments.

If one sees the four theses I listed as the fundamental theses of pragmatism, then one will not be surprised to learn that the several pragmatist arguments for ethical objectivity were related from the beginning to the effort to preserve and perfect the open society, and to preserve what was right in the epistemological critiques of authoritarianism and apriorism that appeared on the scene together with modernity.

"Indispensability Arguments" in Science and in Ethics

As I just remarked, pragmatists believe that, in "a certain sense," practice is primary in philosophy. It is necessary to say a little more about what that means, and doing so will bring us to the first of the arguments I have in mind. In philosophy of science, the most celebrated example of an appeal to practice in the course of a metaphysical argument is due to Quine; I am referring to what I have elsewhere[3] called his "indispensability argument" for the acceptance of the conceptual scheme of set theory. Quine ignores the problem which goes back, in part, to Plato, as to how we can know that abstract entities exist unless we can interact with them in some way. Instead of arguing that we *can* causally interact with abstract entities, as one or two philosophers have,[4] or contending that we have some sort of supercausal or noncausal interaction with abstract entities (perhaps with the aid of the faculty of "reason"), Quine deliberately displaces the discussion to a more humanly accessible region. Quine replaces questions about the "mystery" of interaction with abstract entities with the question "Why do we need the conceptual scheme of sets?"[5] Quine's argument is that the conceptual scheme of set theory is *indispensable* to mathematics, and indeed to physical science[6] as well, and what is indispensable to our best paradigms of knowledge cannot, Quine argues, be criticized from some supposedly "higher" philosophical viewpoint; for there is no "first philosophy" above and outside of science.

To be sure, Quine is in many ways a most atypical pragmatist. Although Morton White has argued early and late[7] that given Quine's own doctrines, in particular Quine's rejection of the "dualism" of analytic and synthetic, Quine *ought* to reject the fact/value dichotomy, Quine has stubbornly refused to "go along" with his old friend White. Indeed, Quine seems to have rejected one dichotomy (the dualism of analytic and synthetic) only to replace it with another (the dualism of science, or rather science as formalized in the notation of symbolic logic, and everything that Quine regards as of only "heuristic" value, including intentional idioms and value idioms). Although these elements of Quine's philosophy are more reminiscent of Viennese positivism than of American pragmatism, *within* the sphere of science Quine does give an account which is strongly influenced by pragmatism. I am thinking not only of the "indispensability argument," but also of Quine's insistence[8] that the scientific method is not an algorithm, but an informal matter of "trade-offs" between such desiderata as preservation of past doctrine, predictive efficacy, and simplicity. This account is strikingly reminiscent of, for example, that of William James.[9]

In any case, the classical pragmatists—Peirce, James, and Dewey—whatever their disagreements, did not hesitate to apply to the topic of values exactly the kind of indispensability argument that Quine applies to the topic of scientific ontology. Just as Quine displaces the traditional worry as to the mystery of our "interaction" (if any) with abstract entities such as sets and numbers, the classical pragmatists displaced the equally ancient worry as to the nature of our "interaction" (if any) with ethical properties and with value properties and normative properties generally. Like Quine, they found it fruitful to replace metaphysical conundrums with the more humanly accessible question "What function does this discourse serve?" According to the pragmatists, normative discourse—talk of right and wrong, good and bad, better and worse—is indispensable in science and in social and personal life as well. Even relativists and subjectivists frequently concede this; we make and cannot escape making value judgments of all kinds in connection with activities of every kind. Nor do we treat these judgments as matters of mere *taste;* we argue about them seriously, we try to *get them right,* and, as philosophers have pointed out for centuries, we use the language of objectivity in our arguments and deliberations—for example, we use the same laws of logic when we reason about an ethical question that we use when we reason about a question in set theory, or in physics, or in history, or in any other area. And, like Quine, the classical pragmatists do not believe that there is a "first philosophy" higher than the practice that we take most seriously when the chips are down. There is no Archimedean point from which we can argue that what is indispensable in life *gilt nicht in der Philosophie.* Here at least, pragmatism rejects *revisionary* metaphysics.[10]

Of course, there is an obvious difference between set theory and ethics: there is a wide body of accepted doctrine in set theory (even if nominalists and intuitionists reject it), and there is a vast amount of

disagreement about values in the modern world. The fact that pragmatists offer indispensability arguments in both areas does not mean
that pragmatism fails to take moral disagreement seriously. For pragmatists like John Dewey, moral disagreement of the kind that we find
in an open society was not a metaphysical problem but a political
problem—a problem and a challenge. The problem is to keep moral
disagreement within the bounds of community and productive cooperation, and the challenge is to make moral disagreement serve as a
stimulus to the kind of criticism of institutions and values that is
needed for progress toward justice and progress in enabling citizens to
live in accordance with their various conceptions of the good life.
Pragmatism anticipated an idea that has become a commonplace in
contemporary moral philosophy,[11] the idea that disagreement in individual conceptions of the good need not make it impossible to approximate (even if we never finally arrive at) agreement on just procedures and even agreement on such abstract and formal values as
respect for one another's autonomy, non-instrumentalization of other
persons,[12] and such regulative ideas as the idea that in all our institutions we should strive to replace relations of hierarchy and dependence by relations of "symmetric reciprocity."[13] Both Ruth Anna Putnam and I have written elsewhere[14] about the ways in which the
classical pragmatists attempt to justify these ideas, and I shall also
speak about this in what follows.

An Important Objection

Before we proceed any further, however, it is necessary to face a very
important objection to the whole idea of "the primacy of practice in
philosophy." The objection is most easily presented in the form of
a parody, a parody of the "indispensability argument." Here is the
parody:

> If we find the belief that p is "indispensable," for any reason, then
> that is all the justification we need for saying that p is true—never
> mind that in our more reflective moments we may realize that p can-
> not possibly *be* true.

The parody carries the accusation that pragmatism does not care
about truth, but cares *only* about "successful practice." A well-known
variant of that accusation is that pragmatism dodges the whole issue
by simply *identifying* truth with successful practice. To see how this

accusation can be rebutted it is useful to look again at Quine's indispensability argument.

The problem that Quine ignored—I said that he "displaced" it—is that (one hears it said) even if there were such things as sets, we could not possibly *know* of their existence (in a variant of the argument,[15] one could not so much as *refer* to them) because (it is said) knowledge (and reference) require causal interaction. Since we do not interact with sets causally, we cannot know anything about them (and we cannot refer to them). While Quine does not explicitly discuss this argument, I think I can guess what he would say. He would say that the premise of the argument is, in fact, the whole argument. And the premise is a "dogma." The philosopher who advances such an argument claims that whatever does not fit a certain paradigm is not knowledge (or not reference) at all. But this claim is not supported by anything one might call evidence; it is simply a metaphysical dogma. If we do not let ourselves be trapped by an appeal to what is "evident to reason," we shall see that we do have evidence of a kind for set theory. Pragmatists do not urge us to ignore sound arguments against what we believe, when such arguments are advanced; they do urge us not to confuse the "intuitions" of metaphysicians with genuine arguments.

It is pretty easy to see, on reflection, that Quine is right about set theory.[16] Philosophical arguments against set theory do depend on some "fishy" metaphysical premises. But can we say the same about the well-known materialist arguments[17] against the very possibility of ethical knowledge? As those arguments were set out by John Mackie, in particular, they are strikingly similar to the arguments against set theory alluded to above. According to Mackie, moral properties would be "ontologically queer." What he meant by this was that they would not fit into the picture of the world provided by modern science; and Mackie assumes not only that the picture of the world provided by modern science is approximately correct (which the pragmatists would not challenge) but that it is approximately *complete* (an assumption that they would challenge). Moreover, even to show that the existence of ethical properties (or of value properties in general) *is* incompatible with the world-view of physics, Mackie needs to employ some pretty substantial premises, not all of which are made explicit. Value properties are, according to Mackie (this is supposed to be a conceptual truth), such that if something has a positive value property, then anyone who fully recognizes that it does is thereby moved to approve of the thing or action in question. They are, in a very strong sense, *action guiding*. But it is part of the world-view of physics (according to Mackie) that one can know that something has a property without feeling either approval or disapproval. (In effect, Mackie seems to read the world-view of *economics* into modern physics.)

Mackie's argument, like the argument against the truth of set theory, rests on a number of metaphysical "intuitions" which look more and more suspicious as one begins to probe them. For example, is it really a *conceptual* truth (that is, a conceptual truth viewed from within moral language) that if I know that an action is good, then I will approve of it? After all, a person may perform a good action, but I may disapprove, because I think the person could have done something much better. It is also no contradiction at all to think that somebody's action is good, and not to approve of a similar action in another case (in particular, not to be moved to perform a similar action myself). This is so both because different cases require different actions and because, as Agnes Heller observes,[18] there are different ways of being good, and another person's way may simply not be my way. (And there is also the rare but unfortunately not nonexistent case of the person who does evil *because* it is evil; such a person knows that he is an enemy of the good, but he does not approve of the good.) But these are not the grounds on which I wish to criticize Mackie's argument.

Let us reformulate Mackie's incautious claim by saying that positive moral properties, if any such really exist, are conceptually required to be such that when one knows that something possesses one of them, then *ceteris paribus* that very knowledge will produce in one feelings of approval, and negative moral properties are conceptually required to be such that when one knows that something possesses them, then *ceteris paribus* that very knowledge will produce in one feelings of disapproval. Mackie's argument (whether or not we modify the premise by inserting *ceteris paribus* clauses as I just have) is that these conceptual requirements show that moral properties (if there be such) are "ontologically queer." But do they really?

It is easy to see that some properties whose existence we do not find at all incompatible with the world-view of physics are, in fact, "action guiding" in somewhat the way Mackie claims moral properties (and value properties generally) are conceptually required to be action guiding. I am thinking in particular of *pain*. The knowledge that something is extremely painful may not keep me from wanting it, or wanting to do it, under special circumstances, but it is certainly true that "other things being equal" the very knowledge that something is painful will lead me to disapprove of it, to recommend against it, and so on. In some sense, this seems to be "conceptually linked" to pain, even if there are no "analytic truths" in the old metaphysical sense in this area. And we don't find this at all "queer." On the positive side—and this example brings us closer to moral properties—consider the property of being *intelligent*. People who are themselves intelligent value their intelligence, other things being equal. If an intelligent person were offered a million dollars provided that he or she agreed to undergo a brain operation which reduces IQ by 60 points, then he or she would have to be seriously disturbed or depressed even to consider saying "yes." Again, we don't find this fact particularly remarkable.

Of course, an unintelligent person might not care about losing or gaining in intelligence; but an unintelligent person does not have a good idea of what intelligence *is*. What makes this example relevant to the moral domain is that an ancient tradition in ethics, the Greek tradition, did in fact think that virtue was in these respects like intelligence; it held that only the virtuous have an adequate idea of what virtue is, and that those who have an adequate idea of what virtue is do not *ceteris paribus* wish to lose their virtue. Perhaps most people do not believe any longer that the Greek tradition was right; but it is not clear that this disbelief is based on some piece of "scientific knowledge" that we have gained in the meantime.[19]

Mackie would have replied that even if it is true, as a matter of empirical fact, that those who are highly intelligent do not (unless they are disturbed or depressed) wish to *lose* their intelligence, still there is no *logical* contradiction in the idea of a highly intelligent (and not mentally disturbed or depressed) person who has an adequate idea of what intelligence is and simply values something *more* than keeping his intelligence. But there is, according to Mackie, a *logical* contradiction in saying that one recognizes that something is good, but one does not approve of it and one would not under any circumstances recommend acting in that way (if the thing in question is an action). The problem with this argument is that it assumes the metaphysical notion of analytic truth. Mackie himself may have been a firm believer in a sharp distinction between conceptual truth and empirical truth (and may have further believed that these are the only sorts of truths there are); but pragmatism was in large part an attack on the analytic/synthetic dichotomy. Once again we see that what was supposed to be a rational argument against the objectivity or cognitivity of ethics turns out to depend on a lot of suspect metaphysical baggage.

Perhaps a better line for a defender of Mackie's position to take today would be to argue that the value of intelligence (to animals possessing it) was originally a purely instrumental value. It may indeed be that, as a result of evolution, intelligence has acquired a quasi-instinctual value for members of our species, or for members who possess it to a high degree, but there is no corresponding story to be told about virtue, and that is why the claim that there are action-guiding virtue properties is, or should be, suspect from a naturalistic point of view. But this argument is extremely "blurry." The story about the process by which intelligence was transformed from an instrumental value to a terminal value[20] is itself speculative, and, moreover, there is no reason to think that a parallel story could not be told in the case of at least some of the basic virtues; indeed, some writers have suggested that one can be told. More important, the supposed fact that intelligence was originally an instrumental value, and that it became a terminal value as a result of evolution, says nothing about whether that process was a rationally laudable process or one that we should rationally criticize and, if possible, try to reverse. Of course, it could be a premise of the argument that I just suggested that the transformation of values from instrumental values into terminal values is merely a "psychological" process, that is, a process which cannot be rationally criticized; if so, then the premisse is as strong as the desired conclusion. If we assume a sharp fact/value as one of our premises, it is not surprising that we can pull out a sharp fact/value dichotomy as our conclusion.

In summary, I have just replied to the charge that pragmatism was anti-intellectual by trying to show that pragmatists do not seek to suppress or downplay genuine intellectual difficulties with any of our beliefs, or with the justifications of any of our actions. What pragmatism does argue is that the criticisms of our beliefs and actions which are associated with various kinds of intellectualistic metaphysics,[21] and with equally intellectualistic skepticism, will not stand up to close scrutiny. This is not something the classical pragmatists asked us to take on faith; on the contrary, every one of them was concerned to carry out a detailed criticism of the better-known metaphysicians of his own time. Pragmatism goes with the criticism of a certain style in metaphysics; but the criticism does not consist in wielding some exclusionary principle to "get rid of metaphysics once and for all." Indeed, as Strawson[22] has reminded us (and as Dewey remarked many years earlier),[23] revisionary metaphysics is not always bad, and we owe many insights, in science and in morals and in politics, to various kinds of revisionary metaphysics. But if revisionary metaphysics is not always bad, neither is it always good. It does spawn more than one intellectual bugaboo; and the criticism of these intellectual bugaboos is a permanent task of the pragmatist philosopher.

So far, then, I have rehearsed a *negative* argument for the objectivity of values: the negative argument is that the belief in the cognitive status of value judgments underlies an enormous amount of our practice (indirectly, perhaps, the whole of our practice), and that metaphysical arguments that say that *notwithstanding* the indispensability of the "realist" stance that we adopt toward value disputes in practice, realism with respect to values cannot *possibly* be right, are themselves unsupported by anything more than a collection of metaphysical dogmas. It is time now to consider more positive arguments.

Instrumental Rationality and Topic-Neutral Norms

I now want to present and discuss an argument to the effect that instrumental rationality would be impossible if there were not topic-neutral norms whose claim to rational acceptability is not derived *simply* from the fact that they help us to achieve particular goals a certain percentage of the time. This argument is an important part of the case for the view that objective values of a kind (though, so far, not *ethical* values) are presupposed by science itself.

First a word on my choice of terminology. I have chosen to speak of "topic-neutral norms" rather than to employ some traditional language, for example, the language of "intrinsic values," for a number of reasons. For one thing, talk of "intrinsic values" is associated in the history of philosophy with many doctrines that pragmatists have always viewed with suspicion. For example, the pragmatists have typically been hostile to the natural law tradition, and especially to the form of that tradition according to which there are norms somehow built into the very structure of reality, norms which "the wise" (as opposed to "the many") have always been able to discern. That tradition is riddled with appeals to "what is agreeable to reason," and pragmatists have always distrusted such appeals unless they are tempered by a healthy dose of fallibilism and experimentalism. Dewey, in particular, loved to point out that the discourse of "natural law," "what is agreeable to reason," and so forth, has provided rationalizations for the interests of privileged groups. Again, talk of "intrinsic values" has sometimes gone with ethical intuitionism, in the style of G. E. Moore, and that is also a tradition that pragmatists distrust. Since I am trying to argue in the spirit of American pragmatism, even if the arguments I am giving are *only* "in the spirit" of American pragmatism (they are not arguments found in the pages of American pragmatists in the form in which I give them, in spite of their obvious debt to the arguments of Peirce, Dewey, and James), I do not wish to use a terminology which presupposes just the sort of metaphysics that pragmatism was instrumental in overthrowing. There are topic-neutral truths, to be sure (the truths of deductive logic are a well-known example), but even topic-neutral truths emerge from experience, or, better, from *practice* (including reflection on that practice), and belong to conceptual schemes which have to show their ability to function in practice (which does not mean that they are "empirical").[24] In the same way, I shall argue, there are topic-neutral norms; but they too emerge from practice and have to show their ability to function in practice, as do all norms and values. The topic-neutral norm I wish to discuss applies to behavior that is directed toward a concrete goal, and applies in circumstances in which it makes sense to think of the alternative actions as having known or fairly well estimated probabilities of reaching the goal. The norm is, moreover, one whose justification *at first blush* seems to be entirely instrumental. It is simply this: *Act so as to maximize the estimated utility.*

This norm is, of course, a famous rule of decision theory; and while there is controversy as to whether it applies in *every* situation (of goal-oriented behavior with known probabilities), there is no question that it applies to the great majority of such cases. In particular, it applies to cases of the kind that Peirce discussed in "The Doctrine of Chances."[25] These are cases in which I must, *on one single occasion,* perform one of two actions, and one of the actions has a high probability of giving me an enormous benefit and the other has a high probability of giving me an enormous loss. In these situations, the rule, of course, directs me to perform the action which is associated with a high probability of an enormous benefit. But why is the justification of this rule not entirely instrumental ("if you follow the rule, you will get an enormous benefit a high percentage of the time")? Note that I say that the justification of the rule is not *entirely* instrumental. Obviously, *part* of its justification is instrumental. Whenever I (or a group to which I owe loyalty) has to engage in a series of repeated wagers (with known probabilities), we can say (or it *looks* as if we can say—Peirce raises an important problem here too) that obeying this norm will yield a better "payoff" in the long run, and in many cases payoff in the long run is exactly what we are interested in. But, as Peirce pointed out, there is a very special problem about the single case. If what I am interested in is *not* success in some long run, but success in one, un-repeatable, single case,[26] I cannot justify performing the action with the higher estimated utility by saying that I know that that action will succeed, because I do *not* know which action will succeed (if I knew which action would succeed, I wouldn't need to talk of probabilities). And if I justify it by saying that I know which action will *probably* succeed, then I am simply saying that I am justified in performing the action which has the higher estimated utility *because it has the higher estimated utility;* for "will probably succeed" is just an imprecise way of saying "has the higher estimated utility." (Indeed, Peirce develops his argument directly in terms of the rule that, in cases where the benefits are as described, one should perform the action with the higher probability of gain, rather than in terms of the notion of esti-mated utility. Peirce's point is that, for a self-interested player who has no long run to look forward to, the justification of *this* rule cannot be "if you follow it in the long run, you will succeed in a large percentage of the cases.")

Nor is the problem restricted to the unrepeatable[27] single case. Peirce points out[28] that when we say that the practice of betting on the action with the higher estimated utility will succeed in a high percentage of the cases in the long run, we had better not mean any given *finite* long run. For if we do, then what we are doing is, again, betting on an unrepeatable single case. If, for example, the entire future experience of the human race is contained within a time period of, say, a million years, then *the statement that the percentage of the time that the rec-ommended strategy (of betting on actions with a high estimated util-ity, or of performing actions whose probability of success is high) will succeed will not, in this one single run of cases, be improbably far below its expected value* is itself a statement about a single case. And what was just said about the justification of betting that the action with the higher estimated utility will probably succeed in a single case applies here too. Knowing the *probability* with which a policy will succeed in one particular unrepeatable finite "long run" is not the same as knowing the percentage of the time (that is, the *frequency*) with which the policy will succeed in that one finite period of time; it is only knowing the *expected value* of that percentage. To bet that the actual value of that percentage will be close to the expected value is precisely to rely on the norm whose justification we are considering.

In *The Many Faces of Realism*, I said[29] that I found Peirce's own solution to the problem he raised to be unbelievable. Peirce believed that there was no problem about the *infinitely* long run, because he accepted the frequency theory of probability, according to which the probability just *is* the limit of the relative frequency in the infinite long run; he dealt with the problem of the single case (which is also the problem of any given finite "long run") by arguing that the purpose of a rational person, in any action, should be not to benefit himself, but to act in accordance with the policy that would benefit all rational beings in the infinitely long run. A person who is not interested in the welfare of all rational beings in the infinitely long run is, according to Peirce, "illogical in all his inferences."[30] Even if I am facing a situation in which the alternatives are "eternal felicity" and "everlasting woe," on Peirce's view my belief that I, in this one unrepeatable situation, am somehow more rational if I perform the action that will probably lead to felicity than if I perform the action that will probably lead to everlasting woe is fundamentally just a fictitious transfer[31] of a property which has to do only with what happens in the infinitely long run to a single case. What is true, and not fiction or projection, however, is that my fellows, the members of the ongoing community of inquirers with which I identify myself, will have eternal felicity 24 times out of 25 (or whatever),[32] if they follow the recommended strategy; or, more generally, it is true that even if this one particular situation is never repeated, if in all the various uncorrelated cases of this kind or of any other kind that they find themselves in, they always perform the action with the higher estimated utility, then in the infinitely long run they will experience more gains and fewer losses. But, as I asked in *The Many Faces of Realism*, is it really true that the reason that I would make the choice that is likely to give me eternal felicity and not everlasting woe is that I am *altruistic?*

Peirce's argument is that I ought to choose the arrangement that will give me eternal felicity for what one might describe as "rule-utilitarian" reasons: in choosing this arrangement I am supporting and helping to maintain a norm which will benefit the community of rational investigators *in the infinitely long run*. But is this really what is in my mind when what I am facing is *torture?* Obviously, it isn't. What

Peirce himself attempts is to give a completely *instrumental* justification for the norm. In order to push through his instrumental justification, not only does he need an incorrect theory of probability (very few students of the subject would today subscribe to the claim that probability can be *defined* as the limit of a relative frequency in the infinitely long run); but he also needs two further dubious assumptions: (1) the assumption that the motive for all of my actions, insofar as they are rational, is entirely altruistic; and (2) the assumption that there will be rational investigators in the indefinitely far future, that is, that the community of rational investigators is literally immortal. But even if Peirce failed to provide a satisfactory solution to his own problem, it remains the case that he was the philosopher who called our attention to its importance and its *depth*.

It is just because the problem Peirce raised is so deep that I want to examine it again, and to go further than I did when I discussed it in the closing pages of *The Many Faces of Realism*. In those pages, I discussed only the part of Peirce's argument that refers to extreme choices in unrepeatable situations. I did not discuss Peirce's claim that the problem of relying on knowledge of probabilities to guide our actions in the finite long run poses the same problem; and, indeed, I think that there are objections to this claim of Peirce's. One possible objection is this: while we can easily imagine that in any ordinary "single case" an improbable event happens, imagining that improbable events happen "across the board" for a very long time (a million years) may, in fact, go beyond what is conceivable. Can we really make sense of the notion that *almost all* events might be improbable "flukes" for the next million years?[33] I won't try to decide this question here, but even if we assume, for the sake of Peirce's argument, that the answer is "yes," there is still a further objection. For one might plausibly claim that the fact is that we firmly believe that this will not happen; that is, we don't just think it is *improbable* that the whole statistical pattern of events in the next million years (or even in the next ten years) will be a "fluke"; perhaps we find it *inconceivable* that in a run that long, the frequency *won't* be near its expected value. (When the time period is large enough, it may be that the very notion of "probability" crumbles if we assume that all or most of the statistics we encounter are "flukes.") But, if that is so, relying on the norm of expecting what is probable to happen, and on the norm of performing the action with the higher estimated utility, does have an *instrumental* justification when our interests really are in success in the *very* long run, and not in success in some small number of unrepeatable cases, or even in one moderately long series of cases. But—and this speaks in Peirce's favor—even if this is true, the problem of the single case is still worse than it looks at first. The problem does not arise only in cases which are literally unrepeatable.

To see this, consider any case whatsoever—and such cases are familiar enough—in which I am tempted to perform an action whose success is "against the odds." Let us say that I have a strong "hunch" that I am going to be lucky, so strong that I am tempted to stake my life's savings or my family's savings on it. I may perfectly well agree that if everyone followed the policy of relying on such hunches, then in the long run this would cause an enormous amount of suffering; but I am not recommending that other people follow that policy in the future. I do not even intend to follow that policy myself in the future; I only intend to follow it in this single case, let us assume.

It may be true that if I follow this policy in this single case, then I am bound to follow the same policy in the future, and that even if my hunch is correct this time, sooner or later "the odds will catch up with me." But it could be that I know myself well enough to say truthfully, "I am going to gamble just this once; win or lose, I am not going to risk going against the odds again." If that is my fixed intention, then even if I know that I *would* lose money if I made this "gamble" many times in the future, or that other people would lose money if they made such gambles many times in the future, that knowledge is *relevant* to the question "Will this risky gamble achieve my goal?" *only on the assumption that probability is relevant to single actions,* that is to say, only if the topic-neutral norm is in place.

Some theorists would, no doubt, try to get around the whole problem in the following way: They would argue that deciding what to do can be broken into two steps, namely, the fixation of belief and the choice of an action. With respect to the first, the fixation of belief, it might be said that the operative norm is simply a norm of rationality: a rational man, it is said, proportions his *subjective degrees of belief* (his "subjective probabilities") to the relevant objective statistical probabilities when those are known or assumed, which is the case that Peirce is discussing. (Note that Peirce is *not* discussing "the problem of induction," that is to say, the problem of whether we *can* know the objective statistical probabilities when those relate to future events). In the Peirce thought experiment, the agent knows that the *objective* probability that he will achieve "eternal felicity" and avoid "everlasting woe" if he follows the recommended policy is 24/25ths. If he is rational, he will therefore proportion his subjective degree of belief in the proposition "I shall obtain eternal felicity if I follow the recommended policy" to this objective probability; that is, he will *almost believe* that if he performs the recommended action (choosing a certain deck of cards) he will gain eternal felicity. He does not absolutely believe that he will obtain eternal felicity if he performs the action, but he believes it to the very high degree 24/25ths. Given that he believes (almost) that if he performs the action he will be successful, he would be irrational *not* to perform the action. In this way, performing the action is instrumentally justified.

In fact, however, this justification is not a completely instrumental justification. It is not, because it assumes a norm of rationality which is itself not instrumentally justified: the norm that one should "proportion one's subjective degrees of belief to the objective statistical probabilities when they are known." That norm, like the norm that one should perform the action with the higher estimated utility, has a partial instrumental justification; in situations in which what we are interested in really is long-run success, then one can argue that conforming to the norm will achieve the goal. (However, to argue so, as we observed above, we must assume that in that particular "long run" frequencies will be close to their expected values, an assumption which—Peirce would say—presupposes the very norm we are "justifying"). But in any case, to say that it is "rational" to conform to the norm even when what we are interested in is not success in the very long run, is just another way of saying that one *ought* to conform to that norm in those situations, and this, for reasons just rehearsed, is a belief which cannot be instrumentally justified.

At this point, if I am not mistaken, two objections to what I have been maintaining will occur to various of my readers, though probably not to the *same* readers. The first objection, which I shall call "the naturalism objection," runs as follows: "The norms you describe, like all norms, have evolved because they have a high of degree of long-run utility, to communities if not always to individuals. (When I use the word 'evolved' in stating the objection, philosophers who are prone to sociobiological speculation may even think that Darwinian evolution is involved here; however that may be, social evolution is certainly involved.) But if we can understand perfectly well what the origin of these norms is, and what the origin is of the compulsion that each of us feels to conform to them, even when we don't know that that conformity will in fact bring us success in any particular individual case, then what's the problem?"

The objection is serious because it rests on an assumption which is undeniably correct; to say, as I have, that the norms cannot be *completely* justified instrumentally is not to deny that they do have long-run instrumental value to communities. And the pragmatists certainly believed that the metaphor of "evolution" is an appropriate one, in cases like these. The pragmatists also believed—and here I am thinking more of James and Dewey than of Peirce, perhaps—that one must take the agent point of view seriously, and not look at everything from the third-person descriptive point of view. It is quite true that from a third-person descriptive point of view there is no difficulty in understanding the origin of topic-neutral norms like the ones I have been describing; that is, there is no difficulty in understanding the existence of such norms *as a mere psychological fact.* But if I as an agent put to myself the question *What should I do?* in a situation of the kind we have been discussing, then the knowledge that I feel some compulsion to act one way, as a psychological fact about myself, does not answer my question. Indeed, if I also have a strong compulsion to "be irrational for once," to act on a "hunch," I may also be able to find some naturalistic explanation of the existence of *that* compulsion. Each compulsion is a brute fact; that I have both compulsions doesn't tell me what to do. The factual descriptive questions are certainly legitimate questions. But *so are the normative first-person questions.*

Here is the second of the objections that I mentioned: "Your question is really just why it is rational to do certain things, to act in accordance with probabilities (or, more precisely, estimated utilities), or to proportion one's subjective degrees of belief to probabilities. But it is just a *tautology* that these are rational things to do. To be 'rational' is just to obey certain rules, for example, the rules of deductive logic and the rules of rational betting. So what's your problem?"

One problem (a decisive one) with this objection is that to say that something is rational is not *merely* to describe it as in accordance with some algorithm or quasi-algorithm or other.[34] If I say that believing something or acting in a certain way is rational, then, other things being equal, I am *recommending* that belief or that course of action. To say that it is rational to bet in accordance with the probabilities (more precisely, the estimated utilities) is to say that, other things being equal, one *ought* to bet in accordance with the probabilities (the estimated utilities). In short, the fact that something is rational is *pre-*

cisely the sort of fact that Mackie regarded as "ontologically queer"; it is an *ought-implying fact.*

Instead of creating spurious philosophical problems for ourselves by insisting that the causal-descriptive world-view *must* be "complete," in a sense which is never satisfactorily defined,[35] the pragmatists urged that the agent point of view, the first-person normative point of view, and the concepts indispensable to that point of view should be taken just as seriously as the concepts indispensable to the third-person descriptive point of view.

In closing this part of my argument, I want to compare once more the conclusion I have reached with the conclusion Peirce reached. What our arguments have in common—and, of course, mine is built out of the very materials Peirce provided—is that we both agree that the norm of acting in accordance with the probabilities or estimated utilities cannot be justified instrumentally if the only goals considered are the goals of the agent himself. Peirce concludes that all rational goal-directed activity must be altruistic and personally disinterested, a conclusion that fits well with his own moral outlook, which tended to stress the "Buddhistic"[36] virtues of self-abnegation and freedom from personal interest. As I have said, I cannot go along with this conclusion; we are, after all, talking about *goal-oriented activity,* and in the case of goal-oriented activity our aims are usually not disinterested. The conclusion I draw from Peirce's problem is, rather, that even when I seek to attain a goal (in a situation in which risk is involved either way), the rational decision as to what I must do to attain my practical goal depends upon my acknowledging the binding force of norms which do not possess a satisfactory instrumental justification in terms of my own goals. This conclusion is not incompatible with Peirce's; but it is not as metaphysically daring as Peirce's.

Finally, to the inevitable question "How would I justify norms like the one we have been considering, if a complete instrumental justification cannot be given?" I would reply that the alternative to instrumental justification here is not transcendent knowledge but *reflection.* Norms like the estimated utility rule were discovered not by mere trial and error, but by *normative reflection on our practice.* Kant was right in urging us to realize that reflection on the possibility of gaining knowledge from experience is itself a source of knowledge, even if he was wrong in considering such reflection to be an infallible source (when properly conducted). Kant was further right in supposing that we must reflect not only on the presuppositions of learning from experience, but also on the presuppositions of acting in the ways in which we do act. Most puzzles about the very "possibility" of normative knowledge spring from a too narrowly empiricistic picture of how knowledge is gained and how actions are justified.

"Oughts" and Belief Fixation in Pure Science

I have described the facts that certain actions and beliefs are rational as "ought-implying facts"; by including *beliefs* here I mean to indicate that this allegedly "ontologically queer" phenomenon is one that appears not only in the context of goal-oriented activity, and in the context of moral activity, but also in the context of "pure" scientific activity. In *Reason, Truth, and History,*[37] I described some of the terms we use in appraising scientific theories, for example, the terms "simple," "elegant," and "well confirmed," as having just this character; for to describe a theory as simple, elegant, or well confirmed is to say that, other things being equal, we *ought* to accept the theory or at least consider it seriously. Although these ought-implying characteristics are not *ethical* characteristics, they share many of the properties of the so-called[38] thick ethical characteristics. Just as no nonethical term seems to have exactly the same descriptive range as the term "cruel," so no non-normative term applied to theories seems to have exactly the same descriptive range as the term "confirmed."

It might be claimed, however, that, even though there are "oughts" connected with rational belief and rational action, these "oughts" (at least in the case of rational *belief*) are of quite a different *kind* from the "oughts" that we encounter in connection with justice and in connection with morality. As far as I know, only one reason is ever given for suggesting that the ontological status of pure cognitive values is completely different from the ontological status of normative values, and that is, once again, that it is thought that at least the sorts of cognitive values I just mentioned—elegance, simplicity, predictive power, the conservation of past doctrine, and so on—are justified purely instrumentally (relative to truth as the goal of inquiry), and that the "oughts" connected with them are thus purely hypothetical "oughts." To say that one ought to consider seriously theories which have striking predictive power or simplicity is, on this view, just to say that *if you follow the policy of taking theories with these virtues seriously, in the long run you will arrive at a higher percentage of true or approximately true theories.* (Roderick Firth devoted his presidential address to the Eastern Division of the American Philosophical Association[39] to criticizing this view.)

We can see that it is not the case that we believe we ought to accept justified theories in each single individual case *only* because we believe that doing so leads to the acceptance of a higher percentage of truths "in the long run"; for if that were the complete justification for our reliance on these cognitive norms, then we would run into exactly the "problem of the single case" that we ran into in connection with choosing an action. There are "ought-implying facts" in the realm of belief fixation; and that is an excellent reason not to accept the view that there cannot be "ought-implying facts" anywhere. If the *sole* reason the opponents of moral objectivity (or "moral realism") have for believing that "there cannot be 'ought-implying facts' in ethics" is that "such facts cannot exist anywhere," then they had better rethink.

But What Does Any of This Have to Do with Ethics?

Perhaps the most detailed case for the view just defended, the view that all inquiry, including inquiry in pure science, itself presupposes values, is made by Dewey, in his *Logic*. Ruth Anna Putnam and I have analyzed Dewey's argument elsewhere;[40] here, I want only to discuss one aspect of Dewey's view, the insistence on a very substantial overlap between our cognitive values and our ethical and moral values.

I have already examined the claim that there is a fundamental *ontological* difference between cognitive or "scientific" values and ethical values, and found that the reasons offered for believing that claim fail. But even apart from the "ontological" question, a view like Dewey's will not be intelligible if one starts with what I may call a Carnapian view of the scientific method. For this reason, I need to say a few words about the differences between the way in which a philosopher like John Dewey viewed the scientific method and the way in which a philosopher like Rudolf Carnap did. First of all, it is noteworthy that in Carnap's great work on inductive logic,[41] the work to which he devoted almost all his energy in the last two decades of his life, there is virtually no reference to *experiment*—the word does not even occur as an entry in the index to *The Logical Foundations of Probability*. Scientific theories are confirmed by "evidence" in Carnap's systems of inductive logic, but it is immaterial (that is to say, there is no way to represent the difference in the formalism) whether that evidence—

those "observation sentences"—is obtained as the result of intelligently directed experimentation, or whether it just happens to be available. Passive observation and active intervention are not distinguished, and the question whether one has actually tried to *falsify* the hypotheses that have been "highly confirmed" is not a question which can asked or answered *in* the languages Carnap constructed. Even more important, for our purposes, is the fact that the term that Carnap used to characterize his own stance in *Logische Aufbau der Welt,* the term "methodological solipsism," could also be applied, though in a different sense, to this later philosophical work of Carnap's. For just as it makes no difference from the point of view of Carnapian inductive logic whether our observation is passive or active, whether we just look or whether we intervene, it also makes no difference whether observation is *cooperative* or not. Fundamentally, the standpoint is that of a single isolated spectator who makes observations through a "one-way mirror" and writes down observation sentences. Appraising theories for their cognitive virtues is, on this picture, simply a matter of using an algorithm to determine whether a sentence has a mathematical relation to another sentence (the conjunction of the observation sentences the observer has written down). The scientific method is reconstructed as a method of *computation,* computation of a function like Carnap's famous "c*."[42]

Dewey's picture is totally different. For Dewey, inquiry is cooperative human interaction with an environment; and both aspects, the active intervention, the active manipulation of the environment, and the cooperation with other human beings, are vital. The first aspect, the aspect of intervention, is connected with pragmatist fallibilism. Of course, Carnap was also a fallibilist, in the sense of recognizing that future observation might disconfirm a theory which is today very well confirmed; but for the pragmatists this was not fallibilism enough. Before Karl Popper was even born, Peirce emphasized that[43] very often ideas will not be falsified unless we go out and actively *seek* falsifying experiences. Ideas must be put under strain, if they are to prove their worth; and Dewey and James both followed Peirce in this respect. In what follows, however, I want to focus on the other aspect of Dewey's thought, that is, the conception of scientific inquiry as a form of cooperation.

For the positivists—for example, for both Carnap and Reichenbach—the most primitive form of scientific inquiry, and the form that they studied first when they constructed their (otherwise very different) theories of induction, was induction by simple enumeration. The model is always a single scientist who determines the colors of the balls drawn successively from an urn, and tries to estimate the frequencies with which those colors occur among the balls remaining in the urn. For Dewey, the model is a *group* of inquirers trying to produce good ideas and trying to test them to see which ones have value.

One more point must be mentioned at the very outset of any discussion, however brief, of Dewey's conception of inquiry: the model of an *algorithm,* like a computer program, is rejected. According to the pragmatists, whether the subject be science or ethics, what we have are maxims and not algorithms; and maxims themselves require contextual interpretation. Furthermore, the problem of subjectivity and intersubjectivity was in the minds of the pragmatists from the beginning. They insisted[44] that when one human being in isolation tries to interpret even the best maxims for himself and does not allow others to criticize the way in which he or she interprets those maxims, or the way in which he or she applies them, then the kind of "certainty" that results is always fatally tainted with subjectivity. Even the notion of "truth" makes no sense in such a "moral solitude" for "truth presupposes a standard external to the thinker."[45] Notions such as "simplicity," for example, have no clear meaning at all unless inquirers who have proven their competence in the practice of inquiry are able to agree, to some extent at least, on which theories do and which theories do not possess "simplicity." The introduction of new ideas for testing likewise depends on cooperation, for any human being who rejects inputs from other human beings runs out of ideas sooner rather than later, and begins to consider only ideas which in one way or another reflect the prejudices he has formed. Cooperation is necessary both for the formation of ideas and for their rational testing.

But—and this is the crucial point—that cooperation must be of a certain kind in order to be effective. It must, for example, obey the principles of "discourse ethics."[46] Where there is no opportunity to challenge accepted hypotheses by criticizing the evidence upon which their acceptance was based, or by criticizing the application of the norms of scientific inquiry to that evidence, or by offering rival hypotheses, and where questions and suggestions are systematically ignored, the scientific enterprise always suffers. When relations among scientists become relations of hierarchy and dependence, or when scientists instrumentalize other scientists, again the scientific enterprise suffers.[47] Dewey was not naive. He was aware that there are "power plays" in the history of science as there are in the history of every human institution. He would not have been surprised by the findings of historians and sociologists of science; but he differs from them (or from some of our contemporary ones) in holding that it makes sense to have a *normative* notion of science.

Moreover, it is not just that, on Dewey's conception, good science requires respect for autonomy, symmetric reciprocity, and discourse ethics—that could be true even if scientific theories and hypotheses were, in the end, to be tested by the application of an algorithm, such as the inductive logic for which Carnap hoped—but that, as already observed, the very *interpretation* of the *non*-algorithmic standards by which scientific hypotheses are judged depends on cooperation and discussion structured by the same norms. Both for its full development and for its full application to human problems, science requires the *democratization of inquiry.*

What I have just offered is, in part, an *instrumental* justification of the democratization of inquiry. But Dewey opposes the philosophers' habit of dichotomization. In particular, he opposes both the dichotomy "pure science/applied science" and the dichotomy "instrumental value/terminal value." Pure science and applied science are interdependent and interpenetrating activities, Dewey argues.[48] And similarly, instrumental values and terminal values are interdependent and interpenetrating. Science helps us to achieve many goals other than the attainment of knowledge for its own sake, and when we allow inquiry to be democratized simply because doing so helps us achieve those practical goals, we are engaged in goal-oriented activity. At the same time, as we saw above, *even when we are engaged in goal-oriented activity* we also are guided by norms of rationality which have become terminal values for us, and which cannot be separated from the modern conception of "rationality" itself. Moreover, we are not—nor were we ever—interested in knowledge *only* for its practical benefits; curiosity is coeval with the species itself, and pure knowledge is always, to some extent, and in some areas, a terminal value even for the least curious among us. And just as the norm I discussed in connection with Peirce's problem has become inseparable from the modern conception of "rationality," so the norms Dewey discusses have become inseparable from the modern conception of proceeding "scientifically," inseparable, that is, from our *normative* conception of what it is to be scientifically rational. It is not, *for us*, any longer just a sociological-descriptive fact that choosing theories for their predictive power and simplicity, and fostering democratic cooperation and openness to criticism in the generation and evaluation of theories, are part of the nature of scientific inquiry; these norms describe the way we *ought* to function when the aim is knowledge. Saying this is not the same as saying that inquiry which follows these norms produces knowledge in the way fire produces warmth; we are not dealing with mere empirical correlation here. Nor is it "analytic" that inquiry which does *not* meet these standards does *not* produce justification and knowledge; "knowledge" and "justification" are not the sorts of words that can be analytically defined once and for all. Concepts of knowledge are essentially contested concepts; they are always open to reform. What we can say is that the applicability of our present conception to practice is constantly being tested (it is not *a priori* that, for example, the concept of "probability" can be successfully used in practice) *and* that that conception itself is partly constituted by norms which represents values which are now terminal but not immune to criticism. And this "messy" state of affairs is one that, I would say, Dewey wanted us to see as typical.

Was Dewey Trying to Derive Ethics from the Logic of Science?

But it would be a mistake to see Dewey's project in the *Logic* as "deriving an ethic from science" (or from the theory of inquiry). What Dewey's argument does show is that there is a certain overlap between scientific values and ethical values; but even where they overlap, these values remain different. Scientific values are not simply instrumental (the relation between the "means"—scientific justification—and the "goal"—knowledge—is too "internal" for that story to work), but they are relativized to a context—the context of knowledge acquisition—and knowledge acquisition itself is something that can be criticized ethically.[49] Yet there *was* a close connection between inquiry and ethics, in Dewey's view, for more than one reason.

First, all cooperative activity involves a moment of inquiry, if only in the ongoing perception that the activity is going smoothly/not going smoothly. What is essential to the rational—or, to use the word that Dewey preferred, the *intelligent*—conduct of inquiry is thus, to some extent, essential to *the intelligent conduct of all cooperative activity*. Perceiving this can help us understand why, as the modern conception of rationality gains the upper hand, one sees an insistence on extending democratization to more and more institutions and relationships.

Second, *ethics* itself requires inquiry. Experiencing ourselves as ethical fallibilists, as persons who do not inherit values which cannot be questioned, as persons who *have,* in fact, criticized many inherited values (even if we have not all criticized the *same* inherited values), we more and more see ethical disputes as disputes to be settled, if possible, by intelligent argument and inquiry, and not by appeals to authority or to *a priori* principles. Now nothing Dewey wrote, and nothing James wrote, or Peirce wrote, can *prove* that there are objective ethical norms, ideals, rules of thumb, or even situation-specific values; but—and here I state the argument in a more "Kantian" way than Dewey himself would—*if* there are ethical facts to be discovered, *then* we ought to apply to ethical inquiry just the rules we have learned to apply to inquiry in general. *For what applies to inquiry in general applies to ethical inquiry in particular.*

If this is right, then an ethical community—a community which *wants* to know what is right and good—*should* organize itself in accordance with democratic standards and ideals, not only because they are good in themselves (and they are), but *because they are the prerequisites for the application of intelligence to the inquiry.* It is true that some inquiries can be conducted with only partial democratization; a tyrant, for example, may allow his physicists a freedom of discussion (in certain areas) that is generally forbidden in the society. But—and this is an empirical presupposition of Dewey's argument—any society that limits democracy, that organizes itself hierarchically, thereby limits the rationality of those at both ends of the hierarchy. Hierarchy stunts the intellectual growth of the oppressed, and forces the privileged to construct rationalizations to justify their position.[50] But this is to say that hierarchical societies do not, in these respects, produce solutions to value disputes that are rationally acceptable.

At this point it may look as if Dewey is "pulling himself up by his bootstraps." For even if we assume that inquiry into values should be democratized, that the participants should, *qua* seekers after the right and the good, respect free speech and the other norms of discourse ethics, not instrumentalize one another, and so on, what *criteria* should they use to tell that their inquiry has succeeded?[51]

This objection overlooks another feature of the pragmatist position; we do not, in fact, start from the position of "doubting everything." As long as discussion is still possible, as long as one is not facing coercion or violence or total refusal to discuss, the participants in an actual discussion always share a large number of both factual assumptions and value assumptions that are not in question in the specific dispute. Very often, parties to a disagreement can agree that the disagreement has, in fact, been resolved, not by appeal to a universal set of "criteria," but by appeal to values which are not in question in *that* dispute. (Recall again Peirce's distinction—which all the pragmatists accepted—between real and "philosophic" doubt.) It may, of course, happen that the criteria accepted by even one of the participants are in conflict with themselves; but in that case, rational reconstruction is called for. Pragmatism is not against rational reconstruction; but it sees rational reconstruction as one among other tools to be used in resolving problems, not as a route to a set of universal principles applicable to all situations.

Moreover, Dewey stressed[52] that one does not always need a set of *criteria* to tell that a problem has been resolved. We have all had the experience of discovering that the satisfactory resolution to a problem in our own lives was one that would not have counted as satisfactory by any of the "criteria" we had in mind at the beginning of our search for a solution. (A corollary to this is that when we *have* solved a collective or an individual problem we may not, at the end, know whether it was an "ethical" problem or some other kind of problem that we solved; and is that a bad thing?) And finally, believing that ethical objectivity is possible is not the same thing as believing that there are no undecidable cases or no problems which, alas, cannot be solved. The point is that once we give up the metaphysical claim that *there cannot be* such a thing as ethical objectivity, and once we observe that objectivity in other areas is strongly connected with values, we can begin to see not just that ethical objectivity might be possible, but, more important, that investigating ethical problems requires just the values that have come to be linked with the open society.

In closing, I want to say just a word about my reasons for writing this paper. Besides my long-standing interest in the problem of moral objectivity there was, as I indicated, another reason: to combat the idea that there is no intellectual structure worth taking seriously to the arguments of the American pragmatists. I have laid out some of that structure here in my own way, and without a lot of scholarly apparatus, because my interest was in the living relevance of what American pragmatism bequeathed to us, and that is something one can only explain in one's own words, because they are the only words one can take full responsibility for.

In particular, I hope to have shown that the appeal to the primacy of practice (for example, the "indispensability arguments") in pragmatism is always accompanied by critique of those metaphysical criticisms of practice that make it look "irresponsible" to take practice as seriously as pragmatists do.[53] I have tried to give some sense of the range, the complexity, and the depth of the investigations of the pragmatists into such questions as the value presuppositions of goal-oriented activity and pure science, and the overlap (though never the identity) between science and ethics. If this leads other students of these questions to take the pragmatists seriously, I shall feel this all too brief account of some of their thought was well worth the effort it took me to present it.

Notes

The Conference on Human Capabilities (for which this paper was written) took place in Helsinki at the World Institute for Development Economic Research on August 15–22, 1991.

1. See Jürgen Habermas, *The Theory of Communicative Action,* T. McCarthy translation (Boston: Beacon Press, 1984).

2. I have chosen to speak of "moral objectivity" rather than to use the currently fashionable term "moral realism" because "realism" is entangled in so many metaphysical and language-philosophical disputes at this time. Of course, talk of "objectivity" is also open to metaphysical construals of various kinds; when I speak of objectivity here and in what follows, what is at stake is "objectivity humanly speaking," the objectivity of what is objective from the point of view of our best and most reflective practice.

3. See my "Philosophy of Logic," reprinted as the final chapter in the second edition of *Mathematics, Matter, and Method* (New York: Cambridge University Press, 1979).

4. This view has been defended in a series of papers by Penelope Maddy.

5. Quine identifies all the abstract entities needed in science, including numbers, with sets.

6. This has been challenged by Hartry Field in his *Science without Numbers* (Oxford: Oxford University Press, 1980) and elsewhere. Field's controversial arguments, even if we concede that they are correct as far as they go, do not apply at all to modern quantum mechanics (for reasons unconnected with the "measurement problem," by the way), and thus do not really show that physics *can* dispense with quantification over numbers and sets, however.

7. In *Towards Reunion in Philosophy* (Cambridge: Harvard University Press, 1956) and in "Normative Ethics, Normative Epistemology, and Quine's

Holism" in *The Philosophy of W. V. Quine,* ed. L. E. Hahn and P. A. Schilpp (La Salle, Ill.: Open Court, 1986), pp. 649–662.

8. See "Two Dogmas of Empiricism" in Quine's *From a Logical Point of View* (Cambridge: Harvard University Press, 1953).

9. In *Pragmatism,* James repeatedly mentions usefulness for prediction and control of experience ("extraordinary fertility in consequences verifiable by sense," p. 91), conservation of past doctrine ("we keep unaltered as much of our old knowledge, as many of our old prejudices and beliefs, as we can," p. 83; "A new belief counts as 'true' just in proportion as it gratifies the individual's desire to assimilate the novel in his experience to his beliefs in stock," p. 36), and simplicity ("what fits every part of life best and combines with the collectivity of experience's demands, nothing being omitted," p. 44). That success in satisfying these desiderata simultaneously is a matter of trade-offs rather than formal rules is also a Jamesian idea: "Success in solving this problem is eminently a matter of approximation. We say that this theory satisfies it on the whole more satisfactorily that that theory; but that means more satisfactorily to our selves, and individuals will emphasize their points of satisfaction differently. To a certain degree, therefore, everything here is plastic," p. 35. All quotations are from *Pragmatism and the Meaning of Truth* (Cambridge: Harvard University Press, 1978).

10. For the distinction between "revisionary metaphysics" and "descriptive metaphysics" see P. F. Strawson's *Individuals* (London: Methuen, 1959).

11. See, for example, the works of John Rawls, Agnes Heller, and Jürgen Habermas.

12. Although I describe this as a "formal value," Agnes Heller, in *A Philosophy of Morals* (Oxford: Basil Blackwell, 1990), derives a number of quite substantive "rules of thumb" from the idea of non-instrumentalization.

13. This is one of Heller's "rules of thumb" that I referred to in n. 12.

14. See my "A Reconsideration of Deweyan Democracy," *The Southern California Law Review,* 63 (1991), 1671–1697; Chapter 10 of the present volume; and "William James's Ideas" (with Ruth Anna Putnam), reprinted in my *Realism with a Human Face* (Cambridge: Harvard University Press, 1990).

15. This variant is due to Paul Benacerraf; see his "What Numbers Could Not Be," reprinted in *Philosophy of Mathematics: Selected Readings,* ed. Paul Benacerraf and Hilary Putnam (Englewood Cliffs, N.J.: Prentice-Hall, 1964), pp. 272–294.

16. I ignore here a difference between Quine's position and my own; my own view is that we should speak not of evidence for the *truth* of set theory, but rather of evidence for the *applicability* of the concepts of set theory in practice. I argue in Chapter 12 of the present volume that the *falsity* of set theory or arithmetic (apart from the possibility of its turning out to be inconsistent, omega inconsistent, or something of that kind) is not something

that has any clear present *content*. But discussing this difference between my position and Quine's would lead us away from the present topic.

17. See John Mackie, *Ethics: Inventing Right and Wrong* (New York: Penguin, 1977), and Bernard Williams, *Ethics and the Limits of Philosophy* (Cambridge: Harvard University Press, 1985).

18. Heller, *A Philosophy of Morals,* pp. 28ff.

19. The claim that the person who does not engage in the *practice* of virtue cannot have a fully adequate idea of what virtue is may seem queer to many contemporary sensibilities, but the similar-sounding claim that the person who does not engage in musical practice cannot have a fully adequate idea of what great music is does not sound so queer. In fact, something like this view has been defended in a well-known series of papers by John McDowell.

20. The terminology of "instrumental" and "terminal" values, and the idea that the line between these two constantly shifts in the course of inquiry, are both John Dewey's, of course.

21. The pejorative notion of *intellectualistic* metaphysics is one I take from William James, who employed it early and late.

22. Strawson, *Individuals.*

23. For example, in *Reconstruction in Philosophy* (reprinted by Beacon Press, Boston, in 1948) and in *Ethics* (with James Hayden Tufts), reprinted as vol. 5 of *John Dewey: The Middle Works, 1899–1924,* ed. Jo Ann Boydston (Carbondale: Southern Illinois University Press, 1978).

24. For the reasons why it is a mistake to identify a scheme's showing its ability to function in practice with its being "empirical" see "It Ain't Necessarily So," in my *Mathematics, Matter, and Method, Philosophical Papers,* vol. 1, "Language and Philosophy," in my *Mind, Language, and Reality, Philosophical Papers,* vol. 2 (both volumes published by Cambridge University Press, 1975), and Chapter 12 of this volume.

25. Reprinted in *Collected Papers of Charles Sanders Peirce,* vol. 2, ed. C. Hartshorne and P. Weiss (Cambridge: Harvard University Press, 1931), pp. 389–414.

26. I review Peirce's argument briefly in *The Many Faces of Realism* (La Salle, Ill.: Open Court, 1987), pp. 80–86.

27. Peirce ensures unrepeatability by imagining a case in which the alternatives are "eternal felicity" and "everlasting woe"; in *The Many Faces of Realism,* I modify Peirce's argument by imagining a case in which the choice is between an easy death and a hard death.

28. "The Doctrine of Chances," pp. 396ff. (paragraph 2.653).

29. See p. 84.

30. "The community . . . must reach, however vaguely, beyond this geological epoch, beyond all bounds. He who would not sacrifice his own soul to save the whole world, is, as it seems to me, illogical in all his inferences, collec-

tively. Logic is rooted in the social principle." Peirce, "The Doctrine of Chances," paragraph 2.654.

31. The term "fictitious transfer" comes from Reichenbach's discussion of single case probabilities. See *The Theory of Probability* (Berkeley: University of California Press, 1940), pp. 372ff.

32. The probability involved in Peirce's example is 24/25ths.

33. The discussion of the limits of conceivability in Wittgenstein's *On Certainty* (ed. G. E. M. Anscombe and G. H. von Wright [Oxford: Basil Blackwell, 1969]) is on my mind here.

34. Although for Carnap it was! Carnap at one time held the view that to say that a hypothesis is *confirmed* to a certain degree r is *just* the same as saying that a certain algorithm yields the number r when applied to the evidence. On this view, anyone who knows that a certain mathematical function has the value r on a certain argument *ipso facto* knows something about rational belief; but this is clearly wrong.

35. I am reminded here of Wittgenstein's distrust of philosophical "musts." When I say that the metaphysical notion of a "complete" description has never been satisfactorily defined, I am thinking, among other things, of Quine's claim that the description given by physics is complete because no change of any kind can take place without a *physical* change taking place. However, it is also true that no change of any kind can take place without a change in *the gravitational field* taking place; but not even Quine would maintain that I have "completely" described the world if I have only described the gravitational field! The combination of a "must" with a concept that only *looks* as if it has been defined is characteristic of the philosophical phenomenon Wittgenstein wanted us to attend to.

36. In a letter to James dated March 13, 1897, Peirce wrote, "Undoubtedly, its [philosophy's] tendency is to make one value the spiritual more, but not an abstract spirituality. It makes one dizzy and seasick to think of those worthy people who try to do something for 'the Poor,' or still more blindly, 'the deserving poor.' On the other hand, it increases the sense of awe with which one regards Gautama Booda." This letter appears in the Introduction (p. 9) to the text of C. S. Peirce, *Reasoning and the Logic of Things: The Cambridge Conferences Lectures of 1898,* ed. Kenneth Laine Ketner and Hilary Putnam (Cambridge: Harvard University Press, 1992).

37. *Reason, Truth, and History* (New York: Cambridge University Press, 1981), p. 136.

38. On the notion of a "thick" ethical characteristic see Bernard Williams, *Ethics and the Limits of Philosophy,* and my discussion in "Objectivity and the Science/Ethics Distinction," in *The Quality of Life,* ed. Martha Nussbaum and Amartya Sen (Oxford: Oxford University Press, 1992) (this essay is also reprinted in my *Realism with a Human Face*).

39. "Epistemic Merit, Intrinsic and Instrumental," in *Proceedings and Ad-*

dresses of the American Philosophical Society, 55, no. 1 (September 1981), 5–23.

40. In Chapter 10 of the present volume.

41. See Rudolf Carnap, *The Logical Foundations of Probability* (Chicago: University of Chicago Press, 1950), and *The Continuum of Inductive Methods* (Chicago: University of Chicago Press, 1952).

42. See *The Logical Foundations of Probability,* pp. 294ff.

43. See "Methods for Attaining Truth," pp. 399–422 in the *Collected Papers of Charles Sanders Peirce,* vol. 5. Note in particular p. 419 (paragraph 5.599).

44. The omnipresence of this theme in Peirce's philosophy is the subject of K. O. Apel's *C. S. Peirce: From Pragmatism to Pragmaticism* (Amherst: University of Massachusetts Press, 1981). See also James, "The Moral Philosopher and the Moral Life," in *The Will to Believe and Other Essays in Popular Philosophy* (Cambridge: Harvard University Press, 1979), and Dewey, in *Experience and Nature,* chap. 5, "Nature, Communication, and Meaning" (Mineola, N.Y.: Dover, 1958) (first published in 1925 by Open Court, La Salle, Ill.).

45. James in "The Moral Philosopher and the Moral Life."

46. This is the approach to ethics made famous by Habermas, and Apel. See Habermas' *The Theory of Communicative Action,* 2 vols. (Boston: Beacon Press, 1985 and 1989), and Apel's *Diskurs und Verantwortung: Das Problem des Übergangs zur Postkonventionellen Moral* (Frankfurt am Main: Suhrkamp, 1985). For a comparison of discourse ethics and pragmatism see "A Reconsideration of Deweyan Democracy."

47. I have used the vocabulary of Agnes Heller's *A Philosophy of Morals* in this sentence to bring out the "ethical" tone of the norms governing scientific inquiry.

48. This is discussed in Chapter 10 of this volume.

49. See My "Scientific Liberty and Scientific License," in *Realism with a Human Face.*

50. See "A Reconsideration of Deweyan Democracy."

51. This objection was suggested by Harry Frankfurt.

52. This is gone into in Chapter 10 of this volume.

53. This may be a part of what Dewey meant when he defined philosophy as "the critical method of developing methods of criticism" in *Experience and Nature,* p. 437.

9. Pragmatism and Relativism: Universal Values and Traditional Ways of Life

In recent years, philosophers such as Stuart Hampshire, Bernard Williams, and Alasdair MacIntyre (responding, perhaps, to arguments by anthropologists such as Clifford Geertz and political scientists such as Michael Walzer) have given increasing centrality to the question whether ethics should be universalistic or should rather be rooted in the forms of life of particular traditions and cultures. I want to consider that question in the following light: On the one hand, John Rawls—whom I consider to be the greatest living social ethicist—has said that he is not discussing the "foundations" of ethics, but rather addressing the main question confronting Western bourgeois democracies after the French Revolution, that is, the tension between equality and liberty.[1] This suggests that Rawls is pessimistic about the prospects for "universalistic" ethical theory (perhaps more so than when he wrote A Theory of Justice). On the other hand, George Steiner has suggested that after the Holocaust it may be impossible to believe that the values of the West have any vitality at all.[2] But to understand this thought it is necessary to understand how Steiner is using the notion of "the Holocaust."

Steiner is not using the phrase in its accepted denotation, the execution (I write "execution" to bring out the horrible "legality" of the proceeding, as contrasted with a mere "slaughter") of six million Jewish women, men, small children, and even infants. Instead, and very tellingly, he is using the term to cover the killing, by war, genocide, and so on, of *seventy million people* in the thirty-seven years beginning with 1914. He is, for example including the slaughter of Europe's youth in World War I, itself one of the most suicidal acts by any civilization in history, and also the purges of Stalin, the deportations of peoples, the planned starvations, and so on.

Elsewhere, Steiner connects the self-destructive proclivities of European civilization with a loss of the concept of "tragedy" and with an alarming loss of what he calls "flexibility."[3] Putting these remarks—Rawls's and Steiner's—together, I find myself in the following "bind": If Rawls is right, ethical theory seems to require the framework of a tradition to give its questions substance, and to provide a shared framework of assumptions within which questions can be discussed. Yet the horrors to which the regnant Western tradition have led call into question, at least for some, the possibility of doing what Rawls suggests, that is, just assuming the basic values of the Enlightenment and calmly discussing how to adjudicate tensions between them.

Before saying something about these dilemmas, let me get out of the way a reason that may occur to any liberal person for not taking seriously enough this thought of Steiner's. The obvious reason one might give for dismissing Steiner's views is that there is nothing wrong with the great Enlightenment *values;* it is just the West's *compliance* with those values that is faulty. In a sense, this is perfectly true. I, for one, cherish and want others to cherish the Enlightenment values of liberty (expanded by Kant and others to include autonomy and toleration), fraternity, and equality. And the events of the Holocaust—in Steiner's extended sense—were a violation of those values, even if some of the participants in the extended Holocaust claimed that their actions would bring about the reign of those very values on earth in due course.

But the distinction between our values and our "compliance" is too simple, and in two different ways. In the first place, our values are not all that *clear.* This is the problem to which Rawls's work is addressed. In the real world, our values of liberty and of equality conflict, and the conflicts are difficult to adjudicate. In principle, I suppose, one could have perfect economic equality (equality of political power is a far more difficult notion). At one time, the more left-wing kibbutzim in Israel required all their members to have the same *furniture* in their apartments, to make sure that no invidious inequalities would arise. Most of us would feel that this degree of equality requires an inadmissible interference with individual freedom. On the other hand, the wide-open "freedom" of economic enterprise on which the United States and England today pride themselves has led to massive inequalities, including the inequality between the homed and the homeless.

In the second place, the massive and long-continued failure of the West's societies to comply with their own supposed values suggests that large numbers of people find them insufficient in some way. If the Enlightenment were a recent event, one might say, "Well, naturally people are nostalgic for old verities, old faiths, old ways, however superstitious or unjust. Give them time." But the Holocaust—I am using the term now in it narrower sense—took place two centuries after the Enlightenment, and was perpetrated by a nation that prided itself on its contributions to Western philosophy, literature, music, science, and so on. If there is a felt dissatisfaction with Enlightenment values, we must not turn our eyes away from that fact.

Two Meanings of "Universal Ethic"

In a conversation, my old friend Sidney Morgenbesser once remarked that many philosophers confuse the notion of a "universal ethic" with the notion of a "universal way of life." Thinking about the present topics has caused me to wonder whether that confusion may not be intrinsic to the Enlightenment itself or, perhaps, even to Western philosophy itself. Aristotle's *Politics* poses the question as "What is the best constitution for a *polis*—for *any* group of civilized human beings?" And it is undeniable that many Enlightenment thinkers framed the question in the same way. As Isaiah Berlin recently put it, "Voltaire's conception of enlightenment as being identical in essentials wherever it is attained seems to lead to the inescapable conclusion that, in his view, Byron would have been happy at table with Confucius, and Sophocles would have felt completely at ease in *quattrocento* Florence, and Seneca in the *salon* of Madame du Deffand or at the court of Frederick the Great."[4]

This tendency, the tendency to think that the right ethical principles must be concretized in the form of an "ideal society" or an "ideal way of life"—I know that these are not the same, but a blueprint for one tends to become a blueprint for the other—has been reinforced by the successes of science, successes that went far beyond even what the most optimistic Enlightenment thinkers expected. In the wake of those successes, it was inevitable that some thinkers, if not by any means the majority, would begin to suggest that human welfare, too, was a problem which could benefit from a technical solution. A special case of this is the development of the nineteenth-century socialist movement in a particular direction, a direction heavily influenced by

Karl Marx's notion that he had taken socialism from its "Utopian" phase to its "scientific" phase.

In the light of these facts, is it to be wondered at if many people began to feel that much of what they valued in their traditions—and above all their religious beliefs and their sense of their own history— was in peril? To be sure, such feelings are especially likely to arise if one is superstitious or chauvinist or racist or all three at once, but is it fair to *equate* such a worry with superstition and chauvinism and racism? This, I think, is the question that will not go away. As communitarian thinkers like Michael Sandal and Charles Taylor have recently been pointing out, to dismiss such feelings as "reactionary" is to hand a potent issue—in the long run, perhaps the most potent of all issues— over to reactionaries.

The Wealth of Cultural Diversity

But even posing the issue of cultural diversity, and of the sense that cultural diversity is in tension with the Enlightenment, in terms of "religions" (perhaps the concept of "religions" is itself a uniquely Western concept)[5] and "history" (a notion that has come to have a special sense in the West in the last two or three centuries) is itself unduly parochial. Perhaps we in the West have far too narrow a sense of the wealth of human cultural diversity, and perhaps this makes it easier for some of us to contemplate the idea of a world with one language, one literature, one music, one art, one politics—in a word, one culture.

Let me make it clear that I am not saying that most, or even many, Enlightenment thinkers would endorse such an idea. But some have done so and some still do. Rudolf Carnap—a philosopher whose stature both as a thinker and as a human being were undeniable—felt strongly that for all x, planned x is better than unplanned x. I know this from conversation with him, and it is also evident in his intellectual autobiography.[6] Thus the idea of a socialist world in which everyone spoke Esperanto (except scientists, who, for their technical work, would employ notations from symbolic logic) was one which would have delighted him. And I recently had a conversation with a student who remarked quite casually that it would not really be so bad if there were only one language and one literature: "We would get used to it, and it might help to prevent war."

Part of what lies behind such attitudes is a simple failure to appreciate the real wealth of cultural diversity in the world, a failure to appreciate *what* we are in danger of losing as the result of cultural *Gleichschaltung*. My own awareness was recently heightened by reading Ben Ami Scharfstein's description[7] of a number of cultures whose way of life is *really* "different" from any I have personally experienced, and in an unexpected way—in the artistic creativity and spontaneity that is normal in those cultures. Permit me to quote a short passage from Scharfstein's book:

> In Chattisgarh, a great, mostly arid plain of northeastern India, every subject goes into poetry, much of which, for that reason, is prosaic; but much is sensitive and eloquent. Many of the songs are known to everyone, and gifted individuals continue to augment their number. "Life in Chattisgarh is hard, dusty and unrewarded; it might well be hopeless were it not for the happiness that song brings to the meanest hovel."[8]

Scharfstein goes on to describe a number of other peoples in whose ways of life the arts of poetry and song play a role which is almost incomprehensible to my contemporaries, for whom "poetry and song" almost always are products produced by "artists" and enjoyed by consumers few of whom are "artists." I quote Scharfstein again: "In the Andaman Islands, everyone composes his own songs, even the small children. To end this disorderly paragraph, I repeat the sneer of an Eskimo woman at a rival, 'She can't dance, she can't even sing,' the latter part of the sneer meaning, 'She can't even compose songs.'"

The possibility of making oneself conscious of other modes of human fulfillment and the terrible difficulty of doing this are themes to which I shall return later in this essay.

Individualism and Egotism

In addition to the confusion between the idea of a universal ethic and the idea of a universal way of life, there is another confusion of ideas which is associated with the Enlightenment, and that is the confusion between individualism and egotism. That the confusion (or identification) exists has long been noticed, as witness the following remark by Horace Greeley in 1853: "This is preeminently an age of Individualism (it would hardly be polite to call it Egotism) wherein the Sovereignty of the Individual—that is the right of every man to do pretty nearly as he pleases—is already generally popular and is visibly gaining ground daily."[9]

Again, let me make it clear that I am *not* joining the host of critics of "bourgeois individualism." "Individualism" is not the name of one single thing, and some of the ideas that go under the name of individualism are to be cherished. For example, individualism can mean, simply, the idea that individuality is precious—even sacred. In the Jewish tradition, one often quotes the parable about Rabbi Zusiah, who, on his death bed, told his grieving disciples that he was terrified of the judgment of his Maker. "But you are a holy man," the disciples protested. "You have been as faithful as Abraham; you have been as holy as Moses; you have been as learned as Hillel." "The Lord is not going to ask me, 'Have you been Abraham?' 'Have you been Moses?' or 'Have you been Hillel?'" was the sage's reply. "The Lord is going to ask me 'Have you been Zusiah?'"

Again, individualism can mean the doctrine of individual rights; and this is a precious doctrine. Those who attack this doctrine as bourgeois ought to reflect more on what happens when individual rights are suppressed in the name of a supposed solution to all human problems (a useful case, in that it reveals how two tendencies of the Enlightenment can conflict: the emphasis on individual rights and the emphasis on finding a solution to the problems of life by the use of reason). But there is no doubt that the doctrine of individual rights easily becomes popularized as "the right of every man to do pretty nearly as he pleases."

There have been philosophers for whom the confusions and excesses of the Enlightenment have constituted the Enlightenment itself. I am thinking especially of Heidegger. For Heidegger, the desire for the Esperanto-speaking planned society and the world of capitalist greed and competitiveness are both manifestations of the same thing: the Enlightenment is simply the pretty face of an age whose real inner compulsion is to ends-means rationality, unbridled subjectivity, and the will to power. I am the last to say that there is nothing to Heidegger's critique; yet, even if Heidegger himself had never joined the Nazi movement, the critique would remain hopelessly one-sided. As a one-sided critique it has real power, however (as does Marx's *Capital,* from a different direction); what Heidegger focuses on are just the issues that I have located as the points of greatest dissatisfaction with Enlightenment values.

To locate dissatisfactions is very different from offering solutions, however, and I do not intend here to try to solve these problems. Indeed, I do not think that one can solve them in the study. Durkheim remarked that the problem of alienation can be solved only in life, not in the study, and that the thing to do to hasten a solution is to eliminate concrete injustices and exclusions,[10] and one can only applaud his wisdom. But part of eliminating injustices is to eliminate the injustices we do to the interests and sentiments of others by too hastily labeling those interests and sentiments "reactionary." We have to become more aware of the enormous value of cultural diversity, we have to recognize the need for and the value of cultural roots, and we have to know and *say* that if everyone *should* have the *legal* right to "do pretty nearly as he pleases," it does not follow that one *deserves* that right as a matter of course. Some people are *morally* undeserving of rights that it would be wrong to take away from them. Some of one's rights should be *earned,* morally speaking.

The Return of Relativism

There is another side to the coin, however. If the idea of a universal ethic leads (however invalid the logic!) to the idea of a universal way of life, then there are many thinkers who would advocate *modus tollendo tollens:* since a universal way of life is a bad idea, so is a universal ethic. (Bernard Williams' *Ethics and the Limits of Philosophy* is a recent example of this way of thinking, and, philosophically speaking, one of the most powerful. Of course, Williams also believes on metaphysical grounds that a universal ethic with objective validity is an impossibility.)[11]

The relativist position faces a problem which is simultaneously obvious and deep. Relativism is not itself an ethics but a metaethics, one which, as Bernard Williams is aware, is corrosive of all ethical positions and views. That *reflection destroys ethical knowledge* is something Williams tells us again and again; this could be the motto of his whole book. To the extent that the relativist wants to be more than just a *meta*ethicist, he is in a difficult position. As I said, Williams is aware of this problem, and one way in which he tries to meet it is the following. He accepts the now familiar dichotomy between "thick" and "thin" ethical concepts. "Thick" ethical concepts (the terminology comes, I believe, from anthropology) have a heavy descriptive content. The importance of such concepts, though not the terminology, was already familiar to Ortega y Gasset: "Language evinces—for deep reasons which we cannot go into in this essay—an economizing tendency to express phenomena of value by means of a halo of complementary signification that surrounds the primary, realistic signification of words. . . . Similarly [Ortega has just discussed the word 'noble' as an example of this] the words 'generous,' 'elegant,' 'skillful,' 'strong,' 'select'—as well as 'sordid,' 'inelegant,' 'gauche,' 'weak,' 'vulgar'—mean simultaneously realities and values. What is more, if we explored the dictionary in order to gather all the words with a completely evaluative sense, we would undoubtedly be astonished by the fabulous decantation of characters and tinges of value in ordinary language."[12] By "thin" ethical concepts, Williams means such abstract ethical concepts as "right," "wrong," "good," "bad," "virtue," "vice," "duty," and "sin."

Following the lead of John McDowell,[13] Williams rejects the view that "thick" ethical concepts can be explicitly factored into a "descriptive component" and an "evaluative component"; that is, he rejects the view that, for each thick ethical concept (see, for example, Ortega's little list that I just quoted) one can construct a value-free concept which has exactly the same extension. McDowell's argument—which Williams considers to be probably correct—is that a speaker cannot tell how these concepts will be applied to hard cases, or just to novel cases, by skilled speakers unless he or she is able to identify imaginatively with the values of the group whose concepts they are.[14]

But Williams goes still further, and denies that there are any *entailments* connecting "thick" and "thin" ethical concepts. He considers a hypertraditional society which he imagines as lacking our thin ethical concepts altogether, and he argues that when someone in that society says, for example, that some action is "sordid" his statement does not *entail* that the action is *wrong*: after all, "wrong" is *our* notion, and it is a kind of logical parochialism (Williams claims) to hold that all valuations in all languages implicitly involve *our* thin ethical concepts.

I think Williams' conclusion is right but the argument is terrible! There *are* circumstances in which it would not be self-contradictory to say, "That was a sordid thing to do, but it had to be done" (where the "had to be done" clearly has the force of "was morally required"); that is why I agree that (for example) "sordid" does not *entail* "morally wrong." But the *fact that a concept does not belong to some language does not show that statements in our language containing that concept cannot be entailed by statements in the other language*; "I have one pear in each hand" entails "I have an even prime number of pears in my hands," whether or not the concepts "even" and "prime" belong to the language in which the first statement was made.

Williams needs this complicated philosophical machinery because he wants to argue that, in a hypertraditional society, ethical truths (expressed in the thick ethical vocabulary of that society) can be *true* (in accordance with the rules of the local language game) without having any *universal* implications whatsoever. In effect, Williams' machinery is designed to allow precisely what some critics of the Enlightenment seem to want: a number of local ethical outlooks, each of which can be regarded as "true" by its adherents, but whose truth does not have any universalistic implications whatsoever.

An example may make it clearer how this works. Suppose we have lost an ethical concept ("chastity," I fear, is a good example). Then even if that concept is alive and well in society S, if society S's way of life is too "distant" from ours, if we could not adopt that way of life without being brainwashed or going mad, and if, in the same sense, our way of life is too "distant" from society S's, then, if all these conditions are met, according to Williams, the knowledge of people in S that some forms of behavior are "unchaste" is simply *irrelevant* to us. (In Williams' jargon, any confrontation between our outlook and the outlook of S is *notional* and not *real*.) Indeed, if we have really lost the concept, we will be "disbarred" from even expressing what people in S can express by saying that those forms of behavior are "unchaste." (Here Williams is using the machinery of "incommensurability" introduced into the philosophy of science by Kuhn.) Nor does the truth of the statement that those forms of behavior are unchaste (made by a member of society S) entail that those forms of behavior are "morally reprehensible" (something we *can* express), for such an entailment would be just the sort of "thick to thin" entailment that Williams is at pains to deny.

One wonders, however, to just *what* societies Williams' doctrine, imagining it to be correct, would ever apply? Examples are hard to come by in Williams' writing: the three that I remember are a "bronze age chieftain," a "medieval samurai," and the Aztecs!

It seems appropriate here to comment on the inclusion of the "medieval samurai." As we know, the medieval samurai was extremely likely to be a student of Zen Buddhism and possibly also of Confucianism. As such, he may not have been inclined to use our Western "thin" ethical concepts, but he was certainly acquainted with an abstract vocabulary suitable for making universalistic claims. When a Zen Buddhist says that one way of life leads to *satori* and another way of life leads to pain, he is making a claim of universal significance: that is, so to speak, the *point* of Buddhism. And when Confucius tells us how we should treat our family members, our superiors, and our subordinates, it is, I recklessly say, fair to use the words "should" and "ought" in explaining his thought in English even if the uses of these words in English do not exactly line up with their uses in Chinese (the language in which Confucianism was studied in Japan). Certainly, by the time of the "medieval samurai," rich systems of *thin* ethical concepts had become widely known in Japan.

Indeed, the whole idea of a culture which has only "thick" ethical concepts and no "thin" ones is a philosopher's myth. Homer tells us a lot about "bronze age chieftains" and *they* certainly had "thin" ethical concepts, starting with χρή, meaning "it is right and proper"; "one must, one ought to." Again, I am not claiming that χρή is *synonymous* with any of these dictionary entries; but any philosophical doctrine which requires for its defense the claim that this common Greek word is totally *uninterpretable* in English is as bankrupt as the bugaboo of total "incommensurability" itself, while the claim that the use of it was restricted to class-bound obligations (so that an aristocrat could not even express—or think—the thought that *anyone,* including commoners, "ought to" defend his home or feed his children) is pure fabulation. As for Nahuatl (the Aztec language), even though I wrote my senior paper for Zelig Harris on the Nahuatl plural many years ago, I no longer know (if I ever did) what the Nahuatl ethical vocabulary was like, but I would be astounded if it, too, did not have its "thin" as well as its "thick" concepts.

The problem, in short, is that traditional societies—the traditional societies that actually have existed, not Williams' fictitious "hypertraditional society"—don't just have "thick" ethical concepts; they also have *philosophical* conceptions, conceptions about how *everyone* should live, and attach great importance to those conceptions. What we in the West refer to as the "religions" of traditional peoples, for example, are concerned with problems that are meant to *transcend* the culture-bound, as well as with problems that arise in particular "traditional" cultures. The impossibility of discussing ethical problems without assuming the value framework of a particular culture, if it is an impossibility, suggests the impossibility of any significant notion of a "universal" or "eternal" existential problem. Yet every sane person does believe deep down that there are universal human problems.

That Williams himself does not think that his doctrine of a "relativity of distance" helps us very much *today* is indicated by his remark (*Ethics and the Limits of Philosophy*, p. 163) that "relativism over merely spatial distance is of no interest or application in the modern world. Today all confrontations between cultures must be real confrontations."

Isaiah Berlin on Relativism

If Williams' version of relativism is ultimately unsatisfying, it is in part because the *constraints* he places on an adequate ethical outlook seem so very weak. True, he often says that such an outlook must be such that we could "live reflectively and stably in it"; but he often expresses a certain pessimism as to whether *any* ethical outlook can really survive very much reflection. Apart from that, the only standard of human flourishing that he mentions is "the ecological standard of the bright eye and the bushy tail"—a revealing bit of reductionism, that!

A very different conception arises when one begins to see that there are alternative good ways of life, alternative fulfilling conceptions of the good, in (if you please) a "thicker" sense of "fulfilling." I should like to quote Berlin again:

> Communities may resemble each other in many respects, but the Greeks differ from Lutheran Germans, the Chinese differ from both; what they strive after, and what they fear or worship is scarcely ever similar.
>
> This view has been called cultural or moral relativism. . . . It is not relativism. Members of one culture can, by the force of imaginative insight, understand (what Vico called *entrare*) the values, the ideals, the forms of life of another culture or society, even those remote in time or space. They may find those values unacceptable, but if they open their minds sufficiently they can grasp how one might be a full human being, with whom one could communicate, and at the same time live in the light of values different from one's own, but which nevertheless one can see to be values, ends of life, by the realization of which men could be fulfilled.[15]

To say with Berlin that one can *entrare* the "values, the ideals, the forms of life" of another society is not to say that one must regard all "values, ideals, forms of life" as equally good. Berlin spoke of "another culture or society," but very often what is hard to "enter" is our own culture, or our own culture as it conflicts with itself inside each of us. These conflicts are hard to bear; but the refusal to understand imaginatively one or another part of one's own culture is often a re-fusal to understand oneself. Wittgenstein once said that "to imagine a language is to imagine a form of life." Citing this passage, Stanley Cavell has written,

> In philosophizing, I have to bring my own language and life into imagination. What I require is a convening of my culture's criteria, in order to confront them with my words and life as I pursue them and may imagine them; and at the same time to confront my words and life as I pursue them with the life my culture's words may imagine for me; to confront the culture with itself along the lines in which it meets in me.[16]

This form of philosophy, Cavell adds, may be called "education for grown ups."

Pragmatism and Pluralism

Is there a danger of relativism in the wider and deeper knowledge of traditions (including the traditions of one's ancestors) with which one does not fully identify? To some, Berlin's denial that his position amounts to "cultural and moral relativism" might seem a little facile. After all, he condemns moral absolutism in sharp terms. "I conclude that the very notion of a final solution is not only impracticable but, if I am right, and some values cannot but clash, incoherent also. The possibility of a final solution—even if we forget the terrible sense that these words acquired in Hitler's day—turns out to be an illusion, and a very dangerous one. For, if one really believes that such a solution is possible, then surely no cost would be too high to obtain it; to make mankind just and happy and creative and harmonious forever—what would be too high a price to pay for that? To make such an omelette, there is surely no limit to the number of eggs that should be broken—that was the faith of Lenin, of Trotsky, of Mao, for all I know, of Pol Pot."[17] Or, if Berlin is not a relativist, is he not just saying that there are a number of optimal moral and political and religious philoso-phies around, and that one must just make one's own subjective choice from among the optimal ones?

Berlin is certainly defending pluralism, but pluralism should not be confused with naive cultural relativism. Since he does not discuss this issue in detail, I shall close by looking at a thinker who had a lifelong preoccupation with these questions—William James. James, just as much as Isaiah Berlin, defended pluralism and condemned dogmatism and absolutism. At the same time, James famously (or notoriously, depending on your point of view) defended the right to believe.

> Our passional nature not only lawfully may, but must, decide an option between propositions, whenever it is a genuine option that cannot by its nature be decided on intellectual grounds, for to say under such circumstances, "Do not decide, but leave the question open," is itself a passional decision—just like deciding yes or not—and is attended with the same risk of losing the truth.[18]

How does James reconcile the right to believe with "passion" with his condemnation of dogmatism and authoritarianism?

For pragmatists the answer lies in the following reflection. The notion that history has thrown up a number of "optimal" ways of life—optimal but irreconcilable—is much too simple. Every way of life, every system of values, traditions, and rituals that humans have so far invented has defects as well as virtues. Not only are there imperfections that can be exposed from within the way of life, imperfections that a reflective person of good will can point out and try to change from within, but there are defects that we come to see from the outside, as the result of increased knowledge and/or a widened sense of justice (from what James called "listening to the cries of the wounded").[19] For example, all historical ways of life suffer from male chauvinism, from prejudice against homosexuals, and from other kinds of insensitivity or cruelty. Simply to declare any way of life perfect is to violate a maxim which should govern the search for truth in *every* area of life: do not block the path of inquiry! That truth cannot be secured once and for all by revelation applies to ethical and religious truth just as much as to scientific truth. Our problem is not that we must choose from among an already fixed and defined number of optimal ways of life; our problem is that we don't know of even one *optimal* way of life.

In this predicament, we have no choice but to try to reform and improve the ways of life we have, as well as to try new ones if we believe them to be better; but these trials must not be at the expense of the right of others to make their trials. There is nothing wrong with the choice of the person who chooses to stay within a traditional way and to try to make it as good and as just and as fulfilling as possible—as long as he or she does not try to force that way on everyone else. This is, of course, a democratic idea; for pragmatists, however, it follows not just from the idea of democracy, but, more fundamentally, from the recognition that a truth worthy of the name has to be world-guided and subject to public discussion.[20] This is what William James meant when he wrote that "the practical consequence of such a philosophy is the well-known democratic respect for the sacredness of individuality. . . . [It] is, at any rate, the outward tolerance of whatever is not itself intolerant. . . . Religiously and philosophically, our ancient national doctrine of live and let live may prove to have a far deeper meaning than our people now seem to imagine."[21]

When Berlin describes what "all these views" (Platonism, traditional theology, the Enlightenment, progressive thought in the nineteenth century) had in common he writes:

> What all these views had in common was a Platonic ideal: in the first place that, as in the sciences, all genuine questions must have one true answer and one only, all the rest being necessarily errors. In the second place, that there must be a dependable path toward the discovery of these truths. In the third place, that the true answers, when found, must necessarily be compatible with one another and form a single whole, for one truth cannot be incompatible with another—that we know *a priori*. This kind of omniscience was the solution of the cosmic jigsaw puzzle. In the case of morals, we could then conceive what the perfect life must be, founded as it would be on a correct understanding of the rules that governed the universe.

Pragmatism agrees with Berlin in rejecting the first and third items in this list: the idea of one true answer (which does not really apply to science either,[22] except in an oversimple picture of what science is like) and the resulting idea of a single set of rules which describe both the universe and what would be a "perfect life." Pragmatism does not believe that there can be an "ethical theory dogmatically made up in advance," James tells us;[23] and it requires that we tolerate pluralism. But pragmatism's attitude toward Berlin's second point—the idea of "a dependable path toward the discovery of these truths"—is nuanced. There is no *algorithm* or mechanical procedure, no set of fixed ahistorical "canons of scientific method," which will lead us to the truth in every area, or in any, but there is the imperfect but necessary "path" of struggling for and testing one's ideals in practice, while conceding to others the right to do the same.

The ethic to which this conception of truth leads is, it seems to me, the ethic that is needed to combine the great Enlightenment value of tolerance with the respect for the particularity of tradition, and with the recognition of the need for thick conceptions of the significance of life whose absence in Enlightenment thought left people feeling a huge void. To some this ethic will seem dull—a mere restatement of "liberalism." To this the reply must be that the desire for views which are "exciting," "original," "radical," views which "deconstruct" everything which we thought before, is not in general the same as the desire for truth. The clash of traditions and conceptions of the good will certainly continue. If that clash is not accompanied and tempered by the effort to understand values and conceptions of the good which are not our own and by the willingness to compromise, our worst fears will certainly come true. Writing of the very failing I have been discussing, the failure to understand (James calls it a "blindness") the "values and meanings" of others, James says, "No one has insight into all the ideals. No one should presume to judge them off-hand. The pretension to dogmatize about them in each other is the root of most human injustices and cruelties, and the trait in human character most likely to make the angels weep."[24]

Notes

1. See Rawls's "Justice as Fairness: Political not Metaphysical," *Philosophy and Public Affairs,* 14, no. 3 (Summer 1985).
2. I am referring to a lecture Steiner gave a few years ago at the Van Leer Foundation in Jerusalem.
3. In *The Death of Tragedy* (New York: Knopf, 1963).
4. "On the Pursuit of the Ideal," *New York Review of Books,* March 17, 1988, p. 14.
5. This was suggested by Wilfred Cantwell Smith in *The Meaning and End of Religion: A New Approach to the Religious Traditions of Mankind* (New York: Macmillan, 1963); see esp. chap. 2, "Religion and the West."
6. See *The Philosophy of Rudolf Carnap,* ed. P. A. Schilpp (La Salle, Ill.: Open Court, 1963).
7. See chap. 3 of Scharfstein's *Of Birds, Beasts, and Other Artists* (New York: New York University Press, 1989).
8. In the last sentence, Scharfstein is quoting from V. Elwin, *Folk Songs of Chattisgarh* (Bombay, 1946), p. 1.
9. Greeley was thinking about divorce, but the remark has, of course, much wider pertinence (quoted in N. M. Blake, *The Road to Reno: A History of Divorce in the United States* [New York: Macmillan, 1962; rep. Westport, Conn.: Greenwood, 1977]).

10. At the end of *Of the Division of Labor,* trans. George Simpson (New York: Free Press, 1964).

11. For a detailed critique of Williams' arguments, see my "Objectivity and the Science/Ethics Distinction," in my *Realism with a Human Face* (Cambridge: Harvard University Press, 1990).

12. "Introducción a la estimativa," *Obras Completas,* vol. 6 (1923), pp. 317, 320–321.

13. See McDowell's "Are Moral Requirements Hypothetical Imperatives?" *Proceedings of the Aristotelian Society,* suppl. vol. 42 (1978), and "Virtue and Reason," *Monist,* 62 (1979).

14. For a somewhat different argument to the same effect, see my *Reason, Truth, and History* (New York: Cambridge University Press, 1981).

15. "On the Pursuit of the Ideal," p. 14.

16. *The Claim of Reason* (Oxford: Oxford University Press, 1979), p. 125.

17. "On the Pursuit of the Ideal," p. 16.

18. "The Will to Believe," in *The Will to Believe and Other Essays in Popular Philosophy* (Cambridge: Harvard University Press, 1979).

19. See "The Moral Philosopher and the Moral Life," in *The Will to Believe and Other Essays.*

20. This pragmatist idea of a connection between democratic ethics and scientific method has recently been revived and elaborated by two famous Frankfurt philosophers: Jürgen Habermas and Karl-Otto Apel. For a discussion of their work and its relation to pragmatism see my *The Many Faces of Realism* (La Salle, Ill.: Open Court, 1987), pp. 53–56.

21. *Talks to Teachers on Psychology and Some of Life's Ideals* (Cambridge: Harvard University Press, 1983), pp. 4–5.

22. On this, see my *Realism and Reason, Philosophical Papers,* vol. 3 (New York: Cambridge University Press, 1983).

23. This is the first sentence of "The Moral Philosopher and the Moral Life."

24. "What Makes a Life Significant?" in *Talks to Teachers on Psychology,* p. 150.

10. Dewey's *Logic:*
Epistemology as Hypothesis

With Ruth Anna Putnam

The last words in John Dewey's *Logic: The Theory of Inquiry* are "failure to institute a logic based inclusively and exclusively upon the operations of inquiry has enormous cultural consequences. It encourages obscurantism; it promotes acceptance of beliefs formed before methods of inquiry had reached their present estate; and it tends to relegate scientific (that is, competent) methods of inquiry to a specialized technical field. Since scientific methods simply exhibit free intelligence operating in the best manner available at a given time, the cultural waste, confusion and distortion that results from the failure to use these methods, in all fields in connection with all problems, is incalculable. These considerations reinforce the claim of logical theory, as the theory of inquiry, to assume and to hold a position of primary human importance."[1] This is the claim to which we refer in our title, the claim that, in the spirit of Dewey, we take to be a hypothesis. Briefly reformulated, we claim that (a) Dewey's philosophy of science enables him to give a more adequate account of what used to be called "the moral sciences" than do rival theories; (b) he is able to show that policy decisions can be evaluated with respect to the rationality of their goals, and not only with respect to the efficiency of means; and (c) if one accepts the relevance to social practice of "free intelligence operating in the best manner available at a given time," one can offer an empirical argument in favor of the sort of social democracy that Dewey favored.

Our strategy will be as follows. First, we will provide a quick sketch of Dewey's theory of inquiry, both as a reminder and in order to emphasize the points that are most relevant to the claim under consideration. Second, we will examine the implications of that theory for the dispute about whether there can be rational choice of ends. Then we will consider a number of objections to Dewey's position, objections which we believe would naturally occur to someone conversant with the present-day literature in philosophy and the social sciences, and show that Dewey possesses the resources to deal with those objections. In the course of doing this, we will show how the theory of inquiry both serves and is served by democratic politics.

Logic as the Theory of Inquiry

Logic as the theory of inquiry is itself the result of an inquiry. Thus what Dewey says about inquiry in general is true of inquiry into inquiry, that is, it begins in an indeterminate situation. An indeterminate situation is characterized by the fact that "*things* will come out differently according to what is done" (p. 107). Dewey believes that what will happen in the world, and particularly in the social world, depends (in part) on our understanding of what goes on in inquiry. He shares this conception with J. S. Mill,[2] but holds that Mill "disastrously compromised" his case because he based his logic on "psychological theories that reduced 'experience' to mental states and external associations between them, instead of upon the actual conduct of scientific inquiry" (p. 81).

Early in the *Logic* Dewey asserts that "the outstanding problem of our civilization is set by the fact that common sense in its content, its 'world' and methods, is a house divided against itself" (p. 78). We approach the problems that concern us most intimately, in particular social problems, unscientifically, yet "scientific" is in our culture an honorific term. The problems of everyday life arise, at least in part, because of the advances of science—the degradation of the environment may serve as an example—and, to some extent, we look to scientists to solve them; the tension, or split, results from the fact that we have an entirely instrumental view of science. Although it provides the means to our ends, science, so it is claimed, is incompetent to evaluate the ends. We cannot, says Dewey, overcome this schizophrenia of modern life unless we come to see every problem as an invitation to inquiry, to understand all inquiry as of one pattern, and to abandon the demands for ends that are beyond all evaluation.

Yet Dewey begins with the claim that "rationality is, according to the position here taken, as well as in ordinary usage, an affair of the relation of means and consequences" (p. 9). If so, it has appeared to many that rationality has nothing to say about the value of the consequences. Thus Hans Reichenbach argued[3] that an individual's ultimate ends cannot be rationally evaluated. Of course, one cannot deny that human beings value certain things, that they seek food, shelter, clothing, beauty, friendship, knowledge, but in a Reichenbachian world nothing more can be said about these ends, or their more specific instantiations. There is nothing rational or irrational in our valuing them; we can inquire only into the means to their satisfaction; only what Reichenbach called "entailed decisions" can be evaluated. Dewey responds to such claims in several ways. First, we are misled by the existence of what he calls "generic" ends, for example, the items we just listed. Because we seek something specific that falls under one of these rubrics, we fail to see that the goods, in so far as we seek them, function as means and can be evaluated. Thus, in an affluent and health-conscious society, we have come to understand that there are good and bad foods, we understand that eating has consequences beyond the appeasement of hunger which may be such that it would be better to refrain from eating a particular food. Nevertheless, in a world in which thousands die of starvation each day only a monster would deny that an adequate food supply fairly distributed is one of our most urgent goals. This goal is difficult to achieve, and it may be too general and too ambitious to direct conduct; pursuing more modest goals (developing grains that will flourish in India, limiting the population growth in China) may be more efficacious. Ends are neither laid up in a Platonic heaven nor the mere whims of individuals; they are, rather, ends-in-view, they guide conduct; in that capacity they are themselves means to solving a problem and as such rationality is competent to pronounce judgment on them. "In framing ends-in-view, it is unreasonable to set up those which have no connection with available means and without reference to the obstacles standing in the way of attaining the end" (pp. 9–10). Nor are ends-in-view ultimate termini; once achieved, they become the situation in which we live and in which new problems will arise. In retrospect we may well say that we would have done better to have pursued a different goal.

The existence of generic ends, and we do not gainsay their usefulness, is misleading also because we tend to think that such ends are just good, absolutely good. Thus describing a more specific goal as falling under one of these rubrics, for example as knowledge, may mislead us into thinking that it is permissible to pursue it, but there is knowledge that we ought not to seek (how to torture people); even knowledge worth having may not be obtained by all means—witness restrictions on experiments with human subjects. Once again, means-ends rationality enables us to evaluate ends, here in terms of the cost of the means required to achieve them.

Here an objector may wonder why we are encouraged to pursue one investigation rather than another because the former is more likely to appease some actual hunger in the near future than the latter. In Deweyan language, this objector maintains that without valuings there can be no evaluations, a point which Dewey will readily grant, and that our valuings introduce an ineradicably subjective, nonrational element, a point which Dewey denies. Any valuing can become evaluated, although we cannot ever be in a position in which all valuings have been evaluated. The objector seeks a foundation, but for Dewey there are no foundations; we can only start from where we are. Where we are includes both our sufferings and enjoyments (our valuings) and our evaluations, the latter coming both from our community and from ourselves. Our sufferings or enjoyments become appreciations, involve evaluation, only when they are the results, the completions, of our activities (physical or intellectual). Dewey sometimes seems even to suggest that an enjoyment which simply comes to us without any effort on our part, which is not the fulfillment of some striving, has no value. This is not the place to examine this claim in full generality; it suffices here to say that such an enjoyment has, at any rate, no cognitive value, unless indeed it stimulates our curiosity so that we are prompted to inquire how to prolong it, or how to bring it about again. More needs to be said in support of Dewey's claim that value judgments can be as warranted as can any other judgments. We shall return to this topic shortly.

First we want to say something about Dewey's relationship to Peirce, to whose logical writings he acknowledges a "great indebtedness" (p. 9n). The notion that inquiry begins in an indeterminate situation and is completed when the situation has become unified is, of course, a restatement of Peirce's claim that inquiry begins with doubt and ends with settled belief. But it is characteristic of Dewey that he eschews the "subjective" or "idealist" language of doubt and belief: "*We* are doubtful," he says, "because the situation is inherently doubtful. Personal states of doubt that are not evoked by and are not relative to some existential situation are pathological" (pp. 105–106). Peirce had said that the aim of inquiry is settled belief, that to fancy that we seek a true opinion is "groundless," but Peirce also held that any belief which is not true will become "unsettled," will lead to unsuccessful action and thus to new doubt. For Dewey the end of inquiry ("end" both in the sense of goal and in the sense of terminus) is a unified, or settled, situation; it is belief if that word is taken to refer to "the settled condition of objective subject-matter, together with readiness to act in a given way when, if, and as, that subject-matter is present in existence" (p. 7). But the word "belief" tends to be understood as a mere personal, mere mental state, so Dewey prefers the term "warranted assertion" because of its explicit reference to "inquiry as that which warrants the assertion" (p. 9). It is worthwhile here to point out that contrary to a widespread misapprehension, which we have shared in an earlier essay, Dewey does not substitute warranted assertibility for truth; rather he quotes Peirce's well-known statement that "the opinion which is fated to be ultimately agreed to by all who investigate is what we mean by truth, and the object represented by this opinion is the real" (quoted on p. 345n).

Inquiry is carried out by human beings who live and inquire not only in a physical but in a social environment, and the latter influences every step in the inquiry. Although a hungry person will be hungry no matter what, whether we see the hunger of others (and of *which* others) as our problem and what possible solutions we are able to envisage and attempt to bring about depends as much on where and when we are as on the extent of hunger in the world, and even the hungry individual's behavior is shaped by her culture. The hungry individual's problem is not a scientific problem; it is what Dewey calls a "problem of use and enjoyment" or a "common sense" problem; its desired solution, its end-in-view, is not the attainment of knowledge for its own sake. That is how common-sense inquiry is distinguished from scientific inquiry, or how we come to distinguish between the practical and theoretical. But scientific inquiry grows out of common-sense problems, though the connection may be more or less remote, and it provides ultimately expanded means for the solution of problems of use and enjoyment.

Philosophers and others (for instance, methodologists) seek patterns of inquiry which experience has shown to lead to warranted assertions, that is, assertions which remain (relatively) stable under continued inquiry. Logic as the enunciation of such a pattern is itself the result of an inquiry into inquiry; thus Dewey seeks paradigmatic examples of inquiry. It comes both as somewhat of a surprise and as reassurance to find that for Dewey, as for other philosophers of science up to his time and well beyond, physics is the paradigmatic science. Physics is paradigmatic because of the stability of its results—that stability is by no means called into question by the scientific revolutions of the twentieth century, but to defend that claim would lead us too far beyond the confines of our topic. Taking physics as paradigmatic has both advantages and disadvantages. One advantage is that it is quite obvious that the description of a situation in terms of the values of physical magnitudes is a redescription of a common-sense situation. Attention is thus drawn to the role of our concepts in the apprehension and appreciation of a situation. Dewey's emphasis on what one might call the unity of form and content has borne rich and well-known fruits; we cannot pursue this topic here.[4] A second advantage is that in physics and other "hard" sciences one sees most clearly the so-called hypothetical-deductive pattern. The pattern is familiar: at a certain stage in the inquiry scientists formulate hypotheses, further observational consequences are deduced from these, and if they are found to be true, the hypothesis is confirmed. Dewey points out, as, incidentally, did Reichenbach, that the formulation just given suggests that the scientific method is merely a combination of guesswork and the fallacy of affirming the consequent. The account just given omitted the role of experiment both prior to the formulation of an hypothesis and afterward, as well as the fact that the deductions in question always employ a host of so-called auxiliary hypotheses. One of the advantages of the established sciences is that they consist of a body of knowledge which guides practitioners to the sort of selective observation combined with collection of data that is most likely to suggest relevant hypotheses; similarly, the established sciences provide the information that enables the scientist to devise and carry out experiments which test the hypothesis under investigation and eliminate plausible rivals. Dewey prevents the ordinary methods of scientists from falling afoul of the methods of deductive logic not by applying an unrealistic falsification criterion but by insisting on the fact that the hypothetical-deductive (that is, inductive) phase of inquiry draws on the results of previous experimental inquiry. As a famous scientist once wrote Karl Popper, "You wouldn't think that science is a matter of always testing the most falsifiable hypothesis if as many crazy theories crossed your desk every week as cross mine."

Using the history of the discovery of the cause of malaria, Dewey illustrates brilliantly how very complex the processes of discovery, elimination of rival hypotheses, and testing actually are. More important, he points out that the ultimate practical application stemming from the discovery—the draining of swamps, which led to the disappearance of the disease in those areas—is itself one of the crucial tests since it eliminates rival hypotheses concerning the transmission of the disease.

Science cannot limit itself to the establishment of generalizations. In fact, "the content and validity of the general proposition hangs wholly upon the contents of the singular propositions in which it is grounded. This grounding depends in turn upon the nature of the operations by which these contents are instituted" (p. 436). Dewey's point here is twofold. On the one hand, a generalization is warranted only if the sample on which it is based has been chosen so as to be representative of the kind of thing concerning which we wish to establish the generalization. We do not expect to discover any geological "law" based on the collection of pebbles a child has gathered on the beach. On the other hand, the very process of selecting objects or events as of interest ("instituting singulars" in Dewey's phrase) presupposes that these objects are part of a larger situation that prompts inquiry. Dewey insists repeatedly that we cannot point *at* an object as *this,* since anything in the line of sight might be what we are pointing at. Yet, in a problematic situation, say, when seeking means to prevent malaria, we may well identify this (this swamp) as a breeding ground for mosquitoes. Here we take swampiness as a quality given in observation, which serves as ground for the classification of the swamp as a breeding ground for mosquitoes. Further observations and controlled experiments, such as determining that draining the swamp is followed by a disappearance of mosquitoes, will provide further warrant for the identification. Scientific generalizations are established only between such deliberately constructed properties, as is most evident when one thinks of laws of physics, for the description of a situation using the magnitudes of physics is always a deliberate redescription.

If one were to be misled by the fact that we think of physics as a collection of "laws" to claim that science is concerned only with the establishment of generalizations, one would be led to deny that what engineers and physicians do when they *apply* scientific generalizations to particular cases is science. Such a denial, Dewey points out, "obliterates, logically, the enormous difference between activities that are routine and those that are intelligent; between actions dictated by caprice and the conduct of arts that embody technologies and techniques expressing systematically tested ideas. Even more to the point is the fact that it involves logical suicide of the sciences even with re-spect to generalizations"; for no line can be drawn between tech-niques of experimentation and the use of the same techniques for practical ends. Finally, "no hard and fast line can be drawn between such forms of 'practical' activity and those which apply their conclu-sions to humane social ends without involving disastrous conse-quences to science in its narrower sense" (p. 439). For drawing such a line would deprive science of a large part of the experimental testing that was just shown to be a necessary step in the pattern of inquiry, and one would erect an invidious distinction between theory and practice, between pure and applied science, that would in the end lead to undesirable consequences. Those consequences might be contempt for applied science, but might equally well be a cut-off of funding for "pure" science.

Once it is realized that knowledge or warranted assertion is not the final end of scientific inquiry, but is rather an end-in-view which is itself a means both as a guide to inquiry and as a pathway to applica-tions, a step is taken toward seeing that no science can be value-free in the sense envisaged by Reichenbach. That takes us a certain way to-ward a legitimization of the moral sciences. Another such step was taken by Dewey when he remarked that if the *only* object of scientific inquiry were the establishment of general principles, then one would have to question the scientific status not only of history but of major parts of biology and geology as well (p. 438).

Dewey's Rejection of the Fact/Value Dichotomy

Let us return to Dewey's assertion, quoted above, that "rationality is, according to the position here taken, as well as in its ordinary usage, an affair of the relation of means to consequences" (p. 9). When we couple this conception of rationality with Dewey's understanding that means and ends form a continuum, his rejection of the fact/value di-chotomy follows. A future event is a possible consequence of actions one might now take; that same event once it has taken place is a means to further consequences. As a means to an envisaged end a situation can be evaluated as better or worse, as more or less efficient, as having more or less other undesirable or desirable consequences. As an end-in-view a situation is evaluated both in terms of the means necessary to its realization and in terms of its future consequences. All these evaluations are rational in the sense defined by Dewey. Dewey does not deny that we value things, states of affairs, and so on, without consideration of their status as means or consequences, but he holds that while such valuings, like the qualitative observations of everyday life, may and do initiate inquiry, they are not its outcome.

What has just been said undermines the fact/value distinction by showing that paradigmatic value judgments are as amenable to rational-experiential warrant as are means-consequences judgments. But Dewey points out also that paradigmatic factual assertions—descriptions of the situation which suggest possible solutions, possible ends-in-view—are the result of selective attention and of deliberately chosen experimental procedures. We judge which features are relevant, we judge what information will be helpful and how precisely it must be determined, and so on. Our paradigmatic factual assertions are inextricably intertwined with value judgments.[5]

Finally, what sort of situations appear to us to be problematic, especially in the public realm or in the sciences, is a matter that is almost entirely a function of the values we already embrace, what we care about. As long as AIDS appeared to be a disease confined to the community of gay males, it was difficult to find financial support for research into its causes, prevention, and possible cure.

Once it is acknowledged that science cannot avoid dealing with what Dewey calls "singulars" and that it cannot avoid evaluations, it can be admitted that historians can be scientific (or, to be sure, non-scientific) in their studies of the past. Again, once it is acknowledged that even in the hard sciences, scientists select the data guided by the problem that concerns them, it is clear that the goal to find out and present "wie es eigentlich gewesen war" is chimerical. In fact, historiography is subject to a double process of selection. Prior generations selected what they wanted us to know about them, or what they thought were things worth preserving for posterity. We select from that storehouse on the basis of questions which we have chosen to ask.

Today, fifty years after Dewey wrote his *Logic,* we can elaborate on these brief remarks. Computers have recently enabled historians to deal with large collections of data. That has enabled historians to answer, and hence made it sensible to ask, questions concerning the lives of the masses. History need no longer confine itself to the lives of individuals who happened to play crucial roles or occupy highly visible positions, nor need it deal only with world-shaking events. Our understanding of the past is enriched and altered in this way. A particular kind of knowledge became an end-in-view when the means to attain it were at hand. Another illustration of the general point made here is that with the rise of feminism historians have become interested in asking about the roles and accomplishments of women, questions which simply were not asked in an earlier time.[6] Some may fret that in this case "political considerations" are "distorting" the direction of research, but surely this does not differ from the "distortion" in research that resulted from the large investments in computer research by the Defense Department, also a decision based on political considerations. Dewey summarizes this point by saying, "The notion of the complete separation of science from the social environment is a fallacy which encourages irresponsibility, on the part of scientists, regarding the social consequences of their work" (p. 489). And, we may add, it prevents philosophers from appreciating the ways in which science is dependent on the social environment in terms of the questions it knows to ask, in terms of the research that brings prestige, in terms of the work that receives public funding, and so on.

The point just made opens Dewey's inquiry into the backward state of the social sciences, an inquiry in which he engages in order to "test the general logical consequences which have been reached. For the results of discussion of the topic may show that failure to act in accord with the logical conditions which have been pointed out throws light on [their] retarded state" (p. 487).

Science is itself a social activity not only in the sense that the results of an individual scientist, or team of scientists, must be corroborated by others in the scientific community, but in the sense that scientific results have social consequences and at times exacerbate social conflicts. "These conflicts," writes Dewey, "provide presumptive evidence of the insufficiency, or partiality, or incompleteness of conclusions as they stand" (p. 490). That is an extremely radical claim. It implies, for example, that we cannot rest content having discovered techniques for surrogate motherhood but must develop legislation which will protect women from being exploited as a result of the new techniques. In particular, Dewey suggests that the social sciences have failed to solve social problems because they have attempted to isolate problems in the manner in which physicists attempt to isolate a physical system. But the social consequences of the application of social science results and thus the inadequacy of partial answers is more immediately evident than in the physical sciences.

From the research side of the question there appears to be an asymmetry. One can, of course, investigate a physical system without reference to social or psychological factors, but one cannot, Dewey insists, understand social phenomena without "extensive prior knowledge of physical phenomena and their laws" (p. 492), where biological laws are included under the heading "physical." Although this seems to be an excessively radical claim, it becomes plausible if one remembers that for Dewey mere understanding is never the end of inquiry. For example, the (social) problem of famine was solved in India by the (biological) development of new grains (the green revolution), in Egypt by the (physical) building of the Aswan dam, in many places by the (chemical) development of new fertilizers.

The basic difficulty for social inquiry must in any case be sought elsewhere, namely, *in the idea that social inquiry in order to be scientific must abstain from social practice.* The result has been a radical separation of social theory from social practice. It seems to us that, presumably under the influence of Dewey, that separation is no longer quite as radical as it was fifty years ago; every administration since the days of Roosevelt has raided the universities and transformed experts in various fields into policy makers, or at least policy advisors. Nevertheless, when an acute social problem arises, we still tend to rush into a solution without a careful prior investigation. A glaring example of how things go awry is the current debacle concerning long-term medical care for the elderly.

The deeper philosophical problem lies, however, in the demand that science be value-free. Of course, physicists—whatever they may profess—evaluate data, methods, hypotheses, research projects, and so forth, but these, they would insist, are not moral evaluations, the only kind that scientists must eschew. Because the data, hypotheses, and problems of social scientists concern human beings and human social structures and behavior, that distinction is untenable in the social sciences. Social scientists agree with Dewey that "harm has been wrought by forming social judgments on the ground of moral preconceptions" (p. 495), but they fail to understand that the kind of moral blame or approval that leads to harmful exclusion of data, to the rejection out of hand of possible ends-in-view, "rests on some preconception of *ends* that *should* or *ought* to be attained" (p. 496). Only the false view that all evaluations are preconceptions leads social scientists to the false conclusion that they must eschew all evaluation. Actually, if social scientists were to rule out all evaluation, they would be unable to select relevant information, for without an end-in-view, a working hypothesis, one would not know what to look for by way of data. "One 'fact' would be just as good as another—that is, good for nothing in control of inquiry and formation and in settlement of a problem" (p. 497).

In the physical sciences inquiry often begins with problems internal to the relevant science. Nevertheless Dewey insists that to be scientific social inquiry must "grow out of actual social tensions, needs, 'troubles,'" and be related to some "plan or policy for existential resolution of the conflicting social situation" (p. 499). Facts must then be determined as resources for or obstacles to reaching this solution, but always with the understanding that social facts are part of a history. Although a physicist builds, needless to say, on the work of other physicists and depends on their corroboration of his results, he can carry out his investigation in the privacy of his laboratory. In contrast, social scientists depend at every step on the cooperation of others because "any hypothesis as to a social end must include as part of itself the idea of organized association among those who are to execute the operations it formulates and directs" (p. 503).

Dewey's approach to social science is troubling. His attempt to rescue the social sciences from sterility and irrelevance, an irrelevance that would make "experiment" and hence "science" impossible, has driven him to insist on a greater degree of "relevance" to actual social problems than seems healthy. Surely, in the social sciences as in the physical sciences, there must be room for conceptual clarification and for the search for large-scale hypotheses that will unify many smaller-scale solutions. But in the social sciences, or perhaps one should say in social philosophy, Dewey is deeply suspicious of large-scale hypotheses, for they seem to him to be advanced always as being universal rather than historically limited, or as being normative rather than descriptive, and to be employed not to direct the selection of data but to prejudge them.[7] There is ample empirical justification for Dewey's misgivings. We have made little if any progress toward solving pressing social problems, and we tend to be in the grip of ideologies that blind us to possible solutions, and hence to possible resources. Nevertheless, Dewey's criticisms of social science seem to us exaggerated; it may well be that Dewey could not resist the temptation to build his own preference for a piecemeal approach to social problems into this very theory of inquiry.

Dewey's worries are most justified when social scientists become policy advisors, or advocates of particular policies. Then they seem to fall into two large classes, conservatives versus liberals, or even reactionaries versus radicals, though a given person may well be on one side with respect to one social question and on another with respect to another issue. Dewey, it seems to us, is right in suggesting that it would help if influential underlying ideologies were explicitly formulated. "For only explicit formulation stimulates examination of their meanings in terms of the consequences to which they lead and promotes critical comparison of alternative hypotheses. Without systematic formulation of ruling ideas, inquiry is kept in the domain of opinion and action in the realm of conflict" (p. 508). That is surely correct, but, alas, even with systematic formulation conflict continues. The force of tradition or special interest seems often greater than that of reasonable discussion. Nevertheless, reasonable discussion and acknowledgment that any social policy is to be regarded as a kind of experiment to be halted if it turns out badly are our last best hope, and Dewey has helped us see that we can proceed in this way, that we need no final ends. Rejection of the fact/value distinction and recognition of the means-ends continuum have been shown by Dewey to be intimately connected with a proper appreciation of the methods of science, of the continuum of inquiry.

To be sure, a number of objections to Dewey's arguments will occur to anyone who has been brought up on the literature of present-day analytic philosophy. As we said at the beginning, we believe that Dewey has the resources to meet these objections, and that by raising the objections against Dewey and seeing how he might answer them we can get a much better understanding of the depth of his position as well as of its difference from more standard views.

A Psychological Objection

The first objection comes from philosophical psychology—we say "philosophical" psychology and not simply psychology because the psychology in question has been held to be *a priori* and not empirical (notably by Donald Davidson). This psychology, which has been incorporated into the very mathematics of modern economics and decision theory, holds that an end can be *rationally* revised on the basis of undesired consequences only if the undesirability of those consequences is established by reference to another end or combination of ends which is ranked higher than the end being revised. Since justificatory "cycles" (justifying an end A by reference to an end B and B in turn by reference to A) are held to be irrational, it follows that any "rational preference ordering" must contain what Dewey would call "final ends"; that is, ends or combinations of ends which are not subject to rational criticism. In one formalization of this idea, due to von Neumann, every possible combination of things one could value (every "commodity bundle") is assigned a weight on each of a finite number of dimensions; the sum of these weights is the total utility of the combination. The dimensions themselves, and (up to certain arbitrary scale factors) the weights assigned to commodity bundles on those dimensions, represent the, so to speak, final ends of the person whose preference ordering is so represented.[8] In this representation, what happens when a person achieves an "end-in-view" and then decides that she doesn't like the "commodity bundle" she receives is that the consequences of the action taken have such low values on dimensions *other* than the ones corresponding to the end-in-view that the total value of the "commodity bundle" obtained is lower than the value of other bundles she could obtain which fail to achieve the original end-in-view. Of course it could also happen that the agent decides that she doesn't value the original "end-in-view" at all (and not just that the cost of getting it is too high); but then she must either have lacked self-knowledge (not have known what her preference ordering really was) or have changed her preference ordering because of an empirical change in her nature (something by definition neither rational nor irrational).

Just this psychology was one of Dewey's targets from almost his earliest pragmatist writings on. To see why Dewey is not convinced by the claim that the rational abandonment of an end *requires* that there be higher-ranked ends or combinations of ends, let us try to imagine a concrete case. A student enters a graduate program in philosophy. The student does extremely well, gets As, is regarded as "promising" by her professors; yet, after a couple of years, the student begins to wonder whether philosophy is what she "wants to do." Perhaps the student takes a leave of absence. Of course some students go through this and discover that philosophy is what they want to do after all; but let us imagine a case in which the student finally opts for a life of social service, rather than a life in a philosophy department. What is the "higher-ranked end" for which philosophy was given up in this case?

One answer, a very old one, is that the student wants "satisfaction." But the idea that all more specific ends are really valued for some common quality of "satisfaction" (so that even Joan of Arc is aiming for the greater quantity of "satisfaction" when she goes to the stake rather than recanting) has been repeatedly attacked as an utterly empty bit of hedonist dogma ever since the eighteenth century, if not earlier.

Another answer, Donald Davidson's, is that the question is not empirical at all: it is simply an *a priori* requirement on *interpretation* that in explaining the student's choice in action-theoretic terms we must ascribe to her ends which were higher ranked than the original ends in terms of which a career in philosophy appeared desirable. If there is a certain indeterminacy in how we are to do this, then that is simply something like the general "indeterminacy of interpretation." But Dewey rejected the idea of *a priori* truth in philosophy and believed that his work represented an alternative picture of how rational value change is possible.

Before we expand on this, let us consider one last alternative. In our story, the student eventually decided that she wanted to be more immediately helpful to distressed and oppressed people and opted for social service. *That* goal, being immediately (that is, face-to-face) helpful to distressed and oppressed people, it may be said, must have been the "higher-ranked end." To reject this explanation, as Dewey does, is not to deny that it can *sometimes* be right. It is to deny that this *must* be the correct explanation. (There are times when Dewey, like Wittgenstein, is concerned to free us from "the grip of a picture," to free us, that is, from the illusion that a philosophical theory *must* be right, and this is nowhere more the case than with the illusion that there *must* be final ends.) In the case we imagined, the student finds that her life as a philosopher is no longer satisfying, it seems to be aimless, there seems to be no end-in-view rather than an already available alternative. In this indeterminate situation she was not concerned with the question "How shall I achieve such and such an end-in-view?" Rather she had to discover the origin of her malaise and to institute the problem "What end-in-view shall I now pursue?" The formulation of the new end-in-view of social service was itself the resolution of that problematical situation. The conventional philosophical psychologist misdescribes the situation by making it seem as if the decision to give up (or at least interrupt) the study of philosophy were explained by the student's becoming aware of a conflict of the ends-in-view, whereas what actually explained the interruption of the study of philosophy was that the student found herself in a problematical situation—a situation in which she could not go on—and the new end-in-view was the provisional solution to this problematical situation, not its cause.

This example illuminates Dewey's alternative picture of how rational value change is possible. The pursuit of an end-in-view, even of an end-in-view to which efficient means are available, can lead not only to the frustration of other ends-in-view that the agent already possesses, but to a state of "dissatisfaction"; and it is the worst kind of *a priori* psychologizing, in Dewey's view, to see dissatisfaction as just the frustration of a (very general) *end*. The better way of describing this kind of "dissatisfaction" is to say that the pursuit of an end-in-view has led to a problematical situation which requires the formulation of a different end-in-view. Nothing is an end except in so far as it is someone's end-in-view; all of one's ends-in-view are means to the conduct of one's life, or, in another Deweyan image, ends and means lie on a continuum. In this picture, just what is inconceivable on the traditional picture—that ends should be just as subject to empirical testing as means—is the most obvious thing in the world.

We should like to emphasize the significance of the term "end-in-view" by reference to the importance in pragmatism of the theme of *control*: control over habits of inquiry and action in general. "Logic," in Peirce's sense as well as in Dewey's, is concerned with the achievement and employment of such control. What is under our control is subject to evaluation and criticism. To blur the distinction between ends which are really formulated by the agent and intentionally used to guide her conduct and "unconscious ends," which may of course be present, but which are not subject to intelligent criticism as long as they remain unconscious, and worse, to blur the distinction between ends which are genuinely ends-in-view for an agent and ends which are simply "read in" by a philosopher determined to hang on to a metaphysical picture, is to adopt a language which is useless from the point of view of logic as the theory of inquiry. Thus Dewey's "ends-in-view" are not merely what all other philosophers call "ends"; they are those ends which the agent herself uses at a certain moment in inquiry and action as means to conduct her life.

The Significance of Dewey's Picture for the Fact/Value Debate

A second objection to Dewey's arguments comes from philosophers who might well accept Dewey's criticism of decision theory and "rational psychology." These philosophers might agree that, in the way just outlined, there can be rational criticism of ends, and that a life rationally lived need neither be guided by nor culminate in a set of "final ends." Yet such a philosopher may still defend a "science/ethics" dichotomy.[9] After all, such a philosopher might say, there is no reason to think that people who follow Dewey's method will come to agreement on values, even if each person separately leads what we might regard as a rational life. Deweyan agents might still find that their values are subjective in a way in which their opinions about physical fact are not.

Of course Dewey would not deny that this *might* happen: Dewey is not in the business of making *a priori* claims. The question is whether the assumption that it *would* happen is the only reasonable one. And to investigate that question we must remember that Dewey's conception of inquiry is social; the *relevant* question is not what would happen if *individuals* followed Dewey's recommendations, but what would happen if individuals *and communities* followed Dewey's "scientific method" or "method of intelligence."

Here certain things must be kept in mind. The first is that the communities in which we live are concerned with what they themselves describe as "the common good."[10] The second is that disagreements over values which rise to the level of open conflict, loss of solidarity, or anomie are themselves experienced by individuals and communities as problematical situations requiring resolution.

The point of keeping these things in mind is that if the intelligent conduct of lives by individuals leads to conflicts—and of course it sometimes does—that is only a special case of the general fact that the resolution of some problems can lead to other problems. It does not follow that it must lead to *unresolvable* problems, even if there is no *a priori* guarantee that the problems it leads to are resolvable.

Here Dewey can sound unreasonably optimistic if one does not keep in mind the range of different things that can count as the resolution of a problem. If you and I disagree in our "values" a resolution need not take the form of a universalistic principle that you and I and all other persons can accept as valid. If the value disagreement concerns only our separate lives, then the apparent disagreement may be resolvable by simply relativizing the judgments in question; it may be the case that it is well for you to live your life in one way and for me to live mine in another. A similar situation sometimes arises in exact science; when we discovered that the simultaneity judgments of different observers could be incompatible, we resolved the resulting problem by adopting a theory according to which such judgments are relative to the state of motion of the observer. The idea of ethical objectivity is not the same as and does not presuppose the idea of *a universal way of life*. Dewey supports the former and consistently opposes the latter. Not only individuals but also communities and nations may have different but satisfactory ways of life.

Of course, not all ethical conflicts are subject to resolution in this way; when they are not, we face not a problem calling for a universal philosophical solution but rather an existential problem calling for practical settlement. Perhaps not all such problems can be settled; not all problems in physics or mathematics or geology or history can be settled either, but that does not support the idea that warranted assertibility and truth exist in one domain but not in another.

Pragmatism and Democracy

Once again, an example may help flesh out this abstract account. Defenders of democracy have long faced the following dilemma: If the defense of democracy is based on a metaphysical theory of human nature, that is to say, a prior decision as to what interests human beings have *qua* human beings, or a prior decision as to what is due to human beings *qua* human beings, then, like all metaphysical theories of an aprioristic kind it will rest ultimately on what Peirce called "the method of what is agreeable to reason," and that is just what (pragmatists claim) experience has taught us *doesn't work*. And if we try to rely on an empirical psychology rather than an *a priori* one, it is not clear that we have (or that we will ever have) a sufficiently well established and sufficiently penetrating "science of psychology" to deliver a defense of any particular set of political institutions. The traditional alternative has been to defend democracy on consequentialist grounds, as, for example, utilitarians do. But utilitarians assume "final ends" that are to be "maximized." Dewey, as we have said repeatedly, rejects the former, and there are well-known difficulties with the latter notion. Yet the defense and elaboration of what we may call a *critical conception of democracy* was early and late a central concern of Dewey's. Such a conception is to be used to criticize and reform present democratic institutions, and not merely to praise them.[11]

Dewey's strategy is to assume a "thin" theory of human nature, one which does not pretend to describe our interests or our rights "*qua* human beings" (and one which is of course revisable in the course of inquiry; like the account of the scientific method itself, the account of good in Dewey is a hypothesis). A key assumption is that what human beings value, and not only value but need, is not some passive state of satisfaction or pleasure but productive activity. Human conceptions of the good are indeed various, but what we most want is to bring about what we conceive to be our good through our own activity, and not to be "given" it. There is an obvious relation here to Aristotle: Aristotle's dictum that human well-being (eudaimonea) consists in the *activity* of the psyche in the complete life according to arete contains a fundamental insight. There is also a relation to the early Marx (whose writings were, of course, not known when Dewey was writing), in particular to the young Marx's thought that we both discover who we are and become who we are through productive and unalienated labor. Dewey uses this conception of our needs in a powerfully stated comment on the futility of "benevolent despots":

> History shows that there have been benevolent despots who wish to bestow blessings on others. They have not succeeded, except when their actions have taken the indirect form of changing the conditions under which those live who are disadvantageously placed. The same principle holds of reformers and philanthropists when they try to do good to others in ways which leave passive those to be benefited. There is a moral tragedy inherent in efforts to further the common good which prevent the result from being either good or common— not good, because it is at the expense of the active growth of those to be helped, and not common because these have no share in bringing the result about.[12]

What Dewey is concerned to argue, early and late, is that democracy is the precondition for the application of intelligence to the solution of social problems. We need the method of intelligence ("the scientific method") to find what our ends-in-view should be, as well as to find what means are to be used. And democracy is a precondition for the use of the method of intelligence in social life.

That this is so is not something Dewey argues on *a priori* grounds.[13] But neither are the premises Dewey uses drawn from "psychology." Here it is instructive to recall Peirce's (as well as Dewey's) arguments for the scientific method itself: in the two famous articles in *Popular Science Monthly* in which Peirce launched the pragmatist movement,[14] he argued that we have *learned from experience* that the method of authority, the method of tenacity, and the method of what is agreeable to reason don't work. In a similar vein, Dewey's *Logic* conceives of the theory of inquiry as a product of the very sort of inquiry that it describes: *epistemology is hypothesis*.

The need for such fundamental democratic institutions as freedom of thought and speech follows, for Dewey, from requirements of scientific procedure in general: the unimpeded flow of information and the freedom to offer and to criticize hypotheses. Durkheim offered similar arguments up to a point, but came to the conclusion[15] that political opinions should rest on "expert opinion," those without expertise being required to defer to the authority of the experts (and especially to sociologists). While Dewey may not have known of Durkheim's essay, he did consider and reject this view, and he did so for frankly empirical reasons: "A class of experts is inevitably so removed from common interests as to become a class with private interests and private knowledge, which in social matters is not knowledge at all."[16] Here Dewey links up with another of his themes, that privilege inevitably produces cognitive distortion: "All special privilege narrows the outlook of those who possess it, as well as limits the development of those not having it. A very considerable portion of what is regarded as the inherent selfishness of mankind is the product of an inequitable distribution of power—inequitable because it shuts out some from the conditions which direct and evoke their capacities, while it produces a one-sided growth in those who have privilege."

Thus, if a value as general as the value of democracy is to be rationally defended in the way Dewey advocates, the materials to be used in the defense cannot be circumscribed in advance. There is no one field of experience from which all the considerations relevant to the evaluation of democracy come.

The dilemma facing the classical defenders of democracy arose because all of them presupposed that we already know our nature and our capabilities. In contrast, Dewey's view is that we don't know what our interests and needs are or what we are capable of until we actually engage in politics. A corollary of this view is that there can be no final answer to the question "How should we live?" and that we should, therefore, always leave it open to further discussion and experimentation. And that is precisely why we need democracy.

Justification without Foundations

The last objection we shall consider comes from "noncognitivists" in ethics. These philosophers will argue that Dewey has not explained how there can *be* value facts. John Mackie in his *Ethics: Inventing Right and Wrong,* and more recently Bernard Williams in *Ethics and the Limits of Philosophy,* have argued that value facts are "ontologically queer" (Mackie), that they have no place in "the absolute conception of the world" (which, Williams says, we may think of as resembling the conception we get from present-day physics). The heart of these positions is the idea that ordinary epistemological practice counts for nothing if it does not square with some philosophical conception of what is allowed to be "really there," in short, the idea that the philosopher can tell us what the true world is, and that our ordinary practice is a wandering in appearance. Dewey responds to this idea in many places, but nowhere more eloquently than here:[17]

> [Philosophy's] primary concern is to clarify, liberate, and extend the goods which inhere in the naturally generated functions of experience. It has no call to create a world of "reality" *de novo,* nor to delve into secrets of Being hidden from common sense and science. It has no stock of information or body of knowledge peculiarly its own; . . . Its business is to accept and to utilize for a purpose the best available knowledge of its own time and place. And this purpose is criticism of beliefs, institutions, customs, policies with respect to their bearing upon good. This does not mean their bearing upon *the* good, as something itself formulated and attained within philosophy. For as philosophy has no private store of knowledge or of methods for attaining truth, so it has no private access to good. As it accepts knowledge of facts and principles from those competent in science and inquiry, it accepts the goods that are diffused in human experience.

We formulate ends-in-view on the basis of experience, and we appraise these on the basis of additional experience. For a pragmatist that suffices to establish the "existence" of warranted assertibility in this area. And to engage in the practice of making claims that are warrantedly assertible and of criticizing such claims is to be committed to the existence of truth. Democracy is a social condition of such practice, and therein lies its justification.

Notes

This paper was originally presented in a symposium at a meeting of the Society for the Advancement of American Philosophy in conjunction with a meeting of the Eastern Division of the American Philosophical Association, December 28, 1989, in Atlanta, Georgia.

1. John Dewey, *Logic: The Theory of Inquiry* (New York: Henry Holt,

1938), p. 535. All subsequent references to this work will be given in parentheses.

2. Mill wrote that "the backward state of the Moral Sciences can only be remedied by applying to them the methods of Physical Science, duly extended and generalized." These are the opening words of Book VI of Mill's *A System of Logic* (1843), 8th ed. (New York, 1881).

3. Hans Reichenbach, *Experience and Prediction* (Chicago: University of Chicago Press, 1938), pp. 9–16.

4. Hilary Putnam discusses the significance of the unity of form and content for ethics in "Objectivity and the Science/Ethics Distinction," in *The Quality of Life,* ed. Martha Nussbaum and Amartya Sen (Oxford: Oxford University Press, 1992; collected in *Realism with a Human Face* (Cambridge: Harvard University Press, 1990).

5. For a contemporary discussion in the same direction, see Ruth Anna Putnam, "Weaving Seamless Webs," *Philosophy,* 62 (1987), 207–220, and Hilary Putnam, *Reason, Truth, and History* (New York: Cambridge University Press, 1981), as well as the paper cited in n. 4.

6. For more discussion of these issues, see Ruth Anna Putnam, "Understanding Lincoln," *American Philosophical Quarterly,* 25 (1988), 261–268.

7. Just this case against one of the social sciences, classical sociology, has been made by an "insider," Geoffrey Hawthorn, in *Enlightenment and Despair,* 2nd ed. (Cambridge: Cambridge University Press, 1987).

8. Hilary Putnam criticizes the assumptions required for von Neumann's proof of the possibility of this representation in "Rationality in Decision Theory and in Ethics," in *Rationality in Question,* ed. Shlomo Biderman and Ben-Ami Scharfstein (Leiden: E. J. Brill, 1989).

9. As Bernard Williams does in *Ethics and the Limits of Philosophy* (Cambridge: Harvard University Press, 1985).

10. The notion of "the common good" is discussed in Part III of John Dewey and James H. Tufts, *Ethics* (in a section written by Dewey), rev. ed. (New York: Henry Holt, 1932), esp. pp. 382–387.

11. Hilary Putnam discusses this aspect of Dewey's thought in "A Reconsideration of Deweyan Democracy," op. cit. We are indebted to Geoffrey Hawthorn for valuable comments on this paper, which are reflected in our formulations in the present essay.

12. Dewey and Tufts, *Ethics* (Part III), p. 385.

13. In this respect Dewey differs radically from Habermas, who in many ways agrees with Dewey that democracy is a prerequisite for rational social decision making with respect to ends as well as with respect to means, but wishes to establish this by a "transcendental argument." For a comparison of Dewey and Habermas in this regard see the article by Hilary Putnam cited in n. 8.

14. "How to Make our Ideas Clear" and "The Fixation of Belief," reprinted in

Collected Papers of Charles Sanders Peirce, vol. 5: *Pragmatism and Pragmaticism,* ed. Charles Hartshorne and Paul Weiss (Cambridge: Harvard University Press, 1965).

15. Emile Durkheim, "Individualism and the Intellectuals" (1898), with an introduction by Steven Lukes, *Political Studies,* 17 (1969), 14–30.

16. Quoted in James Gouinlock, *The Moral Writings of John Dewey* (New York: Free Press, 1976), p. 245 (originally from *The Public and Its Problems,* pp. 206–209).

17. *Experience and Nature* (La Salle, Ill.: Open Court, 1926), pp. 407–408.

11. Education for Democracy

With Ruth Anna Putnam

In 1915 Dewey began the Preface to *Democracy and Education*[1] as follows, "The following pages embody an endeavor to detect and state the ideas implied in a democratic society and to apply these ideas to the problems of the enterprise of education." One may say, without doing too much violence to historical accuracy, that in that volume Dewey provided a reasoned defense of what was called progressive education, although even then he was aware of the excesses of some of its champions. In 1938, in *Experience and Education,* Dewey remarked that educational theory has always been subject to an either/or mentality, and that at that time the alternatives that were being treated in this "either/or" fashion were traditional education and progressive education. Moreover, he noted that in a period of intellectual, emotional, and economic insecurity, people tend to long for a return to traditional methods. Dewey, characteristically, rejected both the either/or stance and the possibility of a successful return to traditional methods, describing the latter idea as so out of touch with the conditions of modern life that it would be "folly" to seek salvation in that direction.[2] He called for a middle way between the extremes of authoritarian traditionalism and undirected progressivism (we hasten to add that these epithets are ours). In particular, he claimed that progressivism's greatest failure is in the area of curriculum[3] while traditional education fails to take the child's experience and interests seriously. He concluded by saying that the issue is not traditional versus progressive education but "what anything whatever must be to be worthy of the name *education.*"

We recount this little bit of educational history because it seems to us that we stand today at a place very much like that occupied by Dewey in 1938. What corresponds to the demands of progressivists is the demand for multiculturalism. Indeed, multiculturalism is an issue

221

with which Dewey was well acquainted, even if that issue appeared to have subsided in the 1930s.[4] In the 1880s and 1890s in the United States there were major controversies concerning the right of German children to receive instruction in German. (Such teaching was well established in Cincinnati, St. Louis, and other places where large communities of German immigrants existed.) World War I, and its attendant anti-German hysteria, finished off the acceptance of such bilingual instruction. Woodrow Wilson (following the earlier example of Theodore Roosevelt) attacked "hyphenated Americans," meaning people who considered themselves "Hebrew-Americans," "Irish-Americans," "German-Americans," "Italian-Americans," and so on. In response, Dewey, speaking to the National Education Association in 1916, defended the value of cultural pluralism: "Such terms as Irish-American or Hebrew-American or German-Americans are false terms, because they seem to assume something which is already in existence called America, to which the other factors may be hitched on. The fact is, the genuine American, the typical American, is himself a hyphenated character. It does not mean that he is part American and that some foreign ingredient is added. It means that . . . he is international and interracial in his make-up. He is not American plus Pole or German. But the American is himself Pole-German-English-French-Spanish-Italian-Greek-Irish-Scandinavian-Bohemian-Jew—and so on. The point is to see to it that the hyphen connects instead of separates. And this means at least that our public schools shall teach each factor to respect every other, and shall take pains to enlighten us all as to the great past contributions of every strain in our composite make-up."[5] Failure to recognize and appreciate "that the peculiarity of our nationalism is internationalism" would, Dewey thought, be divisive rather than unifying. He was as concerned to combat a splitting of American society into rigid classes—these were the years when both the whether and the how of "industrial education" were hotly debated—as to combat the division into ethnic groups; indeed, the two issues were intimately linked, since the children of the poor were also the children who came from non-Anglo backgrounds.

Dewey and his followers[6] lost the battle for multiculturalism at that time: following World War I, there was a wave of postwar chauvinism which led to the deportation of East Europeans, to the banning of mass immigration in 1924, and to the rise of the Ku Klux Klan. Nebraska even passed a law (later found unconstitutional by the Supreme Court) banning the teaching of all foreign languages before the eighth grade.[7] But it was inevitable that, in a society as pluralistic as ours, the issue could not and would not go away for keeps.

Just as traditionalists in 1938 reacted to the excesses of progressivism by demanding a return to traditional education, so traditionalists today react to the excesses of the advocates of multiculturalism by advocating a return to the traditional curriculum and canon. We say "excesses of the advocates of multiculturalism" rather than "excesses of multiculturalism" since multiculturalism in education is still largely in the planning stages; we do not know what its excesses, if any, will be in practice. Just as Dewey sought an educational philosophy that would transcend the traditional/progressive dichotomy while yet being education for a future more democratic society, so we seek in Dewey's philosophy the resources to transcend the Eurocentric/multicultural dichotomy while advocating, as Dewey himself did in 1916, education for a future more pluralistic society. Let us begin, then, with a short review of that philosophy.

Philosophy as Education

In *The Claim of Reason,* Stanley Cavell imagines[8] that a child "little or big, asks me Why do we eat animals? or Why are some people poor and others rich? or What is God? or Why do I have to go to school? or Do you love black people as much as white people? or Who owns the land? or Why is there anything at all? or How did God get here?" and he goes on to describe confronting such questions—confronting them in a thoughtful way, as opposed to repeating "foregone conclusions"—as "a task that warrants the name of philosophy." "It is also the description of something we might call education," he adds.

John Dewey would certainly have applauded these words. Indeed, writing in 1915,[9] he anticipated Cavell's identification of philosophy with education, writing, "If a theory makes no difference in educational endeavor, it must be artificial. The educational point of view enables one to envisage the philosophical problems where they arise and thrive, where they are at home, and where acceptance or rejection makes a difference in practice. If we are willing to conceive education as the process of forming fundamental dispositions, intellectual and emotional, philosophy may even be defined as *the general theory of education.*"

To better understand Dewey's thought, we wish to trace the way in which this identification of education (or the general theory of education) with philosophy comes about in Dewey's philosophy. If one wishes to pursue just about any topic in Dewey's thought, it is, however, necessary to keep Dewey's thoroughgoing radicalism in mind at all times. Although Dewey was not an economic determinist (or, indeed, a determinist of any kind), he did see philosophical ideas and their conflicts as products of the conflicts and difficulties of social life. Members of a privileged ruling class cannot be expected to see the world in the way it is perceived by those having to struggle for their bare existence. A commercial and manufacturing society cannot be expected to see "the needs and possibilities of life" as they would be seen by a feudal society or a society like that of ancient Athens, and a society which has experienced a series of crises and upheavals cannot be expected to see them in the same way as a society whose conditions have been static for a long time.[10] In particular, Dewey suggests that the prevalence of various dualisms in the theory of knowledge is the product of the hard and fast walls which mark off social groups and classes within a group, for example, rich and poor, men and women, nobles and base-born, ruler and ruled.[11] Dewey's argument is that such barriers mean the absence of fluent and free intercourse, and that this absence results in a kind of sealing off of different types of life experiences from one another, "each with isolated subject matter, aim, and standard of values. Every such social condition must be formulated in a dualistic philosophy, if philosophy is to be a sincere account of experience." Among the dualisms that Dewey wished to account for in this way are the dualisms of inner and outer, mind and body, reason and emotion, action guided by self-interest and action guided by principle, and still others. As evidence that these dualisms will not fade away as long as the social divisions that engender them are still with us Dewey points out that the old soul/body or mind/body dualism still survives in a scientific age as a dualism between "the brain and the rest of the body."[12] Any one familiar with the philosophy inspired by today's "cognitive science" will appreciate the justice of this remark (made in 1915).

To these dualistic theories of knowledge, Dewey opposed his own conception, based on a thoroughgoing continuity between action and intelligence (conceived of as the intentional reorganization of experience through action), as well as a continuity between fact and value and between the intellect and the emotions. Dewey describes the educational views of those under the influence of the intellect/emotions dichotomy with a dry wit:

The intellect is a pure light and the emotions are a disturbing heat. The mind turns outward towards the truth; the emotions turn inward to considerations of personal advantage and loss. Thus in education we have that systematic depreciation of interest which has been noted, plus the necessity in practice, with most pupils, of recourse to extraneous and irrelevant rewards and penalties in order to induce the person who has a mind (much as his clothes have a pocket) to apply that mind to the truths to be known. Thus we have the spectacle of professional educators decrying appeal to interest while they uphold with great dignity the need for reliance upon examinations, marks, promotions and emotions, prizes, and the time-honored paraphernalia of rewards and punishments. The effect of this situation in crippling the teacher's sense of humor has not received the attention it deserves.[13]

What Is Education?

For Dewey, education has many of the functions that Hegel ascribed to the family; above all, it is the method by which civil society reproduces itself. The education that Dewey recommends is designed to overcome the dualisms that he attacks, not by explicitly instilling a better philosophy, but by serving the aim of beginning to eradicate the very barriers that he described as responsible for those dualisms, barriers between social classes, and between rulers and ruled.

According to Dewey's normative description of education, these functions are to be served by that "reconstruction or reorganization of experience" which (1) adds to the meaning of experience and (2) increases the students' ability to direct the course of their post-classroom experience.[14] "Meaning" is a quasi-technical term in *Democracy and Education,* and is identified with the perception of connections, as, for example, the connections between facts and facts, between ends and means, and between facts and values.

At first blush (1) and (2) represent different perspectives on the process of education, the former being social and the latter individualistic. But Dewey points out quite quickly that "reconstruction" may be social as well as individual. In particular, "progressive communities"[15] do not try to educate the young with the aim of simply reproducing current ways, but rather try to shape the experiences of students so that better habits will be formed, and thus the future adult society will be an improvement on their own. We shall return to this notion of *social* reconstruction, but we must first take a brief look at Dewey's notion of "reconstructing" the *child's* experience.

Dewey uses the example of learning one's first language to illustrate the respective functions of nature and nurture. One would not learn to speak any language if one lacked the necessary physical organs, but what language one speaks, indeed whether one will speak any language at all, depends on one's environment, in particular one's social environment. The same example serves to illustrate the roles of child and "educator" in learning. The child has a natural impulse to communicate but whether that impulse is encouraged or frustrated depends on the adults with whom she interacts. Finally, learning to speak one's first language is a prime example of learning at its best, namely, learning in order to learn more, for *the aim of education is to enable individuals to continue their education.*[16]

That the aim of education is to enable individuals to continue their education is an ideal which often fails to be realized. All education instills habits. Although we often think of habits as mere routine responses to stimuli, in Dewey's use of the term there are habits of judging and reasoning and experimentation, as well as of using instruments or carrying out familiar activities. Nevertheless, there is a constant danger that habits will become routine, and it is only by constructing a learning environment which teaches *the use of intelligence in forming habits* that this tendency can be counteracted. In particular, as Dewey pointed out in the remark attacking the dualism of emotion and intellect, education will not have this aim if the student's mind is thought of as a "pocket" to be filled by the facts and theories that the teacher already possesses. The student needs to learn how to utilize her own and humanity's past experience, how to formulate hypotheses and how to test them.

The emphasis on *testing* both "facts" and "values" is no accident. Dewey sees the human being as an organism, which learns in the only way it is possible to learn, by constructing hypotheses and testing them in practice. The experimental method, Dewey claims,[17] understood in this generous way, is as old as action, although scientific knowledge of that method is a very recent acquisition. In sharp contrast to the positivists, Dewey insists that value judgments as well as facts can be tested "experimentally" (we shall say more about this below). But this testing is not something to be carried on by some elite (say, by social scientist "savants," as Auguste Comte urged).[18] In a democracy, it is something that every citizen must learn to do. Indeed, Dewey's ideal aim of education—"to enable individuals to continue their education"—is applicable to all members of society *only* in a democratic society. For, Dewey points out, when social relationships are hierarchical, what some persons take to be their aims will be merely means to the ulterior aims of others.[19]

If the capacity for inquiry and the capacity for testing are to be learned, facts, values, and theories supplied by the teacher must make sense by connecting to the child's own experience. By the time the student reaches high school or college, the connection will often be to an earlier educational experience, while for the first-grader or pre-schooler it will almost always be to an out-of-school experience. But not all experiences are educative, alas; many school experiences fail to prepare the student for future experiences, and even encourage rigidity and obtuseness in the face of experiences that don't fit what the student has been taught to expect. The slogan Dewey adopts in his late work *Experience and Education,* "education of, by and for experience,"[20] consciously echoes Lincoln. The echo emphasizes the ever present connection between the themes of education and democracy in Dewey's philosophy; it also prepares the way for the idea that a philosophy of education presupposes a philosophy of experience.

Dewey continually stresses the continuing interactive nature of experience. What experience one has now depends on what experiences one had in the past, not only because one's present situation is the result of past experiences, but because, even in the very short term, what one *attends* to depends on what one has just experienced and on what one has just *done.* And what experience one has now will, for the same reasons, shape one's future experiences. In particular, although Dewey rejects erecting the distinction between "subjective inner conditions" and "objective outer conditions" into a dualism, he recognizes the distinction as a distinction between factors which interpenetrate and continuously modify each other. A theory of education which places too much emphasis on one of these factors at the expense of the other will lead the teacher to shape her pupils' experiences so that they are mis-educative rather than educative. Traditional education failed to pay sufficient attention to the internal factor, to the experiences and interests of the child; it attempted instead to mold individuals that would fit into preconceived social roles. But Dewey's alternative is not to let children run wild. "The ideal aim of education," according to *Education and Experience,* "is creation of the power of self-control." This does not contradict the overriding goal of enabling individuals to continue their education. Without self-control a person cannot transform her impulses and desires into settled purposes, into ends-in-view, for to do that she must stop and think before she acts. Ideally, the educator's greater experience enables her to understand what experiences her students have; this requires sympathetic attention. It also enables her to foresee the consequences of her pupils' experiences. Her greater maturity (again, ideally) give her the right and the responsibility to shape these experiences, through shaping the school environment, through selection of subject matter, and so on, so that they will be educative rather than stifling or distorting.

In 1915, Dewey had already written that the school environment is designed to serve these functions: "simplifying and ordering the factors of the disposition it is wished to develop; purifying and idealizing the existing social customs; creating a wider and better balanced environment than that by which the young would be likely, if left to themselves, to be influenced."[21] Three quarters of a century later we can still see how short we fall of this ideal. Rather than purifying and idealizing existing social customs, we seem to have brought more and more of the problems of the adult world into the school environment. We think not only of drugs and violence but of the fact that many schools are laboring under such severe economic constraints that teaching and learning are adversely affected. Again, while the intention of Brown v. Board of Education and subsequent decisions to desegregate the schools was to create a wider and better balanced environment for our children, economic segregation undermines that goal for many of our children, to the detriment of both the affluent and the economically deprived.

In a similar vein, we note Dewey's remark that "the increasing complexity of social life requires a longer period of infancy" in which to acquire the powers needed to deal with these complexities.[22] On this point our society seems now at odds with itself. We have adopted longer years of schooling as the norm, yet we have allowed infancy to be shortened for many through earlier sexual activity and earlier involvement with drugs and violence. We are inclined to think that Dewey would have been amazed and saddened could he have foreseen that at the very end of the twentieth century the views of education he developed at its beginning still represent an unrealized ideal rather than an accomplishment upon which a yet better educational approach could be based.

Dewey's Experimentalism about Values

It is evident from what we have said that Dewey does not hold the view that the schools should just "teach facts and skills" and regard "value judgements" as, so to speak, personal idiosyncrasies. But neither, as we shall see, does he think the schools should "teach values" in the sense of teaching "a scheme of separate virtues." What the schools should teach is *the experience of applying intelligence to value questions.*

After what has been said, the method by which Dewey suggests this is to be accomplished should not come as a surprise. Dewey holds that an education which is to subserve the ends of breaking down the dualisms, and the social "barriers" and forms of possession and dispossession which are responsible for those dualisms, must be responsible to the nature of the human being as a social, interest-creating being whose intelligence is rightly conceived of not as a bunch of "faculties" but as an ongoing activity of reorganization of experience through action. In its moral dimension, what this means is that people are to be seen not as originally self-centered little creatures who have to be bribed and threatened into a semblance of social concern, but as communal beings who will learn to think in social terms if they are allowed to participate in the practice of forming and testing collective goals and means. As Dewey puts it in the closing paragraph of *Democracy and Education,* "under such conditions, the school becomes itself a form of social life, a miniature community and one in close interaction with other modes of associated experience beyond school walls. All education which develops power to share effectively in social life is moral."

But we need to say a word about the picture of human nature that underlies Dewey's belief in the possibility of applying intelligence to the assessment of values.

Dewey's picture of human nature is Darwinian and naturalistic, but not reductionist. As we said, he views the human being as an organism, which learns in the only way it is possible to learn, by constructing hypotheses and testing them in practice. One aspect of Dewey's antireductionism is an insistence that the distinction between needs and mere desires, and likewise the distinction between "values" (which have been intelligently appraised in the course of experience) and mere satisfactions, is essential to understanding human action.[23] This does not mean that ethics is a "special science," the science which seeks to appraise satisfactions in order to discover what is *valuable;* rather, for Dewey, *every* inquiry tests values as well as facts.

We have analyzed elsewhere[24] the arguments Dewey employs to support this last claim. Here it may be helpful to recall Dewey's disagreement with the standard decision-theoretic picture, according to which every rational choice presupposes a rank ordering of "preferences" which cannot be *rationally* altered. (We believe that that picture is behind much, if not all, of the popularity of noncognitivism in ethics.) In our "Dewey's *Logic:* Epistemology as Hypothesis" (Chapter 10, above), we illustrated Dewey's very different picture by imagining a graduate student of philosophy who finds herself increasingly frustrated with the subject. We imagined that after considerable reflection and experimentation this student discovers that a life of social service is more satisfying. According to the conventional decision theorist, becoming aware of a conflict of ends-in-view explains why the student finds herself in a problematical situation; in contrast, we maintained that the student's problem was that she found herself without any aim, and the new end-in-view was the provisional solution to this problematical situation, not its cause.[25] Nor, as we pointed out, would Dewey accept the following redescription of this case: the student had the very general end *avoid dissatisfaction,* and she discovered empirically the means to *that* end. Not only does this description introduce an *a priori* psychology (so that even Joan of Arc's going to the stake can be described as her "avoiding dissatisfaction"), but it sweeps under the rug the important distinction between ends which really guide our conduct ("ends-in-view") and the tension that we experience when we are seeking such ends. In Dewey's alternative psychology ends and means lie on a continuum, and in the course of an inquiry we may revise our means or our ends or both. As we wrote in "Dewey's *Logic:* Epistemology as Hypothesis,"[26] on this picture just what is inconceivable on the traditional decision-theoretic picture— that ends should be just as subject to empirical testing as means—is the most obvious thing in the world.

Commenting on our argument in "Epistemology as Hypothesis," one friendly critic[27] responded by asking for "more argument" for the claim that the student's problematical situation requires the formulation of a different "end-in view," and went on to ask, "Is there any way in which her resulting end-in-view can be rationally defended other than that it gives her something to do?"

This question seems to assume a traditional philosophy of mind, in which being in a problematic situation is conceived as a having a *feel-ing* of, say, frustration, and resolving it is just "having something to do." But just as a great many philosophers in this century have re-jected the idea that we directly perceive only our sense data and only know of material objects by means of a problematic "infer-ence," so Dewey rejects the idea that we directly perceive only our feelings and only know whether our interactions with the social and physical environment are going well or are in trouble by means of an "inference." Perceiving that one has a problematical situation which is not being resolved by just looking for better means to ex-isting ends-in-view is perceiving something *objective* in Dewey's ac-count (for example, in *Logic: The Theory of Inquiry*), and perceiv-ing that a new end-in-view enables one to function effectively is likewise perceiving something objective. But functioning effectively is not just "having something to do," nor is it something one al-ways judges in terms of some fixed criterion like the classical utilitarian's "pleasure"; one inevitably brings one's whole charac-ter (which is to say, the product of one's knowledge and values to date) to such a judgment. If the critic's demand is that the student be able to justify her judgment that the new end-in-view is valuable in terms of criteria she would have acknowledged *before* she made her decision, then that demand may well be impossible to meet; but that demand is frequently impossible to meet in science as well.[28] We realize, of course, that merely offering an account like Dewey's does not *refute* noncognitivism; but neither does merely offering a noncognitivist account refute cognitivism. Dewey's achievement is to have given a richly detailed picture of a holistic cognitivism which does not recognize any hard and fast dichotomy between the factual and the evaluative.

The rejection of the fact/value dichotomy illustrates the way in which Dewey wants us to replace *one* of the traditional dualisms by a continuity; in a fuller discussion of Dewey's philosophy, we would have to explain how each of the dualisms listed earlier receives a sim-ilar treatment. But understanding the way in which Dewey avoids a fact/value dualism is of particular importance in reading any of his works. If this is not grasped, then his emphasis on learning to bring about changes in the world, on confirming and disconfirming our ideas through experimentation, and so on, can easily be assimilated to positivism, and Dewey will be seen as a conventional social engineer (like Auguste Comte). But this would be a profoundly mistaken reading.

A Brief Comparison of Dewey with Habermas

Elsewhere[29] one of us has compared Dewey's conception of democracy with Jürgen Habermas'. Because Dewey and Habermas often discuss the very same issues, we shall risk digressing to consider just how a Habermasian might see *Democracy and Education*. When we warned against seeing Dewey as a Comtean social engineer, we were, in fact, thinking of the danger of identifying Dewey's notion of "intelligence" with what Habermas calls "instrumental rationality" *(Zweckmittelrationalität)*. In the scheme put forward in Habermas' *Knowledge and Human Interests,*[30] human nature is conceived of as involving three fundamental "interests": (1) *Zweckmittelrationalität,* an interest in choosing the most efficient means given fixed (usually self-interested) goals; (2) a *social* interest, which manifests itself in the establishment of communities and norms, and in communication and interpretation; and (3) an *emancipatory* interest, which is an interest in *transcending* the framework of conventional understandings and norms (in any and all areas of our collective and personal life). We are *convention-transcending animals,* in Habermas' philosophical anthropology. This emancipatory interest of ours has its pathologies, to be sure, and political Utopianism and philosophical fantasy are among them; but it is absolutely essential to our humanity, and both political progress and philosophy itself are among its products.

While there is much that is right in this philosophical anthropology, we believe that Dewey would object to the rigidity of the scheme. It cannot be called a dualism, because it has three components rather than two, but otherwise it resembles (and indeed presupposes) a number of the traditional dualisms. For example, Habermas presupposes an absolutely sharp division between "norms" and "facts," and between *Zweckmittelrationalität* and the discursive rationality that is involved in the rational establishment of a norm in a community. In contrast, Dewey would argue that the social interest and the emancipatory interest require the use of intelligent experimentation if their fruits are not to be fantastic or totalitarian, and that, as we just explained, instrumental rationality in Dewey's sense, if not in the decision theorists' sense, involves a constant sensitivity to value questions. The three interests all interpenetrate, in Dewey's philosophical anthropology, and the intelligent pursuit of any or all of them requires the experimental method.

At bottom, then, the difference between the two pictures is this: although Habermas does not actually deny the need for experiment in the establishment of norms, he rarely mentions it. His picture is one in which communities arrive at norms by mere discussion, while they arrive at "facts" by experimentation. Moreover (although Habermas has been moving away from this of late),[31] the methodology that is supposed to guide the norm-producing discussion is itself derived *a priori*, via a "transcendental pragmatics." Dewey, we believe, would welcome Habermas' notion of an "emancipatory interest," but he would wish to break down all of the dualisms and reject all of the apriorism implicit in Habermas' scheme.

Better and Worse Communities

Education, we saw, is the way a society renews itself. But as societies may be good or bad, or rather better or worse, so are the results of the socialization that education accomplishes. Dewey sets out, therefore, to seek a standard by which to measure the progress of societies, for, as we mentioned above, in a progressive society the aim of education is to make the future society better by making the future adults better. In order to be sure that the standard will be practicable, Dewey seeks to base it on actually existing positive traits of social life. "Now in any social group whatever, even in a gang of thieves, we find some interest held in common, and we find a certain amount of interaction and co-operative intercourse with other groups."[32] Generalizing these traits, Dewey's view is that the more interests are shared and the freer the interaction with other groups, the better the society.

Dewey's two criteria may be understood so as to be in conflict, however, and it is at this point that we make contact with the multi-culturalism debate, both in Dewey's time and in ours. If we think that more interests being shared means more uniformity of interests, and that free interaction with other groups primarily makes for diversity of interests within the home-group, then we will feel that one can have one or the other but not both. The old ideal of American society as a melting pot, an ideal which meant in practice that the home-cultures of citizens and would-be citizens were to be submerged in an Anglo or at best Anglo-American culture, takes it that a uniform culture will generate uniformity of interests and hence shared interests. On this view, to be a "hyphenated American" is not to be a proper American at all, and therefore the aim becomes for every American to purge himself or herself of every characteristic on the left side of the hyphen and to become culturally indistinguishable from every other American.

To be sure, in theory, one might conceive of a "melting pot" as producing an amalgam in which all the best features of all the constituent cultures would form a coherent whole, though even then the image suggests that the various ingredients would no longer be clearly discernible. In practice, the culture of the melting pot reflected the fact that the original settlers were English. Not only did these settlers suppress the native Americans they found already here, but they were able to impose their culture on the successive waves of immigrants and on the descendants of the Africans they had imported. Hence the culture was predominantly English as late as 1837, when Emerson delivered what Justice Holmes was to call "our intellectual Declaration of Independence," the address titled "The American Scholar." Emerson and his fellow Transcendentalist Theodore Parker both bemoaned the absence of "originality" in American letters, but Parker was to point out that America had produced one form of literature that was unique to this country and could have been produced only here, namely, slave narratives. To be sure, Parker failed to recognize these narratives as literature worthy to be included in a canon.[33] When African-Americans turned to forming their own canon, some of them reiterated the claim that their literature, indeed *only* their literature, was truly American. We believe that Dewey would have objected to that claim just as he explicitly repudiated the corresponding claim of "Englandism," going so far as to say that anyone who insisted that American culture must conform to one of its constituent cultures "no matter how early settled in our territory, or how effective it has proved in its own land," would be "a traitor to an American nationalism."[34] (Strong words during World War I—a period of nationalist hysteria!)

An American culture that would reflect the diversity of our population would, as we suggested earlier, include the best from a variety of traditions. As Dewey wrote in 1915, "One would not expect a ruling class living at ease to have the same philosophy of life as those who were having a hard struggle for existence."[35] To the extent that our literary canon is English or at best Anglo-American and our philosophical canon is European, both will reflect the philosophy of "a ruling class living at ease" and fail to include the philosophy of those who had to struggle for survival whatever the color of their skin, the continent of their origin, or, indeed, their gender. The teaching of literature and of philosophy is, as Henry Louis Gates, Jr., points out, the teaching of values. In order to teach the values our students will need as citizens of a pluralistic democracy and a "global village," we shall inevitably have to engage in a certain amount of what Gates calls "canon deformation."[36]

Cultural Diversity in Education

The need for this sort of educational reform derives from the fact that over the past two centuries the dominant group failed to interact in a cooperative spirit with the many other groups present in this country. In so far as education perpetuates a one-sidedly Anglo-American culture and polity, it fails to be progressive in Dewey's sense. Unfortunately, members of what we call "minorities" still see their children return from school ignorant of their own cultural heritage yet not accepted by what is called the "majority." Insofar as the dominant group fails to interact cooperatively with other groups, the society as a whole fails to have shared values developed through democratic inquiry. When values and the choices among alternative values are imposed from the outside, individuals do not make these values their own. One piece of evidence which suggests the existence of widespread alienation of this sort among citizens of the United States is the fact that almost half the eligible voters do not vote. Yes, most of us speak English more or less well, but that does not mean that we understand one another, let alone respect one another. Education has failed to overcome the barriers between rich and poor, men and women, those of European descent and persons of color—indeed, even the contributions of non-English Europeans to our so-called Eurocentric culture are not adequately recognized.

What has been said so far suggests how one might argue for a policy of multiculturalism on the basis of Dewey's conception of education. Since ours is a population which consists of members of many different ethnic identities (and since indeed a single individual frequently has roots in more than one cultural group), education should prepare the next generation to live and function in a pluralistic society. Just as Dewey saw that a truly democratic society must overcome class barriers, saw that the schools must provide an environment in which differences in economic class carry no weight, neither privilege nor stigma, and saw, further, that "the typical American, is himself a hyphenated character," so we must see that a truly democratic society must overcome ethnic barriers and barriers of color and hence differences of color or ethnicity must not confer differential benefits or burdens on our students. Current demands for a multicultural curriculum in the elementary and secondary schools or for a multicultural requirement in colleges represent only first and halting steps toward that goal. For a long time to come, pupils whose home language is English, whose home religion is Christianity, and whose skin is white will find that what they are taught relates to their experiences, connects with matters that are familiar from home more often than not, while children for whom one or more of these conditions fails to obtain will have this experience proportionately less often. Dewey's first principle, that education must take the experiences and interests of the child seriously, virtually requires that the curriculum be cognizant of the variety of homes from which the children come. Although we have spoken of children, what has just been said is true of young adults in college as well.

The importance of a culturally diverse curriculum goes far beyond making schooling less alien and alienating, however. The aim, as we said before, is to prepare the future citizens of a pluralistic society. A pluralistic society, as we understand the term, is not simply a society in which many different racial, ethnic, and religious groups can be found; it is not simply a society in which all these groups enjoy equal civil and political rights; rather, a pluralistic society is a society in which members of each group respect the cultures and values of the other groups. Respect, unlike mere tolerance, requires some knowledge of the other culture; one cannot respect what one does not know at all. Obviously, in as plural a society as ours, that knowledge will be extremely superficial with respect to most other groups, but one would hope that everyone would have some nonsuperficial knowledge of the history, tradition, art, or literature of at least one group not his or her own. John Rawls has expressed the hope that persons with widely divergent conceptions of the good might nevertheless come to agree on a common conception of political and social justice through what he calls an overlapping consensus.[37] We are suggesting that such an overlapping consensus requires that members of the society can communicate with one another concerning the values by which they live. What that requires is more than simply sharing a language: it requires a willingness to find out where the other person "comes from." The slang expression has got it exactly right. Just as I cannot understand your joy when it rains until I find out that you come from a part of the world that suffers from severe droughts, so I cannot understand why you react with anger to some expression I use until I find out that it has been used historically to denigrate people like you. So, there will be conflicts between us. I may think that you want to limit my academic freedom when you tell me what I must not say, and you may think that I am a racist because I object to your demand that I eliminate certain expressions from my vocabulary. Some feminists think men are sexists when they object to ordinances banning pornography; some men and women think that people who want to enact ordinances banning pornography are totalitarian enemies of free speech. Only when we try to understand where each of us comes from, what baggage of sufferings and of preconceptions we carry with us, can we hope to achieve an overlapping consensus.

Some Objections to Multiculturalism

Finally we must consider some objections that have been raised to multiculturalism. One objection with which we agree is this: Because the drive for multiculturalism has been instigated and led by people of color, it has tended to overlook that United States culture is Anglophone rather than European. Thus when Italians, or Poles, or Greeks have suggested that their cultures too have been ignored, that their cultures too need to be brought into the center, that request has often been rejected on the grounds that the point of multiculturalism is to combat Eurocentrism. We reject this understanding of multiculturalism.

We reject it for two reasons. First, to return to Dewey's point that the school should take the experiences of the child seriously, a child from one of these backgrounds may feel just as alien in an overwhelmingly Anglo-American classroom as a Cambodian child, she may be subject to just as much teasing and mistreatment from the other children as a Hispanic youngster. Those children will learn to accept this child if they find that the teacher takes this child's different traditions, songs, stories seriously by giving them a place in the curriculum.

Second, the long-range aim of multiculturalism as we understand it is to produce adults who respect one another regardless of their ethnic, racial, or religious heritage. When multiculturalism is reconceived, or rather misconceived, as anti-Europeanism, it fails to produce that mutual respect; it will generate centrifugal forces of contempt, distrust, and fear rather than the ability to form a set of shared values.

Some critics of multiculturalism seem to fear that the very idea of a multicultural society inevitably will result in a balkanization. Arthur Schlesinger, Jr., believes that what underlies the demand for a culturally diverse education is the view that "ethnicity is the defining experience for most Americans, that ethnic ties are permanent and indelible, that the division into ethnic groups establishes the basic structure of American society, and that a main objective of public education should be the protection, strengthening, celebration, and perpetuation of ethnic origins and identities."[38] Against this Schlesinger maintains, "Obviously the reason why the United States, for all its manifest failure to live up to its own ideals, is still the most successful large multiethnic nation is precisely *because,* instead of emphasizing and perpetuating ethnic separation, it has assimilated immigrant cultures into a new *American* culture."[39] We have already acknowledged that Europhobia is no better than Afrophobia or Asiaphobia, but Schlesinger thinks that students should be encouraged to develop an understanding and respect for "American culture" rather than for their own cultural heritage. Why are these seen as mutually exclusive alternatives? Is it not rather the case that just as individuals who do not respect themselves generally fail to respect others, so individuals who do not appreciate the cultures of their parents will fail to appreciate the culture of the United States? Moreover, to the extent that cultural diversity is an important characteristic of American society—to the extent that "the typical American is himself a hyphenated character"—failure to encourage an appreciation of that diversity will amount to a failure both to adequately socialize the student and to properly honor what is "typically American" in each of ourselves. In short, it will undermine Schlesinger's professed aim of saving the unity of the United States.

Like Schlesinger we are dismayed by the fragmentation of our society. With Schlesinger we hope for integration, not disintegration. Unlike Schlesinger we believe that the fragmentation that troubles him, including the Europhobia that we too regret, is the result of a long American tradition of racism and of disdain for non-English speakers and their cultures. Unlike Schlesinger we do not identify integration (that is, pluralism) with total assimilation (that is, the submerging of all our differences). We belong, each of us, to more than one community; yet all of us belong to the large community called the United States of America. It is important, Dewey has taught us, that there be many shared interests within that large community, and it is also important that that large community engage in fruitful interaction with the smaller communities within it and that those smaller communities interact cooperatively with one another. In fact, unless these latter interactions take place, the large community will be unable to develop sufficiently strong bonds of shared interests. Multiculturalism is one way, though by no means the only way, to aid in this process.

But there are those who think that opening the canon—expanding the received conception of the humanities—will create a tower of Babel where there used to be a *uni*versity: that far from improving communication, it will increase incomprehension. This would, indeed, be the case, if we did not also modify the ways in which we teach, the ways in which we do research, the ways in which we think. In the course of making a similar point against opponents of opening the canon, Gates wrote, "in the humanities, facts and values don't exist in neatly disjoint realms of knowledge"[40]—to which we add: not only in the humanities but in life.

This is not the only way in which advocates of multicultural education adopt a Deweyan point of view. The authors of the report of the New York State Social Studies Review and Development Committee, titled *One Nation, Many Peoples: A Declaration of Cultural Interdependence* list among their guiding principles the following characteristically Deweyan tenets: "the subject matter content should be *treated as socially constructed* and therefore tentative—as is all knowledge" and "the teaching of social studies should *draw and build on the experience and knowledge that students bring to the classroom*" (emphasis in the original). Throughout the report these authors emphasize that "a multicultural perspective must necessarily be a multiple perspective."[41] We can do no better than to end with a thought of John Dewey's, "pluralism is the greatest philosophical idea of our times," and his question, "How can we bring things together as we must without losing sight of plurality?"[42]

Notes

Originally presented to the Association for Philosophy of Education, December 28, 1992, in Washington, D.C.

1. *Democracy and Education* (New York: Macmillan, 1916). Dewey dated the Preface "1915"; the copyright is 1916. The sentence quoted is on p. iii.
2. *Experience and Education,* in *John Dewey: The Later Works,* vol. 13, ed. Jo Ann Boydston (Carbondale, Ill.: Southern Illinois University Press, 1988), p. 57.
3. Ibid., p. 52.
4. We are indebted to Nathan Glazer for instruction on the early history of the multiculturalism debate.

5. John Dewey, "Nationalizing Education," in *John Dewey: The Middle Works,* vol. 10, ed. Jo Ann Boydston (Carbondale, Ill.: Southern Illinois University Press, 1988), p. 205.

6. Horace Kallen, whose essay "Democracy versus the Melting-Pot" appeared in *The Nation,* February 18, 1915, pp. 190–192, and February 25, 1915, pp. 217–220; Randolph Bourne, who published a similar essay (titled "Trans-national America") in *The Atlantic,* July 1916, pp. 86–97, took similar pro-pluralist positions.

7. Nathan Glazer suggested to us that these events should be seen as parts of a single chauvinist trend in that period. He also points out that Nebraska exempted Greek, Latin, and Hebrew, "all presumed safely dead."

8. *The Claim of Reason* (Oxford: Oxford University Press, 1979), p. 125.

9. *Democracy and Education,* p. 328.

10. Ibid., pp. 324–327.

11. Ibid., chapter 25. (In particular, pp. 333–4.)

12. Ibid., p. 336.

13. Ibid., pp. 335–6.

14. Ibid., p. 76.

15. Ibid., p. 79.

16. Ibid., p. 100.

17. Ibid., pp. 338–339.

18. See *The Crisis of Industrial Civilization: The Early Essays of Auguste Comte,* ed. Ronald Fletcher (London: Heinemann Educational Books, 1974), p. 212.

19. Ibid., pp. 100–101.

20. *Experience and Education,* p. 14.

21. *Democracy and Education,* p. 22.

22. Ibid., p. 46.

23. See, for example, Dewey's *The Quest for Certainty: A Study of the Relation of Knowledge and Action* (New York: Minton, Balch, 1929), pp. 260–261.

24. See Chapter 10 of the present volume.

25. According to the decision-theoretic picture, either the student all along had the aim of helping distressed and oppressed people, she merely discovered that philosophy was not an efficient means to this end, and so she chose a different career, or the student came to see that she could not realize her always present aim of helping the downtrodden while also pursuing the aim of being a philosopher. Following Dewey, whose account we were illustrating, we denied that the end of helping distressed and oppressed people *must* all along have been the student's higher-ranked end. In our story, the student finds that her life as a philosophy student seems to be aimless, there seems to be *no* end-in-view rather than an already available alternative. In this indeterminate situation she was not concerned with the question "How shall I achieve my higher-ranked end?" Rather she had to dis-

cover the source of her malaise, and to institute the problem "What end-in-view shall I now pursue?" The formulation of the new end of social service is the resolution of that problematical situation.

26. Chapter 10 of the present volume, p. 213.

27. We thank Henry Richardson for raising these questions.

28. For example, it is doubtful if one could convince a Newtonian physicist that quantum mechanics is even a scientific theory at all, let alone a better theory, by criteria already accepted in Newtonian science!

29. "A Reconsideration of Deweyan Democracy," the last chapter of Hilary Putnam's *Renewing Philosophy* (Cambridge: Harvard University Press, 1992).

30. Jürgen Habermas, *Knowledge and Human Interests* (Boston: Beacon Press, 1971).

31. See the closing chapter of his *Theory of Communicative Action*, vol. 2 (Boston: Beacon Press, 1989).

32. *Democracy and Education*, p. 83.

33. See Henry Louis Gates, Jr., *Loose Canons: Notes on the Culture Wars* (New York: Oxford University Press, 1992), pp. 22–23.

34. "Nationalizing Education," p. 204.

35. *Democracy and Education*, p. 327.

36. *Loose Canons*, p. 35.

37. John Rawls, "The Idea of an Overlapping Consensus," in his *Political Liberalism* (New York: Columbia University Press, 1993).

38. "A Dissent on Multicultural Education," *Partisan Review*, 58, no. 4 (1991), p. 630.

39. Ibid., p. 631, emphasis in the original.

40. *Loose Canons*, p. 118.

41. *One Nation, Many Peoples: A Declaration of Cultural Interdependence*, the report of the New York State Social Studies Review and Development Committee, June 1991.

42. Quoted without reference in Gates, *Loose Canons*, p. 119.

IV

Essays after Wittgenstein

12. Rethinking Mathematical Necessity

We had been trying to make sense of the role of convention in *a priori* knowledge. Now the very distinction between *a priori* and empirical begins to waver and dissolve, at least as a distinction between sentences. (It could of course still hold as a distinction between factors in one's adoption of a sentence, but both factors might be operative everywhere.[1]

A consequence of Quine's celebrated critique of the analytic-synthetic distinction—a consequence drawn by Quine himself—is that the existence of mathematical entities is to be justified in the way in which one justifies the postulation of theoretical entities in physics. As Quine himself once put it,[2]

> Certain things we want to say in science may compel us to admit into the range of variables of quantification not only physical objects but also classes and relations of them; also numbers, functions, and other objects of pure mathematics. For mathematics—not uninterpreted mathematics, but genuine set theory, logic, number theory, algebra of real and complex numbers, and so on—is best looked upon as an integral part of science, on a par with the physics, economics, etc. in which mathematics is said to receive its applications.

As I read this and similar passages in Quine's writings, the message seems to be that in the last analysis it is the utility of statements about mathematical entities for the prediction of sensory stimuli that justifies belief in their existence. The existence of numbers or sets becomes a hypothesis on Quine's view, one not dissimilar in kind from the existence of electrons, even if far, far better entrenched.

It follows from this view that certain questions that can be raised about the existence of physical entities can also be raised about the existence of mathematical entities—questions of indispensability and questions of parsimony, in particular. These views of Quine's are views that I shared ever since I was a student (for a year) at Harvard in 1948–49, but, I must confess, they are views that I now want to criticize. First, however, I want to present a very different line of thinking—one which goes back to Kant and to Frege. This line is one that, I believe, Carnap hoped to detranscendentalize; and in Carnap's hands it turned into linguistic conventionalism. My strategy in this essay will be to suggest that there is a different way of stripping away the transcendental baggage while retaining what (I hope) is the insight in Kant (and perhaps Frege's)[3] view; a way which has features in common with the philosophy of the later Wittgenstein rather than with that of Carnap.

Kant and Frege

What led me to think again about the Kantian conception of logic was a desire to understand an intuition of Wittgenstein's that I had never shared. For the early Wittgenstein it was somehow clear that logical truths do not really say anything, that they are empty of sense (which is not the same thing as being nonsense), *sinnlos* if not *unsinnig*. (There are places in the *Investigations* in which Wittgenstein, as I read him, confesses that he still feels this inclination, although he does not surrender to it.) *Obviously,* sentences of pure logic are statements with content, I thought; if proved, they are moreover *true* statements, and their negations are *false* statements. But I felt dissatisfaction; dissatisfaction with my own inability to put myself in Wittgenstein's shoes (or his skin) and to even imagine the state of mind in which one would hold that truths of logic are "tautologies," that they are *sinnlos*. It was then that I thought of Kant.

   Kant's lectures on logic[4] contain one of his earliest—perhaps the earliest—polemic against what we now call "psychologism." But that is not what interests me here, although it is closely related to it. What interests me here is to be found in *The Critique of Pure Reason* itself, as well in the lectures on logic, and that is the repeated insistence that illogical thought is not, properly speaking, thought at all. Not only does Kant insist on this, both in the lectures on logic and in the *Critique,* but his philosophical arguments in the *Critique* employ this doctrine in different ways. One employment has to do with the issue of thought about noumena. Kant allows that noumena are not in space and time. They are not related as "causes" and "effects." They may not be "things" as we creatures with a rational nature and a sensible nature are forced to conceive "things." But we are not allowed to suppose that they violate laws of logic; not because we have some *positive* knowledge about noumena, but because we know something about thought, and the "thought" that the noumena might not obey the laws of logic is no thought at all, but rather an incoherent play of representations.

This is in striking contrast to Descartes's view that God could have created a world which violated the laws of logic.

But Kant's view goes further than this. A metaphysician who thinks of "logical space" as a Platonic realm of some sort might agree with Kant: logical laws hold not only in "the actual world" but in all the other "possible worlds" as well. On such a view, logical laws are still descriptive; it is just that they describe *all* possible worlds, whereas empirical laws describe only some possible worlds (including the actual one). This opens the possibility of turning Kant's flank, as it were, by claiming that while indeed the laws of logic hold in all possible worlds, *God could have created an altogether different system of possible worlds.*

On my reading of the first *Critique,* there are points in that work at which Kant at least entertains the idea that talk of "noumena" is empty, that the notion of a noumenon has only a kind of formal meaning. But even when he entertains this possibility, Kant never wavers from the view that even *formal* meaning must conform to the laws of logic. It is this that brought home to me the deep difference between an *ontological* conception of logic, a conception of logic as descriptive of some domain of actual and possible entities, and Kant's (and, I believe, Frege's) conception. Logic is not a description of what holds true in "metaphysically possible worlds," to use Kripke's phrase. It is a doctrine of *the form of coherent thought.* Even if I think of what turns out to be a "metaphysically impossible world," my thought would not be a thought at all unless it conforms to logic.

Indeed, logic has no metaphysical presuppositions at all. For to say that thought, in the normative sense of *judgment which is capable of truth,* necessarily conforms to logic is not to say something which a metaphysics has to *explain.* To explain anything *presupposes* logic; for Kant, logic is simply prior to all rational activity.

While I would not claim that Frege endorses this view of Kant, it seems to me that his writing reflects a tension between the pull of the Kantian view and the pull of the view that the laws of logic are simply the most general and most justified views we have. If I am right in this, then the frequently heard statement that for Frege the laws of logic are like "most general laws of nature" is not the whole story. It is true that as *statements* laws of logic are simply quantifications over "all objects"—and all concepts as well—in *Begriffsschrift*. There is in Frege no "metalanguage" in which we could say that the laws of logic are "logically true"; one can only assert them in the one language, *the* language. But at times it seems that their *status,* for Frege as for Kant, is very different from the status of empirical laws. (It was, I think, his dissatisfaction with Frege's waffling on this issue that led the early Wittgenstein to his own version of the Kantian view.)

It was this line of thinking that helped me to understand how one might think that logical laws are *sinnlos* without being a Carnapian conventionalist. Laws of logic are without content, in the Kant-and-possibly-Frege view, insofar as they do not *describe* the way things are or even the way they (metaphysically) *could* be. The ground of their truth is that they are the formal presuppositions of thought (or better, *judgment*). Carnap's conventionalism, as interpreted by Quine in "Truth by Convention" (in *From a Logical Point of View*), was an *explanation* of the origin of logical necessity in human stipulation; but the whole point of the Kantian line is that logical necessity neither requires nor can intelligibly possess any "explanation."

Quine on Analyticity

In a certain sense, Quine's attack on analyticity in "Two Dogmas of Empiricism" (in *From a Logical Point of View*) does not touch the truths of pure logic. These form a special class, a class characterized by the fact that in them only the logical words occur essentially.[5] If we define an "analytic" truth as one which is either (a) a logical truth in the sense just specified, or (b) a truth which comes from a logical truth by substituting synonyms for synonyms, then the resulting notion of analyticity will inherit the unclarity of the notion of *synonymy;* and this unclarity, Quine argued, is fatal to the pretensions of the philosophical notion in question. But if we choose to retain the term "analytic" for the truths of pure logic, this problem with the notion of synonymy will not stop us.

But what would the point be? The definition of a logical truth as one in which only logical words occur essentially does not imply that logical truths are *necessary.* And Quine's doctrine that "no statement is immune from revision" implies that (in whatever sense of "can" it is true that we can revise any statement) it is also true that we "can" revise the statements we call "logical laws" if there results some substantial improvement in our ability to predict, or in the simplicity and elegance of our system of science.[6]

This doctrine of the *revisability of logic* would of course be anathema to Kant and to Frege (who says that the discovery that someone rejects a logical law would be the discovery of a hitherto unknown form of madness).

The idea that logic is just an empirical science is so implausible that Quine himself seems hesitant to claim precisely this. There are two respects in which Quine seems to recognize that there is something correct in a more traditional view of logic. In the first place, he suggests that the old distinction between the analytic and the synthetic might point to a sort of continuum, a continuum of unrevisability ("There are statements which we choose to surrender last, if at all"),[7] or of bare behavioristic reluctance to give up, or of "centrality." We were wrong, the suggestion is, in thinking that any statement is absolutely immune from revision, but there are some we would certainly be enormously reluctant to give up, and these include the laws of traditional logic. And in the second place, Quine sometimes suggests that it is part of translation practice to translate others so that they come out believing the same logical laws that we do.[8] Thus revising the laws of logic might come to no more—by our present lights—that *changing the meanings* of the logical particles. It is on the first of these respects that I wish to focus now.

It seems right to me that giving up the analytic-synthetic dichotomy does not mean—that is, *should not mean*—thinking of all our beliefs as empirical. (To think that way is not really to give up the dichotomy, but rather to say that one of the two categories—the analytic—has null extension.) "There are no analytic sentences, only synthetic ones" would be a claim very different from "There is no epistemologically useful analytic-synthetic *distinction* to be drawn." Saying that there is an analytic-synthetic *continuum* (or rather, an *a priori–a posteriori* continuum—since Quine identifies the rejection of the analytic with the rejection of the a priori in his writing)[9] rather than an analytic-synthetic *dichotomy* is a promising direction to go if one wishes to reject the dichotomy as opposed to rejecting the analytic (or the *a priori*). But does the idea of "reluctance to give up" capture what is at stake, what is *right* about the idea that logical truths are quite unlike empirical hypotheses?

Consider the following three sentences:

(1) It is not the case that the Eiffel Tower vanished mysteriously last night and in its place there has appeared a log cabin.
(2) It is not the case that the entire interior of the moon consists of Roquefort cheese.
(3) For all statements p, $\ulcorner -(p \centerdot -p) \urcorner$ is true.

It is true that I am much more reluctant to give up (3) than I am to give up (1) or (2). But it is also the case that I find a fundamental difference, a difference in kind, not just a difference in degree,[10] between (3) and (2), and it is this that Quine's account(s) may not have succeeded in capturing. As a first stab, let me express the difference this way: I can imagine finding out that (1) is false, that is, finding out that the Eiffel Tower vanished overnight and that a log cabin now appears where it was. I can even imagine finding out that (2) is false, although the reluctance to trust our senses, or our instruments, would certainly be even greater in the case of (2) than in the case of (1). But I cannot imagine *finding out* that (3) is false.[11]

It Ain't Necessarily So

But is talk about "imagining" so and so not gross psychologism? In some cases it is. Perhaps I could be convinced that certain describable observations would establish to the satisfaction of all reasonable persons that the interior of the moon consists entirely of Roquefort cheese. Perhaps I could be convinced that my feeling that it is "harder to imagine" the falsity of (2) than to imagine the falsity of (1) is just a "psychological fact," a fact about *me*, and not something of methodological significance. But to convince me that it is possible to imagine the falsity of (3) you would have to put an alternative logic in the field;[12] and *that* seems a fact of methodological significance, if there is such a thing as methodological significance at all.

To explain this remark, I would like to review some observations I made many years ago in an essay titled "It Ain't Necessarily So."[13]

In that essay, I argued against the idea that the principles of Euclidean geometry originally represented an empirical hypothesis. To be sure, they were not necessary truths. They were *false*;[14] false considered as a description of the space in which bodies exist and move, "physical space," and one way of showing that a body of statements is not necessary is to show that the statements are not even true (in effect, by using the modal principle $-p \supset -\Box p$). But, I argued, this only shows that the statements of Euclidean geometry are synthetic; I suggested that to identify "empirical" and "synthetic" is to lose a useful distinction. The way in which I proposed to draw that distinction is as follows: call a statement *empirical relative to a body of knowledge B* if possible observations (including observations of the results of experiments people with that body of knowledge could perform) would be *known* to disconfirm the statement (without drawing on anything outside of that body of knowledge). It seemed to me that this captures pretty well the traditional notion of an empirical statement. Statements which belong to a body of knowledge but which are not empirical relative to that body of knowledge I called "necessary relative to the body of knowledge." The putative truths of Euclidean geometry were, prior to their overthrow, simultaneously synthetic and necessary (in this relativized sense). The point of this new distinction was, as I explained, to emphasize that there are at any given time some accepted statements which cannot be overthrown merely by *observations,* but can only be overthrown by thinking of a whole body of alternative theory as well. And I insisted (and still insist) that this is a distinction of methodological significance.

If I were writing "It Ain't Necessarily So" today, I would alter the terminology somewhat. Since it seems odd to call statements which are false "necessary" (even if one adds "relative to the body of knowledge B"), I would say "*quasi*-necessary relative to body of knowledge B." Since a "body of knowledge," in the sense in which I used the term, can contain (what turn out later to be) false statements, I would replace "body of knowledge" with "conceptual scheme." And I would further emphasize the nonpsychological character of the distinction by pointing out that the question is not a *mere* question of what some people can imagine or not imagine; it is a question of what, given a conceptual scheme, one *knows* how to falsify or at least disconfirm. Prior to Lobachevski, Riemann, and others, no one knew how to disconfirm Euclidean geometry, or even knew if anything *could* disconfirm it. Similarly, I would argue, we do not today know how to falsify or disconfirm (3), and we do not know if anything could (or would) disconfirm (3). But we do know, at least in a rough way, what would disconfirm (1), and probably we know what would disconfirm (2). In this sense, there is a qualitative difference between (1), and probably (2), on the one hand, and (3) on the other. I do not urge that this difference be identified with analyticity; Quine is surely right that the old notion of analyticity has collapsed, and I see no point in reviving it. But I do believe that this distinction, the distinction between what is necessary and what is empirical relative to a conceptual scheme, is worth studying even if (or especially if) it is not a species of analytic-synthetic distinction. Here I shall confine myself to its possible significance for the philosophy of mathematics. First, however, I shall use it to try to clarify, and possibly to supplement,[15] some insights in Wittgenstein's *On Certainty*.

Some Thought Experiments in *On Certainty*

There are a number of places in *On Certainty* at which Wittgenstein challenges the very conceivability of what look at first blush like empirical possibilities. I will consider just two of these. The statement that water has boiled in the past, that is, that it has on many occasions boiled, or even more weakly that it has boiled on at least *one* occasion, looks like a paradigmatic "empirical statement." The conventional wisdom is that its degree of confirmation should, therefore, be less than one; its falsity should be conceivable, even given our experience so far. But is it? Can we, that is to say, so much as make sense of the possibility that we are deceived about *this;* conceive that our entire recollection of the past is somehow mistaken, or (alternatively) that we have all along been subject to a collective hallucination?[16]

A different kind of case: Can I be mistaken in thinking that my name is Hilary Putnam,[17] in thinking, that is, that that is the name by which I am called and have been called for years?

To take the second case first: Certainly I can imagine experiences as of waking up and discovering that what I call my life (as Hilary Putnam, as husband, father, friend, teacher, philosopher) was "all a dream." One might "make a movie" in which just that happened. And Wittgenstein (who, of course, wrote "Ludwig Wittgenstein" and not "Hilary Putnam") admits[18] that such experiences might *convince* one. (Of course, they might not convince one; one might break down mentally, or one might commit suicide—there are many ways of telling such a story.) But, Wittgenstein points out, saying that such experiences might convince one is one thing; saying that they *justify* the conclusion that it was all a hallucination, that I am not Hilary Putnam, is something else. Why should I not say that *those* experiences are the hallucination (if I come to have them)? If experiences call into question *everything* that I take for granted—including the evidence for every single scientific theory I accept, by the way—then what is left of notions like "justification" and "confirmation"?

The question Wittgenstein raises here has a significance that reaches far beyond these examples. There is a sense in which they challenge not just the truth but the very intelligibility of the famous Quinian slogan that no statement is immune from revision. Can "Water has sometimes boiled" be revised? Can I (rationally) revise my belief that my name is Hilary Putnam?

In one sense, of course, we can revise the *sentences*. We could change the very meaning of the words. In that sense it is trivial that any *sentence* can be revised. And, since Quine rejects talk of "meaning" and "synonymy" at least when fundamental metaphysical issues are at stake, it might seem that the very question Wittgenstein is raising cannot even make sense for Quine (when Quine is doing metaphysics), depending, as that question does, on speaking of "beliefs" rather than "sentences." But things are not so simple.

Quine's Philosophy of Logic

The reason they are not so simple is that Quine himself has at times suggested[19] that it is difficult to make sense of the notion of revising the laws of classical logic. The problem is that—at least in the case of truth-functions—the fact that a translation manual requires us to impute violations of these laws to speakers calls into question the very adequacy of the translation manual. By so much as raising this question, Quine has opened the door to the sort of question I saw Wittgenstein as raising two paragraphs back. Can we now conceive of a community of speakers (1) whose language we could make sense of, "translate," in Quine's sense, who (2) assent to a sentence *which we would translate as* "Water has never boiled"? Can we now conceive of a community of speakers whom (1) we could interpret and understand, and who (2) assent to a sentence *which we would translate as* "7 + 5 = 13"?

Well, suppose we cannot. What significance does it have if we admit that we cannot do this? Here I would like to recall again what I wrote in "It Ain't Necessarily So." In my view, if we cannot *describe* circumstances under which a belief would be falsified, circumstances under which we would be prepared to say that -B had been confirmed, then we are not presently able to attach a clear *sense* to "B can be revised."[20] In such a case we cannot, I grant, say that B is "unrevisable," but neither can we intelligibly say "B can be revised." Since this point is essential to my argument, I shall spend a little more time on it.

Consider a riddle. A court lady once fell into disfavor with the king. (One easily imagines how.) The king, intending to give her a command impossible of fulfillment, told her to come to the Royal Ball "neither naked nor dressed." What did she do? (Solution: she came wearing a fishnet.)

Concerning such riddles, Wittgenstein says[21] that we are able to give the words a sense only after we know the solution; the solution bestows a sense on the riddle-question. This seems right. It is true that I could translate the sentence "She came to the Royal Ball neither naked nor dressed" into languages which are related to English, languages in which the key English words "naked" and "dressed" have long-established equivalents. But if I didn't know the solution, could I *paraphrase* the question "How could she come to the ball neither naked nor dressed?" *even in English itself?* I would be afraid to make *any* change in the key words, for fear of losing exactly what the riddle might turn on. Similarly, I would be afraid to translate the riddle into a foreign language which was not "similar" to English in the sense of having obvious "equivalents" to "naked" and "dressed." And if someone asked me, "In what sense, exactly, was she neither naked nor dressed?" I could not answer if I did not know the solution.

But are we not in the same position with respect to a sentence like "In the year 2010 scientists discovered that 7 electrons and 5 electrons sometimes make 13 electrons"? Or with respect to "In the year 2010 scientists discovered that there are exceptions to $5 + 7 = 12$ in quantum mechanics"? If this is right, and I think it is, then perhaps we can see how to save something that is right in the Kant-Frege-early Wittgenstein line that I described earlier.

Kant-Frege-Wittgenstein (Again)

Before trying to say what might be saved of the position I attributed to Kant, possibly Frege, and the early Wittgenstein at the beginning of this essay, it is important to specify what is metaphysical excess baggage that should be jettisoned. According to these thinkers, logical (and mathematical) truths are true by virtue of the nature of thought (or judgment) as such. This is a highly metaphysical idea, and it receives a somewhat different inflection in the writings of each of them.

In Kant's case, the metaphysics is complicated by the need to distinguish the truths of logic not only from empirical truths, but also from synthetic *a priori* truths. In the case of a synthetic *a priori* judgment, say, "Every event has a cause," Kant tells us that what makes the judgment true is not the way the world is—that is, not the way the world is "in itself"—but the way our reason functions; but this talk of the function and constitution of human reason has to be distinguished (by Kant) from talk of the nature of thought, and of the (normative) laws of thought, alluded to above. There is, according to Kant, such a thought as the thought that there is an event with no cause; but I can know *a priori* that that thought is false, because the very constitution of my reason ensures that the data of the senses, as those data are represented to my mind, will fit into a certain structure of objects in space and time related by causality. There is a sense in which the negations of synthetic *a priori* truths are no more descriptions of a way the world could be than are the negations of logical truths. Yet there is an enormous difference (for Kant) between the negation of a synthetic *a priori* truth and a logical contradiction. The negation of a synthetic *a priori* truth is thinkable; and the reason such a statement could never turn out to be a truth is explainable—to provide the explanation is precisely the task of the *Critique of Pure Reason*. The negation of a logical truth is, in a sense, unthinkable; and it is unthinkable precisely *because* it is the negation of a logical truth. Explanation goes no further. "Logical truth" is, as it were, itself an ultimate metaphysical category.[22]

Frege's views are less clear, although he too seems to have retained the notion of synthetic *a priori* truth.[23] At the same time, Frege prepares the way for Wittgenstein by identifying the Kantian idea of the nature of thought with the structure of an ideal language. The early Wittgenstein, however, tried (if my reading is correct) to marry a basically Kantian conception of logic with an empiricist rejection of the synthetic *a priori*. For the Wittgenstein of the *Tractatus,* the opposition is between logical truths and empirical truths, not between logical truths and synthetic truths in the Kantian sense. The problem of distinguishing the way in which the structure of thought (which, as just remarked, becomes the structure of the ideal language) guarantees the unrevisability of logic from the way in which the structure of reason guarantees the unrevisability of the synthetic *a priori* no longer arises, because either a judgment is about the world, in which case its negation is not only thinkable but, in certain possible circumstances, confirmable, or it is not about the world, in which case it is *sinnlos.*

My suggestion is not, of course, that we retain this idea of a nature of thought (or judgment, or the ideal language) which metaphysically guarantees the unrevisability of logic. But what I *am* inclined to keep from this story is the idea that logical truths do not have negations that we (presently) understand. It is not, on this less metaphysically inflated story, that we can say that the theorems of classical logic are "unrevisable"; it is that the question "Are they revisable?" is one which we have not yet succeeded in giving a sense. I suggest that the "cans" in the following sentences are not intelligible "cans": "Any statement can be held true come what may, if we make drastic enough adjustments elsewhere in the system. Even a statement very close to the periphery can be held true in the face of recalcitrant experience by pleading hallucination or by amending certain statements of the kind called logical laws. Conversely, by the same token, no statement is immune from revision."

A Few Clarifications

Let me spend a few moments in explaining how I am using some key terms, to prevent misunderstandings. I have already illustrated the idea that a question may not have a sense (or, at any rate, a sense we can grasp), until an "answer" gives it a sense, with the example of the riddle. And I want to suggest that, in the same way, saying that logic or arithmetic may be "revised" does not have a sense, and will never have a sense, unless some concrete piece of theory building and applying *gives* it a sense. But saying this leaves me open to a misunderstanding; it is easy to confuse talk of "senses" with talk of meanings in the sense in which translation manuals are supposed to be recursive specifications of meanings. But the word "sense" (in "In what sense do you mean *p*?") is much broader and much less specific than the term "meaning." When I learned the sense of "She came to the ball neither naked nor dressed" I did not learn anything that would require me to revise my dictionary entries for either the word *naked* or the word *dressed*.[24] Knowing the "sense" of a statement (or a question) is knowing how the words are used in a particular context; this may turn out to be knowing that the words had a "different meaning," but this is relatively rare. (Yet knowing the sense of the question or statement is connected with our ability to paraphrase discourses intelligently.) I may know the meaning of words, in the sense of knowing their "literal meaning," and not understand what is said on a particular occasion of the use of those words.

It follows that "giving words a sense" is not always a matter of giving them a new literal meaning (although it can be). "Momentum is not the product of mass and velocity" once had no sense; but it is part of Einstein's achievement that the sense he gave those words seems now *inevitable*. We "translate" (or read) old physics texts homophonically, for the most part; certainly we "translate" *momentum* homophonically.[25] We do not say that the word "momentum" used not to refer, or used to refer to a quantity that was not conserved; rather we say that the old theory was wrong in thinking that momentum was exactly *mv*. And we believe that wise proponents of the old theory *would* have accepted our correction had they known what we know. So this is not a case of giving a word a new meaning, but, as Cavell put it (using a phrase of Wittgenstein's), "knowing how to go on."[26] But that does not alter the fact that the sense we have given those words (or the use we have put them to) was not available before Einstein.

A different point of clarification. There is an old (and, I think futile) debate about whether contradictions are "meaningless." When I suggested that Frege was attracted to (and the Wittgenstein of the *Tractatus* held) the position that the negation of a theorem of logic violates the conditions for being a thinkable thought or judgment, I do not mean to exclude contradictions from "meaning" in the sense of well-formedness in the language, or in an ideal language. (For Kant, of course, it would be anachronistic to raise this issue.) The point is rather that a contradiction cannot be used to express a judgment by itself. Frege would perhaps say that it has a degenerate *Sinn,* that a contradiction functions as a mode of presentation of the truth value $\perp$ (falsity). (This would explain how it can contribute to the meaning of a complex judgment, say, $q \supset (p \cdot -p)$, which is just a way of saying $-q$.) But for Frege, as for Kant, the notion of *thinking that* $(p \cdot -p)$ makes no sense (except as "a hitherto unknown form of madness").

In any case, it is well to remember that part of the price we pay for talking as if science were done in a formalized language is that we make it harder to see that in every language that human beings *actually* use, however "scientific" its vocabulary and its construction, there is the possibility of forming questions and declarative sentences to which we are not presently able to attach the slightest sense. If we formalize English, then in the resulting formal idiom, "John discovered last Tuesday that $7 + 5 = 13$," or the formula that corresponds to that sentence in regimented notation, may be "well formed," but it does not follow that one could *understand* that sentence if one encountered it.

Arithmetic

One last point of clarification: it may seem that, given any p of the kind I have been discussing, any p that has the status of being "quasi-necessary relative to our present conceptual scheme," there must be a fact of the matter as to whether p is *merely* quasi-necessary or truly "necessary." But a review of the considerations I have employed should dispel this impression. Whether a given statement, say, the parallels postulate of Euclidean geometry, or some formulation of determinism, or an ordinary arithmetic truth "could be revised" depends on whether an "alternative theory" could really be constructed and confirmed (and on whether or not we would translate p homophonically into our present language, were such an alternative theory described to us); and all of the crucial terms—"theory," "confirmation," "acceptable translation manual"—have far too much indeterminacy to make application of the principle of bivalence convincing. The illusion that there is in all cases a fact of the matter as to whether a statement is "necessary or only quasi-necessary" is the illusion that there is a God's-Eye View from which all possible epistemic situations can be surveyed and judged; and that is indeed an illusion.

We can now, perhaps, see how the position I have been suggesting differs from the position of Rudolf Carnap. On Carnap's position, an arithmetic truth, say $5 + 7 = 12$, or a set-theoretic truth for that matter, is *guaranteed* to be unrevisable—guaranteed by a recursive linguistic stipulation.[27] We *know* that the truths of mathematics are unrevisable (that any revision would be a change of meaning), and we know this because we have *stipulated* that they are unrevisable (and changing the stipulations just *is* changing the meaning of the terms). As Quine has pointed out,[28] Carnap wanted a notion of analyticity that would have epistemological clout! By contrast, what I have suggested is simply that, as a matter of descriptive fact about our present cognitive situation, we *do not know* of any possible situation in which the truths of mathematics (as we take them to be) would be disconfirmed, save for situations in which the meanings of terms are (by our present lights) altered. To insist that these statements *must* be falsifiable, or that *all* statements must be falsifiable—is to make falsifiability a third (or is it a fourth by now?) dogma of empiricism.

It might be argued,[29] however, that there must be more to the truth of the theorems of mathematics than my story allows, for the following reason: even if the theorems of mathematics are consequences of principles whose negations could not, as far as we now know, intelligibly be true—principles such that the idea of *finding out that they are false* has not been given a sense—still there are statements of mathematics whose truth value no human being may ever be able to decide, even if more axioms become accepted by us on grounds of "intuitive evidence" or whatever. Certainly there are (by Gödel's theorem) sentences whose truth value cannot be decided on the basis of the axioms we presently accept. Yet, given that we accept the principle of bivalence, many of these sentences are true (as many as are false, in fact). And nothing *epistemic* can explain the truth of such undecidable statements, precisely because they *are* undecidable. To this objection, I can only answer that I am not able to attach metaphysical weight to the principle of bivalence; but a discussion of *that* issue would take another essay at least as long as this one.

The Existence of Mathematical Objects

It is time to consider the effect of the position I am considering (and tentatively advocating) on the issues with which this essay began. Some of Quine's doctrines are obviously unaffected if this line of thinking is right. What I have called the metaphysical analytic-synthetic distinction, that is, the idea of a notion of "analyticity" which will do foundational work in epistemology, is still jettisoned. Indeed, I have made no use of the idea of "truth by virtue of meaning," and the only use made of the notion of sense is the claim that there are some "statements" to which we are presently unable to attach any sense—something which I take to be a description of our lives with our language, rather than a piece of metaphysics. The principal effect of this line of thinking is on the idea, described at the beginning of this essay, that the existence of mathematical entities needs to be justified.

To begin with, let me say that, even apart from the issues I have been discussing here, talk of the "existence" of mathematical entities makes me uncomfortable. It is true that when we formalize mathematics, we at once get (as well-formed formulas, and as theorems) such sentences as "Numbers exist," in addition to sentences which might really occur in a mathematics text or class, sentences like "There exist prime numbers greater than a million." For Quine, this shows that arithmetic commits us to the existence of numbers; I am inclined to think that the notion of "ontological commitment" is an unfortunate one. But I will not discuss that issue here. What is clear, even if we accept "Numbers exist" as a reasonable mathematical assertion, is that if it makes no sense to say or think that we have discovered that arithmetic is *wrong*, then it also makes no sense to offer a reason for thinking it is not wrong. A reason for thinking mathematics is not wrong is a reason which excludes nothing. Trying to justify mathematics is like trying to say that whereof one cannot speak one must be silent; in both cases, it only looks as if something is being ruled out or avoided.

If this is right, then the role of applied mathematics, its utility in prediction and explanation, is not at all like the role of a physical theory. I can imagine a "possible world" in which mathematics—even number theory, beyond the elementary counting that a nominalist can account for without difficulty—serves no useful purpose. (Think of a world with only a few thousand objects, and no discernible regularities that require higher mathematics to formulate.) Yet imagining such a world is not imagining a world in which number theory, or set theory, or calculus, or whatever is *false;* it is only imagining a world in which number theory, or set theory, or calculus, or whatever, is not *useful.* It is true that if we had not ever found any use for applied mathematics, then we might not have developed pure mathematics either. The addition of mathematical concepts to our language enlarges the expressive power of that language; whether that enlarged expressive power will prove useful in empirical science is an empirical question. But that does not show that the truth of mathematics is an empirical question.

The philosophy of logic and mathematics is the area in which the notion of "naturalizing epistemology" seems most obscure. The suggestion of this essay is that the problem may lie both with "naturalize" and with "epistemology." The trouble with talk of "naturalizing" epistemology is that many of our key notions—the notion of understanding something, the notion of something's making sense, the notion of something's being capable of being confirmed, or infirmed, or discovered to be true, or discovered to be false, or even the notion of something's being capable of being stated—are normative notions, and it has never been clear what it means to naturalize a normative or partly normative notion. And the trouble with talk of epistemology in the case of mathematics is that this talk depends on the idea that there is a problem of *justification* in this area. But perhaps mathematics does not require justification; it only requires theorems.

Notes

I am indebted to Warren Goldfarb and Charles Parsons for valuable discussions of previous drafts of this paper.

1. W. V. Quine, "Carnap on Logical Truth" *Synthese* (1960), p 364.

2. "The Scope and Language of Science," *British Journal of the Philosophy of Science,* 8 (1957), 16.

3. I am aware that many people (for instance, Michael Dummett) read Frege as a Platonist rather than as a Kantian. However, two of my colleagues at Harvard, Burton Dreben and Warren Goldfarb, convinced me long ago that this is a mistake. For a reading of Frege which is close to the views of Dreben and Goldfarb, see Joan Weiner's *Frege in Perspective* (Ithaca: Cornell University Press, 1991).

4. Immanuel Kant, *Logic,* trans. R. Hartman and W. Schwarz (Mineola, N.Y.: Dover, 1974).

5. A term F is defined to "occur essentially" in a sentence (after that sentence has been "regimented" in the style of quantification theory) if there is a term G of the same syntactic class (e.g., a monadic predicate if F is a monadic predicate, a dyadic predicate if F is a dyadic predicate . . .) such that replacement of every occurrence of F in the sentence by an occurrence of G results in a sentence with a different truth-value. Notice that this Quinian definition of "occurs essentially" uses no *modal* notions.

6. Quine himself draws this conclusion, for example on p. 40 of "Two Dogmas of Empiricism" in *From a Logical Point of View* (Cambridge: Harvard University Press, 1953): "Any statement can be held true come what may, if we make drastic enough adjustments elsewhere in the system. Even a statement very close to the periphery can be held true in the face of recalcitrant experience by pleading hallucination or by amending certain statements of the kind called logical laws. Conversely, by the same token, no statement is immune to revision. Revision even of the logical law of the excluded middle has been proposed as a means of simplifying quantum mechanics; and what difference is there between such a shift and a shift whereby Kepler superseded Ptolemy, or Einstein Newton, or Darwin Aristotle?"

7. "Truth by Convention," pp. 350–351, in Benacerraf and Putnam, eds., *Philosophy of Mathematics: Selected Readings,* 2nd ed., ed. Hilary Benacerraf and Hilary Putnam (Cambridge: Cambridge University Press, 1984).

8. For example, in "Carnap on Logical Truth" Quine writes (p. 354), "Deductively irresoluble disagreement as to logical truth is evidence of deviation in usage (or meanings) of words" (emphasis in the original). In *Word and Object* (Cambridge: MIT Press, 1960), it is part of translation practice to translate others so that the verdict-tables for their truth functions come out the same as ours (otherwise, one simply does not attribute truth func-

tions to them) and so that "stimulus analytic" sentences have stimulus analytic translations. Indeed, in *Philosophy of Logic,* 2nd ed. (Cambridge: Harvard University Press, 1986), Quine seems to hold that one *cannot* revise propositional calculus without losing simplicity; but he has later rejected this view.

9. On this, see my "Two Dogmas Revisited," in *Realism and Reason,* vol. 3 of my *Philosophical Papers* (New York: Cambridge University Press, 1983).

10. I recall that Herbert Feigl asked me once, shortly after the appearance of "Two Dogmas," "Is the difference between a difference in kind and a difference in degree a difference in kind or a difference in degree?" This essay is, in a way, a return to this issue.

11. I do not claim, by the way, that *no* revisions in classical logic are conceivable. I myself have expressed sympathy for both quantum logic (which gives up the distributive law) and intuitionist logic. But the principle of contradiction seems to me to have quite a different status. On this see "There Is at Least One A Priori Truth" in my *Realism and Reason.*

12. I am aware that some people think such a logic—paraconsistent logic—has already *been* put in the field. But the lack of any convincing application of that logic makes it, at least at present, a *mere* formal system, in my view.

13. Reprinted in *Mathematics, Matter, and Method,* vol. 1 of my *Philosophical Papers* (New York: Cambridge University Press, 1975).

14. One way to see that they were false, regarded as descriptions of the space in which bodies are situated, is that they imply that space is infinite, whereas, according to our present physics, space is finite. See the discussion in "It Ain't Necessarily So."

15. In my view, the propositions Wittgenstein calls "grammatical" are often better conceived of as necessary relative to our present conceptual scheme. The use of the term "grammatical," with its strong linguistic connotations, inevitably suggests to many readers something like the notion of analyticity.

16. *On Certainty,* ed. G. E. M. Anscombe and G. H. von Wright (Oxford: Basil Blackwell, 1969), §§338–341.

17. Ibid., §515.

18. See ibid., §517.

19. See n. 8 above for references.

20. The way I expressed this in "It Ain't Necessarily So" (in *Mathematics, Matter, and Method*), using the example of Euclidean geometry, was to say that prior to the construction of an alternative geometry plus physics, the statement "There are only finitely many places to get to, travel as you will" did not express anything we could conceive.

21. In an unpublished manuscript cited by Cora Diamond in *The Realistic Spirit* (Cambridge: MIT Press, 1991), p. 267. Readers of that book will see

how much my thinking has been influenced by Diamond's brilliant essays on Frege and Wittgenstein.

22. I do not, of course, use the word "category" here in the sense of the Kantian table of categories.

23. For example, Frege never doubted that the truths of *geometry* are synthetic *a priori*.

24. But see Donald Davidson on "passing theories" in "A Nice Derangement of Epitaphs," in *Truth and Interpretation: Perspectives on the Philosophy of Donald Davidson*, ed. Ernest Lepore (Oxford: Basil Blackwell, 1984), p. 446.

25. Likewise, we treat "place" (in "There are only finitely many places to get to, travel as you will" homophonically, when we are relating the Euclidean view of the world—infinite space—with the Einsteinian. Cf. "It Ain't Necessarily So," p. 242. That is why I wrote, "Something that was literally inconceivable has turned out to be true."

26. See Cavell, *The Claim of Reason* (Oxford: Oxford University Press, 1979), pp. 121–122.

27. See Quine's "Truth by Convention."

28. See Quine's "Reply to Geoffrey Hellman," in *The Philosophy of W. V. Quine*, ed. L. E. Hahn and P. A. Schilpp (La Salle, Ill.: Open Court, 1986).

29. I argued this way myself in "What Is Mathematical Truth?" in *Mathematics, Matter, and Method*.

13. Does the Disquotational Theory of Truth Solve All Philosophical Problems?

Two well-known philosophers, Paul Horwich and Michael Williams,[1] guided by what they say is a reading of Wittgenstein, have (in separate publications) suggested a novel way of treating the dichotomy between statements which have "truth conditions" in the realist sense and those which have only "assertibility conditions." Rather than rejecting the dichotomy, these philosophers say we should regard one side of the dichotomy as empty. *Every* statement has assertibility conditions they say; it is by knowing these that we understand the statements we make (knowing them in the sense of having the practical ability to recognize when they are fulfilled; the theoretical ability to *state* them is not what is in question). The idea that we understand statements by grasping assertibility conditions is taken to be what Wittgenstein was driving at with his metaphor of conceptual schemes as "language games"; the assertibility conditions are the "rules of the game" on this interpretation.

What of "truth conditions"? To say a statement is true is not to ascribe *any* property to it, according to these philosophers. To say a statement is true is to make the statement over again (or to endorse it, if someone else made it, or if it is being considered "in the abstract"); the only substantive kind of rightness our statements (the ones that meet our highest cognitive standards) possess is warranted assertibility. What does "Snow is white" is true mean? Just "disquote" the sentence mentioned (erase the quotation marks), and you get the answer: it means *Snow is white!*

In my view, however, we do have a notion of truth, even if we don't have an enlightening account of "the nature of truth" in the high

264

metaphysical sense, and in my view truth *is* a property of many of the sentences we utter and write—a characteristic we want those sentences to have when we are not trying to deceive each other (or ourselves). If asked why I hold on to this idea, in the face of our lack of success with the high metaphysical enterprise, I would answer that we can recognize many clear cases of truth, as well as of falsity. It is true that sugar is soluble, true that philosophy is hard, true that all men are mortal; and false that there were men living on the moon in 1914, false that most women are fickle, false that children always do what one wants them to do. What I propose we do is *accept* the "vulgar" notion of truth and *forget about* the question whether sentences have "truth conditions" or "assertibility conditions," since the dichotomies on which the question is based belong to a circle of ideas which have failed.[2] It is those dichotomies against which the charge may justly be leveled that no one has been able to build a successful metaphysical theory on them. It is not the notion of truth that has let us down, but rather a particular conception of how that notion is to be philosophically founded (and improved).

This line may be effective against realists, but against the neo-Wittgensteinians just mentioned it "runs through open doors." Michael Williams and Paul Horwich agree with me in rejecting the traditional metaphysical dichotomies I have discussed and dismissed in this connection, for instance, noumenal *versus* phenomenal, or fact *versus* value. Our difference concerns the best way of effecting the rejection.

What they maintain is that the best way of giving up the dichotomies in question is to *give up* the notion of truth as a *property*. The word "true" is still useful, even on their view, since we frequently have occasion to endorse one another's statements, to reaffirm our own statements, and so on. Certainly it is true that all men are mortal and true that sugar is soluble; but to say this is not to say that the *sentences* "All men are mortal" and "Sugar is soluble" have a "substantive property," but just to reaffirm the platitudes that all men are mortal and that sugar is soluble.

The attraction of this view is that it promises an account of how we understand our language, an account which avoids entanglement with the problem of the nature of truth. But this very attraction should make us suspicious: in the history of philosophy, attempts at *showing* a problem to be a "pseudo-problem" have often encountered the very same difficulties that have beset attempts to *solve* the problem. Metaphysics—especially empiricist metaphysics—frequently appears disguised as the rejection of metaphysics. In the present case, we should be doubly suspicious because the very notion these neo-Wittgensteinians hope to use, and not just to use but to give pride of place to, the notion of an *assertibility condition,* is one that seems to presuppose the very notion these philosophers want to reject, the notion of a genuine "truth condition" in the realist sense.

Recall, for the moment, the use John Mackie made[3] of the idea that dispositional statements (Sugar is soluble, etc.) have "assertibility conditions." Mackie's idea was that the following statements are *true* ("simply true") of appropriate objects x_1, x_2 . . .

x_1 is a piece of sugar;	x_1 was put in water and dissolved.
x_2 " " " " "	x " " " " " " . . .
x_3 " " " " "	" " " " " " " . . .
etc.	

The *truth* of these statements (and of other relevant statements, including the statement that *Sugar is of a uniform chemical composition* and the statement that *If two things have the same chemical composition and one of them dissolves in water, then the other will dissolve under the same physical circumstances*), and the fact that the conditions were what we regard as "normal" in all of the cases listed, justify our "licensing" one another to predict that *x will dissolve* given that *x is sugar which has been put in water,* and given that the conditions seem "normal" to us (notwithstanding all the physically possible cases I mentioned in *The Many Faces of Realism* in which sugar which is put in water does *not* dissolve). This "licensing practice" is not infallible, but it fails so rarely that we would be foolish to abandon it; the success of this practice is what is really "behind" our calling the statement "sugar is soluble" *true,* on Mackie's account.

The structure of the account is: A statement is said to be *assertible* if certain "justificatory" statements are "simply true." *The notion of assertibility, as used by Mackie, presupposes that some statements are "simply true"; it would make no sense, in Mackie's account, to suggest that no statement has "truth conditions," that all statements have only "assertibility conditions."* The notions of assertibility and truth take in each other's wash; the notion of assertibility presupposes the notion of truth; it cannot be used to supplant it.

But we do not need to refer to Mackie's use of the notion to see this. Consider an ordinary "observation statement," say, *There is a chair in front of me.* Suppose the neo-Wittgensteinians are right, and this has "assertibility conditions" rather than truth conditions. What could such an "assertibility condition" possibly look like?

For an old-fashioned empiricist the answer is easy; but Wittgenstein's aim was, in large measure, to refute old-fashioned empiricism, not to repeat its moves. An empiricist of an older generation might have said that what makes "There is a chair in front of me" warrantedly assertible is *the fact that I have chair-shaped sense data in my visual field*. But what makes "I have chair-shaped sense data in my visual field" warrantedly assertible? Obviously, what makes "I have chair-shaped sense data in my visual field" warrantedly assertible, when it is, is the fact that I do have chair-shaped sense data in my visual field; but this is not just an "assertibility condition"; it is precisely the *truth condition* for this sentence. In the case of perceptual reports in sense-datum language, the notion of an "assertibility condition" reduces to the classical notion of a truth condition.

Of course, this would not have discomfited old-fashioned empiricists. They had no qualms about using the realist notion of truth in connection with what they claimed to "directly observe," that is, their own sense data. Sense-datum reports were supposed to be "incorrigible"; in their case we are supposed to have direct access to truth itself, and not merely to assertibility.

But the neo-Wittgensteinians are not out to revive sense-datum epistemology. However, just what they *do* have in mind with their talk of "warrant," "assertibility," etc., is not clear. When Wittgenstein himself gives examples of "language games" at the beginning of the *Investigations,* these are presented in straightforward *physicalistic* language, not in sense-datum language. (Someone says "slab" and his partner hands him a slab.) This suggests that the "assertibility conditions" for "There is a table in front of me" might go like this: *there must be a table in front of the speaker; the speaker must see the table;* ... Certainly these are the sorts of conditions that the "slab game" involves. But these are sufficient conditions for the *truth* of "There is a table in front of me," and not merely for its *assertibility!* If people see a chair in front of them, then *there* is a chair in front of them. Or should the assertibility condition be "There *appears* (to the speaker) to be a chair in front of him or her" (as in "language of appearance" epistemology)? This would ignore Wittgenstein's well-known aversion to describing ordinary unproblematical cases of perception as cases of something "appearing" to be so and so. Wittgenstein wouldn't say there *appeared* (to Susan) to be a table in front of her; he would say Susan *saw* a table.

That it is difficult to spell out what "assertibility conditions" are supposed to be in a Wittgensteinian framework is no accident. The notions of "warrant" and "assertibility," like the notion of "appearance," belong to the classical epistemological tradition, with its deep methodological skepticism. Wittgenstein's conscious policy of describing his language games in physicalistic language is part and parcel of his rejection of methodological skepticism as the right procedure in philosophy. The neo-Wittgensteinians face a dilemma: if they are to say what "assertibility conditions" are, they must either use "objective" language *(seeing a table in front of one)*, in which case they face the objection that what they have actually given is a *sufficient condition* for the *truth* of the statement in question—but the whole point of the notion of "assertibility" was that assertibility conditions were *not* sufficient for truth, which was why assertibility was thought to *contrast* with the (more problematical) notion of truth—or else they must revive some form of classical epistemology—sense-datum language, or language of appearance, or something of that sort—in which case the classical dichotomies will be back in full force.

The dilemma is clear when the sentence whose "assertibility conditions" are to be described is an observation report in physicalistic language. It might be thought that there is still room for a semantics of assertibility conditions in the case of so-called theoretical sentences, such as *There is an electric current flowing through the wire.* To know the meaning of this sentence, it might be held, is to know (to have practical knowledge of) the rules which determine when it is confirmed or infirmed. The sentences which describe the evidence that confirms or infirms this sentence would not themselves contain theoretical terms. Rather they would be observational reports in "thing language." *(The needle of the meter is displaced.)*

Up to now I have treated Williams' and Horwich's views together, but at this point, since Horwich has developed his view at greater length in his new book, I shall focus on *it*.

On Horwich's view, as on Williams', a language game is to be understood as consisting of sentences for which (if we confine attention to assertoric language) there are "assertibility conditions." These conditions specify that under certain observable conditions a sentence counts as true or at least as "confirmed." (Think of these conditions as stipulating that under certain observable conditions we are allowed to utter certain noises, or write certain marks, and also to expect certain observable events or certain reactions from others.) This model is similar to Carnap's or Reichenbach's model of a speaker-hearer of a natural language.[4] The key idea (as in positivism) is that if you know under what conditions a statement is confirmed, you understand the statement. "Truth," as already explained, is not a property on this view, but is to be understood "disquotationally": to say that a statement is true is just to make an equivalent statement. More precisely, the Tarski biconditionals tell us all we need to know about the notion of truth.[5] Note that this account differs from Malcolm's well-known interpretation of Wittgenstein on "criteria" in that the "criteria" which govern our use of words provide (in some cases) for degrees of assertibility less than certainty. Still, speakers who understand their language in the same way and who have the same evidence should all agree on the degree of assertibility of their sentences, in this model.

The assumption that underlies this picture is that the use of words can be described in terms of what speakers are allowed to say and do in observable situations. "Use" is a theoretical notion, and there is a standard way of describing the use of expressions in an arbitrary language game. Let me call this *the positivistic interpretation of Wittgenstein.*

A very different interpretation (one suggested, or very nearly suggested, by Peter Winch in *The Idea of a Social Science*) is the following: the use of the words in a language game cannot be described without using concepts which are related to the concepts employed *in* the game. Winch has discussed the case of the language games of "primitive" peoples; but I believe the same point applies to scientific language games. Consider, for example, the language game of a good electrician. He learns to employ sentences such as the theoretical sentence I mentioned earlier, "An electric current is flowing through the wire." On the positivistic interpretation of Wittgenstein, Wittgenstein must hold (with Bridgeman and the early Carnap) that the electrician understands this sentence by knowing that, for example, it is assertible if the voltmeter needle is deflected, and he recognizes that something is a voltmeter by recognizing that it has a certain appearance (and it has VOLTMETER printed on it, perhaps).

I tried many years ago to explain what is wrong with this picture in my debates with Malcolm.[6] A good electrician relies on "criteria" in this sense, to be sure: but when things go wrong (and anyone who has ever repaired his own appliances or fixed a car knows how much can go wrong when one is dealing with the real world!) he also knows to distrust the criteria, and *the knowledge of when to distrust the criteria is not itself something which is learned by rules.* Rather, we can say here what Wittgenstein said about learning to tell if another person is feigning a feeling he does not have (*Philosophical Investigations,* II, § 11, p. 227; I have rectified the translation):

> Is there such a thing as "expert judgment" about the genuineness of expressions of feeling? Even here there are those whose judgment is "better" and those whose judgment is "worse."
>
> Correcter prognoses will generally issue from the judgments of those who understand people better *(des besseren Menschenkenners).*
>
> Can one learn this knowledge? Yes; some can. Not, however, by taking a course in it, but through "experience." Can another be one's teacher in this? Certainly. From time to time he gives him the right *tip.* This is what "learning" and "teaching" are like here. What one acquires is not a technique; one learns correct judgments. There are also rules, but they do not form a system, and only experienced people can apply them right. Unlike calculating rules.

Here we see that Wittgenstein recognized that even within one language game there may be truths which not every one can see, because not everyone can develop the skill of recognizing the "imponderable evidence" (*unwägbare Evidenz;* p. 228) involved.[7] Some people are just better at telling what is going on. Nothing could be further from the picture of a language game as an automatic performance, like the execution of an algorithm.

I want to apply to this case a remark that Habermas makes at a number of points in *The Theory of Communicative Action:* Someone who does not see the "point" of the language game, and who cannot imaginatively put himself in the position of an engaged player, cannot judge whether the "criteria" are applied reasonably or unreasonably in it. Someone who described the game by saying that the players (the electricians) make certain noises in certain observable situations would not be able to make head or tails of what is going on.

In contrast, consider the following description of the use of "electric current is flowing through the wire" (the one I would give): "One uses a voltmeter, or some such, to tell if electric current is flowing through the wire. A voltmeter is constructed in such and such a way (here, imagine an explanation of how a voltmeter 'works'—*not* in observation language). In using a voltmeter it is important to be sure that no electromagnetic fields be present which might effect the accuracy of its readings . . ."

Knowing the "use" of "Current is flowing through the wire" is knowing things like *this*. Of course, much else is presupposed—in fact, acculturation in a technical society, with all that that entails. *Understanding a language game is sharing a form of life.* And forms of life cannot be described in a fixed positivistic metalanguage, whether they be scientific, religious, or of a kind that we do not have in Western industrial societies today.

Note that, on this reading of Wittgenstein, the famous remark[8] that, in a large class of cases, we may say that the meaning of a word is its use in the language is not a *theory* of meaning (although it is the expression of a point of view from which one can question whether it makes sense to ask for a "theory of meaning," in any sense in which a "theory of meaning" might be metaphysically informative).

In this connection, I should like to make two further observations. (1) To know under what conditions a statement (not a "sentence") is assertible is to know *under what conditions it is certainly true or liable to be true*. The idea that assertibility conditions are conditions for making a *noise* is a total distortion of Wittgenstein's meaning. "Assertibility" and "truth" are internally related notions: one comes to understand both by standing inside a language game, seeing what Wittgenstein calls its "point,"[9] and *judging* assertibility and truth. (2) After 1936, Rudolf Carnap often advocated one form or another of the very position Horwich ascribes to Wittgenstein (and defends on his own behalf as well). And a problem, which was sharply pointed out by Quine (in correspondence and conversation with Carnap as early as 1936, and in print in Quine's celebrated "Two Dogmas of Empiricism" in 1950) is that the sentences which confirm or infirm "There are electrons flowing through the wire," or any other theoretical sentence, themselves depend on what our body of auxiliary belief looks like (for example, what the currently accepted theory of the electron is). If we count each change in the body of background knowledge as a change in the meaning of the theoretical term "electron," or whatever, then we may as well abandon the notion of "meaning" altogether. To say (as Carnap ended up saying) that each change in "total science" is a change in the meaning of *every* theoretical term whose assertibility conditions are, however indirectly, affected would require us to say that the distinction between *changing the meaning of one's terms* and *changing one's factual beliefs* has to be given up. (In addition, Quine might have pointed out, one could no longer require, as a principle of applied practical logic, that a *correct answer to a question must use the relevant terms with the same meanings that they had in the original question,* for almost every scientific inquiry will "change the meanings" of the terms that were used in the question that the inquiry was meant to answer, on such a theory of meaning.) If we must really abandon the distinction between change of theory and change of term-meaning, we may as well just abandon the notion of "meaning."

Let us apply these lessons from philosophy of science to Horwich's proposal: To draw a distinction between an assertibility condition which has the status of a "rule of the language game" and one which has some other status (say, "empirical consequence of a theory") would just be to advance the old "analytic/synthetic" distinction in a feeble new disguise. To suppose that *this* is what the later Wittgenstein was propounding would be to assimilate his philosophy to Rudolf Carnap's, that is, to the sort of position he was so instrumental in overthrowing.

Williams' Way Out

Michael Williams, at least, seems to be aware of the possibility of just this charge.[10] In his discussion-review of my *Reason, Truth, and History* he suggested that I myself have provided the way out: we need, he says, to distinguish between changes in assertibility conditions which are *merely* "changes" and changes which are actually *reforms*. Such a distinction will, of course, be unacceptable to positivists, because "reform" is a value-laden notion; but my purpose in *Reason, Truth, and History* was to argue that *all* our notions are ultimately value-laden (which is why the positivists "fact/value" dichotomy is untenable), and Williams agrees with me so far. If we are not concerned to do philosophy of language in a "value-free" way, or in a reductionist way, why should we not avail ourselves of the notion of a reform? he asks. (And I would in turn agree, so far.) And it is part of good interpretive practice *not* to count a word as having changed its meaning (even though the assertibility conditions for some of the sentences containing that word have changed) if the changes in the assertibility conditions represent *reforms* and not mere changes of our linguistic practice. (Here too I agree.) Thus, Williams argues, we can accept the criticism of positivist philosophy of science just reviewed without committing ourselves to any notion of truth beyond a "disquotational" one.

But this rejoinder employs the notion of "reforming" a language game as though that were a *fixed* notion available to the theorist. To know what counts as a reform in the language game of the electrician one must know the point of his game: to figure out how circuits are behaving, and how to repair them when they need repairing, or to install them, or to design them. If you think of the language game as nothing but a game of making noises in certain observable situations in the hope that making those noises will help you get the lights to go on, then the only notion of "reforming" the rules you will be able to give is a narrowly positivistic one: in effect, we will be back to "the aim of science is prediction and control." While that may look plausible in the case of applied electricity, it will give you no understanding at all of most of human language. (In general, as I argued in *Reason, Truth, and History,* the purposes of a language game are not statable without using the language of that game or of a related game.)

If this is true even of scientific language, these ideas become especially important in understanding Wittgenstein when we turn to Wittgenstein's various discussions of forms of language other than scientific, to his discussion of religious language, of "primitive" language games, and of differing "forms of life" in *On Certainty.* In the "Lectures on Religious Belief," Wittgenstein makes it clear that he, standing outside religious language (or affecting to), cannot say that religious language is cognitive or non-cognitive; all he can say is that, from the "outsiders" perspective, the religious man is "using a picture." But he adds that in saying this he is not saying that the religious man is *only* using a picture, or only "expressing an attitude." I take Wittgenstein to be saying here that the possibilities of "external" understanding of a different form of life are sometimes extremely limited.

Disquotation in Wittgenstein

Last but not least: what is the textual justification for ascribing a "disquotational theory of truth" to Wittgenstein? Kripke (who agrees with the neo-Wittgensteinians in ascribing a disquotational theory of truth to Wittgenstein) cites the occurrence of the formula "p" is true $\leftrightarrow p$ as conclusive evidence. But Wittgenstein makes clear in this very passage that a *Satz* (sentence, proposition) in his sense is not simply an arbitrary grammatical sentence. Instead of saying that "p is true" amounts to p, Wittgenstein tells us, we could just as well take "true" as the already understood notion and say that a *Satz* is what "fits" the predicates "true" and "false."[11] If there is disquotation in this passage, it is disquotation of truth as applied to *Sätze, not to Tarskian, "senten-ces." Indeed, Wittgenstein also tells us that, queer as it sounds, part of being a Satz is sounding like a Satz.*

As Charles Travis has emphasized,[12] Wittgenstein *rejects* the famil-iar post-Russellian distinction analytic philosophers make between a "sentence" (in the sense of a row of letters) and the "proposition" expressed by the sentence. A *Satz,* in Wittgenstein's sense, consists of words (so, in that sense, it is a "syntactic object") *and* it says some-thing (it doesn't just "have" a meaning, it *speaks* to us, as it were.)[13] To say that calling a *Satz* S true is just to affirm S is not to put forward an informative philosophical theory (as it is an informative—if mis-guided—philosophical theory to say that to call a "string of pho-nemes" S true is just to display a disposition to say "yes" to the string of phonemes); for the notion of a statement *(Satz)* and the notion of truth (and, for that matter, the notion of "affirming") are equally "in-tentional." They are on the same level. And this is exactly what Wittgenstein says in the passage Kripke cites.

Consider the case of talking about a chair in front of me. When I say, "The chair is blue," then, Wittgenstein says elsewhere, my state-ment "corresponds to a reality."[14] Does this sound like the Wittgen-stein these philosophers have imagined, who thinks such a statement has only "assertibility conditions"? The neo-Wittgensteinians would perhaps answer that they do not intend the notion of an "assertibility condition" to be the classical epistemological notion. "You are trying to saddle us with empiricist baggage we too reject," they might say. "Sometimes, indeed, an assertibility condition can be a condition for what would classically be called the 'truth' of a statement. That just means that in such a circumstance a speaker can be *certain* that the statement is true. We still don't need the notion that truth is a substan-tive property. *That* is where you, Hilary, went wrong in your *Reason, Truth, and History.*"

Truth and the Past

What is right in this rejoinder is that one cannot fully see what is at issue when one confines attention to just present-tense statements about what John Austin charmingly called "middle-sized dry goods." What is at issue appears more clearly when we change the tense to the past. Suppose I say, "There was a rabbit where my house now stands at such-and-such a time (2000 years ago)." What does it mean to say that this *Satz* has only "assertibility conditions," that the notion of a "truth condition" is a bit of bad metaphysics?

I think it is quite clear what picture these philosophers are gripped by. In their picture, there is no normative property of "rightness" and "wrongness" that statements have over and above warranted assertibility in various contexts. But what is it to be assertible in a context?

If a statement can be "assertible" even when no speaker is actually present, and if assertibility is *not* independent of truth (as it was on the classical epistemological conception, at least when the statement involved medium-sized dry goods), then presumably the statement "There was a rabbit where my house now stands at such-and-such a time (2000 years ago)" could have been "assertible" at that time in the sense that a *sufficient condition for its truth* obtained. On such an interpretation, "assertibility" virtually collapses into *truth*, at least for statements about middle-sized dry goods in normal conditions.

But this is not, I believe, what these philosophers mean at all. Horwich, for example, compares assertibility to *confirmation*. The picture is that assertibility requires the presence of an *assertor;* this is why Williams criticizes my notion of *idealized* rational acceptability; the objectionable feature, from his point of view, is precisely that I allow talk of what *would be* assertible were someone sufficiently well placed, and not just of what is/is not assertible in the positions people are actually in.

So the picture is this: the statement about the past may or may not be assertible right now. If it is not, we of course say, "The statement is either true or false," but when we say this, we are not saying that the statement about the rabbit has one of two exclusive properties. We say this, rather, because a *different* sentence—"Either there was a rabbit where my house now stands at such-and-such a time or there was no rabbit where my house now stands at such-and-such a time"— is (trivially) always assertible. (Just why the theorems of classical logic are trivially always assertible is something of a mystery on this picture, but I shall let this pass.) If the statement is not assertible and its negation is not assertible (right now), then there is *no* substantive kind of rightness or wrongness that the statement has right now. (A similar point can be made with respect to statements about the future.) Technicalities of the formulation aside, is this so different from the positivist tendency to treat statements about the past as disguised statements about present experiences (methodological solipsism of the present instant)? True, the claim that a statement S has the same *meaning* as the statement "S is assertible" is no part of the position of Williams and Horwich. But the statement S, I repeat, never has any kind of *substantive rightness or wrongness* beyond being assertible or having an assertible negation, on this picture. If it "corresponds to a reality," it is the reality expressed by the statement "S is assertible," and no other.

Pictures and Philosophy

I have tried to bring out the way in which these neo-Wittgensteinians are in the grip of a positivistic picture, a picture that situates the connection of our words with reality at the point of contact with the speaker, the point at which the speaker undergoes something which makes a sentence "assertible." These philosophers are terrified of the idea that there is a property that a sentence can have that depends on something distant from the speaker. Truth, conceived of as such a property, is something "mysterious" (and mysteries are, of course, just what we want to get rid of). I urge that we reject this solipsistic picture.

But should we not equally reject the realist picture, the picture of truth as a property (one which sometimes depends on what is distant from us)? Was not Wittgenstein telling us to reject *all* pictures in philosophy? Should not a proper Wittgensteinian say, "A plague on both your houses—Putnam's house as well as Williams' "?

The answer, I think, is that there are pictures and pictures. Consider the sentence "Caesar crossed the Rubicon." I think it is undeniable, as a fact about the lives we actually lead, that our ordinary linguistic practice in connection with such a statement is deeply informed by a "realist" picture. For an educated person, it is virtually as if we had *seen* Caesar crossing the river. That the statement is just something we "utter" in response to *present-day* (or even present and future) "assertibility conditions" is an idea infinitely remote from our actual form of life.

And this makes a difference. Wittgenstein's objection to many philosophical pictures is not just that they are unexplanatory; it is that they *do* nothing for us. They have no *point.* (To this extent, Wittgenstein *is* a pragmatist.) Regarding my utterances about Caesar as utterances about a real human being is essential to what Stanley Cavell would call *acknowledging* Caesar. To think of "Caesar-talk" as *just* a language game which enables me, let us say, to predict what I will find when I read ancient documents, history books, and so on, is not at all the same as acknowledging Caesar as a "fellow passenger to the grave."

The point is that some forms of skepticism *matter*. Consider the following difference, in essence the one pointed out by Cavell in *The Claim of Reason:* (1) Suppose I were to be convinced by some brilliant philosophical argument that the phenomenalist program can actually be carried through, and that all sentences about "material objects" can be translated into a phenomenalist language. This would be exciting stuff, intellectually speaking, but it would make virtually no difference to our *lives*. (2) Suppose, instead, that I were to be convinced that *other people* were just logical constructions out of my sense-data (or, alternatively, that talk about other people is just a game that is useful for predicting my future sense impressions); this would make an enormous difference to my life. (The whole question of hurting other people would be "displaced"; and so would the whole question of companionship.) As Cavell put it, skepticism about other minds can be (and, in a way, often is) a real problem, while skepticism about "middle-sized dry goods" is an utterly unreal problem.

I am saying that our "realism" (note the small "r") about the past, our belief that truth and falsity "reach all the way to" the past, and "do not stop short," *is* part of a picture, *and the picture is essential to our lives.* As Cora Diamond has pointed out in another connection,[15] the fact that a picture is not an "explanation" doesn't mean that the picture is *wrong.* As Wittgenstein himself puts it (in the Lecture on Religious Belief), a picture can have human weight. That truth is not *just* "disquotational," that truth genuinely depends on what is *distant,* is part of a picture with enormous human weight. As Wittgenstein himself writes,[16] "It is true that we can compare a picture that is firmly rooted in us to a superstition; but it is equally true that we *always* eventually have to reach some firm ground, either a picture or something else, so that a picture which is at the root of all our thinking is to be respected and not treated as a superstition."

Notes

1. I am thinking of Michael Williams' discussion-review of my *Reason, Truth, and History (Journal of Philosophy,* 81, no. 5 [May 1984], 257–260) and of Paul Horowitch's recent *Truth* (Oxford: Basil Blackwell, 1990).
2. That these ideas have failed is argued in my first Carus Lecture, in *The Many Faces of Realism* (La Salle, Ill.: Open Court 1987).

3. In *The Cement of the Universe* (Oxford: Oxford University Press, 1974).

4. I analyzed those models in "Dreaming and Depth Grammar," reprinted in my *Mind, Language, and Reality* (New York: Cambridge University Press, 1975). See pp. 320–324.

5. There is a well-known problem (which Horwich tries to finesse) with this claim: from a knowledge of the truth of the Tarski biconditionals it does not even follow that "is true" is *defined* when the subject is a pronoun or a variable, rather than a fully quoted sentence.

6. See "Dreaming and Depth Grammar" and "Brains and Behaviour," both reprinted in my *Mind, Language, and Reality*.

7. "It is certainly possible to be convinced by evidence that someone is in such-and-such a state of mind, for instance that he is not pretending. But 'evidence' here includes imponderable evidence." *Investigations* (Oxford: Basil Blackwell, 1958), II, §11, p. 228.

8. §43 of the *Investigations*.

9. See §563–564 of the *Investigations*.

10. See n. 1.

11. §136 of the *Investigations*.

12. See Charles Travis, *The Uses of Sense* (Oxford: Oxford University Press, 1989).

13. The whole section on "reading" in the *Investigations*—which otherwise looks like a strange bit of Husserlian phenomenology—is virtually devoted to just this point.

14. See Lecture 25, *Wittgenstein's Lectures on the Philosophy of Mathematics*, ed. Cora Diamond (Ithaca: Cornell University Press, 1976, Chicago University Press 1989).

15. In "The Face of Necessity," reprinted in Diamond's *The Realistic Spirit* (Cambridge: MIT Press, 1991).

16. *Culture and Value* (Oxford: Basil Blackwell, 1980), p. 83.

14. Realism without Absolutes

In *The Pursuit of Truth* W. V. Quine repeats and restates a doctrine for which he has become famous, the doctrine of ontological relativity. "What is empirically significant in an ontology," Quine tells us, "is just its contribution of neutral nodes to the structure of a theory. We could reinterpret 'Tabitha' as designating no longer the cat, but the whole cosmos minus the cat" (p. 33). There is no fact of the matter as to what any of our terms refer to.[1] Further explaining his doctrine, Quine tells us,

> Kindly readers have sought a technical distinction between my phrases "inscrutability of reference" and "ontological relativity" that was never clear in my own mind. But I can now say what ontological relativity is relative to, more succinctly that I did in the lectures, paper, and book of that title. It is relative to a manual of translation.[2] To say that "gavagai" denotes "rabbit" is to opt for a manual of translation in which "gavagai" is translated as "rabbit," instead of opting for any of the alternative manuals.
>
> And does the indeterminacy or relativity extend also somehow to the home language? In "Ontological Relativity" I said it did, for the home language can be translated into itself by permutations that depart materially from the mere identity transformation, as proxy functions bear out. But if we choose as our manual of translation the identity transformation, thus taking the whole language at face value, the relativity is resolved. Reference is then explicated in disquotational paradigms analogous to Tarski's truth paradigm; "rabbit" denotes rabbits whatever *they* are, and "Boston" designates Boston. (pp. 51–52)

Whatever *they* are, indeed! Quine is not expressing some doubt about our scientific or common-sense knowledge concerning rabbits. He is claiming that there is no fact of the matter as to whether "rab-

279

bit" refers to those little creatures with long ears and funny little tails
or to each thing that is the mereological complement of a rabbit, that
is, the whole cosmos minus a rabbit. Quine does not mean, of course,
that *in my own language* there is any doubt as to whether I should
accept the sentence "Rabbits are identical with mereological complements of rabbits." Within my language, that sentence is false. But that
only means that it is false on each admissible interpretation of my
language. If M is one admissible interpretation of my language, then
the model in which the "rabbits" of M and the "mereological complements of rabbits" of M are "switched" is just as admissible a model.
Moreover, even *within* my language, or rather, within my metalanguage, I can define truth and reference in such a way that

"Rabbit" refers to rabbits in my object language

comes out true, or in such a way that

"Rabbit" refers to mereological complements of rabbits in my object language

comes out true, without altering the set of true sentences of my object
language in any way, and without altering the truth conditions for
observation sentences as wholes; and in such a case, Quine tells us,
there is no fact of the matter as to which reference/truth definition is
correct. If I adopt the second definition of truth and reference, I shall
in a sense be flouting Tarski's "Convention T,"[3] but there is no fact of
the matter, from Quine's point of view, as to whether the Convention
T itself is correct. It is simply convenient.

In *Reason, Truth, and History* I used an argument similar to
Quine's, but drew an opposite conclusion (thus illustrating the well
known maxim that one philosopher's *modus ponens* is another
philosopher's *modus tollens*). I argued there that metaphysical realism
leaves us with no intelligible way to refute ontological relativity,[4] and
concluded that metaphysical realism is wrong. And I still see ontological relativity as a refutation of any philosophical position that leads
to it. For what sense can we make of the idea that the world consists
of objects any one of which is a quark in one admissible model, the
Eiffel Tower in a second admissible model, myself in a third admissible model, but is no more intrinsically any one of these than any
other? Surely, the very notion of an "object" crumbles if we accept
this. The reason that Quine does not see that it does is, I think, his
belief that the laws of quantification theory by themselves give enough

content to the notion of an object to render notions like "object" and "ontology" usable in metaphysics.[5]

I am happy that most of the readers of *Reason, Truth, and History* (though regrettably not all) understood that my argument was meant as a *reductio*. But I recognize that I did not say enough there about how the absurd conclusion of the *reductio* can be avoided. What is the right way to answer these "permutation arguments"?

Reference and Perception

What I did not appreciate when I wrote *Reason, Truth, and History* was the importance of connecting the issues about reference and the classical issues about perception. At bottom they are the same issue, the issue of the relation of thought to the world.

Assume that perception requires a nonphysical intermediary, a sense datum, and you have the problem of perception in its classical form. But the problem can arise for physicalists as well. In contemporary cognitive science, for example, it is the fashion to postulate that the brain is a computer, and to hypothesize the existence of "representations" in the cerebral computer. If one assumes that the mind is an *organ*,[6] and one goes on to identify the mind with the brain (if it's an organ, what else could it be?), it can become irresistible to think of some of the "representations" (that is, some of the brain-computer's "representations," now thought of as parts of the mind) as *data* for the mind (the cerebral computer, or "mind," makes *inferences* from at least some of the "representations," the outputs of the perceptual processes), and, second, to think that those "'representations" are linked to the external objects in the organism's environment only causally, and not cognitively. In *The Modularity of Mind* by Jerry Fodor, for example, the mind/brain is pictured as making inferences from the outputs of "perception modules." (These inferences are described as "unmodularized," that is, not automatic, and as involving background knowledge and "general intelligence.") The modules themselves are not supposed to make inferences or to draw on background knowledge; they are conceived as relatively stupid semi-automatic devices which incorporate quick and dirty recognition algorithms of various sorts. The result is a picture which is startlingly similar to the sense-datum theory. Sense data were supposed to be linked to the external world (if the philosopher believed that the external world was more than a construction out of the subject's sense data) only causally. The coffee table sense datum, as it might be, I am having cannot be *justified* by the fact that there is a coffee table in front of me; it can only be *caused* by the fact that there is a coffee table in front of me (given a variety of other contributory causes as well); inference begins with the sense datum and not with the external object.[7]

McDowell has argued, in his John Locke Lectures,[8] that this picture, whether in its classical version or in its modern materialist version, is disastrous for just about every part of metaphysics and epistemology. The key element responsible for the disaster is the idea that there has to be an "interface" between our conceptual powers and the external world; our conceptual powers cannot reach all the way to the objects themselves. In both of the theories just described, this interface is *inside* us and not outside us.

Quine's picture of our "speech dispositions" may seem to be a different matter. After all, Quine's "stimulus meanings" are dispositions to respond to the firings of neurons on the surface of our bodies, not to the "reports" of modules inside the brain. However, Quine has made it clear that he adopted surface neurons as stand-ins for presently unavailable central processes; and, in any case, surface neurons, even if outside the brain, are certainly not outside the nervous system. The Quinian model of language exactly parallels the classical model of perception (in its materialist version). Stimulations of nerve endings are caused (or "prompted") by external things, and knowledge of what those external things are is not available to the organism. The organism has only dispositions to respond (linguistically and otherwise) to stimulations of its nerve endings, or as Quine says with deliberate irony, to its "surface irritations." Once those surface irritations have occurred, complex processing takes place, leading to the issuing of all kinds of verbal reports, indeed to the whole edifice of science. Given the lack of any *rational* connection between the surface irritations and what is outside (or inside) the skin, it is not to be wondered at that language ends up without any determinate reference to reality.

I did not see the problem in this way when I wrote "Realism and Reason" and "Models and Reality," and if I had, I would not have been content with the appeals to what I called "verificationist semantics" in those essays. There I was content to urge that we think of our understanding of our language as consisting in our mastery of its use. And I went on to say, "To speak as if *this* were my problem, I know how to use my language, but now how shall I single out an interpretation? is nonsense. Either the use of the language *already* fixes the 'interpretation' or *nothing* can."[9]

It is not, I hasten to say, that I now think that that is false. But it is much too easy. What I did not see was that the notion of "use" can itself be understood in different ways. I was still a functionalist when I wrote those words, and the notion of use as I understood it then was the cognitive scientist's notion, that is, use was to be described largely in terms of computer programs in the brain. To be sure, even then I did not think the notion of "use" could be exhausted by reference to computer programs in the brain. As an "externalist" about reference, I thought one would not only have to talk about the functional organization of the language user's brain, but would also have to specify the sort of environment in which the language user was embedded. In short, I was a "socio-functionalist." But the picture of use was a portmanteau affair. There was the computer program in the brain, and there was the description of the external causes of the language user's words. My conclusions were the reverse of Quine's, but my picture of mental activity was very similar.

But there is another, fundamentally different, way to conceive of "use." On this alternative picture, which, I believe, was that of the later Wittgenstein,[10] the use of words in a language game cannot, in general, be described without employing the vocabulary of that very game. If one wants to talk of the use of the sentence "There is a coffee table in front of me," one has to talk about seeing and feeling coffee tables, among other things. In short, one has to mention *perceiving* coffee tables. By speaking of perceiving, what I have in mind is not the minimal sense of "see" or "feel," the sense in which one might be said to "see" or "feel" a coffee table even if one hadn't the faintest idea what a coffee table is; rather I mean the full achievement sense, the sense in which to see a coffee table is to see that it is a coffee table that is in front of one.

There is, of course, a sort of cultivated naiveté about the move I just described. I mentioned Wittgenstein in connection with it; I could also have mentioned Strawson or Austin or, going back earlier in the century, William James.[11] The difference between these two understandings of the slogan "meaning is use" is stark. Taken in the scientistic way, the slogan fits nicely into the Cartesian *cum* materialist picture I have been describing; the use of an arbitrary sentence is something that can be described in a fixed metatheoretic vocabulary, in terms of dispositions to respond to "mental representations" or "surface irritations." If I am right about where the problems "How can we so much as perceive things outside our own bodies?" and "How can we so much as refer to things outside our own bodies?" come from, then the slogan "Meaning is use" will not help one bit with those traditional problems if one understands the notion of "use" in *that* way.

Of course, there are also problems if one understands the slogan in the way I attributed to Wittgenstein et al. (And, by the way, the slogan should not really be "Meaning is use" but *understanding is having the capacity, or better the system of capacities, which enables one to use language.*) The problem is not "How does perceiving objects enable us to refer to them?" I take it that no one thinks that *that* is a problem. The difficulty is in seeing how such a move in the direction of deliberate "naiveté" can possibly help after three centuries of modern philosophy, not to mention a century of brain science and now cognitive science. The problem now is to *show the possibility* of a return to what I called "deliberate naiveté," or what James called "natural realism." Nevertheless, it seems to me that that is the direction in which we need to go.

The answer to Quine's argument seems to me, then, to be as simple as this: when we use the word "Tabitha," we can refer to Tabitha and not to the whole cosmos minus Tabitha, because after all we can see the cat, and pet her, and many other things, and we can hardly see or pet the whole cosmos minus Tabitha.

Causal Semantics and Semantic Nihilism

A very different response to Quine's problem was foreshadowed by Michael Devitt's response to my own version of Quine's model-theoretic argument.[12] Devitt argued that there is no problem here, because our words are attached to their referents by "causal connection." A more elaborate version of this response has recently been defended by Jerry Fodor, who has tried to define reference in terms of a certain kind of causal connection.[13] Other versions of this "causalist" response to permutation arguments (and related "model-theoretic" arguments) have been produced by Richard Boyd[14] and others. And oddly enough, the same fact—the fact that our linguistic behavior has a *causal* explanation—has been used by Richard Rorty to argue *against* the idea that there is a genuine relation of reference between words and objects in the world.[15] "We are connected to the world causally, not semantically," I have heard Rorty say more than once.

What Rorty is building on is an argument against the "given" used by Wilfrid Sellars.[16] Sellars pointed out that any given phenomenal report, for instance "I am experiencing E now," must have a multitude of causes, and there is nothing in any one of those causes, qua cause, to single it out as "the appropriate" cause of my verbal response or my verbalized thought. Even if my verbal report (or my thought) is caused, in part, by the very quality of the sense datum I am trying to describe (assuming the existence of sense data), it may still be a misreport; for my report cannot causally depend on *just* the quality of my "sense datum." If it is to be a report in a language with stable meanings, it must also depend on my prior linguistic conditioning, on attention, on "set," and so on. Like Rorty, Sellars thought that to postulate a semantic relation between linguistic items and nonlinguistic objects which determines when I am successfully "referring" is to postulate a mystery relation.

Rorty generalizes Sellars' argument—and, indeed, once one accepts it, it invites immediate generalization—and concludes that if we are connected to the world "causally but not semantically" (a fair summary of Sellars' view), then our words have no determinate real counterparts. (As we have seen, this is also Quine's conclusion, though not his argument.) Sellars attempted to avoid going so far by postulating a holistic relation he called "picturing" between our conceptual schemes and reality, postulating further, in Peircean fashion, that with the progress of science our schemes come to "picture" the world more and more accurately; but Rorty rejects Sellarsian "picturing" on the grounds that it is as occult a relation as "reference" allegedly is.

Now Rorty and Sellars are right in saying that any given event can be traced to a multitude of different causes. As William James wrote in a different context,[17]

> Not a sparrow falls to the ground but some other remote conditions of his fall are to be found in the Milky Way, or in our federal constitution, or in the early history of Europe. That is to say, alter the Milky Way, alter the facts of our federal constitution, alter the facts of our barbarian ancestry, and the universe would so far be a different universe from what it is now. One fact involved in the difference might be that the particular little street boy who threw the stone which brought down the sparrow might not find himself opposite the spar-

row at that particular moment, or finding himself there he might not be in that particular serene and disengaged mood of mind which expressed itself in throwing the stone. But true as all of this is, it would be most foolish of anyone who is inquiring the cause of the sparrow's fall to overlook the boy as too personal and proximate, and so to speak anthropomorphic an agent, and to say that the true cause of the sparrow's fall is the federal constitution, the westward migration of the celtic race, or the structure of the Milky Way. If we proceeded on that method, we might say with perfect legitimacy that a friend of ours, who slipped on the ice upon his doorstep and cracked his skull, some months after dining with thirteen at the table, died because of that ominous feast.

Causalists, as I shall call them, attempt to meet this difficulty in different ways. Jerry Fodor, for example, determines the appropriate cause (the one that fixes the reference) by a complicated appeal to counterfactuals. But it is not difficult to show that his attempt does not succeed.[18] In any case, the idea is misguided from the start, for counterfactuals themselves lie squarely within the domain of meaning. Yet Fodor's avowed aim was to reduce the intentional to the non-intentional.

Richard Boyd proposes that to constitute a referential connection a cause must be the sort of cause that enables us to gain *knowledge*. The kind of causal connection that exists between our use of the word "gold" and gold constitutes reference because it is the kind of causal connection that enables us to have knowledge about gold. To avoid circularity, Boyd assumes that knowledge and reference can be described together, in a socio-functionalist way. But in *Representation and Reality* I have tried to show that these functionalist and "socio-functionalist" programs have no more chance of success than did earlier reductionist programs in philosophy.

If the program of reducing the realm of meaning to the realm of what McDowell in his Locke Lectures provocatively calls "disenchanted nature" has not met with any success, a number of thinkers—in addition to Richard Rorty, one might mention the Churchlands and Stephen Stich—have proposed that perhaps the very existence of intentionality is an illusion. Quine's position skirts the edge of this "eliminationist" stance. For Quine, there is no such thing as reference absolutely speaking, but a mysterious act of "taking one's home language at face value" (or simply "acquiescing" in it) makes it all all right anyhow. Quine's picture of the speaker as constructing theories which are nothing more than devices for predicting his or her own surface irritations obviously poses the threat of solipsism. To say that by taking my own language "at face value" I can be a "robust realist" is no answer at all, if there is no fact of the matter as to whether the "face-value" interpretation of my own language is the right one (and if even the face-value interpretation amounts to no more than disquotation—remember that "whatever *they* are"!). But Rorty's more radical nihilism is no help either. Even Rorty has his "robust realist" moments. He wants to say, "Of course there's a world; we're connected to it causally not semantically." But Rorty here is treating causality as Kant treated his pseudo-causal notion of a "ground" or "basis" for the world of experience—he is treating it as a transcendent relation connecting the story which we and our cultural peers make up with a world in itself. Rorty cannot have it both ways; causality cannot be just one more relation within a story which is seen as just a device for making ourselves "happy" and avoiding "pain," and also be a transcendent relation which connects the whole story (or at least the words "Of course there is a world") to a robust reality. Quine's picture is basically a materialist version of Hume's; Rorty's picture is, in this respect, a materialist version of Kant's transcendental metaphysics.

As one would expect, causalism and nihilism also appear in the philosophy of perception. The nihilist version (thinly disguised) may be found in Daniel Dennett's recent book on consciousness.

Does Natural Realism Require Immaculate Perception?

Recently I mentioned to a friend who is a world-famous cognitive psychologist that I am a "direct realist" about perception, and without blinking an eye he wisecracked, "Oh, so you believe in immaculate perception!" I explained that when I say that perception need not involve mental intermediaries of the sorts postulated by either sense-datum theory or its materialist imitations, I am not saying that perception is not a conceptual activity. I am saying rather that the conceptual activity does not begin with the arrival "in the mind" of some nonconceptual datum which we then "process." When I explained my view, my friend eventually withdrew the charge, but his first response may help us to understand why causalism and nihilism have seemed the only possible views concerning the relation of mind to the world. Once one has identified the mind with an organ, be it the brain or be it an immaterial organ, obvious facts (joined, as always, with fashionable views)—the fact that light rays are involved in visual perception, the fact that the eye, the ear, and the other sense organs are involved in perception, the fact that the nervous system is involved, the probable fact that semi-automatic computational "devices" in the brain ("modules") are involved, the (cloudy) doctrine that "representations" in the cerebral computer are involved—all seem to rule out any possibility of perception being "direct."

To be sure, part of the problem lay with my use of the unfortunate word "direct." As John Austin pointed out,[19] it is only in very special situations that the question "Did you perceive that directly or indirectly?" makes any sense. But the unfortunate word does not bear *all* the responsibility. Already in James's day, the idea of point-to-point correlations between brain events and mental events was popular, and James devotes some of the most prescient sections of his great *Principles of Psychology* to criticizing that idea. (James points out, for example, that the same "memory trace" in the brain may very well, when activated, give rise to phenomenologically different "memories," depending on what is going on in the rest of the brain—a possibility recently exploited by Gerald Edelman in his neural theorizing.) Yet in Fodor's *The Modularity of Mind,* the outputs of "perceptual modules" are identified with *appearances.* If this were literally correct, then if the module that enables me to recognize, say, telephones could be kept intact in a vat, and stimulated so as to fire, one would have a sense datum in a small group of neurons! But this is complete nonsense. The module is part of what gives me the capacity to recognize telephones, if the modularity hypothesis is correct, but its output is not yet a perception or even an "appearance." To use McDowell's language, a perception—or even an appearance—is the exercise of a capacity, and events in the brain are not identical with exercises of mental capacities, although they are necessary for us to have those capacities. (Moreover, if the module were left intact in my brain, while I lost my whole fund of knowledge about the function of telephones because of some brain damage[20]—it is this sort of possibility that makes "point-to-point correlation" so natural—it might happen that when I saw a telephone I would still have a "feeling of recognition"— but a moment later, I would realize that I didn't have the faintest idea what *that thing* was!) Thus the modularity hypothesis does not, contrary to Fodor, undermine the importance of general intelligence to perception, even though it may change our understanding of how the brain works in certain ways.

Reductionist naturalism is very tempting if one is a cognitive scientist because it is much more exciting to tell the world "I am discovering how the mind works" than to say "I am modeling the brain functions that enable an organism to have the mental capacities we have." A sane view recognizes that human beings are a part of nature, and their mental capacities require a certain specific sort of material embodiment (see Chapter 2 of the present volume). But once one sees that perception, in the strong achievement sense of the word, involves our conceptual powers, it is not difficult to see that the arguments against functionalism as a reductive theory of intentionality also apply to reductive theories of perception. Seeing an object should not be thought of a two-part affair: a "non-cognitive" interaction between the object, the light rays, and the eye, as the first part, followed by "cognitive" processing in the brain. The whole affair is cognitive; the events in the brain are a part of my cognitive and perceptual activity *only* because I am a creature with a certain kind of normal environment, and with a certain history of individual and species interaction with that environment. Brain events are not intrinsically "cognitive" nor are events that take place between the telephone and the eye intrinsically "non-cognitive." As John Dewey would have said, what is cognitive is the *interaction*.

Free-standing Semantical Facts?

What goes for perception goes as well for conception, and hence for reference.[21] Our ability to refer is not one ability but a whole complex of abilities, including our perceptual abilities. And again, as I argued in *Representation and Reality,* our brains are involved in reference, but that does not mean that a point-to-point reduction of our referential capacities to the computational properties of our brains is possible or necessary.

Simon Blackburn[22] has raised the objection that such a view postulates "free-standing semantical facts"; such facts are, according to him, incompatible with the "determination" of the mental by the physical.

> One could see Putnam as poised to accept it [the view that there are non-reducible or "self-standing" semantic facts] since the drift of his work is to refuse to grant especial ontological privilege to any particular kind of fact, and that would include facts from the Base Totality.

But there is a cost . . . the real difficulty is not epistemological, but ontological. For Quine appears to put into the base totality everything we could possibly want in order to determine reference and meaning. If we say he did not, we are making an ontological claim. We are denying that semantics *supervenes* on the extensional facts about things. (emphasis added)

In this passage, saying that facts in the Base Totality (Blackburn's term for the "non-intentional facts") do not "determine" reference and meaning *means* asserting that there can be a difference in semantical facts without any difference in physical facts. But there is a very different sense of "determine" that Blackburn should have considered. When Moore—a philosopher Blackburn has thought about a great deal—denied that natural facts determine moral facts he was not asserting that there can be a *difference* in moral facts without any difference in physical facts, and likewise when John McDowell and I both deny, from our respective points of view, that facts in the Base Totality determine semantic facts, we are not asserting that there can be a *difference* in semantical facts without any difference in physical facts. The point is rather that if you want to understand *why* semantic facts are "supervenient" on facts in the Base Totality (accepting, for the moment, this way of talking), you must, so to speak, *look from above*—you must look at the (allegedly)[23] "non-intentional" facts about how we use words (for example, We often assert "There's a rabbit" when a rabbit is present, and not very often when there is no rabbit present, or when we don't see the rabbit) from the standpoint of your intentional notions, rather than trying to explain from below—trying to use physics, or behavior science, or computer science, or whatever, to explain why words refer. The analogy with ethics may be helpful here. If you want to know why two people who do the same things and think the same thoughts cannot differ in moral worth, you should ask a moral philosopher, not a physicist. If you want to know why two people who causally interact with the same things (both directly and through the medium of their culture), think the same words, have the same dispositions, and so on, cannot be referring to different things (apart from the trivial case of indexicals), you should ask a philosopher of language, not a physicist (or a computer scientist).

In particular, if you want to know why it does not make sense to imagine a world in which people use their words just as we do but in which the reference of all the words is systematically permuted in such a way that the truth conditions of whole sentences are unaffected—so that "cat" refers to cats*, etc.[24]—part of the answer is that it is easy to *perceive* that something is a cat, and difficult (without the aid of mental calculation) to perceive that something is a cat*. Another part of the answer is that using words in the way we do (not saying "There is a cat in front of me" when I see that there is no cat in front of me, for example) is what we *call* "using 'cat' to refer to cats and not to cats*," and so forth. (Note that this answer employs the intentional notion of "calling something a so and so," that is, *referring,* as well as the intentional notion of *perceiving that something is a so and so.* That is why this is an answer "from above" and not an answer "from below.")

However, I would now reject the claim that I made in *Realism and Reason* (p. 225) that intentional relations are not "in the world."[25] Today I would say that if in certain cases what we take a word as denoting or what we take to be "the cause" of an event depends upon both the context and our interests, what that shows is that there are sometimes alternative right descriptions of the world with respect to reference and causality, but not that reference and causality are "not in the world." What we should not do is absolutize any one of the alternative right descriptions.

Indeed, it is precisely our desire to absolutize one description—the description of the world in terms of the "primary qualities" as a perfected physics might be imagined to list them—that makes it seem somehow illegitimate to use words like "perceive" in answering the question "How does thought relate to the world?" Yet the vocabulary of physics, it should be remembered, is selected with one very special purpose in mind: the purpose of providing the mathematically most elegant account of the time-development of particle/field parameters in an arbitrary closed system. Again, it is Quine who has made himself the spokesman for the view that the facts needed for *that* purpose are all the facts there are. One of Quine's best-known arguments is the following:[26]

> If the physicist suspected there was any event that did not consist[27] in a redistribution of the elementary states allowed for by his physical theory, he would seek a way of supplementing his theory. Full coverage in this sense is the business of physics, and only of physics.

But as Christopher Hookway has asked,[28]

> Why should we take the point about "full coverage" to show that the physical facts exhaust the facts at all? If statements drawn from eco-

nomics or cognitive psychology provide us with an understanding of phenomena which we could not obtain from physics, and if we have means for settling disagreements in these areas in a reasonably reliable fashion, why shouldn't we claim that they reveal to us a facet of reality that is not revealed to us by physics? In spite of full coverage, there are non-physical facts which we would allude to in making sense of ourselves and our surroundings. That all change *involves* physical change does not entail that every fact *is* a physical fact.

Notes

1. "Suppose now we shift our ontology by reinterpreting each of our predicates as true rather of the correlates *fx* of the objects *x* that it had been true of. Thus where '*Px*' originally meant that *x* was a '*P*,' we interpret '*Px*' as meaning that *x* is *f* of a *P*. . . . The observation sentences remain associated with the same sensory stimulations as before, and the logical interconnections remain intact. Yet the objects of the theory have been supplanted as drastically as you please." *Pursuit of Truth* (Cambridge: Harvard University Press, 1990), pp. 31–32.

2. For a criticism of the idea that reference is *literally* relative to a translation manual, see Chapter 17 of this volume, "A Comparison of Something with Something Else."

3. Instead of getting as a theorem "There is rabbit in the lettuce patch" is true if and only if there is a rabbit in the lettuce patch, I shall now get "There is a rabbit in the lettuce patch" is true if and only if there is a mereological complement of a rabbit in the set of things which have a mereological complement in the lettuce patch. This is only flouting Convention T "in a sense" because, if we assume the axioms of mereology (the calculus of parts and wholes), we can still deduce Tarski's original T sentence from this.

4. For an account of this argument as I now see it, see Chapter 18 of this volume, "Model Theory and the 'Factuality' of Semantics."

5. I argue against this view in the first lecture in *The Many Faces of Realism* (La Salle, Ill.: Open Court, 1987).

6. The idea that the mind is neither a material nor an immaterial organ but a system of capacities is strongly urged by John McDowell in an article titled "Putnam on Mind and Meaning" in an issue of *Philosophical Topics*, 20, no. 1 (Spring 1992), devoted to my work. (McDowell draws, in turn, on the insights of Gareth Evans in *Varieties of Reference*, a book whose importance I regret having failed to appreciate when I reviewed it in the *London Review of Books* some years ago). Although I do not wish to hold McDowell responsible for my formulations here, I want to acknowledge the pervasive influence of his work, which has reinforced a standing interest of mine in natural realism in the theory of perception (one originally awak-

ened by thinking about the views of both William James and John Austin on the topic of the theory of perception in recent years).

7. The Vienna Circle added a wrinkle; according to their doctrine, inference cannot even begin with the sense datum, but only with the proposition that I am having a sense datum of such and such a kind! The sense datum can cause such a proposition to be believed, but it cannot justify the belief—a view which is the ancestor of Davidson's doctrine that experience is related to belief only causally. For a penetrating criticism of this doctrine, see the discussion of Davidson in McDowell's John Locke Lectures, when they are published.

8. Given in 1990. These lectures will be published by Harvard University Press under the title *Mind and World*.

9. See p. 24 of "Models and Reality," reprinted in my *Philosophical Papers*, vol. 3, *Realism and Reason* (New York: Cambridge University Press, 1983).

10. See Chapter 13 of the present volume for this reading of Wittgenstein, as well as chaps. 7 and 8 of my *Renewing Philosophy* (Cambridge: Harvard University Press, 1992).

11. See "James's Theory of Perception" in my *Realism with a Human Face* (Cambridge: Harvard University Press, 1990).

12. Michael Devitt, *Realism and Truth* (Princeton: Princeton University Press, 1984).

13. Jerry Fodor, *A Theory of Content* (Cambridge: MIT Press, 1990).

14. Richard Boyd, "Materialism without Reductionism: What Physicalism Does Not Entail," in *Readings in Philosophy of Psychology*, vol. 1, ed. Ned Block (Cambridge: Harvard University Press, 1980).

15. Richard Rorty, "Pragmatism, Davidson, and Truth," in *Truth and Interpretation*, ed. Ernest Lepore (Oxford: Basil Blackwell, 1986).

16. Wilfrid Sellars, "Empiricism and the Philosophy of Mind," in *The Foundations of Science and the Concepts of Psychology and Psychoanalysis*, ed. Herbert Feigl and Michael Scriven, Minnesota Studies in the Philosophy of Science, 1 (Minneapolis: University of Minnesota Press, 1956).

17. Pp. 163–164 in "Great Men and Their Environment," in *The Will to Believe and Other Essays* (Cambridge: Harvard University Press, 1979).

18. For details, see chap. 3 of *Renewing Philosophy*.

19. See *Sense and Sensibilia* (Oxford: Oxford University Press, 1964).

20. According to Fodor's "modularity hypothesis" this general knowledge is *not* part of the perceptual module.

21. Here I discuss only reference to observables; for a discussion of reference to unobservables, see Chapter 13 in the present volume.

22. Simon Blackburn, "Enchanting Views," in *Reading Putnam*, ed. P. Clarke and R. Hale (Oxford: Basil Blackwell, 1993).

23. I say "allegedly" non-intentional facts because as we saw earlier *seeing*

something is an "intentional" notion. Quine's notion of "stimulus meaning" is, of course, an attempt to dodge this very issue. If facts about "seeing" are not included in the Base Totality, then it is unclear why Blackburn wants to claim that "Quine appears to put into the base totality everything we could possibly want in order to determine reference and meaning."

24. See Chapter 3 in the present volume, pp. 67–68.

25. There I wrote, "If the materialist cannot define reference, he can, of course, just take it as *primitive*. But reference, like causality, is a flexible, interest-dependent notion: what we count as referring to something depends on background knowledge and our willingness to be charitable in interpretation. To read a relation so deeply human and so pervasively intentional into the world and to call the resulting metaphysical picture satisfactory (never mind whether or not it is 'materialist') is absurd."

26. *Theories and Things* (Cambridge: Harvard University Press, 1981), p. 98.

27. Note the similarity between Quine's use of "consist" and Blackburn's use of "determine"!

28. Christopher Hookway, *Quine* (Oxford: Basil Blackwell, 1988), p. 214.

15. The Question of Realism

Although Auguste Comte deserves the title of the father of positivism, his positivism was in certain respects quite unlike any of the twentieth-century views that have associated themselves or been associated by others with that name. Comte's lasting legacy and the source of his enormous influence on European and American thought is the particular conception of "positive knowledge" that he bequeathed to us. On that conception the knowledge that human beings can aspire to not only does not extend to the ultimate nature of things; it does not even extend to a knowledge of "causes" in any sense of "cause" in which to know causes is to know more than certain empirical relations of invariant correlation. What we can know, according to Comte, are invariable relations of similarity and succession—*period*.

This can sound like empiricism, and all twentieth-century positivists have *also* called themselves empiricists. But in many ways the description is misleading when applied to Comte. It is not that Comte was anti-empiricist. The problem is that many of the problems of empiricism were of no concern to Comte. For example, the great question of realism—"How does mind or language hook on to the world?"—is one he would have dismissed as hopelessly metaphysical. Indeed, Comte was criticized by Mill for his utter lack of interest in individual psychology; and the question I called the great question of realism cannot be discussed without entering explicitly or implicitly into an account of mind. Nor is it that Comte was "philosophically naive"; in many ways he was more sophisticated than later empiricists typically were. On Comte's account, for example, each science develops methods appropriate to its own subject matter, methods that we can study only if we engage in historical study of that science; the empiricist search for an ahistorical universal "inductive logic" is utterly foreign to Comte. And for Comte the observation of a fact did not mean the observation of Machian sensations or Carnapian *Elementarerleb-nisse:* an observation, for Comte, must be connected, at least hypo-thetically, with some scientific law, and Comte is aware of the "circu-lar" interdependence of observation and hypothesis, although this did not lead him to post-Kuhnian doubts about the very possibility of pos-itive knowledge.

Yet, in retrospect, it is not surprising that his positivist successors were very much concerned with the problem of realism, or rather with showing the problem of realism to be a pseudo-problem. For without at least some discussion of that problem, the Comtean doctrine that all we can know is relations of invariable similarity and succession appears as mere dogma—or at best, perhaps, as an induction from the failure of past attempts at a convincing "solution."

This latter possibility would not, I think, have bothered Comte. He might have been content to rest his case for positivism on a mere in-duction from the failure of past attempts at metaphysical knowledge. For Comte's aims were social and political. The real argument against continuing metaphysical discussion, in his view, is that experience shows that it doesn't pay off; in this respect, however different his recommendations, Comte very much resembles that most recent "end-of-philosophy" philosopher Richard Rorty. To be sure, Rorty would disagree with Comte's highly technocratic conception of a just and stable society run by expert "sociologists," and he would recom-mend creating "new vocabularies" rather than just seeking relations of similarity and succession among observable facts. But like Comte, he denies that we can penetrate to the ultimate nature of things; or rather (and here too Comte would have agreed) he denies that know-ing the "nature" of things is a task that makes sense, outside the exact sciences, where (I suspect) he would agree with Comte that the sense it makes is given by the success of those sciences in predicting and systematizing "relations of similarity and succession of observable facts." And it sometimes appears as if Rorty, again like Comte, is pre-pared to rest his case (for "postmodernism," however, rather than "positivism") on a mere induction from the history of philosophy. At other times, however, Rorty's own way of dismissing the history of philosophy appears to presuppose the existence of deep results—re-sults concerning, for example, the possibility of representation— which have recently been attained in philosophy of language and mind (although his rhetoric officially disavows the possibility of such philosophical "results"). What I want to do here is examine one of these philosophical "results" that Rorty's dismissal of philosophy seems to me to presuppose.

Although I would agree with Comte and Rorty that the question as to how thought and language hook on to the world is a muddled one, I am not willing to conclude that discussing it has proved to be a waste of time. Indeed, I would argue that even if we never find a "solution," discussion of this issue has led to some of the deepest and most fertile thought of the last two centuries. However, I am not going to pursue that argument at this time. Instead, what I want to do is consider how satisfying we should find Rorty's way of attempting to dismiss the question of realism.

Rorty's Short Way with the Question

I have discussed Rorty's work in my undergraduate courses on more than one occasion, and to my dismay I have found that in their final examinations students often quote with conviction and approval an argument of his that I find terrible. This argument is supposed to show that the whole idea that our words and thoughts sometimes do and sometimes do not "agree with" or "correspond to" or "represent" a reality outside themselves ought to be rejected as entirely empty. The reason given is that it is impossible to "stand outside" and compare our thought and language with the world. The only access we have to the world is to the world as it is represented in thought and language. Rorty concludes that speaking of some of our words and thoughts as "true" or as "in agreement with the facts" is only a "compliment" that we pay to our own intellectual creations (the ones that help us "cope").

If the question of realism could be disposed of so simply, then many other philosophical issues which are entangled with it could be disposed of as well. I agree with Rorty that we have no access to "unconceptualized reality." As John McDowell likes to put it, you can't view your language "from sideways on" in the way that the idea of looking at one's language and the world and comparing the two suggests. But it doesn't follow that language and thought do not describe something outside themselves, even if that something can only be described by describing it (that is by employing language and thought); and, as Rorty ought to have seen, the belief that they do plays an essential role *within* language and thought themselves and, more important, within our lives.

To see why Rorty's short way with realism cannot be accepted, consider the following two instances of exactly the same argument form:

Argument 1: The idea that other people really exist and that I can know what they are thinking and feeling is empty, because I can't stand outside my own mind and compare my thoughts about the thoughts of other people with the thoughts and feelings of other people as they are in themselves. Suppose someone took this argument seriously, and decided that she did not have to worry about the thoughts and feelings of other people, except insofar as what she did to them might lead to experiences—*her* experiences—which she wouldn't like to have! Would we not be more than a little disturbed by such a person? Yet how would this person's reasoning differ from Rorty's?

This person would have adopted a version of "methodological solipsism," a doctrine according to which the best way for me to think of concepts purporting to refer to other people is for me to think of them simply as intellectual devices which are useful for the purpose of predicting and systematizing my own experiences. It is a serious question in just what sense such a solipsism should be regarded as just "methodological." If, as Rorty is fond of claiming, talking and thinking is just a matter of producing "marks and noises" which help *us* "cope," then how does his position really differ from methodological solipsism? How does it differ from saying that what I call "talking about other people" simply *is* producing "marks and noises" for the purpose of enabling *me* to "cope"? Even if he says, "I am not just interested in my own happiness, I am interested in the happiness of other people as well," doesn't that in the end, on Rorty's view, just come to producing more marks and noises? And how can one justify to oneself producing those "marks and noises" beyond seeing whether they enable *oneself* to "cope"?

Argument 2: Here I borrow an argument against (what Reichenbach himself deprecatingly called) "positivism" from Reichenbach's classic *Experience and Prediction*: Suppose someone were to say, "Talk about a future after my own death is simply an intellectual device whose real function is just to enable me to predict my experiences while I am alive. After all," this person might say, "you can't stand outside your language and thought and compare your language and thought with the future after your own death." (Reichenbach simply asked, why should such a person buy life insurance?)[1]

Reflecting on these two further instances of Rorty's argument form, we see that if "realism" is understood simply as the idea that thought and language can represent parts of the world which are not parts of thought and language, then no one should be convinced that realism in that sense is an incoherent idea by the mere thought that we do not and cannot have "direct access" to the world outside of thought and language—unless one is also prepared to be convinced that one should act as a solipsist would be committed to acting with respect to other people and with respect to the future. And (contrary to Wittgenstein's celebrated remark in the *Tractatus* about consistent solipsism and realism coming to the same thing), there is a difference—*a difference in what justifications of conduct make sense viewed from within our language and thought,* and not from some impossible Archimedean point—between regarding other people merely as convenient intellectual devices for coping with one's own experiences and (to borrow a term from Stanley Cavell) *acknowledging* them. This is the difference the later Wittgenstein tries to capture with his remark "My attitude towards him is an attitude towards a soul. I am not of the *opinion* that he has a soul."[2]

In stating the argument that I just criticized, I said that it is impossible to stand outside and compare our thought and language, on the one hand, with the world on the other; and, indeed, this is the way Rorty puts matters. But if we agree that it is *unintelligible* to say, "We sometimes succeed in comparing our language and thought with reality as it is in itself," then we should realize that it is also unintelligible to say, "It is *impossible* to stand outside and compare our thought and language with the world." (In a sense it is even *more* unintelligible than to say that we do sometimes do it: for in this case to say that it is impossible to do "*p*" not only involves a "*p*" which is unintelligible but also introduces the peculiar philosophical "impossible"—a variant of what Wittgenstein calls "the philosophical 'must.'") Rorty seems to be telling us of an impotence, in the way the physicist tells us of an impotence when he says, "You can't build a perpetual motion machine," but it turns out on examination that the impotence is a mirage, or even less than a mirage—that it is chimerical.[3]

But why is Rorty so bothered by the lack of a *guarantee* that our words represent things outside themselves? Evidently, Rorty's craving for such a guarantee is so strong that, finding the guarantee to be "impossible," he feels forced to conclude that our words do not represent anything. It is at this point in Rorty's position that one detects the trace of a disappointed metaphysical realist impulse. I think the trouble here comes when one does not properly explore the sort of "impossibility" which is at issue when one concludes—with Rorty—that such a guarantee is indeed impossible. What I want to emphasize is that Rorty moves from a conclusion about the unintelligibility of metaphysical realism (we cannot have a guarantee—of a sort that doesn't even make sense!—that our words represent things outside of themselves) to a skepticism about the possibility of representation *tout court*. We are left with the conclusion that there is no metaphysically innocent way to say that our words *do* "represent things outside themselves." Failing to inquire into the character of the unintelligibility which vitiates metaphysical realism, Rorty remains blind to the way in which his own rejection of metaphysical realism partakes of the same unintelligibility. The way in which skepticism is the flip side of a craving for an unintelligible kind of certainty (a senseless craving, one might say, but for all that a deeply human craving) has rarely been more sharply illustrated than by Rorty's complacent willingness to give up on the (platitudinous) idea that language can represent something which is itself outside of language. While I agree with Rorty that metaphysical realism is unintelligible, to stop with that point without going on to recover our ordinary notion of representation (and of a world of things to be represented[4]) is to fail to complete that journey "from the familiar to the familiar"[5] that is the true task of philosophy.

Rorty's Davidson and Davidson's Davidson

Rorty reads Donald Davidson's celebrated rejection of "the scheme-content distinction" as a rejection of the very idea that *things* make our sentences true, and thus as support for his rejection of the whole idea of representation. To distinguish the morals I draw from Davidson's celebrated address to the American Philosophical Association from the ones Rorty draws, it may help to point out that in the very last sentence of an essay of Davidson's[6] that Rorty is fond of praising, Davidson speaks of "the familiar objects whose antics make our sentences and opinions true or false." This remark would seem to suggest that Davidson doesn't mean to deny that objects, be they near or be they distant from us in space or time, sometimes *make* our sentences true. (If he had, I should now be quarreling with Davidson, as well as with Rorty.) Rather, Davidson's point seems to be that we must not think that true sentences correspond one by one to special objects which "make them true," call them "states of affairs"; for to do that would be to bloat our ontology with what Collingwood called "a kind of ghostly double of the grammarian's sentence."[7]

Whether a descriptive sentence is true depends on whether certain things or events satisfy the conditions for being described by that sentence—conditions which depend upon the ongoing activity of using and reforming language. I agree with Davidson that this should not be thought of as the correspondence of the sentence to a unique sentence-shaped thing in the world. The distribution of mammals in this room is such that the sentence "There is no elephant in the room" is true, but I feel no need to invent some *thing* called "the absence of elephants in the room" for that sentence to "correspond to."[8] (However, I do not agree with Davidson that it is *verboten* to speak of "states of affairs" at all; if we can, as Davidson urges we should, think of "events" as individuated in such a way that they are describable by different and inequivalent sentences, why should we not think of "states of affairs" in a similar way? The meaningful question—that is, the one that *does* make sense—is not whether states of affairs "really exist" or not, but whether notions like "state of affairs" are to be conceived of as having a single determinate meaning or whether they are more happily conceived in terms of an open and ever extendable family of uses. A version of this question should be asked about other philosophical favorites as well: "object," "event," and so on.)

But Rorty's real worry is this: How can one say that sentences are "made true" by objects if objects aren't "what they are independent of my way of talking"?[9] And my reply[10] is that Rorty's very vocabulary contains philosophical assumptions that one should not accept. Talk of "independent existence" makes little sense when what is at stake is neither ordinary causal nor ordinary logical independence. That the sky is blue is causally independent of the way we talk; for, with our language in place, we can certainly say that the sky would still be blue even if we did not use color words (unless, of course, we affected that color in some ordinary causal way, say by producing more smog). And the statement that the sky is blue is, in the ordinary sense of "logically independent," logically independent of any description that one might give of our use of color words. For these reasons, I have, especially in recent years, tried *not* to state my own doctrine as a doctrine of the dependence of the way things are on the way we talk (perhaps Rorty's retention of this way of speaking betrays his deep linguistic idealism). In any sense of "independent" I can understand, whether the sky is blue is independent of the way we talk.[11]

There is, however, a way in which Rorty himself has put things else-where that seems much happier to me. Even if we (*with* our language in place) must say that the sky is blue, and even if we must allow that that fact is (causally and logically) independent of how we talk, we do not have to concede that there would be a thing called "the proposi-tion that the sky is blue" even if we did not talk that way. It is state-ments (not abstract entities called "propositions") that are true or false, and while it is true that the sky would still have been blue even if language users had not evolved, it is not true that *true propositions* would still have existed. If language users had not evolved, there would still have been a world, but there would not have been any *truths*. But recognizing that fact—and it is an important one—does not require us to say that the sky is not blue independently of the way we speak. What it does require us to do—and here I do agree with Rorty—is to give up the picture of Nature as having its very own lan-guage which it is waiting for us to discover and use. I agree with Rorty that there is no one metaphysically privileged description that was al-ways waiting to be written down. There are many ways of describing things, some better and some worse and some equally good but simply different, but none which is Nature's own way. If I say, "There is a blue chair in front of me," and my statement happens to be true, I have described a part of the world just as truly as if I had said, "There is a large collection of fermions." Both descriptions describe what is before me; neither describes it "in itself," not because the "in itself" is an unreachable limit, but because the "in itself" doesn't make sense.

We make up uses of words—many, many different uses of words—and the senses of "agree" in which our various sentences "agree" with reality, when they do, are plural indeed. Yet for all that, some of our sentences *are* true, and—in spite of Rorty's objections to saying that things "make" sentences true—the truth of "I had cereal for breakfast this morning" *does* depend on what happened this morning.

Rorty's Putnam and My Putnam

Rorty reads my "model-theoretic arguments" in *Reason, Truth, and History* and in two essays of mine—"Realism and Reason"[12] and "Models and Reality"[13]—as strong support for his view that the whole idea of "representing" a reality external to language has col-lapsed. From what I have said previously, it should be evident that I do not wish to endorse his reading of those essays.

Up to now I have been defending common-sense realism: the realism that says that mountains and stars are not created by language and thought, and are not parts of language and thought, and yet can be described by language and thought. But there is a more metaphysical version of realism which tries to defend this insight by reformulating it with the aid of a great deal of supposedly explanatory machinery. The nature of that machinery varies from metaphysician to metaphysician (from Plato's forms to Aristotle's substances, to Descartes's vortices in a substantial space plus minds, to Hume's ideas, to the modern materialist's points in a four-dimensional space-time plus sets); but what is common to all versions of this more metaphysical realism is the notion that there is—in a philosophically privileged sense of "object"—a definite Totality of All Real Objects and a fact of the matter as to which properties of those objects are the intrinsic properties and which are, in some sense, perspectival.

The chief aim of the essays of mine that Rorty cites was to argue that this metaphysical kind of realism is "incoherent." I did not mean by that that it is inconsistent in a deductive logical sense, but rather that when we try to make the claims of the metaphysical realist precise, we find that they become compatible with strong forms of "antirealism." Thus attempts at a clear formulation of the position never succeed—because there is no real content there to be captured. My aim in those essays, therefore, was not to argue for the truth of a metaphysical counter-thesis (one which could be identified with the negation of metaphysical realism), but rather simply to provide a *reductio ad absurdum* of metaphysical realism by teasing out the consequences of its own presuppositions.

My strategy for showing that there was no real content there to be captured was to examine what I regarded as the most tenable current form of metaphysical realism, that being advocated at that particular time by Richard Boyd (and defended by myself in my John Locke Lectures).[14] According to Boyd (and to me in the Locke Lectures), metaphysical realism can be reformulated as an over-arching empirical theory about the success of science, namely the (meta)theory that the success of the theories of the mature physical sciences is explained by the fact that the terms used in those theories typically *refer* (refer to subsets of the Totality of All Objects, that is) and that the statements that constitute the basic assumptions of those theories are typically *approximately true.*

Today there is a commonly heard objection to this view, namely, that the notion of approximate truth cannot (so it is claimed) be made precise. This was not my objection.[15] Instead my strategy was to suppose that we could actually spell out the details sufficiently to give substance, as it were, to the over-arching meta-explanation of scientific progress just referred to. I argued that the truth of this theory, should it prove to be true, could be accounted for on either a realist understanding of truth or an antirealist understanding of truth. But if both the metaphysical realist and his opponent can agree that the "scientific realist" metatheory of scientific progress is true, that shows that the "theses" about which they disagree are not captured by that "scientific realist" metatheory; and, by parity of reasoning, I argued, no attempt to capture metaphysical realism by a set of over-arching empirical claims can possibly succeed. However, the suggestion that metaphysical realism might be *nonempirically* true is a possibility I did not—and still do not—take seriously.

My original antirealist (in "Realism and Reason") assumes a set of operational constraints and a set of theoretical constraints. (These latter need not be known to us in advance—they are allowed to possibly become clear only in an ideal limit of inquiry.) She conceives of "truths" as simply sentences that, in the limit of inquiry, satisfy the constraints. For good measure, I went on to consider a third, intermediate, position. In this intermediate position there are, again, operational and theoretical constraints, but these are not used to directly single out the class of truths. Rather, they are used to define a class of "intended models" (in the sense of "model" employed in modern mathematical logic), and the "truths" are the sentences that are satisfied by all intended models. One of my arguments was that the same sentences could be true on all three conceptions of truth. Another argument was that (it is possible to show that) there always exists at least one "correspondence" relation such that, if we take it to be *the* correspondence relation, metaphysical realist truth will coincide with truth on the other two conceptions. And if the same sentences are true on all three conceptions, the difference between the conceptions cannot be captured by any sentence in the language that they speak about.

The second idea that I defended in "Realism and Reason" is that all situations have many different correct descriptions, and that even descriptions that, taken holistically, convey the same information may differ in what they take to be "objects"; this was part of my case against the idea of a Totality of All Objects. If there isn't one single privileged sense of the word "object" and one privileged totality of "intrinsic properties," but there is only an inherently extendable notion of "object" and various properties that may be seen as "intrinsic" in different inquiries, then the very notion of a totality of all objects and of the *one* description that captures *the* intrinsic properties of those objects should be seen to be nonsense from the start. I subsequently referred to this idea, the idea that there are many usable extensions of the notion of an object, and many alternative ways of describing objects, as "conceptual relativity," and I went into it at greater length in a little book and a number of papers.[16]

But there was a third idea in "Realism and Reason" and "Models and Reality" that I now think was dead wrong; that idea is the picture of the mental states of what I called "a speaker-hearer of a natural language" as simply the internal computational states of a finite automaton. That picture, which became widely known (and indeed widely accepted) under the name "functionalism," sees language as something inside the head (inside the computer); and by doing so, it inevitably makes it mysterious how any item in language can refer to what is outside the head, or outside the computer. (I think that one sees this consequence in the writings of Daniel Dennett.) Subsequently, I gave up the functionalist picture[17] and moved to an alternative that John McDowell has long been urging: that is, not to think of the mind as an *organ* at all, but to think of it as a structured system of object-involving abilities. I would add to McDowell's picture that since the notion of an object is inherently extendable, so is the notion of the mind. Not only can these abilities not be described without speaking of the things outside the organism that they involve, but, as I argued repeatedly in the papers and books I published from *Reason, Truth, and History*[18] on, they cannot be described in language which does not avail itself of intentional and normative notions. The mind cannot be "naturalized."[19]

Now Rorty is not functionalist (although he did once remark to me in a conversation, "I was sorry that the functionalist program didn't succeed"). But, as he himself has recognized, he does retain strong traces of his physicalist past. Certain passages in his *Philosophy and the Mirror of Nature* seem to assume that mind talk can just be replaced by brain talk when science becomes sufficiently advanced. And in spite of Rorty's frequently expressed admiration for Dewey, he seems not to have noticed Dewey's wonderful remark that the old soul/body or mind/body dualism still survives in a scientific age as a dualism between "the brain and the rest of the body."[20] In any case, Rorty's response[21] to the statement I just made (the statement that our mental abilities cannot be described in language which does not avail itself of intentional and normative notions) is to say that while it is true, understood simply as a claim about the non-reducibility of one "vocabulary" to another, nothing about reality follows from non-reducibility—an odd move indeed for some one who claims the very vocabulary/reality distinction has to be given up!

In sum, it seems to me that while I have moved from versions of "internal realism" I put forward after I left physicalism to a position which I would describe as increasingly realist—though without going back to the latter-day version of fourteenth-century semantics known as "metaphysical realism"—Rorty has moved from his physicalism to an extreme linguistic idealism which teeters on the edge of solipsism.

"Representation"

Up to now I have followed Rorty in not distinguishing between the claims that garden-variety true thoughts are "represensions" of reality (or representations of the "antics" of familiar objects) and the claim that sentences are. There is, however, one important difference between the two cases; if, as I have just urged, we think of our thoughts as exercises of object-involving abilities, then their relation to what they describe is too "internal" to fit the metaphor of "representations." Here again I follow the lead of John McDowell, who puts the point very well in a paper[22] in which he sympathetically discusses a view which I have long defended (indeed, a view which is essential to thinking of thoughts as exercises of object-involving abilities): namely, the view that the content of our thoughts is individuated in part by the sort of environments we inhabit, and therefore (as I put it in "The Meaning of 'Meaning'") "meanings aren't in the head."[23]

McDowell points out that there are two different ways someone who accepts my Twin Earth argument may be tempted to apply it.

One way (the way followed by many in the cognitive science community)[24] is to think of thoughts as representations which can be individuated in two different ways: "narrowly," by their roles in an internal computational system, and "widely," by the way in which they are related to things outside the system. Against this "duplex conception," McDowell argues that from the fact that thinking, say, that one hears the sound of water dripping is representing that one hears the sound of water dripping, it does not follow that thinking that one hears the sound of water dripping must in itself consist in the presence in the mind of a symbol; something into which the significance that one hears the sound of water dripping can be read, as it can be read into the sign-design "I hear the sound of water dripping," although in both cases the symbol's bearing that significance is extraneous to its intrinsic nature. Putnam's solid point [McDowell means the upshot of my Twin Earth argument] cannot dislodge the possibility that thinking that one hears the sound of water dripping is a mental representation, in the sense of a mental representing that intrinsically represents what it represents.[25]

The deep point that McDowell is making is that if we think of our thoughts as *symbols,* then indeed nothing except magic could constitute their referential directedness at the world, and this, I believe, is precisely the line of thinking that leads Rorty to conclude that a healthy refusal to invoke magic in philosophy requires that we renounce the whole idea that our thoughts *possess* referential directness at the world; but there is a possibility that Rorty misses, the possibility (to borrow a phrase of McDowell's) of "representation without representations."

If we follow McDowell's line, as I am convinced we should, then we can even agree with Rorty that the idea that there is a genuine problem about "how language hooks on to the world" is one we should get over; but we should not get over it by reviving Bergson's[26] unfortunate idea that, since language is rightly viewed as a product of evolution, our statements and verbalized thoughts should be viewed as simply tools which enable us to survive *as opposed to* correct representations. Rather we should reject the assumption that thinking is manipulating items with no intrinsic relation to what is outside the head.

As McDowell points out, the rejection of that assumption is not just to be identified with the postulation of mysterious powers of mind.

The proper target of that accusation is a way of thinking in which we try to combine conceiving the mind as an organ of thought, so that what an episode of thinking is in itself is a mental manipulation of a representation, with supposing that an episode of thinking has its determinate referential bearing on the world intrinsically. Putnam's cogent point is that this combination pushes us into a magical picture of the reference of the supposed mental symbols, and hence into a magical picture of the powers of the mind. But the conception I am urging needs no appeal to a magical theory of reference, precisely because it rejects the supposed mental symbols. My aim is not to postulate mysterious powers of mind; rather my aim is to restore us to a conception of thinking as the exercise of powers possessed, not mysteriously by some part of a thinking being, a part whose internal arrangements are characterizable independently of how the thinking being is placed in its environment, but unmysteriously by a thinking being itself, an animal that lives its life in cognitive and practical relations to the world.

Rorty sees as well as McDowell and I do the need to avoid postulating mysterious powers of the mind; but failing to see any room for a middle course, he recoils into an extreme denial of representation itself.

Conceptual Relativity Again

Earlier I remarked that I would add to McDowell's picture the observation that, since the notion of an object is inherently extendable, so is the notion of the mind. To some it will seem that this introduces a jarring note. They will want to ask: Is the idea that our thoughts have determinate reference to objects not undercut by the idea of a growing variety of concepts of an "object"?

To see why I believe that the answer is in the negative, it is well to consider an example.[28] We count the objects in a room (a lamp, a table, a chair, a ballpoint pen, and a notebook) and come up with the answer "five." But (taking the same things to be the atomic individuals, and not considering the parts of the lamp or the pages of the notebook as "objects"), we are told to count again, this time considering mereological sums of objects to be objects, and we come up with the answer $2^5 - 1 = 31$ (if the "null object" is excluded). Now, suppose we are asked to explain why the sentence "There are 31 objects in the room" is true, in the conceptual scheme of mereology, and not to refer to mereological sums in our answer.

One way to do this is to point out that the language of mereology is so set up that the number of "objects" is always equal to the number of nonempty *sets* of individuals. This explanation does not say what a "mereological sum" *is*. But it does provide a "definition in use" for the expression "the number of objects is n" as that expression is used in mereology. That the definiens is not "synonymous" with the definiendum does not prevent this definition in use from answering the question how one counts using mereological sums.

The point of this example is that the fact that one can describe the same room using two different vocabularies (vocabularies which are not interdefinable in the trivial way in which "vixen" and "female fox" are interdefinable) does *not* mean that one cannot talk about how those vocabularies relate to the familiar objects in the room; one can do that in a variety of ways, depending on what resources are available in the metalanguage, and what the purpose of the explanation is.[29] Given a definite language in place and a definite scheme of "objects," the relation between "words and objects" is not at all indescribable; but it does not have a single *metaphysically privileged* description any more than the objects do. In sum, we can think of our words and thoughts as having determinate reference to objects (when it is clear what sort of "objects" we are talking about and what vocabulary we are using); but there is no one fixed sense of "reference" involved. Accepting the ubiquity of conceptual relativity does not require us to deny that truth genuinely depends on the behavior of things distant from the speaker, but the nature of the dependence changes as the kinds of language games we invent change.

In the preceding discussion I have been reflecting upon what is right and what is misguided in the impulse to metaphysical realism. I believe that such a task of reflection—the task of teasing out the kernel of truth which underlies a metaphysical impulse from the confusions in which it becomes entangled—is a distinctly *philosophical* activity. I further believe that any attempt to get free and clear of metaphysical realism by means of a shortcut (in particular, one which seeks to dispense altogether with the exigencies of such reflection) will inevitably sink back into the very morass of philosophical confusion it seeks to dispel.

The sort of philosophical reflection I have been engaging in is just the sort of reflection that both Comte and Rorty see as *pointless*. For Comte such reflection is a throwback to a prescientific age; for Rorty, a reluctance to fully enter into a postmodern one. Some of you will probably agree with one or another of these thinkers. But in my view reflection on just what it is that makes thinkers like Rorty doubt the very idea of representing the world—and I think there is a Rorty in each of us as well as a Comte in each of us, however suppressed—is part of understanding ourselves, and not just part of understanding certain sophisticated and influential thinkers. For what is common to Rorty and Comte is the idea that much of what we think we know cannot have the status it seems to have. For Richard Rorty the recommended response is to take a more "playful" attitude to what we think we know; and for Auguste Comte it is to sternly restrict ourselves to "positive knowledge." But understanding the temptations and seductions of the idea that Comte and Rorty share, so that we can live with those temptations and seductions without succumbing to them, is far more important—and more valid as a response—than pretending that the world is either just a playpen or just a scientific laboratory.

Notes

An earlier version of this paper was given as the Auguste Comte Lecture at the London School of Economics on February 2, 1993. It has been substantially improved by the friendly but merciless criticism of Jim Conant.

1. "The insufficiency of a positivist language in which talk of events after my death is construed as a device for predicting my experiences while I am alive is revealed as soon as we try to use it for the rational reconstruction of the thought processes underlying actions concerned with events after our death, such as expressed in the example of the life insurance policies" (*Experience and Prediction* [Chicago: University of Chicago Press, 1936], p. 150). In spite of this trenchant argument, Reichenbach also maintains that the choice of realist as opposed to positivist language is a non-cognitive "volitional decision"; I discuss this tension in his thought, and related problems in Carnap's thought, in "Logical Positivism and Intentionality," Chapter 4 of the present volume.

2. *Philosophical Investigations* (New York: Macmillan, 1953), p. 178.

3. I further explore this idea (that the negation of something unintelligible is not a kind of impossibility) in "Rethinking Mathematical Necessity," Chapter 12 in the present volume. See also James Conant's profound examination of this issue in "The Search for Logically Alien Thought," in *The Philosophy of Hilary Putnam*, *Philosophical Topics*, 20, no. 1 (Spring 1992).

4. As Wittgenstein remarks, "if the words 'language,' 'experience,' 'world' have a use, it must be as humble a one as that of the words 'table,' 'lamp,' 'door.'" (*Philosophical Investigations*, §97.)

5. See J. Wisdom, "Metaphysics and Verification," *Mind*, 67, no. 188 (October 1938).

6. Donald Davidson, "The Very Idea of a Conceptual Scheme," in *Inquiries into Truth and Interpretation* (Oxford: Oxford University Press, 1984), p. 198.

7. Collingwood's *Autobiography* (Oxford: Oxford University Press, 1939, 1978), p. 34. Collingwood was speaking of postulating "propositions" as meanings of sentences, but the same point applies to "states of affairs."

8. If we were to reify the distribution of color properties over books in the room, say, for example, by identifying it with the function whose value on each book in the room is the color of that book, it would be extremely implausible to say that the sentence "There is no purple book in the room" "corresponds" to *that* object in the sense of the correspondence theory of truth, although that mathematical object indeed contains enough information to determine the truth of that sentence.

9. See Rorty's "Putnam on Truth," *Philosophy and Phenomenological Research,* 52, no. 2 (June 1992), 416.

10. See my "Truth, Activation Vectors, and Possession Conditions for Concepts," in *Philosophy and Phenomenological Research,* 52, no. 2 (June 1992).

11. See my discussion of the different senses of "independent" whose intelligibility I do/do not wish to challenge in my "Replies" in *The Philosophy of Hilary Putnam,* pp. 366–368.

12. This was my presidential address to the annual meeting of the Eastern Division of the American Philosophical Association (December 1976). It is reprinted in my *Meaning and the Moral Sciences* (London: Routledge and Kegan Paul, 1978).

13. This was given as my presidential address to the Association for Symbolic Logic (December 1977). It is reprinted in *Philosophical Papers,* vol. 3, *Realism and Reason* (New York: Cambridge University Press, 1983).

14. Reprinted in *Meaning and the Moral Sciences.*

15. For it is not inconceivable that the notion of "approximate truth" should someday be made precise at least as applied to physical theories. (Of course, if the claim is that there is no hope of a notion of "approximate truth" which is both precise and applicable to all forms of human discourse I agree; but why must a notion always be precise to be usable, especially if the notion concerns discourse which is not itself precise?) If scientific revolutions ever stop taking place in the fundamental physical sciences, we might someday have good reason to believe that any correct physical theory must be stated in terms of certain particular magnitudes, and that the laws of any correct physical theory must have certain particular mathematical forms. In that case, the idea that previous theories in those sciences had been good approximations to this "final" theory, or theory-sketch, could doubtless be given a precise sense, just as we can now give a precise sense to the claim that Newtonian physics is approximately true from the standpoint of General Relativity.

16. *The Many Faces of Realism* (La Salle, Ill.: Open Court, 1987) and the papers collected in *Realism with a Human Face* (Cambridge: Harvard University Press, 1990).

17. In this connection, see my *Representation and Reality* (Cambridge: MIT Press, 1988).

18. Published by Cambridge University Press in 1981.

19. The "naturalism" I reject is, of course, scientistic and reductionist. That, in a *non*-reductionist sense of "nature," we and our abilities are part of nature is undeniable.

20. John Dewey, *Democracy and Education* (New York: Macmillan, 1916), p. 336.

21. In "Putnam and the Relativist Menace" (published in French in *Lire Rorty* (Paris: Editions de l'Éclat, 1992), and in English in the *Journal of Philosophy* 90, no. 9 (Sept. 1993).

22. "Putnam on Mind and Meaning," in *The Philosophy of Hilary Putnam*.

23. I argued, in particular, that we could imagine humans who would be neuron for neuron identical, but who still thought different thoughts. I did this by imagining a planet called Twin Earth on which the liquid called "water" by the inhabitants had the same superficial properties as our water but a different chemical constitution, say XYZ, and argued that the Twin English word "water," and the thoughts of Twin English speakers involving this word, should be thought of as referring to XYZ while our thoughts should be thought of as referring to H_2O. See "The Meaning of 'Meaning,'" in my *Philosophical Papers*, vol. 2, *Mind, Language, and Reality* (New York: Cambridge University Press, 1975).

24. McDowell supposes that this was my view in *Reason, Truth, and History;* in fact, as I point out in my reply (in *The Philosophy of Hilary Putnam,* pp. 358–361), he misreads certain passages in that book. Although I was a functionalist in *Reason, Truth, and History,* I did not identify thoughts with particular brain events there or elsewhere.

25. "Putnam on Mind and Meaning," p. 43.

26. This idea occurs repeatedly in Bergson's writings. See, for example, *Matter and Memory* (London: Swan Sonnenschein, 1911). "That which is commonly called a fact is not reality as it appears to immediate intuition, but an adaptation of the real to the interests of practice and the exigencies of social life" (pp. 238–239).

27. "Putnam on Mind and Meaning," p. 45.

28. I used this same example in chap. 7 of *Representation and Reality*.

29. I discuss this point at more length in "Truth and Convention," reprinted in my *Realism with a Human Face*.

V

Truth and Reference

16. On Truth

Analytic philosophers today can be divided roughly into two classes. In one class there are philosophers of a number of different persuasions who see truth as a substantial notion which still remains to be philosophically explicated in a satisfactory way or which cannot be satisfactorily explicated, but must in that case be simply taken as primitive. Donald Davidson (who takes the notion of truth as primitive), Michael Dummett (who wants to identify truth with justification), and many, if not all, metaphysical realists share the view that truth is what I shall call a "substantial notion." In the second class are philosophers who feel that the problem of truth, if there ever was one, has been solved. These philosophers tend to call themselves "disquotationalists." Very often, though not always, they refer to the work of Alfred Tarski and to the semantical conception of truth. The purpose of this essay is to refute the views of the philosophers of the second class. The idea that the philosophical problems surrounding the notion of truth have been solved once and for all either by the idea of disquotation, or by the semantical conception of truth, or by some combination of these two is simply an error. It is a very important error, because if one commits it, and especially if one appeals to the work of Alfred Tarski, then one is liable to have the illusion that the major problem of philosophy—the problem of the way language and thought "hook on" to the world—has been solved by modern mathematical logic. It seems to me a task absolutely essential to repairing many of the gaping errors and confusions that fill the literature of contemporary analytical philosophy to show that this is not the case.

It is not the purpose of this essay to say anything positive about the notion of truth. My aim here is simply and purely destructive: I hope to show that a certain attitude toward the significance of scientific results for a major philosophical problem, the classical problem of truth, is misguided.

One may see the importance of what I am trying to do by seeing how it affects the argument put forward by Richard Rorty in a recent book.[1] In this book Rorty argues that all the classical problems of philosophy, at least from the time of Descartes, are "optional." One of the problems that he lumps under the general name of the problem of "representation" is precisely the problem of the nature of truth. Rorty's own solution to this problem is that what is true is what could be established to the satisfaction of one's "cultural peers." I have pointed out elsewhere that this is a self-refuting view. But one who believes that Tarski (or the "disquotational theory," whatever that is) *solved* the problem of truth might nevertheless agree with Rorty that all the classical problems were "optional," while criticizing the particular argument that Rorty gave. If neither Rorty's "solution" to the problem of truth nor any of the alternative fashionable solutions really works then at least one major problem in the history of philosophy is not "optional." But this is enough to destroy Rorty's entire argument.

Tarski's Theory of Truth

Tarski provided logicians with a method for defining a predicate which is coextensive with the predicate "is true," or rather which is coextensive with that predicate when that predicate is restricted to the sentences of a particular interpreted formalized language. Unfortunately, Tarski also wrote some philosophical essays in which he made various philosophical claims about the significance of his work as a conceptual analysis of the notion of truth. He claimed, for example, that it was philosophically neutral, and also that it explicated the grain of truth in the classical correspondence theory of truth. These various claims have resulted in Tarski's being acclaimed as the solver of the classical problem of truth by some realists (notably Karl Popper) and some antirealists (notably W. V. Quine). It is these philosophical claims advanced by Tarski, or advanced by others on behalf of Tarski, that I wish to refute. I do not deny that a properly defined "truth predicate" is, indeed, coextensive with the predicate "is true" (in the way just explained), at least in the case when the object language does not contain any vague (semantically undecided) sentences. What I deny is that the so-called truth predicate that Tarski defines is in any way similar in meaning to the intuitive predicate "is true." If there is a problem of conceptually analyzing our intuitive notion of truth,[2] then Tarski's work does not speak to it.

To see why it does not speak to it, it is useful to ignore the technical complications involved in the actual construction of a truth definition for languages with infinitely many sentences, and see what a Tarskian truth definition looks like when the language in question has only finitely many sentences. (This idea was originally suggested to me by Rudolph Carnap, who used to illustrate Tarski's idea in just this way.) Let "mond-shaped" be a predicate which applies to all and only those inscriptions which have the shape "Der Mond is blau." Let "schnee-shaped" be a predicate that applies to all and only those inscriptions which have the shape "Schnee ist weiss." Call a sentence *mond-good* if and only if it is the case both that the sentence in question is mond-shaped and that the moon is blue. Call a sentence *schnee-good* if and only it is the case both that the sentence is schnee-shaped and that snow is white. Finally, call a sentence *L-true* if and only if the sentence is either mond-good or schnee-good.

The property of being L-true just defined is the property that would correspond to the truth predicate for a language which contained just the two sentences "Der Mond ist blau" and "Schnee ist weiss" with their standard German meanings. If we have a language ML which contains the two sentences that make up the total stock of well-formed formulas of the object language L and which in addition contains devices for spelling and for talking about the shapes of sentences, and has quantifiers ranging over sentences and standard truth functions, then in such a language ML we can easily formalize the above definitions of the predicates "mond-shaped," "schnee-shaped," "mond-good," "schnee-good," and "L-true."

In such an ML the following two theorems are easily proved (assuming standard axioms for syntax and logic):

"Der Mond ist blau" is L-true if and only if der mond ist blau.
"Schnee ist weiss" is L-true if and only if schnee ist weiss.

If instead of taking "Schnee ist weiss" and "Der Mond ist blau" as primitive sentences of ML we take their translations into English, say "The moon is blue" and "Snow is white," and modify the "truth definition" in ML in the obvious way, then we can prove in ML the two sentences:

"Der Mond ist blau" is L-true if and only if the moon is blue.
"Schnee ist weiss" is L-true if and only if snow is white.

That these two sentences are theorems of ML shows that the "truth definition" is "adequate," according to Tarski.

Notice that the property L-true is defined in a way that makes no reference to *speakers* or to *uses* of *words*. Whether or not an arbitrary string of letters is or is not "L-true" depends on just three things: how that string of letters is composed (the *spelling*, in other words) and whether or not snow is white and whether or not the moon is blue. If we know the spelling of a string of letters and we know whether or not snow is white and whether or not the moon is blue, then we can decide *in any possible world* whether or not that string of letters is "L-true." In particular then, the string of letters "Schnee ist weiss" has the property of being L-true in all worlds in which snow is white, *including* worlds in which what it means is that water is a liquid. The property "L-true" is not a *semantical* or even a *pragmatic* property of utterances (except in Tarski's specially constructed sense of "semantic"). It is easy to imagine counterfactual situations in which a sentence would have the property of being L-true and not be true. Thus the notion of truth has not been conceptually analyzed at all.

The same objection applies to the more complicated truth definitions that Tarski's procedure yields when the object language has infinitely many sentences. The property "L-true" that we obtain by the Tarskian procedure always is a property that depends solely on the spelling of the objects to which it is applied and on facts about the world describable by the sentences of L. If the sentence to which the predicate "L-true" is applied is one which itself does not talk about speakers or their use of words, then whether or not the sentence has the property of being L-true will be independent of speakers and their use of words. But "is true" as that notion is *pre-analytically understood* is a predicate whose truth conditions do not depend only on the spelling of the objects to which it is applied and on such facts as the color of the moon and the color of snow, but do depend crucially on whether or not speakers *use* the object to which the predicate is applied in such a way that it *means*, say, that the moon is blue or that snow is white. A property which by its very meaning has nothing to do with the way speakers use and understand language cannot be seriously offered as having the same *meaning* as the predicate "is true," even if it is coextensive with the predicate "is true" in the actual world.[3]

The Convention T

So far I have considered the view that it is the truth definition for an individual language that is supposed to give us some kind of analysis or understanding of the notion of truth. It may be urged, however, that this is to misunderstand what Tarski's philosophical claims actually were. It might be thought that what is supposed to tell us the meaning of "truth" is not the individual truth definitions for the various individual languages, but rather the "criterion of adequacy," Tarski's famous "Convention T."

Convention T has, however, experienced remarkably little textually faithful philosophical investigation or discussion. Philosophers often write as if the *following* were the Convention T: all substitution instances of the following schema must be true if *L-true* is to be an adequate truth predicate for a language L:

"*P*" is L-true if and only if *P*.

This however would be flagrantly circular, since in this form (which is not Tarski's) the Convention T would itself contain the word "true." If we know that all instances of the above schema are true, then of course we know the predicate L-true is coextensive with the predicate "true in L." To say this may be to say something informative about the notion of truth; but since to say this we have to use the notion of truth (in the language ML), we have not really successfully answered any of the deep philosophical worries about what truth really comes to.

What Tarski really required was not that the instances of the above schema should all be true, but rather that they should all be *theorems* of the language ML. But this will not do either; if the language ML is ω-inconsistent, then it may be the case that some instances of the above schema are theorems of ML although (in the metametalanguage) one can easily see that they are not all (in the intuitive sense) *true*. The fact that all instances of a schema are provable in some language or other does not mean that all instances of that schema are *true*. A third possibility is the following: it might be held (although Tarski himself never, as far as I know, suggests this) that we understand the word "true" by knowing that a predicate is coextensive with "true" just in case all instances of the above schema are *assertible*. This idea would try to combine an idea which often arises in connec-

tion with the so-called redundancy theory of truth,[4] or "disquotational theory of truth," the idea that we understand our language by
mastering or "internalizing" assertibility conditions, rather than truth
conditions in the realist sense, with the idea that the meaning of the
word "true" is somehow fixed by the Convention T. Whether or not
anyone has actually held it, the hybrid view just suggested would have
two advantages: It would overcome Tarski's own objection to the "redundancy theory," namely, that *that* theory does not tell one how to
use the word "true" with variables and quantifiers, in the way suggested by Tarski himself. We know how to use the word "true" with
variables and quantifiers, because we know how to find a predicate
which is coextensive with "true" and which *can* be used with variables and quantifiers. (Of course this would be very strange as a description of how people on the street use "true" in ordinary language.)
Second, the objection that the Convention T is either circular or incorrect (the objection that I just made) would be overcome by saying that
what we really require is not that all instances of the above schema be
true (which would be circular) and not that all instances of the above
schema should be theorems (which ignores the possibility that ML is
incorrect), but that all instances of the above schema should be assertible. On this view there are no philosophical problems with truth;
all the real philosophical problems concern the notion of *assertibility*.

Asserting as Uttering

That a disquotational account of truth, either in the sense of Ayer's
"redundancy theory" or in the sense of an attempted combination of
the redundancy theory with more or less of Tarski's work along the
lines just sketched, finds its proper home in an account according to
which our understanding of our language consists in the mastery (or
"internalization") of so-called assertibility conditions is widely recognized. One might expect, therefore, that there would be a considerable
literature devoted to the analysis of *assertibility*. But one would be
disappointed. Notions of "assertibility conditions" appear here and
there in the literature, as if some agreed-upon account of assertibility
existed, but in fact there exists no such account (no account that is
sufficiently clear and noncontroversial to justify using the notion of an
"assertibility condition" as if this, itself, were an unproblematic notion).

In fact, at least three notions of "assertibility" seem to be present in contemporary philosophical writing. Sometimes "assertibility" is used in a very "thin" sense. In the thinnest possible sense to "assert" something is merely to *utter* it (without provoking what Quine calls a "bizarreness reaction") or, perhaps, to "subvocalize" it (if we allow that one can assert things in thought, without saying them out loud). If "assertibility" is taken in this thin behaviorist sense, then the idea that the mastery of our language consists in the internalization of assertibility conditions comes to no more and no less than the claim that a complete account of our understanding of our language would simply be a description of the noises that we utter together with a description of the actual causal processes by which we produced those noises (or subvocalizations).

Although Quine, in particular, seems tempted by the idea that such a pure cause-effect story is a complete scientific *and* philosophical description of the use of a language, the problem with such a view is obvious. If the cause-effect description is complete from a philosophical as well as from a behavioral-scientific point of view; if all there is to say about language is that it consists in the production of noises (and subvocalizations) according to a certain causal pattern; if the causal story is not to be and need not be supplemented by a normative story; if there is no substantive property of *warrant* connected with the notion of *assertion;* if truth itself is not a property (the denial that truth is a property is, in fact, the central theme of all disquotational theories); then there is no way in which the noises we utter (or the subvocalizations that occur in our bodies) are more than mere "expressions of our subjectivity," as Edward Lee put it in a fine paper describing similar ideas[5] advanced by Protagoras. A human being speaking and thinking resembles an animal producing various cries in response to various natural contingencies, or even a plant putting forth now a leaf and now a flower, on such a story. Such a story leaves out that we are *thinkers.* If such a story is right, then not only is *representation* a myth; the very idea of *thinking* is a myth.

Can any philosopher think that *so* reductionist a story is really right? Even Quine emphasizes that such a story is right only from the standpoint of what he calls "our first-class conceptual scheme"; he has often said in lectures and conversations that the first-class conceptual system needs to be supplemented by a vague, informal, but nonetheless indispensable notion of "justification" or "coherence." (But if these are *indispensable* notions, what is the point of calling them "second-class"?)

Such a view falls, in fact, before the arguments that Frege deployed against the naturalism and empiricism of *his* day. On such an account, we cannot genuinely disagree with each other: if I produce a noise and you produce the noise "No, that's wrong," then we have no more disagreed with each other than if I produce a noise and you produce a groan or a grunt. Nor can we agree with each other any more than we can disagree with each other: if I produce a noise and you produce the same noise, then this is no more *agreement* than if a bough creaks and then another creaks in the same way.[6] Frege's point was that the *data* in philosophy are not limited to *sensations;* my knowledge that, for example, *I am thinking the same thought that I thought a little while ago* or my knowledge that *I disagree with what you just said,* is also knowledge that is as sure as any that we have. Such knowledge must be taken seriously by philosophers, not treated as an illusion to be explained away.

I am not advocating that we all become metaphysical realists; in fact, I don't agree with Dummett that Frege was a metaphysical (or "Platonic") realist. What I think is that we have to recognize that there are *some kind of* objective properties of rightness and wrongness associated with speaking and thinking, before we can even face the question whether we should take them as primitive, give a metaphysical realist account of them, give an "idealist" account of them, or seek a new response altogether. I suspect that most philosophers today would agree with this, and that very few would, accordingly, be willing to regard Tarski's work (or the disquotational theory) as having "solved" (or "dissolved") the philosophical problem of truth if they believed that accepting the solution (or the "dissolution") required them to accept the further idea that to say of what another person says that it is "right" or "warranted" or "justified" or . . . is only to express the disposition to say "yes" to what has been said, or something of that kind.

"Cultural" Accounts of Warranted Assertibility

Sometimes the solution to the problem just pointed out is thought to be quite simple. My own past idea, that psychological states should be identified with functional states of the organism, is sometimes alleged to solve just about all the problems there are (the nature of truth, the nature of reference, the nature of justification, the nature of explanation . . .).[7] In particular, someone who wants to hold fast to a disquotational account of truth, while avoiding the extreme behaviorism of Quine's "first-class" account, might, it is thought, get the sort of account he is looking for by saying that to "assert" p is not merely to produce the noise p as the result of any physical causes whatever, but is rather to produce the noise p in accordance with a certain "program," in accordance with the requirements of a certain "functional organization." (Think of us as computers and of the "functional organization" as a program that we are able to instantiate.) The notion of "functional organization," whatever its merits in other contexts, is of little help with *these* problems, however. In the context of any deep philosophical worry about truth or justification (warrant) it is fatally ambiguous. Any actually existing thing, and, in particular, any actually existing organism, can be viewed as realizing, and (even more easily) as approximately realizing, infinitely many different "machine tables." One functional description of any organism is that which predicts the actual response probabilities of the organism in any situation (including those produced by errors, slips, biological breakdowns, and so on). Such an assignment of a functional organization to an organism has the property that if we assign *that* functional organization as the organism's "conceptual-role semantics," then *everything* the organism says is "competent" (and even "warranted," if being in accordance with the program is identified with being warranted). Under such a description, the organism makes no "performance errors" at all.

This is not, however, the normal way of assigning a functional organization to something—to look for a "program" that predicts actual behavior. Generally what one looks for is a "machine table" or whatever, which the actual computer only approximately obeys. When a speaker, in particular, performs according to his hypothetical "machine table," then Chomskians say he is performing up to his "competence"; when he disobeys the machine table they say he has made a "performance error."

Clearly there are infinitely many descriptions of the functional organization of an actual organism which could be used to divide the actual behavior of that organism into what is in accordance with competence and what is "performance error." What singles out the "true" functional organization of the organism, or the class of "best" descriptions of or assignments of functional organization?

If we say that the "correct" description of the functional organization of the organism is the description that best *explains* what the organism does, then we have assumed an objective intentional notion, namely, the notion of *explanation*. If our aim, in trying to give an account of truth, was to avoid the need for unreduced intentional notions in philosophy, then, in this respect at least, no progress will have been made.

It is perhaps for this reason that some philosophers have recently suggested that the distinction between what is said *rightly,* either in the sense of being true or in the sense of being meaningful or in the sense of being justified, and what is not said rightly makes no sense in the case of a single organism considered in isolation from any community to which that organism belongs. The suggestion is that these "normative" properties of utterances are properties that utterances possess only when considered as utterances by a (member of a) linguistic community. This view has been read into the later Wittgenstein by Saul Kripke[8] and has been explicitly espoused by Richard Rorty in *Philosophy and the Mirror of Nature.*

On these "cultural" views, what we say has any kind of rightness or wrongness only when it is produced in accordance with (respectively, deviates from) a pattern of speech production (perhaps a "functional organization") which leads us to agree with our community sufficiently often or in sufficiently many paradigmatic cases. There is, on such views, an objective property of rightness (though not necessarily of *truth;* the predicate "is true" is itself explained disquotationally in the way I have described), and that objective property of rightness is identified with a culturally relative property.

Meaningfulness in a public language is indeed a culturally relative property; but warranted assertibility cannot be identified with a culturally relative property any more than truth can be, for reasons which I am sure are familiar and which I shall not rehearse here.[9] I do not believe that very many philosophers would regard the problem of truth as *solved* if they had to agree that the solution involves the notion that rightness (in any objective sense) is a culturally relative property. (In particular, the cultural relativists themselves do not stop believing that their own views are right just because they cannot get the agreement of *their* "cultural peers" that their relativist views are right.)

Warranted Assertibility as Degree of Confirmation

The final suggestion I shall consider is that the assertibility (or the "rightness") of an utterance, to the extent that "rightness" *is* a property, might be identified with its *degree of confirmation*. The idea would be that degree of confirmation is itself an objective property, an objective degree of rightness or wrongness that particular utterances enjoy, whereas truth is not a property. "To say a sentence is true is to reaffirm the sentence," as Quine has put it, whereas to say that a sentence is highly confirmed is to ascribe a substantive property to the sentence, on this view (not Quine's).

In part, this view has the same problems that the "functional organization" view has. There are many possible definitions of "degree of confirmation" that might be associated with a particular language, dialect, or idiolect. What singles out a particular definition of degree of confirmation, a particular inductive logic or "conceptual-role semantics" as the *right* one?

If the answer is some kind of agreement with the dispositions of a culture, then we are back in cultural relativism. In addition, the use of dispositions in these accounts (cultural accounts, I mean) involves us in such notions as "similarity of possible worlds"; and it seems to me that the notion that some non-actual situations are "more similar" to the actual situation than others is an intentional notion on the face of it.

Suppose, however, that the advocate of this view is willing just to take "degree of confirmation" as an unreduced normative notion. It is not wholly clear why he would not just take the notion of *truth* as an unreduced normative notion, but let that pass. Could such a view—the view that degree of confirmation is an objective and substantial property but truth is not—possibly be the correct view?

Such a view might have a certain attraction. One can say, as on Tarski's theory, that "Snow is white" is true if and only if snow is white (this sentence would have degree of confirmation 1 on every evidence *e*); and, by uttering this sentence, one might claim to have recognized that what is true "depends on the world." It is a little more complicated, but one can even give a sense to "The truth value of 'snow is white' would be different, even if snow were still white, if our use of the language were sufficiently different." One might point out that one has not said, in the account that I described as a mixture of Tarski's ideas and disquotational ideas, that the Tarski "truth predicate" for the language L is *synonymous* with "true." One has said only that Tarski's procedure provides one with a procedure for discovering a predicate that is *coextensive* with "true" as restricted to L. If one imagines counterfactual situations in which the words are used differently, then one has to ask whether the language as used in those counterfactual situations is to be translated into our "home language" homophonically or in some other way. If the use is sufficiently different from the use in the actual world, then we will not translate the words "snow is white" homophonically any more. We might even translate them by the words "the kettle is on the stove." If we adopt this translation, then the criterion of adequacy (in this special case) becomes that we should not accept a predicate "L-true" as a "truth predicate" for L as *used in the situation* unless we are willing to accept the sentence

"Snow is white" is L-true if and only if the kettle is on the stove.

Since one can say that "Snow is white" would not be true if the world were different (if snow were not white), and one can say that "Snow is white" would not be true if the use of the language were different (if the translation of that sentence into our actual language were "The kettle is on the stove"), then can we not say everything that a "realist" should want us to say?

In a sense, yes, and yet this account cannot, I think, be accepted either. For one thing, the account contains no answer to the question "What is the nature of the property *truth?*" Rather, we are told that although the question "What is the nature of the property *electrical charge?*" is a perfectly legitimate question, the question "What is the nature of the property *truth?*" is a confused question. The description of the assertibility conditions (in the sense of confirmation conditions) for sentences containing the word "true" tells us all there is to know about truth, although a description of the assertibility conditions for sentences containing the words "electrical charge" would not (unless we are operationalists) tell us all there is to know about electrical charge. In this way, the account, whether it asserts or denies the sentence "Truth is a property," reveals that truth is still not thought of as any kind of *substantive* property of the things we say.

But if truth is not a substantive property of some of the things that we say, if "to say that a sentence is true is just to reaffirm the sentence," then is the picture not like the picture that Reichenbach once flirted with[10] in which everything that we say is built up from a reduction basis of the experience of a single speaker at a single instant? The *picture* is, after all, that a language speaker is a device which says things and which appraises the things that it says and hears at each instant for a property (degree of confirmation) that *depends only on the present memory and experience of the speaker.* Even if the speaker says "the truth or falsity of a sentence does not depend, in general, only on my present memory and experience," that too is a *noise* which the speaker processes by ascertaining whether it (the noise) possesses a sufficiently high "degree of confirmation" (possesses a property which depends only on the present memory and experience of the speaker). If the noise in question (the noise that sounds like the avowal of a "realistic" philosophy) possesses the property (the methodologically solipsist property, the one which depends only on the present memory and experience of the speaker), then it possesses the only kind of objective rightness the view allows for. Such a picture of language speaking, leaving out, as it does, any property of rightness that goes *beyond* methodological solipsism, is simply disastrous.[11] And one cannot turn a solipsistic picture into a realistic picture by merely adding a "disquotation scheme."

To recapitulate, the idea that there is such a thing as an "assertibility-conditions" account of language falls before the simple fact that nobody has ever given a theory of what "assertibility conditions" are. The only candidates I have been able to find in the literature plunge us at once into the disastrous picture of Skinnerian behaviorism or the disastrous picture of cultural relativism or the disastrous picture of methodological solipsism of the present instant. That any of the exhibits in this philosophical horror show constitutes a solution to the problem of the nature of truth, cannot be and should not be believed.

Notes

This paper was prepared for the Festschrift of Sidney Morgenbesser, entitled *How Many Questions?* Sidney Morgenbesser, when he was himself a graduate student, was my first teacher in the philosophy of science. Two of the ideas that he made a living reality for me were the idea that the responsible discussion of philosophical problems requires an adequate familiarity with modern logic and the idea that fashionable solutions to philosophical problems are to be viewed with a certain cynicism. If the present paper is not directly about the work of Sidney Morgenbesser, I hope that the attitude of mind that it expresses is one that is still congenial to him. It was a great pleasure to contribute this paper to the Festschrift for my teacher and friend.

1. *Philosophy and the Mirror of Nature* (Princeton: Princeton University Press, 1979). I criticize Rorty's relativism in "Why Reason Can't be Naturalized," in *Realism and Reason,* vol. 3 of my *Philosophical Papers* (New York: Cambridge University Press, 1983).
2. A philosopher who has denied that there is, is Charles Chihara, who in

"The Semantic Paradoxes: A Diagnostic Investigation," *Philosophical Review*, 88, no. 4 (October 1979), 590–618, opts for the view that our intuitive notion of truth is simply inconsistent. The argument of the present essay leads me to respond that if the intuitive notion is inconsistent, then I don't know just what notion Tarski is supposed to have put in its place. Just as Tarski's "truth predicates" are properties that do not depend on the speaker's use of the language in any way, so Tarski's reference relations ("satisfaction" relations) likewise do not depend on the speaker's use of the language in any way. But, then, how any one of these is singled out as the way that language "hooks on" to the world is left a mystery. Perhaps the idea of a world/language dichotomy is what leads us astray; but *this* is a deep philosophical issue to which Tarski's "truth definitions" hardly speak.

3. I use the traditional language of "meaning," "conceptual analysis," etc., here for simplicity of exposition. Even if these notions are not well defined (and I don't think they are well defined), there is still a difference between an account of a predicate which intends to give a perspicuous picture of the way the predicate is employed in practice, an account which should also be correct in hypothetical situations we have some handle on (even if we don't believe in a definite totality of *all* "possible worlds"), and an account which merely aims at specifying the extension the predicate happens to have in the actual world in any way whatsoever. Giving up the analytic/synthetic distinction isn't the same thing as giving up the distinction between a philosophical analysis of a notion and a description of its extension, or, at least, it isn't giving up *that* distinction altogether.

4. The "redundancy theory," as put forward by A. J. Ayer in *Language, Truth, and Logic,* is that "is true" is "redundant" in such sentences as *"Snow is white" is true;* that is, *"Snow is white" is true* just *means* "Snow is white."

5. "Hoist with His Own Petard" in *Exegesis and Argument: Studies in Greek Philosophy Presented to Gregory Vlastos,* ed. E. N. Lee, A. P. D. Mourelatos, and Richard Rorty (Assen: Van Gorcum, 1973), pp. 231–278.

6. Another way of making the same point is that what makes two utterances, say, "Snow is white" and "Snow isn't white" *contradict* each other is that there are various *rightness-properties* that the two utterances cannot both have simultaneously. For instance, if one is true then the other can't be; if one is justified, then the other can't be; if one has probability greater than 0.5, then the other can't have . . . The fact that Quine has to take "assent" and "dissent" as primitive in what is supposed to be a behaviorist account is a symptom of his inability to give an account of agreement and disagreement in judgment.

7. For example, Gilbert Harman argues that the competence/performance distinction solves the problem of the nature of *justification* in his "Metaphys-

ical Realism and Moral Relativism: Reflections on Hilary Putnam's *Reason, Truth, and History*," *Journal of Philosophy*, 79, no. 10 (October 1982), 568–574. I respond to this in Chapter 22 of the present volume.

8. *Wittgenstein on Rules and Private Language* (Cambridge: Harvard University Press, 1982).

9. In this connection, see my article mentioned in n. 1.

10. I should emphasize that Reichenbach flirted with this solipsistic reduction basis ("reports about our personal macroscopic environment (concreta) at a certain moment") in only one place ("The Verifiability Theory of Meaning," reprinted in *Readings in the Philosophy of Science*, ed. H. Feigl and M. Broadbeck [New York: Appleton-Century-Crofts, 1953], pp. 93–102). In his major works he is much more realistically inclined than this.

11. Another way of putting the point is that there is a realist intuition—namely, that there is a substantive kind of rightness (or wrongness) that my statement that I had cereal for breakfast this morning possesses as a consequence of what happened this morning, and not as a consequence of my present memory and experience—which must be preserved even if one finds *metaphysical* realism unintelligible (as I do). Preserving this philosophical intuition is not, of course, just a matter of making it right to utter this *noise*.

17. A Comparison of Something with Something Else

The idea of comparing the views of Willard Van Quine and Richard Rorty may seem a trifle bizarre, not to say dotty, but I have a justification (I think). First of all, this paper was written for a conference at which we were invited to compare issues in literary theory and issues in the philosophy of science (or at least that is how I construed the title of the conference and the announcement that we would "discuss such questions as . . . ," followed by the formidable list of questions that we all received). Now, I don't want to plead complete innocence with respect to literary theory, but I have to admit that this idea made my blood run cold. Yet, there are points at which the ideas of Richard Rorty and the ideas of Van Quine can be compared, and I do think such a comparison can deepen our understanding of both thinkers. Rorty is close to (if by no means identical with) "literary theory," and Quine is certainly a towering figure in "philosophy of science." So I was sort of fulfilling the assignment (as the student says, shame-facedly) by comparing R.R. and W.V.Q.

My purpose is not merely to deepen our understanding of Rortian and Quinian views, however worthwhile that may be. I also hope to explain precisely why I feel compelled to "get off the boat" (both boats) at a certain point. That the reasons that make one philosopher unable to go all the way with Rorty's version of—call it historicism, or deconstruction—are not all that different from the ones that make him unable to go all the way with Quinian scientism may, I imagine, surprise some people. So I hope to bring a novel perspective to the discussion.

My perspective, insofar as it is "novel," arises out of my career as a mathematical logician and a philosopher of language. Someone working in these two fields inevitably finds himself thinking about the problem of truth from two different angles. And I have been dissatisfied for many years with almost everything written about the notion of truth. Quine has also worked in both fields, and he has also thought a great deal about truth. Unlike me, he is *not* dissatisfied with Tarski's work—not dissatisfied with Tarski's work as a solution to the philosophical problem of truth, I mean. (Every logician is satisfied with Tarski's *formal* achievement, which was to show us how to define a predicate of sentences in a formalized language which denotes the true sentences in that language.) And thereby hangs much of our disagreement. But I get ahead of myself.

In *Philosophy and the Mirror of Nature*, Rorty misspoke himself on the subject of truth (as he later admitted). Unnecessarily from the point of view of the position he wishes to defend, he wrote as if truth just *is* intersubjective acceptability in a culture (the agreement of one's cultural peers). In his Introduction to *Consequences of Pragmatism* he makes an important revision: he distinguishes between truth as a purely formal (and, in his view, empty) notion and whatever sort of normative rightness ("paying its way") a sentence may have. To call a sentence "true" is not to ascribe a property, truth, to the sentence; it is just another way of asserting the sentence. (This is a "disquotational view," in the jargon of philosophers of language.) "Snow is white" is true if and only if snow is white, and this is so not because *Snow is white* corresponds to snow's being white, whatever that might mean, but because *saying* " 'Snow is white' is true" is just *saying* "Snow is white" in a different way. We shall see that this is also Quine's view.

On Rorty's amended view, what we are interested in (even if it isn't "truth") is whether a sentence or a whole discourse pays its way by the standards of our fellow "postmodern bourgeois liberals" (the people with whom Rorty is interested in "solidarity," as he explained in his Howison Lecture).[1] *That's* the substantial question. For Quine, in contrast, we are interested in predicting "stimulations of our nerve endings." Evidently, Quine and Rorty, while agreeing on the emptiness of the notion of truth, disagree radically on what we should care about instead. What properties do we want our sentences to have? No one thinks we are out to just write or utter sentences at random.

Great as the differences between Rorty and Quine in some ways are, it is clear from what I have just pointed out that the disagreement presupposes a very large measure of agreement. They agree, in fact, on what *I* find shocking: the idea that "truth" is an empty notion. In order to explore this interesting agreement—far more interesting, I think, than their predictable disagreement—I shall begin by examining Quine's reason for holding a disquotational view and then turn to Rorty's reasons.

The "Definability" of True-in-L

I have given an elementary exposition of the technical part of Tarski's work in other places, and I shall not attempt to reproduce it here. But this much must be said: Tarski claims that if the metalanguage is "stronger" than the object language in the sense of containing, for example, appropriate sets and sets of sets that are not in the universe of discourse of the object language, then, in the meta-L in question, one can define "true-in-L" *ex nihilo.*

What I mean by defining "true-in-L" *ex nihilo* (of course, Tarski did not use this language) is defining "true-in-L" without using any primitive notions that are not among the primitive notions of L itself. The only exception to this rule is that, as I just mentioned, the language we use may have a larger universe of *sets* than L itself does: the notion of a "set" is not considered to be a "descriptive" notion, however, but belongs to the purely logical vocabulary along with the words *all, and, or, if-then, not,* and so on. So the language in which we define "true-in-L" (the metalanguage) does not contain any primitive "descriptive" notions that are not notions of L (the object language) itself. In particular (assuming L itself does not contain any primitives standing for such intentional notions as *believes, desires, refers to, thinks that,* and so on), "true-in-L" is to be defined in *nonintentional* terms. A "semantical" notion is to be defined using no semantical primitives! Truly, Tarski's name for his theory, "The Semantical Conception of Truth," is highly misleading! It would have been more revealing to call the theory the "*Non*semantical Conception of Truth." (And it would have produced a more enlightened philosophical discussion than we actually witnessed.) If *I* had to name the theory, I would call it the "Look No Semantics! Conception of Truth"; then no one could miss the startling claim Tarski made.

Of course, if the theory had gone out into the world under the name I just suggested, philosophers might have thought there was something fishy about it. And I think there is. Suppose, for example, that "Snow is white" is a sentence of L. Tarski himself points out that the following is a theorem (provable, of course, in meta-L): (1) *"Snow is white" is true in L if and only if snow is white*. From a mathematical logician's point of view, what this says can be better explained if we replace the quotation marks by the device of spelling which Tarski actually employed: (2) *(for any sentence X) If X is spelled S-N-O-W-SPACE-I-S-SPACE-W-H-I-T-E, then X is true in L if and only if snow is white*.

Now, pay close attention, please! This is just where, it seems to me, philosophers have been asleep at the opera for a long time! Since (2) is a *theorem of logic* in meta-L (if we accept the definition—given by Tarski—of "true-in-L"), since no axioms are needed for the proof of (2) except axioms of logic and axioms about spelling, (2) holds in all possible worlds. In particular, since no assumptions about the *use* of the expressions of L are used in the proof of (2), (2) holds true in worlds in which the sentence "Snow is white" does not mean that snow is white. In fact, "true-in-L," as defined by Tarski, is a notion which involves only the primitive notions of L itself, as I said and as Tarski himself stressed. So if L does not have notions which refer to the *use of linguistic expressions,* there is no way in which "true-in-L," or, rather, the notion to which Tarski gives that name, *could* involve the *use* of expressions in any way. The property to which Tarski gives the name "true-in-L" is a property that the sentence "Snow is white" has in every possible world in which snow is white, *including worlds in which what it means is that snow is green.*

From the point of view of formal applications of Tarski's theory in mathematical logic this doesn't matter, because all that a logician wants of a truth definition is that it should capture the *extension* (denotation) of "true" as applied to L, not that it should capture the *sense*—the intuitive notion of truth (as restricted to L). But the concern of philosophy is precisely to discover what the intuitive notion of truth is. As a philosophical account of truth, Tarski's theory fails as badly as it is possible for an account to fail. A property that the sentence "Snow is white" would have (as long as snow is white) no matter how we might use or understand that sentence isn't even doubtfully or dubiously "close" to the property of truth. It just isn't truth at all.

A question which is related to the point just made is the following: If, as Tarski claims, it is a tautology that the sentence "Snow is white" is true if and only if snow is white, then how can it be the case that we learn to understand our language by learning the truth conditions for its sentences (as traditional "realist" views seem to require)? Can it really be the case that I learn my native language by learning a bunch of tautologies?

While this objection rests on a dubious premise (that we learn our first language *by* learning "truth conditions"), it does voice a concern to which any substitute for the realist view must speak: an account which denies that truth and falsity *are* the central notions in any adequate philosophical account of language must tell us what it is that we learn when we learn to use a language if it *isn't* truth conditions.

One possible reaction to my criticism of Tarski's account as an account of our intuitive notion of truth would be to dismiss the intuitive notion as something of no real interest. If Tarski's notion isn't the intuitive one, so much the worse for the intuitive one! someone might say. Tarski has given us a substitute for the intuitive notion that is adequate for our scientific purposes (if we don't consider the theory of speech acts or intentional semantics to be part of "science"), and one that is defined in a precise way. From now on, Tarskian truth is all the truth we shall want or need.

Quine

This would be the reaction of Quine. Quine would, in any case, not take talk of the "meaning" of the word *true* seriously, nor would he regard my counterfactual remarks about what would be the case if we used words differently, or my talk of "possible worlds," as sufficiently intelligible to bother about. The task of philosophy is not the examination of our intuitive notions, in Quine's view, but rather the construction of a substitute for those notions based on first-class science.

This leaves the question about how we learn our language. Quine, of course, does not believe that we learn our language by learning truth conditions. We don't, in his view, understand sentences as isolated units. What we understand is, strictly speaking, the language as a whole; and that understanding is a complex, multi-tracked *disposition*. I "understand" the sentence "Snow is white" in the sense that using that sentence in response to certain stimuli (including internal stimuli explained by the "interanimation of sentences") is part of the complex, multi-tracked disposition which is my understanding of the language as a whole. That complex, multi-tracked disposition could, Quine claims, be described (in principle) in purely physicalistic terms, without any reference to intentional states or properties at all.

The aspects of Quine's view that I have so far discussed are ones which more often interest philosophers of science and philosophers of language than literary theorists. But bear with me! In accordance with our "assignment" (to compare issues in philosophy of science and in literary theory), which I have not forgotten, I shall turn now to Quinian doctrines which have attracted the attention of all students of interpretation. What is too often not realized by people who write about Quine's doctrine of the indeterminacy of translation is that that doctrine rests upon the Tarskian theory of truth and on the multi-tracked disposition view of understanding that I have just described.

Suppose, to use Quine's famous example, a speaker of a "jungle language" is disposed to assent to "gavagai" when she sees a rabbit (at least she is disposed to assent under the conditions in which the linguist and the native informant meet). We could translate "gavagai" in many ways, compatibly with this speech disposition (we could translate it as "undetached rabbit part," as "rabbit slice," as "Rabbithood again!" or as "rabbit," for example). Quine showed that, in principle, there are infinitely many ways of assigning reference conditions to sentence parts and truth conditions to whole sentences which are compatible with "the totality of the native's speech dispositions"—compatible, that is to say, with the entire multi-tracked speech disposition which constitutes the informant's understanding of her language, in Quine's view.

Some of these translations might seem to be ruled out by "simplicity" considerations. Thus it might seem highly *improbable* that a translation according to which "gavagai" means "undetached rabbit part" should be correct. But to argue this way (and many critics have) would be to miss Quine's point. *Simplicity,* and other nonexperimental principles of theory selection, apply only when we have theories which make scientific sense before us. When the question is whether a theory is scientific at all, to argue that the theory is "simpler" than some rival (whose scientific intelligibility is also under challenge) is to mistake the issue. Quine claims that the theory that the native "really means" *rabbit* and not *undetached rabbit part* makes no sense given our (materialist) scientific world view. If both theories agree on the native's multi-tracked speech disposition, then they agree on all the facts there are to describe. If either is right, both are. They are mere notational variants. To postulate a further fact, *what the native is referring to,* which is not determined by the totality of her dispositions to verbal behavior, is to postulate a mystery relation.

It might seem that Quine is in trouble. Quine holds that Tarski has rehabilitated the notion of truth (and of reference). He also holds that there is no fact of the matter as to what the truth conditions of a sentence in an arbitrary "alien language" are. How can he reconcile these views?

This is the most subtle question in the whole of Quinian philosophy. I can only sketch the answer here. First of all, one must know a further fact about the Tarskian procedures. They do not apply directly, in their uncorrupted set-theoretic purity, except when the object language is "contained" in the metalanguage. Suppose that the object language is one language, say French (or a formalized version of French, call it F), and the metalanguage is a quite different language, say English (or a formalized part of English, meta-E, set-theoretically rich enough for the purpose). If we treated F (French) as if it were *contained* in meta-E (the relevant part of English) and applied Tarskian procedures straightforwardly, we would get a definition of "true-in-F" which contained a mixture of English and French words, and, on the basis of that definition, we would write out a "derivation," also containing a mixture of French and English words, of the statement: *"La neige est blanche" is true in F if and only if la neige est blanche.*

But this is not a sentence of English (or meta-E), but rather a sentence of franglais! If we want to define "true in French" (true-in-F) in *English,* as opposed to franglais, we must replace each and every French word in the franglais definition of "true-in-F" with its English translation (and do something about differences in word order and syntax). The result wanted is a definition of "true-in-F" which *is* in English, and a derivation, also in English, of the theorem *"La neige est blanche" is true in F if and only if snow is white.*

To know that this definition is *correct,* however, we have to know that we did replace the French words by their *correct* English translations. That this is the case is not something logic can certify. Indeed, it is precisely Quine's claim that there is no fact of the matter as to what is the "correct" translation of a French word. (No fact of the matter from the standpoint of "first-class science," this means; Quine does not deny that there are correct and incorrect translations in a sense defined by *custom.* Notice that he is both "deconstructing" the notion of correct translation *and* refusing to say that this "deconstruction" is a simple abandonment of what is deconstructed.)

In sum, sentences in French are true and false only relative to a translation scheme into English (or the interpreter's "home language"). This is Quine's startling conclusion. The idea that truth and falsity are substantive properties which sentences in any language possess independently of the point of view of the interpreter must be given up.

What of the "home" language? I can think of my own language as if it were an alien language; then it will seem to me that it consists of dispositions to verbal behavior and no more than dispositions to verbal behavior. It will seem that there is no relation of "reference" between sentence parts and items in the world, and no property of truth which its sentences have or fail to have. But as soon as I view my home language from within—as soon as I "acquiesce" in it, in Quine's phrase—the situation changes.

Here is how Quine himself describes the situation:

> If questions of reference make sense only relative to a background language, then evidently questions of reference for the background language make sense in turn only relative to a further background language. In these terms the situation sounds desperate, but in fact it is little different from questions of position and velocity. When we are given position and velocity relative to a given coordinate system, we can always ask in turn about the placing of origin and orientation of axes in that system of coordinates; and there is no end to the succession of further coordinate systems that could be adduced in answering the successive questions thus generated.
>
> In practice of course we end the regress of coordinate systems by something like pointing. And in practice we end the regress of background languages, in discussions of reference, by acquiescing in our mother tongue and taking its words at face value.[2]

What Quine says here may seem, however, not to meet the problem. What is it to "acquiesce" in my "mother tongue"? And how can "acquiescing" and taking my mother tongue's words at "face value" bring it about that there is a relation between my sentence "Snow is white" and a substance out there in the world being a certain color, if no such relation is to be discerned by an impartial observer who speaks a different "mother tongue" (say, an ideal linguist from Mars)?

Quine's response to such questions is remarkable:

> Very well; in the case of position and velocity, in practice, pointing breaks the regress. But what of position and velocity apart from practice? What of the regress then? The answer, of course, is the relational doctrine of space; there is no absolute position or velocity; there are just the relations of coordinate systems to one another, and ultimately of things to one another. And I think that the parallel question regarding denotation calls for a parallel answer, a relational theory of what the objects of theories are. What makes sense to say is not what the

objects of a theory are absolutely speaking, but how one theory of objects is interpretable or reinterpretable in another.[3]

There are not in the world such things as positions or velocities; there are only relative positions and relative velocities. And similarly there are not in the world such things as denotations; there are only relative denotations. The word *snow* refers to an X which is relative to both the choice of a background language and the choice of a function that maps English onto that background language. If I accept a coordinate system, I can speak of the table as having a position and a velocity without explicitly mentioning that coordinate system each time. And if I accept a background language *and a translation of the background language into itself,* I can speak of a word's having a reference or of a sentence as being true if and only if such and such is the case, without explicitly mentioning that background language and that translation scheme each time, or so Quine is saying.

It may seem surprising that a translation manual is involved even when I speak of reference or truth in the case of my own language. But recall: what we call a language (a "mother tongue") is, from a Tarskian point of view, an infinite series of formalized languages (or rather this is what our mother tongue becomes when it is "regimented" by formalization). English is an object language (E), plus a metalanguage (meta-E), plus a metametalanguage (meta-meta-E), and so forth. When I define "true-in-E" in meta-E in such a way that *"Snow is white" is true in E if and only if snow is white* is forthcoming as a theorem of meta-E, I am implicitly deciding that each sentence of E is to be translated "homophonically" into meta-E; that is, that each sentence of E is to be its own translation into meta-E. This is the reason that Quine thinks the adoption of Tarski's procedure presupposes a "translation scheme," albeit a peculiarly transparent one (the "homophonic" or "disquotational" translation procedure), even in the case in which the object language is contained in the metalanguage. There is, in Quine's view, no fact of the matter as to whether the object language *is* contained in the metalanguage. The decision that each sentence of the object language is a sentence of the metalanguage *and* has the very same reference and truth conditions in the metalanguage as in the object language (which is what it means to say that the object language is "contained" in the metalanguage) is a decision that involves *interpretation.* And there is no "fact of the matter" as to which of infinitely many incompatible interpretative schemes is "correct," even in this case, according to Quine.

Still, when one is speaking a natural language, one treats a sentence as the same sentence whether it occurs in what a logician might view as the metalanguage or in what a logician might view as the object language. This is what Quine calls taking one's language at face value, or "acquiescing" in one's language. To "acquiesce" in one's language is to translate it homophonically into its own metalanguage.

Here is how Quine puts all this in the lead paper ("Things and Their Place in Theories") of his book *Theories and Things:*

> The conclusion I draw is the inscrutability of reference. To say what objects someone is talking about is to say no more than how we propose to translate his terms into ours; we are free to vary the decision. ... The translation adopted arrests the free-floating reference of the alien terms only relatively to the free-floating reference of our own terms, by linking the two.
>
> The point is not that we ourselves are casting about in vain for a mooring. Staying aboard our own language and not rocking the boat, we are borne smoothly along on it and all is well; "rabbit" denotes rabbits, and there is no sense in asking "Rabbits in what sense of 'rabbit'?" Reference goes inscrutable if, rocking the boat, we contemplate a permutational mapping of our language on itself, or if we undertake translation.[4]

A problem may seem to remain. When I say that the sentence "Snow is white" is true, I am accepting my own language, or, in a Tarskian reconstruction, the part of it I take as the metalanguage, as a given (I am not rocking the boat), and I am taking "Snow is white" in the metalanguage to be the translation of "Snow is white" in the object language (I am taking "Snow is white" at face value). This enables me to accept *"Snow is white" is true if and only if snow is white.* But how can I ever decide that snow is white? That question, Quine replies, belongs to epistemology and not to theory of truth. Whatever may lead me to say that snow is white will also lead me to accept " 'Snow is white' is true." "Truth is immanent and there is no higher. We must speak from within a theory."[5]

But how can there be an epistemology in connection with truth if there is no truth to be found? It is at this point that one notices a defect in the analogy that Quine employed in *Ontological Relativity and Other Essays,* the analogy between a coordinate system and a background language. There may be no such thing as absolute position, but there is such a thing as relative position, and relative position (in pre-relativistic physics) is absolute or, better, invariant. An impartial observer should agree with any other impartial observer on the relative positions of all bodies at a time, no matter which coordinate systems they individually use. But an impartial observer (say, the ideal linguist on Mars) will not be able to say whether a sentence in English (viewed as an "alien" language) is true or false relative to the choice of the "alien" meta-English (meta-E) as a background language and homophonic translation as the translation scheme connecting the two "alien" languages. Even though we have fixed the background language to be used (meta-E) and fixed the translation scheme (the identity mapping, or "homophonic translation"), there is still no "fact of the matter," from the linguist's point of view, as to the truth value of any English sentence—no fact of the matter, because the background language we named does not happen to be the one the linguist "acquiesces in." In geometry, by contrast, I can say what the position of a body is relative to a coordinate system C even if that coordinate system does not happen to be *my* rest system (the one I, so to speak, "acquiesce in"). Even relative truth value and relative reference are inscrutable—dependent on the choice of an interpretation of meta-E by the Martian linguist. Lacking such an interpretation, the Martian linguist can say that *snow* in E has the *same* reference (relative to the specific translation manual) as *snow* in meta-E; but this is not to *interpret* reference in E as a word-to-thing relation at all, not even as a *relative* word-to-thing relation. As soon as the Martian linguist assumes a translation of meta-E into Martian, he can say, "Relative to the homophonic translation of E into meta-E, the word *snow* refers in E to *glub*," where *glub* is the Martian translation of the word *snow* in meta-E, but this statement is not an absolute statement because its truth value depends on the translation scheme used to translate meta-English into the linguist's "home language." In short, relative reference (that is, the relation *word W in language L refers to the set of objects C, relative to background language B and translation rule R connecting L with B*) and relative truth or falsity (that is, the relation *sentence S in language L is true, relative to background language B and translation rule R connecting L with B*), unlike relative position and relative velocity, have no absolute reality. Only if the background language happens to be one I "acquiesce" in will the specification of a translation scheme make truth or reference determinate from my standpoint ("immanently" determinate, as Quine might say).

This difficulty, or one closely related to it, was pointed out a number of years ago in an important paper by Stephen Leeds,[6] but Quine has not, to my knowledge, responded to it. The only solution consonant with Quine's general position that I can see would be to abandon the geometrical analogy and to say that in the case of my own language calling a sentence "true" is doing no more than reaffirming the sentence. I am not ascribing any property, not even a relative property, to the sentence when I say that it is true; I am just assenting to the sentence. Quine himself puts the matter this way when he says that "to say that a sentence is true is to reaffirm the sentence." On this interpretation, to say, as Quine does, that there is only "immanent truth" is—as close as makes no difference—to say *il n'y a pas de hors texte*. That Quine has not used the coordinate analogy for some years, and that he has a number of times described his view by saying that he knows no truth but "immanent truth," suggest that this is the resolution of the difficulty that he himself has adopted.

In a notorious review of Jonathan Culler's *On Deconstruction: Theory and Criticism after Structuralism,* John Searle dismissed Derrida as a second-rater. In the same paragraph, Searle wrote that we live in "something of a golden age" in philosophy of language. "It is not only the age of the dead giants, Frege, Russell, and Wittgenstein, but also the age of [list of names] . . . and a dozen other first-rate writers."[7] While I am pleased to have been included in Searle's list, I wonder at the particular way in which he distinguishes between what is "intellectual weakness" and what is "first-rate philosophy." If Derrida really denies that "texts represent, at least sometimes, the real world" (Searle's interpretation of "il n'y a pas de hors texte"), then Searle's indignation is intelligible. Someone who simply denied that we ever talk about anything except language would, one presumes, be pulling our leg. But Derrida does not deny that *viewed from within,* texts talk about many things. That texts refer to all sorts of things—to Dracula and Frankenstein, to the proletariat and the downfall of the West, to the libido and the superego, *in the sense of immanent reference*—is certainly not something Derrida denies. If, however, the crime with which Derrida is charged is to deny that there is any absolute sense, any sense except the immanent one, in which texts stand in a relation of reference to the "real world," surely Quine belongs in the prisoner's box along with Derrida. Somehow the change of language from "il n'y a pas de hors texte" to "truth is immanent" changes intellectual pretenders to first-rate philosophers. But I digress.

Let me remark that Quine's position has repeatedly been misunderstood. Thus, one book on Quine's philosophy, highly praised (on the dust jacket) by Quine himself, compares Quine's use of Tarski's work to Popper's.[8] But Popper subscribes to the traditional idea that truth depends on a *correspondence* between bits of language and bits of the "real world," a correspondence which is absolute in the sense of being "there" independently of interpreters, choices of "background language," and free choices of translation manuals. When Popper says that this view of truth has been rehabilitated by Tarski, he simply doesn't know what he is talking about. And Davidson tends to play down the difference between his own views, on the one hand, and those of Quine and Tarski, on the other, although the move of taking truth as a primitive idea (in fact, as the *one* primitive idea which is indispensable for the description of linguistic behavior—which is the key move in Davidsonian philosophy) is incompatible with Tarski's approach (no matter how similar a Davidsonian "meaning theory" may be to a Tarskian "truth definition" in formal *structure*). But I do not have the space to elaborate on these remarks. For now, the thing that must be kept in mind is that in Quine's hands the Tarski theory becomes very similar to the "redundancy theory"advocated by Ayer in *Language, Truth, and Logic*. That theory was technically defective, and the logical work of Tarski shows how to repair the defects (Quine thinks). But, if I am right, Quine does *not* view truth as an objective property (which Tarski showed us how to define), but views it simply as a predicate which enables us to "ascend semantically," that is, a predicate which, when suitably defined, enables us to "reaffirm" any sentence by simply coupling that predicate to the quotation of the sentence. The difference between Quine and Popper is precisely that for Popper there is, and for Quine there is not, an interpreter-independent fact of the matter as to whether an arbitrary sentence is *true*. Quine has deconstructed the notion of truth by making it something "immanent" rather than something "transcendent." Of course this deconstruction is not a simple throwing away. But it isn't a simple throwing away for Derrida either.

Rorty

I have spent a long time on Quine because I think his views are widely misunderstood. Quine's description of himself as a "realist" and even a "robust realist" has contributed to this confusion. Rorty's views also have their nuances, however, and it is to these I now turn.

Rorty is not a materialist as Quine is, but the adequacy (or equal adequacy) of materialism plays a key role in the argument of *Philosophy and the Mirror of Nature*. Rorty argues that the whole mind/body dichotomy is "optional," and his principal way of showing this is to argue that an adequate (or equally adequate) language could dispense with this dichotomy altogether. He tells a science fiction story in which an intelligent race on another planet, the Antipodeans, say "I have Z362 in area 00–236–50019," or something of that kind, instead of "I have a blue patch against a white ground in my visual field." When a member of this species encounters the argument that there is something it is like to have a blue patch against a white ground, but nothing it is "like" to have stimulation Z362 in area 00–236–50019, we may imagine him to be simply astounded. "Of course there is something it is like to have Z362 in area 00–236–50019," we can imagine him retorting with indignation. "What is that Earthian talking about!" For both Quine and Rorty, the failure of first-class science to come up with anything that corresponds to the traditional idea of the "mental" and the possibility (in principle) of dispensing with our intuitive notion of the "mental," and with "meanings," and with the pre-Tarskian notion of "truth" play an important role in the argument. This is not to downplay an important difference: Quine thinks we should dispense with our intuitive notions (when they cannot be rehabilitated scientifically) and stick to first-class science (the first-class/second-class dichotomy is from Quine's *Word and Object,* by the way), while for Rorty, once truth goes "immanent," there is no reason to privilege science over literature, or over ethics, aesthetics, and so forth.

I find this "deconstructive" use of the appeal to science interesting, but it is not the principal point at which I wish to make a comparison between Quine and Rorty. The principal point at which I want to compare them has to do with a certain ambivalence I find in both of them toward the idea of metaphysics, or, in Rorty's jargon, the idea of a "metastory."

Rorty often says that "metastories"—intellectually satisfying accounts of the furniture of the universe, of the noumena and our epistemic relation to them—are impossible. The separation between noumena and phenomena, and the picture of the mind as "representing" or "mirroring" the noumena, have to be given up as unnecessary predicaments we blundered into, "optional" problems we should now opt out of. The noumena/phenomena distinction is no more forced upon us than is the mind/body distinction. And if we reject the distinction, then no function is left for a metastory.

The problem is that Rorty defends these views by appealing to what look very much like metastories. I have mentioned the story about the Antipodeans, which seems at least to flirt with the metastory that there are just brains and the neurological processes that go on in them, and no "sensations" over and above these (the Quinian metastory?). A much more pervasive story (metastory?) in Rorty's writing is a "cultural" story, however. In this story there are people, cultures, and dispositions—including dispositions to agree. "Truth" makes no sense unless it is taken as a predicate we apply to a sentence when we wish to express agreement with it (recall Quine's "To say that a sentence is true is to reaffirm the sentence"). The only kind of rightness that a sentence has which transcends the speaker's own subjectivity is inter-subjective rightness. We should not, Rorty tells us, be ashamed of seeking the agreement of our fellow postmodern bourgeois liberals and we should not pretend that we seek that agreement because it is an index of some kind of objective truth.

If I agree that there are people, dispositions, and acts of agreeing (and, accordingly, dispositions to perform acts of agreeing), and that it is "metaphysics" in the pejorative sense to think that there is *truth* (construed *not* à la Quine or à la Ayer, but as an interpreter-independent property that assertions have or lack depending on two things: [1] how they are used and [2] how the nonlinguistic world is), or that there are *facts,* or that there is such a thing as *rational acceptability,* then perhaps I will find Rorty's view coercive. But if the whole project of saying how the world is, as opposed to saying what sentences we utter, has collapsed, then why are *dispositions,* of all things, in better shape than *truth?* The philosophical problems associated with disposition talk (including counterfactual talk) are just as formidable as the philosophical problems associated with the notion of truth. It looks—to me at any rate—as if Rorty says "no more metastories" and tries to convince us by telling us a higher-level metastory of his own, a cultural relativist or cultural imperialist metastory. But if you go with Wittgenstein so far as to say "no more metastories," then you had better not tell me a metastory—not even a metametastory!

Rorty will probably reply that his use of this metastory is purely dialectical, like Wittgenstein's. Wittgenstein, Rorty might remind us, often undermines a philosophical move by pointing out alternative philosophical moves, not to support those alternatives, but to destroy the coerciveness of the move being undermined by showing that move to be, in Rorty's word, "optional."

This tactic is a good one, but only against highfalutin ("philosophical") ways of talking. Wittgenstein never suggests that our ordinary ways of talking and thinking—our *ordinary* talk of "following a rule," or our *ordinary* talk of "seeing as," or our *ordinary* "understanding"—are shown to be mere *mythology* by the fact that our accounts of what it is to follow a rule, or to see something as a duck, or to understand a sentence run thin. (On this, there is a beautiful paper by Cora Diamond, "Realism and the Realistic Spirit.")[9] We walk on thin ground, but we do walk. Rorty, however, does suggest that even ordinary talk of objectivity, or rational acceptability, or truth is somehow mythological. To show this by the technique of telling alternative metastories would require one to produce an adequate scientific metaphysics, or something like it. But then philosophy would be reconstructed, not deconstructed!

Let me be as clear and explicit as I know how to be. I think that talk of "dispositions" is perfectly fine as part of ordinary language, or spontaneous phenomenology, or our *Lebenswelt,* or what have you. In discussions of metaphysical issues at the depth at which Quine and Rorty are both working—and they are certainly two of our leading metaphysicians—I think such talk is irresponsible. Dispositional talk is counterfactual talk, and Nelson Goodman showed us a long time ago that such talk depends on the notion of a *relevant condition*—a notion, which is thoroughly anthropocentric (and, I would add, thoroughly intentional).[10] To reject talk of "meanings" as mythology—as do both Quine and Rorty—while rejoicing in talk of the totality of the informant's speech dispositions (Quine), or in talk of dispositions of one's fellow "postmodern bourgeois liberals" to agree (Rorty), is irresponsible. If we should now let the project of saying what the noumena are, and whether or not there are noumena, and whether or not the whole question was a mistake, have a long respite, well and good! A moratorium on the cut between the phenomena and the noumena! But that is quite different from saying that we have achieved a coherent standpoint from which we can see what is and what is not mythological. Such a standpoint would be, to all intents and purposes, a noumenal one. If there is no Archimedean point, then the dispositions-to-agree of my fellow postmodern bourgeois liberals are not an Archimedean point either. One cannot show that a "line" between what is "really real" and what is at least partly a projection cannot be drawn by drawing one!

Moreover, if we are allowed to go on using dispositional idioms without a metaphysical account of how dispositionality "emerges" in the world (without a "foundation"), then why should we be forbidden to talk of true and false, right and wrong, rational and irrational, in exactly the same way? The failures of metaphysics as an enterprise are not a proof of the correctness of either Quinian materialism or Rortian culturalism.

Quine Again

If there is a structural principle unifying Quine's bewildering variety of philosophical doctrines and claims ("ontological relativity," "indeterminacy of translation," "epistemology naturalized," "holism," "immanent truth," "robust realism"), it is perhaps this: the ontological notions of reality and fact, in short, the notion of *existence,* are now seen to be "parochial." "Parochial" and "inscrutable" are dual terms in Quine's system of thought: what is inscrutable in the case of an alien language is parochial in the case of my own. Thus an alien's notion of reality is inscrutable, that is, nonexistent apart from some choice of a translation manual, but my own notion of reality is parochial: obvious from within, but inscrutable from without. Nevertheless, Quine claims, the ontological notions of reality and fact (reality and fact as determined by science, needless to say) should lose none of their authority over our thought by being seen to be parochial.

What this means is that the notion of what really exists, what there really is a "fact of the matter" about, continues to be taken seriously by Quine—as seriously as if these continued to be "transcendent" notions. At bottom, as we have seen, his reason for denying any reality to "meanings" (apart from translation schemes) is that no objects recognized by "first-class" science could play the role of meanings. There is, as Quine puts it over and over again, no "fact of the matter" about meanings. But *can* a notion of existence which is seen to be parochial have this kind of metaphysical authority?

The traditional notion of "reality" as that against which all our claims have to be squared was correlative with certain other notions. The idea of squaring a claim with reality went with the notion that our claims were *about* reality. But Quine wants to drop any and every notion of intentionality except a purely disquotational or immanent notion. Can one really keep reality and drop intentionality?

From a parochial point of view, Quine says, he is a "robust realist." There are tables and chairs, galaxies and black holes, and "black hole" refers to black holes. But as we have seen, reference is not a relation that possesses total intersubjectivity, in Quine's view, not a relation which is singled out in a way which is open to discovery by all scientists, no matter what background language they speak and no matter what arbitrary conventions they choose. Even *relative reference*—reference relative to a background language and a translation scheme—is not there intersubjectively, unless the community of scientists is restricted to speakers of the background language in question.

Quine is asking us to think that there is something about which we should be "realists" *and* telling us that the relation between our thoughts and that something is purely "immanent," that is, internal to our language and theory; that that language and theory do not have a relation to that something which is singled out in a way that can be scientifically determined by rational inquirers independently of how or whether *we* interpret them. This sounds like saying that there is a reality, but you aren't really thinking about it, you only pretend you are thinking about it. Or like saying there isn't a reality, but you pretend there is one whenever you think, and you have to take seriously the reality you pretend there is. Or still more like Hume saying that when he is in his study he sees that total skepticism is correct, but whenever he leaves his study he is a "robust realist." (Hume didn't use those exact words.) Quine's denial of "transcendent reality" is the denial of reality as traditionally, metaphysically conceived. Quine's claim is that "immanent" reality, the reality internal to our text contains a part—the "first-class" part—that is certified by science, and therefore deserves to be just as authoritative, just as coercive, as the metaphysician's reality ever was. But why should the "reality" of science be more coercive than our reflective intuition that what we say is true or false? Is not the failure of present-day science even to sketch a non–question-begging way of dealing with intentionality as good a reason as one could wish for retaining our common-sense scheme, retaining the common-sense scheme *in addition* to our scientific theories, not as a *refutation* of those theories in any way? We do not have to choose between being worshipers of science or opponents of science, after all.

To this question too Quine has an answer. Quine takes it that the whole purpose of cognition is to predict sensations (or, in a "naturalistic" reconstruction based on neurology, to predict stimulations of nerve endings).[11] Only by sticking to science as our criterion of rationality do we fulfill this purpose with maximum effectiveness. But surely this positivist notion of THE "aim of science" does not have to be taken seriously? Moreover, even the authority of perception is undermined by Quine's moves. The entire image—the image of a world of linguistic communities desperately trying to arrive at good expectations with respect to the stimulation of their nerve endings—is still "immanent." Stimulations of nerve endings are not something outside language, Quine emphasizes (he says all this is "immanent epistemology"), but just one more part of our evolving doctrine. Quine's view is that neither the authority of ontology nor the authority of epistemology is impaired in any way by being seen to be "immanent." In my view, whatever authority they had depended entirely on our conceiving of reality and sensations as, respectively, the makers-true and the makers-justified of the sentences we produce—not the makers-true and the makers-justified from within the story, but the things outside the story that hook language onto something outside itself. If Quine is right, then Rorty is right. If the makers-true and the makers-justified have really turned out to be "immanent," then they have also become "optional." Quine's talk of what is "first-class" and what is "second-class" becomes mere rhetoric.

Rorty Again

Rorty may not disagree with my saying that "if Quine is right, then Rorty is right." Presumably he thinks this is the case on independent grounds. Rorty has not himself tried to lean on the word *fact,* as Quine has, nor has he described himself as a "robust realist," even with respect to his "parochial" beliefs. Still, I do not think he entirely escapes the same sort of problem. If "solidarity" is to do the work that Rorty wishes it to do, then the picture to which the notion of solidarity belongs has to be taken seriously—I mean, of course, the picture of there being a certain number of other people in the world one cares to argue with ("postmodern bourgeois liberals") and of there being a fact of the matter, at least sometimes, as to what is and what is not a good argument by the lights of this group of people. But other people (not to mention *dispositions to agree*) are as "noumenal" from a metaphysical point of view as material objects and causes. Rorty may reply, however, that it is not real "external" people and real dispositions but only people (and dispositions) in his own historicist (meta-?)story that he cares about. Fictional solidarity with fictional characters is enough; or rather, the very opposition between "real" people and "fictional" people is now seen to be old hat. But I won't try to explain this further, because this is where I get off the boat.

What Rorty and Quine and a certain quasi-fictional philosopher I call "Kripgenstein" have in common is this: All three tell a story about how all there is is speakers and speech-dispositions, and about how we don't need any "metaphysical" notions of truth or warranted assertibility. All three soften this austere Protagorean picture by telling us that we can, in fact, recover a surrogate for truth and rationality—as much truth and rationality as we need—from "solidarity" (Rorty), or from the practice of scientists (Quine), or from the communal practice of deciding that certain people have "got," and certain people have failed to "get," various concepts (Kripgenstein). All three insist that their stories are *self-applicable:* that talk of the dispositions of, respectively, postmodern bourgeois liberals, scientists, and speakers who share a form of life is itself to be thought of not as a description of what is "out there," but simply as a part of our evolving doctrine. I say this sort of transcendental Skinnerianism has got to stop! If all there is is talk and objects internal to talk, then the idea that some pictures are "metaphysical," or "misleading," and others are not is itself totally empty. If you really believe that language is about Nothing, that may give you a certain *frisson,* but I can't take you seriously. However, as soon as you shift into your "it isn't as bad as you think" mode, you begin to privilege one story within the vast array of stories that our culture has produced in just the way you criticize other philosophers for doing. As Aristotle long ago pointed out, if a philosopher's doctrine won't allow him to say *anything,* then you don't have to refute him. And if he goes on not saying anything, he's "no better than a plant," Aristotle added. But the minute a philosopher starts trying to persuade one that some views are misleading, that giving up some notions isn't as bad as one thinks, and so forth, then he admits that there really is such a thing as getting something *right.* And if talk of "solidarity," or whatever, is an explanation of how (and to what extent) anything can be right at all, then you had better not fall back on the metametametastory that your metametastory is mere talk (*or* mere "writing," *pace* Derrida).

Notes

1. This lecture was given at the University of California, Berkeley. The argument is repeated, in virtually the same language, in Rorty's "Solid erité ou

Objectivité," *Critique,* 39, no. 439 (December 1983), 923–940. This is a review of my *Reason, Truth, and History* (New York: Cambridge University Press, 1981). It is reprinted in English as "Solidarity and Objectivity" in *Post-Analytic Philosophy,* ed. John Rajchman and Cornel West (New York: Columbia University Press, 1985).

2. Willard Van Quine, *Ontological Relativity and Other Essays* (New York: Columbia University Press, 1969), p. 49.

3. Ibid.

4. Willard Van Quine, *Theories and Things* (Cambridge: Harvard University Press, 1981), pp. 19–20.

5. See the title essay of *Theories and Things* (on p. 23) and the declaration on p. 180 that "immanent truth, a la Tarski, is the only truth I recognize."

6. Stephen Leeds, "How to Think about Reference," *Journal of Philosophy,* 70, no. 15 (September 1973), 485–503.

7. John R. Searle, "The World Turned Upside Down," *New York Review of Books,* October 27, 1983, pp. 74–79.

8. George D. Romanos, *Quine and Analytic Philosophy* (Cambridge: MIT Press, 1984).

9. In *Ludwig Wittgenstein: Critical Assessments,* ed. V. A. Shankar and S. G. Shanker (Amsterdam: Croom Helm, 1986). Diamond's essay is also reprinted in her *The Realistic Spirit* (Cambridge: MIT Press, 1991).

10. Nelson Goodman, *Fact, Fiction, and Forecast,* 4th ed. (Cambridge: Harvard University Press, 1983). See especially "The Problem of Counterfactual Conditionals," pp. 13–30.

11. Thus, the first sentence of Quine's *Theories and Things* reads, "Our talk of external things, our very notion of things, is just a conceptual apparatus that helps us to foresee and to control the triggerings of our sensory receptors." For a discussion of this "positivist" strain in Quine's views see Chapter 17 of the present volume.

18. Model Theory and the "Factuality" of Semantics

Although I first met Noam Chomsky over forty-five years ago, we really became friends in 1959, when he spent a year at Princeton University, where I was teaching. I remember the excitement of learning about "transformations" for the first time, and the long discussions we had about semantics (we were often joined by Paul Benacerraf and Paul Ziff), as well as about the sad state of the world (which has not gotten any less sad in the intervening years). Chomsky is, of course, a major philosopher as well as a great linguist, and he has often discussed philosophical issues, especially the ones surrounding Quine's thesis of the indeterminacy of translation. It is a great pleasure to contribute to his Festschrift and to wish him the traditional Jewish "hundert un zwanzig yohr" (may you live to be a hundred and twenty—the age Moses reached in the Bible).

In this essay I hope to clarify the nature and purpose of my model-theoretic argument against realism. This may seem a far cry from anything Noam Chomsky has written about; but a connecting link to his work is provided by Chomsky's well-known criticism of Quine's attack on the factuality of semantical claims.[1] This link should not really occasion surprise; Quine himself has often linked the issues of indeterminacy of translation and ontological relativity, and the latter issue is directly connected with the model-theoretic argument.

The Model-Theoretic Argument

I set out my model-theoretic argument in four publications,[2] beginning with my Address to the American Philosophical Association in 1976, and related issues continue to occupy my attention even today.[3]

351

For the sake of readers who may not be familiar with it, I shall give a brief summary. The argument assumes that we have somehow succeeded in formalizing our language.[4] A function which assigns extensions to the individual constants and to the predicate and function symbols of the language is called a *reference relation*. Such a function might assign Aristotle to the individual constant "*a*," the class of cats to the predicate "$C(x)$," the class of ordered pairs $\{<x,y>|$ x is a parent of $y\}$ to the predicate "$P(x,y)$," and so on. Tarski showed how such a reference relation can be extended by an inductive definition to complex predicates (that is, formulas with free variables), so that we can say, for instance, that under the reference relation just described the one-place predicate "$(\exists x)(C(x)\cdot P(x,y))$" has as its extension the class of just those y such that y is the offspring of a cat. Once this is done, one can also define the set of "true" sentences of the given language (that is, the set of sentences that would be true if that reference relation were used to interpret the language): a sentence S is true, assuming a reference relation, just in case the predicate "$x = x\cdot S$" refers to at least one thing.

The metaphysical realist pictures the world as a totality of language-independent things, a totality which is fixed once and for all; and, at least in the case of an ideal language, one (and only one) reference relation connecting our words with that totality is supposed to be singled out by the very way we understand our language. This description is meant to capture two features of traditional metaphysical realism: its insistence on a unique *correspondence* (to a fixed, mind-independent Reality) as the basis of truth and falsity, and its insistence that there is just One True Theory of the fixed mind-independent Reality. If we insist that our formalization of the language must be a formalization within classical two-valued logic, then we will have the third great feature of the traditional metaphysical realist picture: its commitment to bivalence.

Now, suppose that a theory I contains all (and only) those statements that we would accept in the ideal limit of rational inquiry (scientific or otherwise). Metaphysical realists—as opposed to pragmatists like Peirce—do not agree that such a theory would necessarily be *true*. According to metaphysical realists, the world could be such that the theory we were most justified in accepting would not really be true in the realist sense. (We might all be Brains in a Vat.) Rational acceptability—even in the ideal limit—is one thing, and truth is another. In this sense, the metaphysical realist views truth as radically non-epistemic.

Although metaphysical realism separates truth and rational acceptability (even idealized rational acceptability) in this way, the metaphysical realist does *expect* rationally acceptable statements to be consistent with one another in the long run. He admits that it is logically possible that we will have to live with a number of empirically equivalent systems of the world, or theories which equally well satisfy all our operational and theoretical constraints even as scientific inquiry continues indefinitely, but he does not really expect this to happen. In short, he expects scientific inquiry to converge to *one* ideal theory. (In this respect, he agrees with Peirce.)

A "model-theoretic argument against realism," in my sense, begins by showing—that one can show this is, today, an undisputed result of modern logic—that if there is such a thing as "an ideal theory," then that theory can never implicitly define its own intended reference relation. In fact, there are always many different reference relations that make *I* true, if *I* is a consistent theory which postulates the existence of more than one object. Moreover, if *I* contains non-observational terms (no matter how the line between the observational and the non-observational may be drawn), then there are reference relations that assign the correct extensions to the observation terms and wildly incorrect extensions to the non-observation terms and *still* make *I* come out true, as long as *I* does not actually imply a false observation sentence. As I put it in "Models and Reality," one can always find a reference relation that satisfies our observational constraints and also satisfies such theoretical constraints[5] as simplicity, elegance, subjective plausibility, and so on, under which such a theory *I* comes out true.

The problem this poses for the realist is the following: If *all* his realism requires is that there be *a* reference relation (a "correspondence") between items in the language (individual constants, function and predicate symbols) and items in the language-independent world which satisfies all our operational and theoretical constraints, then the model-theoretic results just described *show* that such a relation exists. But such reference relations are *not* unique (so the correspondence between words and the world is not "singled out" in the sense of being singled out *uniquely*). Moreover, if there should be more than one "ideal theory" (if there should be alternative equally rationally acceptable "systems of the world")—and realists, as I said, regard this as a logical possibility, although an unlikely one—then there would be "correspondences" making *each* of them true (so the idea that there is just *one* True Theory of the World would have to be given up). Finally, every ideal theory in the sense described above is guaranteed to possess a "correspondence to the world"—a reference relation satisfying all our operational and theoretical constraints under which it comes out *true*. So the idea that even an epistemically ideal theory could in reality be false makes no sense, if truth and falsity are identified with truth and falsity under reference assignments which satisfy our operational and theoretical constraints.

The upshot is this: If the realist wants to be a *metaphysical* realist— if he wants to hold on to the picture of the reference relation as (1) unique; (2) associated with a unique True Theory (note that there are two sorts of uniqueness involved in metaphysical realism—uniqueness of the True Theory and uniqueness of the reference relation); and (3) radically non-epistemic (in the sense that even an ideal theory can be false under the reference relation); then he must insist that it is something *other* than operational and theoretical constraints that singles out the right reference relation. But this, I argued, is an incoherent idea.

Incoherence and Inconsistency

Notice that I said "incoherent" not inconsistent. What is consistent or not is a matter of pure logic; what is coherent, or intelligible, or makes sense to us, and what is incoherent, or unintelligible, or empty, is something to be determined not by logic but by philosophical argument. Suppose it were the case, as a matter of contingent fact, that the number of elementary particles of a certain kind, say "gluons," in an arbitrary token of a word always equaled the number of particles of another kind, say "chromons," in every one of the things the word referred to. If this were so, then each token of the word "cat" would have just as many gluons as there were chromons in each cat; each token of "house" would have just as many gluons as there were chromons in each house, and so on. In such a world, there would be a simple physicalistically definable relation between tokens of terms[6] and the extensions of those tokens:

> For any token T of a term, T refers to x just in case the number of chromons in x is equal to the number of gluons in T.

However, if there were no *explanation* of how we use the words to refer which involved this fact, if this fact were just a weird coincidence, then the fact that there was such a simple physicalistic definition of the extension of the reference relation would shed no light at all on the way in which the reference relation is singled out. It would only add to the mystery.

Why is this? Because we simply would not be able to understand how such a relation connects with the activity of *denoting*. Now, the model-theoretic argument shows that for any physicalistic relation you like (satisfying the operational and theoretical constraints) there is another which does just as well. If someone says, "Well, one of these is just *intrinsically* identical with reference; it is the *essence* of reference that, say, a term *T* refers to whatever has the same number of chromons as the token of *T* has gluons," we would not be able to say, "You are inconsistent," for the speaker would not have contradicted himself; but we would feel that we had received nothing but scholastic-sounding noises as an answer to our puzzlement.

Explanation and Reference

Up to this point the problem does not look very serious. The example I used to illustrate our problem seems to point the way to a solution (and, indeed, this was the way I myself thought of the situation for some years, before I decided to "go public" with the model-theoretic argument). If the incoherence or unintelligibility of the suggestion that the physicalistic relation described above just happens to be the reference relation "by the very nature of reference itself" arises from the fact that the behavior we call "denoting" is not *explained* (in the possible world we imagined) by the fact that the thing denoted has just as many "chromons" as the token denoting it has "gluons," then surely the alternative is not to give up the search for a physicalistic theory of the reference relation, but rather to look for a physicalistic relation which has *explanatory value*. If there is a relation between our tokens and the things they refer to whose presence *explains* the way we behave with those tokens, our observable actions and their observable results, then the suggestion that we identify that relation with the relation of reference would make good scientific sense. And is this not precisely the program of semantic physicalism: to discover just such a physicalistic relation?

I will illustrate the obstacle to such a solution using the familiar nomological-deductive model of explanation, but it is easy to show that the suggestions that have been made for improving the nomological-deductive model—namely, to add pragmatic constraints to the requirements for an explanation, and to weaken the requirement that the *explicandum* actually be *deducible* from the *explicans,* desirable as they may be on other grounds—would not affect the difficulty I am about to explain. (In the nomological-deductive model, the premises in a complete and correct explanation are required to consist of laws and initial conditions; the statements which constitute the premises are all required to be true; the laws are required to be nomological [physically necessary truths] and not merely accidentally true; and the conclusion [the statement of the fact explained] is required to follow deductively from the premises.)[7]

In fact, there is more than one difficulty with the suggestion that the existence of an *explanation* of certain facts from the supposition that R is the correct reference relation is what singles out R as "the" reference relation for the language. One difficulty—the one I stressed in my first papers on the model-theoretic argument—is that this requirement uses the notion of *truth*. Our problem, remember, was to explain how a particular reference relation—and that means, also, a particular extension for the notion of truth—gets attached to our words. To say that what does the attaching is the fact that certain sentences (even if they are sentences in the metalanguage[8] and not in the object language) are *true* (and that certain additional conditions are met) is flagrantly circular. The problem, of course, is that what the semantic physicalist is trying to do is to reduce intentional notions to physicalist ones, and this program requires that he not employ any intentional notions in the reduction. But *explanation* is a flagrantly intentional notion.[9]

As I mentioned, there is more than one difficulty with using the notion of explanation to counter the model-theoretic argument. Here is the second difficulty—one to which considerably less attention has been paid in the literature.[10] Suppose we have fixed which sentences (in both the object language and the metalanguage) are true. In *Reason, Truth, and History* (1981)[11] I showed that even if we do this in *every possible world* (as opposed to just fixing the set of sentences which are true in the actual world), still the *reference* of individual constants, predicate symbols, and function symbols is far from being fixed. Even if the referent of some terms (the observation terms) is taken to be fixed (by the "operational constraints"), all the other objects in the universe can be permuted as you will, and the permutation will generate a new reference relation which has the strange property that a sentence will keep its truth value (in all possible worlds), *in spite of* the change in the reference relation. I illustrated the idea (1981, pp. 33–35) in the following way: I defined properties I called "cat*" and "mat*" in such a way that (1) in the actual world the things which are cats* are cherries and the things which are mats* are trees; and (2) *in every possible world,* the two sentences "A cat is on a mat" and "A cat* is on a mat*" have the same truth value. A consequence of this is that if instead of considering the two sentences just mentioned, we consider just the one sentence "A cat is on a mat" and allow its interpretation to change by using first the standard reference relation and then a nonstandard relation which assigns the set of cats* as extension to "cat" (in every possible world) and the set of mats* as extension to "mat" (in every possible world), the truth value of "A cat is on a mat" will not change—it will be the same as before *in every possible world.* This illustrates the way in which two different reference relations may assign not just the same extension, but the same *intension* to a sentence. The model-theoretic argument in the Appendix to *Reason, Truth, and History* shows that this technique can be extended to the totality of the sentences of a language.

A way of seeing what is happening here is to notice that while the sentence "A cat is on a mat" would receive a different translation into a fixed language if we changed the reference relation in the way described, the new translation would be *logically equivalent to the old one.* Indeed, the two sentences "A cat is on a mat" and "A cat* is on a mat*" are such a pair of "translations."

Now, any sentence which is logically equivalent to a nomological sentence is also nomological. Also, the property of truth and the relation of logical consequence are preserved under logical equivalence. In short, *nomological deductive explanations are preserved under changes of interpretation of the kind just described.* What follows? Simply this: Any observable event that can be *explained* (in the sense of the nomological-deductive model of explanation) from the fact that the relation R holds between certain tokens and the things those tokens bear R to can also be explained (in the sense of the nomological-deductive model) from the fact that those tokens bear R^* to whatever they bear R^* to, where R and R^* are related as in the model-theoretic argument of the Appendix of *Reason, Truth, and History.* In short, the suggestion fails even apart from the problem of circularity.

In presenting this second difficulty, however, I have made essential use of the assumption that the requirements on an explanation are those of the nomological-deductive model. What happens if we impose pragmatic constraints—plausibility, preservation of past doctrine, simplicity—as additional requirements on a good explanation?

At this point we run into the first difficulty again. What is expressed by the "simpler," "more plausible," etc., sentences in the metalanguage depends on what the *real* reference relation for the metalanguage is; and our problem, for the metalanguage as much as for the object language, was how we supposed this could be singled out. Remember, we are not addressing a practical problem of translation. It is not that we can suppose that we possess a metalanguage whose reference relation has somehow already been fixed, and the problem is to determine the best *translation* of the object language into the part of the metalanguage that corresponds to it. The problem is rather (to speak the language that metaphysical realists often use nowadays) how a reference relation is fixed "from the point of view of the universe." Simplicity, plausibility, and preservation of past doctrine make sense from the point of view of the universe only *if* the metalanguage has a singled-out reference relation "from the point of view of the universe." Appeal to these notions to explain *how* a reference relation is singled out "from the point of view of the universe" is flagrant anthropomorphism.

And this, indeed, is why I spoke of "incoherence." If the universe is supposed to be informed by Platonic Ideas, which attach something intentional to every particular, or if in some other way we manage to inhabit a world-view quite other than the world-view of modern physical science, then we may not see anything incoherent in the idea that what is outside our minds somehow *interprets our languages for us.* But the modern physicalist should not ascribe powers to nature for which his own image of nature has no room.

Reference and Causal Connection

A variant of the idea that "explanation" is what fixes reference is the idea, put forward vigorously by Michael Devitt (1981) as well as by a host of others, that "reference is causal connection." Since causal connection is supposed by these philosophers to be a language-independent relation between events in the world, it might seem that this suggestion would avoid the difficulties just described, but this appearance is an illusion. One problem with Devitt's idea (to which I shall return in a moment) is that, if $E(T)$ is the event of someone's using a token of a term T, then there is a good sense of "causal connection" in which *every* event in the backward light-cone of $E(T)$ is "causally connected" to the event $E(T)$; but it will almost never be the case that the term T (or the token in question) *refers* to every event in the backward light-cone of $E(T)$ (and it will typically be the case that the term does refer to things with which the token is *not* causally connected, for instance, future things). Bracketing this objection for the moment, let us simply observe that "A cat is on a mat" and "A cat* is on a mat*" would normally be said to describe the *same* event. (Logically equivalent sentences do not seem to be descriptions of different events so much as equivalent descriptions of the same event; for example, "John put two apples in his pocket" and "John put an even prime number of apples in his pocket" do not seem to be two different events which happened at the same time, but just two different ways of describing one event.) But if this is right and "a cat's being on a mat" and "a cat*'s being on a mat*" are the same event, then they must *have the same causes and the same effects*. If so, then there is no way in which the event $E(T)$ can be causally connected to a cat's being on a mat without being identically causally connected to a cats*'s being on a mat*.

One can point out that, just as we do in the case of statements about what *explains* what, we require statements of causality to satisfy various pragmatic constraints. Such constraints—or, simply, our interests in a particular context—may determine that it would be natural to describe the event one way, to say "A cat is on a mat," and "weird" to say "A cat* is on a mat*." But when the question is not what it is natural to *say*—that is, what *sentences* it is natural to utter—but what is the "natural" way of describing the event *from the universe's point of view*, we run up against the difficulty that the very attribution of any point of view in the matter to the universe is nonsense.[12]

To come back to the objection I postponed: someone might suppose that the universe itself somehow "factors" events into background conditions and bringers-about. And he might say that not every event in the backward light-cone of $E(T)$ is a "bringer-about" of $E(T)$. (The problem of getting a *unique* description of the events which *are* "bringers-about" still remains, of course.) But the distinction between bringers-about (causal agents) and background conditions is rather obviously an interest-relative matter; again, the anthropomorphism of ascribing this distinction to "the universe" is obvious.

One philosopher who has acknowledged this difficulty is David Lewis (1984). Lewis' solution is to give up the "causal connection theory" and to postulate that certain classes of things are *intrinsically* natural. (What 'intrinsically' means in this connection is (1) not by virtue of what we *think* or of how things are described in language and (2) not by virtue of anything like the simplicity of laws—since the laws obeyed by the *-magnitudes[13] are formally the same as the laws obeyed by the "standard" magnitudes.) In short, Lewis claims that certain classes are *natural from the universe's point of view*. While I compliment Lewis on seeing exactly what the problem is, I have to say that I do not see the advantage of adding to our conceptual scheme an unfamiliar metaphysical primitive like "naturalness" over just taking the notion of reference itself as an unreduced primitive notion. Doesn't Lewis' account amount to saying that we-know-not-what fixes the reference relation we-know-not-how?

The Metaphysical Upshot

The upshot of the argument is not (or at least not without further argument) that "realism is false" and "antirealism is true." After all, there are many versions of both realism and antirealism (and positions which may not be easily classifiable as "realist" or "anti-realist," for example, Wittgenstein's). The upshot of *this*[14] model-theoretic argument is simply that semantic physicalism does not work. (However, physicalism seems to be the only sort of metaphysical realism that our time can take seriously.) The way reference is fixed is not intelligibly explained by any sort of physicalist account so far proposed. This conclusion leaves, of course, a wide variety of possibilities: not only the possibility of taking some notion other than reference (for example, rational acceptability)[15] as the base for doing semantics, but also the possibility of taking reference as primitive.[16] What it rules out, if I am right, is the view that reference is fated to be reduced to notions which belong to the world picture of physics.

It is at this point that my discussion makes contact with Quine's philosophy. Quine has expressed qualified agreement with what he calls "Brentano's Thesis"—with the thesis I just expressed by saying that "reference is not fated to be reduced to notions which belong to the world picture of physics." Moreover, his arguments in *Word and Object* and *Ontological Relativity and Other Essays* are, in significant part, model theoretic. (My own treatment differs from Quine's in (1) dropping the concern with "proxy functions" and (2)—in *Reason, Truth, and History*—extending the argument to intensional logic.) But Quine has a way out of the problem very different from any I have ever considered accepting, a way out that involves a fundamental disagreement between himself and Noam Chomsky. Quine's way out is to *deny the existence of objective facts about reference, and also to deny the existence of objective facts about synonymy* (except in the case of observation sentences, and then only when the observation sentences are "taken holophrastically").[17]

In the remainder of this essay I want to explore the nature of this disagreement, using my own model-theoretic argument and its obvious relation to Quine's defense of "ontological relativity" as an entering wedge. Let me begin by saying, however, that I did not perceive the relation of the arguments at the time the model-theoretic argument first occurred to me. The reason Quine's argument did not suggest my own argument to me is precisely that Quine's conclusion was so different—or rather, his conclusions (in the plural) are so different, for, as we shall see, Quine draws more than one conclusion from *his* model-theoretic argument.

Water Imagery in Quine

One conclusion that Quine draws is expressed in a remarkable series of metaphors that all involve the idea of floating on water. That image has been used in philosophy before, of course, notably by Neurath in the famous anti-foundationalist image of knowledge-building as analogous to the task of rebuilding a ship while the ship is afloat on the open sea, but the point of the water imagery in *Theories and Things* (1981) is rather different. In that work, the upshot of the doctrine of the "inscrutability of reference" is expressed by saying that all a translation scheme does is connect the "free-floating reference" of the term being translated with the equally free-floating reference of its translation into the home language. When I say that *lapin* refers to rabbits I do not say what *lapin* refers to "absolutely," Quine is telling us; I am only informing you that *lapin* and *rabbit* are coupled, they float together, presumably remaining side by side as they float. But Quine hastens to reassure us: even though our reference is floating, nothing goes wrong as long as we "acquiesce in our home language" (which means, I take it, as long as we speak it without allowing ourselves to think about it as speculative philosophers) and *don't rock the boat* (1981, p. 20).

In the case of Neurath's image it is clear what the "water" stands for: it stands for the pressures of life and experience which threaten to destroy our "boat" (and with the boat, our very existence) if we try to replace too much of the boat at any one time. But what does the "water" stand for in this passage in *Theories and Things?* As far as I can see, it can only stand for something like a *noumenal reality*.[18] Quine writes as if there were a noumenal reality, and what his model-theoretic argument shows is that our terms have an infinite number of ways of being modeled in it. I argue that at least the naturalistic versions of metaphysical realism land one in precisely such a conclusion as Quine reaches here—and I conclude that there must be something wrong with metaphysical realism! Of course, I am not accusing Quine of metaphysical realism; rather I am suggesting that the familiar Kantian image of our world as a "product" with some kind of noumenal world providing the "raw material" haunts Quine's thought. But metaphysical realism and that sort of Kantianism[19] are made for each other.

Inscrutability of Reference and Indeterminacy of Translation

My emphasis on the model-theoretic route to Quine's doctrine of the inscrutability of reference may appear puzzling. After all, I said I would discuss the dispute between Quine and Chomsky over the question whether there is a "fact of the matter" as to the truth of (certain semantical) claims in linguistics. And, from a logical point of view, one might accept the picture of our terms as sliding freely over the surface of the noumenal waters, accept the picture of our terms as having no fixed "absolute" reference, and not feel committed at all to accepting Quine's thesis of the indeterminacy of translation. That is to say, one might *accept* the doctrine that "there is no saying what our terms refer to absolutely," while *rejecting* the inscrutability of ordinary "relative" reference and the indeterminacy of translation. One might agree with Quine that *lapin* and *rabbit* have no "absolute" reference at all (if a structured system of objects is a candidate for the interpretation of our words, any isomorphic system is an equally good candidate, Quine claims),[20] while insisting that there *is* a fact of the matter that *"lapin" refers to rabbits* (even though all that means is that the two "free-floating references" are coupled in a certain way).[21]

While the objection would be correct as a point of formal logic, I think that one cannot understand Quine's picture of the situation if one simply takes his arguments one by one, independently of one another. Let us remember, first of all, that Quine partly inherits and partly rebels against a tradition, the tradition of Frege (the Frege of *Sinn und Bedeutung*), Russell, and Carnap, in which it is simply taken for granted that meaning (in the sense of "intension" or *Sinn*) determines reference. Also, let us remember that for Frege and (at times) Russell (though not Carnap), meanings were supposed to be directly available to the mind (concepts are "transparent to reason and reason's nearest kin," Frege wrote). Like Carnap, who explicitly rejected the idea that meanings can somehow be the objects of a mental faculty akin to perception, Quine thinks that *if* meanings can be retained at all in science, it must be by identifying them with equivalence classes of synonymous expressions. Meanings as entities whose existence somehow *explains* why it is that certain expressions are synonymous have to go.[22]

If reference is not fixed at all ("absolutely"), if saying that *"lapin"* denotes rabbits only tells us that the two words have the same "free-floating" reference, then, in particular, the idea that reference is fixed by *meaning* is hopelessly wrong, and belief in anything like the traditional picture of the speaker as "grasping" meanings which "determine" reference is akin to belief in magic, to belief in noetic rays or whatever. What ontological relativity by itself tells us is not that synonymy is indeterminate—that requires, indeed, a separate argument—but that the traditional *philosophical* reasons for thinking it must be determinate were terrible reasons. It tells us that *if* the notion of synonymy is to be rehabilitated, it must first be rationally reconstructed.

What does it mean to rationally reconstruct the notion of synonymy? For Quine rational reconstruction has a very particular meaning. A rational reconstruction describes our "first-class" scientific image of the world, the only image we should take with metaphysical seriousness, and it does so subject to certain constraints that are themselves seen as central to the scientific image, notably the principle of bivalence from classical logic and the maxim "No entity without identity"—there must be statable criteria of identity for all entities admitted as values of variables. If synonymy is to be admitted as a notion of first-class science, if synonymy classes are to be admitted as values of variables, then there must be *criteria of identity* for synonymy classes, that is, *there must be a set of criteria which fix precisely the conditions under which two terms may be said to be synonymous.*

It seems to me that *this* is the principle which really does the work in Quine's arguments for the indeterminacy of translation. Consider the structure of those arguments:[23] Quine lays down some criteria for synonymy (or, more precisely, for translation from one language to another). He observes that they do not determine a unique translation. The criteria he lists in the famous Chapter 2 of *Word and Object* (1960) are so weak that this, in itself, is hardly surprising. But he also conjectures that no addition to those criteria would help the situation. And he adds that even if (contrary to what he expects) we *found* criteria which determined a unique translation, this would *still* not establish the factuality of translation-claims.[24] I want to postpone consideration of this last move for a little while, and consider the grounds for Quine's pessimism about the power of criteria to single out the "correct" translation.

That skepticism, it seems to me, is fully justified—no matter what one's view on indeterminacy of translation. What Quine is saying here is something that, in fact, Noam Chomsky also believes—although most discussions of the debate fail to bring this out. Neither Quine nor Chomsky expects *mechanical translation* to succeed. That is, neither Quine nor Chomsky expects us to find a set of criteria which will function as an *algorithm* to determine when one has correctly translated an expression of one language into another language. The idea that *interpretative rationality can be fully exhausted by a finite set of criteria that we will actually succeed in writing down* is Utopian on its face. But this is what Quine is, in effect, demanding—that we succeed in writing down such a set of criteria—before he will accept that we have succeeded in rationally reconstructing the notion of synonymy.

To meet Quine's argument (as I have just interpreted it), to counter it *without* defending the possibility of success in the Utopian project of completely formalizing interpretation, one must do one of two things: either one must show that the factuality of translation-claims does not require that there be exactly *one* rationally acceptable translation manual (and Chomsky has tried to argue that *given Quine's own epistemology* this *is* indeed a defensible position), or one must argue that translation can be determinate even though it is not a set of *criteria* that determines what the correct translation is. But if one takes the latter tack, Quine will, of course, ask how the position that something other than a set of criteria fixes correct translation differs from belief in mysterious "meanings"—how it differs, except verbally, from what he calls the Museum Myth of meanings.

The Question of the "Factuality" of Semantics

According to Quine, even if we knew the totality of all possible correct observation statements, still it is possible that more than one theory would agree equally well with the whole totality. Certainly we do not possess *criteria* which would always single out exactly one theory of the world from the whole set of "empirically equivalent theories" in every such case. Theory is, in this sense, "underdetermined by evidence"—possibly underdetermined by the totality of all possible observations. So—various thinkers have asked Quine—how can you argue that the possibility of alternative translation schemes, all equally in accordance with linguistic observation and the criteria of acceptability we are able to write down, shows that there is "no fact of the matter" as to which translation scheme is right, while at the same time arguing that *there is a fact of the matter* in physics? On your own showing, are not semantics and physics in the same boat?

In a generally excellent recent book, Christopher Hookway (1988) argues that such thinkers (he mentions Chomsky and Rorty) are "misunderstanding" Quine. He writes, "Although the misreading is understandable, it is clear that Quine's point is not primarily epistemological: his claim is not that correct translation is underdetermined by available evidence, but that it is underdetermined by the *facts*. In light of his physicalist conception of 'the facts,' he holds that correctness of translation manuals (and semantic claims generally) is not fixed by physics" (p. 137). But Chomsky (and Rorty) are perfectly well aware that Quine is making a metaphysical (and not just an epistemological) claim. The problem is that Quine's arguments for the metaphysical claim range from bad to worse. Again and again, Quine simply goes from the premise that all facts are supervenient on physical facts to the conclusion that all facts are identical with physical facts. For example, here: "Full coverage is the business of physics and only of physics": "nothing happens in the world, not the flutter of an eyelid, not the flicker of a thought, without some redistribution of physical states" (1981, p. 98). But supervenience does not imply identity[25]—not without further argument. And Quine supplies no such argument.

Were this all there was to say, it would have been charitable not to discuss Quine's position on the factuality of semantics at all. But when a great philosopher makes an *obvious* mistake, there is usually something behind it. Quine makes mistakes when a point is so clear to him, when the burden of proof is so obviously on his opponents, that he becomes impatient. (He has self-mockingly remarked that impatience is, perhaps, his main emotion.) What I am seeking is the line of thinking that makes it just *obvious* to Quine that semantics is not factual.

What I am suggesting is that the line that moves him (or, at least, the

line that originally moved him to his present position) is the following.
Although our fundamental picture of the world, the world picture of
physics, may be underdetermined by the evidence, there is no *further*
or *higher* picture from which we can stand back and say "this is less
than factual." (Although there are tensions in Quine's view, this is
how he himself, recognizing the tensions, sees the matter.)[26] Moreover, *within* our version of the world—even if it should turn out to be
underdetermined by the evidence and, in part, a radical choice—there
are well-defined criteria of identity for all the entities we speak of.[27]
For example, although there are alternative systems of set theory
available to us, *within* each system of set theory there is a simple and
elegant criterion of set identity: x and y are the same set just in case
they have the same members. But even after we have *chosen* a version
of the fundamental facts, the facts of physics and mathematics, we are
unable to state, in the language of physics and mathematics, a *criterion* for synonymy. If we still believed in "meanings" as entities that
explain synonymy, we could, at worst, simply *add them to our physics
as additional fundamental entities*. But since we have given up the
myth, that route is not open to us. We have to reconstruct the notion
of synonymy if we are to employ it without lowering our standards of
scientific rigor, and (for the reasons given above) the prospects for
such a reconstruction are not good ones. I believe that this argument
fits the text of *Word and Object* even if it does not fit all of the "fall-
back arguments" that Quine has developed since he wrote *Word and
Object*. And it does not need the premise that *all* facts are physical
facts (although Quine believes that premise), but only the premise that
postulating irreducible "semantic facts" represents a return to a way
of thinking about meaning that has been seen not to make sense. It
does not make sense, to repeat, because it requires "meanings" to
have properties that are quite magical, properties our scientific image
of the world leaves us with no way of understanding.

Quine's Fall-Back Argument

Unfortunately, there is another way in which Quine sometimes argues. Quine sometimes argues that *even if our canons singled out a
unique translation* there would be no fact of the matter as to whether
or not the *canons themselves* were correct. The only thing there is a
"fact of the matter" about is the "verbal dispositions themselves."
(Recall: "If [simplicity, charity, and 'kindred canons of procedure']

suffice to weed out all conflicting codifications of the natives' verbal dispositions, which is doubtful, I would still say that they confer no fact on the matter"; Hahn and Schlipp, 1986, p. 155.)

Quine's argument seems to be that even if there were criteria of correct translation C which picked out a unique translation manual in each case, we could construct "incorrect" but equally complete alternative criteria C'. Then (as long as the "incorrect" criteria C' did not require us to ascribe verbal dispositions to the natives they don't actually have) we could ask: "What makes C and not C' the correct set of criteria?" The answer couldn't be that criteria C are *analytic* of the notion of correct translation, for analyticity was already "debunked" in "Two Dogmas of Empiricism." Nor could it be any physical facts, since all physical facts are equally compatible with the statements (1) "Criteria C are the correct criteria for selection of a translation manual" and (2) "Criteria C' are the correct criteria for selection of a translation manual." So (unless we are willing to accept "nonphysical facts," which Quine is not), we must regard our preference for C over C' as a matter of practical convenience (which can be explained in various ways, for example, simplicity, utility, our past history and culture, and so on), without serious theoretical implications as to the Furniture of the World.

But this argument is more an immunizing move (in Popper's sense) than a serious argument. The model-theoretic argument against the traditional correspondence picture of meaning and reference is a serious and intricate argument, whether one finally accepts it or not. And it points to a real difficulty with the traditional notion of what a "semantical fact" looks like. But this latter argument simply invokes the principle that all facts are physical facts: a principle for which, as we noted, Quine gives no real argument at all. (And it assumes that we cannot simply say, "Accepting C' rather than C would constitute *changing the meaning of the notion of synonymy*"; that is, it assumes that not only the notion of analyticity but also the notion of synonymy has *already* been discredited. But in that case, we do not *need* any further argument against the factuality of assertions of synonymy.)

Again, Quine often points out that there is *one* kind of linguistic statement that he regards as fully objective: statements about our "verbal dispositions" are fully scientific, in his view. How does my reconstruction of Quine's thinking square with this?

In his writing Quine has suggested that dispositional predicates refer to mechanisms which we presently do not understand, but which are perfectly physical in nature. "We intend in advance that solubility consist precisely in those explanatory traits of structure and composition however ill-pictured or unpictured at the time, that do make things dissolve when in water."[28] As Hookway (1988, p. 108) puts it, explaining Quine's view, "While dispositional terms have an essential heuristic or regulative role in formulating ideas and problems as science progresses—and while they provide an excellent shorthand in alluding to great stretches of theory, and a useful means for covering up our relative ignorance—there is no reason to think they need have a role in formulating the true finished theory of reality." There is no need, in Quine's view, for a general dispositional idiom in science; and if we do use individual dispositional predicates, this is only because we have not yet reached the stage at which they can be eliminated in favor of terms from more fundamental science. (In conversation, however, Quine has sometimes taken the line that it is all right to use dispositional predicates *even if it turns out that we cannot actually give necessary and sufficient conditions for their application* in the language of mathematics and physics. Perhaps this was only a slip; but if Quine were to stick to this line, it would represent another immunizing move in his philosophy of a most unfortunate kind.)[29]

Alexander George's Reconstructions of the Chomsky-Quine Debate

Alexander George (1986) has suggested that the debate is, at bottom, an empirical disagreement about the future of cognitive psychology. And it is true that Quine has sometimes made statements about the nature of the brain processes involved in language learning.[30] But it is a mistake to think that discovering that these statements are wrong, and that the modularity hypothesis is right, would cause Quine to concede the factuality of semantic claims. Even if we imagine that every claim Jerry Fodor makes in *The Language of Thought* were empirically verified, for example, we would only have established the possibility of defining something called "narrow content" in cognitive psychology. But Fodor himself emphasizes that "narrow content" is not *meaning*[31] ("elm" and "beech" may have the same narrow content, for example, but they do not have the same meaning). And Fodor's own suggestions for defining the nonsolipsistic component of meaning—"broad content"—run into a problem Fodor calls "the problem of error," a problem Fodor himself recognizes as a difficulty Quine raised as far back as "Two Dogmas of Empiricism." In any case, it is all but certain that the tremendously strong form of the innateness hypothesis defended by Fodor, which requires that "every word in the Oxford English Dictionary" be innate (as Fodor has put it), is untenable—and untenable for reasons connected with Quine's meaning holism.[32] On *no* psychological theory—excluding ones made up by philosophers—is it going to turn out that whenever two speakers have the same belief the *identical* neurological or computational process is going on in their heads, because, for one thing, our actual notion of "sameness of meaning" *discounts substantial differences in belief and in inference patterns.* So even if we allow criteria that invoke neurological or brain-computational evidence (as has also been urged by Michael Friedman [1975]), we will never be able to write down precise criteria for the selection of a translation manual.[33] True, the Chomsky-Quine debate is not a purely "conceptual" debate; empirical facts are relevant, in the sense in which they are relevant to every philosophical debate; but it is certainly not a straightforward empirical disagreement about, say, modularity versus equipotentiality. Even were Quine to allow neurological, brain-computational, etc., evidence in linguistics, the most this *might* force him to concede is the possibility of defining some notion of narrow content (and, I have argued in *Representation and Reality,* there are good Quinian arguments that such a notion would probably have *no* significant relation to the notion of "sameness of meaning" that guides us in *translation*). To ignore the *conceptual* difficulties facing the program of finding a neurologically *cum* computationally based notion of "narrow content" (one which makes it the case that narrow content is preserved in translation) is to fall for a "scientific" version of the "Museum Myth" of meaning.[34] And is this not what Quine has been telling us?

I have argued that Quine's argument (freed of various "immunizing strategies" that Quine added later) has two parts: it consists of (1) an argument against the "Museum Myth of meaning" which has interesting similarities to my own model-theoretic argument against (naturalistic versions of) metaphysical realism; and (2) an argument that a certain demand (one which Quine thinks we must impose before we admit such a term as "synonymous" into our "first-class" scientific language) cannot be met. An acceptable rational reconstruction of the notion of synonymy will not, Quine claims, turn out to be possible.

We will not be able to give precise criteria for when two terms are/are not synonymous (criteria which are themselves stable in the language of fundamental science).

Although I have some problems with the first part—it is an inconsistency to speak of "the free-floating reference of our own terms" if one also insists, as Quine does again and again, that there is no standpoint outside or above our own language—I agree that the Museum Myth of meaning is untenable, and model-theoretic methods can help to bring this out. But my real difficulties are with the second part of Quine's argument. Asking for precise criteria (whether one also calls them "behavioral" or not is a red herring, I think) for selecting a translation manual is, as I have said, Utopian. And while the request for criteria statable in the language of "fundamental" science has a certain appeal, it is ultimately indefensible. Quine's demands for such criteria lead him to reject not only the existence of an objective relation of synonymy, but also the existence of a fact of the matter as to whether or not two terms (in another language) are the same or different in reference. To avoid having to abandon the notion of reference as he has abandoned the notion of synonymy, Quine must then claim that in his "home language" the situation is different. One can be a "robust realist" with respect to one's home language, and give a nonrealist or antirealist account of the functioning of *every other language*.[35] Most philosophers would regard such an outcome as a *reductio ad absurdum* of the demand that leads to it.

In the end, then, I think Noam Chomsky is right in making this rejoinder to Quine's claims: The underdetermination of semantical descriptions (to the extent that there is underdetermination) has no more and no less significance, epistemologically *or* metaphysically, than the underdetermination of physical theory by evidence—or, for that matter, than the underdetermination of physical theory by *sociology*.

Notes

1. Quine and Chomsky have repeatedly discussed each other's views over the years. Here I focus on just one of their debates, namely, Chomsky's criticism in *Words and Objections* (1969) and elsewhere of Quine's claim that there is no fact of the matter as to the truth or falsity of semantic claims and Quine's reply in the same volume. I do not discuss their disagreement over Chomsky's innateness hypothesis, or over the status of generative grammar.

2. "Realism and Reason" in my *Meaning and the Moral Sciences* (1978),

"Models and Reality" in *The Journal of Symbolic Logic,* 15 (1980), 464–482, the book *Reason, Truth, and History* (1981), and the Introduction to vol. 3 of my *Philosophical Papers, Realism and Reason* (1983). See Chapter 19 of the present volume and chaps. 12, 13, and 16 of *Realism and Reason.* "Models and reality" is also reprinted in *Realism and Reason,* as chap. 1.

3. See, for example, Putnam, 1987.

4. More precisely, assume that we have succeeded in formalizing our language up to some (possibly trans-finite) level of the Tarskian hierarchy of meta-languages (to avoid semantical paradoxes).

5. Nor does my argument depend on this or any other particular list of theoretical constraints, contrary to what Richard Miller contends (1988). To see this, let C be any constraint on theory selection you like—even, if you think you understand the notion, "realist truth." Let ECC (the Epistemic Counterpart of C) be the constraint that *the world is an epistemic counterpart of a world in which C is fulfilled.* (The notion of an epistemic counterpart was introduced by Kripke, 1972. The idea, of course, is that in any epistemic counterpart of a world in which p is true, one's experiences will fully justify one in believing that p is true.) Then ECC represents the part of the constraint C that is really *epistemic.* And any set of constraints that are *epistemic* in this sense will do for my argument. (Nor does this notion of the epistemic require the sense-datum theory, or any other particular theory of what the objects of observation are—as was pointed out in "Models and Reality.")

6. I am restricting attention to terms for physical objects in this example, of course.

7. The *locus classicus* for the deductive-nomological model is Hempel and Oppenheim, 1948.

8. Given an object language, both the construction of a metalanguage and the extension of the reference relation of the object language to that metalanguage are completely straightforward procedures (given, of course, a sufficiently strong set theory—one which must be stronger than what is available in either the object language or the metalanguage). But if a reference relation has not been fixed for the object language, we cannot suppose that one is already available for the metalanguage, without begging the question.

9. For a considerably lengthier discussion of this point, see "Beyond historicism," chap. 16 in my *Realism and Reason* (1983).

10. I also raised this second difficulty in "Information and the Mental," 1986.

11. See the Appendix. In his *Representing and Intervening* (1983), Ian Hacking suggests that my model-theoretic argument may be flawed because it depends on the Skolem-Löwenheim Theorem, which does not apply to Second Order languages. Besides ignoring my discussion of just this point in

"Models and Reality," Hacking's suggestion ignores the fact that the model-theoretic argument of *Reason, Truth, and History*—the book he cited—did *not* employ the Skolem-Löwenheim Theorem, but used a technique—permutation of individuals—which does apply to second-order Logic, modal logic, tensed logic, etc.!

12. For a much fuller discussion of the problems with the causal connection theory see my "Is the Causal Structure of the Physical Itself Something Physical?" (1984), and chap. 3 of my *Renewing Philosophy* (1992).

13. If M is the referent of any term under the "standard" reference relation, M^* may be the referent of the same term under whatever nonstandard reference relation we please (where the model-theoretic argument establishes that such nonstandard reference relations exist). In particular, if M_1, M_2, M_3 . . . are the standard physical magnitudes, then M_1^*, M_2^*, M_3^* . . . will be magnitudes such that *the very same sentences that are nomologically true of the first lot, are also true of the second lot.*

14. Other model-theoretic arguments *do* bear against metaphysical realism, even in its nonphysicalist versions, however. In particular, this is true of the argument from equivalent descriptions, explained in "Realism and Reason" (in *Meaning and the Moral Sciences*, 1978) and developed at length in Lecture 1 in *The Many Faces of Realism* (1987).

15. This is the view I defended in *Reason, Truth, and History* (1981). I no longer regard it as correct: see my replies to Gary Ebbs, John McDowell, and David Anderson in *The Philosophy of Hilary Putnam, Philosophical Topics*, 20, no. 1 (Spring 1992).

16. In *Representation and Reality* (1988), I argue that doing this does not commit one to viewing reference as "simple and irreducible."

17. The idea of taking observation sentences holophrastically—that is, as unanalyzed wholes, thereby finessing Quine's own worries about whether to translate *gavagai* as "rabbit" or as "rabbithood exemplified again"—is emphasized in Quine's reply to me, in Hahn and Schilpp, 1986, pp. 427–431.

18. Speaking at a symposium titled "Ways the World Is" at Harvard's 350th anniversary celebration (June 1986), Quine said that he does not believe in things in themselves, but added, "I do believe in a world in itself. The world in itself is Nature." Note the similarity to James's tendency to treat "pure experience" as a pre-ontological noumenal reality.

19. That sort of Kantianism, I argue in *Reason, Truth, and History* (1981), and also in *The Many Faces of Realism* (1987), is not the only sort. Much more of Kant than is commonly thought not only does not depend on the notion of a noumenal world, but is at odds with the notion.

20. Thus, after pointing out that "it is quantification, with its variables, that embodies reification," Quine goes on to say, "It is startling to reflect that this contribution is purely structural. *Other objects would have served the purpose as well as ours, as long as they were in one-to-one correlation with*

them. No evidence, therefore, could be adduced for the reification of one lot rather than the other" (my italics; the quotation is from *Quiddities*, 1988, p. 182). While Quine speaks here of reification and evidence, rather than of reference, the underlying thought is model-theoretic: it is magical, in Quine's view, to think that science can do more than fix the structure of the world up to isomorphism.

21. "Thus 'London' designates London (whatever *that* is) and 'rabbit' denotes the rabbits (whatever *they* are)" (Hahn and Schilpp, 1986, p. 460).

22. "We could simply identify meanings with classes of synonyms ["if we could admit synonymy"]. Ayer made the same point long ago and so did Russell . . . The point . . . is that the *prior* admission of an *unexplained* domain of objects called meanings is in no way to explain synonymy or anything else" (Hahn and Schilpp, 1986, p. 73).

23. For an analysis of the structure of Quine's arguments see my "The Refutation of Conventionalism" in my *Philosophical Papers*, vol. 2, *Mind, Language, and Reality* (1975).

24. "If [simplicity, charity, and 'kindred canons of procedure'] suffice to weed out all conflicting codifications of the natives' verbal dispositions, which is doubtful, I would still say that they confer no fact on the matter" (Hahn and Schilpp, 1986, p. 155).

25. According to current physics, nothing happens in the world without a change in the gravitational field. But Quine himself would not argue that all facts are gravitational facts. To restate the point: "all facts are supervenient on gravitational facts" is true; "all facts *are* gravitational facts" is false.

26. See his reply to Roger F. Gibson, Jr., in Hahn and Schilpp, 1986, pp. 155–158.

27. Actually, this is not true in quantum mechanics. But I don't suppose that Quine's knowledge of contemporary physics reaches so far.

28. *Ways of Paradox* (1976), p. 72. See also *Word and Object* (1960), pp. 222–225, *The Roots of Reference* (1973), pp. 4ff., 10–15, *Ontological Relativity* (1969a), pp. 130–131.

29. See my discussion of Quine's use of dispositions in "Is the Causal Structure of the Physical Itself Something Physical?" (1984).

30. Quine believes that different people may acquire linguistic competence through entirely different means. "Different persons growing up in the same language are like different bushes trimmed and trained to take the shape of identical elephants. The anatomical details of twigs and branches will fulfill the elephantine form differently from bush to bush, but the overall outward results are alike" (1960, p. 81).

31. As I understand it, Fodor's view is that meaning is something like the ordered pair of what he calls "broad content" and what he calls "narrow content." And "broad content" depends on what the utterer's words *causally co-vary with*—thus not just on what's "in the head." See his *Psychosemantics*, 1987.

32. See my "Meaning Holism" in Hahn and Schilpp, 1986, and the first two chapters of *Representation and Reality* (1988).
33. This is argued at length in my *Representation and Reality* (1988).
34. As Ricketts remarked in his article on the Chomsky-Quine debate (1982): "We simply have no idea as to how such distinctions are to be interpreted within any foreseeable extension of current neural theory" (p. 129).
35. See Hookway, 1988, pp. 208–210. See also Chapter 17 of the present volume.

References

Chomsky, Noam. 1969. "Quine's Empirical Assumptions." In *Words and Objections: Essays on the Work of W. V. Quine,* ed. D. Davidson and J. Hintikka, pp. 53–68. Dordrecht: D. Reidel.

_____ 1975. *Reflections on Language.* New York: Random House.

Devitt, Michael. 1981. *Designation.* New York: Columbia University Press.

Fodor, Jerry. 1987. *Psychosemantics.* Cambridge: MIT Press.

Friedman, Michael. 1975. "Physicalism and the Indeterminacy of Translation." *Nous,* 9: 353–374.

George, Alexander. 1986. "Whence and Whither the Debate between Quine and Chomsky?" *Journal of Philosophy,* 83: 489–499.

Hacking, Ian. 1983. *Representing and Intervening.* Cambridge: Cambridge University Press.

Hahn, L. E., and P. A. Schilpp, ed. 1986. *The Philosophy of W. V. Quine.* La Salle, Ill.: Open Court.

Hempel, C. G., and P. Oppenheim. 1948. "The Logic of Explanation." *Philosophy of Science,* 15: 135–175. Reprinted in *Readings in the Philosophy of Science,* ed. H. Feigl and M. Brodbeck, pp. 319–352 (New York: Appleton-Century-Crofts, 1953).

Hookway, Christopher. 1988. *Quine.* Cambridge: Polity.

Kripke, Saul. 1972. *Naming and Necessity.* Cambridge: Harvard University Press.

Lewis, David. 1984. "Putnam's Paradox." *Australasian Journal of Philosophy,* 62: 221–236.

Miller, Richard. 1988. *Fact and Method.* Princeton: Princeton University Press.

Putnam, Hilary. 1975. *Philosophical Papers,* vol. 2, *Mind, Language, and Reality.* New York: Cambridge University Press.

_____ 1978. "Realism and Reason." Presidential address to the Eastern Division of the American Philosophical Association (1976). Reprinted as Part 4 of *Meaning and the Moral Sciences* (Boston: Routledge and Kegan Paul, 1978).

_____ 1981. *Reason, Truth, and History.* New York: Cambridge University Press.

_____ 1983. *Philosophical Papers,* vol. 3, *Realism and Reason.* New York: Cambridge University Press.

_____ 1984. "Is the Causal Structure of the Physical Itself Something Physical?" In *Causation and Causal Theories,* ed. Peter A. French, Theodore E. Uehling,

Jr., and Howard K. Wettstein, *Midwest Studies in Philosophy*, 19, pp. 3–17 Minneapolis: University of Minnesota Press.

_____ 1986. "Information and the Mental." In *Truth and Interpretation: Perspectives on the Philosophy of Donald Davidson,* ed. E. Lepore. Oxford: Basil Blackwell.

_____ 1987: *The Many Faces of Realism.* La Salle, Ill.: Open Court.

_____ 1988: *Representation and Reality.* Cambridge: MIT Press.

_____ 1992. *Renewing Philosophy.* Cambridge: Harvard University Press.

Quine, Willard V. 1960. *Word and Object.* Cambridge: MIT Press.

_____ 1969a. *Ontological Relativity and Other Essays.* New York: Columbia University Press.

_____ 1969b. "Reply to Chomsky." In *Words and Objections: Essays on the Work of W. V. Quine,* ed. D. Davidson and J. Hintikka, pp. 302–311. Dordrecht: D. Reidel.

_____ 1973. *The Roots of Reference.* La Salle, Ill.: Open Court.

_____ 1976. *The Ways of Paradox and Other Essays* Cambridge: Harvard University Press.

_____ 1981. *Theories and Things.* Cambridge: Harvard University Press.

_____ 1988. *Quiddities.* Cambridge: Harvard University Press.

Ricketts, Thomas. 1982. "Rationality, Translation, and Epistemology Naturalized." *Journal of Philosophy,* 79: 117–136.

19. Probability and the Mental

In *Knowledge and the Flow of Information,* Fred Dretske[1] makes the interesting suggestion that the nature of information and of reference (a belief's being *about* an object) can be explained information-theoretically, by using the notion of probability. The perspective is that of physicalism (metaphysical materialism). In a précis of his book written for *Behavioral and Brain Science* Dretske writes that he wishes to use this idea "to deepen our understanding of mind, the chief consumer of information, in the natural order of things." The purpose of this short essay is to suggest that this program is unworkable.

Probability and Reference

The following is Dretske's suggestion: Let us say that, in a situation *S,* an event *E* gives the "information" that *some cat is on some mat (CM)* if the conditional probability of *CM* relative to *E* (in situation *S*) is one, while the absolute (or "prior") probability of *CM* in situation *S* is less than one. One could argue about the *details* of this account at many points, but this is not the sort of criticism I wish to make here. For example, one could ask whether requiring probabilities of *one* is not unrealistic—an objection Dretske himself discusses at great length. More important, in my view, one could ask whether the probabilities do not depend on what one takes to be the relevant description of the *situation*—an objection Dretske does *not* discuss. For example, if I see an eclipse, we can say—let us concede this, anyway—that the probability that the sun will reappear in a few minutes is one on the condition that I had the perception—*P* (the sun will reappear / I perceive an eclipse) = 1—but to argue that the perception gives me the *information* that the sun will reappear in a few minutes, I need, on Dretske's account, to be able to say that the prior probability that the sun would reappear in a few minutes (after a period of darkness—this is what "reappear" means here) is *less than one*. But if the "situation" is the actual astronomical situation, this is false. The probability that the sun will reappear in a few minutes is one, relative to *that* specification of the situation, whether I have the perception or not. If the "situation" is that I am in the class of all situations in which people look at the sky, then relative to *that* reference class of situations the probability that the sun will reappear in a few minutes is, indeed, much less than one. But this dependence of the probability—and hence the *information*—on what one takes to be the reference class is nowhere allowed for by Dretske.

My purpose is more abstract: I want to show that *no* account of the kind Dretske gives, that is, no account consisting of clauses which refer to probabilities, supplemented by whatever other clauses one likes, provided these employ no nonphysicalist notions (in particular, no notions which might be intentional, with the exception of the notion of probability), can be a correct account of what it is for an event E (say, the uttering of "A cat is on a mat") to refer to something (say, *cats*).

I shall give a simple "impossibility proof." The proof turns on the fact that probability obeys the following *L-Equivalence Rule:*

(To state the rule, I write $p \equiv q$ for p *is logically equivalent to* q.)

(1) $P(A, B) = P(A', B')$ whenever $A \equiv A'$ and $B \equiv B'$

(The rule follows readily from the standard De Finetti/Shimony "coherence" arguments. It is also assumed as a basic rule of inference in the standard mathematical theory of probability.)

From (1) we immediately derive
(2) $P(A, B) = P(A, B')$ whenever $B \equiv B'$ and
(3) $P(A, B) = P(A', B)$ whenever $A \equiv A'$.

What (1), (2), and (3) say is that probabilities cannot distinguish between logically equivalent states of affairs.

In my book *Reason, Truth, and History,* I showed that there are properties which I called "cat*" and "mat*" such that:[2]

(i) The things which possess the property of being cats* in the actual world are *cherries*.
(ii) The things which possess the property of being mats* in the actual world are *trees*.

(iii) *A cat being on a mat* and *a cat* being on a mat** are logically
equivalent states of affairs.[3]

In *Reason, Truth, and History* the purpose of this somewhat bizarre
construction of properties was to argue that the materialist metaphysician (the "physicalist") lacks the resources to explain why the word
"cat" doesn't refer to cats* (doesn't have the set of *cherries* as its extension in the actual world.) Can Dretske meet the challenge?

In a word, the problem is that "A cat is on a mat" refers to cats and
mats, while "A cat* is on a mat*" refers to cats* (which happen to be
cherries, in the actual world) and to mats* (which happen to be trees,
in the actual world). Yet *a cat being on a mat* and *a cat* being on a
mat** are the same state of affairs, up to logical equivalence. Knowing
what state of affairs, up to logical equivalence, a sentence corresponds
to does not tell one what its words refer to. But *probability relations*
only connect words (or rather the event of someone's uttering those
words) to states of affairs ("events" in the jargon of probability theory) not to things. Even if we can determine that the event of
someone's saying "A cat is on a mat" gives the information that some
cat is on some mat by using probability relations, that cannot tell us
that those words referred to cats and mats and not to cherries and
trees. The reason is clear: up to logical equivalence, that a cat is on a
mat is the same information as the information that a cat* is on a
mat*, and no notion that obeys the L-Equivalence Rule can fix states
of affairs more finely than logical equivalence. If you "pack in" a notion that does not individuate states of affairs more finely than logical
equivalence, you will never be able to "pack out" a notion that indi-
viduates these things more finely than logical equivalence. The reference of a sentence depends on *more* than the "information" given by
the uttering of the sentence, in Dretske's sense of "information." The
Dretske approach cannot solve the problem which has come to be
known as Brentano's, the problem of giving a physicalistic account of
reference.

Two Notions of Probability

I shall now turn to the question of the nature of probability itself. *Is*
there a notion of "probability" which is compatible with the world-
view of a "completed physics," as we might now imagine it, and
which is suitable for Dretske's purposes? I shall canvas a number of

possibilities (including ones which Dretske clearly does not have in mind), because I think the question is an interesting one.

The notion of probability does not get employed at all in General Relativity. If the theories of physics are to be appealed to as explanations of the nature of probability—and from where but physics *could* probability arise in nature, if probability is part of "the natural order of things"?—then only two physical theories combine the foundational character and the probabilistic character that a theory would have to have to be able to explain how probability comes to be a part of the natural order of things: these are, of course, statistical thermodynamics and quantum mechanics.

Statistical thermodynamics does not, of course, assert the existence of any objective "propensities" (indeterministic causal tendencies) in nature. The probabilities of Gibbsian thermodynamics are relative frequencies that we expect to be approximated in actual ensembles. Their origin is explained by the laws of time-evolution of the universe (the deterministic laws of Hamiltonian mechanics) together with the fact that certain variables were normally distributed at certain past times. In other words, relative frequencies today are explained by relative frequencies yesterday *and* mechanics. In classical physics probability distributions (relative frequencies) always *come from* probability distributions (at an earlier time). In this sense it is the case that probability is a primitive fact (the laws of thermodynamics cannot be deduced from the laws of mechanics *alone*), and simultaneously the case that probability is merely relative frequency in large ensembles. At least this is how it is in classical physics and statistical thermodynamics.

But, it may be objected, I have ignored the "lawlike character" of the frequency statements of thermodynamics, the fact that they "support counterfactuals," and so on. Surely the truth of the frequency statements is not *coincidence?*

It is *not* coincidence, *given* that appropriate other frequency statements held at a suitable past time. (On this, the long literature on the "reversibility objection" to the Boltzmann H-theorem is relevant). But whether those relative frequencies (in the distant past) are or are not ultimately anything more than "coincidence" is something on which thermodynamics as such is silent. It does *not* assert the existence of *laws* (in a strong sense) that guarantee that the entropy must always (on a cosmological time scale) keep going up; it was speculated in the nineteenth century that we may just be living in the period after a ("coincidental," if you like) entropy low, which is why the "Second Law of Thermodynamics" is valid for our epoch. Of course, one cannot imagine a world in which the "laws" of thermodynamics are different without imagining a world whose *past* has been very different for a long time, and hence a world very "dissimilar" to the actual one. That is why (on the Stalnaker-Lewis theory of counterfactuals) the laws of thermodynamics are strong enough to support counterfactuals. But that is an artifact of the way we use counterfactuals; none of this supports the idea that classical statistical thermodynamics makes any claims about "the natural order" which *require* a notion of probability stronger than relative frequency to state.

Of course, we may some day learn that the relative frequencies which Gibbsian thermodynamics predicts can be explained as arising from quantum mechanical indeterminacy operating at some past time (say, the time of the Big Bang). This would "reduce thermodynamics to quantum mechanics." But unreduced statistical thermodynamics does not, I repeat, appeal to the notion of "propensity" that quantum mechanics employs (according to Karl Popper).

The notion of relative frequency, to stick with that one for a moment, is always (by definition) relativized to an ensemble. If the notion of probability Dretske has in mind is relative frequency, or a special kind of relative frequency ("lawlike" relative frequency), then it has as many values as there are sets of situations the given situation S could be regarded as belonging to. We could, of course, specify that we are to choose an ensemble we regard as "natural," or one with respect to which we possess good statistics, or something of that kind. But in addition to other problems, this faces the fatal objection that the notion of reference ("situation we *regard* [that is, refer to] as 'natural'") has been employed in the explanation of the very notion in terms of which we intend to explicate the notion of *reference*. An intentional primitive would have been smuggled in from the start.

It is for this reason that one reviewer[4] has suggested that Dretske must have "propensities" in mind when he speaks of "probabilities." But "propensities" arise in nature only through the processes described by quantum mechanics.

Quantum mechanics does have to do with indeterminism, and in that sense with "propensity" (or "objective chance"). But Karl Popper's interpretation, that probability just is (a numerical measure of) objective chance, is extremely problematical. The problem is that the actual probabilities predicted by quantum mechanics and confirmed by experiment are incompatible with *realism*.[5] The only ways out appear to be: (1) to give up classical logic or (2) to give up *locality* (the principle that causal signals cannot propagate faster than light, which is one of the most successful basic assumptions of *quantum* field theory itself). Popper wishes to assimilate quantum mechanics to an ideal type of classical stochastic theory, but quantum mechanics has features—the "measurement problem," the problem with locality—that such an account ignores. For this reason, virtually no working physicist or philosopher studying the foundations of quantum mechanics agrees with the "propensity" interpretation.[6] In any case, if realism were to be defended with the aid of notions taken from quantum mechanics, it would first be necessary to show that there exists a satisfactory realistic interpretation of quantum mechanics itself.[7]

Another problem is that quantum mechanics is compatible with a great deal of deterministic prediction. When an eclipse will take place has no significant "indeterminacy" about it, any more than it does in classical physics, nor does the time of the sun's reappearance. Yet an eclipse can give us information. As already pointed out, whenever the probability of an event *and* of what the event is supposed to inform us of are both *one* in a situation (as will be the case whenever the deterministic approximation—the "classical limit"—is valid), it is impossible to see how Dretske's definition of "information" allows us to get information from the event. Yet we *do* get information from events in situations to which quantum mechanical indeterminacy is simply irrelevant.

The upshot is that Dretske has not given us any way of explicating *either* "reference" or "information" in a satisfactory way starting from either of the concepts of probability—relative frequency and quantum mechanical probability—that actually enter into the world picture of physics in a fundamental way.

An "Ordinary" Notion of Probability

So far I have considered only the probability notions of fundamental physics. But in daily life there is a probability notion we use in such statements as

> If someone eats arsenic, the probability that he will die is greater than .9

which seems to have a "dispositional" or "causal" component. The above statement seems to say more than that a certain frequency is greater than .9. It seems to say that eating arsenic would *cause* death in a certain proportion of cases (or, perhaps, that the people who ate arsenic and died would not have died, other things being equal, if they had not eaten the arsenic). On the "possible worlds" semantics for counterfactuals, this might be rendered by saying:

> In all worlds sufficiently similar to the actual world in which people take arsenic the frequency of deaths soon after taking the arsenic is greater than .9.

Granting that we have this kind of "dispositional" notion of probability, the comfort this affords to Dretske's effort has to be small. First of all, counterfactuals also obey the (analogue of the) L-Equivalence Rule under any fixed similarity metric. So a notion of probability based on counterfactuals must also obey the L-Equivalence Rule. And second, as I have argued elsewhere,[8] the notion of "similarity of possible worlds" is intentional on its face. To project this notion into nature is to project the relation of *explanation* into nature, to say that what it is reasonable to take as "other things being equal," what it is reasonable to take as an *important* respect of similarity between hypothetical solutions, and so on, is all "built into" nature. Such a view, I have argued, is not a successful materialist metaphysical picture, but an incoherent mixture of ideas drawn from materialism with ideas drawn from objective idealism, if not from scholasticism. One might as well say *reference* is "built into" nature and be done with it as say "similarity of possible worlds" is built into nature (if anyone is tempted).

Igal Kvart's Suggestion

Igal Kvart has recently proposed[9] that counterfactuals can be explicated without appeal to any notion of similarity of possible worlds. In fact, Kvart, like Dretske, but in a different way, proposes to start from the notion of *probability*. Kvart proposes to solve Goodman's famous problem of cotenability[10] by assuming a Popperian interpretation of quantum mechanics, in which the world is a stochastic process (in spite of the objections referred to above). A counterfactual such as

> If I lived in Boston, I would go regularly to the Boston Symphony

(imagine this said by someone who lives in Calcutta) is true, on Kvart's interpretation, just in case (1) there is a past time at which the world might (compatibly with quantum mechanics) have evolved so that the speaker would now be living in Boston; and (2) the most probable "process" (quantum mechanically speaking) which starts at that past time and results in the speaker's now living in Boston instead of Calcutta would have resulted in the speaker's going to the Boston Symphony regularly.

Does this way of evaluating counterfactuals have anything to do with how we actually evaluate the counterfactuals we hear, or with how we mean hearers to evaluate the counterfactuals we utter, however? I know *nothing* about what the most probable "process" which might have resulted in my Calcutta friend's coming to live in Boston is, and am unlikely ever to have such knowledge of the alternative quantum mechanical histories of the world. Perhaps the most probable process (I shudder to contemplate it!) is that my friend might have gotten very ill and have come to Boston to be treated by a famous doctor at the Massachusetts General Hospital. In that case he would *not* (let us suppose) have gone regularly to the Boston Symphony—he would have been too ill. But does this possibility (which, happily, did not occur) have *anything* to do with what my friend *means* when he says, "If I lived in Boston, I would go regularly to the Boston Symphony"? Surely not! What I have to know in order to know that my friend's statement is true is his musical tastes, and not the alternative quantum mechanical histories of the world from each past time.

I must acknowledge, however, a certain feeling of gratitude that I bear Kvart and Dretske for their suggestions. They have added novel and interesting ideas to the debate; no one had suggested previously using a notion of probability to give physicalistic analysis of (respectively) *reference* and *counterfactuals*. The very failure of their attempts is important philosophically: it further confirms the irreducibility of intentional properties to physicalistic ones.

Honderich and "Nomic Connection"

The notion of probability Dretske has in mind seems, in fact, closer to the ordinary language "dispositional" notion than to Kvart's quantum mechanical world histories. Rather than identify probability with relative frequency *tout court*, Dretske identifies it with "nomic" (lawlike) relative frequency. Only if a relative frequency obtains as a matter of "law" (or is "counterfactual supporting") should we take the relative frequency to be a "probability."

The notion of "nomic connection" is not explicated by Dretske. However, the suggestion that we simply take "lawlike connection" as *primitive* has recently been advanced by Ted Honderich.[11]

But *would this solve any philosophical problems at all?* Given Dretske's aim, at least (I am not sure what Honderich's aim actually is), viz., to show that probability was "there" (in the natural order) before "mind," the answer is "no." *For we understand no better how there could be "lawlike connection" independently of minds than we understand how intentional properties are possible on the world picture of metaphysical materialism.*

The problem is this: Granted that there is *a* notion of "physical necessity" and "physical possibility" that one might take as primitive in a fundamental physical theory, that notion cannot be the one that Dretske and Honderich want. What is "physically necessary" in such a theory is that one whole state of the universe (or of a "closed system") will be followed by another whole state, or that certain properties (say, mass-energy) will be conserved in such a transition, or certain symmetries maintained. But it is *not* "physically necessary" in this sense that a person who eats arsenic will die; that depends on what we specify to be the exact circumstances under which he eats the arsenic, the condition of his body, and so on. If one speaks of a "lawlike connection" between "eating arsenic" and "dying" *so described,* one is talking of an emergent relation (in fact, the relation of explanation). One is certainly not saying that it is *physically impossible* for a human being to eat arsenic and not die (that has happened).

Let me elaborate on this point. Consider an example Honderich himself uses, the conditional "if the door had not been shut, the room would not have gotten warmer." (This is what it means to say "shutting the door caused the room to get warmer" in a situation in which there is no "overdetermination," according to Honderich.) When we make such an assertion, either in those words or by saying "shutting the door caused the room to get warmer," then, according to Honderich, there is an unstated "categorical premise" that "certain conditions exist" (p. 302). "We may say that the windows were not all wide open, and so on, perhaps actually using the words and so on." This does not mean the speaker could actually *supply* the list of conditions which, together with the door's being open, make it physically impossible that the room get warmer. Honderich is explicit about this, and, in any case, it is clear that few speakers who utter such a counterfactual are ever in a position to supply such a list. This is, indeed, just the problem of *cotenability*.

Honderich uses two notions: the notion that a description ("the windows were not all wide open, and so on") *excludes* a state of affairs even if it does not entail (alone or in conjunction with the laws of mechanics) that "excluded" state of affairs does not obtain (thus "the windows were not all wide open and so on" excludes a "catastrophic" event which heats up the room), and the notion of a "simple" relation of lawlike connection.[12]

The first ("exclusion") makes no sense to me in the case where the speaker (or his community) *could not*, in fact, supply the list of conditions that prevent the room from getting warmer. What the conditions would have been if the windows had remained open is a counterfactual question (Goodman's point). To use an unexplained notion of "exclusion" is, in effect, to "solve" Goodman's problem by just taking cotenability as primitive.

To say that there exists a "simple" relation of lawlike connection between *partially specified* events—a door's remaining open and a particular room's not getting warmer—is to say that nature itself knows that a certain *part* of a total state of affairs—the door's being open—is an instigator or a *bringer-about*, as opposed to a "background condition," and knows also what a cotenable set of possible-but-not-actual conditions (a filling out of the "and so on") should have looked like. I see absolutely no difference between this and simply postulating a primitive relation of explanation in the "natural order"—a relation between events, independent of our minds, which picks out "bringers-about," "relevant conditions," and the rest. Honderich himself does not have a metaphysical materialist world picture into which all this is supposed to fit; but if a physicalist tried to take this line, I would have to say this is more a return to the twelfth-century idea of "Substantial Forms" than a successful defense of materialism.

Now, I cannot presume to saddle Dretske with Honderich's views. Dretske himself speaks of "nomic connection" as holding not between single events but between types of events (although he does not see that this makes "probability" relative to a reference class, just as much as the frequency theory does). But the problem is the same: if the classes of events "shutting doors" and "rooms getting warm" are "nomologically connected" (in certain buildings), if the relation is

"counterfactual supporting," then (on Dretske's view) there is a relation in the "natural order" which picks *the door being shut* out of the
total state of the physical system in each case. How this could be so is
even more puzzling than how reference is possible or how counterfactuals could have truth value. We have been handed dark sayings about
certain frequency relations being "lawlike" and this being a fact about
the "natural order." In fact, talk about "nomic connections" being in
"the natural order," like talk about "lawlike connection" being "simple," is . . . just talk.

I can now summarize what I have been saying quite briefly. The
world-views of what we call the "fundamental" physical theories—
quantum mechanics (if we ignore the funny role of the observer) and
Relativity Theory—like the world-views of Newtonian Gravitational
Theory and Maxwellian Electromagnetic Theory, in their time—are
the physicalist's only candidates for "the way the world is." The
whole philosophical *thrust* of physicalism is to turn such a world-view
(as it will be when physics is finally unified) into "naturalized metaphysics."
   What the physicalist does not notice is that these fundamental theories are really atypical even as scientific theories. These theories have
precise notions of "closed system," "state," and "time evolution"—
which is why these theories, and only these theories, can avoid ordinary language talk of "causing," "disposition," "propensity," and so
on. These latter notions bring in the point of view of reason, or rather
of explanation—for that is what talk of "relevant conditions" and
"bringing about" and "lawlike connection" all have to do with. It is
because the materialist does not want to take explanation as primitive
that he tries to reduce everything to the *fundamental* physical picture.
It is because that enterprise fails that he bounces back to the ordinary
language picture, and starts taking "lawlike connection," or "non-
Humean causation," or what have you as primitive (or "simple") notions, or just postulates a "similarity metric," or whatever. What I
contend is that it is neither possible to reduce reference and related
notions to such notions as "probability," "lawlike connections,"
"causation," and the like, *nor* possible to reduce *those* notions to notions that belong to the fundamental theories. In short, even if I *gave*
Dretske, Honderich, Kvart, and others their "probability," their
"nomic connection," and the rest, they could not explain *reference*;
and, what is perhaps more significant, they cannot explain the possi-

bility of these very notions from the pre-critical materialist standpoint Dretske and Kvart adopt.

In sum, I argue that the problem is not just that semantics is not reducible to physics; in my metaphysical picture *geology* (which needs ordinary language disposition talk as much as, say, evolutionary biology does) is not reducible to (fundamental) physics either.

I fear that all this is not as widely understood as it might be because we are still reacting to the logical positivist period. The fact that the Verifiability Theory of Meaning collapsed has given the other sort of scientism—materialism—a spurious respectability. But materialist monism cannot much longer keep itself afloat by just pointing out the problems with the positions of Carnap and Reichenbach. When the day comes that we examine "physicalism" on its own, and not just as an alternative to Vienna, we will soon see that it is even weaker than logical positivism.

Notes

1. Fred Dretske, *Knowledge and the Flow of Information* (Cambridge: MIT Press, 1982).

2. See my *Reason, Truth, and History* (New York: Cambridge University Press, 1981), chap. 2, and Chapter 3 (pp. 67–68) of this volume.

3. See the Appendix to *Reason, Truth, and History* for a generalization of this result.

4. See Barry Loewer's "Review of Dretske," *Philosophy of Science,* 49, no. 2 (1982), 297–300. Loewer's brief review mentions a number of difficulties I discuss in the present essay.

5. An excellent discussion is Bas von Fraassen's fine paper "The Charybdis of Realism: Epistemological Implications of Bell's Inequality," *Synthese,* 52, no. 1 (July 1982).

6. For a discussion of this alternative see my "Quantum Mechanics and the Observer" in *Realism and Reason,* vol. 3 of my *Philosophical Papers* (New York: Cambridge University Press, 1983), pp. 248–270.

7. Most physicists, in fact, regard quantum mechanical probabilities as (expected) frequencies in large ensembles upon which a measurement is performed.

8. See "Why There Isn't a Ready-made World" in *Realism and Reason* and "Why Reason Can't Be Naturalized" in the same volume.

9. See Igal Kvart, *Towards a Theory of Counterfactuals* (Indianapolis: Hackett, 1982).

10. See Nelson Goodman, *Fact, Fiction, and Forecast,* rev. ed. (Cambridge: Harvard University Press, 1983).

11. See Ted Honderich: "Causes and If *p*, even If x still *g*," *Philosophy*, vol. 57.

12. The *grounds* for asserting a subjunctive conditional are complex on Honderich's view, and he spends much time describing these. (Even these—the grounds—need subjunctive conditionals and the notion of "causal sequence" to explain.) But the truth conditions are just that what the conditional says would happen would, in fact, happen, Honderich says. The *meaning* of this is what he calls a "simple" idea (even a "clever monkey" has it, he thinks).

VI

Mind and Language

20. Artificial Intelligence: Much Ado about Not Very Much

The question I want to contemplate is this: Has artificial intelligence (AI) taught us anything of importance about the mind? I am inclined to think that the answer is no. I am also inclined to wonder, What is all the fuss about? Of course, AI may someday teach us something important about how we think, but why are we so exercised now? Perhaps it is this prospect that exercises us, but why do we think now is the time to decide what might in principle be possible? Or am I wrong: Is the "in principle" question really the important one to discuss now? And if it is, have the defenders of AI had anything important to tell us about it?

The computer model of the mind is now associated with AI, but it is not unique to AI (Noam Chomsky is not, as far as I know, optimistic about AI, but he shares the computer model with AI),[1] and the computer model was not invented by AI. If it was invented by anyone, it was invented by Alan Turing. Computer science is not the same thing as AI.

In fact, the idea of the mind as a sort of reckoning machine goes back to the seventeenth century.[2] In the early twentieth century two giants in logic—Kurt Gödel and Jacques Herbrand—first proposed the modern conception of computability (under the name "general recursiveness").[3] Turing reformulated the Gödel-Herbrand notion of computability in terms that connect directly with digital computers (which were not yet invented, however!) and also suggested his abstract computers as a model for a mind.[4] Even if Turing's suggestion should prove wrong—even if it should prove in some way more empty than it seems—it would still have been a great contribution to thinking in the way past models of the mind have proved to be great contributions to thinking—great, even if not finally successful, attempts to understand understanding itself. But AI is not recursion theory, is

391

not the theory of Turing machines, is not the philosophy of Alan Turing, but is something much more specific.

To get to AI, we first have to get to computers. The modern digital computer is a realization of the idea of a universal Turing machine in a particularly effective form—effective in terms of size, cost, speed, and so on. The construction and improvement of computers in terms of both software and hardware is a fact of life. But not everyone concerned with the design of either software or hardware is an AI researcher. However, some of what AI gets credit for—for example, the enormous improvement in the capacities of chess-playing computers—is as much or more due to discoveries of the inventors of hardware as it is to anything that might be called a discovery in AI.

Computer design is a branch of engineering (even when what is designed is software and not hardware), and AI is a subbranch of this branch of engineering. If this is worth saying, it is so because AI has become notorious for making exaggerated claims—claims of being a fundamental discipline and even of being "epistemology." The aim of this branch of engineering is to develop software that will enable computers to simulate or duplicate the achievements of what we intuitively recognize as "intelligence."

I take it that this is a noncontroversial characterization of AI. The next statement I expect to be more controversial: AI has so far spun off a good deal that is of real interest to computer science in general, but nothing that sheds any real light on the mind (beyond whatever light may already have been shed by Turing's discussions). I don't propose to spend my pages defending this last claim (Joseph Weizenbaum has already done a good job along these lines).[5] But I will give a couple of illustrations of what I mean.

Many years ago I was at a symposium with one of the most "famous names" in AI. The famous name was being duly "modest" about the achievements of AI. He said offhandedly, "We haven't really achieved so much, but I will say that we now have *machines that understand children's stories.*" I remarked, "I know the program you refer to" (it was one of the earliest language-recognition programs). "What you didn't mention is that the program has to be *revised* for each new children's story." (That is, in case the point hasn't been grasped, the "program" was a program for answering questions about a specific children's story, not a program for understanding children's stories in general.) The famous name dropped the whole issue in a hurry.

Currently the most touted achievement of AI is "expert systems."

But these systems (which are, at bottom, just high-speed data-base searchers) are not models for any interesting mental capacities.

Of course, the possibility remains that some idea dreamed up in an AI lab may in the future revolutionize our thinking about some aspect of mentation. (Parallel distributed processing is currently exciting interest as a possible model for at least some mental processes, for example. This is not surprising, however, since the model was suggested in the first place by the work of the neurologist D. O. Hebb.)[6] My point is not to predict the future but just to explain why I am inclined to ask, What's all the fuss about *now?* Why don't we wait until AI achieves something and *then* have an issue?

"In Principle"/"In Practice"

Perhaps the issue that interests people *is* whether we can model the mind or brain as a digital computer—in principle as opposed to right now—and perhaps AI gets involved because people do not sharply distinguish the in-principle question from the empirical question "Will AI succeed in so modeling the mind or brain?" It may be useful to begin by seeing just how different the two questions are.

In one way the difference seems obvious: We are tempted to say that it might be possible in principle to model the mind or brain as a digital computer with appropriate software, but it might be too difficult in practice to write down the correct software. Or it just looks as if this difference is obvious. I want to say, "Tread lightly; things are not so simple: in one sense, any physical system can be modeled as a computer."[7] The claim that the brain can be modeled as a computer is thus, in one way, trivial. Perhaps there is another more meaningful sense in which we can ask, "Can the brain be modeled as a computer?" At this point, however, all we can say is that the sense of the question has not been made clear.

But the feeling seems to be that not only is it possible in principle to model the mind or brain computationally, but there is a very good chance that we will be able to do it in practice, and philosophers (and defectors from AI like Joseph Weizenbaum) are seen as reactionaries who might talk us out of even trying something that promises to be a great intellectual and practical success. If this is how one thinks, then the gap between the two questions (and the vagueness of the in-principle question) may not seem very important in practice. Indeed, it may be of strategic benefit to confuse them.

The reasons for expecting us to succeed in practice are not clear to me, however.[8] If we are digital computers programmed by evolution, then it is important to know how to think about evolution. The great evolutionary biologist François Jacob once compared evolution to a tinker.[9] Evolution should not, Jacob wrote, be thought of as a designer who sits down and produces a lovely blueprint and then constructs organisms according to the blueprint. Evolution should rather be thought of as a tinker with a shop full of spare parts, interesting "junk," and so on. Every so often the tinker gets an idea: "I wonder if it would work if I tried using this bicycle wheel in the doohickey?" Many of the tinker's bright ideas fail, but every so often one works. The result is organisms with many arbitrary features as well as serendipitous ones.

Now, imagine that the tinker becomes a programmer. Still thinking like a tinker, he develops "natural intelligence," not by writing a Grand Program and then building a device to realize it but by introducing one device or programming idea after another. (Religious people often reject such a view, for they feel that if it is right, then our nature and history is all "blind chance," but I have never been able to sympathize with this objection. Providence may work through what Kant called "the cunning of Nature.") The net result could be that natural intelligence is not the expression of some *one* program but the expression of billions of bits of "tinkering."

Something like this was, indeed, at one time discussed within the AI community itself. This community has wobbled back and forth between looking for a Master Program (ten or fifteen years ago there was a search for something called inductive logic) and accepting the notion that "artificial intelligence is one damned thing after another." My point is that if AI is "one damned thing after another," the number of "damned things" the tinker may have thought of could be astronomical.[10] The upshot is pessimistic indeed: if there is no Master Program, then we may never get very far in terms of simulating human intelligence. (Of course, some areas that are relatively closed— for example, theorem proving in pure mathematics—might be amenable. Oddly enough, theorem proving has always been a rather underfunded part of AI research.)

A Master Program?

But why shouldn't there be a Master Program? In the case of deductive logic, we have discovered a set of rules that satisfactorily formalize valid inference. In the case of inductive logic, we have found no such rules, and it is worthwhile pausing to ask why.

In the first place, it is not clear just how large the scope of inductive logic is supposed to be. Some writers consider the "hypothetico-deductive method"—that is, the inference from the success of a theory's predictions to the acceptability of the theory—the most important part of inductive logic, while others regard it as already belonging to a different subject. Of course, if by "induction" we mean any method of valid inference that is not deductive, then the scope of the topic "inductive logic" will be enormous.

If the success of a large number (say, a thousand or ten thousand) of predictions that were not themselves consequences of auxiliary hypotheses alone (and that were unlikely in relation to what background knowledge gives us, Karl Popper would add)[11] always confirmed a theory, then at least the hypothetico-deductive inference would be easy to formalize. But problems arise at once. Some theories are accepted when the number of confirmed predictions is still very small. This was the case with the General Theory of Relativity, for example. To take care of such cases, we postulate that it is not only the number of confirmed predictions that matters but also the elegance or simplicity of the theory in question. Can such quasi-aesthetic notions as "elegance" and "simplicity" really be formalized? Formal measures have indeed been proposed, but it cannot be said that they shed any light on real-life scientific inference. Moreover, a confirmed theory sometimes fits badly with background knowledge; in some cases we conclude that the theory cannot be true, while in others we conclude that the background knowledge should be modified. Again, apart from imprecise talk about simplicity, it is hard to say what determines whether it is better in a particular case to preserve background knowledge or to modify it. And even a theory that leads to a vast number of successful predictions may not be accepted if someone points out that a much simpler theory would lead to those predictions as well.

In view of these difficulties, some students of inductive logic would confine the scope of the subject to simpler inferences, such as the inference from the statistics for a sample drawn from a population to the statistics for the entire population. When the population consists of objects that exist at different times, including future times, the present sample is never going to be a random selection from the whole population, however; so the key case is this: I have a sample that is a random selection from the members of a population who exist now (or worse, from the ones who exist here, on Earth, in the United States, in the particular place where I have been able to gather samples, or wherever). What can I conclude about the properties of future members of that population (and about the properties of members in other places)?

If the sample is a sample of uranium atoms, and the future members are in the near as opposed to the cosmological future, then we are prepared to believe that the future members will resemble present members, on the average. If the sample is a sample of people, and the future members of the population are not in the very near future, then we are less likely to make this assumption, at least if culturally variable traits are in question. Here we are guided by background knowledge, of course. This sort of example has suggested to some inquirers that perhaps all there is to induction is the skillful use of background knowledge—we just "bootstrap" our way from what we know to additional knowledge. But then the cases in which we don't have much background knowledge, as well as the exceptional cases in which what we have to do is precisely to question background knowledge, assume great importance; and here, as just remarked, no one has much to say beyond vague talk about simplicity.

The problem of induction is not by any means the only problem confronting anyone who seriously intends to simulate human intelligence. Induction—indeed, all cognition—presupposes the ability to recognize similarities among things; but similarities are by no means just constancies of the physical stimulus or patterns in the input to the sense organs. What makes knives similar, for example, is not that they all look alike (they don't), but that they are all manufactured to cut or stab (I neglect such cases as ceremonial knives here, of course). Thus, any system that can recognize knives as relevantly similar must be able to attribute *purposes* to agents. Humans have no difficulty in doing this. But it is not clear that we do this by unaided induction; we may well have a "hard-wired-in" ability to put ourselves in the shoes of other people that enables us to attribute to them any purposes we are capable of attributing to ourselves—an ability that Evolution the Tinker found it convenient to endow us with and one that helps us to know which of the infinitely many possible inductions we might consider is likely to be successful. Again, to recognize that a Chihuahua and a Great Dane are similar in the sense of belonging to the same species requires the ability to realize that, appearances notwithstanding,[12] Chihuahuas can impregnate Great Danes and produce fertile offspring. Thinking in terms of potential for mating and for reproduction is natural for us, but it need not be natural for an artificial intelligence—unless we deliberately simulate this human propensity when we construct the artificial intelligence. Such examples can be multiplied indefinitely.

Similarities expressed by adjectives and verbs rather than by nouns can be even more complex. A nonhuman intelligence might know what "white" is on a color chart, for example, without being able to see why pinkish gray humans are called white, and it might know what it is to open a door without being able to understand why we speak of opening a border or opening trade. There are many words (as Ludwig Wittgenstein pointed out)[13] that apply to things that have only a "family resemblance" to one another; there need not be one thing all x's have in common. For example, we speak of the Canaanite tribal chiefs of the Old Testament as kings although their kingdoms were probably little more than villages, and we speak of George VI as a king, though he did not literally rule England; we even say that in some cases in history, kingship has not been hereditary. Similarly (Wittgenstein's example), there is no property all games have in common that distinguishes them from all the activities that are not games.

The notional task of artificial intelligence is to simulate intelligence, not to duplicate it. So perhaps one might finesse the problems just mentioned by constructing a system that reasoned in an ideal language[14]—one in which words did not change their extensions in a context-dependent way (a sheet of typing paper might be "white$_1$" and a human being might be "white$_2$" in such a language, where "white$_1$" is color-chart white and "white$_2$" is pinkish gray). Perhaps all family-resemblance words would have to be barred from such a language. (How much of a vocabulary would be left?) But my list of difficulties is not yet finished.

Because the project of symbolic inductive logic appeared to run out of steam after Rudolf Carnap, the thinking among philosophers of science has, as I reported, run in the direction of talking about bootstrapping methods—methods that attribute a great deal to background knowledge. It is instructive to see why philosophers have taken this approach and also to realize how unsatisfactory it is if our aim is to simulate intelligence rather than to describe it.

One huge problem might be described as the existence of conflicting inductions. Here's an example from Nelson Goodman: as far as we know, no one who has ever entered Emerson Hall at Harvard University has been able to speak Inuit (Eskimo). This statement suggests the induction that if any person enters Emerson Hall, then he or she does not speak Inuit.[15] Let Ukuk be an Eskimo in Alaska who speaks Inuit. Shall I predict that if Ukuk enters Emerson Hall, Ukuk will no longer be able to speak Inuit? Obviously not, but what is wrong with this induction?

Goodman answers that what is wrong with the inference is that it conflicts with the "better entrenched," inductively supported law that people do not lose their ability to speak a language upon entering a new place. But how am I supposed to know that this law does have more confirming instances than the regularity that no one who enters Emerson Hall speaks Inuit? Through background knowledge again?

As a matter of fact, I don't believe that as a child I had any idea how often either of the conflicting regularities in the example (conflicting in that one of them must fail if Ukuk enters Emerson Hall) had been confirmed, but I would still have known enough not to make the silly induction that Ukuk would stop being able to speak Inuit if he entered a building (or a country) where no one had spoken Inuit. Again, it is not clear that the knowledge that one doesn't lose a language just like that is really the product of induction; perhaps this is something we have an innate propensity to believe. The question that won't go away is *how much of what we call intelligence presupposes the rest of human nature.*

Moreover, if what matters really is "entrenchment" (that is, the number and variety of confirming instances), and if the information that the universal statement "One doesn't lose one's ability to speak a language upon entering a new place" is better entrenched than the universal statement "No one who enters Emerson Hall speaks Intuit" is part of my background knowledge, it isn't clear how that information got there. Perhaps the information is implicit in the way people speak about linguistic abilities; but then one is faced with the question of how one decodes the implicit information conveyed by the utterances one hears.

The problem of conflicting inductions is ubiquitous even if one restricts attention to the simplest inductive inferences. If the solution is really just to give the system more background knowledge, then what are the implications for artificial intelligence?

It is not easy to say, because artificial intelligence as we know it doesn't really try to simulate intelligence at all. Simulating intelligence is only its notional activity; its real activity is writing clever programs for a variety of tasks. But if artificial intelligence existed as a real, rather than notional, research activity, there would be two alternative strategies its practitioners could follow when faced with the problem of background knowledge:

1. They could accept the view of the philosophers of science I have described and simply try to program into a machine all the information a sophisticated human inductive judge has (including implicit information). At the least, this would require generations of researchers to formalize the information (probably it could not be done at all, because of the sheer quantity of information involved), and it is not clear that the result would be more than a gigantic expert system. No one would find this very exciting, and such an "intelligence" would in all likelihood be dreadfully unimaginative, unable to realize that in many cases it is precisely background knowledge that needs to be given up.

2. AI's practitioners could undertake the more exciting and ambitious task of constructing a device that could learn the background knowledge by interacting with human beings, as a child learns a language and all the cultural information, explicit and implicit, that comes with learning a language by growing up in a human community.

The Natural-Language Problem

The second alternative is certainly the project that deserves the name "artificial intelligence." But consider the problems: To figure out what is the information implicit in the things people say, the machine must simulate understanding a human language. Thus, the idea of sticking to an artificial ideal language and ignoring the complexities of natural language has to be abandoned if this strategy is adopted—abandoned because the cost is too high. Too much of the information the machine would need is retrievable only via natural-language processing.

But the natural-language problem presents many of the same difficulties all over again. Chomsky and his school believe that a "template" for natural language, including the "semantic," or conceptual, aspects, is innate—hard-wired-in by Evolution the Tinker.[16] Although this view is taken to extremes by Jerry Fodor, who holds that there is an innate language of thought with primitives adequate for the expression of all concepts that humans are able to learn to express in a natural language,[17] Chomsky himself has hesitated to go this far. What Chomsky seems committed to is the existence of a large number of innate conceptual abilities that give us a propensity to form certain concepts and not others. (In conversation, he has suggested that the difference between postulating innate concepts and postulating innate abilities is not important if the postulated abilities are sufficiently structured.) At the opposite extreme is the view of classical behaviorism, which explains language learning as a special case of the application of general rules for acquiring "habits"—that is, as just one more bundle of inductions. (An in-between position is, of course, possible: Why should language learning not depend partly on special-purpose heuristics and partly on general learning strategies, both developed by evolution?)

Consider the view that language learning is not really learning but rather the maturation of an innate ability in a particular environment (somewhat like the acquisition of a birdcall by the young of a species of bird that has to hear the call from adult birds of the species to acquire it but that also has an innate propensity to acquire that sort of call). In its extreme form, this view leads to pessimism about the likelihood that the human use of natural language can be successfully simulated on a computer. This is why Chomsky is pessimistic about projects for natural-language computer processing, although he shares the computer model of the mind, or at least of the "language organ," with AI researchers. Notice that this pessimistic view about language learning parallels the pessimistic view that induction is not a single ability but is rather a manifestation of a complex human nature whose computer simulation would require a vast system of subroutines—so vast that generations of researchers would be required to formalize even a small part of the system.

Similarly, the optimistic view that there is an algorithm of manageable size for inductive logic is paralleled by the optimistic view of language learning. This is the idea that there is a more or less topic-neutral heuristic for learning and that this heuristic suffices (without the aid of an unmanageably large stock of hard-wired-in background knowledge or topic-specific conceptual abilities) for learning one's natural language as well as for making inductive inferences. Perhaps the optimistic view is right, but I do not see anyone on the scene, in either artificial intelligence or inductive logic, who has any interesting ideas about how the topic-neutral learning strategy works.

Notes

1. Noam Chomsky, *Modular Approaches to the Study of the Mind* (San Diego: San Diego State University Press, 1983).
2. This is well described in Justin Webb's *Mechanism, Mentalism, and Metamathematics* (Dordrecht: D. Reidel, 1980).
3. The Gödel-Herbrand conception of recursiveness was further developed by Stephen Kleene, Alonzo Church, Emil Post, and Alan Turing. The identification of recursiveness with effective computability was suggested (albeit obliquely) by Kurt Gödel in "On Formally Undecidable Propositions of *Principia Mathematics* and Related Systems I." The German original of this was published in the *Monatsheft für Mathematik und Physik*, 38 (1931), 173–198; the English translation is in *The Undecidable: Basic Papers on Undecidable Propositions, Undecidable Problems, and Computable Functions,* ed. Martin Davis (Hewlett, N.Y.: Raven Press, 1965), pp. 5–38. The idea was then explicitly put forward by Church in his classic paper on the undecidability of arithmetic, "A Note on the Entscheidungsproblem," *Journal of Symbolic Logic,* 1, no. 1 (March 1936), 40–41; correction, ibid., no. 3 (September 1936), 101–102; reprinted in Davis, *The Undecidable,* pp. 110–115.
4. Alan Turing and Michael Woodger, *The Automatic Computing Machine: Papers by Alan Turing and Michael Woodger* (Cambridge: MIT Press, 1985).
5. Joseph Weizenbaum, *Computer Power and Human Reason: From Judgment to Calculation* (San Francisco: Freeman, 1976).
6. See *Parallel Distributed Processing: Explorations in the Microstructure of Cognition,* vols. 1 and 2, ed. David E. Rummelhart, James L. McClelland, and the PDP Research Group (Cambridge: MIT Press, 1986); and D. O. Hebb, *Essay on Mind* (Hillsdale, N.J.: Lawrence Erlbaum Associates, 1980).
7. More precisely, if we are interested in the behavior of a physical system that is finite in space and time and we wish to predict that behavior only up to some specified level of accuracy, then (assuming that the laws of motion are themselves continuous functions) it is trivial to show that a step function will give the prediction to the specified level of accuracy. If the possible values of the boundary parameters are restricted to a finite range, then a finite set of such step functions will give the behavior of the system under all possible conditions in the specified range to within the desired accuracy. But if that is the case, the behavior of the system is described by a recursive function and hence the system can be simulated by an automaton.
8. In his reply to this paper, in *Daedalus,* 117, no. 1 (Winter 1988), Daniel Dennett accuses me of offering an *"a priori"* argument that success is impossible. I have not changed the text of the paper at all in the light of his reply, and I invite the reader to observe that no such *"a priori* proof of impossibility"* claim is advanced by me here or elsewhere! Although

Dennett says that he is going to explain what AI has taught us about the mind, what he in fact does is to repeat the insults that AI researchers hurl at philosophers ("We are experimenters, and you are armchair thinkers!"). On other occasions, when Dennett is not talking like a spokesman for AI but doing what he does best, which is philosophy, he is, of course, well aware that I and, for that matter, other philosophers he respects are by no means engaged in *a priori* reasoning, and that the fact that we do not perform "experiments" does not mean that we are not engaged—as he is—in thinking about the real world in the light of the best knowledge available.

9. François Jacob, "Evolution and Tinkering," *Science,* 196 (1977), 1161–1166.

10. That the number of times our design has been modified by evolution may be astronomical does not mean that the successful modifications are not (partially) hierarchically organized, nor does it mean that there are not a great many principles that explain the functioning together of the various components. To describe the alternative to the success of AI as "the mind as chaos," as Dennett does, is nonsense. If it turns out that the mind is chaos when modeled as a computer, that will only show that the computer formalism is not a perspicuous formalism for describing the brain, not that the brain is chaos.

11. Karl Popper, *The Logic of Scientific Discovery* (London: Hutchinson, 1959).

12. Note that if we had only appearances to go by, it would be quite natural to regard Great Danes and Chihuahuas as animals of different species!

13. See Ludwig Wittgenstein, *Philosophical Investigations* (Oxford: Basil Blackwell, 1958), secs. 66–71.

14. Note that this idea was one of the foundation stones of logical positivism. Although the positivists' goal was to reconstruct scientific reasoning rather than to mechanize it, they ran into every one of the problems mentioned here; in many ways the history of artificial intelligence is a repeat of the history of logical positivism (the second time perhaps as farce).

15. Nelson Goodman, *Fact, Fiction, and Forecast,* 4th ed. (Cambridge: Harvard University Press, 1983).

16. Chomsky speaks of "a subsystem (for language) which has a specific integrated character and which is in effect the genetic program for a specific organ" in the discussion with Seymour Papert, Jean Piaget, et al. reprinted in *Language and Learning,* ed. Massimo Piatelli (Cambridge: Harvard University Press, 1980). See also Noam Chomsky, *Language and Problems of Knowledge: The Managua Lectures* (Cambridge: MIT Press, 1987).

17. Jerry A. Fodor, *The Language of Thought* (New York: Thomas Y. Crowell, 1975).

21. Models and Modules: Fodor's *The Modularity of Mind*

Jerry Fodor's book *The Modularity of Mind*[1] is readable enough to be read in a day and thoughtful enough to inspire reflection for many days. Whether one agrees or not, one will undoubtedly find the model of the mind that Fodor presents a reference point against which to define one's own problems and views. But before considering Fodor's model, I should like to pay tribute to the ease and charm with which he writes. Henry James once said that a story teller should be a person who enjoys life, because story telling is a profession that aims at giving enjoyment. Jerry Fodor obviously thinks that philosophy should be enjoyable, and one senses that he enjoys life. In many ways one feels as if one were in the presence of the author as one reads this clear prose, so free of pomp and academic affectation.

This short book (145 pages, including notes and references) breaks into roughly three parts. The first part (pp. 1–46) provides background and historical antecedents for the view Fodor presents. The middle section (pp. 47–100) gives the evidence for the view, and further explanations of the content of the view, and the last part of the book qualifies and limits the view (and then draws some general morals).

The "modules" with which the book is concerned are "informationally encapsulated" subsystems of the brain; systems of subroutines which subserve special objectives connected with language and with perception, for example, the recognition and parsing of sentences and the recognition of objects and patterns. They are, in effect, special purpose computers which take "inputs" from the body's peripheral neurons, or whatever, and deliver such "outputs" as, as it might be, "there's a penny," "that's red," or "he said, *'Parlez vous français?'*" to the central processes concerned with final perceptual judgment, intelligent thinking, and so forth.

An automaton is "informationally encapsulated," in Fodor's sense, just in case the information it is allowed to use in its data processing is limited to (a) "lower-level" data (for example, the inputs from the body's "transducers") and (b) information stored in the module itself. An "informationally encapsulated" module does not have access to all of a subject's beliefs and desires. Fodor lists a number of other properties of the hypothetical "modules": They are *domain specific* ("I imagine . . . there are highly specialized computational mechanisms in the business of generating hypotheses about the distal sources of proximal stimulations. The specialization of these mechanisms consists in constraints either on the range of information they can access in the course of projecting such hypotheses, or in the range of distal properties they can project such hypotheses about, or, most usually, on both"; p. 47). The operation of these modules is *mandatory* ("You can't help hearing an utterance of a sentence [in a language you know] as an utterance of a sentence, and you can't help seeing a visual array as consisting of objects distributed in three dimensional space"; p. 53). There is only *limited central access* to the mental representations that modules compute ("what might be called 'interlevels' of input representation are, typically, relatively inaccessible to consciousness. Not only must you hear an utterance of a sentence as such, but, to a first approximation, you can hear it *only* that way"; p. 56). Modules are *fast* ("mind-boggling or otherwise, it is clear that shadowing latency is an extremely conservative measure of the speed of comprehension. Since shadowing requires *repeating* what one is hearing, the 250 msec. of lag between stimulus and response includes not only the time required for the perceptual analysis of the message, but also the time required for the subject's integration of his verbalization"; p. 61). *Modules have "shallow" outputs* ("In general, the more constrained the information that the outputs of a perceptual system are assumed to encode—the shallower their outputs—the more plausible it is that the computations that effect the encoding are informationally encapsulated"; p. 87). Modules are associated with *fixed neural architecture* ("Neural architecture, I'm suggesting, is the natural concomitant of informational encapsulation"; p. 99). Modules exhibit *characteristic and specific breakdown patterns* (p. 99). And modules have an ontogeny which exhibits "characteristic pace and sequencing" (although Fodor writes that "the issues here are so very moot, and the available information is so fragmentary, that I offer this point more as a hypothesis than as a datum"; p. 100).

The evidence Fodor cites is of several kinds. He begins with evidence that various sorts of integration (including the recognition of senten-ces as sentences) are (a) extremely fast and (b) not under the control of volition (see the passages just cited from pp. 47, 53, 56, 61). We cannot help hearing speech as speech. We cannot help seeing one line in the Müller-Lyer illusion as longer than the other (even if we have measured the lines ourselves). Perhaps the most important aspect of this section of the book, however, is the criticism and reinterpretation of various experiments that have been taken to support what Fodor calls "New Look" psychology, that is, the theory (associated with Bruner) that there is large-scale determination of appearances by prior belief and by background knowledge in general. A kind of experiment to which Fodor devotes considerable attention is represented by the following example: The subject hears, "Because he was afraid of elec-tronic surveillance, the spy carefully searched the room for bugs." We know from previous research, Fodor tells us, that the response latency for "bugs" (in a word/non-word decision task) will be faster in this context, where it is relatively predictable, than in a neutral context, where it is acceptable but not predictable (has low "Cloze value").

If, instead of measuring reaction time for word/non-word decisions on "bugs," we present (flashed on a screen that the subject can see) a different word belonging to the same "semantic field," for instance, "microphones," then "microphones" too will exhibit facilitation. A New Look psychologist would say that the subject has figured out (using as much background knowledge as necessary) that either the word "bugs" or the word "microphones" could occur in the context he has heard. "But the appearance is misleading," Fodor writes (p. 79), "for Swinney's data show that if you test with 'insects' instead of 'microphones' you get the same result: facilitation as compared to a neutral context. Consider what this means. 'Bugs' has two para-phrases: 'microphones' and 'insects.' But though only one of these is contextually relevant, *both are contextually facilitated*. This looks a lot less like intelligent use of contextual/background information to guide lexical access. What it looks like instead is some sort of associa-tive relation among lexical forms (between, say, 'spy' and 'bug'); a relation pitched at a level of representation sufficiently superficial to be *in*sensitive to the semantic content of the items involved." On Fodor's theory the language-recognition module comes to "know" that "bug-microphone" and "bug-insect" are associated. When the word "bug" is activated (by association with "spy"), the semantically irrelevant word "insect" is also activated just as much as the "relevant" word "microphone." What seemed to be a sophisticated bit of reasoning on the part of the subject turns out to be, so to speak, a "clever hack" (that is, a subroutine that does something that *looks* intelligent), to use the jargon of computer programmers. On Fodor's view, New Look psychology is not totally wrong, but the New Look psychologists badly misconceived the significance of their findings.

The third part of the book argues that "modules" are not going to play much of a role in explaining judgment ("belief fixation"), because of problems posed by the holism of belief fixation (almost any information can, in the right context, become relevant to any judgment), and because of the nonmonotonicity of conformation (if evidence *e* confirms hypothesis *h,* it does not follow that the conjunction of *e* with *e′* will also confirm *h*). Rather than opting for more modules (or for modules which are not "input devices"), which would seem to be the natural guess from a computational point of view, Fodor suggests rather mysteriously that the part of the brain responsible for belief fixation may be characterized by "equipotentiality."

What is one to make of all this? Certainly the evidence for the presence of subroutines, or "clever hacks," is extremely suggestive, and if it proves robust we will have to think of the brain as containing Fodor's "modules." However, certain questions remain.

Fodor speaks of the language module as "cognizing" the "denotations" of words. I found this surprising, since the data and hypotheses just described would seem to me to suggest a different view. Fodor is, after all, trying to explain as much as he can by means of "informationally encapsulated" subroutines. The "bug-microphone-insect" example suggests that the "language recognition module" may well generate plausible "readings" of sentences without having internalized anything like the full conceptual roles of the words those sentences contain. Why then should we attribute anything like knowledge of the meanings *or* denotations of words to the language recognition module itself?

The problem may come into sharper focus if we recall some of the ideas that have become central to much twentieth-century philosophy of language. Three such ideas are:

(1) *Conceptual Linkage*
It would be odd to ascribe to someone the full mastery of the concept *gold* if that person did not know that gold was a metal, or full

mastery of the concept *chair* if that person did not know that chairs
are artifacts, that their "purpose" is to serve as seats for one person,
that they are normally portable, that they always or almost always
have backs, and so on. To have a concept one must have a suitable
range of other concepts. (This is somewhat obscured by the practice
of charity to the linguistically immature. Babies are said to "understand" words they use when very little of their conceptual powers and
relations have in fact been learned.)

(2) *Meaning Holism*

(The label "meaning holism" was suggested—for Quine's views, not
his own—by Michael Dummett.)[2] This doctrine was a reaction
against the idea, which can be suggested by a simplistic interpretation
of conceptual linkage, that the meaning of a term depends on the
knowledge of a set of "analytic sentences" containing the term and
containing, also, the most central of the other terms to which it is
linked conceptually. As developed by Donald Davidson[3] (building on
Quine's doctrines),[4] the doctrine of meaning holism holds that, while
it is true that a speaker must have learned a large number of sentences
and procedures of belief fixation connected with those sentences before we can talk of "meanings" at all in connection with his utterances, there is no single definite set of such sentences which one *must*
be able to use in order to have a particular "concept." Rather, it is a
matter of interpretation. The interpreter implicitly constructs a
"meaning theory" which assigns a particular interpretation to a word,
say, "gold," or "chair," partly on the basis of the meanings assigned
to the *other words in those sentences by that very meaning theory,*
and on the basis of the situations in which those *other* words are used.
Interpretation, according to meaning holists, is a matter of trade-offs,
and these trade-offs are "where rational, pragmatic," in a phrase of
Quine's. There are no precise rules for interpretation.

(3) *Causal Theory of Reference*

According to many theorists, the denotations of words do not depend simply on their "conceptual roles," or inferential powers and
conceptual connections to other words, but on what *causes* one to use
those words (causes either directly or through the mediation of other
speakers). A particular substance—*Au*—has a great deal to do, directly and indirectly, with our using the words "gold," "or" (in
French), "chrysos" (in Greek), and so on, at all, and no account of
how the reference of these words is fixed that ignores the causal links
between bits of *Au* and certain uses of these words can be correct.

· · ·

Now, meaning holism suggests that grasp of typical concepts *(dog, chair)* cannot be attributed to any "organ" less sophisticated than a speaker/believer with a rich fund of other concepts and beliefs. In particular, it suggests that grasp of such concepts should be attributed *not* to the "language module" or the "vision module" itself, but only to the whole person (including the—unmodularized, according to Fodor—belief fixation component). It also suggests that "meanings" and "concepts" have identity conditions that are as vague and context sensitive as the practice of making pragmatic trade-offs in interpretation, that is, they are not suitable constructs for theorizing in a psychology that hopes to link with neurological research, or even in a psychology that hopes to identify its constructs with computational features of the brain. Neither the idea that concepts cannot be attributed to modules, nor the idea that concepts (or "contents," as Fodor prefers to call them) are not (isolable) *entities* at all, is palatable to Fodor. In this book he does not discuss these matters (although his language presupposes definite views), but in a paper written since the book, Fodor[5] argued that, while belief fixation is indeed holistic, the identity conditions for denotations may *not* be. "Suffice it to repeat the lesson that causal semantic theories have recently been teaching us," he writes (p. 12), "*viz.* that holism may not be true. Specifically, it may not be true that (all) the semantical properties of sentences (/beliefs) are determined by the theoretical networks in which they are embedded."

Now, *I* don't think that this is what "causal semantic theories" have been teaching us at all.

Consider the following simplified form of the "causal theory of reference": a word (or token utterance of a word) refers to X only if the word-token is connected to X by a "causal chain of the appropriate type." No one ever believed that this is right for all word-tokens (let alone for complex phrases). Even apart from such deep and controversial cases as the terms "number," "space-time point," and "inaccessible cardinal," there is the mundane fact that we can refer to things with which we are not causally connected. What supporters of the causal theory suppose is that there is a class of basic cases for which the causal idea is correct. And this is not implausible. If I am the nearsighted Mr. Magoo, and I fail to realize that the baby I am baptizing is a pillow, then the name "John" which I bestow will not normally end up being the name of the pillow; what usually happens is that I simply fail to bestow a reference on the name "John" at all. And if tiger-seeings, cases of being "eaten by a tiger," and so on, are all false rumors, lies, illusions, hallucinations, and so on, then the word *tiger* does not refer to anything either. In the case of proper names and natural kind words, there has to be something of the right sort connected to some uses of the word by a causal chain of the appropriate type or the word does not refer.

This observation helps fill a lacuna in the account Quine gives of interpretation. According to Quine (who credits the term and the idea to N. L. Wilson) there is a "Principle of Charity" in interpretation which directs us to interpret one another so that many of the interpretees' beliefs (on certain sorts of topics) come out true. Can the Principle of Charity play the role that is played by the idea that we should require the presence of causal chains of the appropriate type before assigning a referent to a proper name or an extension to a natural kind word? The answer is that it cannot. Even if a reference assignment made *all* of my utterance true, if it did so by assigning to my utterances truth conditions to which, as states of affairs in the world, I have no causal access whatsoever, it would be simply unbelievable.

Of course, from the fact that causal considerations are relevant to interpretation it does not follow that one can really give a causal *theory* of reference, and I do not myself believe in the possibility of such a theory. This is why (in company with Donald Davidson) I would speak of causal *constraints* upon reference rather than a causal *theory of* reference. Even if something *is* the cause of many of my beliefs containing a given word—as, for example, textbooks are the cause of many of my beliefs about "electrons"—it does not follow that that cause is the referent of a word in those beliefs. "Electrons are flowing through wires" does not contain any word that refers to textbooks. Assigning "electron" the class of textbooks as extension would not cohere with an acceptable theory of the language as a whole, a theory which would satisfy the constraints on reasonable interpretation for all of the sentences of the language; so textbooks are not what "electron" refers to. Note what this example shows: causal access does not suffice for certain sentences to be about things; it shows, as Richard Boyd has emphasized, that we need the *sort* of causal access that we are prepared to count as *cognitive* access.

Back to Jerry Fodor. Explaining how causal theories of reference supposedly defeat holism, he writes, "The point is, of course, that their attachment to the world, unlike their inferential role, is something that symbols(/beliefs) have *severally;* so that, when such attachments are at issue, the morals of holism don't apply."[6] Now, the causal process which leads to my uttering "Look out, there's a tiger!" on a given occasion may be non-holistic. I am always prepared to be instructed by psychologists. But it is not true that the external cause which triggers this process admits of only one description, independently of my language and speech dispositions as a whole. I can describe the cause as the presence of a tiger, or as the presence of a large and ferocious wild beast, or as the presence of light rays of a certain kind impinging on my retina, or as tigerhood being exemplified again. (The Shawnee are reported to say "forkpattern being exemplified by hand action mine in the bush," or morphemes to that effect, when they mean to convey what we would convey with "I pull the branch aside.") The "attachment to the world" of my utterance does not determine what it denotes. Even if we regard all the descriptions I mentioned as descriptions of the same event (as a well-known theory of Davidson's would have them be, perhaps), still those descriptions "parse" the event into objects, properties, and relations in different ways. Denotation depends on the appropriate parsing of the "attachment to the world" into objects, properties, and relations; and what is an appropriate "parsing" of an event for the purpose of interpreting a given utterance which describes that event depends on what the reference-assignment we contemplate will do to the interpretation of the other sentences of the language in which those words occur, and on how the other words of the language—words which do not occur in the given utterance at all—will interact with the words which occur in the given utterance when they occur together with those words in still other sentences and contexts.

In (unpublished) lectures and discussions Fodor has suggested meeting the problems just mentioned by (1) restricting the causal theory he has in mind to *Mentalese* ("Mentalese" is the hypothetical innate "language of thought" of Fodor's book by that name) and (2) postulating a fixed "parsing" of events in the world into objects and properties (one that would rule out, for example, "tigerhood being exemplified again!" as a possible "parsing" of the situation of there being a tiger in front of one) which would correspond, in some way, to the structure of Mentalese. This would still leave a problem which Fodor calls the "problem of error": a speaker may be caused to say, "There's a witch," whenever he sees a malign-looking old woman, but it does not follow that the extension of "witch" (or of the corresponding representation in Mentalese) is the class of malign-looking old women; it may be that the intended extension is the (empty) class of old women with magical powers of an evil kind, and that the speaker is making the error of believing that all the malign-looking old women he sees are in this class. To meet this difficulty Fodor suggests that denotation is fixed *not* by the causal attachments which actually obtain between a speaker and the world, but by the causal attachments which *would* obtain under circumstances which are relevantly cognitively ideal for humans. I find counterfactual conditionals about what would trigger an utterance under ideal cognitive circumstances extremely problematical, not to say remote from practice, and I find it difficult to see that such speculations have any "pay-off" for either psychology or philosophy. In any case, it is clear that Fodor's view that an informationally encapsulated subroutine can have "concepts" presupposes a number of doctrines which are not explicitly spelled out in *The Modularity of Mind,* doctrines which many readers who might be sympathetic with aspects of the model would find bizarre.

Let us now examine how Fodor's perceptual modules—say, the visual modules—are supposed to work. This is where I feel most in the dark about Fodor's theory, and where I hope future publications by Fodor may further clarify what the theory is.

I have the impression that the visual module is supposed to have statements—say, "That is a dog"—as outputs. (The reason I hesitate is that Fodor also speaks of "appearances," and "appearance" suggests something like an image.) I will assume that "That is a penny," "That is a book," "That is a dog" are the sorts of "outputs" that the visual module might "print out."

Wherefrom is the "visual perception module" supposed to get these notions? Even if they are innate, they are hardly likely to be *in the module* from birth. What Fodor seems to think is that certain simple and quasi-geometric notions are congenital with the module itself, while certain other "phenomenologically salient" concepts, such as "dog," are somehow constructed by the module out of its primitives. But why *should* the module construct "dog" or "penny"?

Consider the parallel problem for the language module. The language module has to recognize the occurrence of the word "penny" when someone says it (I assume we are dealing with a native speaker of English). Where does it get this notion? Here Fodor gives us the answer: the language module has the capacity to learn the language given enough time. No synchronic process enables the speaker to recognize "penny" instantaneously and without prior exposure to the language, but a slow-moving diachronic process has already been completed in the language organ of an adult English speaker. (That this slow-moving process involves *only* the "language module," and not the "diachronic penetration" of the language module by material from general intelligence, is something which Fodor and I have debated in the past, albeit in a new guise, but I refuse to argue about the innateness hypothesis here.) It seems that, if the visual module is to recognize such cultural artifacts as pennies, books, telephones, and so on, it cannot just rely on its "built-in" stock of notions (built in to the visual module itself, that is); it must, rather, allow itself to be "diachronically penetrated" by material that the language module learns, or selected portions of such material. (Or, perhaps, the visual and other perception modules and the language module all get modified simultaneously and interdependently in the diachronic process of learning the language.)

Anyway, when the diachronic process is completed, and the visual module has acquired the "notion" of a penny, what is it that it has acquired? It has certainly not acquired the full use of the word "penny" in the language, by just the arguments Fodor used to establish encapsulation. (If the visual module had the full use of "equal length" as applied to lines, and every adult speaker had sophisticated knowledge of the Müller-Lyer illusion, then the lines would *look* equal in length, and so on.) It seems that what the module has acquired, and all it can plausibly have acquired, is a procedure for telling that there's a "penny-looking thing" out there. In short—I know that Fodor doesn't like "procedural semantics" but here goes—it looks as if the visual module has a procedural semantics for a primitive replica of the notion of a penny. The visual module *doesn't* have the notion of a penny at all; it *simulates* it (much as a "clever hack" might simulate it in AI).

If all this is right—and I have been speculating madly about what Fodor's model comes to—then it is hard to see what the criticism of "New Look" psychology comes to. "Penny" may be available to the visual module as the result of diachronic penetration, but then "X-ray tube" could be too. Not every word in the language could correspond to a "clever hack" (a subroutine which does something which looks "intelligent") in the visual module, but that is hardly surprising, since not everything has a visual appearance. One doesn't have to agree with Norwood Russell Hanson's wilder statements about how much scientists "observe" to think that one can observe X-ray tubes, nor is there anything in the idea of informational encapsulation to go against the idea that one can observe X-ray tubes. In fact, if someone has spent years looking through electron microscopes, couldn't he have acquired a knowledge of how iron atoms *look? Couldn't* this be encapsulated in this visual module?

Fodor's response would presumably be "no." Fodor seems to think that only the most "phenomenologically salient" categories can be encapsulated. Thus he cites evidence (p. 94 of *The Modularity of Mind*) that "dog" is phenomenologically more "basic" than "poodle" or "mammal." This is why he thinks that "dog" can, so to speak, get into the visual module itself while "poodle" requires more "central" kinds of unconscious inference. This seems totally unconvincing to me. "Mammal" cannot correspond to a recognition-heuristic in the way that, say, "tree" can because there is no such thing as "the" appearance of a mammal. Whales, dogs, and bats do not have enough in common, appearance-wise, for the notion of "the typical look" of a mammal to get off the ground. But poodles *do* have a typical look, and I see no reason to think that it would be harder to build up a subroutine to recognize poodles than it was to build up a subroutine (or family of subroutines—Great Danes and Chihuahuas *don't* have much in common, appearance-wise, either!) for recognizing dogs. Citing experiments to show that "dog" is more "salient" than "poodle" just seems beside the point to me; why couldn't a more salient and less salient category *both* be "informationally encapsulated"?

It might be useful to discuss a case we can all imagine. Those of us who have been playing chess (well or badly) for a while can *see* when our king is in check (well, sometimes). Does Fodor want to claim that the visual module only prints out "There's a rook *there*," "There's a king *there*," "The rook and the king are on the same file," and we then infer (by an *un*encapsulated inference process) that the king is in check? I find this implausible. On the other hand, if one can, as I suppose, "encapsulate" chess perception up to a point as one can encapsulate penny perception and telephone perception, then why not iron atom perception?

Let me review the points made in this discussion so far. The first point is that the denotation of our terms depends on the whole structure of our language and belief system, and not just on the "causal attachments." The second point is that what is in, say, the visual module is not the whole notion of, say, a penny, but at best a procedure for telling when there is a penny there which works in a normal class of cases, a "clever hack." Even such a procedure cannot be in the visual module *ab initio,* but must be developed diachronically. The conclusion I would draw from the two points together is that no presently surveyable limit to the class of "observation concepts" is set by the structure of the visual module (and the other perception modules) itself. Even if the structure of the visual module determines which "appearances" I could learn to recognize, the class of *notions* that might go with those appearances is not limited by anything in the module itself.

Fodor believes that the scientific use of "observe" (and the ordinary language use of "observe") are very different from the notion of observation that is relevant to psychological theory. But if, as I have been arguing, Fodor's theory does not really exclude the possibility of someone's learning to "see iron atoms" (when he is looking through an electron microscope or, perhaps, even in a situation in which he knows it isn't *really* an electron microscope, but still the "appearance" is produced), then mightn't this psychological possibility—if it is a psychological possibility—help illuminate the scientific use of "observe"? And doesn't the scientific use of "observe" (and the painter's use, and the chess player's use) suggest that this sort of inquiry should not be prejudged? Could it end up being the case that, even in Fodor's sense, people "observe" pretty much what they ordinarily *say* they observe?

So far I have granted Fodor something that I now wish to call into question—not really challenge, but just call into question. That is the assumption that what the vision module, to stick to my example, produces is (or determines) "appearances." My problem is this. When I see a TV tube, for example, it is true that I don't see what Hanson would have had me see (for example, that electrons flow from there and strike that and the magnetic field does so and so to the beam and . . .). But the appearance isn't (I am introspecting unashamedly now) just a neutral appearance. There is a sort of "televisiony" *gestalt* associated with the appearance. To shift the example, I can imagine a battery that looks very much like a quarter. But I don't see a quarter (the coin) as a battery—I can't see it as a battery, even when I try. William James expressed this by speaking sometimes of a conceptual "penumbra" around an appearance, and sometimes of appearances as "thought and sensation fused."

Now, if there is anything to this phenomenon, then there are various ways Fodor might account for it. I have already mentioned very simple associations—for example, "bug-microphone" and "bug-insect"—which are supposed to get introjected into the language module itself (another example of "diachronic penetration"). There could be associations of this kind—relatively "encapsulated" associations, or even associations between items in different modules—which account for the feeling of a conceptual penumbra around perceptions (as when I see something as a quarter, or see that my king is in check). But then it might turn out that the output of the visual module is not anything as *conscious* as the word "appearance" suggests. It is dangerous to assume that a phenomenon as complex as an "appearance" is to be accounted for by the automatic action of just one "informationally encapsulated" module.

In conclusion, let me say that the notion of an informationally encapsulated subroutine is an important one, and that Fodor has performed an important service by calling attention to diverse jobs that the notion can do and to psychological phenomena that it may help illuminate. It is the restriction of informational encapsulation to a few systems—the systems Fodor calls "input systems"—and, within those systems, to only a few sorts of recognition tasks—the tasks that go with highest perceptual salience—that I find implausible. Neither the arguments nor the experiments cited in this book seem to me to give one much reason to think that there is not much *more* "informational encapsulation" than Fodor thinks. In particular, the claim that the *central* processes cannot be broken down into subroutines which are, individually, informationally encapsulated must be false if the computational model of the brain is the right one at all. But it is no mean accomplishment to have produced as suggestive a picture as this book presents even if the picture is one that one accepts (as a whole) at one's peril.

Notes

1. This paper was first published as a review of Fodor's book *The Modularity of Mind* (Montgomery, Vt.: Bradford Books, 1983). All page references in the text are to this book.
2. Michael Dummett, "What Is a Theory of Meaning, II," in G. Evans and J. McDowell, *Truth and Meaning* (Oxford: Oxford University Press, 1976).
3. Donald Davidson, "Truth and Meaning," *Synthese,* 17 (1967), 304–323.
4. W. V. Quine, *Word and Object* (Cambridge: MIT Press, 1960).
5. Jerry Fodor, "Observation Reconsidered," written in 1983, but published in Fodor's *A Theory of Content* (Cambridge: MIT Press, 1990).
6. Ibid.

22. Reflexive Reflections

Today conferences on cognitive science regularly feature the presence of philosophers in large numbers. These philosophers have very different visions of the functioning of the mind. Jerry Fodor and Daniel Dennett have represented[1] the different schools of thought with the aid of a geographical metaphor: in the metaphor there is an "East Pole," which is MIT, and views which are less "propositional" or less "digital" (or both) than MIT views are described as being more or less "West Coast" or simply "West," according to the extent of the deviation from MIT Orthodoxy. Cute as this is, it is also seriously misleading. For MIT itself is not a unified entity: if (as Dennett suggests) Jerry Fodor is the Pope of the High Computationalist Church, Noam Chomsky shows alarming signs of heresy! And Fodor himself has many different views, and the controversies which separate him from say, Kosslyn, are not at all the same as the controversies which separate him from Searle, or as the controversies which separate him from Dreyfus.

The first dogma of the High Computationalist Church, as represented by Fodor, pictures the mind as "computing" in a formalized language with a classical or "Fregian" quantificational structure. In addition, the church believes that *standard belief-desire explanations (practical syllogisms, in the Aristotelian sense) correspond (more or less step by step) to reasonings that take place in "Mentalese"* (as the hypothetical "language of thought" is called). But this second dogma of High Computationalism is independent of the first dogma. Finally, Fodor's book *The Language of Thought* suggested that the "contents" which are believed or desired by a human being correspond to the same formulas in the language of thought no matter what natural language the particular human believer-desirer happens to speak. Again, this third dogma of High Computationalism is independent of

416

dogmas *one* and *two*. It would be nice to report that the philosophers at these conferences regularly succeed in distinguishing these three crucial dogmas, but the sad fact is that usually the atmosphere is "all or none": either the brain will compute in a way that satisfies all three dogmas, or it will compute more like an "analog" device than a "digital" one. Or so the disputants seem to believe.

Now, I am not myself terribly interested in guessing what future science will discover. I do not believe that Peter Hempel regards it as the function of a philosopher to become a heated partisan of one side or the other in an ongoing scientific controversy. Here (in what I believe to be the spirit of Hempel) I will rather try to see what philosophical bearing work by computationalist psychologists and artificial intelligence researchers might in principle have. (When I say "in principle," I don't, of course, mean "independently of *all* possible changes in our conceptual scheme." I have argued elsewhere that the philosopher does not have to choose between claiming an *apodictic* status for his work and claiming merely to be making empirical predictions or guesses.)

I want to begin by proving a theorem. The theorem says that if there is a complete computational description of our own prescriptive competence—a description of the way our minds ought to work,[2] where the ought is the ought of deductive logic or inductive logic—then we cannot come to believe that that description is correct when our minds are in fact working according to the description. By "inductive logic" I mean simply the theory of non-demonstrative inference, or rather of demonstrative *and* non-demonstrative inference—for technical reasons, it is useful to treat deductive logic as a part of "inductive logic." (Noam Chomsky objects to the notion of "induction"—like Karl Popper he doesn't believe there is any such thing, though not for Popper's reasons—but even Chomsky doesn't deny that we have a capacity to reason non-demonstratively.) Like everything else, this theorem can be viewed either optimistically or pessimistically. The optimistic interpretation is: *Isn't it wonderful! We always have the power to go beyond any reasoning that we can survey and see to be sound. Reflexive reflection cannot totally survey itself.* The pessimistic interpretation is: *How sad!*

The proof is not hard. For the mathematical case, consider the totality of functions which are provably recursive according to M, where M is a recursive description of our prescriptive mathematical competence. Add a subroutine to M which lists separately the "index," or computational description, of each partial recursive function that M ever proves to be total (as M is allowed to run). Let D be the "diagonal function" corresponding to this effective list of total recursive functions (that is, the function whose value at the argument n is one greater than the value of the nth function in the list of provably recursive functions generated by M on the argument n). A mathematician (even a beginner) can prove infinitely many functions to be general recursive (total partial recursive) functions. So if M is a reasonable simulation of prescriptive human mathematical competence, there will be infinitely many functions that M can prove to be general recursive, and hence infinitely many computational indices listed by the subroutine we added to M. In this case, the diagonal function D will itself be total, as is easily seen. So, if we were able to prove by intuitively correct mathematical reasoning that M is a sound proof procedure, we would also be able to prove that D is a total recursive function. But this proof will not itself be one which is captured by any proof in the proof-scheme M, unless M is inconsistent! (If this proof were listed by M, then D would itself be a function listed by the subroutine, say, the kth. Then, from the definition of D, we would have $D(k) = D(k) + 1$! Note that this is a proof of the Gödel Incompleteness Theorem.) Thus no formalization of human mathematical proof ability can both be sound *and* be such that it is part of human mathematical proof ability to *prove* that soundness.

The more important case for our purposes is the case of our full prescriptive competence: our competence to think thoughts that (from the point of view of a normative notion of justification) are the ones *we should* think on given evidence. In a paper[3] I published back in 1963, I showed that if the relation of confirmation in an inductive logic I is recursive, then, given the computational description of that relation one can effectively produce another inductive logic I' which is more adequate than I, in the sense that by using I' one can discover every regularity that I would enable one to discover and additional regularities that I would not enable one to discover, even if the data went on agreeing with them forever, besides. (Subsequently a number of related theorems were proved by other workers in the field of recursive inductive logic.) Again, the moral is that if I is such that one could discover that I is sound by an intuitively correct (demonstrative or non-demonstrative argument), then one would be justified in using not only I but I', and hence in regarding a certain regularity as well confirmed (if the evidence supported it for a long time), even though the prediction that the next instance one observes will conform to the regularity is not "confirmed" in the sense of I but is only "confirmed" in the sense of I'. Since the conclusion that the regularity is one that we are justified in betting on is intuitively sound, and I does not register this conclusion, then that already shows that I is not a formalization of our *entire* prescriptive inductive competence.

One might think to escape this problem by discovering someday that the logic which formalizes our "inductive" (non-demonstrative as well as demonstrative) reasoning is itself *non-recursive*. If the relation of being confirmed by given evidence (or confirmed to a degree r by given evidence) is not itself a recursive one, then the above theorem may be irrelevant (for example, if the confirmation relation is recursive in the jump of the complete recursively enumerable set, then the inductive logic may, in principle, be strong enough to discover any regularity that is expressible as a Boolean combination of recursively enumerable predicates).[4] But I don't think that this is really a significant "escape hatch."

To see why it isn't (apart from the difficulty of seeing what it would mean *psychologically* to postulate that our "competence" is high enough up in the arithmetic hierarchy to avoid the "diagonal" argument referred to), consider the following version of the Montague-Kaplan "Paradox of the Knower": Let P be a mathematical description of our full (demonstrative and non-demonstrative) prescriptive competence, and consider the "Computational Liar," that is, the sentence:

(I)   There is no evidence on which acceptance of the sentence (I) is justified.[5]

Or rather the sentence of mathematics which is the Gödelian equivalent of (I). (It follows from Gödel's work that there is a sentence of mathematics which is true if and only if P does not accept that very sentence on any evidence, where P is any procedure itself definable in mathematics—not necessarily a recursive procedure.[6]

Now, suppose there is evidence e on which the acceptance of (I) is justified. Then (I) is false. And (I) is a sentence of pure mathematics.[7] So there is a situation in which we are prescriptively justified in believing a mathematically false sentence, if P really is a sound formalization of our prescriptive competence! Many would consider this already to show that a correct P cannot lead to the acceptance of (I) (for example, the standard De Finetti-Shimony requirements rule out assigning a degree of confirmation less than 1 to a mathematical truth on any evidence). But let us go on for a bit. Suppose there is evidence *e* on which the acceptance of (I)'s negation is justified. Then, either there is also (presumably different) evidence on which the acceptance of (I) is justified, or else (I)'s negation is a mathematically false sentence that *P* instructs us to accept on certain evidence. (N.B.: the negation of (I) asserts there is evidence on which the acceptance of (I) is justified.) In the first case (there is different evidence on which the acceptance of (I) is justified), we know by the previous argument that (I) is a mathematically false sentence, and so there is again evidence—the "different evidence" mentioned—on which *P* licenses the acceptance of a mathematical falsehood, namely, (I) itself. In the second case, I just noted that (I)'s negation is a mathematical falsehood that *P* licenses us to accept (an "omega inconsistency"). So, if *P* "converges" on the argument (I), that is, if the question "Is the acceptance of (I) justified or not?" is one to which there is ever an answer (relative to some evidence *e* or other) which we are *P*-justified in giving, then there is evidence relative to which *P* licenses us to accept a mathematical falsehood.

The point about this argument is that it is *obvious*. If there is *anything* that I am "competent" to believe, anything I am "justified" in believing, it is that *P* cannot converge on the argument (I) without licensing me to believe what is mathematically false. So it certainly seems that the following should be accepted as a *criterion of adequacy* on the acceptability of any proposed formalization of our prescriptive competence:

(II) The acceptance of a formal procedure *P* as a formalization of (part or all) of prescriptive inductive (demonstrative and non-demonstrative) competence is only justified if one is justified in believing that *P* does not converge on *P*'s own Gödel sentence (I) as argument.

So if *P* is a description of a procedure the mind uses which is prescriptive for human minds, then we cannot come to see that this procedure *is* prescriptive for us as long as our minds function as *P* says they should.

To spell this out: Suppose our minds are functioning in accordance with *P*. We assume that it is rational to accept the above criterion of adequacy (II). If we come to believe that *P* is a complete and correct description of our own prescriptive competence, then, since we believe

(II), we have to believe that *P* does not converge on (I); but this is just to believe (I)! And, since we believe that this belief is justified and that justified belief is formalized by *P*, we are committed to believing that *P* tells us to believe (I)—that is, *P* converges on (I)! But now we have a contradiction.

So a description of our "competence" which is complete and prescriptive is certainly an impossible task for us. (It might be an interesting task for Alpha Centaurians. Unfortunately, if the Alpha Centaurians figured out what our prescriptive description is, either we could not understand it or we would not be justified in trusting their statement!)

"Competence" and Prescriptive Competence

The natural reaction of a cognitive scientist to all this is, "So what? No one working on computational models of human reasoning aims at anything *like* a complete description of how we *ought* to think. What does any of this have to do with cognitive science?"

I certainly agree that this is the right reaction, or, rather, that it is right as long as "cognitive science" is really pursued as empirical model building and not as philosophy by other means. But it is not at all clear how much "cognitive science" really *is* empirical model building in any serious sense, as opposed to the making of claims about the philosophical significance of various research programs. As soon as someone talks about "explaining what makes thought thought" or "capturing the nature of thought"—and one hears such talk constantly at "cognitive science" get-togethers—it is perfectly legitimate to point out that one thing that "makes thought thought" as opposed to "cows mooing" (in Frege's phrase) is that thought is sound or unsound, that is, thought has normative epistemic properties. Perhaps these properties are not what "makes thought thought" either (although I myself cannot believe that an account of "what makes thought thought" which leaves us in the dark as to the nature and origin of these properties could be correct). Perhaps it is rather semantic properties such as *reference* and *truth* that "make thought thought." But computer models of the *brain* are certainly not going to give us an account of *reference* or *truth*. Can a description of thought which by its own admission does not aim at describing the difference between correct and incorrect ways of thinking (in either an epistemic or a non-epistemic sense of "correct") have relevance to the philosophical problems that worried Frege or the philosophical problem that worried Brentano?

It is important to remember that the Orthodox or East Pole version of computationalism has taken the distinction between "competencee" and "performance" to be *the* fundamental distinction on which cognitive science is based. Now, Gilbert Harman and, at least some of the time (in conversation), Noam Chomsky have *suggested that our idealized or "competence" description is a description of correct thinking in the normative sense.*[8] If they are right, then it follows from what has just been shown that the aim of cognitive science is to describe something that it is in principle impossible for us to describe completely. Some may not be bothered by this: I can agree with the sort of realist who is willing to believe that either there are or there aren't intelligent extraterrestrials, for example, even if it is beyond human competence to know the fact of this matter. But the impossibility of knowing what our "competence description" is looks like a different sort of impossibility, an impossibility of knowing a we-know-not-what. Tying the notion of "competence" which figures in descriptive cognitive science, the notion of a best idealization for predictive and descriptive purposes, to the notion of competence which figures in inductive logic does not look like a good way to go!

Fodor and the Language of Thought

The next subject I want to discuss is an argument I employed a number of years ago[9] against the idea of an innate Language of Thought. (The connection between the subjects in this paper will become evident shortly, I hope.) The Pope of High Church Computationalism—Jerry Fodor—has declared that all concepts are innate (including, obviously, *sparkplug*). His argument in *The Language of Thought* was that the brain must be thought of as containing at least one agent (or "homunculus" in Dennett's widely used terminology) who formulates such hypotheses as

> (III)   When Jones says "the sparkplug needs to be replaced," what he says is true if and only if the sparkplug needs to be replaced.

The homunculus cannot have the ability to formulate arbitrary hypotheses of this kind unless its innate vocabulary (the vocabulary of

"Mentalese") includes *every* concept a human being could learn to understand. So Fodor's incredibly strong version of the Innateness Hypothesis—the thesis that the *Oxford English Dictionary is innate*—must be true.

Criticizing this argument, I argued that the brain need not think the way I do. When I take the "intentional stance" toward my own brain, I may, for example, attribute to it the knowledge that there are certain representations in the left-eye stripes of areas 17 and 18, and certain representations in the right-eye stripes of the same areas, and also attribute to it certain inferences to the existence of external objects with certain colors and shapes at a certain distance from my body, but it would be false to say "Hilary Putnam knows that there are such and such representations stored in such and such places in areas 17 and 18." Similarly, the homunculi in my brain may formulate hypotheses of the following form, even if Hilary Putnam does not:

(IV)   If I want this body to speak like Jones, I should print out "The sparkplug needs to be replaced" whenever I have neural inputs of type blahblah.

And such hypotheses can be stated in a machine language much weaker than the *O.E.D.* An analogy which it is useful to keep in mind in this connection is the analogy to a Turing machine which proves theorems in Zermelo-Fraenkel set theory. The program of such a machine can be stated in machine languages much weaker than set theory.

When I published this argument, Fodor replied, fairly enough, that no one has ever written down rules which will enable an organism to use a language correctly which are stated in such "procedural" terms. Of course he is right. But this is not surprising. If we could state rules for using language without making *any* normative blunders, then we could survey our own prescriptive competence, and I have just argued that we know on Gödelian grounds that we cannot do that. In fact, we have no reason to think we can even come close to describing our own prescriptive competence. How close we can come is, of course, an empirical question; but the Gödelian results remind us that, no matter how smart we may be, it is always possible that we are not smart enough to answer the question "What makes you so smart?" Of course, we may be able to write programs for "reasoning" which simulate the errors that people make on the tests designed by Amos Tversky and Kahneman! But anyone who thinks that such test results show "there isn't much to human intelligence" should consider the well-known difficulties with simulating informal context-bound reasoning in artificial intelligence (the "Frame Problem").

If we cannot solve the "Frame Problem," and we content ourselves with a "menu" of rules for speaking which leads to "printing out" utterances that are irrational, our simulated speaker will look "dumb"; if the utterances are too obviously unwarranted, they will be linguistically "deviant." We will not have "captured understanding." So it's *Catch 22!* Unless we do something which is Utopian, Jerry Fodor can say, "You haven't shown that it is possible to understand a natural language by following rules that are statable in machine language." It doesn't follow from this that what is going on at the cause-effect level is Fodorian inferences (inferences of the form (III) carried out with the aid of a language of thought in which "all concepts are innate").

"Cognitive Science" and Intentionality

I repeat that one thing that none of the programs in "cognitive science" speak to is the problem of intentionality. Of course the *philosophers* who write on issues in cognitive science do have theories of intentionality. Perhaps the best known is Dennett's "intentional stance" theory. If this theory is supposed to extend to semantics—if the idea is that sentences are always true or false only relative to the "stance" of some interpreter or other—then I don't see any way to even understand this without retreating to a "redundancy" theory of truth and reference for the language of the last interpreter in the chain. And such a theory seems to me inherently unstable. Redundancy theories, I claim, collapse into either magical theories of reference or linguistic idealism. (This is a provocative remark.)

The reason that none of the computationalist programs speak to the issue of intentionality, or the problem of the nature of understanding as a deep philosophical problem, is that, as I remarked, the disputants use notions like "competence" in ways that vacillate between modest descriptive ambitions and total emptiness. As I have already pointed out, what it means to speak of "the" competence of human beings in the prescriptive sense is wholly unclear. I don't mean that the common-sense conception of an ability to tell sound from unsound reasoning to some extent is unclear; I mean that the idea that this ability is really something like a "competence" in the Chomskian sense, and thus something to be ideally represented by a computational description, is wholly unclear. Certainly a description of it would be beyond our powers. And even if those Alpha Centaurians do have a description of it, we can restate the problem of intentionality by asking "what singles out *their* description of my brain as *the* competence description?" (as Kripke has emphasized).[10]

Even if we waive the central issue, and even if we pretend that the Alpha Centaurians do have that description D, the description of *their* prescriptive competence isn't D but, say, D'. And the description of beings intellectually powerful enough to find *that* out is D''. And . . . So it seems that the description of the "competence" of an arbitrary physically possible "intentional system" capable of understanding a language would be an infinite disjunction D *or* D' or D'' or . . . and that no physically possible intentional system would be able to survey (give a rule for writing down) *this* disjunction. So the problem, if it is a problem, and it certainly feels like a problem, "What do all instances of understanding have in common?" isn't addressed—isn't either "solved" or "dissolved." Anyone who feels that this is the real issue will have to look to something other than "cognitive science"—to metaphysics[11] or to Wittgensteinian therapy or to the possibility of a new alternative in philosophy. His or her bafflement won't be relieved by any amount of marvelous work in artificial intelligence.

Notes

1. Attributing this geographical metaphor to Fodor "several months ago in a heated discussion at MIT," Dennett writes, "He was equally ready, it turned out, to brand people at Brandeis or Sussex [in England] as West Coast. He explained that just as when you're at the North Pole, moving away from the pole in any direction is moving south, so moving away from MIT in any direction is moving West. MIT is the East Pole and from a vantage point at the East Pole, the inhabitants of Chicago, Pennsylvania, Sussex, and even Brandeis University in Waltham are all distinctly Western in their appearance and manners. Boston has long considered itself the Hub of the Universe; what Fodor has seen is that in cognitive science the true center of the universe is across the Charles, but not so far upriver as the wild and wooly ranchland of Harvard Square." "The Logical Geography of Computational Approaches (A View from the East Pole)," read at the MIT Sloan Conference, May 19, 1984.

2. It might seem to some readers that cognitive science need not be concerned with representing how we *ought* to reason at all (as opposed to describing

how we do reason, "warts and all"). But in *Representation and Reality* (Cambridge: MIT Press, 1988), pp. 11–15, 87–89, and 116–119, I argue that there is an intimate connection between our inductive competence ("general intelligence") and our ability to *interpret* one another's words and sentences. Unless we can say in computational terms when two sentences *should be* interpreted as synonymous, we cannot have a *computational criterion for sameness of belief* (of any other propositional attitude). But such a computational criterion is precisely what is required by functionalist theories of mind.

3. "Degree of Confirmation and Inductive Logic," pp. 270–292 of my *Philosophical Papers,* vol. 1, *Mathematics, Matter, and Method* (New York: Cambridge University Press, 1975; 2nd ed., 1979). First published in *The Philosophy of Rudolf Carnap,* ed. P. A. Schilpp (La Salle, Ill.: Open Court, 1963).

4. The Boolean combinations of recursively enumerable predicates are exactly the k-trial predicates (proved in my "Trial and Error Predicates and the Solution to a Problem of Mostowski," *Journal of Symbolic Logic,* 30 [March 1965], 49–57). It is an easy theorem that the k-trial predicates can be enumerated by a single trial-and-error predicate. The statement in the text follows from the fact (proved in the same paper) that the trial-and-error predicates are exactly the predicates in $\Sigma_2 \cap \Pi_2$; that is, the predicates recursive in the jump of the complete recursively enumerable set. For a general survey of results on the incompleteness of inductive logics belonging to various classes in the arithmetic hierarchy, see Peter Kugel's "Induction, Pure and Simple," in *Information and Control,* 35 (December 1977), 276–336.

5. If the inductive logic P uses the notion of degree of confirmation rather than the notion of acceptance, then one replaces "is justified" by "has instance confirmation greater than 0.5," as in the paper cited in n. 2.

6. The relevant part of Gödel's work is now generally referred to as the "Diagonal Lemma." This says that if $F(x)$ is any one-place predicate definable in the language of a system of mathematics which contains number theory, then there is a sentence of that very language which is true if and only if the Gödel number of that sentence does not satisfy the predicate $F(x)$. In this form, the Diagonal Lemma was not, of course, stated in Gödel's 1934 paper, but all the techniques needed for the proof are present in that paper.

7. Note that if I have evidence on which the acceptance of (I) is justified, then (I) is not only mathematically false but *obviously* so. So even someone who thinks acceptance of a mathematically false sentence is *sometimes* justified should not think that acceptance of *this* mathematical falsehood is.

8. Harman makes this suggestion in "Metaphysical Realism and Moral Relativism: Reflections on Hilary Putnam's *Reason, Truth, and History,*" *Journal of Philosophy,* 79 (1982), 568–575.

9. In "What Is Innate and Why?" in *Language and Learning,* ed. Massimo Piatelli (Cambridge: Harvard University Press, 1980), pp. 287–309.

10. Cf. his *Wittgenstein on Rules and Private Language* (Cambridge: Harvard University Press, 1982).

11. Recent metaphysical ideas suggested in this connection are the idea that the "broad content" of a sentence depends on the state of affairs it "causally covaries with across possible worlds" when the speaker is (in relevant respects) in an ideal epistemic relation to his environment (Fodor in "Narrow Content and Meaning Holism," unpublished), and the idea that certain sets of external things are "elite," that is, that it is in the nature of things that these sets are the ones to which our kind terms have a singled-out correspondence (David Lewis in "New Work for a Theory of Universals," *Australasian Journal of Philosophy,* 61 [1984], 343–377). Notice that these suggestions are purely *philosophical*—they in no way depend on computer modeling!

23. Reductionism and the Nature of Psychology

Reduction

A doctrine to which most philosophers of science subscribe (and to which I subscribed for many years) is the doctrine that the laws of such "higher-level" sciences as psychology and sociology are reducible to the laws of lower-level sciences—biology, chemistry—ultimately to the laws of elementary particle physics. Acceptance of this doctrine is generally identified with belief in "The Unity of Science" (with capitals), and rejection of it with belief in vitalism, or psychism, or, anyway, something *bad*.

In this paper I want to argue that this doctrine is wrong. In later sections, I shall specifically discuss the Turing machine model of the mind—and the conception of psychology associated with reductionism and with the Turing machine model.

I shall begin with a logical point and then apply it to the special case of psychology. The logical point is that from the fact that the behavior of a system can be *deduced* from its description as a system of elementary particles, it does not follow that it can be *explained* from that description. Let us look at an example and then see why this is so.

My example will be a system of two macroscopic objects, a board in which there are two holes, a square hole one inch across and a round hole one inch in diameter, and a square peg, a fraction less than one inch across. The fact to be explained is: The peg goes through the square hole, and it does not go through the round hole.

One explanation is that the peg is rigid and the board is rigid. The peg goes through the hole that is large enough and not through the hole that is too small. Notice that the microstructure of the board and the peg is irrelevant to this explanation. All that is necessary is that, whatever the microstructure may be, it be compatible with the fact that the board and the peg are rigid.

Suppose, however, we describe the board as a cloud of elementary particles (for simplicity, we will assume these are Newtonian elementary particles) and imagine ourselves given the position and velocity at some arbitrary time t_0 of each one. We then describe the peg in a similar way. (Say the board is "cloud B" and the peg is "cloud A".) Suppose we describe the round hole as "region 1" and the square hole as "region 2." Let us say that by a heroic feat of calculation we succeed in proving that "cloud A" will pass through "region 2" but not through "region 1." Have we explained anything?

It seems to me that whatever the constraints on explanation may be, one constraint is surely this: The relevant features of a situation should be brought out by an explanation and not buried in a mass of irrelevant information. By this criterion, it seems clear that the first explanation—which points out that the two macro-objects are rigid and that one of the two holes is big enough for the peg and the other is not—*explains* why "cloud A" passes through "region 2" and never through "region 1," while the second—the deduction of the fact to be explained from the positions and velocities of the elementary particles, their electrical attractions and repulsions, and so on—fails to *explain*.

If this seems counterintuitive, it is for two reasons, I think. (1) We have been taught that to *deduce* a phenomenon in this way is to *explain* it. But this is ridiculous on the face of it. Suppose I deduce a fact F from G and I, where G is a genuine explanation and I is something irrelevant. Is G and I an *explanation* of F? Normally we would answer, "No. Only the part G is an explanation." Now, suppose I subject the statement G and I to logical transformations so as to produce a statement H that is mathematically equivalent to G and I (possibly in a complicated way), but such that the information G is, practically speaking, virtually impossible to recover from H. Then on any reasonable standard the resulting statement H is *not* an explanation of F; but F is deducible from H. I think that the description of the peg and board in terms of the positions and velocities of the elementary particles, their electrical attractions and repulsions, and so on, is such a statement H: The relevant information, that the peg and the board are (approximately) rigid, and the relative sizes of the holes and the peg are buried in this information, but in a useless way (practically speaking). (2) We forget that explanation is not *transitive*. The microstructure of the board and peg may explain why the board and the peg are rigid, and the rigidity is part of the explanation of the fact that the peg passes through one hole and not the other, but it does not follow that the "raw" microstructure—the assemblage of positions, velocities, and so on—explains the fact that the peg passes through one hole and not the other. Even if the microstructure is not presented "raw," in this sense, but the information is *organized* so as to give a *revealing* account of the rigidity of the macro-objects, a revealing explanation of the rigidity of the macro-objects is not an explanation of something which is explained by that rigidity. If I want to know why the peg passes through one hole and not the other in a context in which I already know that these macro-objects are rigid, then the fact that one hole is bigger than the peg all around and the other isn't is a complete explanation. That the peg and the board consist of atoms arranged in a certain way, and that atoms arranged in that way form a rigid body, and so on, might also be an explanation—although one which gives me information (*why* the board and the peg are rigid) I didn't ask for. But at least the relevant information—the rigidity of the board and the peg, and the relation of the sizes and shapes of the holes and the pegs—is still *explicit*. That the peg and the board consist of atoms arranged in a certain way *by itself* does *not* explain why the peg goes through one hole and not the other, even if it explains something which in turn explains that.

The relation between (1) and (2) is this: An explanation of an explanation (a "parent" of an explanation, so to speak), generally contains information I, which is irrelevant to what we want to explain, and in addition it contains the information which *is* relevant, if at all, in a form that may be impossible to recognize. For this reason a parent of an explanation is generally not an explanation.

What follows is that certain systems can have behaviors to which their microstructure is *largely* irrelevant. For example, a great many facts about rigid bodies can obviously be explained just from their *rigidity* and the principles of geometry, as in the example just given, without at all going into why those bodies are rigid. A more interesting case is the one in which the higher-level organizational facts on which an explanation turns themselves depend on *more* than the microstructure of the body under consideration. This, I shall argue, is the typical case in the domain of social phenomena.

For an example, consider the explanation of social phenomena. In *Capital* Marx uses certain facts about human beings—for example, that they have to eat in order to live and that they have to produce in order to eat. He discusses how, under certain conditions, human production can lead to the institution of *exchange,* and how that exchange in turn leads to a new form of production, production of commodities. He discusses how production of commodities for exchange can lead to production of commodities for profit, to wage labor and capital.

I assume that something like this is right. How much is the microstructure of human beings relevant? The case is similar to the first example in that the *specifics* of the microstructure are irrelevant: What is relevant is, so to speak, an organizational result of microstructure. In the first case the relevant organizational result was rigidity. In the present case, the relevant organizational result is intelligent beings able to modify both the forces of production and the relations of production to satisfy both their basic biological needs and those needs which result from the relations of production they develop. To explain how the microstructure of the human brain and nervous system accounts for this intelligence would be a great feat for *biology;* it might or might not have relevance for political economy.

But there is an important difference between the two examples. Given the microstructure of the peg and the board, one *can* deduce the rigidity. But given the microstructure of the brain and the nervous system, one cannot deduce that *capitalist* production relations will exist. The same creatures can exist in pre-capitalist commodity production, or in feudalism, or in socialism, or in other ways. The laws of capitalist society cannot be deduced from the laws of physics plus the description of the human brain: They depend on "boundary conditions" which are *accidental* from the point of view of physics but essential to the description of a situation as "capitalism." In short, the laws of capitalism have a certain *autonomy* vis-à-vis the laws of physics: They have a physical *basis* (men have to eat), but they cannot be deduced from the laws of physics. They are compatible with the laws of physics; but so are the laws of socialism and of feudalism.

This same autonomy of the higher-level science appears already at the level of biology. The laws that collectively make up the theory of evolution are not deducible from the laws of physics and chemistry; from the latter laws it does not even follow that one living thing will live for five seconds, let alone that living things will live long enough to evolve. Evolution *depends on* a result of microstructure (variation in genotype); but it also depends on conditions (presence of oxygen, and so on) which are *accidental* from the point of view of physics and chemistry. The laws of the higher-level discipline are deducible from the laws of the lower-level discipline together with "auxiliary hypotheses" which are *accidental from the point of view of the lower-level discipline*. And *most of the structure at the level of physics is irrelevant from the point of view of the higher-level discipline;* only certain *features* of that structure (variation in genotype, or rigidity, or production for profit) are relevant, and these are specified by the higher-level discipline, not the lower-level one.

The alternative, "mechanism *or* vitalism," is a false alternative. The laws of human sociology and psychology, for example, have a basis in the material organization of persons and things, but they also have the autonomy just described vis-à-vis the laws of physics and chemistry.

The reductionist way of looking at science both springs from and reinforces a specific set of ideas about the social sciences. Thus human biology is relatively unchanging. If the laws of psychology were deducible from the laws of biology and (also unchanging) reductive definitions, then it would follow that the laws of psychology are also unchanging. Thus the idea of an unchanging human nature—a set of structured psychological laws, dependent on biology but independent of sociology—is presupposed at the outset. Also, each science in the familiar sequence—physics, chemistry, biology, psychology, sociology—is supposed to reduce to the one below (and ultimately to physics). Thus sociology is supposed to reduce to psychology, which in turn reduces to biology via the theory of the brain and nervous system. This assumes a definite attitude toward sociology, the attitude of methodological individualism. (In conventional economics, for example, the standard attitude is that the market is shaped by the desires and preferences of individual people; no conceptual apparatus even exists for investigating the ways in which the desires and preferences of individuals are shaped by economic institutions.)

Besides supporting the idea of an unchanging human nature and methodological individualism, there is another and more subtle role that reductionism plays in one's outlook. This role may be illustrated by the effect of reductionism on biology departments: When Crick and Watson made their famous discoveries, many biology departments fired some or all of their naturalists! Of course, this was a crude mistake. Even from an extreme reductionist point of view, the possibility of explaining the behavior of species via DNA mechanisms "in principle" is very different from being able to do it in practice. Firing someone who has a lot of knowledge about the habits of, say, bats, because someone else has a lot of knowledge about DNA is a big mistake. Moreover, as we saw above, you *can't* explain the behavior of bats, or whatever species, *just* in terms of DNA mechanisms—you have to know the "boundary conditions." That a given structure enables an organism to fly, for example, is a function not just of its strength, and so on, but also of the density of the earth's atmosphere. And DNA mechanisms represent the wrong level of organization of the data—what one wants to know about the bat, for example, is that it has mechanisms for producing supersonic sounds and mechanisms for "triangulating" on its own reflected sounds ("echolocating").

The point is that reductionism comes on as a doctrine that breeds respect for science and the scientific method. In fact, what it breeds is physics worship coupled with neglect of the "higher-level" sciences. Infatuation with what is supposedly possible "in principle" goes with indifference to *practice* and to the actual structure of practice.

I don't mean to ascribe to reductionists the doctrine that the "higher-level" laws could be arrived at in the first place by deduction from the "lower-level" laws. Reductionist philosophers would very likely have said that firing the naturalist was a misapplication of their doctrines, and that neglect of direct investigation at "the level of sociology" would also be a misapplication of their doctrine. What I think goes on is this: Their claim that higher-level laws are deducible from lower-level laws and *therefore* higher-level laws are *explainable* by lower-level laws involves a mistake (in fact, two mistakes). It involves neglect of the *structure* of the higher-level explanations, which reductionists never talk about at all, and it involves neglect of the fact that *more than one* higher-level structure can be realized by the lower-level entities (so that what the higher-level laws are cannot be deduced from *just* the laws obeyed by the "lower-level" entities). Neglect of the "higher-level" sciences themselves seems to me to be the inevitable corollary of neglecting the structure of the explanations in those sciences.

Turing Machines

In previous papers,[1] I have argued for the hypothesis that (1) a whole human being is a Turing machine and (2) that psychological states of a human being are Turing machine states or disjunctions of Turing machine states. In this section I want to argue that this point of view was essentially wrong, and that I was too much in the grip of the reductionist outlook just described.

Let me begin with a technical difficulty. A *state* of a Turing machine is described in such a way that the machine can be in exactly one state at a time. Moreover, memory and learning are represented in the Turing machine model not as acquisition of new states, but as acquisition of new information printed on the machine's tape. Thus if human beings have any states at all which resemble Turing machine states, those states must (1) be states the human can be in at any time, independently of learning and memory, and (2) be *total* instantaneous states of the human being—states which determine, together with learning and memory, what the next state will be, as well as totally specifying the present condition of the human being ("totally" from the standpoint of psychological theory, that means).

These characteristics already establish that *no* psychological state in any customary sense can be a Turing machine state.[2] Take a particular kind of pain to be a "psychological state." If I *am* a Turing machine, then my present "state" must determine not only whether I am having that particular kind of pain, but also whether I am about to say "three," whether I am hearing a shrill whine, and so forth. So the psychological state in question (the pain) is not the same as my "state" in the sense of *machine state,* although it is possible (so far) that my machine state *determines* my psychological state. Moreover, *no* psychological theory would pretend that having a pain of a particular kind, being about to say "three," or hearing a shrill whine, all belong to *one* psychological state, although there could well be a machine state characterized by the fact that I was in it only when simultaneously having that pain, being about to say "three," hearing a shrill whine, and so on. So, even if I am a Turing machine, my machine states are *not* the same as my psychological states. My description *qua* Turing machine (machine table) and my description *qua* human being (via a psychological theory) are descriptions at two totally different levels of organization.

So far it is still possible that a psychological state is a large disjunction (practically speaking, an almost infinite disjunction) of machine states, although no *single* machine state is a psychological state. But this is very unlikely when we move away from states like "pain" (which are almost *biological*) to states like "jealousy" or "love" or "competitiveness." Being jealous is certainly not an *instantaneous* state, and it depends on a great deal of information and on many learned facts and habits. But Turing machine states are instantaneous and are independent of learning and memory. That is, learning and memory may cause a Turing machine to go into a state, but the identity of the state does not depend on learning and memory, whereas, no matter what state I am in, identifying that state as "being jealous of X's regard for Y" involves specifying that I have learned that X and Y are persons and a good deal about social relations among persons. Thus jealousy can be neither a machine state nor a disjunction of machine states.

One might attempt to modify the theory by saying that being jealous equals either being in State A and having tape c_1 or being in State A and having tape c_2 or . . . or being in State B and having tape d_1 or being in State B and having tape d_2 or . . . or being in State Z and having tape y_1 . . . or being in State Z and having tape y_n—that is, by letting the individual disjuncts be conjunctions of a machine state and a tape (that is, a total description of the content of the memory bank). Besides the fact that such a description would be literally infinite, the theory is now without content, for the original purpose was to use the machine table as a model of a psychological theory, whereas it is now clear that the machine table description, although different from the description at the elementary particle level, is as removed from the description via a psychological theory as the physico-chemical description is.

I now want to make a different point about the Turing machine model. The laws of psychology, if there *are* "laws of psychology," need not even be *compatible* with the Turing machine model, or with the physico-chemical description, except in a very attenuated sense. And I don't have in mind any version of psychism.

As an example, consider the laws stated by Hull in his famous theory of rote learning. Those laws specify an analytical relationship between *continuous* variables. Since a Turing machine is wholly discrete, those laws are formally incompatible with the Turing machine model. Yet they could perfectly well be correct.

The reader may at this point feel annoyed, and want to retort: Hull's laws, if "correct," are correct only with a certain accuracy, to a certain approximation. And the *exact* law has to be compatible with the Turing machine model, if I am a Turing machine, or at least with the laws of physics (if materialism is true). But there are two separate and distinct elements to this retort. (1) Hull's laws are "correct" only to a certain accuracy. True. And the statement "Hull's laws are correct to within measurement error" is perfectly compatible with the Turing machine model, with the physicalist model, and so forth. It is in this attenuated sense that the laws of any higher-level discipline have to be compatible with the laws of physics: It has to be compatible with the laws of physics that the higher-level laws could be true *to within the required accuracy*. But the *model* associated with the higher-level laws need not *at all* be compatible with the model associate with the lower-level laws. Another way of putting the same point is this. Let L be the higher-level laws as normally stated in psychology texts (or texts of political economy, or whatever). Let L* be the statement "L is approximately correct." Then it is only L* that has to be compatible with the laws of physics, not L. (2) The *exact* law has to be compatible with the Turing machine model (or anyway the laws of physics). False. There need not *be* any "exact" law—any law *more* exact than Hull's—at the psychological level. *In each individual case of rote learning*, the exact *description* of what happened has to be compatible with the laws of physics. But the best statement one can make in the general case, at the psychological level of organization, may well be that Hull's laws are correct to within random errors whose explanation is beneath the level of *psychology*.

The general picture, it seems to me, is this: Each science describes a set of structures in a somewhat idealized way. It is sometimes believed that a non-idealized description, an "exact" description, is possible "in principle" at the level of physics; be that as it may, there is not the slightest reason to believe that it is possible at the level of psychology or sociology. The difference is this: If a model of a physical structure is not perfect, we can argue that it is the business of *physics* to account for the inaccuracies. But if a model of a social structure is not perfect, if there are unsystematic errors in its application, the business of accounting for those errors may or may not be the business of *social science*. If a model of, say, memory in functional terms (for example, a flow chart for an algorithm) fails to account for certain memory losses, that may be because a better psychological theory of memory (different flow chart) is called for, or because on certain occasions memory losses are to be accounted for by biology (an accident in the brain, say) rather than by psychology.

If this picture is correct, then "oversimplified" models may well be the best possible at the "higher" levels. And the relationship to physics is just this: It is compatible with physics that the "good" models on the higher levels should be *approximately* realized by systems having the physical constitution that human beings actually have.

At this point, I should like to discuss an argument proposed by Hubert Dreyfus. Dreyfus believes that the functional organization of the brain is not correctly represented by the model of a digital computer. As an alternative he has suggested that the brain may function more like an *analog* computer (or a complicated system of analog computers). One kind of analog computer mentioned by Dreyfus is the following: a map of the railway system of the United States made out of *string* (the strings represent the railroad lines, the knots represent the junctions). Then to find the shortest path between any two junctions—say, Miami and Las Vegas—just pick up the map by the two corresponding knots and pull the two knots away from each other until a string between them becomes straight. That string will represent the shortest path.

When Dreyfus advanced this in conversation, I rejected it on the following grounds: I said that the physical analog computer (the map) really was a digital computer, or could be treated as one, on the grounds (1) that matter is atomic and (2) that one could treat the molecules of which the string consists as gears which are capable of assuming a discrete number of positions vis-à-vis adjacent molecules. Of course, this only says that the analog computer can be well approximated by a system which is digital. What I overlooked is that the atomic structure of the string is *irrelevant* to the working of the analog computer. Worse, I had to invent a microstructure which is just as fictitious as the idealization of a continuous string of constant length (the idea of treating molecules as gears) in order to carry through the redescription of the analog device as a digital device. The difference between my idealization (strings of gears) and the classical idealization (continuous strings) is that the classical idealization is relevant to the functioning of the device *as* an analog computer (the device works *because* the strings are—*approximately*—continuous strings), while my idealization is *irrelevant* to the description of the system on *any* level.

Psychology

The previous considerations show that the Turing machine model need not be taken seriously as a model of the functional organization of the brain. Of course, the brain has digital elements—the yes-no firing of the neurons—but whether the larger organization is correctly represented by something like a flow chart for an algorithm or by something quite different we have no way of knowing right now. And Hull's model for rote learning suggests that some brain processes are best conceptualized in terms of continuous rather than discrete variables.

In the first section of this paper I argued that psychology need not be deducible from the laws describing the functional organization of the human brain, and in the previous section I used a psychological state (jealousy) to illustrate that the Turing machine model *cannot* be correct as a paradigm for psychological theory.

In short, there are two different questions which have got confused in the literature: (1) Is the Turing machine model correct as a model for the functional organization of the human brain? and (2) Is the Turing machine model correct as a model for psychological theory? Only on the reductionist assumption that psychology *is* the description of the functional organization of the brain, or something very close to it, can these two questions be identified.

My answer to these two questions so far is that (1) there is little evidence that the Turing machine model is correct as a model of the functional organization of the brain and (2) the Turing machine model *cannot* be correct as a model for psychological theory—that is, psychological states are not machine states nor are they disjunctions of machine states. But what *is* the nature of psychological states?

The idea of a fixed repertoire of emotions, attitudes, and so on, independent of culture is easily seen to be questionable. An attitude that intellectuals are very familiar with, for example, is the particular kind of arrogance that one person feels toward other people because he does mental work and they do manual work. An attitude we would find it almost *impossible* to imagine would be the following: one person's feeling superior to others because the first person cleans latrines and the others do not. This is not the case because people who clean latrines are innately inferior, nor because latrine-cleaning is inherently degrading. Given the right social setting, perhaps a kibbutz, this attitude which we cannot now imagine would be commonplace. Not only are the particular attitudes and emotions we feel culture-bound, but so are the *connections*. For example, in our society, the arrogance of mental workers is frequently associated with competitiveness; but in a "mandarin" society it might be associated with the attitude that one is above competing, while being no less arrogant. This might be a reflection of the difference between living in a society based on competition and living in a society based on a feudal hierarchy.

Anthropological literature is replete with examples that support the idea that emotions and attitudes are culture-dependent. For example, there have existed and still exist cultures in which private property and the division of labor are unknown. An Arunha cannot imagine the precise attitude with which Marie Antoinette said, "Let them eat cake," nor the precise attitude of Richard Herrnstein toward the "residue" of low IQ people, which, he says, is being "precipitated," nor the precise attitude which still makes me and thousands of other philosophers feel tremendous admiration for John Austin for distinguishing "Three Ways of Spilling Ink" ("intentionally," "deliberately," and "on purpose"). Nor can we imagine many of the attitudes which Arunha feel, and which are bound up with *their* culture and religion.

This suggests the following thesis: Psychology is as underdetermined by biology as it is by elementary particle physics, and people's psychology is partly a reflection of deeply entrenched societal beliefs. One advantage of this position is that it permits one to deny that there is a fixed human nature at the level of psychology, without denying that *Homo sapiens* is a natural kind at the level of *biology*. Marx's thesis that there is no fixed "human nature" which people have under all forms of social organization was not a thesis about "nature versus nurture."

[Because of its length, the fourth section of the original paper has been omitted. It is a discussion of the social and political biases built into the concept of intelligence, including the technical concept of IQ.]

Psychology Again

If these reflections are right, then it is worthwhile reexamining the nature of psychology. Reductionism asserts that psychology is deducible from the functional organization of the brain. The foregoing remarks suggest that psychology is strongly determined by sociology. Which is right?

The answer, I suspect, is that it depends on what you mean by psychology. Chomsky remarks that "so far as we know, animals learn according to a genetically determined program." While scientific knowledge reflects the development of a *socially* determined program for learning, there can be little doubt that the possible forms of socially determined programs must in some ways be conditioned by the "genetically determined program" and must presuppose the existence of this program in the individual members of the society. The determination of the truth of this hypothesis and the spelling out of the details are the tasks of cognitive psychology. Nothing said here is meant to downgrade the importance of those tasks, or to downgrade the importance of determining the functional organization of the brain. Some parts of psychology are extremely close to biology—Hull's work on rote learning, much of the work on reinforcement, and so on. It is no accident that in my own reductionist papers the example of a psychological state was usually "pain," a state that is strongly biologically marked. Yet if one thinks of the parts of psychology that philosophers and clinical psychologists tend to talk about—psychological theories of aggression, for instance, or theories of intelligence, or theories of sexuality—then it seems to me that one is thinking of the parts of psychology which study mainly societal beliefs and their effects on individual behavior.

That these two sides of psychology are not distinguished very clearly is itself an effect of reductionism. If they were, one might have noticed that none of the literature on intelligence in the past seventy-five years has anything in the slightest to do with illuminating the nature and structure of human cognitive capacity.

Notes

1. "Minds and Machines," "The Nature of Mental States," and "The Mental Life of Some Machines," all in *Mind, Language, and Reality*, vol. 2 of my *Philosophical Papers* (New York: Cambridge University Press, 1975).
2. For an exposition of Turing Machines, see Martin Davis, *Computability and Unsolvability* (New York: McGraw Hill, 1958).

24. Why Functionalism Didn't Work

Starting around 1960, I developed a view in the philosophy of mind based on the analogy between a mind and a digital computer. I gave my view the name "functionalism," and under this name it has become the dominant view—some say the orthodoxy—in contemporary philosophy of mind.

In my book entitled *Representation and Reality*[1] I argue that the computer analogy, call it the "computational view of the mind," or "functionalism," or what you will, does not after all answer the question "What is the nature of mental states?" That book was conceived as a single argument, and I obviously cannot give the entire argument in a brief discussion. But what I hope to do is to explain some of the leading ideas of the argument that led me to abandon my former position.[2]

The computational analogy was itself a reaction against the idea that our matter is more important than our function, that our *what* is more important than our *how*. My "functionalism" insisted that, in principle, a machine (say, one of Isaac Asimov's wonderful robots), a human being, a creature with a silicon chemistry, and, if there be disembodied spirits, a disembodied spirit could all work much the same way when described at the relevant level of abstraction, and that it is just wrong to think that the essence of our minds is our "hardware." This much—and it was central to my former view—I do not give up in my new book, and indeed it still seems to me to be as true and as important as it ever did. What I try to do in the book is the trick attributed to adepts in jujitsu of turning an opponent's strength against himself: I try to show that the arguments for the computational view—in fact, the very arguments I formerly used to show that a simple-minded identification of mental states with physical-chemical states cannot be right—can be generalized and extended to show that a straightforward identification of mental states with *functional*

441

states, that is, with computationally characterized states, also cannot be right.

Although this is not a historical essay, I would like to begin with a historical remark. I think that what we would really *like* to believe, if we could only square such a belief with our scientific consciences, is just what the ancients believed. Ancient philosophers held that things in the world have *Forms*—these are a kind of Reason-in-the-World—and that we have a mental faculty, the active intellect, which is precisely suited to figuring out the Forms of things. The beauty of Greek metaphysics was that *nous* (the Reason in us) and the Forms were made for each other. Since the appearance of modern science and philosophy in the seventeenth century, the notion of a Form and the notion of a special faculty for knowing Forms have ceased to meet our standards of clarity and explanatory value. We are no longer able to believe that Reason-in-the-World and Reason-in-Us fit together like the pieces of a jigsaw puzzle.

Instead, what many philosophers believe is that we have minds (with a small "m"—the "mind" no longer has a distinguished part, the "active intellect" or *nous,* which can be identified with Reason) and that what looks like Reason-in-the-World is produced by our minds by an act of "projection." This was Hume's line (and he has many contemporary successors). Hume, however, assumed that one mental power—the power of *referring*—was relatively unproblematical. In the simplest case, an idea refers to another idea or to an impression by *resembling* it. This "resemblance theory" of the semantic powers of the mind is long dead, and thus Hume's present-day successors have a more difficult task than Hume; if our ascription of Forms (that is, of "natures," or "causal powers," or "dispositions") to things is "projection," then they owe us an account of the faculty of Projection. Other philosophers say, in effect, that there is Reason "out there" (an objective relation of "bringing about" in the world, or objective "dispositions," or objective counterfactuals), and our minds simply have evolved with a propensity to "track" these sorts of facts. The problem is that neither intentional powers in us nor Reason out in the world fits into the world picture of reductive physicalism. Explaining how we can have the ability to refer and to think *if* there is a primitive and objective notion of Explanation built into external reality is of no real interest. Explaining how we can "project" a relation of Explanation into external reality *if* we assume a primitive and objective relation of *reference* is of no real interest. The circle connecting

Explanation and Reference is too short. The task of the reductive physicalist is to show that it is possible to account for *both* Explanation and Reference starting from what he takes to be the ultimate "building blocks" of reality—the distribution of fundamental magnitudes over space-time points, or something of that kind. And this is what I contend he cannot do.

But enough for historical background; now for an account of the difficulties with functionalism.

The first difficulty I encountered with my functionalist views was that they were incompatible with the account of meaning that I myself put forward in "The Meaning of 'Meaning.'" According to the arguments of that essay, the content of our beliefs and desires is not determined by individualistic properties of the speaker but depends on social facts about the linguistic community of which the speaker is a member and on facts about the physical environment of the speaker and of the linguistic community. For example, I pointed out that the fact that experts (or other speakers on whom we rely) are prepared to count certain things as "real gold," certain things as "elm trees," certain things as "aluminum," and so on, helps to fix the extension of these terms. The fixing of extension depends on cooperation and linguistic deference. Reference is not fixed by what is "in the heads" of speakers.

Even experts need not have criteria (in the sense of necessary and sufficient conditions) that determine the extensions of our terms. Given a tradition of investigation into nature, a tradition of theory construction and experimentation that gives sense to such questions as "Is this the same metal as that?" and "Is this the same liquid as that?" one can fix the referent of a term (perhaps with some vagueness, but vagueness need not be fatal) by deciding that it will apply to whatever is *of the same nature* as certain paradigms. (In the "Twin Earth" example that I used in "The Meaning of 'Meaning,'" the word "water" on two different planets turned out to refer to two different liquids even though there was nothing "in the heads" of the individual speakers which was different.) What the nature of something is (not in the metaphysician's sense of "the nature," but in the scientist's or the artisan's) can determine the reference of a term even before that nature is discovered. What *chrysos* (gold) was in ancient Greece was not simply determined by the properties ancient Greeks *believed* gold to have (although many philosophers still make the mistake of thinking that a community's notion of a substance is the *definition* of the substance for that community). If the beliefs ancient Greeks had about chrysos defined what *it is to be* gold (or "chrysos") at that time, then it would have made no sense for an ancient Greek to ask himself, "Is there perhaps a way of telling that something isn't really gold, even when it appears by all the standard tests to be gold?" Remember that this is precisely the question Archimedes did put to himself, with a celebrated result! Archimedes' inquiry would have made no sense if Archimedes did not have the idea that something might appear to be gold (might pass the current tests for "chrysos") while not really having the same nature as paradigm examples of gold. Reference (and "meaning") depend upon the nonhuman *environment* as well as upon society.

The upshot of this new theory of reference for the philosophy of mind is that "propositional attitudes," as philosophers call them, that is, such things as *believing that snow is white, feeling certain that the cat is on the mat,* and so on, are not "states" of the human brain and nervous system considered in isolation from the social and nonhuman environment. *A fortiori,* they are not "functional states"—that is, states definable in terms of parameters that would enter into a software description of the organism. *Functionalism, construed as the thesis that propositional attitudes are just computational states of the brain, cannot be correct.*

One way of meeting this objection has been defended by Jerry Fodor and more recently by Ned Block.[3] This is to divide meaning into an individualistic component (often called "narrow content") and an external component (reference, or reference in possible worlds). The individualistic component *is* a computational state of the brain in the case of each "meaning" and each "propositional attitude," Block would argue. Against this I would argue (in company with Tyler Burge)[4] that there is no *one* physical state or *one* computational state that one must be in to believe that there is a cat on the mat. At the level of spontaneous phenomenology, it is undeniable that we perceive one another as "thinking that the cat is on the mat," or whatever. If we understand a foreign language—say, Thai—we may have such "perceptions" even when the person in question speaks a language very different from ours and comes from a very different culture. For example, I may know that a certain Thai peasant thinks that his cat is on a mat. But it does not follow that the Thai peasant who believes that his "meew"[5] is on a mat is in the same "psychological state" as an English speaker who believes a "cat" is on a mat in any sense of "psychological state" that can be explained without reference to what the Thai peasant and the English speaker *mean*. After all, the Thai peasant does not have the same perceptual prototype of a cat as the English speaker (the paradigmatic Thai cat is what we would call a "Siamese" cat, and the English speaker is unlikely to regard a Siamese cat as a stereotypical cat, even if she happens to have seen Siamese cats); the Thai speaker might have to rely on others to be sure that the English speaker's cat was really a "meew"; Thai beliefs about meews (especially in a village) could be quite different from English speakers' beliefs about "cats"; and so on. Block specifies that "narrow content" is to be a matter of speakers' beliefs and/or inferences that speakers make; yet, as this example illustrates, it seems impossible to specify *which* beliefs and inferences must be the same in order for the "narrow content" of a word to be that of the word "cat." Block and Fodor recognize that the enterprise of trying to produce necessary truths about what a speaker must think in order to mean a given thing by a given word is hopeless; yet they provide no alternative way of fixing the "narrow content" of a word.

Global Functionalism

A different way of trying to reconcile functionalism with the non-individualistic theory of reference defended in "The Meaning of 'Meaning'" might be to extend the computer analogy to a larger system. Why not think of *the entire language community together with an appropriate part of its environment as analogous to a computer* rather than just the individual mind? (This was suggested to me by Richard Boyd.) If the content of a word depends on relations to other speakers, why not try to describe those relations computationally? If the content also depends on the nature of the objects the word refers to, why not try to characterize the relation of *reference*, which links the word to those objects, computationally? Perhaps one would have to use both computational notions *and* physical/chemical notions in the definition of reference; but the point is that one might, in some way, accept the chain of arguments that link meaning to reference and reference to entities (experts and paradigms) "outside the head" of the individual speaker without conceding that the intentional cannot be reduced to the nonintentional. *One can be a reductionist without being a methodological solipsist, after all.* Functionalism may have to become more complicated. We may have to speak of functional (and partly functional) properties of organisms-*cum*-environments and not just of functional properties of individual brains. But functionalism is not yet refuted.

Of course, the question is whether this can be done in principle, not whether it can really be done in practice. It is widely recognized that the interpretation of someone's language must always proceed simultaneously with the ascription of beliefs and desires to the person being interpreted. As the example of the Thai peasant illustrated, such an ascription will rarely, in practice, make the other's beliefs and desires come out exactly the same as ours. We construe one word as meaning *plant,* another word as meaning *water,* still another word as meaning *gold,* in spite of the fact that the beliefs of the speakers we are interpreting, as discovered by this very interpretation (by the "translation manual," as Quine calls it), disagree with ours—perhaps disagree over the nature of plants, the nature of water, the nature of gold. When we ought to count two words as having the same meaning in spite of the difference between *other speakers'* beliefs and *our* beliefs which the very interpretation we are constructing requires us to posit, and when the beliefs we are attributing as the result of our translation are so bizarre as to require revision of the translation, are questions of "reasonableness." *A functionalist definition of synonymy and coreferentiality would "rationally reconstruct" these intuitive judgments of reasonableness.* And there is no reason to think it would be easier to do this than rationally to reconstruct inductive logic or, indeed, human informal rationality itself.

Few philosophers are afraid of being Utopian, however. A philosopher might well insist that all this could be done *in principle.* The philosophical problem, such a philosopher will insist, is to evaluate the claim that a certain type of reduction is "possible in principle."

Appraising Reduction Claims

Appraising reduction claims is something that analytic philosophers have a great deal of experience in doing. Thus, after Carnap's *Der Logische Aufbau der Welt* was published, a great deal of philosophical work went into examining (and, in the end, rejecting) the philosophical claim that "thing language is reducible to phenomenalistic language." Likewise, attempted reductions of mathematical to "nominalistic" language have been and continue to be studied (for example, by Hartry Field in *Science without Numbers*). Appraising the claim that the notion of reference can be reduced to computational or computational-plus-physical notions is an enterprise very similar to appraising these other reducibility claims.[6]

If this is not quite self-evident, it is because these other claims were claims about the *conceptual* or *necessary* relations between concepts, and my own functionalism was explicitly put forward as an empirical hypothesis (although David Armstrong and David Lewis appear to regard some version of functionalism as conceptually necessary). But if one examines the famous arguments against the claim that thing language is reducible to sense-datum language given by Hans Reichenbach or by Wilfrid Sellars, one observes that what those arguments really showed was that there is no *nomological relationship* between such typical statements in thing language as "There is a chair in the room" and any statement in phenomenalistic language. That is to say, the refutation of phenomenalism would have been exactly the same if phenomenalism had been put forward as an "empirical hypothesis" and not as a piece of "conceptual analysis"!

Thus, what we need to examine is the question that is perfectly analogous to the question Reichenbach considered in *Experience and Prediction*: Is there any strict nomological relation between arbitrary statements in the class to be reduced (in the present case, statements of the form X refers to Y) and statements in the reducing class (in the present case, statements in the computational-*cum*-physical vocabulary)?

From familiar considerations applicable to all reduction claims, we know that we must not say that reference has been reduced to some physical-*cum*-computational relation R (defined over organisms-*cum*-environments) unless: (1) reference is coextensive with R in all physically possible systems—coextensive for all physically possible organisms and environments such that those organisms are capable of using language, referring, and so on, in those environments; (2) R obeys (approximately) the "laws" that reference is supposed to obey in intuitive (or anthropological) belief about reference; and (3) the presence of R explains the effects (to the extent that they really exist) that the intuitive or anthropological notion of reference was supposed to explain. Merely finding a functional relation R that is coextensive with referring for those organisms which happen to refer (perhaps, by chance, there aren't any other than human beings) would not be enough.

The requirements (1) and (3) assume that the "definiens" in a reduction must be a property or relation which we can define in the vocabulary of the reducing discipline (allowing as parts of that vocabulary constants for appropriate mathematical objects, for example, tensor or scalar constants, mathematical functions, and so on) where "define" has the normal sense of *define in finitely many words*. (If such a requirement is not imposed, then the question of reducibility becomes trivial, since—if we happened to be blessed with omniscience—we could "define" *any* term that refers to any property or relation that is supervenient on physical facts by just listing all the infinitely many physically possible cases in which the property term applies or the relation obtains.)[7]

Analogues of these considerations were involved in the debate about the reducibility of thing language to sense-datum language. At first the phenomenalists were content to claim that material-thing sentences could be "translated" into *infinitely long* sense-datum sentences; however, it was very quickly pointed out that unless the translation were finite (or the infinitely long translation could be constructed according to a rule that was itself statable in finitely many words), the issues over whether the translation exists, whether it is correct, whether it is philosophically illuminating, and so on, would be essentially undiscussible. The antiphenomenalists said, in effect, "Put up or shut up."

In the same way, I am saying to the functionalists (including my former self), "Put up or shut up." However, the antiphenomenalists did not put all the burden of proof on the phenomenalists. Reichenbach, Carnap, Hempel, and Sellars gave *reasons* why a finite translation of material-thing language into sense-datum language was impossible. Even if these reasons fall short of a strict mathematical-impossibility proof, they are highly convincing, and this is the reason why there is hardly a single phenomenalist left in the world today.[8] In the same spirit, I am going to give principled reasons why a finite reduction of intentional relations and properties in terms of physical/computational relations and properties is impossible—reasons which fall short of a strict proof, but which are, I believe, convincing.

The Single-Computational-State Version of Functionalism

I am going to begin by considering an oversimplified version of functionalism. This is the theory that each state of believing something, desiring something, perceiving something, having a particular emotion, and so on, corresponds to one definite computational state. The identification is to be species-independent: *believing that snow is white* is to be the same computational state for all physically possible organisms capable of having that belief. While it is true that so simple a functionalism has never been defended by anyone, so far as I know, the theory that each propositional attitude, emotion, and so on, corresponds to one particular computational (or computational/physical) state *in the case of each particular organism* is a feature of all the familiar varieties of functionalism. For all of the familiar versions of functionalism—my own and David Lewis'[9] in particular—assume that a propositional-attitude term applies to an organism just in case that system is a model for an appropriate psychological theory, where something is defined to be a "model" of a psychological theory only if it has *nonpsychological*—physical or computational—states that are related as specified in the theory. This clearly assumes that one can find one physical or computational state per propositional attitude in the case of a single organism. Where more sophisticated versions of functionalism differ from our oversimplified version is in allowing that the physical or computational states that serve as the "realizers" of a given mental state may be different (although "functionally isomorphic") in the case of *different* organisms and/or different species.

Consider the following model for a speaker-hearer of a natural language: The "organism" is an information-processing system (it could be a robot) that possesses a way of assigning "degrees of confirmation" to the sentences in its "language of thought" and a "rational preference function" that (together with the degrees of confirmation) determines how it will act in any given situation. Certain semantic distinctions must be marked in any such model: For example, we can tell when a word is *acquired* by the fact that the "c-function" of the organism (the function that calculates the degrees of confirmation) and the rational-preference function are *extended* to a new range of sentences. We can tell when a word is *ambiguous* by the fact that (in the underlying "language of thought") the word is marked by subscripts, or functionally equivalent devices, as, for example, "nap_1" (short sleep) and "nap_2" (nap of a rug). But if all we are given to go on is the current subjective probability metric (the current degrees of confirmation), the current desires (the current "utilities"), and the underlying prior-probability function by which the current subjective probability metric was formed by conditionalizing on the observations of the organism, then at least the first two of these will be different even in the case of speakers whose meanings we are prepared to count as the same. In short (this was the point of a paper I published a number of years ago),[10] there will be no discernible synonymy relation extractable from the model itself, nothing to mark the fact that when I say "bureaucrat" and you say "bureaucrat" we are uttering words with the same meaning.

The problem does not disappear even if we suppose (as Carnap did) that we should include information to the effect that certain sentences are marked *analytic* in the very description of a formal language. Even if certain sentences are marked *analytic* by the model, say, "bureaucrats are officials in large institutions," unless I have a criterion of synonymy to tell me that when I say "official" and you say "official" we mean the same thing, and that when I say "institution" and you say "institution" we mean the same thing, I cannot conclude that "bureaucrat" has the same meaning for both of us from the fact that this *sentence* is analytic for both of us. (Moreover, the word may have the same meaning even if we have a *different* stock of "analytic" sentences. For example, someone who lives in a monarchy may have the sentence "People appointed to high positions by the king are officials" in his stock of "analytic" sentences, while someone who doesn't know what a king is but who is acquainted with presidents will have different "analytic" sentences about officials in his language, but this is not what we count as a difference in the meaning of "official.")

Finally, Quine's celebrated *gavagai* example shows that problems of synonymy can arise even at the level of observation terms. Here is a little bit of evidence in support of Quine's claim. I recall that when I visited China in 1984 I lectured on Quine's views at Fudan University in Shanghai, and sophisticated Chinese told me that they did not think that the Chinese word "mao" (cat) could be determinately translated into English as "cat"/"cathood." What they claimed was that "Are you saying there is a cat or that there is cathood exemplifying itself?" is the wrong question to put to a Chinese speaker. There is no special suffix in Chinese to distinguish "mao" from "maohood" ("mao" is used both in contexts in which we would translate it as "cat" and in contexts in which we would translate it as "cathood"), nor are there articles in Chinese. "Cat there" and "Cathood there" would go into the same sentence in Chinese. If my informants were right, then there may be no "fact of the matter" as to whether a certain Chinese character means "rabbit" or "rabbithood" or neither-of-the-foregoing. In fact, sameness of "stimulus meaning" is not even a necessary condition for synonymy, even in the case of observational terms. A Thai speaker may not associate the same stimulus meaning with "meew" that I do with "cat," but it is still reasonable to translate "meew" as "cat." ("Elm" in English and "Ulme" in German would still be synonyms even if "Ulme" were an observation term for Germans—they all learned to distinguish elms—and not an observation term for English speakers.)

So far I have argued that, in the sort of model of linguistic capacity that seems reasonable given the insights of Quine's meaning holism, there is no way to identify a computational state that is the same whenever any two people believe that there are a lot of cats in the world (or whatever). Even if the two people happen to speak the same language, they may have different stereotypes of a "cat," different beliefs about the nature of cats, and so on (imagine two ancient Egyptians, one of whom believes cats are divine while the other does not). The problems that arise "in principle" become much worse if the two "people" may be members of different "physically possible species."

Even in the case of a single species, the "functional organization" may not be exactly the same for all members. The number of neurons in your brain is not exactly the same as the number of neurons in anyone else's brain, and neurologists tell us that no two brains are literally "wired" the same way. The "wiring" depends on the maturational history and environmental stimulation of the individual brain.

Still, many thinkers would suppose, with Noam Chomsky, that there is some "competence model" of the human brain which all actual human brains can be regarded as approximating. This model would determine the "space" of possible computational states that can be ascribed to humans. The problem in the case of two different species is that in this case there is no reason to assume that the space of possible computational states is the same or that either space can be "embedded" in the other.

Consider, for example, the crucial "belief fixation" component of the model. Even if we assume that the species are ideally rational, this leaves an enormous amount of leeway for different inductive logics (as Carnap pointed out).[11] Carnap introduced the concept of a "caution parameter"—a parameter that determines how rapidly or slowly the logic "learns from experience," as measured by how large a sample size the logic typically requires before it begins to give significant weight to an observed sample mean. Different inductive logics can assign different caution parameters. Different inductive logics can also assign different weights to analogy and count different respects as respects of "similarity." In short, different inductive logics can impose different "prior probabilities." Granting that the need for survival potential will reduce the variability, we must remember that we are talking about all physically possible species in all physically possible environments—that is to say, about all the ways evolution (or whatever—some of these "species" will be artifacts, for example, robots) might work to produce intelligent life, compatibly with physical law, not just about the way evolution actually happened to work in the one physically possible environment that actually exists.

For example, if the species is one whose members are very hard to damage, then they can afford to wait a long time before making an inductive generalization. Such a species might use an inductive logic with a very large "caution parameter." What properties it will be useful to count as "similarities" or respects of analogy will obviously depend upon the contingencies of the particular physical environment. Perhaps in a sufficiently peculiar physical environment a species that projected "funny" predicates (for instance, Nelson Goodman's famous predicate "grue") would do better than a species with our inductive prejudices. Computers that have to compute very different "analogies" or employ very different caution parameters (caution parameters that can themselves be different mathematical functions of the particular evidence e, not just different scalars) may have totally different descriptions either in the Turing machine formalism or in any other formalism. The number of states may be different, the state rules may be different, and there is no reason why either machine should have a table that can be mapped homomorphically into the machine table of the other machine.

For all these reasons, members of different possible species (physically possible organisms with minds and language) who are sufficiently similar in their linguistic behavior in a range of environments to permit us to translate some of their utterances may nevertheless have computational states that lie in quite different machine tables—lie in, so to speak, different "spaces" of computational states. The fact that their way of reasoning is similar to ours in some situations (when we interpret that way of reasoning using a "translation manual" that we have succeeded in constructing) does *not* imply that their states or the algorithms in their brains are literally the same. The idea that there is one computational state that every physically possible being who believes a given proposition p must be in is false.

What about physical states? The reason for introducing functionalism in the first place was precisely the realization that we are not going to find any physical state (other than one defined by the sort of "infinite list" that we ruled out as "cheating") that all physically possible believers have to be in to have a given belief, or whatever. But now it emerges that the same thing is true of computational states. And (finite) conjunctions, disjunctions, and so on, of physical and computational states will not help either. Physically possible sentient beings just come in too many "designs," physically and computationally speaking, for anything like "one-computational-state-per-propositional-attitude" functionalism to be true.

Equivalence

I already said that the one-computational-state version of functionalism is oversimplified and that it is a version that no one has ever actually held. Let me now describe a version which I have seriously entertained. This version still makes the assumption (which is made by all forms of functionalism) that each mental state corresponds to one computational (or computational/physical) state in the case of each single organism (or, in the case of "global functionalism," in the case of each language community of organisms), but it does not assume that different organisms (or different language communities) must be in the *identical* computational state when they have a given belief, desire, and so on. Rather, it assumes that they must be in computational states that are *equivalent* under some computationally definable equivalence relation. Let me explain what I mean by this.

Imagine some definite formalism for computational theory to be fixed—say, for definiteness, the Turing machine formalism. Although each Turing machine has its own "space" of machine states, still one can mathematically describe the totality of these machines—indeed, this is just what Turing and his successors did. One can define predicates that relate the states of different machines in different ways, and the notion of *computability* has been defined for such predicates. What is true in this respect of Turing machines is equally true of any other kind of machine that might be taken as a model in computational theory. Thus, given an equivalence relation (or, indeed, any relation) that is defined on computational states of different machines, the question whether that relation is itself "computable" is well defined. (One can also define classes of predicates which, though not computable, are definable starting from the computable predicates—these form the so-called arithmetic, hyperarithmetic, etc., hierarchies.) But why should one believe that there is a computable equivalence relation that connects the propositional attitudes of a person in one language community and the propositional attitudes of an arbitrary person in a different language community?

Here is an argument of a kind that convinces many people (such arguments are quite common in present-day linguistic theorizing): Suppose Mary Jones is an English speaker, and suppose we wish to ascertain that her word "cat" is synonymous with the Thai word "meew" (or with the word "meew" as used on a particular occasion by a particular Thai speaker). We have to know that the extension of the two terms is (at least vaguely) the same even to consider accepting the *synonymy* of the two terms, and this requires some knowledge of the actual nature of the animals in Mary's environment that she (or experts upon whom she relies in doubtful cases) calls "cats" and some knowledge of the actual nature of the animals that the Thai speaker (or experts upon whom she relies) call "meew." Granted that this decision can involve enormously many factors, not only Mary's speech dispositions and those of her Thai counterpart but also the speech dispositions of other members of the linguistic communities to which they belong, and information about the microstructure and evolutionary history of paradigm "cats" and paradigm "meew"; still, *if* we can make this decision and *we* are Turing machines, *then* the predicate "word W_1 as used in situation X_1 is synonymous with word W_2 as used in situation X_2" must be a predicate that a Turing machine can employ—a recursive predicate or at worst a "trial and error predicate."[12]

This argument makes the basic empirical assumption on which functionalism depends, namely that there is some class of computers (for example, Turing machines or finite automata) in terms of which human beings can be "modeled." If we are willing to make this assumption, then the attractive feature of the argument is that it does not presuppose that the two situations being compared involve identical "machines." All that is necessary is that the entire situation—the speaker-*cum*-environment—be describable in some standardized language. In short, the problem we faced in the preceding section, that it makes no sense to speak of the "same computational state" when the speakers (or the speakers-*cum*-environments) are not machines of the same type, does not arise if what we are asking is, "Does a certain definable *equivalence relation* R (the relation of coreferentiality) hold between an element of the one situation and an element of the other?" States of different "machines" can lie in the same *equivalence class* under an arithmetical relation, and so can situations defined in terms of such states. In short, moving from the requirement that the "states" of speakers with the same reference (or believers with the same belief) be identical to the requirement that they be *equivalent under some equivalence relation that is itself computable, or at least definable in the language of computational theory plus physical science,* gives us enormous additional leeway. What we have to see is whether this leeway will help.

Suppose (to return to the example of Mary Jones and her Thai counterpart) that our biology assures us that the animals that Mary takes to be paradigm "cats" are indeed various sorts of domestic felines *(Felis catus)* and that the same thing is true of the animals her Thai counterpart takes to be paradigm "meew." This does not show that the extension of "cat" is the same as the extension of "meew," for several reasons. First—to be somewhat fanciful—it might be that Thai has an ontology of temporal slices rather than things. "Meew" might mean "cat slice." Second, even if we assume that English and Thai both cut the world up into "things," "animals," and so on, the classification used by scientific biologists might not be one either Mary or her Thai counterpart employs. "Meew" might mean "Siamese cat," for example. We have to know a good deal about the Thai speaker's speech dispositions (or those of others to whom she defers linguistically) to know that she would count non-Siamese cats as "meew." What is at stake, as Quine and Davidson (not to mention European hermeneuticists such as Gadamer) have emphasized, is the interpretation of the two discourses as wholes.

To interpret a language one must, in general, have some idea of the theories and inference patterns common in the community that speaks that language. No one could determine what "spin" refers to in quantum mechanics, for example, without learning quantum mechanics, or what "negative charge" refers to without learning a certain amount of electrical theory, or what "inner product" refers to without learning a certain amount of mathematics. This creates a serious problem for the idea that coreferentiality and "synonymy" are theoretically identical with computable (or at least computationally definable) relations over properly parametrized situations.

The problem is that any theory that "defines" coreferentiality and synonymy must, in some way, survey all possible theories. A theory that figures out what people (or physically possible extraterrestrials, robots, or whatever) are referring to when they speak of "spin" and that decides whether the notion of "spin" in Terrestrial quantum mechanics is or is not the same notion as the notion of "grophth" in Sirian Mootrux mechanics, or an algorithm that would enable a Turing machine to make such a decision (or to reach it "in the limit") given a description of the "situations" on Earth and on Sirius, must, in some way, anticipate the processes of belief fixation on which the understanding of quantum mechanics (including the mathematics presupposed by quantum mechanics) and "Mootrux mechanics" (including the "mathematics" presupposed by Mootrux mechanics) depends. Certainly such an algorithm would have to do more than "simulate" an ability that human beings actually have. For no human being can follow all possible mathematics, all possible empirical science, and so on. This point deserves further discussion, however.

Surveying Rationality

The fact that one cannot interpret a discourse unless one can follow it suggests that an algorithm that could interpret an arbitrary discourse would have to be "smart" enough to survey all the possible rational and semi-rational and not-too-far-from-rational-to-still-be-somehow-intelligible discourses that physically possible creatures could physically possibly construct. How likely is it that there is such an algorithm?

First of all, the restriction to physical possibility is not really helpful. As far as we know, physics does not rule out the possibility of an intelligent being that survives for N years for any finite N whatsoever. For example, some astronomers have suggested that a physically possible intelligent being might have a body that was a gas cloud of galactic size—the being would move with an incredible slowness, so that its time scale would be almost inconceivably slowed down by our standards, but such systems might have arbitrary complexity. The fact that such a being survives N years, for some large N, does not mean that it is "long-lived" by *its* (slowed-down) standards, of course, but it could also be incredibly long-lived by *its* standards. The point I mean this example to illustrate is that we do not *know* of any laws of physics that exclude any finite automation whatsoever from being physically realized and from surviving for any finite number N of machine stages.

Let us begin by considering a somewhat less mind-boggling question. Can we hope to survey (and write down rules for interpreting, perhaps by "successive approximation") the reasoning and belief of all possible *human* beings and societies?

Let us recall that there is no one form in which all human beliefs are cast. The predicate calculus is often treated by philosophers as if *it* were the universal language, but to put beliefs expressed in a natural language into the predicate-calculus format, one must first *interpret* them—that is, one must deal with the very problem we wish to solve. A theory of interpretation which works only after the beliefs to be interpreted have been translated into some "regimented notation" begs the question.

Moreover, the predicate-calculus format itself has problems. What should the variables range over? Analytic philosophers have a preference for material objects and sense data; but there is no guarantee that every human language and sublanguage, including the specialized sublanguages of various professions (psychoanalysis, theology, sociology, cognitive science, mathematics . . .), will employ one of these standard ontologies; in fact, we know that the sublanguages just mentioned, at least, do not. Space-time points are another choice popular with philosophers; but to tell whether someone is quantifying over points in Newtonian space, or in space-time, or in Hilbert space, or in the space of supergravitation theory . . . , one again has to *interpret* his or her discourse. And it is not at all clear how to represent quantum-mechanical discourse in the format of standard predicate calculus. I am thinking not of the possibility that quantum mechanics may best be understood in terms of a nonstandard logic (although that illustrates the point in a different way) but of the problem of interpreting quantum mechanics in its standard ("Copenhagen") presentation. Copenhagen theorists claim that quantum mechanics treats the world not as consisting of objects and observer-independent properties but rather as consisting of two realms: a realm of "measuring apparatus," described by one ontology and one theory (classical physics), and a realm of "statistical states," described by vectors in Hilbert space and projection operators on Hilbert space. The "cut" between these two realms is not fixed but is itself observer-dependent—something the predicate-calculus format has no way of representing. Even if it turns out that quantum mechanics is being presented in the wrong way by its own practitioners, as many philosophers have thought (though without coming up with an agreed-upon better way), to interpret a discourse in existing quantum mechanics one must first realize that the language of those practitioners is of this "nonclassical" kind. What other languages that science (or history, or literary criticism, or . . .) might use of a "nonclassical kind" are waiting to be invented?

Experience tells us that no human society is unsurpassable. For any human society, there is a possible other society that is more sophisticated, that has modes of conceptualizing and describing things which members of the first society cannot understand without years of specialized study. What is often said is true, that all human languages are intertranslatable; but that does not mean that one can translate a current book in philosophy or a paper in clinical psychology or a lecture on quantum mechanics into the language of a primitive tribe without *first* coining a host of new technical terms in that language. It does not mean that we could tell any "smart" native what the book in philosophy, or the paper in clinical psychology, or the lecture on quantum mechanics "says" and have him understand (without years of study). Often enough we cannot even tell members of *our* linguistic community what these discourses "say" so that they will understand them well enough to explain them to others.

It would seem, then, that if there is a *theory* of all human discourse (and what else could a *definition* of synonymy be based upon?), only a god—or, at any rate, a being so much smarter than all human beings in all possible human societies that he could survey the totality of possible human modes of reasoning and conceptualization as we can survey the modes of behavioral arousal and sensitization in a lower organism—could possibly write it down. To ask a human being in a time-bound human culture to survey all modes of human linguistic existence—including those that will transcend his own—is to ask for an impossible "Archimedian point."

The conclusion that I take from these reflections is that we do not know what we *mean* when we speak of such a theory. A theory which we could not possibly recognize as doing what the Master Theory of Discourse (or Master Definition of Reference and Synonymy in Computational Terms) is supposed to do is a "we-know-not-what." The notion of "correctness" for such a theory is less clear than the notion of reference itself, and certainly much less clear than the propositional attitudes in their everyday use.

Notes

1. *Representation and Reality* (Cambridge: MIT Press, 1988).
2. The present paper covers the same ground as, and includes some sentences from, the fifth chapter of *Representation and Reality*.
3. See Block's "An Advertisement for a Semantics for Psychology," *Midwest Studies in Philosophy,* 10, 1986.

4. See his "Individualism and the Mental," *Midwest Studies in Philosophy*, 4 (1979), and "Intellectual Norms and Foundations of Mind," *Journal of Philosophy*, 73, no. 12 (December 1986).

5. "Meew" is the Thai word for "cat."

6. The idea that the problem of reducing intentional notions to nonintentional ones is analogous to the problem of reducing physicalist notions to phenomenalistic ones was advanced by Roderick Chisholm in a famous correspondence with Wilfrid Sellars in the 1950s. See "The Chisholm-Sellars Correspondence on Intentionality," in *Concepts, Theories, and the Mind-Body Problem,* ed. Herbert Feigl, Michael Scriven, and Grover Maxwell, Minnesota Studies in the Philosophy of Science, 2 (Minneapolis: University of Minnesota Press, 1958) (quoted in part in the notes to Chapter 1 of the present volume).

7. For a more detailed discussion of this point, see *Representation and Reality,* pp. 77–78.

8. To my knowledge, Frank Jackson is the only one!

9. See Lewis's *Philosophical Papers,* vol. 1 (Oxford: Oxford University Press, 1983). Lewis' views are discussed in detail in chap. 6 of *Representation and Reality.*

10. "Computational Psychology and Interpretation Theory," in *Realism and Reason,* vol. 3 of my *Philosophical Papers* (New York: Cambridge University Press, 1983).

11. See Rudolf Carnap, *The Continuum of Inductive Methods* (Chicago: University of Chicago Press, 1956).

12. The notion of a "trial and error predicate" was introduced in my "Trial and Error Predicates and the Solution to a Problem of Mostowski," *Journal of Symbolic Logic,* 30, no. 1 (March 1965). Such predicates are limits of recursive predicates; their use is possible if one does not ask that one be able to know for sure when the value of the predicate has converged, but asks only that it will sooner or later converge.

VII

The Diversity of the Sciences

25. The Diversity of the Sciences

When he wrote *Philosophy and Scientific Realism,*[1] Jack Smart said a good deal about the conceptual scheme of modern science, but he did not much use the word "science" itself. The word does not appear in the index, nor (as far as I remember) did Jack avail himself even once of the shibboleth of "The Scientific Method." In this essay, I should like to say why I think this was an extraordinarily wise course for him to take!

Philosophers of science as different as Popper, Lakatos, Carnap, and, to name more recent figures, Wolfgang Stegmüller and Dudley Shapere, have proposed models of theory acceptance which are supposed to fit all of science. Sometimes these models are also supposed to "demarcate" the scientific from the nonscientific, or to "account for the growth of knowledge." I think it is generally recognized that none of these models fits scientific theories perfectly, but that is not, after all, surprising. Even if philosophy *were* a science, one would not expect to be able to *perfectly* model as complex a phenomenon as theory acceptance, even in a single case; and philosophy—dare one say?—is very far from being a science in any sense of "science" which does not border on vacuity. But what I want to call attention to is something that goes beyond the fact of life just mentioned, the fact that our pictures and models fall short of their target in various ways. I believe that, in fact, each of the "global" models just mentioned does have a suggestive kind of "fit" to *some* theories (the ones that suggested the model in the first place), while fitting other theories very badly. I want to point out that certain theories tend, in this sense, to be *extreme cases* for philosophies of science. Among them are Darwin's theory of natural selection, relativity theory and quantum mechanics. What I shall undertake here is not the huge project of trying to elucidate the structure of these theories—and I shall not address any of the usual controversies connected with them (for example, the controversy, in which I have participated, concerning the issue of conventionalism in the case of relativity theory)—but the project of pointing out the features which make them extreme cases for one or another global approach to philosophy of science. By doing this, I hope to suggest something about the nature of the activity of philosophizing about science, and to suggest a way in which philosophers of science may begin to come closer to the actual methodology of science.

Background

In *Reason, Truth, and History,*[2] I discussed the question "If the scientific method is an evolving one, is there some sense in which it gets better and better other than a purely technological one?" In connection with this, I touched on a large "budget of problems," the "main items" being: (1) the interconnectedness of theory appraisal in natural science and theory appraisal in epistemology and metaphysics; (2) the connection between theory appraisal in physical science and theory appraisal in social science; and (3) the question of the existence of an objective notion of rationality and of "convergence" in natural science. I claimed that a formalized scientific method is an unrealistic aim, while defending the idea that rationality is something objective (even if our conceptions of it are always imperfect and historically conditioned in various ways). I argued further that scientific inquiry is by its very nature value-loaded in a number of ways, and used this point to try to show that Max Weber's celebrated argument for a sharp fact/value dichotomy is not well founded. Finally, I connected these questions about theory acceptance with questions about realism.

The argument of the book was necessarily abstract, and dealt rather sweepingly with large areas of our culture—scientific theories, historical and social studies, ideological disputes, and "value judgments." In the present discussion, I shall focus more narrowly on scientific methodology, in order to see what difference such an outlook makes to philosophy of science in a narrower sense.

Inductive Logic Is Not Formal

In *Reason, Truth, and History* I argued, following Goodman,[3] that a purely formal method cannot be hoped for in inductive logic. Goodman has shown that inferences of the same logical form can differ with respect to inductive validity/invalidity, no matter how finely we analyze logical form. The suggestion Carnap[4] made to deal with this problem was to postulate that some properties are in themselves "purely qualitative," and to require that the primitive predicates in the languages to which formalized inductive logic is applied be of this sort. This represents an intrusion of metaphysics into inductive logic—an intrusion, moreover, of the sort of metaphysics which Carnap himself combated in other areas, the sort that throws us back on intuitions of an inexplicable kind.

Goodman's own suggestion was to consider logical form *plus* the history of prior projection of the predicates involved in the inference, as well as certain related matters (for example, "entrenchment" and "overriding").

The problem of a criterion of projectibility is extremely robust; it appears in Bayesian theories of confirmation as an aspect of the problem of the choice of a "prior." Bayes's own solution resembles Goodman's, in spirit if not in detail: Bayes thought the "prior" comes from previous experience. This leads to an obvious regress. The regress may be accepted as unavoidable; but then we give up hope of a global, unchanging formalization.

Goodman's solution is worked out only for very simple cases of inductive inference. Even here it has consequences which I find unacceptable; for example, on Goodman's proposal it would follow that a culture which had *always* projected such "crazy" predicates as his celebrated "grue" would now be perfectly justified in doing so—their inferences would now be "inductively valid"! Let me hasten to say that what I disagree with is not Goodman's claim that fit with past practice is important in induction. While I agree with *that,* Goodman's present system cannot, I think, be regarded as more than a first approximation. It too blatantly neglects the fact that we have other epistemic priorities—call them "prejudices" if you like, but they are part of our notion of reasonableness.

Popper and the Theory of Evolution

One of the main approaches I would classify as "informal" (in spite of the pretensions it sometimes had to being a formal treatment) is Karl Popper's. I criticized this approach in "The 'Corroboration' of Theories," where I argued that Popper's ideas do not well fit *the* paradigm example of a physical theory: Newton's theory of gravitation.[5] Moreover, there is a major theory outside physics that it does not fit even to the extent that it fits physical theories, and that is Darwin's theory of evolution by natural selection.

Popper accepts and even appeals to Darwinian ideas—not, however, as "science," but as a "successful metaphysical research programme."[6] This move shows that even Popper is aware he cannot stretch his schema to cover *this* theory—and most of us would consider it to be one of the central examples of a "scientific theory." What is Popper's difficulty?

It might be useful to begin by making some distinctions which Popper surprisingly fails to draw. The idea of evolution in a non-specific sense (that is, the idea of evolution *minus the causal mechanism*) is pre-Darwinian. This is well known, but perhaps still worth saying because even today (for example in our current replays of the Scopes trial) the suggestion is sometimes encountered that the gradual appearance of more complicated species of organisms—let me refer to this as the *fact of evolution*—depends for its credibility *entirely* on Darwinian theory, as if the discovery that there was something wrong with our present ideas about the *mechanism* of evolution, if it should occur, would suddenly make it an open question whether the geological layers came into existence 5,746 years ago, or whenever. Even the fact of evolution is not "falsifiable" in Popper's narrow sense—the statement that the species came into existence in a certain order, starting with, say, viruses, and were not all created in a seven-day period does not, by itself, imply a "basic sentence"—but it *is* falsifiable in precisely the sense in which Newton's theory of universal gravitation is falsifiable: *in combination with auxiliary statements which are appropriate in the various contexts of geology, palaeontology, and so forth, in which it is applied,* it leads to testable predictions. (Note that "falsifiability" in *this* sense is not sharply distinguished from *confirmability*—nor should it be.)[7] The reason I speak of the *fact* of evolution is that this bit of the natural history of our planet is as well established as any scientific fact *can* be, and has, I think, somewhat the same relation to the theory of evolution by natural selection that phenomenological thermodynamics bears to ergodic theory. Like phenomenological thermodynamics, it can be corrected in detail by the more fundamental theory, but its correctness in broad outline is not dependent upon the confirmation of the more fundamental theory.

When we come to the more fundamental theory—Darwin's theory of evolution by natural selection—there are again epistemological distinctions to be drawn. At the advancing edge of the theory—and this is where I feel most unsure of myself—it becomes, in places, highly mathematical. Hearing a talk by Richard Lewontin a few years ago,[8] I was struck by the extent to which the kind of modeling he was doing looked, in broad outline if not in mathematical detail, like a kind of stochastic mechanics. At still other points on the advancing edge, we get controversies—Stephen Gould[9] is involved in a number of these—which resemble controversies in history rather than in mathematical physics. And, it goes without saying, there are now rich areas of overlap with genetics and molecular biology. But this is not what I want to talk about. The claim that Darwin made—the one that is responsible for the "cosmological" excitement generated by the theory—was not a mathematical claim, not a claim about Mendelian genetics (which Darwin did not know of), nor even a claim of the kind that Gould is so concerned to argue, about gradualism and continuity versus "leaps," but rather a vastly important claim about the origin of the species. Darwin said that the species—*all the species except the primordial one*—came into existence by "natural selection."

This is simultaneously a universal statement and a causal explanation. And it is *this* statement that gives Popper trouble. Why it gives him trouble is easy to see. Even if, under suitable conditions, we could observe the mechanisms that Lewontin is modeling in operation and "corroborate" his theory, this would hardly test Darwin's great causal-cosmological claim.

The question that exercises philosophers is, of course, "What *could* test Darwin's causal-cosmological claim?" The simplest position would be that we can just make an induction. If the evidence supports the propositions that (1) natural selection is operating now as evolutionary biologists claim it is, and (2) no other mechanism capable of producing species is now operating (apart from a limited amount of deliberate human intervention of various kinds, which certainly could not have been responsible for producing species in the first place), then we should, barring contrary evidence, just make the induction that natural selection always operated and that no other mechanism (with the insignificant exception noted) ever operated to produce species. But this is not just too simple for an anti-inductionist like Popper; I suspect it is too simple for *any* philosopher of science to take seriously.

Even when philosophers agree that something is wrong (or "too simple"), they rarely agree on *why* it is wrong, and this case is no exception. Let me, therefore, give my own reasons for thinking that it is too simple, and not pretend to speak for the mythical philosophical community. The first thing worth noticing about the "induction" proposed is that it ignores entirely the way in which our willingness to make inductive projections depends on our estimate of the *lawlikeness* of the proposition being projected. We are sure that all life here on Earth contains DNA; yet I suspect that science fiction readers among us are not willing on that basis alone to accept "all life everywhere in the universe contains DNA" as a law, not because we want a larger sample size, or even because our sample is not drawn from 100 or 1,000 different planets rather than from one (although that would surely help), but because we are not able to see why it should be *physically necessary* that all life contain DNA. Indeed, in *Philosophy and Scientific Realism,* Jack Smart expressed the view that *no* biological generalization is physically necessary,[10] and he may well be right. However, it may be that experts can think of reasons why it should be physically necessary that life contain DNA. If so, I would not be surprised to find that they *were* willing to accept this statement as a law. But that is not surprising: our estimate of the *lawlikeness of a statement* generally depends on knowledge quite remote from the "direct" evidential support for the statement, and can even be non-experimental. Even a person who thought that the first of the two propositions above was sufficiently lawlike to justify extrapolating it back a billion years or two might have the opinion that the corresponding extrapolation of the second proposition ("there was never any other mechanism that operated") is not a law but is just a contingent historical claim. And such a person would regard the induction I mentioned as fishy—as analogous to, say, an attempt to conclude that people always knew how to read and write from the fact that the people we now observe know how to read and write. (Notice that this latter would be a bad induction even in the absence of direct knowledge of a time at which people did not know how to read and write; we have too much "cross inductive" evidence that technological devices, methods, and so on, are the sorts of things that tend to be discovered at a time and then persist.)

What of "simplicity"? We might argue that the other mechanisms for producing speciation that have actually been proposed—Lamarckian evolution and special creation—involve a genetic theory which has been refuted, in the first case, and the postulate of an intelligent being who was in existence prior to all forms of life studied by biology (but is inaccessible to scientific investigation), in the second. This latter postulate is not only unscientific, but would be considered anthropo-morphic by many religious people: in my view, it makes God into a super-humanoid in the world, while appealing to the fact that it is God who is being invoked as an efficient cause, and not, say, Martians, to insulate the theory of special creation from scientific objections.

This line of thought is one I find convincing. But let us examine it a little. It depends on the principle (which, I have argued,[11] underlies even our mundane belief in the existence of a material world) that an important reason—and a *good* reason—for accepting an idea is the absence of any serious alternative, as well as the maxim "Don't pos-tulate in-principle-unobservables." Positivists (and I count Popper as a neo-positivist) apply the first principle tacitly when they accept cer-tain theoretical statements which have never withstood any Popperian test because there was never any "rival hypothesis" (for instance, "Space has three dimensions"). But they are uncomfortable with this sort of argument when the question is a historical one, and it seems clear that the theory of evolution by natural selection does contain elements which resemble historical reconstruction more than they do the statement of universal laws and the derivation of predictions from them. This may, of course, change. In a hundred years (give or take) textbook presentations of evolutionary theory *might* look like text-book presentations of mathematical physics (I doubt that the theory as a whole will ever be reduced to such a form, but it *might be*), and then, presumably, even Popper would grant that the theory has made the transition from pre-science to science. But, in its present form, it depends heavily—the causal-cosmological claim which is the heart of the theory depends heavily—on one's acceptance of the methodologi-cal maxims just mentioned.

But doesn't the acceptance of physical theories depend on the same methodological maxims? Of course it does; but it would be wrong to dismiss the intuition that there is a significant difference between physical theories and the Darwinian theory of speciation. I suspect that the heart of the issue has to do with the—admittedly difficult or impossible to explicate, but still vitally important—notion of "law-likeness." As I mentioned, lawlikeness is connected with "physical ne-cessity." A lawlike statement puts forward a putative physical neces-sity, or at least something which is physically necessary under idealized circumstances. (Dudley Shapere has done a good deal of work on the different sorts of "laws" and "lawlike statements" we find in science, emphasizing in particular the different kinds of descriptive and idealizing functions such statements have.)[12] Now, one of our ways of deciding the lawlikeness of a statement is simply to ask ourselves the question "Is this the sort of statement that I would expect, if true anywhere, to be true *everywhere?*" Newton's inverse square law for gravitation is not *exactly* true anywhere, but it is the sort of statement that, if true in one region of (flat) space-time, we would expect to be true in every region. So, as long as we did not even consider the possibility of curved space-time, let alone space-time of variable curvature, this is a paradigm case of a lawlike statement. Of course, *how we know* that this statement couldn't be true at places not more than, say, a trillion miles from Terra, and false everywhere else, is an interesting philosophical question. It certainly isn't analytic that this couldn't be the case: one could imagine a science fiction story (say, by Robert Sheckley) in which it turned out that we were in a little bubble of space-time which obeyed peculiar laws made up by some extraterrestrial. But in that case there would be a *reason* why those laws obtained only in this little (cosmologically speaking) region. It may be that it is part of the way our minds work that we demand of certain sorts of statements that these should hold everywhere or nowhere, not in the sense of being a Kantian synthetic *a priori,* but in the sense of being what Saul Kripke[13] calls a basic "prejudice." Prejudices in Kripke's sense are not irrational beliefs; rather, they are epistemological ultimates which we conform to unless the price is too high. (Some such idea—the idea of a defeasible synthetic *a priori*—is suggested in some of Reichenbach's early writings.)[14]

An example of a *non*-lawlike statement may help. We are willing to believe that it may be true in some places and not others that people speak English. If asked why, we can give a reason—say, that English evolved from Anglo-Saxon, and Anglo-Saxon was not spoken everywhere, but this, of course, just pushes the question back to the similar question "Why was Anglo-Saxon not spoken everywhere?" We just aren't bothered by the fact that such things are true in some places and not in others in the way we would be if (in a flat space-time) the law of universal gravitation held in a particular region (shaped, let us suppose, like a chilliagon, in its spatial cross-section), and not anywhere else. We don't expect *certain* sorts of regularities to just obtain by accident. That's one of our ultimate Kripkean "prejudices."

But we don't have any similar defeasible "prejudice" to the effect that natural selection must either be the sole cause of speciation at every time or be the sole cause at no time.[15] If there *were* mechanisms other than natural selection capable of producing speciation, why shouldn't they depend on conditions which obtained in the past (or might obtain in the future) but which do not obtain now?

In short, I am suggesting that the reason we don't think that the generalization "only natural selection produces species" *must* be true at every time or at no time (even apart from the problem of what produced the first living material) is that it doesn't quite look "lawlike," or, at any rate, it isn't one of our present-day "prejudices" that this statement is lawlike.

What of the argument that the other mechanisms which have actually been suggested—special creation and Lamarckian evolution—are either hopelessly unscientific or refuted? Isn't this an argument for the lawlikeness of "only natural selection is *capable of* producing species"? Well, yes; but notice the idea that special creation is "hopelessly unscientific" turns on the acceptance of a huge cultural and ideological change that took place in the West starting around the year 1500 and only reached unstoppable momentum in the seventeenth century. The acceptance of this idea—let us admit it—does have something "metaphysical" about it (though not, I think, in a bad sense).

Am I then agreeing with Popper? Is natural selection (including the causal-cosmological claim) a "metaphysical research program" and not science?

Here we come to the nub of the issue. If we limit "science" to the formulation of "laws," and we take these to be statements which, like the familiar differential equations of fundamental physics, we expect to hold true in every region or in no region (at least assuming the fundamental idealizations of the branch of physics in question), if we think the epistemology of science can be reduced to pretending that all scientists do is write down systems of such "laws" and derive "basic statements" from these systems, or these systems plus "coordinating definitions" (Reichenbach), or "initial conditions" (Popper), or whatever; then we should not be surprised if practically nothing but physics turns out to be "science." This model doesn't fit the epistemology of evolutionary theory. But in a less tendentious sense of the term "science," *of course* evolutionary theory is science. I have to ask why on earth we should expect the sciences to have more than a family resemblance to one another? They all share a common heritage, in that they owe allegiance to a minimum of empiricism (they "put questions to Nature"; they are conducted in a fallibilistic spirit; and so on); they frequently depend on very careful observation and/or experimentation (think of the amount of data that evolutionary biologists have collected!); and they interact strongly with other disciplines recognized to be "sciences." But there is no set of "essential" properties that all the sciences have in common.

If evolutionary theory does not, taken as a whole, fit Popperian (or more broadly positivistic) accounts of science, there are other models it does fit. "Inference to the best explanation" accounts would not be disturbed by the way in which facts quite remote from the "subject at hand" enter into our acceptance of evolutionary theory, or even by the way in which general methodological convictions enter. It was the aim of these accounts to allow such things to come into theory acceptance. I shall discuss cases which are "extreme" for "inference to the best explanation" accounts in a moment. But first I want to discuss yet another way of dealing with evolutionary theory.

Lakatosian "Research Programs"

The very important work of Imre Lakatos[16] is, perhaps, *the* vehicle by which neo-Popperian ideas have become part of mainstream philosophy of science (as, for all their popular appeal, Popper's never did). If I do not think they help with the problems discussed in this essay, that is not because they are devoid of interest or significance. It is because they do not, by themselves, give us any guidance in epistemology.

Lakatos thought that the unit of scientific research is not the "theory" (the particular organized set of statements about some set of phenomena), but the evolving sequence of theories and related activities he called a "research program." This idea was put forward much earlier in a different terminology by Stephen Toulmin in *The Philosophy of Science: An Introduction,*[17] but it was re-invented and successfully marketed for the first time by Lakatos. Lakatos also thought that successive theories which belong to the same research program share a common set of assumptions, a "theory core" which can be identified in advance. (Here I demur: I believe, with Hardin and Rohrlich,[18] that we can only tell what is "core" and what is "protective belt" after a theory has been superseded, or, rather, after it has become a "limiting case" of a superseding theory which belongs to a later "research program." One could not say *in advance* that the "core" of Newtonian physics is what it has to say about speeds low relative to the speed of light or about phenomena involving large numbers of quanta. Certainly, there is something important about the idea of the research program, as well as about the notions of theory core and protective belt—these notions have already shown themselves to be "robust," that is, capable of surviving transplantation into a number of different philosophies of science. They do not tell us anything about when we should *accept* theories, however, and they do not say anything about epistemology.

It is when he gets to epistemology that Lakatos shows his Popperian heritage. Like Popper, he believes falsifiability—which he construes more reasonably than Popper, in that he allows auxiliary hypotheses to play an important role—is vitally important. But he does not believe that good theories are always falsifiable. (He and I independently made very similar criticisms of Popper on this score in our papers in the Popper volume.)[19] Lakatos resolves the tension between his desire to keep "making risky predictions," the one-and-only *sine qua non* of science, and his recognition that we must allow a research program to have periods in which it is *not* making risky predictions, by saying that the unit of epistemological assessment is the whole research program and not the theory or statement. (Like the Popperians, Lakatos is totally contemptuous of what we actually *say* about theories and statements; he points out that to speak of theories and statements as "well confirmed," "implausible," "well established," and so on, is "ordinary language philosophy"—an intellectual sin beneath contempt.)

A theory that leads to risky predictions over the long run is called "progressive" in Lakatosian jargon. Now, no knowledgeable person would deny that evolutionary biology taken as a whole is a "progressive research programme" in Lakatos' sense. Many successful predictions (which satisfy the Popper-Lakatos criterion of "riskiness," in that they were not probable already on the basis of background knowledge) have been made in a number of different areas which share the general Darwinian-Mendelian paradigm. It is when we inquire about the *epistemological* significance of this that our problems begin.

Does the progressiveness of a research program really account for, or explicate, the *rationality* of accepting the current incarnation of that research program? Here Lakatos is surprisingly coy. He wants, it seems to me, to save the idea that science is a uniquely rational activity *without* giving the working scientist any substantive advice at all—and while one can understand both desires, they are obviously hard to reconcile.

If a theory or a research program is *supported* by evidence to the extent that it is currently "progressive," if "coherence," "simplicity," and other traditional "inductivist" parameters do not have to be considered at all, then we are going to get very strange results. It may be that, for all I know, Velikovsky's theories are *well supported* by such a criterion; he certainly has been lucky with some risky predictions. Even if we cannot find an actual contemporary example, it is certainly possible that a theory including assumptions which are wildly off the mark leads to a "progressive" research program: just imagine that those particular assumptions don't get tested (perhaps because they are difficult to test), and it is only *part* of the "theory core" that is responsible for the successful predictions. (Historical examples are easy to find; Ptolemaic astronomy was, for a long time, a progressive research program, but the assumption that, in addition to the heavenly bodies and their orbits, there are invisible "spheres" in which the bodies are embedded had nothing to do with the success of the predictions Ptolemaic astronomers made—indeed, their own theory of "epicycles" required planets to pass *through* the spheres that were supposed to "carry" them.)

One way to meet this problem would be to require that a progressive research program make predictions which test *all* of the *core assumptions* of the theory. This would require some way of telling what *are* the "core" assumptions without relying on hindsight. It would also require a way of telling when the "protective belt" has been "adjusted" too often. It seems to me that this leads back to precisely the kind of traditional epistemological problem that Lakatos wants to abandon.

At any rate, the question of whether the predictions evolutionary biologists have made really test the causal-cosmological claim which fundamentalist and other opponents of the theory of evolution attack, is, as we have seen, a difficult one for a Popperian, and I do not see how it is any easier for a neo-Popperian like Lakatos. If the only criterion for being part of a research program is a sociological one, if the *sociological* unity of the community of evolutionary biologists is enough to justify considering all of evolutionary biology one research program, and the "progressive" character of this program justifies accepting *all* of it, then we are, perhaps, justified in accepting evolutionary theory on Lakatosian grounds. But then, by parity of reasoning, we were once justified in accepting the idea of "spheres," even though that idea had nothing to do with the success of science in any period. Such a view gives too much to the idea that only predictive success matters in science, in my opinion. If, on the other hand, we have to show that a "crucial experiment" directly testing the causal-cosmological claim has been performed, or that a "risky prediction" whose success *directly* supports that claim has been made, then, if we become Lakatosians, we shall have as much trouble fitting the acceptance of the real "core" of evolutionary theory, the causal-cosmological claim which is its very heart and soul, into our picture of "scientific rationality" as Popper does. The idea that all there is to rational procedure is making novel predictions still haunts philosophy of science.

Inference to the Best Explanation

The view that Bayes himself held seems to have been revived recently, at least in a qualitative form, by Richard Boyd.[20] The idea of a basically Bayesian picture of theory acceptance (with the "prior" coming from background knowledge about "likely sorts of mechanism") fits a good deal of what Kuhn has called "normal science"; but I would argue that it does not fit some of the major scientific revolutions (the quantum mechanical revolution in particular) without undue "stretching."

Boyd's approach is an instance of what has been called inference to the best explanation epistemology. This approach has not been very much elaborated (in spite of the fact that many philosophers refer to it approvingly). I want to examine it briefly with a special eye to the case of quantum mechanics.

Someone who learned about quantum mechanics only by reading recent articles in *Philosophy of Science* might well think that all the conceptual problems were connected with Bell's Theorem. This is, perhaps, a comment on the peculiarity of the relationship between the philosophy of any science and the science. To be sure, Bell's Theorem is important because it puts "hidden variable" theories at a severe disadvantage (it shows, so to speak, how high the price is for taking the hidden variable approach); but the physical community had almost no interest at all in hidden variable theories even before Bell proved his theorem. The discussion in the literature of philosophy of quantum mechanics has for a long time been remarkably indifferent to the way physics is going.

I obviously do not have space for a technical discussion at this point, but I have to say a few words about the history of the problem of "interpreting" quantum mechanics. The problem is as old as the discovery of the phenomenon of quantum mechanical interference (of which the most famous illustration is the celebrated two-slit experiment). That phenomenon already convinced physicists that the squared norm of the state vector is not a "classical probability"; or, to put the same point in a different way, it convinced them that the peculiar transition from probability to actuality we witness in quantum mechanical experiments is not a mere conditionalization of a previously valid probability to additional evidence. While a few physicists (Bohm, De Broglie) attempted to find classical models for the "reduction of the wave packet" (models involving "pilot waves" in the case of De Broglie and a special force in the case of Bohm's theory), the overwhelming majority of all physicists—and not, by any means, only the operationalists—followed Bohr's advice to simply stop trying to think of quantum mechanical reality in classical terms. That is to say, they took the advice to accept the theory (which has, remember, a higher level of accuracy and a greater quantity of direct experimental evidence in its favor than any previous theory in the history of physical science), *even though there is no "likely sort of mechanism" which we know of which could account for the phenomena the theory postulates.* The problem isn't just that the "prior probability" of the kind of phenomena that quantum mechanics postulates would seem to be as close to zero as empirical probabilities ever get, if prior probabilities are really calculated from background knowledge about "likely sorts of mechanism"; the problem is that we don't even know that a "mechanism" *is* what accounts for those phenomena. Certainly, no one has been able to suggest a mechanism that would not violate constraints that working physicists are not willing to give up. This does not appear to be a case in which we have to look for an *unlikely* mechanism because we have discovered unlikely phenomena; it looks more like a case in which *thinking in terms of "mechanism" is not what is called for.*

What I have just said is not the opinion of very many philosophers of physics. Almost every philosopher of physics has his own "realistic" interpretation of quantum mechanics. This is a game which I know very well—I played it myself for years! What I want to urge is not that we stop playing this game—it *is* a fun game, and some interesting theorems get proved—but that we attach greater importance to the fact that physics goes on quite well without any visible success in this game.

Indeed, even to say that what we are dealing with in quantum mechanics is "unlikely sorts of phenomena" may be making the situation in quantum mechanics look too Bayesian. A Bayesian might say, after all, that what is relevant is not the prior probability of the phenomena we witness in quantum mechanics (provided it isn't actually zero), but the result of conditionalizing that prior probability to the very unlikely observations that we have made—although how that conditional probability is to be determined if our prior probabilities really come from previous experience, Bayesianism does not tell us. What I have in mind is this: If we suppose that there *are* "phenomena" in the standard sense in quantum mechanics, events describable in the language of "pre-theories," to use the terminology employed by a number of authors, which quantum mechanics must simply *explain,* then we are assuming that quantum mechanics is compatible with the existence of a global truth about all phenomena (that all phenomena statements "commute," in other words), and not simply with the existence of a true description of the phenomena that *each* observer can conceivably measure. But no way of rendering this assumption compatible with quantum mechanics is known except "brute force," for example, just assuming that all macro-observables commute, whether simultaneously measurable or not. The radical nature of quantum mechanics is shown by the fact that at least one famous thought experiment (Schrödinger's Cat) challenges even *this* assumption.

In any case, the Bayesian story cannot account for the fact that Einstein's special theory of relativity was accepted by a number of famous physicists (Planck, Lorentz) *before* the realistic "space-time" interpretation of that theory had been proposed by Minkowski. What these physicists—let me add Einstein himself to the list—accepted was *not* just the existence of some "phenomena," some events "describable in the language of pre-theories," which had a low "prior probability," they accepted the statement that *there is no objective two-term bivalent relation of simultaneity between distant events.* If the notion of "prior probability" applies to such statements at all, statements which would have been treated as *a priori* false since the beginning of conceptual thought about these matters, it would seem that this statement had prior probability *zero.* Even if one somehow argues (perhaps on Quinean grounds) that no statement ever has probability exactly *one* or exactly *zero,* why the principles Einstein appealed to (principles of formal symmetry and of rejecting in-principle-unobservables) should have had more weight than the existence of objective simultaneity, when *a priori* they would seem likely to have exceptions, is not explained by "inference to the best explanation" epistemology at all.

Extreme Cases for Philosophy of Science

Briefly (and too simply) put, my position is that quantum mechanics and 1905 relativity fit positivist stories fairly well, but don't fit "inference to the best explanation" accounts (at least without more clarification than we have yet received of what "best" means when a theory doesn't have a generally accepted interpretation, clashes with statements which are "*a priori* relative to background knowledge," and so on). Darwinian evolution seems to fit inference to the best explanation accounts, but doesn't fit positivist or Popperian accounts. In this sense, certain theories are extreme cases for certain philosophies of science. I am suggesting that one should stop hoping for a single pattern which fits all theories. Perhaps one can still say some things about scientific procedure in general, but the time has come to recognize that scientific theories are of different "types" and that informative philosophizing has to descend to a more "local" and less "global" level.

Notes

1. J. J. C. Smart, *Philosophy and Scientific Realism* (London: Routledge and Kegan Paul, 1963).
2. Hilary Putnam, *Reason, Truth, and History* (New York: Cambridge University Press, 1981).
3. Nelson Goodman, *Fact, Fiction, and Forecast* (Cambridge: Harvard University Press, 1955).
4. Rudolf Carnap, *The Nature and Application of Inductive Logic* (Chicago: University of Chicago Press, 1951), and *The Continuum of Inductive Methods* (Chicago: University of Chicago Press, 1952).
5. Hilary Putnam, "The 'Corroboration' of Theories," in *The Philosophy of Karl Popper*, vol. 1, ed. P. A. Schlipp (La Salle, Ill.: Open Court, 1974), pp. 221–240; reprinted in *Mathematics, Matter, and Method*, vol. 1 of my *Philosophical Papers* (New York: Cambridge University Press, 1975).
6. Popper has at various times made a number of different claims about evolutionary theory. Thus, in "Natural Selection and the Emergence of Mind," *Dialectica*, 32 (1978), 339–355, he writes, "I still believe that natural selection works this way as a [metaphysical] research programme. Nevertheless, I have changed my mind about the testability and the logical status of the theory of natural selection; and I am glad to have the opportunity to make a recantation" (p. 345). What is Popper's "recantation"? It turns out that natural selection, far from being unfalsifiable, is actually falsified! ("It is not only testable, but it turns out not to be strictly universally true.") Why is

natural selection falsified? Because "*not* everything that evolves is useful" (p. 346). Two comments: (1) that anyone would take the theory of evolution to *assert* "everything that evolves is useful" is amazing; (2) anyway, Popper *still* thinks that what Ernst Mayr, Stephen Gould, and others call "the theory of evolution"—which, of course, does *not* assert that everything that evolves is an *adaptation*—is a "most successful metaphysical research programme." In his autobiography, *Unended Quest: An Intellectual Autobiography* (La Salle, Ill.: Open Court, 1982), Popper takes the same line: "Darwinism" is "not a testable scientific theory, but a metaphysical research programme." To the extent that it creates the impression that an "ultimate explanation" has been found, it is "not so much better than the theistic view of adaption." However, "it suggests the existence of a mechanism of adaption, and it allows us even to study in detail the mechanism at work. And it is the only theory which allows us to do all that."

7. See Putnam, "The Corroboration of Theories" and "A Critic Replies to His Philosopher," in *Philosophy As It Is,* ed. Myles Burnyeat and Ted Honderich (Harmondsworth: Penguin, 1979) (in reply to Popper's "Putnam on 'auxiliary Sentences,'" called by me "initial conditions" in *The Philosophy of Karl Popper*). I feel that Popper's piece misrepresented my objections to him in an extremely uncharitable fashion. I clarify these matters in "A Critic Replies to His Philosopher."

8. See Richard Lewontin, *The Genetic Basis of Evolutionary Change* (New York: Columbia University Press, 1974).

9. Stephen Gould, *The Panda's Thumb* (New York: Norton, 1980) and *The Flamingo's Smile* (New York: Norton, 1985).

10. Smart, *Philosophy and Scientific Realism*, p. 52.

11. See Putnam, "Language and Philosophy," in *Mind, Language, and Reality*, vol. 2 of my *Philosophical Papers* (New York: Cambridge University Press, 1975), pp. 1–32.

12. Dudley Shapere, *Reason and the Search for Knowledge* (Dordrecht: D. Reidel, 1979).

13. The notion that we have a series of ultimate epistemological "prejudices," which are not unrevisable, but which guide us in theory acceptance, was used by Kripke in his (unpublished) lectures on time and identity at Cornell University in 1978.

14. Hans Reichenbach, *The Theory of Relativity and A Priori Knowledge* (Berkeley: University of California Press, 1965).

15. When I read an earlier version of this chapter to the Philosophy of Science Association, Jerry Fodor suggested that this is explained by the fact that biology is a "special science" (in his terminology) and special sciences don't have strict laws. This is just Smart's view on the status of biology; I find the view plausible, but it would not have been so at any time prior to Galileo. Galileo and Newton could not assume physics was a "fundamental sci-

ence" to justify their inductions; they had to rely on the (unstated) "prejudice" described above. Moreover, even the acceptance of Newtonian physics does not, by itself, rule out the existence of exceptionless biological "laws"; Smart's (and Fodor's) reasoning depends on the acceptance of a Newtonian (or post-Newtonian) *world-view* and not just the acceptance of Newtonian (or post-Newtonian) *equations*. Given such a world view, the distinction between "fundamental" and special sciences looks reasonable; but the acceptance of a world-view is not the sort of thing positivist and neo-positivist accounts (such as Popper's) can give an account of. And that's my point.

16. Imre Lakatos, *The Methodology of Scientific Research Programmes, Philosophical Papers,* vol. 1 (Cambridge: Cambridge University Press, 1978).

17. Stephen Toulmin, *The Philosophy of Science: An Introduction* (London: Hutchinson, 1953).

18. L. Hardin and F. Rohrlich, "Established Theories," *Philosophy of Science,* 50 (1983), 603–617.

19. Schlipp, *The Philosophy of Karl Popper.*

20. Richard Boyd, "Scientific Realism and Naturalistic epistemology," in *PSA 1980* (East Lansing, Mich.: Philosophy of Science Association, 1981), pp. 1–50.

26. The Idea of Science

Poets like to issue statements about the nature of poetry, physicists to issue statements about the nature of physical science, economists to issue statements about the nature of economics—and, of course, philosophers love to talk about the nature of philosophy! Whether any of these activities is materially *advanced* by the issuing of these statements is another matter.

A by-product of this production of manifestoes and ideologies is the endless debate about the exact status of the "social sciences." Are they "empirical sciences" at all? My contribution to this discussion will be modest indeed. I want to suggest that the notion of "empirical science" is not one that can lend itself to clarifying, to "shedding light," on the problems of the special disciplines. The concept is, at bottom, too loose, its own structure too fragile, to support the weight that it is asked to bear in these discussions.

Perhaps this is not such a trivial claim at that! For, to hear people talk, it certainly seems as if "empirical science" is regarded as a firm notion. To ask whether history, or economics, or sociology, is (or, perhaps, could be) an "empirical science" is widely regarded as a perfectly meaningful (if controversial) question. But I do not think this question has a clear meaning at all.

The claim I shall defend is that the notion of an "empirical science" contains from the start a fundamental tension, and that this tension infects every attempt to use the notion to do serious philosophical work.

In saying this I am not saying that the notion has no use at all. Ludwig Wittgenstein taught us that not all concepts have "necessary and sufficient conditions." For many concepts, we have only paradigm cases, and more than one paradigm case at that. I believe that "empirical science" is a concept of this sort.

It is quite clear that the paradigm case par excellence, so to speak, is physics. But what makes *physics* so special? The possibility of divergent answers opens up, and it is these divergent answers that set up the tensions in the concept of an empirical science.

The two answers I am speaking of are answers that have appealed to scientifically minded philosophers from the beginning. Almost every empiricist has been attracted to both of them, and the greatest living empiricist philosopher has, in his own philosophical evolution, displayed the pull of first one and then the other of the two answers, the two purported distinguishing features, in a way that is especially perspicuous. I believe one can show the same tension in Carnap's writing, and especially in the seminar notes that were edited by Martin Gardner and published under the title *Philosophy of Science*.

One of these "answers" to the question "What makes physics so special?" is that the distinguishing feature is *method*. Physics owes its success to a special method; an "empirical science" is, first of all, what uses this celebrated method. This is, perhaps, the root idea behind classical empiricism and classical positivism.

But the rise of a school (or of several schools) of philosophy which "take the results of science seriously," as one says, has had consequences which might even have been foreseeable from the start. If we really take the results of science seriously, then why shouldn't we also take them *literally*? Classical empiricism took the methodology of science immensely seriously, but it felt free to reinterpret the *content* of science in the light of its current doctrines. Scientific talk about atoms and bacteria (and, more recently, about black holes), or whatever the current theoretical entities happened to be, is really only "highly derived" talk about sense impressions, or so empiricists used to be fond of claiming. But were these empiricists not taking their own philosophical theories—their theories of perception, for example—more seriously than science itself? Inevitably, philosophers were bound to ask themselves if a perfectly serious scientific philosopher should not believe science to be literally true (allowing for inevitable errors to be discovered in the future by science itself), or, anyway "as true as anything is." Shouldn't one be a *materialist* rather than some species of subjective idealist, if one really takes science seriously as the best knowledge we have?

In Quine's work one sees these two moments in philosophical reflection very clearly. In his early lecture "On What There Is," material objects were described as "posits" and even as "myths," better than

"Homer's gods" only in point of utility. But from "The Scope and Language of Science" and "Epistemology Naturalized" onward, Quine's claim has been that physics and physics alone gets to (or has the program of getting to) "the true and ultimate nature of reality." And nowadays we even find Quine describing his attitude to physics as "robust realism."

If the root idea of classical empiricism is the idea that method is what distinguishes physics, the idea that revealing the true and ultimate nature of the external world, the properties things have "in themselves," is the hallmark of physics deserves to be called the root idea of classical materialism. What I am saying is that two philosophies, not one, claim and have always claimed to be "scientific philosophy," or "philosophy of science" in a proprietary as opposed to a merely topical sense. And since empiricism leads to a state of mind that finds materialism attractive, empiricism is unstable: the cycle, empiricism–positivism–science worship–materialism–scientific method worship–empiricism . . . repeats itself over and over again.

Another way of putting the point, using terms corresponding to the two relevant subdisciplines of philosophy, is to say that one may think of physics as primarily distinguished *epistemologically* or as primarily distinguished *ontologically*. And the resulting images of science will be very different.

The difference in the images is partly accounted for by a certain vagueness in the notion of "scientific method." Whether science even possesses a procedure clear enough and uniform enough to be called a "method" depends, always, on what alternative procedures are contemplated. In the age of Bacon the alternatives were the aprioristic and tradition-based methods of the late medieval/early Renaissance sciences. Then, it was clear enough to Bacon himself, and to his contemporaries, that he was proposing something radically new in relation to these. Putting questions to Nature, relying on particulars and not on an intellectual intuition of substantial forms, and devising sequences of experiments so that Nature could be forced to answer the questions put to her were revolutionary ideas. Today, all the disciplines which engage in empirical research at all have eschewed *a priori* reasoning (or claim to have eschewed it) as anything more than a heuristic which aids in the construction of hypotheses. And the sort of appeal to authority and revelation that one found in the Middle Ages is a "thing of the past." The minimal Baconian standards for being an empirical science (being a part of Bacon's New Instauration) are met by a wide variety of enterprises, including, or so they claim, the "social sciences." So what is the problem?

The problem is that while one can teach any graduate student in a few years what he or she must do to *make a case* for the acceptance of a scientific theory—he or she must make certain kinds of predictions or retrodictions, must observe and/or experiment, must rule out various kinds of error and statistical artifact—it is by no means the case that everything for which this kind of a case is made should be accepted. (What the graduate student learns is, so to speak, a "premethod" rather than a "method"; a method for bringing things to the point at which the question "should we accept this" can be seriously discussed.) Whitehead's theory of gravitation was not experimentally refuted (nor were a number of other special relativistic gravitation theories experimentally refuted) until the 1970s, for example, but Whitehead's theory was never accepted, and Einstein's General Relativity *was* accepted, simply because Einstein's theory was "plausible" and Whitehead's was judged "implausible." Questions of fit with "physical intuition" come into play in the decision to accept a scientific theory—as I have often remarked in this volume, the scientific method is not an algorithm. It is not a formalized method at all. And so, in an age in which everyone claims he or she is using it, the question who is "really" using "the" scientific method becomes a difficult one.

If one dimension of difficulty arises from the informality of the "scientific method," another arises from disputes over what constitutes observation. Purists in the Vienna Circle wanted to restrict observation to "protocols" in sense-datum language. Were we to agree with these epistemologists, we should have to deny that we observe tables and chairs; and then we might be led to wonder whether our common-sense belief in tables, chairs, ice cubes, and so on, is not a folk theory, as Wilfrid Sellars believed, rather than low-level empirical knowledge, as Karl Popper believes. As Peter Strawson has remarked, positivist epistemology tends to undercut everything that we ordinarily think of as the *evidence* for empirical science itself. For we ordinarily think of the perceptible evidence as the presence of certain continuous bodies, bodies which fill up certain regions of space and which bear colors on their surfaces, and this is what sense-datum epistemology says we do *not* really observe.

The same problem arises in a more acute form when the alleged observations are in intentional language. Normally we think of lexicography, for example, as another sort of low-level empirical knowledge—as "descriptive" knowledge. The statement in the phrase book

"Parlez-vous français" *means* Do you speak French

conveys intersubjective knowledge; but of what sort if not empirical? But how was this knowledge obtained? The lexicographer (if he did not just rely on what he learned in school) might have asked bilingual "native informants." But how do they know?

Just this bizarre-seeming question was asked by Quine in *Word and Object*. Quine rejects the theory that there are such things as "meanings," and he also rejects belief-desire psychology. What we observe, Quine thinks, are forms of behavior. Quine does not say that "meanings" are behavior-dispositions; rather he thinks that meaning-talk belongs to a kind of folk theory which has heuristic value but no theoretical significance. The fact that no one has been able to suggest necessary and sufficient conditions for supposed intentional facts of the forms

"X" means that p
A desires that p
A believes that p,

that is to say, the fact that no one has been able to suggest necessary and sufficient conditions in physicalistic (or broadly behavioral) terms, confirms Quine in thinking that it is just a vestige of our (bad) mentalistic heritage to postulate such entities as meanings, beliefs, and desires.

How then does Quine describe whatever it is that the bilingual knows, if it is not the "meanings" of the words and sentences in his two languages? What he knows is how to find (where possible) a sentence or phrase in one language which he can use in the contexts in which he would use a sentence or phrase in the other, and get much the same effect (much the same in the way of response) as if he had used the sentence or phrase in the other language. I say "where possible" because sometimes this is impossible, or, at least, too difficult for most people to do: sentences and phrases in the context of an idiom or a proverb or a poem are notoriously difficult to translate, for example, not to mention the problem of "contexts" that are familiar to speakers of one language but not to speakers of the other.

Still, if Quine admits that this kind of knowledge is real, then what do his doubts about meanings come to?

Part of the answer is that the practice of correlating expressions with an eye to practical substitutability (when we move from one language group to another) does not really yield a theoretical account of what "sameness of meaning" is supposed to *be*. A famous sentence in Shawnee has the morpheme-for-morpheme translation "forked pattern produced in bush by hand action me." The corresponding "idiomatic" translation would be "I pull a branch of the bush aside." Which translation has the same "meaning" as the original—the "literal translation" (the one I gave first) or the "idiomatic translation"? If we say the latter, we abandon a principle which has been held central to meaning theory: that the meaning of a sentence is a function of the meaning of its parts and of the means of compositions (taxemes) in the language. If we say the former, we abandon the principle we used to characterize "what the bilingual knows": that a sentence and its translation are used in the "same" contexts and to the "same" effect. For we certainly will not get the desired effect if we say to the man on the street, "Forked pattern produced in bush by hand action me"!

We might say that the Shawnee sentence *means* "forked pattern produced in bush by hand action (agent-) me," and that this is understood in Shawnee but not in English because this way of describing a certain state of affairs is familiar to Shawnee speakers but not to English speakers. But then we have not said what *means* means. And this is Quine's point.

But there is another problem. To say that "contexts" are the "same" ignores the fact that the contexts themselves (as well as "responses") are frequently *linguistic*. If we say that a translation is successful if the translation of sentence S can be used in just the "contexts" in which sentence S can be used (and produce similar "responses"), and we intend this not just as a heuristic bit of information but as a theory of synonymy, then we have ignored the fact that the "contexts" and the "responses" are identified as "the same" by the very translation-scheme which is being tested for success.

Quine does not deny that this test is strong enough to disqualify many translation-schemes. What he claims—and this is the celebrated doctrine of indeterminacy of translation—is that this criterion, or any such criterion, is not strong enough to fix a unique translation for any sentence or a unique translation-scheme for any language. It is not even strong enough to determine translation up to truth-functional or extensional equivalence.

Before I sketch his argument, let me make one more point: "Contexts" are identified, very frequently, by reference to beliefs and desires. But in all but the most primitive cases, beliefs and desires are the sort of thing to which we have access only through language. And if the language is not our own, we must, once again, depend on translation.

If we put all these points together, we see why Quine believes that there is "no fact of the matter" as to what a native speaker means by any given (non-observational) utterance. If we adopt a "bizarre" hypothesis as to what the speaker means, then we can still square this with the speaker's totality of dispositions to verbal and nonverbal behavior by making compensatory adjustments in our hypothesis as to what the speaker's beliefs and desires are. Any number of alternative descriptions of the whole "intentional" realm, of the subject's meanings, beliefs, desires, and so on, can be rendered compatible with the totality of the subject's "speech dispositions." And these, the "speech dispositions," are all that is really *there*. Or so Quine claims.

If Quine were alone in going so far as to dispute the objectivity of discourse about the intentional, then we might record this as merely one more instance of the remarkable willingness of philosophers to hold views contrary to common sense. But he has recently been joined by an impressive community of "cognitive scientists." While some cognitive scientists, notably Jerry Fodor, continue to insist on the legitimacy and autonomy of intentional knowledge, many other workers (their philosophical spokespersons include Daniel Dennett, Paul Churchland, and Stephen Stich) have come to the conclusion that talk of "meanings," beliefs, and desires is just "folk psychology." Their reasons may not be as complex as Quine's, but they share with him a common scientific outlook—a common belief in physicalism and a common distrust of whatever cannot be reduced to physical, or at least to computer-scientific, terms. If we have been unable to find any neat way of identifying beliefs, desires, and other ordinary language mental states with programs, computational features, and so on (let alone with neurological structures and activities), then, they suggest, we should not think that is because the problem is too hard, or because another thousand years of research is necessary: it is more likely that the cause is simply that these "crude" ordinary language notions were not really designed for scientific purposes in the first place. The ordinary language notion of colors as intrinsic properties of external things turned out to be wrong; the ordinary language notion of energy has little relation to the scientific notion; the ordinary language notion of work has little relation to the scientific notion; so why should we expect that ordinary language psychological notions would "cut nature at the joints"?

What I want to call your attention to is the uselessness of the question "Is lexicography an empirical science?" as a way of speaking to this dispute. Someone impressed by empiricist-epistemological criteria for deciding what is and what is not "science" might, indeed, point out that not all of Quine's alternative translation manuals are equally simple. And he or she might say that accepting a translation manual on account of its greater simplicity, its fit with past background knowledge, and its instrumental efficacy is doing something very "similar" to what we do when we accept a scientific theory which is simpler, fits better with background knowledge, and is equal or superior in instrumental efficacy to its rivals. Indeed, this is exactly how Rudolf Carnap reasoned. Viewing science primarily through epistemological lenses as he did, he saw no reason not to consider translation (and mentalistic psychology) as "empirical."

But those who, with Quine, view science primarily through ontological rather than epistemological lenses will reply that the standard empiricist criteria of simplicity, minimum mutilation of background knowledge, and instrumental efficacy are not complete: the missing criterion is the (ontological) Unity of Science. Faraday, they will remind us, believed in the "reality" of *lines of force;* but today these are regarded as ideal objects, not as physical objects at all, in spite of the epistemological virtues of Faraday's theory considered in isolation, because considering "lines of force" as real physical entities would not be conducive to the unification of our physicalistic world-view along lines that seem to be most promising. Saying that someone has "wonderful taste in painting" may pass as a good descriptive statement when we are in a culture in which there is reasonable agreement on aesthetic standards, but it would be foolish to accept "good taste in painting" as an objective fact. The integrity of the physicalistic world picture itself has to be the overriding standard to which specific theories must be asked to conform if they are to have the status of what Quine has called "first-class science."

But if the question "Is it an empirical science?" cannot even be answered in the case of knowledge which is (practically speaking) intersubjective (after all, everyone knows what "parlez-vous français" means in French), is it to be wondered at that the question cannot be answered in the case of really difficult intentional disciplines, such as history or sociology? The question cannot be answered not because we do not know what history or sociology is, but because we are divided about what we want "empirical science" to be.

To this point I have played the role of an observer of the passing show, describing tensions and disputes but not attempting to adjudicate them. But many of you know my view: I believe that the project of deciding what is and what is not "science" or "reality" or "the external world in itself" on the basis of ontological criteria derived from seventeenth-century thought (which is what materialist criteria are) is now bankrupt. Quine, for example, rejects intentional notions as "second-class" but admits "dispositions" as "first-class"; but, as I have argued elsewhere, dispositional notions are no more "reducible" to the language of dynamical variables and space-time points (Quine's "furniture of the Universe") than are intentional ones. The ontology of the materialists has left them able to say almost nothing about warrant or justification—about the very topics which most concerned classical empiricism—and what little they have said has betrayed hesitation and extreme tension. Quine's "disquotational" theory of truth is a thinly disguised theory of the emptiness of the notion of truth—"is true" is just a linguistic device we use to "reaffirm" a sentence, and not a way of predicating a normative characteristic, on Quine's view. And all this is the case not because Quine is a bad philosopher, but because he is the best and deepest and most honest representative of his tendency. It is because Quine has pushed classical materialism so far that we can now see its bankruptcy, its inability to account for the cognitive status of the very science it esteems so highly, staring us in the face. As Wittgenstein and Husserl have seen, treating physical science as a description of reality "in itself" is a profound error. Physical science is a product of some of the same interests that underlie our conceptual construction of our *Lebenswelt;* it is no more a description of reality "in itself" than is our everyday talk of colors or of meanings or of desires or of values or of anything else.

But if ontological approaches to "demarcation" are bankrupt and epistemological ones are hopelessly vague (or, in the case of the Popperian criteria, fantastic), what are we to do? The man on the street will not be troubled: he will go on saying that physics is a science, that chemistry is a science (it is close to the paradigm), that evolutionary biology is a science (it collects data meticulously, it has a theory which impresses him, and it has close links with subjects like molecular biology, which resemble the paradigm, even if itself does not), and he will continue *not* calling history or sociology sciences (and being pretty skeptical about economics)—unless, that is, they have successes which impress him in the way physics (and more recently biology) have impressed him. In short, he will use science partly as an honorific notion, as he has been doing for several centuries. But what should we, we philosophers and "social scientists," do?

I suggest that we might do well to ignore the whole question. Collingwood deployed many of Quine's arguments to reach opposite conclusions. For Collingwood, the unavoidability of intentional notions in history, taken together with the fact that knowledge of a past belief or a past desire is never simply "observation" in the physicist's sense, showed that history is *sui generis*. It is "science" in one sense and not in another. Historians have learned that they must "put questions" to nature—they do not get answers if they do not approach data with questions. Historians learned in the nineteenth century to be meticulous with texts and carefully to evaluate evidence, which is why history had succeeded in becoming an ever more important discipline. But if history has gotten better, and will get better in the future, it is for the most part not by applying physics and certainly not by imitating physics. We learn to do better by doing history, not by doing anything else. I suspect the same is true of philosophy, of economics, of sociology.

What does it matter whether what we do is "empirical science"? The question was important as long as it seemed that physics had discovered the key to "objectivity." But there is no key to objectivity. Or rather, the idea of a kind of objectivity that does not spring from and is not corrected by a human practice is absurd. History, philosophy, sociology are human practices. Their standards of objectivity must be created, not found by some transcendental investigation (not even one that calls itself "epistemology naturalized"). But creating standards of objectivity is not, for all that, a matter of proceeding at hazard; whenever we stand within one of these practices, instead of looking for an Olympus from which to look down on them, we know perfectly well that there is a difference between competent and incompetent, informed and uninformed, fruitful and fruitless, reasonable and unreasonable, ways of proceeding. If there is any general advice to be given, it is simply not to abandon what we know perfectly well when we function as doers, practitioners, agents—that there is better and worse "social science" and better and worse philosophy, whether or not it all converges to final "laws" or final theories or whatever—for either the illusory certainties or the illusory skepticisms of the would-be Olympians. The standpoint of agents in an uncertain world and at an uncertain moment in history is not perhaps the one we would have chosen, but it is the one that has been given us to occupy; it is our part to occupy it with responsibility.

27. Three Kinds of Scientific Realism

A. O. Lovejoy once distinguished thirteen varieties of pragmatism. I shall not emulate him by distinguishing thirteen varieties of scientific realism, but it may be helpful if I distinguish *three* and indicate my attitude toward each.

Scientific Realism as Materialism

I cannot follow "physicalists" (for example, Hartry Field) who would agree that "intentional" or semantical properties (for example, reference) can be reduced to physical ones.[1] *A fortiori,* I cannot agree that *all* properties are physical. If "scientific realism" is scientific imperialism—physicalism, materialism—I am no scientific realist.

The leading idea of semantic physicalism is by now familiar: *(at least in "basic" cases) x refers to y if and only if x is connected to y by a "causal" chain of the appropriate type.* The familiar problem is that the physicalist is going to have difficulty specifying what counts as the "appropriate type" without using (unreduced) semantical notions.

I want to discuss a different difficulty. John Haugeland has remarked that identity theorists confuse two different notions of "cause."[2] First, there is the notion used in mathematical physics: "causation" is a precise relation between "states" of a system, involving the existence of a transformation function (derived from the Hamiltonian or Lagrangian description of the situation) which deterministically "carries" the earlier state into the later state. (It is essential that the "states" themselves be mathematically precise objects.) Second, there is the notion of the cause as the "bringer about" or "instigator" of an event. In the second sense, my harsh criticism of a student's paper may be the cause of his depression; but there is not the slightest reason to think (and every reason to deny)[3] that *this* relation of "causation" can be defined in terms of the primitive notions of physics. Indeed, the very division of the total situation into "background conditions" and "bringer about" is interest-relative and rationality-relative.[4] It may be *better* to take the criticism as the "bringer about" and the student's current emotional and physical state as the "background conditions" from the point of view of what we count as explanation, but this has nothing to do with *physics*.

Now a "causal chain of the appropriate type" is a chain of "bringers about," not a causal chain in the state-*cum*-Hamiltonian sense. The notions the physicalist hopes to use in defining reference are *loaded* with nonphysicalist content.

A physicalist could reply that "bringer about" can be elucidated, if not rigorously defined, by *using* the notion of reference. (As I understand it, this is Mackie's tack.) The "bringer about" is the fact we *refer to* as such, the one we *pick out*. (I don't mean that Mackie thinks this is wholly arbitrary, or that there are no constraints.) But even if this is right, it is no help if the project is to *define* reference physicalistically. To define "refers" in terms of a notion of "bringing about" which is itself explained in terms of reference is obviously circular.

Similar difficulties beset "evolutionary epistemology." If we *know* what "rational procedures" are, then we can doubtless study the brain to find out how it executes them and our evolutionary past (if data are available) to find out how the brain mechanisms that execute rational procedures were selected for. But the property of being a *rational* procedure is not the same as the property of being a procedure that promotes human survival, by any means. And I see no reason to believe (and every reason to deny)[5] that "rational" could be defined or elucidated in biological terms.

Alvin Goldman has proposed to identify rationality with the propensity to find truth; but, even if this worked—and it does not—it would require a "substantial" (non-disquotational) notion of *truth,* which is just what the physicalist doesn't have—unless he can define "reference" physicalistically.

I am, then, a dualist or, better, a pluralist. Truth, reference, justification—these are *emergent,* non-reducible properties of terms and statements in certain contexts. I do not mean that they are not supervenient on the physical; of course they are. My dualism is one not of minds and bodies, but of physical properties and intentional properties. It does not even yield an interesting metaphysics. Who wanted *that* sort of "dualism"? Ugh. But, as Kant saw, we are stuck with just the sort of dualism we never wanted—"dualities in our experience," as opposed to experience of duals, distinct substances.

Scientific Realism as Metaphysics

Since we are discussing conceptual questions, let us suppose we live in a Newtonian world. Suppose we know this (as well as one can know any physical theory to be right). Consider two philosophers, one of whom, Jones, maintains that *there really are such things as spatial points,* while the other, Smith, maintains that *there are arbitrarily small finite regions* but *not points* (except as logical constructs).[6] Is there a fact of the matter about who is right?

A "scientific realist" who answers, "There *must* be"—either there are "real" (unconstructed) spatial points or there aren't—has become a "metaphysical" realist. He pretends to a notion of truth which (in a Newtonian world in which all particles are extended) wholly transcends what humans could know. The two theories—Jonesian physics (unreduced points) and Smithian physics (points as constructs)—are mathematically and empirically equivalent.[7] If truth is correct assertibility in the language we actually use, then *both* the Jonesian description and the Smithian description are "true," which does not mean they can just be *conjoined* [see the discussion of conceptual relativity in Chapter 15 of the present volume]. No argument from "convergence" or from "the success of science" can justify (or even give sense to) a notion of truth which goes beyond the sort of correct assertibility which the Smithian and Jonesian versions *both* possess.

Some would reply that *points* are "mathematical objects" and that metaphysical realism is correct for "physical objects"—particles, force fields, radiation, and so on. (Field takes *space-time points as physical* objects.)[8] But the same problem arises. Again, assume a Newtonian world and let Jones be a scientist who comes up with Newton's theory (absolute space plus forces) and Smith be a scientist who comes up with one of the elegant space-time theories which leads to exactly the Newtonian trajectories. (In these theories there is a four-dimensional space-time with the metric of special relativity, *no* notion of "same place at two different times," and a special "affine structure"—a definition of "shortest time-like path"—which singles out the trajectories of freely falling bodies. David Malament has shown that this version of Newtonian physics is, in fact, *the limit of General Relativity as the signal velocity is allowed to become infinite.*)

Now consider the questions:

(a) Is there *really* a difference between these theories?
(b) Is there *really* an absolute space (a sense of "same place at different times"), as Jones claims?
(c) Is there *really* a gravitational force (as opposed to a "warped" affine structure), as Jones claims?

If the "scientific realist" answers "Yes" to (a) (so that questions (b) and (c) have determinate, version-independent answers), he is again stuck with the difficulties of "metaphysical" realism.

Finally, if the "scientific realist" says that theories which are equivalent may have "successor theories" (at a later time) which are no longer equivalent (because of the changed empirical assumptions), and that a successor theory may answer our questions, we must remind him that the one true theory, if there is such, *also* has infinitely many mathematically and empirically equivalent versions, which possess incompatible relative interpretations. (Since the problem is a conceptual one, I have been imagining we already *have* the realist's one true theory, or one of its equivalents.)

I am not a "metaphysical" realist. In my view, truth, insofar as we have the notion, does not go beyond correct assertibility (under the right conditions). What determines which are the right conditions? Many things:—I do not have a general theory.[9] Truth is as plural, vague, open-ended, as *we* are.

Scientific Realism as Convergence

Given the right setting (which includes the rest of the language being in place) the statement that there are electrons flowing through a wire may be as objectively true as the statement that there is a chair in this room or the statement that I have a headache. Electrons exist in every sense in which chairs (or sensations) exist; electron talk is no more derived talk *about* sensations or "observable things" than talk about sensations or chairs is derived talk about electrons. Here I *am* a "scientific realist."

Some philosophers of science would say that "There are electrons flowing through the wire" can be true only in the sense that this statement (in conjunction with theory and auxiliary hypotheses) yields true predictions, or, in a more sophisticated version, in the sense that it has a model satisfying various "constraints" (including the yielding of true predictions). We do not expect that present-day physics will survive without change; we expect that tomorrow's theory will have conceptual and empirical disagreements with present-day theory. Is there any sense in which tomorrow's physics might give us a better description of (what *we* refer to as) *electrons?* Or is the notion of an electron bound to one temporary phase in the history of physics (as Aristotle's notion of "spheres" carrying the planets was)?

Sometimes theorists like Sneed or Lakatos or David Lewis say that successor theories refer to the same entities as predecessor theories just in case the "core" assumptions or the "core" applications (or both) are retained by the later theory. But this is no help. Unless the distinction between "core" and "protective belt" *is drawn from the standpoint of the later theory* it is unlikely to be the case that "core" assumptions (or what looked to be such to the *earlier* theorists) *will* be preserved.

An example may help to clarify this point. Special relativity preserves many notions from Newtonian physics (while making them frame-relative): for example, *momentum, kinetic energy, force.* We can view special relativity as preserving the "core" of Newtonian physics *if* we take the "core" to be the approximate correctness of the Newtonian laws at "non-relativistic" distances and speeds (that is, speeds small in comparison with the speed of light, and distances small in comparison with a light-second). But this would be a totally arbitrary way to define the "core" of Newtonian physics from a *Newtonian* point of view.

There are other thinkers who hold that *no* sense can be made of the idea that terms in incompatible theories (theories with no models in common) refer to the same entities. None of the entities referred to by physicists a hundred years ago can be said to exist at all (since the "empirical claim" of these theories is false—for example, some of their predictions turned out to be false) and there is no sense in which later theories are *about* the entities countenanced by the earlier theories. None of the entities referred to by present-day physics will be properly said to exist at all in a hundred years, if future physical theory is incompatible with ours (as it doubtless will be). Theories are "black boxes" which yield successful predictions, not successive approximations to a correct description of micro-entities, on these views.

These neo-positivistic views pay a high price for their "set-theoretic" account of theories. It has been a constant view of almost all philosophers that science holds to the *ideal of convergent knowledge.* Peirce's *ideal limit of inquiry,* Popper's *growth of knowledge,* and K. O. Apel's *regulative ideal of consensus* are expressions of the same theme. To give up the notion that we ever arrive at a description which is stable, to give up the notion that we accept the ideal of such a description as even one among other regulative ideals, is to abandon a very central part of the scientific outlook—a part which informs scientific methodology in a host of ways.

The neo-positivistic thinkers I referred to would reply that they are *not* giving up the ideal of the growth of knowledge; they are simply limiting it to what can be stated in their language: observation language *plus* set theory. But exactly the same problem arises at the level of observation language.

Why should we say the term "grass" refers to the same entity it referred to a hundred years ago? If you answer, "Because 'grass' is synonymous with 'plant of a certain kind,' and this semantical fact has not changed in a hundred years," you make two mistakes: (1) "grass" is not an analytically definable word; natural kind terms do not have analytic definitions; and (2) the word "plant" itself is connected today with a quite different body of belief from that obtaining a hundred years ago (involving photosynthesis, the possibility of one-celled plants, and so on). If you are willing to say "plant" has the same reference that it did one hundred years ago in spite of the change in collateral theory, why not say the same about "electron"? If you are not, then even if "Grass is a plant" is still an accepted sentence, it does not *mean* what it did one hundred years ago, and so one cannot argue that "grass" means what it did one hundred years ago from the supposed definability of this term with the aid of the word "plant." Equating almost any term in reference across a hundred years of growth of scientific knowledge requires the principle of charity in some form:[10] but limiting the principle of charity to observation language is totally unmotivated.

I see no reason, then, not to accept the principle of charity (that is, the principle that we *should* often identify the referents of terms in different theories so as to avoid imputing too many false or unreasonable beliefs to those we are interpreting). Accepting it is, however, incompatible with accepting the "set-theoretic" view of theories. For, if the term "electron" preserves its reference across (suitable) theory change, then "There are electrons flowing through this wire" can be *right,* in the sense of being the verdict on which inquiry would ultimately settle, *without* its being the case that present-day theory has a completely true "empirical claim." There is no algorithmic equivalence between the truth of a particular statement in the language of a theory and the truth of the predictions of the theory. The search for such algorithmic links is a relic of logical positivism; it is high time it is abandoned.

Notes

1. Hartry Field, "Tarski's Theory of Truth" *Journal of Philosophy,* 49 (1972), 347–375. The "reduction" Field seeks is an *empirical* one; "physicalism" in this sense must not be confused with the logicist reductionism defended by Carnap.
2. John Haugeland, "Weak Supervenience," *American Philosophical Quarterly,* 19 (1982).
3. I argue that causation in this sense is not a *physicalistic* relation in "Why There Isn't a Ready-made World" in *Realism and Reason,* vol. 3 of my *Philosophical Papers* (New York: Cambridge University Press, 1983). [See also chap. 4 of my *Renewing Philosophy* (Cambridge: Harvard University Press, 1992).]
4. The doctrine of interest-relativity in connection with explanation and causation is explained in my *Meaning and the Moral Sciences* (London: Routledge and Kegan Paul, 1978). See also Alan Garfinkel, *Forms of Explanation* (New Haven: Yale University Press, 1981). In the lecture cited in the preceding note, I make the further point that the division of situations into what is a "background condition" and what is an instigating cause is not built into nature, but is rather a feature of our notion of *rational explanation.*
5. I argue that "rational" is not a physicalistic notion (not "reducible" in Field's sense) in "Why Reason Can't Be Naturalized" in *Realism and Reason.*
6. Kant proposed that points are not individuals but are only *limits.* One way of formalizing this (due to Whitehead) is to identify points with sets (of, say, convergent spheres).
7. For a discussion of the notion of empirical *equivalence,* see "Equivalence" in *Realism and Reason.*
8. Hartry Field, *Science without Numbers* (Oxford: Oxford University Press, 1980).
9. As is apparent from this language, when I wrote this essay, I still believed that truth could be *identified with* assertibility under ideal epistemic conditions; subsequently I gave this up. (See the replies to Ebbs, McDowell, and Anderson in *The Philosophy of Hilary Putnam, Philosophical Topics,* 20, no. 1 (Spring 1992), and my 1994 Dewey Lectures.
10. Or better, the principle of benefit of the doubt; Cf. my "Language and Reality," in *Philosophical Papers,* vol. 2, *Mind, Language, and Reality* (New York: Cambridge University Press, 1975), pp. 272–290.

28. Philosophy of Mathematics: Why Nothing Works

Instead of describing the main trends in the philosophy of mathematics, I have decided to begin with the theme "why nothing works." But I am not simply being perverse: explaining why and how it seems that "nothing works," that is, why and how it is that *every* philosophy seems to fail when it comes to explaining the phenomenon of mathematical knowledge, *will* involve saying something about each of the "main trends." And it will also, paradoxically, serve to point out why philosophy of mathematics is such a crucial field. If there is such a thing as "philosophical progress"—and I confess to an unregenerate faith that this is not a chimera—then it comes from focusing the attention of philosophers on areas and problems where their pet ideas run into trouble, areas where "nothing works." We will not get beyond the present philosophical discussion by arguing one more time whether or not there are "canons of scientific method," or by dragging out the familiar examples from the history of physics; we may get to a new plateau by taking seriously the idea that there are real problems for *all* the standard views—and no area is more likely to make us aware of this than the philosophy of mathematics.

Logicism

Logicism—the view that "mathematics is logic in disguise" and that *that* is what accounts for its certainty—appears to be defunct as far as having present adherents goes. However, it is often overlooked that something of permanent value came out of logicism. I shall not repeat the objections to logicism here—they are too well known to need repetition, I believe—but instead I shall make the following observation:

499

Since the work of Frege and Russell,[1] we are all much more aware of how much mathematics can be done in logistic systems which are set up to codify deductive logic. Those philosophers who would count second-order logic as logic—and there are some—would hold that *all* of standard mathematics can be formalized within logic (for it can be formalized within second-order logic),[2] even though they would not claim that this makes the epistemology of mathematics any easier (perhaps it makes it harder!); while even if we follow what seems to be the majority fashion, and limit the term "logic" to first-order logic, we still have to recognize that a good deal of what any mathematician would recognize as "mathematics" can be coded into "logic." For example, the whole first-order theory of groups is a fragment of first-order logic. Perhaps all analytic philosophers now recognize that "the nature of logical truth" and "the nature of mathematical truth" are *one* problem, not two—and this is itself a victory for the standpoint of Russell, whose most moderate conclusion was that henceforth it would never be possible to draw a sharp line between logic and mathematics. (Russell changed his view a number of times; but he did not originally believe that "reducing" mathematics to logic showed that mathematics was analytic—unlike Frege, who did believe this, although he employed a notion of analyticity different from Kant's.)

Logical Positivism

For a number of years the logical posivitists made fashionable the view that held that mathematical truths are true simply by virtue of "rules of language." If we take a "rule of language" to be anything like a convention (taking the model for a convention to be something laid down by explicit stipulation), then the view runs into a problem pointed out independently by both Wittgenstein[3] and Quine: the truths of logic (and mathematics) are infinite in number. So "logical truths are true by convention" cannot mean that they are *individually* true by convention (one act of stipulation per logical truth); it can only mean that they *follow* from conventions—that is, that logical (and mathematical) truths are true by convention in the sense of being the *logical consequence* of conventions. But the use of the notion of *logical consequence* makes such an account of logical truth viciously circular.

   In order to avoid this difficulty, Wittgenstein seems to have held that the model of convention has to be replaced by the model of a bare behavioristic practice, a "form of life." But what could the practice *be?* In order to support his view that logical and mathematical truths have *no* descriptive content, the practice would have to be holding certain truths absolutely immune from revision. While such an account overcomes the previous objection (because a practice, like a habit, can be *general*—holding infinitely many truths immune from revision can be the result[4] of finitely many habits), it seems to be a distortion of actual mathematical practice. Consider the statement that a logistic system is *consistent,* for example. We do *not* hold such a statement absolutely immune from revision. In fact, no matter how good my "proof of consistency" may be, I will give up the claim that the system is consistent if I actually *derive a contradiction.* Thus the *observation that a calculation actually has a certain result* has a kind of "brute fact" character (somewhat analogous to the character of an observation statement in empirical science) which enables it, in certain circumstances, to overthrow (or force modification in our statement of) even the best entrenched general principles. The fact is that there is a certain "synthetic" element in at least *combinatorial* mathematics, and it is the failure of "rule of language" accounts to acknowledge this that ultimately makes them simply unbelievable. However, once we grant that there is at least *one* mathematical fact which is not simply our stipulation (nor yet our "form of life")—that, for example, the *consistency* of our stipulations/practices is not itself just another stipulation or practice—then logical positivist/Wittgensteinian accounts of logical and mathematical truth are seen to be bankrupt.

[*Added in 1993: This is not my present reading of Wittgenstein, for which see Chapter 12 of the present volume.*]

Formalism

The formalists did not really attempt to provide an epistemology of logic, or even an epistemology of finitist combinatorial mathematics. Hilbert seems to have thought the former was too evident to *need* an epistemology while the latter dealt with properties of concrete objects (marks on paper) that were likewise so evident that little or no epistemological discussion was needed. It was set theory and non-constructive mathematics that needed some kind of commentary, and the commentary Hilbert provided would have it that these are just "ideal" (and in themselves meaningless) extensions of "real" (finite combinatorial) mathematics.

While there are many objections to formalism that are well known (and they will not be reviewed here), there is one difficulty that is not well known and that deserves a brief exposition.

This difficulty arises from the fact that the locutions of set theory are employed in empirical as well as mathematical statements. Suppose I say, for example, "There are just as many stars in galaxy A as in galaxy B." On the most natural reading, this means that *there exists a one-to-one correspondence between the stars in galaxy A and the stars in galaxy B.* Indeed, suppose the statement is true. Then on a realist conception of truth, there has to be something that makes it true—and the obvious candidate for the "something" is just the *one-to-one correspondence* (or any one of them, since there will be many). But if such objects as sets, relations, one-to-one correspondences, and so on, are just *fictions,* then this "something" (or these "somethings") don't really exist. So there *isn't* really "something" that makes the statement true, after all. So how can it *be* true?[5]

In short, the formalist seems to be really a kind of philosophical nominalist—and nominalism is (it is generally believed) inadequate for the analysis of empirical discourse. Even so simple a statement as "The distance from electron A to proton B is d" would appear difficult for a nominalist/formalist to explicate. If *numbers are marks on paper,* then does the statement just mentioned say that two elementary particles stand in a certain relation to some marks on paper? *What* relation? (An extreme operationist might not be embarrassed by this question, but the difficulties with operationism in the philosophy of empirical science are decisive. And they will be inherited by formalism if the formalist takes an operationist tack.)

Platonism

In view of the difficulties with formalist and logical positivist accounts, it is not surprising that there has been a certain revival of *realism* in the philosophy of mathematics as well as in the philosophy of empirical science. This revival is also, in part, a product of a certain feeling that formalist and logical positivist accounts have little to do with actual mathematical practice. Hao Wang expresses this very well in his *From Mathematics to Philosophy.*[6] To the working set theorist it does not seem at all that the axioms of set theory (the axioms which describe the so-called iterative conception of set), including replacement and choice, are in any way either "meaningless" or mere "conventions." The more one works in set theory, the more it seems that these axioms are *forced upon one,* as Wang puts it. The problem (as he recognizes) is to come up with an account that justifies this feeling that particular axioms are "forced."

The most straightforward realist account is the one advanced by Kurt Gödel.[7] According to Gödel there really are mathematical objects, and the human mind has a faculty different from but not totally disanalogous to perception with the aid of which it acquires better and better intuitions concerning the behavior of the mathematical objects.

The trouble with this sort of Platonism is that it seems flatly incompatible with the simple fact that we think with our brains, and not with immaterial souls. Gödel would reject this "simple fact," as I just described it, as a mere naturalistic prejudice on my part; but this seems to me to be rank medievalism on *his* part. One does not have to be an "identity theorist" in the philosophy of mind (that is, one who holds that sensations, intuitions, and perceptions are identical with brain events) to recognize the difficulties with the kind of dualism that Gödel believes in. We cannot envisage *any* kind of neural process that could even correspond to the "perception of a mathematical object." And if we hold that mental events (such as the event of "intuiting" a new mathematical fact) may not even correspond to brain events (which is Gödel's position, as I understand it), then how do we account for the large role the brain is *known* to play in *ordinary* perception, not to mention *memory,* speech processing, and so on? The idea that the brain is a cybernetic device which stores information, computes from that information, and controls the body—all without interference from a mysterious "soul"—is based on a vast amount of progress in a half-dozen sciences. To say, as I did, that we "think with our brains," does *not* seem to me to be foot-stamping naturalism after three hundred years of progress in physics and biology (not to mention more recent sciences). To me it seems that Gödel is trying to escape into traditional ideas because of the difficulty of coming up with new ones which will account for the phenomenon of mathematical knowledge; but I cannot believe that the solution *will* come in such a return to the past.

Holism

The argument against formalism that I gave above—that formalism/nominalism is inadequate for the ontological needs of *empirical* science—is not in Quine's work in quite the form in which I stated it, but it is in the spirit of much of Quine's writing.[8] Quine has all along contended that mathematics has to be viewed not all by itself but rather as a part of the corpus of total science, and that the necessity for quantification over mathematical objects (Quine would say: quantification over *sets*) if we are to have a language rich enough for empirical science is the best possible reason for taking the "posit" of sets exactly as seriously as we take any other ontological "posit"—say, the posit of material objects. Sets and electrons are alike for Quine, in being objects *we need to postulate* if we are to do science as we presently do it. Perhaps we will find some other way to do science in the future; but then we can change our philosophy as our science changes.

This sort of holistic pragmatism is attractive in that it (1) recognizes what the logicists were for a long time alone in recognizing, that we must account for the use of mathematical locutions in empirical statements, not only in statements of pure mathematics, and (2) provides a good reason for being a realist about the existence of sets without postulating mysterious immaterial souls, or mysterious faculties of *perceiving* sets or other mathematical objects; but upon closer examination it too runs into serious difficulties. Quine seems to be saying that science *as a whole* is one big explanatory theory, and that the theory is justified *as a whole* by its ability to explain *sensations*. Even if we think that Quine's own reductionism (that is, his insistence that all mathematical objects *must* be identified with *sets*) is not really entailed by his holism, but is an independent view of his, the idea that what the mathematician is doing is contributing to a scheme for explaining *sensations* just doesn't seem to fit mathematical practice at all. What does the acceptance or non-acceptance of the Axiom of Choice (or of a known-to-be-consistent but *not* accepted principle like the axiom "V = L" that Gödel once proposed but later gave up) have to do with explaining sensations?

Quasi-Empirical Realism

It seems to me that Quine's account is too attractive simply to jettison, in spite of the difficulty just pointed out, because it does indicate a direction in which one can move if one wishes to be a realist without being a metaphysician. Thus I once tried to develop an account which might be called "quasi-empirical realism" (in "What Is Mathematical Truth?"). There are two main modifications which this account makes in the holist story.

The first modification is to add *combinatorial facts* to *sensations* as things we wish mathematical theorems to explain and to subsume under general "laws." The principle of mathematical induction, for example, bears the same relation to the fact that when a shepherd counts his sheep he always gets the same number (if he hasn't lost or added a sheep, and if he doesn't make a mistake in counting) no matter what order he counts them in, that any generalization bears to an instance of that generalization. (That a finite collection receives the same "count" no matter what order it is counted in is *equivalent* to the principle of mathematical induction.) People have the capacity to notice combinatorial facts and the capacity to generalize them. If empirical science is, as Quine says, a "field with experience as its boundary conditions," then why should we not view mathematical science as a field with combinatorial facts which can actually be noticed by the calculating mind (or brain) as *its* boundary conditions?

This suggestion does *not* commit one to Mill's view that such a principle as the principle of mathematical induction is known to be true by *Baconian* "induction."[9] For, as Wittgenstein points out, Mill's account (Wittgenstein does not mention Mill by name, but he clearly has him in mind) may be correct as a description of how we first came to believe some form of a mathematical truth (for example, that the cardinal number of the sheep doesn't depend on the order in which we count them), without being correct as a description of the *present status* of that truth. Yet as Quine points out, we can recognize that such a principle as the principle of mathematical induction has a special status—that it would take something virtually unimaginable to cause us to revise it (such as discovering a contradiction in the first-order theory of natural numbers?)—without conceding that the status is the status Wittgenstein calls being a "rule of description" (that is, being *analytic,* though Wittgenstein doesn't use the term). A sophisticated "quasi-empirical realist" can grant that mathematical truths attain the status of being "*a priori* relative to our body of knowledge," as some physical laws do, without conceding that *that* status is the same as the logical positivists' "rule" status. We can be empiricists without being either Millians or positivists.

The idea that there is something *analogous* to empirical reasoning in pure mathematics has also been advanced by Lakatos and even by Gödel, who is much too sophisticated to think that acts of "perception" are *all* that is involved in mathematical "self-evidence," "plausibility," and so on. The fact that two philosophers as radically opposed on fundamentals as Quine and Gödel have both been led to recognize the presence of such an element—an element which resembles "hypothetico-deductive" reasoning in empirical science—in pure mathematics is certainly striking and suggestive.

Quine recognizes that even in empirical science there are considerations other than predicting sensations which play an important role. He speaks of "conservatism"—the desire to preserve principles that have long been "central" to the "field"—and of "simplicity," which occasionally makes us fly in the face of "conservativism" when a radical change at the center leads to far-reaching simplifications of the whole system.

The second modification I propose to make in Quine's account is to add a third non-experimental constraint to his two constraints of "simplicity" and "conservatism." (Of course these are not really *single* constraints.) The constraint I wish to add is this: *agreement with mathematical "intuitions,"* whatever their source.

On my view, mathematical "intuitions" are not mysterious "perceptions" of mathematical objects, nor do they have a single source. The Mill-Wittgenstein story—that mathematical induction (in the form of the "sheep-counting principle") started out as a Baconian induction and was elevated to a different status along the line—seems right for mathematical induction, but not for set theory. Quine himself gives a plausible account of the origin of the "self-evidence" of the comprehension axioms of set theory (these say that every condition determines a set, if we ignore the problem of avoiding the Russell Paradox). In *Ontological Relativity and Other Essays,* Quine points out that quantification over predicate letters occurs in natural language quite unconsciously as a mere device for avoiding awkward repetition of whole predicate expressions. In effect, the use of what Quine calls "virtual" classes (that is, class abstracts which can easily be *eliminated* from discourse) leads automatically to quantification over predicates (which commits us to at least *predicative* set theory); and quantification of predicates leads to precisely one of Cantor's two notions of a set: *the extension of a predicate.* The fact that the origin of the idea that every condition determines a set may have been something as mundane as everyday linguistic habits of avoiding the repetition of long expressions does not mean that the existence of sets must be questioned even after we have erected a successful theory (which, we hope, avoids the paradoxes). "To the enlightened mind, illegitimacy of origin is no disgrace," Quine wryly comments.

Quasi-empirical realism, if it succeeded, would have two striking virtues: (1) the virtue that "intuitions" can be *explained* (no *monolithic* notion or mysterious faculty); and (2) the virtue of directing attention not only to the various reasons for which and processes by which new axioms are adopted in mathematics (a remarkably neglected topic!), but also to the various forms of "plausible reasoning" short of proof that occur in mathematics (a topic Polya was extremely interested in).

I said at the beginning of this report that "nothing works." This applies, alas, to my own ideas—which isn't to say that I propose to give them up, I hasten to add, but to say that I see great difficulties which show that this can't be the *solution* to the problem of mathematical knowledge, even if it is right as far as it goes, as I believe it is.

The problem is that it is totally unclear what satisfying *this* sort of non-experimental constraint—agreement with "intuitions" whatever their source—has to do with *truth*. Having accepted the stance of realism—which means that we do regard mathematical statements as true or false—and having given a description, however vague, of how mathematical statements come to be accepted, we cannot duck the question: what is the link between *acceptibility* and *truth?* Gödel's mysterious "perceptions" would at least constitute such a link; it is not clear how mathematical "intuitions" do, if at bottom they are just generalizations from the finite on the basis of human psychology, reified forms of grammar, and so on.

"To the enlightened mind, illegitimacy of origin is no disgrace," Quine says. *Why isn't it?* Presumably because adult performance—which, in the case of set theory, means *utility for physics*—is what we judge by, not "origin." But if "origin" is no justification, if only utility for physics—or, ultimately, for explaining sensations—counts, then set theory is just as good *without* the Axiom of Choice, or, alternatively, *with* "V = L." Quine, apparently, would not be disturbed by such a relativist conclusion, but any working set theorist would. We are back with the unsatisfactory version of "holism" discussed in the previous section if we do *not* regard conformity to our intuitions as something of *methodological* significance, and not just psychological significance; we are stuck with a serious epistemological worry—how to explain its methodological significance—if we do so regard it.

Modalism

One objection to Platonism has always been the strangeness of postulating a universe bifurcated into two sorts of entities: physical things and "mathematical objects" (the modern equivalent of Plato's Forms). But the mathematical realist is not really committed to *this* sort of Platonism, with its attendant problem of how we can succeed in thinking about and referring to entities we can have no *causal* transactions with. As I pointed out some years ago[10] and as Charles Parsons has recently pointed out,[11] we can reformulate classical mathematics so that instead of speaking of sets, numbers, or other "objects," we simply assert the *possibility* or *impossibility* (in the sense of *mathematical* possibility or impossibility) of certain structures. "Sets are permanent possibilities of selection" was the slogan. The structures whose possibility or impossibility is talked about can themselves be predicates of physical objects, or predicates of unspecified objects, or even—if one has nominalistic scruples against admitting even first-order properties into one's ontology—concrete things. Mathematics, on this view (which I called "mathematics as modal logic"), has a special *notion*—the notion of possibility—but no special *objects*. While "modalism" has therapeutic virtues (it explains how mathematics is possible without assuming Plato's Heaven), and while Parsons and I both believe it can shed light on the so-called iterative conception of set, it does not speak to the *epistemological* problem. If we give a "quasi-empirical realist" account of how we *know* modal facts, then the problems will be just the same whether we accept the "mathematics as modal logic" picture or the "mathematics as theory of mathematical objects" picture. Once again, "nothing works."

Intuitionism

Since formalism doesn't work and, on the other hand, the various versions of realism we have considered run into apparently insuperable epistemological problems, it may be worthwhile to reconsider intuitionism, which accepts mathematical statements as meaningful while rejecting the realist assumptions about truth (for example, "bivalence"—every statement is true or false) which I have so far presupposed.[12] But there are at least three difficulties with intuitionism: First, intuitionism is apparently an extension of operationism to mathematical language, in content if not in historic origin, and presupposes that *non*-mathematical language can be analyzed in an operationist or verificationist way. The difficulty is not that intuitionists cannot derive the theorems of enough mathematics to "do" physics— Bishop has convincingly shown that they can[13]—but that the interpretation of the logical connectives assumed by intuitionism doesn't "fit" a non-operationist physics. For example, ⊃ ("if-then") is interpreted by intuitionists as meaning that there is a procedure for going from a *proof* of the antecedent to a *proof* of the consequent. While the assumption that there are such things as verifications ("proofs") of isolated statements may be all right in mathematics, it is not in physics, as many authors have pointed out. So what does ⊃ mean in an *empirical statement?*

Second, intuitionists assume a distinction, familiar from phenomenology and neo-Kantian philosophy, between *empirical* facts about the mind and transcendental or *a priori* facts about the mind. For example, the statement "Every number has a successor" does not mean (when interpreted by an intuitionist) that it is actually possible for the empirical mind to "construct" arbitrarily many numbers; it means, roughly, that it is not *a priori* impossible to construct arbitrarily many numbers (and that *this* fact is itself phenomenologically "evident"). To empiricists like myself this appeal to *a prioricity* and to mysterious phenomenological "evidence" is as objectionable as Platonism. Aren't the intuitionists just saying after all that it is *self-evident* that arbitrarily long finite sequences are *possible?* And how is *this* claim *either* an analysis of what possibility comes to *or* an account of the faculty by which we know these *"a priori"* truths?

Third, the problem of the *consistency* of the mind is shrugged off by intuitionists just a little too easily. If there is such a thing as the transcendental structure of the mind, why couldn't it be inconsistent? "It's *evident* that it isn't" is hardly an answer.

What Directions Should Be Pursued?

After this depressing survey of "why nothing works," you may expect me to recommend *giving up* on philosophy of mathematics (and perhaps on philosophy altogether). But it seems to me that while things are dark they are not altogether hopeless. I have already said that there is something that seems to me worth pursing in "quasi-empirical realism" as an approach to philosophy of mathematics, for example. The epistemological difficulty I pointed out might be met, I think, by pointing out that "truth" cannot be taken on the old "transcendental realist" model (as Kant called it) for many reasons. If we instead think of truth as *ultimate goodness of fit*, in a phrase due to Ullian, then the connection between our *criteria* of fit, even if they be partly aesthetic, and *truth* may not appear quite so mysterious. To be sure, this is a program of work and not a "solution." One thing one has to see, if this program is right, is that a simple copy theory of truth is also wrong in empirical science, and that partly "aesthetic" criteria of truth enter there too. Even more important, while one's first reaction to such an account of mathematical truth (let alone empirical truth) may be that it leads back to Quinian relativism, it will turn out, I believe, that the more one works with mathematics and set theory, the less often it will seem the case that there is a genuine "choice" of which system to accept. Wang's observation that the axioms seem to be "forced upon us" may yet find its explanation.

Such a view has affinities with several of the positions I have discussed. Its indebtedness to Quine's holism is obvious. It has an affinity to Intuitionism in abandoning the idea that truth is independent of even ideal verification, but it gives up the idea of fixed *a priori* structures in the mind. It accords well with modalism and with the logicist insistence that our account of logical and mathematical truth be unitary. Perhaps it is even "Wittgensteinian."

Nor need such a view fall into mere idealism or phenomenalism. It is not being denied that there is a "real world" nor affirmed that all there "really is" is sensations and their relations (sensations too are part of "the web of belief"). What is rather being claimed is that knowledge is necessarily a representation of the world, not a Doppelgänger of the world, and that any representation must be the joint product of the world and human psychology (or Alpha Centaurian psychology, or Betelguesian psychology, or . . .). Thus my view is a soft Kantianism—Kantian in insisting on the mind-dependence of all knowledge, but empiricist in rejecting Kant's distinction between the transcendental and the empirical mind and the unrevisable "synthetic *a priori*." Far from being antirealist, it is my claim that such a view is even compatible with a certain version of a correspondence theory of truth—though not one which supports full bivalence. But that goes far beyond this report.

While this approach too may "not work," it seems clear that what is needed in philosophy of mathematics is work that is *philosophical* and not primarily technical.[14] Investigations in the philosophical foundations of intuitionism, investigations in the history of mathematics which shed light on the processes by which mathematics grows and changes, and investigations into "plausible reasoning" in mathematics are among the areas which invite study. Above all, philosophy of mathematics, like philosophy of science generally, must link up with philosophy of language, and especially with the discussion of the deep metaphysical issue of realism as a theory of truth and reference.

Notes

1. Gottlob Frege, *Foundations of Arithmetic*, trans. J. L. Austin (Oxford: Basil Blackwell, 1950), and Bertrand Russell, *Introduction to Mathematical Philosophy* (London: G. Allen, 1919), and *The Principles of Mathematics* (London: G. Allen, 1903).

2. Frege—and Russell-Whitehead—needed at least third-order logic, but different "translations" are known which translate all of set theory into second-order logic (in the sense that each set theoretic statement is true *if and only if* its "translation" into second-order logic is *valid*).

3. Ludwig Wittgenstein, *Remarks on the Foundations of Mathematics*, ed. G. H. von Wright, R. Rhees, and G. E. M. Anscombe, trans. Anscombe (Oxford: Basil Blackwell, 1956).

4. Strictly speaking, the notion of "result" *is* just the notion of *logical consequence* in disguise, and the difficulty mentioned is *not* avoided. On the other hand, if "results" means what the habit would *actually* lead us to do, then no circularity is involved, but references to the actual infinite *or even the very large finite* have to be construed as a sort of mathematical fiction. This is, I believe, Wittgenstein's stand. To ask if a logistic system is *consistent* is not always meaningful from such a hyper-finitist standpoint. But what of the statement that *there is no contradiction with fewer than* 10^{100} lines? This is true or false, even from a hyper-finitist standpoint, and *not* just a question of our "form of life."

5. In "Steps to a Constructive Nominalism," *Journal of Symbolic Logic,* 12 (1947), 97–122, Goodman and Quine proposed a nominalist analysis of "there are exactly as many cats as dogs." But their analysis not only was extremely artificial, but involved the notion "bigger than" (in volume) which is not easily explainable without reference to volume elements, *counting,* and so on.

6. Hao Wang, *From Mathematics to Philosophy* (London: Routledge and Kegan Paul, 1974).

7. Kurt Gödel, "What is Cantor's Continuum Problem?" *Philosophy of Mathematics: Selected Readings,* ed. Paul Benacerraf and Hilary Putnam (Englewood Cliffs, N.J.: Prentice-Hall, 1964), pp. 258–273.

8. See especially *Ontological Relativity and Other Essays* (New York: Columbia University Press, 1969) and "On What There Is," *Review of Metaphysics,* 2 (1948), 21–38, reprinted in *Ontological Relativity;* "Truth by Convention," in *Philosophical Essays for A. N. Whitehead,* ed. O. H. Lee (New York: Longmans, 1936), reprinted in his *The Ways of Paradox* (Cam-

bridge: Harvard University Press, 1976); and "Two Dogmas of Empiricism," *Philosophical Review*, 60 (1951), 20–43, also reprinted in *Ontological Relativity*.

9. J. S. Mill, *A System of Logic Ratiocinative and Inductive* (London: Longmans, Green, 1961; originally published in 1843).

10. In "Mathematics without Foundations," *Journal of Philosophy*, 64 (1967), 5–22; reprinted in my *Philosophical Papers*, vol. 1, *Mathematics, Matter, and Method* (New York: Cambridge University Press, 1975), pp. 43–59.

11. Charles Parsons, "What Is the Iterative Concept of a Set?" in *Proceedings of the Fifth International Congress for Logic, Methodology, and Philosophy of Science*, ed. R. E. Butts and J. Kontikka (Dordrecht: D. Reidel, 1977), pp. 335–367.

12. See particularly Michael Dummett, *Mathematical Intuitionism* (Cambridge: Cambridge University Press, 1977).

13. E. Bishop, *Foundations of Constructive Analysis* (New York: McGraw-Hill, 1967).

14. I am not denying that *some* technical work is highly philosophically relevant (for example, the work of Georg Kreisel and that of Harvey Friedman), but most technical work by philosophers of mathematics is of a low quality *and* of doubtful philosophical significance.

29. The Cultural Impact of Newton: Pope's *Essay on Man* and Those "Happy Pieties"

Too, too late for the fond believing Lyre,
When holy were the haunted forest boughs,
Holy the air, the water and the fire:
Yet even in these days so far retired
From happy pieties, thy lucent fans,
Fluttering among the faint Olympians,
I see and sing by my own eyes inspired.

Keats, "Ode to Psyche"

Keats, in a letter dated February 3, 1818, criticized Wordsworth for leading poetry in a disastrous direction, a direction characterized by subjectivity and particularity. Wordsworth, Keats said, is producing a poetry of his "life and opinions." But writing to the same correspondent exactly three months later, Keats admitted that the old magisterial position is one that a latter-day poet cannot hope to occupy. Milton's verse, for example, depended upon particular "resting places" in the "intellectual world" to which we can no longer return.

One sees in these letters the particular manner in which Keats came to feel that the position of the poet is a problematic one. But it was not the first time that "resting places" and "happy pieties" had been taken away. In *The Burden of the Past and the English Poet,* Walter Jackson Bate argued that it was in the age of Pope that the "burden of the past," the burden of self-consciously comparing one's work with a great canon, became agonizing. Bate accepted (and modified) an explanation put forward by Hume, the idea that it is the requirement that the writer be "original" which created the morbid pressure. As Bate put it, "These two relatively new ideals of 'originality' and 'sincerity' (new at least for art) were henceforth to lie heavily on the shoulders of almost every English-speaking writer, and very soon almost every Western artist."

To these burdens, the loss of "happy pieties" and the burden of the past, one might, perhaps, add a third which has to do with the future. If the aspiration to be a member of an "immortal freemasonry," in Keats's phrase, can help us to rise above cultural fatigues and declines (as Bates suggests it helped Keats to do), it can also expose us to the fact that artistic work (and philosophical work) inevitably becomes dated. Of course, works that become part of the canon are not often thought of as "dated." But how many writers really think that they have it in them to be "immortal" in the sense in which Shakespeare and Milton are said to be immortal? Keats himself chose the bitter epitaph "His name was writ in water." The idea that creative work can have value even though it is impermanent is difficult to accept. There is a burden in impermanence, a burden of the future, as well as a burden of the past.

Pope was aware of the burden of the past, but he seems, on a superficial look, to be unaffected by the weight of the other two burdens. He does, after all, take on the high Miltonic task, and even echoes Milton's words, when he speaks of vindicating God's ways to man. But, I want to claim, this appearance of serenity and authority is misleading. Pope's endless revising of his own work, and his great concern with the details of editing and publishing it, show a keen awareness of the burden of the future, and it is a mistake (an all-but-universal one) to think of him as unaffected by the slipping away of intellectual "resting places."

The issue interests me because I think that the history of philosophy resembles the history of the arts in these respects. But if I find this similarity between the history of literature and the history of philosophy significant, it is not, let me hasten to add, because I agree with Richard Rorty that all that is left for philosophy is to become literature. The arts, including the literary arts, and philosophy share a common history for reasons some of which are fairly obvious, after all. The collapse of the great cultural synthesis which existed from the fall of Rome to the Diet of Worms, the rise of science, the crisis of faith, the secularization of Western culture, and the appearance of the various modernisms (including the one that calls itself "postmodernism") have been forces to which philosophy and the arts have both had to respond. Some of those responses have been very similar at certain times and in certain places, but others have been very different. One respect in which the situation of philosophy is very different from that of the arts is that philosophy is under the constant temptation to pretend that it has become a science or, alternatively, to abdicate its responsibilities to one or another science. (This is usually thought to be a recent development, but Gilson, in his 1934 William James Lectures, argued that all of medieval philosophy was haunted by the same temptation. The medieval "sciences" of logic, theology, and psychology were supposed, at various times, to provide solutions for the problems of philosophy.) Certainly, post-Galilean philosophy has been preoccupied with the question of the scientific status of the subject, and Anglo-American philosophy today often uses the slogan "naturalism" as shorthand for the widely accepted idea that philosophy is simply (in Locke's phrase) an "under-laborer" to the sciences.

If I subscribed to this consensus, I would not have written the present essay. This is not the place to argue against the consensus, but I will simply say that, like Stanley Cavell, I do not see the problems of philosophy as ones that admit of a "scientific" solution. The most important similarity between philosophy and the arts—a similarity which cuts so deep that it becomes imperative to take Cavell's advice and to start thinking about literary and other artistic issues in a philosophical way without denying or abridging the differences between philosophy and the arts—is that both deal with problems, or better issues, which can neither be "solved" nor simply renounced. And I think that the *Essay on Man* is a beautiful illustration of the way in which philosophical issues can penetrate a literary work.

The *Essay on Man*

The *Essay on Man* is usually described as a theodicy. The editors of the Twickenham text pointed out the traditional theological ideas in the essay, while many readers observed the deist elements, and indeed the text does contain both a version of the Great Chain of Being and the notion of God as a scrupulous avoider of miracles (God "works not on partial but on general laws"). Pope was a Catholic, even if a most anti-dogmatic one, and from the fact that he had done a poetic paraphrase of some lines of Thomas a Kempis as early as 1700 (when he was twelve years old) we might guess that traditional thinking about the "problem of evil" was not unknown to him. And he was an enthusiastic admirer of Bolingbroke and of Bolingbroke's deistic philosophy.

On a close reading, the *Essay* reveals still further strands and complexities. Indeed, the *Essay* seems to cry out for a reading by the late

Paul de Man. Deconstructionists like de Man point out the manner in which the tropes in a work contradict the "semiotic level," and they suggest that the whole notion of a "message" evaporates as one reads a literary work closely. This claim does not fit every literary work, but it fits the *Essay on Man* quite nicely.

Here is an example, one out of many that might be chosen: Pope tackles the problem of evil on a number of different lines: (1) People are, in general, happier than pessimists think, according to Pope. The beggar enjoys capering about for coins, the peasant thinks peasants are the salt of the earth, and so forth. (2) People are borne up through adversity by hope. (3) In any case, true happiness is—barring misfortunes, which are inevitable, since it is beneath God's dignity to work miracles—available to all through the practice of virtue. The tropes that Pope employs in the lines that set forth this optimistic doctrine are at once ironic and depressing. For example, Pope illustrates our general contentment with our lot by comparing us to sheep being fattened for the slaughter.

> Which sees no more the stroke, or feels the pain,
> Than favoured Man by touch etherial slain.

Again, Pope insists that "Whatever IS, is RIGHT," but the subsequent verses point out that what is RIGHT from a God's-eye view is no more concerned with man's special good than with that of the "pampered goose." The celebrated lines about God

> Who sees with equal eye, as God of all,
> A hero perish or a sparrow fall,
> Atoms or systems into ruin hurled
> And now a bubble burst and now a world

fail to contain a word of reassurance on the subject of human good as humanly perceived.

So much for theodicy. Pope himself described the *Essay* as "some pieces on Human Life and Manners," and its "Epistles" as constituting a "Book on Ethic." Read as "Ethic" it is, however, just as full of tension as it is when read as theodicy. The psychology, for example, has a pleasantly modern ring. Reason and passion are not hierarchically ordered, as they were by Plato, nor even as they were (in the opposite way) by Hume, but rather are seen as jointly necessary and equally important ("not this a good nor that a bad, we call"). But it soon turns out that everyone has a ruling passion, and this ruling passion is pictured as invariably able to subvert reason. First the ruling passion is described as "The Mind's disease," while

> Reason itself but gives it edge and power
> As Heaven's blessed beam turns vinegar more sour . . .

Then, a few lines later, the "disease" becomes a "friend":

> Yes, Nature's road must ever be preferred;
> Reason is here no guide, but still a guard;
> 'Tis hers to rectify, not overthrow,
> And treat this Passion more as friend than foe.

Pope's argument is that the ruling passions of various men lead them to various activities and virtues: avarice to mercantile activities and to prudence; sloth to scholarship and philosophy(!); lust to "gentle love"; and so on. Not only is there an internal contradiction in the idea that Reason can "rectify" our ruling passion if Reason is only a "weak queen" and

> We, wretched subjects, though in lawfull sway
> To this weak queen, some favorite still obey . . .

but this picture of human beings as governed by their "ruling passions," and consoled by the "livelier play-thing" appropriate to their stage in life, contradicts the argument of the fourth epistle. The claim that constitutes the argument of the final epistle is that virtue (which is equated with happiness) is available to all; we just have to realize that gold, fine clothes, honors, sexual love, and all those things don't really matter! In fact, the argument of the final epistle is close to the thought of Thomas a Kempis, rather than to the "modern" outlook of the rest of the *Essay*.

So far I have mentioned a contradiction between an avowal that virtue is possible for all,

> See! The sole bliss Heaven could on all bestow;
> Which he who but feels can taste, but thinks can know . . .

and a very Swiftian sort of pessimism, as well as a contradiction between viewing God as a comfort and viewing God as unthinkably remote and abstract. In 1899, Leslie Stephen suggested that the contradictions in the essay were due to the amateurishness in Pope's philosophy and in that of his philosophic mentor Bolingbroke. Pope's "rapidly perceptive mind was fully qualified to imbibe the crude versions of philosophic theories which float upon the surface of ordinary talk, and are not always so inferior to their proto-types in philosophic qualities as philosophers would have us believe," Stephen tells us. Be that as it may, the tensions just mentioned must have been agonizingly real for Pope's readers, and the *Essay* would not be the work of art that it is had it failed to express them.

The tension between wanting to think of God as a comfort and thinking of God "rationally," as a remote and inaccessible principle, is the best-known difficulty in deistic thought after Newton. Newton himself thought that his doctrine provided comfort in two ways: by combating mechanism (Newton thought of the gravitational attraction as something opposed to mechanism, something perhaps even spiritual in nature) and by requiring the constant intervention of God to keep the *vis viva* of the universe from "running down." In Koyre's words, "At the end of the century, Newton's victory was complete. The Newtonian God reigned supreme in the infinite void of absolute space in which the force of universal attraction linked together the atomically structured bodies of the immense universe and made them move around in accordance with strict mathematical laws. Yet it can be argued that this victory was a Pyrrhic one, and the price paid for it disastrously high."

Universal attraction came to be seen as a purely natural force, rather than as a manifestation of God's action in the world. Newton had postulated a finite physical universe in an infinite absolute space; but the physical universe came to be conceived of as filling absolute space. "Last but not least," Koyre adds, "the world-clock made by the Divine Artifex was much better than Newton had thought it to be. Every progress of Newtonian science brought new proofs for Leibniz's contention: the moving-force of the universe, its *vis viva,* did not decrease; the world-clock needed neither rewinding nor mending."

The upshot is that God might as well have put an end to Himself at the instant of creation, if the deist view is right. For if "God acts not on partial but on general laws," as Pope keeps repeating, then only one act of His—the act of Creation itself—impinges on our lives. The tension here, if not its historically particular form, is one which is still very much with us. It is the tension between the world-view of what we refer to as "science" (taking cosmology and atomic physics to be all of "science," as we still tend to do when we philosophize) and the world-view of agency and moral responsibility. It is this tension that— in a much more "professional" way than Pope and Bolingbroke—Hume wrestled with and that Kant erected his mighty metaphysical system to resolve.

The God of the Scientist

The lack of serious discussion of Newton's attitudes toward theology and science by professional philosophers amounts to an intellectual scandal, the more so since Newton was a better "philosopher of science" than most of the professionals who later claimed that title for themselves. Newton was a man of his time, and he had a number of ideas that have become "dated," as well as some ideas that were strange even in his own time. In spite of this, he saw clearly the need to distinguish questions of science (which he called "experimental Philosophy") from what we would call "metaphysical" questions (for example, questions about the ultimate ontological nature of the gravitational attraction). This distinction was essential to the whole enterprise of Newtonian physics, as was Newton's insistence that the gravitational law itself was not, and did not need to be, a necessary truth, but was only the result of deducing certain consequences from the phenomena known to astronomers and "rendering them general by induction." Newton even foresaw, and warned against, the possibility of carrying the insistence upon operational significance in "experimental philosophy" to the extreme to which it was so often carried in later centuries, writing that "those defile the purity of mathematical and philosophical truth, who confound real quantities with their relations and sensible measures."

Newton indicates some of the questions that are in the scope of "experimental Philosophy" when he writes that "there are therefore Agents in Nature able to make the Particles of Bodies stick together by very strong Attractions. And it is the business of experimental Philosophy to find them out." At the same time, "How these Attractions may be performed, I do not here consider. That I call attraction may be performed by impulse, or by some other means unknown to me." As Samuel Clarke put it in the controversy with Leibniz, "It is very unreasonable to call *Attraction a Miracle* and an unphilosophical Term after it has been so often distinctly declared, that by that Term we do not mean to express the Cause of Bodies tending *towards each other,* but rarely the *Effect,* or the *Phenomenon itself,* and the *Laws* or Proportions of the *Tendency,* discovered by *Experience.*"

To put it briefly, Newton and his supporters distinguished between what was a matter for philosophical speculation, namely, "the Cause of Bodies tending towards each other," for example the nature of gravitation in a "philosophical" sense, concerning which Newton said *"Hypotheses non fingo,"* and what was a matter for experimental science, namely, "the Laws or Proportions of that Tendency."

What confuses the situation for us and our contemporaries is that Newton and Clarke did not exclude assumptions about *God* and about God's governance of the physical world from discussions concerning the tenability of Newton's system. On the contrary, in the debate between Leibniz and Clarke, both sides use either a point about inertial effects or a theological point about whether it accords with the dignity of God to think of space as his "sensorium" as if the two kinds of consideration were absolutely on a par. In fact, for Newton and Leibniz they *were* on a par. The existence of God was not a *speculation* for either of these thinkers. Leibniz was sure he could demonstrate the existence of God *a priori,* while for Newton the design argument was conclusive. (He asks, in a famous passage, whether one can suppose that the designer of the ear knew no acoustics or that the designer of the eye knew no optics.) In short, to put ourselves in the proper frame of mind to read these authors, let us try to imagine that the existence of God is a *scientific fact,* while imagining at the same time that we are just beginning to draw something like our present distinction between what is and what is not a scientific question.

If we can manage to do this, then we can see a little more of what is happening in Pope's *Essay on Man.* At one point (lines 73–74 of the first epistle), Pope desperately needs to use the existence of an afterlife as a given, but can only use it as a hypothesis, to the obvious detriment of his argument. We know that Pope himself was aware of this, because in a letter to Carlyle, dated March 8, 1733 (before he publicly admitted his authorship of the *Essay*), Pope writes, "Nothing is so plain as that he (the anonymous author) quits his proper subject, this present world, to assert his belief of a future state, and yet there is an *if* instead of a *since* that would overthrow his meaning." In the Twickenham text, an editor's note remarks, "But Pope could not have changed *if* to *since* without appealing to Revelation, which, as his remark to Carlyle shows, he was determined not to do, and which lay outside the terms of his poem."

But why was "Revelation" to be avoided, when what we would regard as the most peculiar parts of Newtonian theology (for example,

the idea that space is the "sensorium" of God) were embraced? Precisely because Newtonian theology had the authority of science. In the
time of Pope, revelation had ceased to have that sort of authority.
Leslie Stephen decried Pope's substitute for revelation as "abstract
theology dependent upon argument instead of tradition. . . . Its deity
was not a historical personage, but the name of a metaphysical conception." This charge expresses the point of view of the end of the
nineteenth century—but this was *not* the point of view of Pope or of
Bolingbroke. For them, God—the God of Newton and Leibniz, if not
the God of Scripture—was an established fact, a scientific and not a
"metaphysical" conception.

Pope's Attitude to Theology and Philosophy

What I suggest is that Pope was quite deliberately avoiding reliance
upon traditional theology, that is, upon "pre-scientific" theology. In
fact, it would have been difficult for Pope to rely upon the theology of
the churches, even had he wished to do so. An open reliance upon
Catholic theology would have been out of the question in Protestant
England, even if Pope had believed Catholic dogma, and he was very
far from doing that. In the *Essay,* Pope suggests that there is no way
to show who are the "good guys" and who are the "bad guys" among
the theologians:

> One thinks on Calvin Heaven's own spirit fell
> Another deems him instrument of hell;

writes Pope, and again

> For Modes of Faith let graceless zealots fight
> His can't be wrong whose life is in the right.

But "post-scientific" theology—that is, general deistic belief—could
not answer the question with which the *Essay* concludes, namely, how
and where happiness is to be found. Here too, Pope wishes to be independent of technical philosophy and abstruse reasoning.

> Who thus define it, say they more or less
> Than this, that Happiness is Happiness?

asks Pope, with obvious sarcasm, and continues:

> Take nature's path and mad Opinion's leave,
> All states can reach it, and all heads conceive.

Pope wished to solve traditional philosophical problems—the problem of evil, the problem of the true nature of human happiness—and to instruct his own age as Milton had instructed his, but without relying on the happy pieties of revelation or the intellectual resting places of dogmatic theology. He used materials from deistic philosophy, because that philosophy was modern and scientific. Where those materials gave out, he fell back on what he took to be good sense (not noticing its source in Thomas a Kempis and other traditional authors). What makes this so interesting is that this has been the plight of philosophers ever since. Ever since Bacon called for a "New Instauration," that is, a total new beginning in human knowledge, philosophy has lacked the status and authority of a science. All attempts to give it that authority—by identifying it either with the science of the mind, as Hume attempted to do, or with a science of language, as more recent thinkers have wished to do, or with a special sort of transcendental inquiry, as others, following Kant, have sought to do—have failed. That a poet like Pope could try to solve philosophical problems while scorning traditional philosophy as "mad Opinion" is an indication of the way in which the position of philosophy had become problematical in the seventeenth century. But the fact that the position of philosophy as a discipline became (and has, of course remained) problematical does not mean that philosophical issues can or should be dismissed as "optional." The ultimate philosophical issue, as Pope saw, is the position of man in the world. Pope could not put together a moral image of man that can command our allegiance out of the materials that he chose to work with; but, in the words of Rabbi Tarphon, "The task is not yours to finish, but neither are you free to desist from it."

References

Bate, W. J. 1970. *The Burden of the Past and the English Poet*. New York: Norton.

Koyre, A. 1958. *From the Closed World to the Infinite Universe*. New York: Harper.

Stephen, L. 1899. *Alexander Pope*. New York: Harper.

Credits

Chapter 1

Originally published in *Exploring the Concept of Mind*, ed. Richard M. Caplan (Iowa City: University of Iowa Press, 1986).

Chapter 2

Originally published in *Essays on Aristotle's "De Anima,"* ed. Martha Nussbaum and Amalie Rorty (Oxford: Oxford University Press, 1992).

Chapter 3

Originally published in *Modern Thinkers and Ancient Thinkers*, ed. Robert W. Shaples (London: UCL Press, 1993).

Chapter 4

Originally published in *A. J. Ayer Memorial Essays*, ed. A. Phillips Griffiths, Royal Institute of Philosophy Supplement, vol. 30 (Cambridge: Cambridge University Press, 1991). Copyright 1991 by and reprinted with the permission of Cambridge University Press.

Chapter 5

Originally published in *Erkenntnis*, 35, nos. 1–3 (July 1991), 61–76. Copyright 1991 by Kluwer Academic Publishers and reprinted with their permission.

Chapter 6

Presented to the Reichenbach Centennial Conference, sponsored jointly by the Harvard University Department of Philosophy and the Boston Colloquium for the History and Philosophy of Science, at Harvard University on April 2, 1991.

Chapter 7

Originally published in *Proceedings of the Ninth International Congress of Logic, Methodology, and Philosophy of Science, August 7–14, 1991* (Amsterdam: Elsevier Science Publishers, 1993).

Chapter 8

To appear in *Women, Culture, and Equality: A Study in Human Capabilities* (papers presented to the Conference on Human Capabilities sponsored by the World Institute for Development Economics, Helsinki, August 15–22, 1991), ed. Martha Nussbaum and Jonathan Glover (Oxford: Clarendon Press, forthcoming).

Chapter 9

Originally published under the title "The French Revolution and the Holocaust: Can Ethics be Ahistorical?" in *Culture and Modernity: The Authority of the Past—East-West Philosophical Perspectives* (proceedings of the Sixth East-West Philosophers' Conference), ed. Eliot Deutsch (Honolulu: University of Hawaii Press, 1992).

Chapter 10

Originally published as "Epistemology as Hypothesis" in *Transactions of the Charles S. Peirce Society*, 26, no. 4 (Fall 1990), 407–433.

Chapter 11

Originally published in *Educational Theory*, 43, no. 4 (Fall 1993).

Chapter 12

This paper was presented at the Conference on the Philosophy of W. V. Quine at the University of San Marino in May 1990 under the title "On the Slogan 'Epistemology Naturalized,'" and will appear under that title in the proceedings of that conference, to be titled *On Quine*, ed. Paulo Leonardi and Marco Santambrogio (Cambridge: Cambridge University Press, forthcoming).

Chapter 13

Originally published in *Metaphilosophy*, 22, nos. 1–2 (January–April 1991), 1–13.

Chapter 14

Originally published in English in *International Journal of Philosophical*

Studies, 1–2 (September 1993). Also published in Spanish under the title "Atando Cabos" in *Diánoia* (1992), pp. 1–15.

Chapter 15

Presented as the Auguste Comte Lecture to the London School of Economics, February 2, 1993.

Chapter 16

Originally published in *How Many Questions? Essays in Honor of Sidney Morgenbesser*, ed. Leigh S. Cauman, Isaac Levi, Charles Parsons, and Robert Schwartz (Indianapolis: Hackett Publishing Co., 1983).

Chapter 17

Originally published in *New Literary History*, 17 (1985–86), 61–79.

Chapter 18

Originally published in *Reflections on Chomsky*, ed. Alex George (Oxford: Basil Blackwell, 1989).

Chapter 19

Originally published in Jadavpur Studies in Philosophy, vol. 5: *Human Meanings and Existence*, ed. D. P. Chattopadhyaya (New Delhi: Macmillan India, 1983).

Chapter 20

Originally published under the title "Much Ado about Not Very Much" in *Daedalus*, 117, no. 1 (Winter 1988), 269–281. Reprinted by permission of *Daedalus*, the Journal of the American Academy of Arts and Sciences, from the issue entitled "Artificial Intelligence."

Chapter 21

Originally published under the title "Models and Modules" in *Cognition*, 17, no. 3 (1984), 253–264.

Chapter 22

Originally published in *Erkenntnis*, 22, nos. 1, 2, and 3 (January 1985), 143–154. Copyright 1985 by Kluwer Academic Publishers and reprinted with their permission.

Chapter 23

Originally published in *Cognition*, 2 (1973), 131–146.

Chapter 24

Originally published under the title "Why Functionalism Failed" in *Inference, Explanation, and Other Philosophical Frustrations*, ed. John Earman (Berkeley: University of California Press, 1992).

Chapter 25

Originally published under the title "The Diversity of the Sciences: Global versus Local Methodological Approaches" in *Metaphysics and Morality: Essays in Honour of J. J. C. Smart*, ed. P. Pettit, R. Sylvan, and J. Norman (Oxford: Basil Blackwell, 1987).

Chapter 26

Originally published in Midwest Studies in Philosophy, vol. 15: *The Philosophy of the Human Sciences*, ed. P. French, T. Uehling, and H. Wettstein (Notre Dame: University of Notre Dame Press, 1990). Copyright © 1990 by the University of Notre Dame Press; used by permission.

Chapter 27

Originally published in *The Philosophical Quarterly*, 32 (July 1982), 195–200.

Chapter 28

Originally published under the title "Philosophy of Mathematics: A Report" in *Current Research in Philosophy of Science: Proceedings of the P.S.A. Critical Research Problems Conference*, ed. P. D. Asquith and Henry Kyburg, Jr. (East Lansing: Philosophy of Science Association, 1979).

Chapter 29

An earlier version of this paper was presented to the English Institute, September 2–5, 1983, at a session on the *Essay on Man* organized by Stanley Cavell. It was originally published as "Pope's *Essay on Man* and Those 'Happy Pieties'" in *Pursuits of Reason: Essays in Honor of Stanley Cavell*, ed. Ted Cohen, Paul Guyer, and Hilary Putnam (Lubbock: Texas Tech University Press, 1993).

Index